Writing Against

Ronald Hayman

WRITING AGAINST
A Biography of Sartre

Weidenfeld and Nicolson · London

Contents

Illustrations

'Poulou' with his mother Anne-Marie (Documentation Obliques)
Sartre at the Ecole Normale Supérieure (Bibliothèque de l'Ecole Normale Supérieure)
Sartre as a private soldier during the Second World War (author's collection)
Sartre working as a schoolteacher at the Lycée Condorcet (photo Yves Colin)
Paul Nizan (Documentation Obliques)
Sartre in 1939 (photo Gisèle Freund/John Hillelson)
Simone de Beauvoir in 1955 (photo Elliott Erwitt/Magnum, from John Hillelson)
Wanda Kosakiewicz at the première of *Nékrassov* (photo George Henri)
Sartre and de Beauvoir with Boris and Michelle Vian (photo Yves Manciet)
Albert Camus (Documentation Obliques)
Sartre at the Pont-Royal with Dolorès Vanetti, Jacques-Laurent Bost, Jean Cau and Jean Genet (photo Jacques de Poitier/Paris Match)
Sartre and de Beauvoir with Claude Lanzmann (photo Brinon-Gamma)
Sartre with François Mauriac (Agence France-Presse)
Sartre at the Théâtre de la Renaissance with Evelyne Rey and Serge Reggiani during rehearsals for *Les Séquestrés d'Altona* (photo Lipnitzki-Viollet)
Sartre with Arlette Elkaïm (Keystone)
Sartre with Tito in Yugoslavia (Agence France-Presse)
Sartre addressing a meeting held to protest against the Vietnam War (photo D. Berretty/Magnum, from John Hillelson)
Sartre in court waiting to appear as a witness at the trial of Roland Castro (photo Henri Bureau/Sygma, from John Hillelson)
Sartre speaking outside the Renault works at Billancourt (photo Bruno Barbey/Magnum, from John Hillelson)
Sartre with Daniel Cohn-Bendit and Klaus Croissant at a Stuttgart press conference (photo Alain Nogues/Sygma, from John Hillelson)

Acknowledgments

In the four years I have been working on this biography I have become greatly indebted to many people who have helped in different ways. The first words of thanks must go to George Weidenfeld, who suggested I should write it, to Simone de Beauvoir, who was generous with both time and encouragement, and to the Arts Council of Great Britain, which gave me welcome financial support.

I am grateful to all the friends, colleagues, acquaintances and critics of Sartre who talked to me in Paris, including Colette Audry, Simone de Beauvoir, Roland Castro, Jean Cau, Michel Contat, Anne-Marie Cazalis, Robert Gallimard, Roger Grenier, Geneviève Idt, Serge July, Robert Misrahi, Albert Palle, Marcel Péju, J.-B. Pontalis, Jean Pouillon, David Rousset, Nathalie Sarraute, Olivier Todd and Michelle Vian. I also learned a good deal about Sartre and the history of the period from conversations with Ronald Aronson, Catharine Carver, Howard Davies, Val Doulton, Maurice Druon, Shusha Guppy, Quintin Hoare, Douglas Johnson, Leo Labedz, Richard Mayne, David Pryce-Jones, George Steiner and Paul Webster.

I am especially grateful to Lisa Appignanesi, Ronald Aronson and Catharine Carver who at various stages read all or part of the book in typescript and gave me their comments; Juliet Gardiner, my editor at Weidenfeld, has been extremely helpful throughout with constructive criticism. I'd also like to thank Linden Lawson for help on both text and pictures and Elspeth Henderson for help on pictures.

I am grateful to Gilles Chouraqui, the French Cultural Counsellor, who gave me letters which gained me entry to the Bibliothèque Nationale and to various archives in Paris. I must thank Mme Boulez and Mme Dauphragne who helped me to find archive material at the Ecole Normale Supérieure, and all those who helped me in the Lycée Louis-le-Grand.

I would not have been able to read the unpublished second part of Sartre's *Critique de la raison dialectique* but for Robert Gallimard's kindness in consenting and that of Patrick Camiller (Verso Books) in lending me a typescript. I am grateful to Howard Davies for letting me read his unpublished doctoral thesis on *Les Temps modernes* and to Quintin Hoare for lending me Jean Pierre's unpublished memoir of experiences with Sartre in the army. For giving me books and offprints of articles I am indebted to the kindness of Howard Davies, Geneviève Idt and Paul Webster; for putting me in touch with people who could be helpful I should like to thank Ronald Aronson, Simone de Beauvoir, Judith Bumpus, Annie Cohen-Solal, Michel Contat, Rémy Dreyfus, Maurice Farhi, Shusha Guppy, Gabriel Josipovici, Olivier Todd, Paul Webster and Martin Woollacott.

The translations from the French are my own.

	Year		Sartre		World events
p. 27	1913	autumn	Sartre starts at Lycée Montaigne	17.1	Poincaré becomes President and 21.1 Briand forms cabinet
		22.10	paternal grandfather Eymard Sartre (b. 1837) dies	3.2–23.4	Second Balkan War
				19.5–10.8	Third Balkan War
p. 27	1914		attends communal school at Arcachon and later the Poupon school in Paris	28.6	assassination of Austrian Archduke Franz-Ferdinand at Sarajevo
				30.7	socialist leader Jean Jaurès assassinated in Paris
				1–23.8	declarations of war involving major European powers and Japan
p. 30	1915		after a period of private tuition Sartre is sent in October to the Lycée Henri IV	22.4	Germans use poison gas
p. 31	1916		in the *cinquième* Paul Nizan becomes a classmate	29.1	first Zeppelin raid on Paris
				15.9	British use tanks for first time on the Western front
				7.12	Lloyd George becomes prime minister of British coalition government
p. 33	1917		Anne-Marie marries Joseph Mancy and settles with him at La Rochelle	2.4	US declares war on Germany
		Nov.	Jean-Paul moves in with them and starts at the lycée there	15.5	Pétain made French commander-in-chief
				12.9	Paul Painlevé forms cabinet
				15.9	Russian republic proclaimed with Kerensky as premier
				7.11 (26.10 old style)	Bolshevik revolution in Russia
				8.11	Lenin becomes chairman of Council of People's Commissars

		16.1	Clemenceau succeeds Paul Painlevé and forms cabinet
		5.12	Germans and Russians sign armistice, and 21.12 peace negotiations start
p. 37	1918	writes a novel about Goetz von Berlichingen	
		16.7	execution of Tsar Nicholas II who had abdicated 3.17
		12.10	Germany and Austria agree to withdraw troops before armistice is signed
		9.11	republic proclaimed in Bavaria and revolution in Berlin
		11.11	Allies sign armistice with Germany
p. 38	1919	**spring** steals money from his mother	
		5–11.1	Spartacist revolt in Berlin
		28.6	peace treaty signed at Versailles; Alsace-Lorraine returned to France
p. 40	1920	**autumn** returns to Lycée Henri IV in Paris	
		10.1	League of Nations founded
		Feb.	German Workers' Party (which had six members when Hitler joined in 1919) changes its title to National Socialist Party
		29.12	socialist congress at Tours votes in favour of affiliation with Moscow International. Minority withdraws, splitting party. *Humanité* taken over by communist majority
p. 42	1921	**June** passes first part of *baccalauréat*	
		8.3	French troops occupy some Ruhr towns because Germany delays reparations
		28.3	British Independent Labour Party refuses to affiliate with Moscow
		30.9	French troops evacuate Ruhr

p. 43	1922	June	passes second part of *baccalauréat*	6.10	Franco–German agreement on reparations in kind
			writes the story 'L'Ange du morbide' and the unfinished novel *Jésus la Chouette*	15.2	Court of International Justice holds first sessions at the Hague
		autumn	moves to the Lycée Louis-le-Grand as a day-boarder, living with mother and step-father in the square Clignancourt	30.10	Benito Mussolini invited by the king to form fascist government
p. 45	1923		publishes 'L'Ange du morbide' and several chapters of *Jésus la Chouette* in *La Revue sans titre*	11.1	French and Belgian troops occupy the Ruhr because of non-payment of reparations
		summer	writes two chapters of *La Semence et le scaphandre*	10–13.8	strikes and riots in Germany
				8–9.11	Hitler attempts a putsch in Munich
p. 52	1924		starts at the Ecole Normale Supérieure	Jan.	Kuomintang Congress admits communists to the Party and encourages Russian 'advisers'
				13–15.6	Gaston Doumergue becomes French president and Eduard Herriot chosen as premier
				30.11	Franco-Belgian evacuation of the Ruhr completed
p. 60	1925			16.1	Trotsky dismissed as chairman of Military Council
				10.4	Herriot defeated; Paul Painlevé becomes French premier
		Sept.	meets Simone-Camille Sans (later known as Simone Jollivet)	25.4	Hindenburg elected president of Germany
				27.11	Briand forms ministry

Page	Year	Month	Sartre's life	Date	Historical events
p. 63	1926			4–12.5	general strike in Britain
					Briand ministry overturned by financial crisis
		Sept.	Nizan's departure for Aden cements Sartre's friendship with Guille and Maheu	15.7	Poincaré premier again
				23.7	franc devalued and sinking fund established
				10.8	Trotsky and Zinoviev expelled from Politburo
				Oct.	
p. 66	1927	May	Nizan returns	13.5	'Black Friday': breakdown of German economy
			Sartre writes thesis on 'L'Image dans la vie psychologique'	20–21.5	Lindbergh's transatlantic flight
		summer	in Usson-en-Forez. Unofficial engagement to daughter of a grocer	27.12	Trotsky expelled from Party
p. 68	1928	July	fails agrégation	22.4	union of left parties wins French elections
p. 70	1929	July	meets Simone de Beauvoir; comes top in agrégation exam; she comes second	31.1	Trotsky exiled
				27.7	Poincaré resigns; Briand premier again
		Nov.	begins 18 months' military service at St-Cyr	28.10	Wall Street crash, followed by European financial crisis
p. 76	1930	Jan.	transferred to St-Symphorien; inherits money when his grandmother dies	12.3	Gandhi starts campaign of civil disobedience in India
				30.6	last Allied troops leave Rhineland
				12.12	last Allied troops leave the Saar
p. 79	1931	28.2	demobilized	27.1	Pierre Laval premier
		April	teaching job in Le Havre	Feb.	Oswald Mosley forms his New Party
		June	La Légende de la vérité published in Bifur	13.7	all German banks closed
		summer	holiday in Spain with de Beauvoir	1.8	Franco-US loan to Britain

			Sartre		World events
			starts 'Factum sur la contingence' (first version of *La Nausée*)	21.9	Britain abandons gold standard. Pound falls from $4.86 to $3.49
p. 89	1932	Easter	in Brittany with de Beauvoir in Morocco and Spain	21.2	André Tardieu forms ministry
		summer		10.4	Hindenburg re-elected German president with 19 million votes against Hitler's 13 million
		Oct.	de Beauvoir takes teaching job in Rouen	1.5	left parties win French elections
				4.6	Herriot forms ministry
				31.7	nazis win majority in German elections
				10.8	Sanjurjo attempts coup in Spain
				18.12	Herriot resigns and Paul Boncour forms cabinet
			Aron talks to Sartre about Husserl and phenomenology	30.1	Hitler appointed chancellor
p. 92	1933	Easter	in London with de Beauvoir	31.1	Daladier becomes French premier
		summer	with her in Italy	27.2	Reichstag fire; civil liberties and freedom of press suspended
		Sept.	starts a year's study at the French Institute in Berlin	April	nazi persecution of Jews begins
				22.11	Camille Chautemps forms ministry
				Dec.	Stavisky scandal. Maurras's *Action française* denounces corruption: a Jewish swindler has been protected by highly placed friends. When Stavisky is found dead, Chautemps comes under suspicion
			completes second version of *La Nausée* and writes *La Transcendance de l'Ego*	30.1	After resignation of Chautemps Daladier forms ministry
p. 95	1934	Easter	in Paris	8.2	after rioting in Paris, encouraged by the reactionary league Croix-de-Feu, Paul Doumergue forms coalition government
		summer	with de Beauvoir in Germany, Austria, Prague and Alsace	12–13.2	general strike in France
		Oct.	resumes teaching in Le Havre		

			Biography		World events
p. 108	1935	Feb.	injected with mescalin	19.8	Hitler voted *Führer* by plebiscite
		21.3	Charles Schweitzer dies, aged 91	7.3	Saar restored to Germany after plebiscite of 13.1
		summer	holiday with mother and step-father in Norway followed by hiking with de Beauvoir in France	4.6	Pierre Laval forms ministry
		autumn	triangular friendship with Olga Kosakiewicz	27.7	government granted extraordinary financial powers
		Christ-mas	in Switzerland with de Beauvoir		
p. 112	1936		*L'Imagination* published by Alcan writes story 'Erostrate'	22.1	Albert Sarraut succeeds as French premier
		3-5	does not vote at elections	3-5	Popular Front wins French elections
		summer	with de Beauvoir in Italy writes story 'Dépaysement'	4.6	Léon Blum forms ministry
		July	starts new teaching job in Laon	12.6	40-hour week introduced
				30.6	Croix-de-Feu suppressed
				18.7	Spanish Civil War begins
				2.10	devaluation of the franc
p. 119	1937		*La Transcendance de l'Ego* published in *Recherches philosophiques*	Jan.	show trials start in Moscow; Karl Radek among accused
		July	*Melancholia* accepted by Gallimard story 'Le Mur' published in *Nouvelle Revue française*	27.2	French ministry of defence created, Maginot Line extended and Schneider-Creusot factory nationalized
		summer	with de Beauvoir and Bost in Greece	21.6	Blum resigns; Chautemps forms radical socialist government
		Oct.	starts teaching job in Neuilly		
p. 123	1938		writes 400 pages of *La Psyché* stories 'La Chambre', 'Intimité' and 'Nourritures' (formerly 'Dépaysement') published	2-15.3	trial of Bukharin in Moscow
		April	*La Nausée* published	13.3	Blum forms Popular Front ministry
				10.4	Daladier forms ministry with Blum's support
				19-20.5	France and Britain support Czechoslovakia against Hitler

		July	finishes story 'L'Enfance d'un chef'	12.8	Germany mobilizes
		summer	with de Beauvoir in Morocco	7.9	French reservists called up
		autumn	starts *L'Age de raison*	29.9	Munich conference: Sudetenland given to Hitler; Czech frontiers guaranteed
				4.10	end of Popular Front in France
p. 131	1939	Feb.	publishes *Le Mur*	27.2	France and Britain recognize Franco's government
		Easter	with de Beauvoir in Provence	15–16.3	German army occupies Czechoslovakia
		May	meets Ilya Ehrenburg at anti-fascist conference	28.3	Spanish Civil War ends with surrender of Madrid
		summer	in south of France		
		2.9	called up	23.8	non-aggression pact between Hitler and Stalin
				1.9	Germany invades Poland
				3.9	France and Britain declare war
		Dec.	*Esquisse d'une théorie des émotions* published		
p. 156	1940	Feb.	on leave in Paris	20.3	Paul Reynaud replaces Daladier as premier
		March	*L'Imaginaire* published	7.5	Churchill replaces Chamberlain as British premier
		April	on leave again; awarded the Populiste prize		
		23.5	Nizan killed in action	14.5	Dutch army surrenders
		21.6	Sartre taken prisoner	28.5	Belgium surrenders
				14.6	Germans enter Paris
		24.12	*Bariona* staged in Stalag	16.6	Marshal Pétain takes over from Reynaud
				22.6	concludes armistice with Germany
				23.8	German blitz on London begins
p. 170	1941	March	escapes from Stalag	14.5	Vichy government supports Admiral Darlan's commitment to give Hitler naval help
		April	resumes teaching in Neuilly; founds resistance group 'Socialisme et liberté'		
		21.6	article on *Moby Dick* published in *Comoedia*	22.6	Hitler invades Russia

			Sartre		World events
		summer	finishes *L'Age de raison*	12.7	Anglo-Russian alliance
		Oct.	cycling holiday in Free Zone with de Beauvoir	7.12	Japanese bomb Pearl Harbor
			teaching job at Lycée Condorcet	8.12	Britain and US declare war on Japan
			dissolves 'Socialisme et liberté'	11.12	US declares war on Germany and Italy
		Dec.	works on *L'Etre et le Néant*		
p. 175	1942	summer	finishes *Les Mouches*; starts *Le Sursis*	Sept.	US bombers raid France
			cycling holiday in Free Zone with de Beauvoir; they then stay at La Pouèze	8.11	Allies land in French North Africa
		Oct.	completes *L'Etre et le Néant*	24.12	Darlan assassinated
p. 197	1943	Jan.	Sartre joins Comité national des écrivains and contributes to underground papers	30–31.1	German army defeated at Stalingrad
				12.5	German army in Tunisia surrenders
		2.6	*Les Mouches* premiered; meets Camus	4.6	French Committee of National Liberation formed
		autumn	writes *Huis clos* in two weeks		
		Nov.	finishes *Le Sursis*	26.7	Mussolini loses control of Italy
		Dec.	finishes *Réflexions sur la question juive*		
p. 204	1944	May	meets Genet	6.6	'D-Day': landings in Normandy
		27.5	*Huis clos* premiered	15.8	Allied forces land on the Riviera
		July	escapes from Paris with de Beauvoir	25.8	Allied troops enter Paris
		Aug.–Sept.	reports for *Combat* on the liberation of Paris	23.10	Allies recognize de Gaulle as head of French provisional government
		Sept.	forms editorial committee for *Les Temps modernes*		
p. 220	1945	12.1	refuses the Légion d'honneur	4–11.2	Yalta conference: Churchill, Stalin and Roosevelt agree spheres of influence
			flies to the US. Meets Dolorès Vanetti		
		21.1	Joseph Mancy dies	12.4	Roosevelt dies; succeeded by Truman
		May	returns to France	30.4	Hitler dies in bunker

	summer	holiday with his mother in the country and with de Beauvoir at La Pouèze. Writes *Morts sans sépulture*	8.5	V.E. Day
			5.6	Germany divided by Allies into four zones
	autumn	'existentialism' is suddenly a catchword	26.7	Conservatives defeated in Britain: Attlee replaces Churchill
	Oct.	lectures on existentialism in Brussels and in Paris at the Club Maintenant	6–9.8	atomic bombs dropped on Hiroshima and Nagasaki
	12.12	returns to the US	14.8	Japan surrenders
			9.10	Laval sentenced to death for collaborating
			21.10	left triumphant in French elections
			13.11	de Gaulle elected president of provisional government
			20.11	trials begin at Nuremberg of nazi war criminals
p. 232 1946	April	returns to France; meets Boris and Michelle Vian	20–22.1	de Gaulle resigns as president. Félix Gouin succeeds him
	May–June	lectures in Switzerland on existentialism	6.3	France recognizes Vietnam as a free state
	June	lectures in Italy	5.5	referendum rejects French draft constitution
	June–July	publishes 'Matérialisme et révolution' in *Les Temps modernes*	June	MRP wins majority in French elections
	Sept.	stays in Rome to work on *Huis clos* screenplay	19.6	Georges Bidault elected president
	Oct.	moves to flat, 42 rue Bonaparte, with his mother	13.10	revised constitution adopted
	8.11	*Morts sans sépulture* and *La Putain respectueuse* premiered	10.11	in elections communists win 186 seats, MRP 166, socialists 103
	Nov.	trip to Holland	16.12	Blum forms socialist government
p. 240 1947	Feb.– July	*Baudelaire* published	16.1	Vincent Auriol elected president
		Qu'est-ce que c'est que la littérature? published in *Les Temps modernes*	21.1	Blum resigns, Ramadier forms coalition government

	Sartre		World events
July	visit to London for double bill	29.3	revolt against France in Madagascar
Aug.–Sept.	trip to Sweden and Lapland with de Beauvoir	14.4	de Gaulle heads anti-communist Rassemblement du peuple français (RPF)
Sept.	Les Jeux sont faits presented at Cannes Film Festival	May	series of strikes in France
Oct.	Situations 1 published	5.6	George Marshall, US secretary of state, announces programme of economic aid for Europe
Oct.–Nov.	series of radio programmes La Tribune des Temps modernes	19–26.10	RPF triumphs in municipal elections
Christmas	with de Beauvoir at La Pouèze. Starts Les Mains sales	14.11	UN recognizes Korean independence
		19–23.11	Ramadier resigns; Robert Schuman forms ministry with support of MRP and socialists
p. 248			
1948 Feb.	joins Rassemblement démocratique révolutionnaire (RDR)	25.2	communist coup d'état in Czechoslovakia
2.4	Les Mains sales premiered	31.3	US Congress passes law for Marshall Aid
May	Situations 2 published	24.6	Russians blockade West Berlin; air-lift starts
summer	with de Beauvoir in Algeria	28.6	Yugoslavia expelled from Cominform
30.10	Sartre's books put on Index by Vatican	29.7	Tito defies charges and wins support of Party in Yugoslavia
Dec.–June 49	La Mort dans l'âme published in Les Temps modernes	15.8	Republic of Korea proclaimed under Syngman Rhee
		9.9	North Koreans proclaim republic and claim whole country
		10.9	Henri Queuille, radical, forms ministry
		7.11	RPF succeeds in French elections
p. 254			
1949 March	stays at Cagnes working on ethical notes and novel	Jan	Kravchenko trial
	Situations 3 published	8.3	France recognizes non-communist Vietnam as independent state
June	convenes and subsidizes meeting of RDR	4.4	North Atlantic Treaty signed

		Biography		World events
	summer	South American holiday with Dolorès Vanetti. Meets Hemingway in Cuba	**5.5**	Council of Europe established
			12.5	end of Berlin blockade
	6.10	resigns from RDR	**23.5**	German Federal Republic established
	Nov.–Dec.	excerpts from *Drôle d'amitié* published in *Les Temps modernes*	**15.9**	Heuss and Adenauer elected as president and chancellor
			1.10	People's Republic of China proclaimed
			7.10	German Democratic Republic established under Pieck (president) and Grotewohl (minister-president)
			28.10	Henri Queuille resigns and Bidault forms coalition
			30.12	France gives Vietnam sovereignty
p. 262	**1950 Jan.**	Sartre and Merleau-Ponty denounce Soviet labour camps	**8.3**	Soviet Union reveals it has atomic weapons
	spring	with de Beauvoir to Sahara and black Africa	**21.3**	Adenauer proposes Franco-German economic union
	June	breach with Dolorès	**24.6**	Bidault resigns
	July	starts publishing series of six articles on Genet in *Les Temps modernes*	**25.6**	North Koreans invade South Korea
			11.7	René Pleven forms government after Queuille has tried (2.7) unsuccessfully
			15.9–1.10	UN forces land in South Korea and advance to beyond 38th parallel
p. 265	**1951 Jan.**	works on *Le Diable et le Bon Dieu*	**28.2**	Pleven's coalition defeated
	7.6	premiere of play	**10.3**	Queuille forms ministry
	summer	with de Beauvoir in Norway, Iceland, Scotland	**18.4**	treaty for single coal and steel authority in Western Europe
			17.6	French elections: Gaullists win 117 seats, communists 104, socialists 101

Page	Year	Date		Date	
				11.8	Pleven forms centrist coalition
				10.9	NATO foreign ministers consider use of German troops
p. 276				13.12	National Assembly approves plan for single coal and steel authority
	1952	Jan.	agrees to work with communists in protest over Henri Martin affair	7–22.1	Pleven's ministry falls; Edgar Fauré forms coalition after collapse of Fauré's ministry,
				29.2	Antoine Pinay assumes power
		June	reads *Le Coup du 2 Décembre* by Guillemin	30.3	anti-French rioting in Tangier
		July	*Saint Genet* published; works on novel	28.4	General Ridgway replaces Eisenhower as Supreme Allied Commander in Europe
		July and Oct.–Nov.	publishes *Les Communistes et la paix* Parts 1 and 2 in *Les Temps modernes*	27–31.5	Paris signature of treaty for European Defence Community (EDC)
		Aug.	publishes reply to Camus in *Les Temps modernes*	28.5	communist demonstrations in Paris; Dubois arrested
		summer	in Italy	25.7	European Coal and Steel Community established
				5.10	first postwar Party Congress in USSR
				27.11	Slansky (former Party secretary) tried in Czechoslovakia
				12.12	communist peace congress in Vienna
	1953	April	publishes 'Réponse à Claude Lefort' in *Les Temps modernes*	12.1	Tito elected president of Yugoslavia
p. 284		May	Merleau-Ponty withdraws from *Les Temps modernes*	14.1–10.2	constitution drafted for European Political Community
		June	Sartre stays in Venice; condemns execution of Rosenbergs	24.2	conference of foreign ministers on EDC
				5.3	Stalin dies
				17.6	rising in East Berlin

Nov.	*Kean* opens	
		19.6 Rosenbergs executed as atomic spies in US
		26.6 Joseph Laniel forms ministry
		6.8 new series of strikes starts in France
		12.9 Khrushchev becomes first secretary of Central Committee
		20.10 Adenauer forms new government
		23.12 René Coty elected president of France
		L.P. Beria (former Soviet minister of internal affairs) shot as traitor
p. 288	1954	
Jan.–Feb.	makes speeches in protest against European Defence Community	25.1–18.2 Soviet and Western foreign ministers meet in Berlin. USSR vetoes idea of free elections in Germany
Feb.	meets Brecht at international writers' conference	
April	*Les Communistes et la paix* Part 3 published in *Les Temps modernes*	9.3 centre and right victorious in French elections
24–5.5	attends Berlin meeting of World Peace Conference	18.4 Colonel Nasser becomes Egypt's premier
		7.5 French defenders of Dien Bien Phu in North Vietnam defeated by communist Viet-Minh
26.5–23.6	first visit to USSR	18.6 Pierre Mendès-France becomes premier
summer	in Italy. Meets Togliatti. Travels with de Beauvoir in Germany, Austria, Czechoslovakia. Returns to Italy	2.7 French retreat in Indo-China
		20–23.7 settlement in Indo-China: Cambodia, Laos and Vietnam given independence
Dec.	becomes vice-president of Franco-Soviet Association	22.8 French intransigence sabotages Brussels negotiations on EDC treaty
		3.10 West Germany invited to enter NATO
		8.10 communists occupy Hanoi, capital of Vietnam
		23.10 4-power agreement to end occupation of Germany; 9-power agreement on West European union

		26.10	economic and cultural agreement between France and West Germany
		3.11	terrorist activity in Algeria
		Dec.	20,000 French troops sent to Algeria
1955	Jan.	*Les Temps modernes* starts campaign in support of Algerian rebels	
		25.1	Jacques Soustelle appointed governor-general of Algeria
	spring	Sartre starts working on biography of Flaubert	
	8.6	*Nekrassov* premiered	
	26.6	at peace conference in Helsinki; meets Lukács	
		5–23.2	Mendès-France resigns; Edgar Fauré forms ministry
	June	Merleau-Ponty's *Les Aventures de la dialectique* published with a chapter attacking Sartre for 'ultra-bolshevism'. Revival of *Huis clos*; Sartre meets Evelyne Rey, who plays Estelle	
		11–27.3	Treaty for European Union ratified
		5–6.4	Churchill resigns; Anthony Eden succeeds him
		5.5	occupation of Germany ends
		15.6	Anglo-American atomic energy agreement
		2.10	France withdraws from UN, angered at Algerian interference
	Sept.–Nov.	to China with de Beauvoir	
	Nov.	starts working on screenplay of Arthur Miller's *The Crucible*	
		23–6.10	referendum in South Vietnam: emperor deposed, republic proclaimed

		Jan.	East German army formed
		Feb.	Guy Mollet forms ministry
1956	Feb.	controversy with Pierre Hervé and Pierre Naville about Communist Party	
		14.2	20th Party Congress in USSR; Khrushchev denounces Stalin
	March	meets Arlette El Kaïm	
		12.3	communists in Assembly vote to give government special powers in Algeria
	26–31.3	takes part in communist-organized cultural congress in Vienna	
	summer	with Michelle Vian, Simone de Beauvoir and Claude Lanzmann in Italy, Yugoslavia and Greece; then long holiday in Italy till November	
		June	rioting brutally crushed in Poznan
		26.7	Nasser seizes Suez Canal
	Nov.	condemns Soviet intervention in Hungary and Anglo-French intervention in Suez	
		22–25.10	demonstrations in Hungary; Soviet intervention

p. 306	1957	Jan.	to Poland for Polish premiere of *Les Mouches*	**31.10** Anglo-French bombing of Egyptian airfields
		summer	To Rome and Capri with Michelle Vian. Writes introduction to Gorz's *Le Traître*	**4.11** Soviet attack on Budapest
				5.11 Soviet threat to use rockets unless Britain and France accept Middle East cease-fire
		Sept.	Claude Faux, a Party member, succeeds Jean Cau as Sartre's secretary	**8.12** general strike in Hungary; martial law proclaimed
		Sept.–Oct.	*Questions de méthode* published in *Les Temps modernes*	**25.3** Rome treaties signed for Common Market and Euratom
				21.5 Mollet resigns
		10.12	appears as witness in trial of Ben Sadok	**12.6** Maurice Bourgès-Manoury, a radical, forms ministry
				30.10 Felix Gaillard, a radical socialist, forms ministry
				8.12 Union de la Gauche socialiste formed
p. 314	1958	March	Reviews Alleg's *La Question* in *L'Express*. Paper seized by police	**5.4** in Cuba Fidel Castro opens battle against Fulgencio Batista's government
		spring	works on *Critique de la raison dialectique*	**16.4** Gaillard resigns
		May	accepts commission to write a screenplay for John Huston's film about Freud	**14.5** Pierre Pflimlin (MRP) forms ministry
				29.5 de Gaulle forms government of national safety
		22.5	publishes anti-Gaullist article in *L'Express*	
		30.5	participates in press conference about violation of human rights in Algeria	**28.9** referendum on constitution for Fifth Republic
		16.6–15.9	in Italy; works on *Les Séquestrés d'Altona*	**5.10** 'Yes' vote strengthens de Gaulle
		Sept.	campaigns in *L'Express* for a 'No' vote in the referendum	**30.11** Gaullist victory in elections
				12.12 Salan made inspector-general of national defence in Algeria
		Oct.	cardiac illness	**21.12** de Gaulle elected president

		Date		Date	
p. 337	1959	May	completes *Critique* Part I, and works on Freud screenplay	1–2.1	Batista flees Cuba and Manuel Urrutia is appointed provisional governor but Castro postpones elections
		summer	interviewed by Jeanson for *Vérités pour . . .* in Rome and Venice	8.1	de Gaulle becomes president with Michel Debré as prime minister
		Aug.	completes *Les Séquestrés d'Altona*	16.2	Fidel Castro made Cuban premier
		24.9	*Les Séquestrés d'Altona* premiered in Paris	16.9	de Gaulle broadcasts on Algeria's future
		Sept.	stays with John Huston in Ireland		
p. 340	1960	7.1	article on Camus in *France-Observateur*	24.1–1.2	rioting in Algiers
		22.2–20.3	in Cuba with de Beauvoir. Writes preface to new edition of Nizan's *Aden-Arabie*	Mar.–June	10-power disarmament committee meets in Geneva
		May	visits Yugoslavia	16–19.5	Khrushchev, de Gaulle, Eisenhower and Macmillan meet in Paris
		Aug.	is one of 121 signatories of manifesto favouring civil disobedience	14.6	FLN agrees to negotiate ceasefire but rejects de Gaulle's terms
		Aug.–Nov.	visits Brazil with de Beauvoir	30.6	Lumumba becomes premier of newly independent Congolese republic
		1.12	press conference advocating 'No' vote in referendum	Aug.–Sept.	Belgian troops evacuate Congo
				5–9	Lumumba dismissed by President Kasavubu
				8.11	Kennedy elected US president
				13.12	Lumumba arrested
p. 354	1961	Feb.	Péju 'secretary-general' of new editorial committee of *Les Temps modernes* including Bost, Gorz, Lanzmann, Pingaud, Pontalis and Pouillon	6–8.1	massive support for de Gaulle's referendum on Algeria
		May	Merleau-Ponty dies	17.1	execution of Lumumba; danger of civil war in Congo
		June	Sartre installs Mme Mancy in a hotel and moves into a flat with de Beauvoir	17.4	Castro defeats 'Bay of Pigs' invasion
				21–26.4	army revolt in Algeria
				17–18.8	Berlin Wall built

19.7	bomb attack on Sartre's flat, 42 rue Bonaparte	27.8	provisional government formed in Algeria under Ben Khedda
July–	stays in Rome; writes essay on Merleau-Ponty and meets Frantz Fanon	8.11	negotiations begin for Britain to enter Common Market
Oct.	takes part in pro-Algerian demonstrations		
Nov.	lectures on 'Subjectivity and Marxism' at Istituto Gramsci, Rome		
Dec.	resumes work on Flaubert biography		
p. 359 1962			
7.1	second bomb attack on flat in rue Bonaparte; Sartre moves to flat in Quai Blériot, and later to 222 boulevard Raspail	Feb.	riots in Paris against the OAS
14.3	elected vice-president of Congrès de la Communauté européene des écrivains (COMES)	14.3	France boycotts Geneva disarmament conference attended by 17 foreign ministers
June	Péju sacked and replaced by Jeanson	18.3	ceasefire in Algeria; provisional FLN government established
1–24.6	to Russia with de Beauvoir	14–15.4	Debré resigns and Georges Pompidou forms ministry
9–14.7	returns to Moscow for peace conference; makes speech	3.7	after referendum France gives Algeria independence
autumn	stays in Rome; works on adaptation of Euripides' *Alcestis*	16.8	Algeria admitted to Arab League
28.12–13.1	returns to Moscow	Oct.–Nov.	crisis over installation of Russian missile base in Cuba
		2–3.11	base dismantled and missiles removed
p. 368 1963			
July	essay on Lumumba published in *Présence africaine*	22.1	Franco-German treaty of co-operation
Aug.–Sept.	COMES conference in Leningrad; received by Khrushchev in Georgia	29.1	de Gaulle vetoes British entry to Common Market
Sept.	André Puig replaces Claude Faux as Sartre's secretary	15.10	Adenauer succeeded by Erhard as German chancellor
		22.11	President Kennedy assassinated

	Date	Life events	Date	World events
	Oct.–Nov.	publishes *Les Mots* in *Les Temps modernes*		
	12–14.II	visits Czechoslovakia with de Beauvoir		
p. 370	**1964**			
	21.4	lectures for UNESCO on Kierkegaard	27.I	France enters into diplomatic relations with China
	23.5	lectures on morality and society at Istituto Gramsci	7.7	France starts selective military service
	1.6–10.7	visit to Russia	2.8	fighting begins in North Vietnam
	July–Sept.	stays in Rome; works on *Les Troyennes*	15.10	Khrushchev is replaced by Brezhnev and Kosygin
	16–22.10	refuses Nobel Prize	16.10	China explodes atom bomb
	19.II	gives interview for first issue of *Le Nouvel Observateur*		
p. 373	**1965**			
	25.1	applies to adopt Arlette Elkaïm as his daughter	7.2	US air raids on North Vietnam begin
	10.3	*Les Troyennes* premiered cancels lecture at Cornell	21.3	US spacecraft lands on moon
	March	campaigns against Gaston Defferre's proposals for amalgamation of SFIO and MRP	19.6	President Ben Bella of Algeria deposed by Houari Boumedienne, who forms new government
	June		10.7	Hungarian president Kadar resigns.
	July	to USSR and Helsinki	25.6	Succeeded by Gyula Kallai
	6.10	speaks at a COMES meeting about the meaning of 'avant garde'	10.7	World Peace Congress in Helsinki
	Dec.	gives qualified support to Mitterrand in elections	11.11	Ian Smith's Unilateral Declaration of Rhodesian Independence
			5.12	de Gaulle gets only 44 per cent of votes but is re-elected president, defeating Mitterrand
			19.12	
	1966			
	Feb.	writes preface for *La Promenade du dimanche* by Georges Michel, who becomes a friend	10–14.I	Sinyavsky and Daniel tried and sentenced to 7 and 5 years respectively in labour camps

		Date	Event	Date	Event
		May	gives limited support to communist candidate in presidential elections	10.6	International Red Cross suspends operations in Nigeria–Biafra war
		June	abstains from voting in second round	15–20.6	Pompidou becomes president and Jacques Chaban-Delmas prime minister
		summer	to Yugoslavia and Italy; meets student leaders in Rome	17.7	General Franco names Prince Juan Carlos as his eventual successor
		11.12	appears on French television to denounce My Lai massacre	21.10	Willy Brandt becomes chancellor as SDP and FDP form coalition
		19.12	chairs press conference on massacres	12.11	Solzhenitsyn expelled from Soviet Writers' Union
				19.11	My Lai massacre exposed
p. 405	1970	23.2	appears as witness at trial of Roland Castro	15.1	unconditional surrender of Biafra to Nigeria
		April	becomes nominal editor of La Cause du peuple	14.2	Tvardovsky removed from editorship of Novy Mir
		May	Pontalis and Pingaud resign from Les Temps modernes	23–28.5	Portuguese troops destroy guerrilla centre in Angola
		27.5	gives evidence at trial of two previous editors of La Cause du peuple	27.5	Gauche prolétarienne (GP) banned by French government
		11.6	Secours rouge founded	12.6	twelve Russians (including several Jews) try to hijack an aeroplane at Leningrad airport
		20 and 26.6	distributes La Cause du peuple in the street	28.6	US troops begin withdrawal from Cambodia
		26.6	visits Norway	28–29.9	Nasser dies, succeeded by Anwar Sadat
		July	assumes nominal editorship of other extremist papers	9.11	de Gaulle dies
		Sept.	makes speech to Renault workers outside factory	20.12	Gomulka replaced by Edward Gierek as first secretary
		21.10	takes part in a people's trial charging State with responsibility for industrial accidents		
		12.12			
p. 411	1971	15.1	starts contributing regularly to new paper J'accuse	5.2	US manned spacecraft Apollo 2 lands on moon

	13.2	takes part in attempt to occupy Sacré-Coeur	
	18.2	Secours rouge dissolved	
	April	breaks with Fidel Castro	
	14.5	*L'Idiot de la famille* vols 1 and 2 published	
	June	takes over *Révolution* and helps to found Libération press agency	
	summer	in Rome	
	7 and 27.11	joins in demonstrations against racism in Goutte-d'Or district	
p. 45	**1972 Feb.–March**	gives long filmed interview	
	14.2	ejected from Renault factory with group of militants	
	4.3	attends funeral of Pierre Overney, Renault worker killed by guard	
	summer	in Italy	
	Nov.	starts conversations with Benny Lévy and Philippe Gavi	
	winter	involved in preparations for launching daily paper *Libération*	
p. 418	**1973 Jan.**	publishes 'Elections, piège à cons' in *Les Temps modernes*	

25.4	200,000 protesters march on Capitol in Washington, DC, against Vietnam War
3.5	in East Germany Ulbricht succeeded by Hönecker as first secretary
8.6	Sinyavsky released
12.11	Nixon announces withdrawal of 45,000 soldiers from Vietnam and end of US offensive role
3–17.12	Indo-Pakistan War
25–27.2	Israel bombs South Lebanon in reprisal for guerrilla raids
1–15.5	Ulrike Meinhof and six other urban guerrillas arrested in West Germany
22.5	Nixon visits Moscow – first US president to do so
27.6	PCF and socialists agree on joint policy
5.7	Chaban-Delmas succeeded by Pierre Messmer as premier
17.7–11.8	trial of political dissenters in Prague: 46 of them gaoled
5.9	terrorists kill Israeli Olympic athletes at Munich airport
8.9	Israeli planes attack guerrilla bases in Syria and Lebanon
7.11	Nixon re-elected
18–30.12	US resumes heavy bombing of North Vietnam

Feb.	*Spiegel* interview condemning imprisonment of Baader-Meinhof gang
	Libération on sale
22.5 June	Sartre's eyesight deteriorates in Italy
summer	
autumn Oct.	Benny Lévy becomes his secretary moves from boulevard Raspail to larger flat in boulevard Edgar-Quinet
8.10	sued by the weekly *Minute* he appears in court and is fined 1 franc
Dec.	campaigns to rescue *Libération* from financial problems

p. 424 **1974**

April	recommends 'revolutionary abstention' in elections
May	publication of *On a raison de se révolter*
21.5	withdraws from some of the papers he had taken on
summer	holiday in the south of France and Italy; records long interview with de Beauvoir
Nov.	plans for television series
4.12	meeting with Andreas Baader in Stammheim prison

16–22.6	Nixon–Brezhnev summit in US; pact against nuclear war
30.6	Nixon makes television statement on Watergate and accepts responsibility for bugging
6–8.8	accidental US bombing of friendly villages in Cambodia
6.10	Arab states attack Israel on Yom Kippur
11.11	Israel and Egypt sign cease-fire agreement
13.2	Solzhenitsyn deported and deprived of Soviet citizenship
28.2	Heath succeeded by Wilson as minority Labour government takes office
2.4	Pompidou dies
25.4	military coup overthrows Dr Caetano's regime in Portugal
8.5	Willy Brandt resigns after spying incident involving aide
15.5	civilian government installed in Portugal
16.5	Helmut Schmidt becomes chancellor
19.5	Giscard d'Estaing defeats Mitterrand in presidential elections
27.5	Jacques Chirac becomes premier
8.8	Nixon announces resignation
9.8	Gerald Ford sworn in as president

p. 434	1979	14.3	speaks at colloquium organized by Benny Lévy and *Les Temps modernes* for Israelis and Palestinians to discuss peace
		June	Françoise Sagan's open 'love letter to Sartre' published in *Le Matin*
		20.6	takes part in press conference to help Vietnamese boat people
		26.6	received by Giscard d'Estaing with other delegates from committee helping boat people
		16.1	Shah and family leave Iran
		1.2	Ayatollah Khomeini returns after 15 years of exile and takes power
		4.5	Thatcher becomes prime minister with majority of 44 seats
		28.5	British government offers homes to 982 Vietnamese boat people
		7.6	voting for first directly elected European Parliament
		12.10	Castro addresses UN General Assembly
		23.10	six Czech dissidents including Václav Havel sentenced
		25.12	USSR invades Afghanistan
p. 437	1980	10, 17 and 24.3	conversations with Lévy published in *Nouvel Observateur*
		20.3	taken to Broussais hospital
		13.4	sinks into coma
		15.4	dies at nine p.m.
		19.4	buried in cemetery of Montparnasse
		23.4	cremated at Père Lachaise; ashes buried again at Montparnasse
		11.1	Castro and his brother Raúl assume greater powers
		22.1	dissident physicist Andrei Sakharov exiled from Moscow
		6.3	the first woman is elected to the French Academy – Marguerite Yourcenar
		6.5	after relaxation of emigration 10,000 Cubans seek political asylum at Peruvian embassy

Glossary of Abbreviations

bac	*baccalauréat*
CFDT	Confédération française démocratique du travail (second largest union, originally Christian)
CGT	Confédération générale du travail (largest union, dominated by the PCF)
CNE	Comité national des écrivains
COMES	Congrès de la Communauté européene des écrivains
CP	Communist Party
CVN	Comité Vietnam national
ENS	Ecole Normale Supérieure
FAC	Front pour l'action et coordination (anti-fascist organization)
FEN	Fédération de l'éducation nationale (main federation of teachers' unions)
FFI	Forces françaises de l'intérieur
FLN	Front de libération nationale
GP	Gauche prolétarienne (Maoist amalgamation of UJC(ML) and M22M)
JCR	Jeunesse communiste révolutionnaire (Trotskyist)
JEC	Jeunesse étudiante chrétienne
MCF(ML)	Mouvement communiste français (marxiste-léniniste) (Maoist)
MFA	Armed Forces Movement (Portuguese)
MRP	Mouvement républicain populaire
M22M	Mouvement du 22 mars (Maoist)
NRF	*Nouvelle Revue française*
OAS	Organisation de l'armée secrète
PCF	Parti communiste français
RDA	Révolution démocratique africaine
RDR	Rassemblement démocratique révolutionnaire
RPF	Rassemblement du peuple français (Gaullist)
SFIO	Section française de l'internationale ouvrière
SNESup	Syndicat national de l'enseignement supérieur (university teachers' union, controlled by left)
TNP	Théâtre National Populaire
UEC	Union des étudiants communistes
UJC(ML)	Union des jeunes communistes (marxistes-léninistes) (Maoist)
UNEF	Union nationale des étudiants de France
VLR	Vive la révolution (libertarian)

Introduction: Life Begins Tomorrow

When Jean-Paul Sartre was buried on 19 April 1980 a crowd of over fifty thousand converged on the procession and on the cemetery of Montparnasse, while even more people watched on television. No philosopher has ever had a bigger audience for his funeral, though it was not his philosophy that had made him famous. In France, a country where intellectuals are still honoured, he had for thirty-five years been the most celebrated intellectual. His face was familiar to people who had never seen him; his sayings were quoted by people who had never read his books. Witold Gombrowicz called him the Eiffel Tower of French culture. As a philosopher he was less original and less influential than Wittgenstein or Heidegger, but Sartre's importance does not rest on any single area of activity: we can say of him what he said of Proust – that his genius lies in the totality of his work considered as 'the totality of the manifestation of the person'.

As a playwright Sartre was highly successful but less innovative and less significant than Beckett or Ionesco. As a novelist Sartre completed only one work, *La Nausée* (*Nausea*), his other three novels being parts of an unfinished tetralogy. The bulk of his writing time was devoted to political journalism and biography, but he can hardly be called a journalist, while his biographies of Baudelaire, Genet and Flaubert are not biographies in the usual sense of the term. 'Writer' might look like the best one-word description of Sartre, but it is inadequate. Quantitatively his output was prodigious – his bibliographers have calculated that he averaged twenty pages a day throughout his long life[1] – but it was only when he was briefly in the army that he wholeheartedly pitched most of his time into writing. Before the war he would have liked to be a professional writer, but he had to earn his living as a schoolteacher until 1944, when he was almost forty. After the war his working life had two centres. He never enjoyed himself more than when he was philosophizing in his study, but his conscience was easier when he was functioning as a partyless politician, agitating, using his influence to champion the international underdog, fighting capitalism and imperialism, making speeches, editing a review, demonstrating, attending meetings, helping to organize political movements, travelling around the world, writing articles and books calculated to influence communism from outside.

This part of his life was governed by his fame and his eagerness to be useful. Because he attracted so much attention from the media, his presence was constantly in demand, and he was generous with it, but a discontinuity grew up between his public life and his writing. The young Sartre cared enormously about his relationship with his readers. He revised, reshaped, rewrote energetically, often following Simone de Beauvoir's canny advice, and in 1946 he maintained that the author's work is incomplete until the reader has collaborated by letting the book slowly disclose itself until it is 'a unified object'.[2] But once Sartre had become a public man his needs changed. Some energy went into maintaining his image. Should he visit the US during the Vietnam War? Should he reject the Nobel Prize? Should he declare himself in favour of Israel's survival as an independent state? These decisions were not taken without careful calculation about how his supporters would react. No longer depending on books to give him a relationship with the public, he no longer worried about whether readers would – or could – collaborate with him. Writing had become a private activity. He even took to working in his room instead of writing in cafés. He had always been careless about losing manuscripts; he became less interested in whether his books were published, or if published, read, or if read, understood. Few people can have read the million and a quarter words that make up his Flaubert biography and still fewer can have digested them. There was no question, latterly, of cutting, revising, reshaping to make a book more accessible; what mattered to Sartre was the relationship he had with his own intellect while sitting at his desk.

Though the best of his work is important, his importance depends no less on his central position in European intellectual history since the vogue for existentialism, which started in 1945. He could not have remained in this position thirty-five years if he had been averse to either inconsistency or opportunism. His uneven trajectory illustrates the problem of the intellectual caught between the impossibility of having and the impossibility of not having a relationship with the Communist Party. Even his philosophical pronouncements were liable to be adulterated by *Realpolitik*. In 1957, when he decreed that existentialism could hand itself over to Marxism if only Marxism would 'take on the human dimension (i.e the existentialist project) as the basis for anthropological knowledge',[3] he was behaving like the leader of a small country offering to make a deal with an irresistibly aggressive neighbour – he was an ideological Dollfuss trying to negotiate with a communist Hitler. Wanting to change Marxism, Sartre believed that his best chance lay in offering a conciliatory package; had he succeeded, his main importance would have been as a political philosopher, but he failed.

Even if he solved none of the problems he tackled, he plunged into them more deeply than anyone of comparable intellectual acuity, and it will go on being impossible to ignore him as a model. He confronted not only the difficulties created by the divergence of Soviet practice from Marxian theory but also the problems produced by the disintegration of the great empires, while he experimented in different ways of making both his literary activity and his physical presence into political weapons. Like Brecht but unlike Flaubert or D.H.Lawrence, he cared too much about public issues to immerse himself in fiction about personal relationships. Though he theorized authoritatively about commitment in literature, he became – no less than other committed writers – a rope in a tug-of-war between the compulsion to develop his artistic potential and the obligation to exert influence through didactic writing and political action.

He was not ineffectual. In France he had more influence than anyone else over intellectual opinion. He raised the temperature of anti-American feeling, made it harder for anti-semitism to surface and improved the intellectual standing of the Communist Party. He played a major role in politicizing a whole generation of French students, and the leaders of the 1968 rebellion had mostly absorbed Marxism through a Sartrean filter; during the same year his influence contributed – Czech witnesses tell us – to the slackening of oppression during the Prague Spring.

Though he managed to complete nine original plays, seven short stories and several screenplays, nearly all his other major projects in literature and philosophy were abandoned. How could the subject be closed? Why should it be? If energy had not been diverted into political action, he might have tried harder to complete literary and philosophical projects, but this is by no means certain. He deeply disliked bringing anything to a conclusion. In 1938, as soon as *La Nausée* appeared in the bookshops, he started planning to revive the central character, Antoine Roquentin, in a sequel. At the end of both his major philosophical books, *L'Etre et le Néant* and *Critique de la raison dialectique*, he indicates that the work is not to be regarded as complete. The gesture appears to be made more for his sake than the reader's, though there are those who applaud his failure to finish projects: he is shattering 'the myth of the coherently finished text, the myth that the contradictions that gave rise to the work have been resolved by an apparently cohesive textual narrative'.[4] But he tried hard not to leave his promises unredeemed. After ending *L'Etre et le Néant* (1943) by offering to follow it with a book on ethics, he went on until 1949 struggling with the problem of goodness: the notebooks contain even more words than the book, but he finally gave up. After finishing the first volume of the *Critique* in 1959, he wrote 782 pages (about 200,000 words) of the second.

All this unpublished work was not entirely wasted. Some of the material from the abandoned book on ethics went into *Saint Genet*; some of the ideas from the unfinished second volume of the *Critique* went into the Flaubert biography. The ideal way to read Sartre's work is not as a series of separate books but as a discontinuous and open-ended whole.

In the tetralogy *Les Chemins de la liberté* (a title which is misleadingly translated as *The Roads* to *Freedom*) he had relatively little difficulty in completing the first three volumes: nothing needed to be concluded. He wrote 223 pages of the last volume, *La Dernière Chance*, and he did not give up hope of finishing it until nine years after publishing the third volume, *La Mort dans l'âme* – the title is mistranslated as *Iron in the Soul*. Other uncompleted projects include the autobiography, the enormous biography of Flaubert, *La Psyché* (a phenomenological psychology), a book on Mallarmé, one on Tintoretto, *Les Communistes et la paix* (an apologia for the Party, abandoned in 1956 after Soviet tanks invaded Hungary) and *Pouvoir et liberté*, a collaborative book based on conversations with Benny Lévy (Pierre Victor).

Towards the end of Sartre's life interviewers often questioned him about the mass of unfinished work, but less is to be learnt from his answers than from the sequence in *La Nausée* when with an exquisite mixture of pleasure and pain Roquentin decides to give up his work on a historical biography. 'The true nature of the present stood revealed. It was what exists, and everything that was not present did not exist. The past did not exist ... For me the past was only a retreat: it was another way of living, a holiday, passivity.' But Roquentin can now picture the subject of his abandoned book, the Marquis de Rollebon, more vividly than ever before. 'I sighed, let myself lean back against my chair with a feeling of unbearable deprivation.' His immediate future will contain no holiday in the past.

Two of the crucial questions about Sartre are 'Why did he keep changing tack?' and 'Why did he go on committing himself to labours that even he – and no-one has been more of an intellectual Hercules – couldn't possibly have accomplished?' I cannot believe anybody has ever written more greedily and sensually than Sartre did. Even when he was in his twenties his satisfaction when a woman yielded him her virginity was almost eclipsed by the satisfaction of plucking words out of the air to describe the seduction, moment by moment, in a long letter to Simone de Beauvoir. He was never more impatient than just before starting to write. According to Jean Cau, who worked as his secretary from 1946 to 1957, he would come into the flat, when he had slept elsewhere, and immediately sit down on the hard chair at his desk, never stopping to take off his jacket and tie.[5] He never typed, and the fountain pens he used – his friend Michelle

Vian has kept several of them – feel as strongly impregnated with his physical presence as the stems of the pipes he smoked.

When he was writing letters, diaries and short articles, his pleasure was unalloyed; when he worked at long-term projects, it was tarnished by ambivalence. Alternative work would be clamouring for his time, and simultaneously he would feel guilty about enjoying words instead of taking action. Something survived from his passionate boyhood identification with the heroes of adventure stories, from his fantasies of himself as the dashing rescuer of beautiful victims, and this helped to colour his abortive adult forays into the Resistance and political activity. His constant restlessness derived partly from a mixture of romantic optimism and jaded guilt feelings. Even when he was writing about politics he felt that he should be fighting more actively against injustice; he also believed that he was wasting his talent as a writer. In 1969 he grumbled that almost everything he had written was 'exactly the opposite of what I wanted to write'.[6] He felt as though he had spent the major part of his life working, like a hack, to commission, or like a journalist, in response to current events. This feeling is relevant to all those moments of conflict which had been prefigured by Roquentin's triumphant surrender – moments of reluctantly fending off a seductive alternative to keep faith with the project in hand, or moments of deliciously treacherous capitulation.

The betrayal was fourfold – a betrayal of his readers and his intentions, combined with a more conscious betrayal of literature and his talent for it. If anyone in France was qualified to succeed Gide, Claudel and Valéry, it was Sartre, who instead took a principled pleasure in refusing to support literature as an establishment or as a way of life, treating it rather as a myth in need of demolition. According to Roland Barthes, Sartre's importance lies partly in his being the man 'situated at the precise historical point of literature's disintegration'.[7] If the reason Leonardo da Vinci failed to complete any of his works is that he had such a high regard for the greatness of art, Sartre failed for the opposite reason.

Not that he could possibly have succeeded. His Flaubert biography was intended to swallow the ocean of available data. 'We have at the outset no assurance that such a summary is possible and that the truth is not multiple.' His object in the second part of the Critique was nothing less than to prove that history added up to a single truth, a single meaning which could be explained without postulating a divine, extraterrestrial observer. The Marxist viewpoint was valid, Sartre believed, only if dialectical materialism could be made to reveal the unity of history. Could its 'diverse multiplicities' be viewed as 'connected and merged in their very oppositions and diversities by an intelligible totalization from which there is no appeal'?

No doubt Sartre would have achieved less if he had not set himself impossible tasks; he poised himself in a highly unusual way between the past and the future. He pictures consciousness as a blank, aimed like an arrow at the task ahead. This idea derives from Husserl, but we need to look at Sartre's temperament to see why Husserl's intentionality appealed to him so strongly. It is no accident that one of his favourite words was *dépasser* (go beyond, subsume, transcend): like a runner, waiting for the starting pistol with his weight poised forward, or like a child trying to fall asleep on Christmas eve, Sartre found it almost unbearable that the future hadn't already begun. *La vie commence demain.* Simone de Beauvoir has written shrewdly about his indifference to the present and the past. 'Sartre refuses to admit that he has any identity connecting him with his past ... He rarely reminisces.' He could talk with complete critical detachment about what he had said, written or done: 'The truth is that he has already stopped recognizing himself in the old Sartre he is talking about. What he really is, he believes, exists in the future, and in consequence he never feels any vanity about what he has done in the past ... On the other hand he displays immense pride when he talks about what he's expecting to do. This is the metaphysical and unpersonal pride of a liberty which tries to be absolute, which refuses to be constrained by circumstances.'

He was afraid of possessions, afraid they would possess him or anchor him to one place, one situation, one identity. Had he been inclined to keep the money he earned, he could have become extremely rich; instead he not only spent, gave and tipped with compulsive generosity, but supported a small retinue of dependants. The busier he became, the easier he found it to give money rather than time, attention or sympathy. Nor did he ever want to own space. For much of his life he made his home in hotels or in his mother's little flat, where his room was so small that he could not have kept many books in it, even if he had not been in the habit of discarding them as soon as he had read them. (His formidable memory had been strengthened by a lycée education, which involved learning long passages by heart.) The narrow divan became his bed at night, and in the morning, when Jean Cau arrived, 'a fearsome smell of tobacco and nocturnal breathing, spread into an atmosphere you could cut with a knife, jumped at my face and into my throat'.[8] Cau then worked at a table which had to be cleared for lunch if Sartre was going to eat with his mother.

But with space on paper Sartre was lavish. He never squeezed additions or alterations into a margin, and whenever he had to cross words out he started a new sheet. He was in Italy with Michelle Vian when he wrote the preface to André Gorz's *Le Traître*. Arriving at the post office to mail the manuscript to the Paris publisher, she found that the cost of postage would have left them without enough cash to pay their hotel bill. With a pair of scissors she snipped off the unused paper from each page.[9]

Sartre felt most at home in cafés and restaurants where he could annex space by dominating the conversation and exhaling smoke. He noticed that pipe-smoking made him feel like settling wherever he was, watching people and talking through reassuring clouds of smoke. But, like Kafka, he never felt more free than when he was writing, creating an imaginary space. Paper as magic carpet; pen as wand. But if he felt uncomfortable with the literary conquest of imaginary space, his discomfort had one of its roots in the awkward relationship his mind had with his body. After a paradisal infancy centred on the belief that he was beautiful, he huffily but systematically tried to reject his body. To reassure his mind that it had nothing to fear from sibling rivalry with his maltreated body he consistently ignored all the messages it sent out. He resisted fatigue, treated pain as if it were a challenge. To step up his productivity he made reckless use of drugs and stimulants, taking sedatives when he needed to relax. He resented the time he had to spend on washing, shaving, cleaning his teeth, taking a bath, excreting, and he would economize by carrying on conversations with Cau through the bathroom door. He had no personal vanity, took no pleasure in buying clothes. His shoes were bought for him by his mother – his small feet were the same size as hers. When his smoke-stained teeth began to decay, he refused to waste time on seeing a dentist, but even when his face was swollen with an abscessed gum, he would stubbornly settle down to work at his desk. He took immeasurable pride in his intellect – 'I've got a golden brain'[10] – but the punitive attitude to his body was based on the feeling that it could be written off. Occasionally he took exercise to keep fit, but the interest flickered only briefly and he did not want to have his squint corrected surgically. If his constitution had not been exceptionally strong, he could not have treated it so ruthlessly. Throughout his life he smoked excessively, overworked exorbitantly, ate and drank carelessly. He had no hankering for the kind of balance W.B.Yeats craved:

> Labour is blossoming or dancing where
> The body is not bruised to pleasure soul ....

Sartre went on bruising the body to pleasure mind, trying incessantly to outpace himself. When he defines man as the creature who is not identical with himself, he has Heidegger's philosophy as one of his models and his own habits as the other.

Nietzsche observed that all philosophy is 'the confession of its author and a kind of involuntary unconscious memoir'. With his pronouncements the philosopher is pointing to the 'relative positioning of the innermost drives in his nature'.[11] Sartre's declaration of war against the idea of the self points to his hostility against the self as represented by the body. Even his insistence on free will and his resistance to determinism hinge on his refusal to see his own existence as conditioned by uncontrollable physical characteristics. The body, which he had not chosen, could be disregarded: his contempt for it encouraged him to believe that the individual self had no existence. Throughout his career he would find various ways of escaping from the first person singular – into a partnership, into fictional characters, into groups, into political movements, into theories about the collective, into the self-oblivion induced by drink or drugs or extreme fatigue. In 1956–7 he made his most extremist pronouncements against the individual ego, praising Soviet man for subordinating his identity to the group and questioning whether anyone can ever accurately say 'I did it'. Sartre's fanatical faith in the powers of the conscious intellect and his resistance to Freudian ideas about the unconscious are equally rooted in the same inner drive. Needing to believe that the human mind was capable of anything and everything, he was irked by the notion that it might be incapable of coming fully to grips with itself.

Privately he was more interested in dominating a group than in subordinating himself. Almost invariably friendly, he liked the effects he could have on other people more than he liked other people, and in conversation he took pleasure in pleasing. With his musical voice and his quick mind he had a genius for the chats that ranged between fantasy, gossip and practical suggestions. As a companion he was charming, droll, endlessly entertaining. He talked rapidly, trying to catch up with his racing thoughts. With new acquaintances he seldom failed to make a favourable impression, but in a foreign city he was reluctant to ask a stranger the way, wanting neither to be seen as a middle-class tourist nor to 'inflict a disagreeable presence' on anyone in the street.[12]

Though the drug-taking habit had its origins in a campaign to increase output, he began to take pleasure in the violence he was doing himself. For about twenty years he 'abused drugs a great deal' (as he put it) but never so much as while writing the *Critique.* He was taking corydrane and orthodrine. The unpublished Part Two, which was more ambitious, could hardly have failed, had he completed it, to be his most important philosophical work, but not content with sabotaging his chances of writing in a lucid and organized way, he was deliberately putting his life at risk: 'As soon as one passed a certain point, one began to be destroyed, and the risk was a reality. One liked having blurred ideas which were vaguely interrogative and which then disintegrated. It also meant one could drop dead, but there was no knowing when.'

Like Nietzsche, Sartre took an almost religious pleasure in the sense of battling against himself. There could be no complete dichotomy, of course, between mortifying the flesh and fighting the brain. In the same way that he resisted fatigue, he resisted his own ideas, challenged them, questioned whether it wouldn't be better to turn them upside down. Philosophically the habit of dialectical reversal was picked up from Hegel. Karl Marx, who had also picked it up, found, like Sartre, that it encouraged him to leave books unfinished. Both Marx and Sartre tended to define their position by making someone else's untenable and later to make their own untenable. They were both liable to start a book on the basis of convictions that were repudiated before it was finished.

Without setting out to provide a rationale for this habit of leaving projects uncompleted, Sartre does this in the *Critique*, arguing that human action always tends to become something different from what was intended. When a man looks back at his work, simultaneously recognizing and failing to recognize himself in it, acknowledging that it isn't what he wanted to do but that he couldn't have done it any better, he is being forced 'by an immediate dialectical movement to acknowledge necessity as freedom's destiny in exteriority'.[13] This is a form of alienation, which invariably begins as soon as the individual objectifies himself in action. Other people can immediately rob him of his intention. Sartre was basing his ideas about human activity on his own activity as a writer, and there may be a connection between his misgivings about stolen or deflected intentions and his pleasure in abandoning positions he had formerly maintained. Inevitably this involved him in betraying friends, admirers and supporters who had rallied around the idea as soon as they saw it flying from his flagstaff, but since their support had helped to rob him of his intention, they deserved to be punished.

Even when he was young, his attitude to fans and supporters was highly ambivalent. Following the loss of his infantile omnipotence, the loss of his mother when she remarried left him with an uncomfortable awareness of a dichotomy between the impression he had of himself and the impression other people had of him. His strongest need was to be in command of their reactions to him. Lusting for fame, which could bring this power, he was aware of his brain as an aggressive weapon. Part of his need to keep shifting positions was the need to bring the weapon constantly into play. The boxer can never afford to think about what he did in the last round: what matters is what he is doing now. If other people got stuck with yesterday's ideas, that was because they were the audience. He was the champion.

But that's not all there is to it. Working and living are not separate in this man whose main activity is writing. Long before he took to using the ugly word 'totalization' he was practising an instinctive dialectic in which each part of his life must relate to the whole and the whole to each part, while the living subject makes his peace with the image he tries to form of himself from outside. Sartre's passion for biography starts out of an impulse, already strong in childhood, to visualize his own experience from the viewpoint of posterity. He tries to live biographically. He can never surrender himself to the experience of the moment without remembering that it is already sliding into the past. As he says in *Les Mots*, 'Try as I might to throw myself into whatever I took on, into work, anger, friendship, I'm always about to deny the self in me that wants it. I'm betraying myself in the middle of passion by the jubilant anticipation of my future treachery.' With one eye on the biography that remains obstinately in the future, he can never enjoy the present. The book he's writing, the woman he's kissing, the words he's saying can never engage his full attention. The part belongs to the whole and the alternative futures never stop trying to push each other out of the way. Like Roquentin he comes closest to being himself at the moment of changing his mind. The commitment to betrayal and self-betrayal leads to a certain passivity, but it is closely intertwined with activity in liberating himself from attachments in day-to-day living. Nauseated or not, Roquentin's self-critical consciousness is the part of him that functions best; Sartre similarly observes himself observing, while the revulsion from emotional commitment is encouraged by identification of the self with consciousness as he portrays it – something which has no ballast and no substance. Nothing in his life must be allowed to obstruct transparency. Austerely puritanical and ruthlessly ambitious, he sacrifices himself, his projects, his lovers again and again while the destruction fuels his self-aggrandizement. His political passions are generous and the generosity is genuine but compromised. He condemns givers of gifts as aggressors seeking power over those who accept, but he gives relentlessly while remaining endlessly on guard to protect himself against the generosity of others. When given presents, he gives them away; borrowing ideas he conceals his indebtedness, even from himself, knowing anyway that he will soon discard what he has taken.

His capacity for change was heightened by his awareness that we must never expect to recognize ourselves in our completed work, that books and actions deviate like children from parental intentions. Sartre had an extraordinary capacity for change. Disliking the idea of the static self and refusing to be tethered philosophically, politically or personally to any commitment, he believed he could transform his life like a snake sloughing off dead skin.[14] Even physically he changed more than most people do, the slight, narrow-shouldered boy growing into the wide, squat man who was dubbed by his American friends 'Mr Five-by-five'. When he was twenty-four, his ambition, he told Simone de Beauvoir, was to become both Stendhal and Spinoza; later, applying philosophy to politics and *Realpolitik* to philosophy, he tried to negotiate a peace treaty between Marx and Freud. When this diplomacy failed, he fell back on a gigantic biography of Flaubert founded on a combination of Marxist and Freudian insights. By then the young Sartre who never voted had turned into the radical knight-errant who rode on international airlines. The mature Sartre never tired of demonstrating, agitating, signing manifestos, making political speeches, attending rallies, though, to seasoned politicians, he still seemed politically immature, incurably naive. Despite his formidable intellect, he never quite arrived at what he called 'the age of reason', at adult stability, though the young writer who made up his mind that success would never induce him to spend less time on cafés, cinemas or girls, had grown into the compulsive worker who always wore moccasins to avoid wasting time on tying up shoelaces.[15] But the young man who declared that all anti-communists were swine had turned into an old man who declared that the Communist Party was the worst enemy of freedom, and the champion of individual freedom had denied freedom to the individual.

But while he took an almost perverse pleasure in asserting his own freedom through protean self-transformation, he could neither learn from his mistakes nor keep hold of his most valuable insights. He had so much faith in his ability to form new theories that he forgot the old ones: rather than build higher on an old foundation he would start all over again with a new one.

He had two styles of writing because he had two methods of writing. When he wanted to achieve a polished prose, as in *Les Mots*, he would fill only the first three lines on each page, leaving space for multiple revisions of each sentence. Nor would he ever take drugs while writing what he considered to be 'literary' works. But for him the distinction between 'literary' and 'philosophical' books was less meaningful than the distinction between work which demanded painstaking writing and work which did not. If he approximated, while talking, teaching or lecturing, to thinking out loud, he approximated in most of his writing to talking, teaching or lecturing. His predominant feeling was that style should take care of itself, and that a writer should not waste time on painstaking revision of each sentence. He still enjoyed the process of finding the right words and arranging them in the right order but forbade himself to believe that the task of writing was any more than the task of extricating sentences from himself, as if the book already existed inside his consciousness. Drugs not only had the effect of encouraging this illusion: they seemed to be speeding the process of extrication, and, as he went on working in this hurried way, Sartre came to depend less and less on either observation or research: he wrote as if everything he needed was already present inside his brain.

This was something he increasingly needed to believe as he grew older. The future was shrinking as demands on his time were increasing. Always unrealistically optimistic about completing at least some of the projects that were in abeyance, he had more and more reason to hurry. The quality of his writing deteriorates as he relies less on new observation, information, research, more on knowledge he has accumulated, and more on drugs that seemed to make him go faster. In chasing after his ideas, he was also chasing after the creativity that had deserted him.

Much of his better, earlier, writing had depended on his ability to chronicle the play of consciousness, dovetailing the drama into accurate description of external circumstances. Some of his best prose is to be found in *La Nausée*, which is written in the form of a diary, and in his army diaries, *Carnets de la drôle de guerre*. In these fictional and factual journals the pulse of the sentences excitingly follows the rhythm of Sartre's thinking, whereas the latter part of the Flaubert biography is written in amorphous sentences with flaccid rhythms. Judging by the number of words he was producing each day, the army diaries were not written any more carefully, but the life Sartre was living then was more conducive to good writing, though he never shut himself entirely off from new experiences and new social contacts, on which observations could have been based. While he was teaching he was alert to the people around him; *Les Chemins de la liberté* rests on his prewar friendships in Paris and on his experience in the army and the Stalag; his later writing is not nourished to any comparable extent by the life that was going on all round him. He was allowing himself to be seduced by his own powers of analytical improvisation, rather like a composer who refuses to compose except by improvising. Sartre's fluency was prodigious, but even in his earliest fictions the narrative impulse was liable to be overtaken by impulses towards description, analysis and satire. At the same time as chronicling the movements of a consciousness, he was not only philosophizing about the nature of consciousness and the nature of reality, he was competitively measuring himself against other chroniclers. The crude feeling 'anything you can do I can do better' was elaborated into a sophisticated game of pastiche. But once he had proved that he was capable of becoming the greatest French novelist since Proust, he lost interest in both artistry and art. 'Artistic activity', he wrote in *L'Idiot de la famille*, 'consists of devaluing the real by realizing the imaginary.'[16] Though he had been moving towards this position since his early work on the image, it does not seem that his sabotage of his own artistry was entirely deliberate, even if destructive and self-destructive tendencies were at work. Is he rationalizing these tendencies in himself or justifiably exposing them in Flaubert when he condemns the great novelist for making the world unreal by making himself into an artist?

The activity of philosophizing had never been entirely separate for him from forming theories based on generalizations. Travelling when he was young to new countries, he would start to formulate theories about them before he had given himself time to observe what was going on around him; later on, at editorial meetings of *Les Temps modernes*, he would talk authoritatively and at length about books he had not read and films he had not seen, constructing elaborate theories on the basis of what he had been told by a friend.[17] This tendency is paralleled in his later books by the pronounced drift towards abstraction. On a minimum of observation and research he erects a vast superstructure of theory. At the same time his growing distaste for literary artistry accompanied a growing aversion to subjectivity, interiority and individuality. Temperament and political conviction both pushed him towards the collective. A glance at the essays collected in the ten volumes of *Situations* shows how as time passed he concerned himself less and less with literature, art and the private self, more and more with politics and public issues. His mind was such that almost any experience or observation would prompt theoretical generalization but he is at his best as a writer when he is drawing more on recent memories of experience and observation than on his reflective abstractions. In *L'Etre et le Néant* the brilliant analysis of interpersonal relationships seems no further removed from Sartre's private experience than the examples based on observation of café life. But implicit in his later, much more grandiose idea of totalizing history is the dismissal of private experience as irrelevant. This is requisite anyway if the intellectual is to do what Sartre said he must do – put himself entirely in the service of the masses.

In this introduction I have approximated to the method Sartre uses in his biographies. I have tried to give a synchronic impression of the whole man, summarizing tendencies and generalizing about traits which remained more or less constant while providing only the sketchiest indications of development from one phase of his life to the next. He stuck more rigidly than most men do to the strategies he evolved for dealing with everyday life. He worked, for instance, between fixed hours and regularly went abroad at the same time each year. But one of his reasons for needing rigid patterns was that he cultivated discontinuity so assiduously. He loved changing his mind, rejecting principles that had been vital, making a fresh start. He was consistent in nothing – not even in his love for freedom. But the full story of his divagations needs to be told chronologically.

For a Private Future
(1905–31)

ONE · *Poulou*

The 1964 autobiography *Les Mots* is a distorting mirror. Sartre trusted his theories more than he trusted facts and he had been trying for more than fifty years to push his childhood out of the way. He felt neither love nor respect but hatred towards its events, and it would have been out of character for him to do what most autobiographers do – reconstruct by interviewing surviving relatives and other people who remember the background, hunting through attics and drawers for old diaries, letters, notebooks, school reports, photographs, scrapbooks, newspaper clippings. Sartre was less interested in the past than in his present interpretation of it, and what emerges is the myth of a gifted child whose gifts came from nowhere. He liked to think of himself as self-created, indebted to no-one.

He congratulates himself on being only fifteen months old when his father died. 'The death of Jean-Baptiste was my greatest piece of good fortune ... Had he lived, my father would have lain down on top of me with all his weight and squashed me ... I didn't even have to forget him: taking French leave, Jean-Baptiste had denied me the pleasure of meeting him. Today I am still astonished at how little I know about him.'[1] Sartre knew a great deal more than he was willing to admit: as in conversations and interviews, he kept his knowledge to himself.

Jean-Baptiste Sartre was a naval officer, and in a passage that was to be discarded from *La Nausée* the son identifies with the father's need to cut loose from France and the family: 'Stayed a year at Tokyo and Osaka, saved some money, then I left to wander round Java, Shanghai, Indo-China – My last links with France were broken ... I was really alone in the world: of my family one cousin was supposed to be left in Périgord.'[2] The son inherited the father's need for adventure and independence, but Jean-Paul Sartre was an adventurer of a different sort.

His brilliance and his diminutive stature were also inherited. Sartre was five foot two, and his father, who was about half an inch shorter, had excelled himself at the prestigious Ecole Polytechnique, volunteering for the navy when he graduated in 1897. After embarking on the frigate *Melpomène* at the beginning of October, he was in Senegal by the end of the year and soon afterwards in China.[3] Since the Sino-Japanese war of 1894–5, Britain, France, Germany and Russia had been vying with each other for concessions in China, which was unfortunate for Jean-Baptiste Sartre: it was there that he contracted the enterocolitis which was to cut his life so short. He appeared to have recovered his health by 1903, and when he was in Cherbourg another old *polytechnicien*, Georges Schweitzer, now a naval engineer there, introduced him to his pretty twenty-one-year-old sister, Anne-Marie, whose nickname was 'You'.[4] Within weeks the young officer was asking her to be his wife. They were married in Paris on 5 May 1904 when he was twenty-nine and she was nearly twenty-two (not nineteen as Sartre says in *Les Mots*).

Georges and Anne-Marie were cousins of Albert Schweitzer. Schweitzer is the German word for Swiss and the family seems to have had this name since moving from Switzerland to Alsace after the Thirty Years War. Albert Schweitzer's grandfather was a francophile protestant schoolteacher who opened a grocery store on the ground floor of his house in Pfaffenhofen, twenty-two miles from Strasbourg. The youngest of his three sons, Louis, who became a pastor, was Albert's father. Anne-Marie's father was the oldest of the three brothers, Karl, who had refused to become a pastor. After passing his *agrégation* he made a career as a German teacher, working in Mâcon, where he married a girl five years his junior, Louise Guillemin, daughter of a catholic lawyer. At the age of forty-two Karl Schweitzer produced a thesis on the sixteenth-century poet Hans Sachs and thirteen years later another thesis, in Latin, on Guillaume IX, the troubadour and Duc d'Aquitaine (1071–1127). A pioneer of the direct method of teaching foreign languages, Schweitzer published textbooks for teaching German, English and French, collaborating with another teacher, Emile Simonnot, on a series, *Deutsche Lesebücher*. The first of the four children Louise bore him was a girl who died in infancy; the other three, two boys and a girl, she brought up as catholics, so their father had little to do with their education. The daughter, Anne-Marie, was the youngest.

Books had been written on both sides of Sartre's family. Eymard Sartre, Jean-Baptiste's father, was a country doctor in the Dordogne and had written a medical book while in his twenties. He married a pharmacist's daughter and their relationship never recovered from his post-nuptial discovery that far from being rich landowners, her family was penniless. For forty years husband and wife scarcely spoke to each other.

By joining the navy their son Jean-Baptiste had escaped from this unhappy home, and in the winter of 1904, wanting to leave the navy, he applied for six months of unpaid leave. After this was granted, he stayed with his wife throughout most of her pregnancy, but his leave ended in the middle of May, before the birth of the baby which was due at the end of May or the beginning of June. When a boy was finally born on 21 June he was given the names Jean-Paul-Baptiste-Eymard. The father was trying to extricate himself from the navy. He applied for a year's unpaid leave to 'recover his health', but this was refused. When he at last came home in November, he was delighted with his infant son: 'He laughs at everything,' Jean-Baptiste reported, 'moves incessantly, wriggles, yells at the top of his voice, laughs at noises but never cries. His look is curious, intelligent and very gentle... He's very advanced for his age.'[5] But the happiness of the trio was interrupted by a recrudescence of the enterocolitis together with bronchitis. The baby was nine months old when his twenty-three-year-old mother discovered that her husband was dying. They went to a small farm near Thiviers, his birthplace, where he died on 17 September 1906, eight weeks after his thirty-second birthday.

To qualify for a widow's pension Anne-Marie had to convince the navy that her husband had died from the enterocolitis contracted in China, and it would take her nearly a year to do this.[6] With no income, no career, no means of earning, she took refuge in the home of her parents in Meudon, half way between Paris and Versailles, where the baby's presence did not protect her from being treated like an adolescent. There were three bedrooms in the flat: the one that Anne-Marie shared with her son was known as the children's room, and when she was invited out to dinner, she had not only to ask permission in good time but to be home before ten. As he learned to talk, the boy was encouraged to call his grandfather Karl and his grandmother Mamie. Their authority was superior to his mother's. 'Karl and Mamie are waiting.' The boy was nicknamed Poulou – a name his mother was to go on using throughout her life.

Sixty-two years old, Karl Schweitzer had still been working when his son-in-law died, but had applied for retirement and had moved to Meudon from Mâcon before his daughter came home; to earn food for the two extra mouths he reversed his decision about retiring. Anne-Marie took over the job of running the house, while her father, providing money for household expenses, provided none for clothes.

Charles Schweitzer's self-esteem was fortified by other people's reactions. Though his handsome white beard was stained with tobacco, he looked like God the Father, and in the parish church worshippers had sometimes flung themselves at his feet.[7] At mealtimes he would be served by the women, and when he wanted the salt or the bread, he would point silently with his forefinger.

Lying between the Vosges mountains and the Rhine, Alsace had been a battleground since the Roman period, and it was to change hands many times after Louis XIV annexed it in 1648. Lutheran pastors had to surrender part of their church permanently to the catholics, and to make the whole of it available for mass during stipulated periods on Sundays. Rivalry between catholics and protestants revolved around this enforced sharing of churches. In 1871, when the Franco-Prussian war ended and most of Alsace-Lorraine was integrated into Bismarck's empire, Karl Schweitzer, opting for France, had become Charles Schweitzer, but he often revisited Günsbach and Pfaffenhofen, taking Poulou with him. Charles's brother Louis was pastor at Günsbach, a predominantly protestant community, but the catholic presence was permanently visible in the small chancel, where two gilt statues stood above the gilded altar.[8] Patriotically Alsatian, or at least passionately anti-Prussian, Charles Schweitzer alarmed both the boy and the two women with his outbursts against German railway officials and waiters.[9]

Growing up without a father, and with a mother subject to the tyrannical authority of 'Charlémamie', as they were jointly called, Poulou was dominated no less than the two women were by the strong-willed old man. He shouted to get his own way, and instead of resisting, the grandmother withdrew into her migraines, her bedroom, her bed. She was even resigned to Charles's infidelities. He had always been proud of his looks and the admiration they won from female pupils. He was sixty-five when a former pupil – an unmarried teacher – became his mistress. He was seen going into hotels with her and the affair continued until she left to take up a teaching job in Algeria.[10] Perhaps the relationship played a part in giving Anne-Marie a revulsion against sexuality. She saw few men. Cuddles with her small son had to suffice, and her attentiveness may have strengthened his tendency to be passive. One of the Germans who came to lunch with her father was a bald doctor, who regularly tried to kiss her; when she complained to Charles, she was made to feel guilty: she was either fantasizing or making her father seem inhospitable by resisting.

Sartre would later remember the tall patriarch as in a photograph, wearing a panama hat, a cream flannel suit with black stripes, a white piqué waistcoat with a watch-chain across it and a pince-nez dangling at the end of a cord. In the evening, when they went to meet him from the overhead railway, he would strike an attitude, 'beard to windward, body straight, feet at right angles, chest expanded, arms open wide ... I rushed foward, carrying fruit and flowers, and to my grandfather's delight, arrived at his knees, feigning breathlessness; he picked me up, lifted me at arm's length towards the clouds, clutched me to his heart, murmuring: "My little treasure!"'[11]

Sartre's squint and his defective vision dated from a cold caught at the seaside resort of Arcachon, near Bordeaux when he was only three or four. It led to a disease in his right eye, which was left with only ten per cent vision. This was no hindrance to early happiness. He had everything done for him – he was washed, dressed, undressed, his shoes were put on, his hair brushed. He seldom cried, was never noisy.[12] It was easy to win praise from his mother. 'I enjoyed the princely freedom of an actor who can keep the audience in suspense while improving on his own performance. I was adored, I was adorable ... I was told I was good-looking, and I believed it.' He was fair and rosy-complexioned, with plump cheeks and curls. Endless photographs of him were taken; his mother retouched them with crayons. If Sartre was later to understand the dim mental processes of Flaubert's childhood, it was partly by dint of reconstructing his own: the child is not compelled to be active; instead he 'makes giddying capitulations to the established nature he feels inside himself as the product *of Other people* ... I escape from you by becoming, to spite you, what you wanted me to be.'[13] The reasons for wanting to escape are different, but the refuge in placidity is comparable: from early childhood the boy fails either to surface comfortably into adult activity or to withdraw into animal wellbeing. Poulou's domain, like the young Gustave's, is pathos. Life is too frightening – a rough game for older boys. One layer of emotionality is affected and therefore painless; the deeper layer is painful, but not for long. Disguised and failing to assert themselves, the emotions cannot survive.[14] Able neither to challenge the paterfamilias nor to tolerate his own powerlessness, the boy withdraws into inertia, which is reinforced, like Flaubert's, by the mother's inclination to treat the young boy as if he were a girl.

As the only female among the surviving children, Anne-Marie must have longed for a sister, and with her ageing mother more involved than her aged father in handling the baby, the inevitable tendency was to emphasize the feminine side of his nature. If Flaubert's mother was like a daughter to the husband who was nine years her senior, Sartre's mother was still being a daughter to her parents while bringing up her son as if her were a daughter. His curly hair was allowed to grow long. His clothes were girlish. Eventually the adult Sartre would force himself into a mode of living diametrically opposed to Flaubert's. Refusing to be a mere artist or intellectual, Sartre would do his utmost to show that life did not scare him and to prove himself as a man of action, rejecting his inclination to inertia as violently as he reviled his bourgeois childhood. But as a child he was as disinclined as Flaubert was to rebel, though it may be inferred from the beginning of his story 'L'Enfance d'un chef' that there were attendant anxieties. Lucien is frightened he may really be in danger of changing into a girl.

In 1911, finally obliged, at the age of sixty-seven, to retire from the school at Meudon, Charles Schweitzer took his three dependants to Paris. Indefatigable, he founded an institute for teaching French to foreign students.

It was obvious that most of his pupils would be German, but anti-German sentiment had to be subordinated to economic necessity. In arguments about whether France should recover Alsace by fighting for it, he took a pacifist stance. The family settled into a sixth-floor flat at 1 rue le Goff, near the Gare du Luxembourg. In 'L'Enfance d'un chef' when the Fleurier family moves to Paris, it is 'like a magnesium flash' for the child. He 'could no longer sleep because of the cinemas, cars and streets'.

Though they did not go regularly to mass on Sundays, Poulou was being brought up as a catholic. Neither Charles's protestantism nor Louise's catholicism was deep; it was mainly to spite him that she insisted on bringing up her three children as catholics. At mealtimes religion was still the main battlefield: when Charles mocked, Louise would rap him over the knuckles: 'Stop it, papa.' Almost no religious memories would stay in Sartre's mind, except for the vague feeling that only God could see him when, with a match, he set fire to the net curtains.[15] He was taken to church, but mainly to hear the organ music at St-Sulpice or Notre-Dame.[16] If he came to associate the mass with good behaviour, it was partly because Anne-Marie told him that in church a really good boy could stay as still as a statue. He exerted himself to stop his chair from creaking and made no noise with his feet, but he hated having to kneel because it hurt his knees.[17]

His tendency to inertia was encouraged by the sense of being treasured, cosseted, idolized not only by the women but by the godlike old man, who began to take more interest as the boy became more articulate. Charles's two sons, who had never recovered from his indifference to them, were irked, when they visited the flat, to find him besotted with the child, but it is not uncommon for a man who has never let his own children sit on his lap to spend hours dandling a grandchild. Charles would relax in the garden, sitting in a deckchair, a glass of beer in his hand, while he watched the boy playing. Poulou's childish pronouncements were taken with a seriousness that encouraged him to give a non-stop performance. The appreciative old man always sided with the boy when Louise told him to stop his monkey-tricks, and the grandmother flounced off to shut herself in her bedroom.

Poulou was about five when he became scared of death. On the quai Voltaire a tall old woman in black clothes was madly mumbling as she passed him: 'I'm going to put that boy in my pocket.' During a long holiday at Arcachon, he was playing in the garden outside the house of a dying man, when he saw a 'gloomy hole, the cellar which had been opened; I was blinded by an indescribable loneliness and horror'.[18] At night in bed he would lie on his left side, facing the wall, waiting fearfully for the image that would unfailingly appear – a skeleton with a scythe. Once he'd seen it, he could turn on to his right side and sleep peacefully.[19]

But in the daylight, he would be reminded of the old hag by a picture in a book, or by a song his mother sang. In 'L'Enfance d'un chef', the boy Lucien conjures up for himself an image of something round, white, soft as a cloud. Trying to see it, he feels as though he were falling into it, head first, and has to struggle back to the room he is in, as if from a trance.[20] For Poulou the danger was that a dark mouth might open anywhere, in broad daylight, to snap him up.

Most of his experiences, though, were more in harmony with the big anniversary party to celebrate the opening of Charles Schweitzer's institute. Poulou was dressed as an angel in a blue muslin dress with stars in his fair curly hair and his wings; he moved angelically among the guests, offering them oranges from a basket, and being patted. He was doing, as always, what was required of him. Looking back on his childhood, Sartre felt he had tried to keep reinventing himself in a series of vain attempts not to feel superfluous. He was bitterly jealous of his grandfather's fifty-year-old collaborator, Emile Simonnot, an ugly man who waxed his moustache, dyed his forelock and came to lunch every Thursday. One evening, when a party was held at the institute and Anne-Marie was playing Chopin in the flickering gaslight, Charles said: 'Someone's missing: it's Simonnot.'[21] Did anyone ever say: 'Someone's missing: it's Poulou'? He resolved to make himself indispensable and the resolution never wavered. Later, as he admitted, he would let himself be drawn into love affairs by the need to be needed, and fame never killed the compulsion to make himself useful. Meanwhile Poulou was jealous whenever Charles praised a teacher or an editor as irreplaceable.

Pulled in opposite directions by his grandfather and his mother, the boy was bound to suffer; gradually he realized that the old man was hostile to the girlishness his mother was cultivating. 'I was to have the sex of angels, indeterminate but feminine around the edges.'[22] His most vulnerable point was his long hair. 'You're making a girl of him', complained Charles. 'I don't want my grandson to be a sissy.' After sustained verbal onslaughts had failed to make any impact on his daughter, he took the child by the hand, saying that they were going out for a walk. Poulou made no protest when he was taken into a barber's shop. 'We'll give your mother a surprise.' Most family surprises led to exclamations of delight, to hugging and kissing, but this one led to weeping from behind the closed door of his mother's bedroom. Without his long blond curls, Poulou's ugliness was undeniable. 'Even my grandfather seemed taken aback: he had been entrusted with a wonder-child and come back with a toad. Anne-Marie was kind enough to conceal from me the reason she was upset … But I was feeling ill at ease.'[23] According to a letter Sartre wrote in 1925, this occurred when he was five; Les Mots makes it happen when he was seven. Finding it was no longer so easy to charm the grown-ups, he tried harder – often too hard. Unaccustomed to failure, he became jealous and spiteful when other children outshone him.

His grandfather's study was full of books, which were sacrosanct against dusting, except once a year. Long before he could read them, Poulou respected them, and he was impressed when the old man pointed to some volumes bound in brown cloth: 'Your grandfather wrote those, my boy.'[24] Defective eyesight was no obstacle to Poulou's early fixation on books, but whereas *Les Mots* gives the impression that he taught himself to read by taking precocious advantage of the books in his grandfather's library, the truth is that his whole development was conditioned by the early education his grandfather gave him. Teaching and music were the two traditions in the Schweitzer family. Seven generations of Schweitzers had taught in Alsatian village schools.[25] By deviating eccentrically into grocery Charles's father had interrupted the continuity and after resuming it, Charles, frustrated when his sons were diverted by their mother into the hands of the Dominicans, found enormous pleasure in tutoring his responsive little grandson. In a letter written when he was seventy – the boy was nine – Charles wrote: 'I've made myself the schoolmaster of my little man, to whom I teach history and geography while learning them myself. Really nothing is so delicious as cultivating and planting seeds in these little intelligences.'[26]

The soil was fertile and the little intelligence had given signs of being literary as soon as the education began, which was long before Poulou was nine. Sartre's dating is unreliable but probably he was not much more than seven when he began to exchange letters in verse with his grandfather. In the summer, when Poulou was taken to Arcachon, Charles would write three times a week – two pages for Louise, a postscript for Anne-Marie, a whole letter in verse for Poulou. After Anne-Marie bought a manual on versification, he replied to Charles in verse. He received a reply in verse by return post, and a new habit was formed. He had found another way of winning praise from the grown-ups. Presented with a copy of La Fontaine's *Fables choisies*, he started to rewrite them in alexandrines. Modulating into prose, he constructed adventure stories. Using violet ink, he wrote novels in exercise books; for the first, *Pour un papillon*, he took title, characters and story from an adventure story about an explorer, a professor and his daughter who were sailing up the Amazon in quest of a rare butterfly. Sartre's literary career had begun early.

Reading Jules Verne Poulou skipped lengthy descriptions; writing his own stories he stuffed the action with them, helping himself to information from Larousse. He was even given a small typewriter by his uncle Emile.[27] His second story 'Le Marchand de bananes' was lovingly copied out by his mother and handed around for admiration. In *Les Mots* enthusiasm for literature would be condemned as escapist and neurotic, while the blame for inflicting psychological damage on the young boy would be laid entirely on Charles Schweitzer, but Anne-Marie did no less to encourage Poulou to regard himself as a future writer. As a dedicated teacher Charles could not but delight in his gifted young disciple. 'His kind of aptitude is characteristically verbal... he dreams of nothing but adventures and poetry, but these are pretty useless in this twentieth century. Aggressive and eloquent, he's got more of the wherewithal, alas, for becoming a lawyer or a Deputy. In the meantime he's healthy and has the happiest character in the world, he sings all day long.'[28]

Most of the books in the old man's library were French and German classics. The boy would lie on his stomach, facing the windows with either a classical novel or the Grande Larousse encyclopaedia open in front of him, a jam sandwich on a plate to his left, a glass of water with a dash of wine to the right.[29] Charles lavished time on the boy unstintingly, but his devotion was to be memorialized in the autobiography as if he contributed little more than a few patriotic history lessons and a library. His influence was clearly formative: Poulou acquired a far better education than he would have been given at a school. Though *Les Mots* never admits that the boy modelled himself on the septuagenarian, he had no other model, and the reaction against the old man did not set in until later. Even Sartre's refusal to collect a library of his own may have belonged to the exertions he went on making to be unlike his grandfather. Generally the autobiography is unbalanced by its refusal to separate Poulou's valuation of Charles Schweitzer from the mature Sartre's.

Wanting her son to be educated, but not appropriated, by his grandfather, Anne-Marie fought back. One day, taking Poulou to the Jardins du Luxembourg, she stopped, as if accidentally, at a kiosk that sold boys' comics. It was easy to get the child addicted to serial adventure stories – *Cri-Cri*, *L'Epatant*, *Les Vacances*, *Les Trois Boy-Scouts*, *Le Tour du monde en aéroplane*. Rabelais and de Vigny quickly became matters of less urgent concern than the Eagle of the Andes and the iron-fisted boxer. At the same time Anne-Marie found books of adventure stories. Obediently Poulou tried to be secretive about his new reading matter, and it was some time before Charles discovered that he had been betrayed. The women then pretended that the boy had taken the initiative.[30] No veto was imposed and Sartre would go on throughout his life enjoying thrillers.

Another weapon at his mother's disposal was the cinema. Braving her father's disapproval, she took Poulou to the Panthéon on the other side of the rue Soufflot, where violet light bulbs glowed against the wall and a badly-tuned piano accompanied the current instalment of the silent thriller serial. She also took him to the boulevard cinemas – the Kinérama, the Folies Dramatiques, the Vaudeville, the Hippodrome. He saw *Fantômas* and *Les Mystères de New York*. He saw beautiful young girls rescued just in time from deadly perils, handsome horsemen galloping across the steppes, while their sweetheart waited, bound, helpless, but not hopeless, despite the flame that was moving inexorably along the fuse towards the keg of gunpowder.

In the early evening Charles would be teaching at the institute, Louise would be in her room, reading novels, the maid would be in the kitchen preparing the dinner, while Anne-Marie, at the piano, would unwittingly be providing background music for the adventure story Poulou was acting out in her father's study with his ruler and paper-knife as stage properties. Taking his rhythm from the music and mouthing his lines silently, copying the movie actors, he would play all the parts himself – heroes, villains, victims, lovers. But his grandfather hated tyrants, and Poulou's heroes were all *sansculottes*. Every day in *Le Matin* he read Michel Zévaco's serial stories about heroic men of the people. 'The greatest of all, Pardaillan, was my master: planted proudly on my chicken legs I have often imitated him by slapping Henri III and Louis XIII in the face.'[31] In later life Sartre, consistent in refusing fealty to his most august contemporaries, would go on committing intellectual treason.

There was no continuity between Poulou's games and the games of children he saw playing in the Jardins du Luxembourg. Desperate to join in, he would lean against a tree, waiting to be asked, but the invitation never came. Was it because of his size? The uncertainty tormented not only him but his tall mother. At home she could come to terms with his smallness – it made him easier to carry, prolonged his infancy, reminded her of Jean-Baptiste. In the gardens she could not hide her distress. What was he waiting for? Why didn't he ask them to let him play with them? Should she speak to their mothers for him? He begged her not to, but, holding him by the hand, she would accost strange ladies. In 'L'Enfance d'un chef' Lucien becomes self-conscious about the opposite affliction: other boys tease him because of his height. Poulou's grandmother would dolefully predict: 'He'll have the build of a Sartre.' Looking at him uncertainly, the old man would retort: 'He's growing.' Despair and self-disgust increased Poulou's dependence on the invisible camera that whirred approvingly, not just at his performances in the study but at almost everything he did – except when he was guiltily comforting himself in bed.

He soon learned that it was possible to win love by putting on performances. He was about eight when his mother bought him a set of glove puppets, and whenever he had enough money, he treated himself to a new one. He had a Jew, a policeman, Punch, a character called Bu-Ba-Bo and several others. In an old children's book called *Monsieur le Vent et Madame la Pluie* (*Mr Wind and Mrs Rain*), which had probably belonged to his mother, one of the characters had magic puppets who came to life if they were touched three times with a ring, and Poulou's imagination responded to the idea that puppets could enjoy independent life. He began to write plays for them. At first he performed these in the bathroom, but soon he began taking the puppets to the Jardins du Luxembourg. Choosing a seat in the English Gardens, he transformed it into a little stage, crouching behind it and making the puppets appear on his raised hands between the verticals in the back of the seat. He spoke in a high voice as if he were performing only for himself, but his secret desire was to draw other children away from their games to form an audience. In this way he made friends with a freckled girl of his own age, Nicole. Like the hunchback who won the favour of the princess in *Les Bouffons* (*The Jesters*), the romantic verse drama by Miguel Zamacoïs, he had succeeded by virtue of a performance.[32] (But it was characteristic of the fifty-eight-year-old Sartre that he should exclude this success story from *Les Mots*, in which the portrayal of childhood is blanketingly negative.)

Consciousness of being small intensified his pleasure at being able to look down on other people from his sixth floor balcony. 'Everyone has his natural place', he writes in *Les Mots*. 'Mine is a sixth floor in Paris with a view of the rooftops … The universe spreading itself at my feet and each thing was humbly begging for a name. To bestow one was like creating it and taking it.'[33] The short story 'Erostrate' is revealing. Characterizing the man whose ambition it is to kill six passers-by at random, Sartre situates his childhood at a level which is only slightly higher: 'You really need to look at people from above … Whoever considered the shape of a bowler hat viewed from the seventh floor? … They don't know how to combat this great enemy of humanity, the downward look… I have placed myself above the human within me, and I study it.'[34] This is what the boy had already begun to do.

In 1913, when Charles took him to meet the headmaster of the Lycée Montaigne, Poulou was recommended as advanced for his age. After being put in the eighth class, he made so many spelling mistakes in his first dictation that Charles was told he ought to be in the tenth. Concluding that he had disgraced himself deliberately, the old man took him away from the lycée. A Parisian tutor, M.Liévin, was engaged to come almost every day for private lessons, until the family left for a long stay at Arcachon, where Poulou was sent to the école communale. His grandfather told the teacher: 'My dear colleague, I am entrusting my most precious possession to you.' M.Barrault had a small beard, pince-nez and halitosis. He made Poulou sit at a special desk next to his rostrum; even during break he had to stay with M. Barrault instead of playing with the rough working-class boys.

In the autumn Anne-Marie took Poulou to the Poupon school, where they found their way to a room in which the mothers, seated behind the semi-circle of children, were watching the teacher, who had to be careful not to praise one child at the expense of another. Poulou stayed only for a term. Next his mother engaged a girl with pince-nez, who depressed her pupil by confiding in him about her loneliness. She felt worn out, and she would give anything to have a husband. Anyone at all.

The tutors who succeeded her were less memorable. At school the boy had made little contact with children and now he made virtually none. The old man and the two women were using him to give them an image of their identity: Charles was the devoted grandfather, Louise the long-suffering grandmother, Anne-Marie the patient mother. In puberty the boy was more aware than in childhood of the void where his father should have been. Of Jean-Baptiste's intentions for his son, Anne-Marie could remember nothing but the admonition that Poulou must not join the navy.[35] There were no paternal footsteps to follow, no blueprint. This made him more vulnerable to his self-effacing mother's nervousness. He was never to forget the way she restrained him from boisterousness in public places: 'Careful! We're not at home!' But even in his grandparents' flat neither of them could feel entirely at home: they were there under suffrance.

Finding he could retreat into writing, the boy became addicted to it. He wrote so fast that his wrist ached, but seldom completed stories, and took no precautions against losing them. Since Charles did not read them, the activity was an end in itself. Reality was the butterfly to be caught in the net of words. If he saw a plane tree in the Jardins du Luxembourg, he would not try to observe it closely: he would wait for it to yield itself to him in the form of a phrase. Or was it he, the writer, who was transforming himself into a thing – ink on a page? He was becoming something other than himself. Success would multiply him into books that would be treasured on shelves like his grandfather's, printed words that would leap up from the page into other people's eyes. The price was a kind of death: 'I had killed myself in advance because the dead are the only ones to enjoy immortality. Between the ages of nine and ten I became entirely posthumous.'[36] This is the disapproving fifty-eight-year-old Sartre recalling childhood intimations of immortality without trying to recreate their form or reconstitute the quality of his early thinking, but no doubt the idea of posterity bulked large.

Reading a book his uncle Georges had won in 1885 as a second prize in arithmetic, *L'Enfance des hommes illustres*, he was aware of seeing the childhood of Rousseau, Bach, Raphael, Molière in relation to his own. Trivial incidents seemed to indicate future greatness; anticipated strongly enough, his own future greatness cast a violet shadow that rescued each event from insignificance. He had not shut himself off from the intrusive gaze of other people; he had exposed himself to posterity. A thousand years later, a boy would be looking at him through a book. The adult Sartre represents the child as fixated on posterity, but the fixation seems to belong mainly to the adult, who is trying to distance himself from it by using the child as scapegoat.

From 3 August 1914, when Germany declared war on France, Charles was no longer regarded as an Alsatian: the surge of patriotism engulfed all Frenchmen. Poulou was swept along in the excitement: 'our friends harvested simple but noble saying from their concierges, postmen and plumbers, relayed them to us, and everyone declaimed prophetically'.[37] But it soon became evident that Jean-Paul's life would continue much as before, except that many of his favourite weeklies disappeared from the stalls. He had only recently discovered Buffalo Bill, Sitting Bull and Texas Jack; where were they? Charles explained that the publisher was German. By hunting diligently with his mother at second-hand bookstalls on the *quais*, he acquired about five hundred of the instalments which had appeared. He would spend hours looking at the coloured pictures on the fading covers and recite the titles to himself: *Un Crime en ballon, Le Pacte avec le Diable, Les Esclaves du Baron Montoushimi.*

Writers, such as Jean de la Hire, had recast their adventure stories. Intrepid schoolboys were replaced by more topical heroes; regimental mascots cropped up frequently together with orphans from Alsace and the children of soldiers. Occasionally a heroic schoolboy would fire a few shots with a rifle picked up from beside a soldier's corpse, but the writers entrusted the serious fighting to professionals. Courage became a collective virtue: battles were won by regiments. In October at Arcachon Poulou tried to resurrect individual heroism by writing a novel of his own. Private Perrin captured the Kaiser, challenged him to single combat and, with a knife at the vanquished Wilhelm's throat, forced him to sign an ignominious treaty, restoring Alsace-Lorraine to the French. In reality the war continued, and the humiliated author buried his exercise book on the beach.

But the war years were the happiest in his childhood: he experienced a new closeness with his mother, who gradually eclipsed Charles in importance. She called Poulou her attendant knight, her little man. He could confide in her unreservedly: 'We acquired the habit of recounting to each other in epic form the details of our life as they occurred ... in public we had our little conspiracies ... In a shop or a café the assistant would strike us as funny and on the way out my mother would say: "I didn't meet your eyes: I was afraid I'd burst out laughing in her face".[38] Holding hands with Anne-Marie, he was her protector; intuitively he shared her fear of the brash males who might accost her in the street. He never forgot the pasty complexion of a plump man with a waxed moustache and a straw hat: when he came up to them near a bookstall one day, they recoiled together.[39] Poulou was unequivocally on her side, hostile to males, oblivious of his own maleness.

Not that he forgot it consistently. At the age of ten, holidaying with his grandparents at Vic-sur-Cère, he went for walks with them, accompanied by the vice principal of the local school, his wife and Mme Lebrun, a young woman whose husband had been called up. To impress her Poulou invented a story about a girl who had hurt him and made him want to take vengeance on the whole sex. Sartre never forgot her reaction: 'I'd like to see the boy at twenty: I'm sure all the girls will be mad about him.'

For two years he had not needed to compete with other children. Except for brief intervals at the école communale in Arcachon and at the Poupon school he had been isolated, pampered, tutored privately like a much older child. But in October 1915, four months after his tenth birthday, he was finally sent to school. His grandfather's choice was the Lycée Henri IV, where he started as a day-boy in the sixième. Naturally he found it disconcerting that Monsieur Ollivier, his principal teacher, divided his attention among the whole class. Nor was it easy to compete with boys accustomed to competition: in class the others could answer questions more promptly and satisfactorily; in written work he did badly. With his first essay he came bottom of the class. Charles was soon threatening to take him away from the school, but Anne-Marie arranged an appointment with M. Ollivier. In 'L'Enfance d'un chef' Lucien's mother speaks in a musical voice when she is angry and wants to conceal it; in *Les Mots* Mme Sartre speaks in a musical voice during her meeting with M. Ollivier. Poulou was more studious, she explained, than would be apparent from his homework: he had learned to read by himself and he wrote novels. The teacher refused to give him any private lessons, but agreed to keep an eye on him. Basking in what he thought was preferential treatment, the boy began to relax, began adapting himself to his new situation.

He was surprised at how easy it was to make friends. Unlike the children in the Jardins du Luxembourg, the boys in the sixième accepted him as an equal. After school each afternoon they would run about, shouting, in the Place du Panthéon, and they played ball between the Hôtel des Grands Hommes and the statue of Rousseau. After trying so hard to be special he wanted nothing more than to be like the others. He joined in their laughter, repeated their jokes, echoed their catch-phrases, accepted their values. The group had its unwritten laws and its ways of enforcing them. Jeering and insults were prohibited; offenders would be surrounded by the group and coerced into apologizing.[40] Most of the mothers knew each other, and Mme Sartre was told by Mme Malaquin that, according to her André, 'Poulou puts on airs'. But the relationship between the boys was not affected.[41]

At the end of Poulou's first term M. Ollivier called him an 'excellent child, but not at all thoughtful. Hardly ever gives the right answer first time. Must accustom himself to thinking more.' He did: by the end of the school year he was pronounced to be 'excellent in all respects'.[42] The boy who came top of the class was the day-boarder, Bénard, who 'looked like a baby chick'. The son of a dressmaker who was not on visiting terms with the other mothers, he was sensitive to the cold, always wore a long woollen scarf, and was not allowed to join in outdoor games. He waved to the others through the window. In class he never raised his hand to answer a question, but always knew the answers when asked. At the end of the winter he died, and forty boys sobbed behind his coffin.[43]

For the others the routine continued unchanged. During his first year at the school Poulou acquired his long-lasting enthusiasm for the classics and for ancient history. The boys were taught about Egypt, Greece and Rome, and he enjoyed the nineteenth-century historian Victor Duruy's *Histoire des Romains* which was full of good stories. He consumed books voraciously, sometimes understanding only a small part of what he read – as with Henri Barbusse's novel *Enfer* (*Hell*) which had appeared in 1908, creating a scandal. The narrator is a man who lives in a hotel room with holes in two walls which enable him to see what is going on in the adjoining rooms. Many of the incidents are erotic, and the family was shocked that Poulou had read the book.

A few weeks after the autumn term had begun, the form master of the cinquième, M. Durry, was in the middle of a Latin lesson when the door opened and the porter ushered in a boy who looked so much like Bénard that Sartre thought it was a ghost. 'We recognized his steel spectacles, his muffler, his slight aquiline nose and his resemblance to a chick who must be protected from the cold.' But when the new boy was asked his name and his father's profession, he said that he was Paul-Yves Nizan, the son of an engineer. When Sartre spoke to him during break, there was an immediate rapport. The squint which differentiated Nizan from Bénard gave him something else in common with Sartre, but the appearance of virtue and shyness was deceptive. 'Overwhelmed with violent, passive emotions, he did not shout out, but we saw him go white with anger and stammer: what we mistook for gentleness was only a momentary paralysis.'[44]

He seemed more sophisticated than the others, cultivating a cynical object-ivity and referring ironically to the parents whom secretly he adored. His Breton father, a railwayman throughout his working life, had been an engine driver before becoming an engineer.[45] Nizan had read widely and wanted to be a writer; Sartre spent a lot of time chatting with him, but scarcely had time to think of himself as a writer during his first two years at the lycée. Exercise books were for dictation, composition, logical analysis and arithmetic. He made a particularly good impression on his French teacher, M. Noël: 'Among the best in the class at French... already a store of literary knowledge and a very alert memory.'[46] But he had not liberated himself from his literary vocation: 'my mission determined my character, my delirium left my head to flow into my bones'.[47] Later on he would try to convince himself that he had no Super-ego, but it had taken control of his Ego like an occupying army.

TWO · *Nitre and Sarzan*

When Poulou lost his father he had not lost anything he had been aware of having, but when his mother married again in April 1917 after letting the boy monopolize her for nearly twelve years, he sustained a loss from which he never entirely recovered. His anger and resentment would last throughout his life and be carried beyond the grave: not wanting to be near his step-father, he left instructions that he was not to be buried next to his mother. He had felt totally safe with her, totally secure in his possession of her. The only male rival had been Charles, and as the boy drew closer to adolescence, the old man was growing more feeble, less dangerous. The young mother and the boy had been natural allies – 'the children'. Anne-Marie had flowered only briefly into womanhood, retreating after Jean-Baptiste's death into the home she had only just left. Suddenly, at the age of thirty, she was no longer one of 'the children'; horrifyingly she was no longer Madame Sartre. She was Madame Mancy. Describing Baudelaire's reaction (at the age of seven) to his mother's second marriage, Sartre would later write: 'A moment ago he was still quite immersed in the unanimous and religious life of the couple he formed with his mother. This life has ebbed like a tide, leaving him alone and dry; he has lost his *raison d'être*. He discovers shamefully that he's separate, that he has been brought to life for nothing. With his rage at having been evicted is mixed a sense of profound failure.'[1]

Precocious though he was, Poulou would have been incapable of understanding the complexity of his mother's motives, even if she had tried to explain them. The paternal grandfather, Dr Eymard Sartre, had been the boy's deputy guardian, but when he died at the age of seventy-seven in October 1913, his son Joseph had succeeded to the position. Anne-Marie had never been on good terms with him and after convening a family meeting in April 1917 she arranged for her new husband to take over the role. Joseph Mancy was the champion who could displace both her father and her brother-in-law as rival authorities over her son as well as solving all her financial problems; what she miscalculated was the extent to which Poulou would feel betrayed.

For the moment his routine would continue uninterrupted, except by her absence. He could stay on with his grandparents while she moved into a flat with her new husband. The boy did not want to believe that his mother could love this stranger; the mature Sartre would tell himself that she had married to free her ageing father from the burden of supporting her. 'My mother certainly did not marry my step-father from love. Moreover, he was not very lovable. A tall, thin fellow with a black moustache, a rather furrowed face, a very big nose, rather beautiful eyes, black hair.'[2] Mancy was a naval engineer who had graduated, like Jean-Baptiste, from the Ecole Polytechnique. In fact the two men had known her at the same time in Cherbourg, but though Mancy paid court to her, he would not, as the son of a railwayman, have been considered a suitable match. Twelve years later, he was working in Paris as a manager at the Delaunay-Belleville factories, and he got in touch with her again.

Writing of Flaubert, Sartre uses the phrases 'golden age' and 'expulsion from paradise'. No longer allowed to accompany his doctor father on his rounds, young Gustave felt, according to Sartre, that he was living under a paternal malediction. Poulou's golden age ended when his mother moved out of the flat in rue le Goff. When Mancy was appointed as head of the Delaunay-Belleville shipbuilding yards in La Rochelle he settled there with his new wife, and in November the boy moved into their flat. No doubt he felt that he was living under Mancy's disapproval, but this was partly because of his own hostility. In later life Sartre would alternate between abusing Mancy ('He was the most futile of men... His flesh was an abstraction') and praising him ('He was a good man, really impeccable').[3]

Leaving Paris, leaving his school, losing his friends – there would have been a big upheaval in his life even if he had not had to confront the man, and, worse still, the new image that his mother presented as the subservient wife of a domineering stranger. Mancy's intentions were honourable. Viewing his new step-son as overeducated in classics and literature but undereducated on the scientific side, he devoted time after dinner to tutoring him in geometry. But to the boy it seemed that the man was making him forget what little geometry he knew.[4] It was worse when his mother was present. One evening his insolent tone made her storm out of the room. In her absence the lesson proceeded more peacefully but after her rage had gathered momentum in the kitchen she came back to slap her son twice across the face. Infuriated by her intervention, Mancy shouted at her; the child, still in pain, walked out of the room. Like Genet, as Sartre would later describe him, Poulou felt rejected by everyone, by life. He had never worried so much about his ugliness; he felt certain he was unlovable. Anne-Marie's identity depended now as much as her surname on a man Poulou could never accept as his father. At the dinner table, as Mancy held forth about the responsibilities of an employer, he seemed intolerant, prejudiced, narrow-minded. Sartre's experiences in La Rochelle were quite different from those of the catholic girlhood Simone de Beauvoir describes in her autobiography but both children were being imbued with a lifelong hatred for the way of life they were intended to emulate.

There was a grand piano in a large drawing-room which was used mainly for receptions, and his mother played a good deal; so did Poulou, learning to read the scores of operettas and to play duets with his mother. Soon he graduated to Schumann, Beethoven, Bach, not worrying about the fingering but trying to get the tempo right. He never troubled with five-finger exercises but by going patiently over the same passages again and again he improved his technique sufficiently to cope with more difficult pieces including Beethoven Sonatas and work by Chopin. He also enjoyed singing, accompanying himself.[5]

Starting at the co-educational lycée in La Rochelle, Poulou, in his smart Parisian knickerbockers, felt like an outsider. The boys were unexpectedly tough, partly because La Rochelle was a port town. 'The boys there would hang around ships and sailors and so on – an atmosphere which instilled in them more than the ordinary amount of energy and violence.'[6] The lycée boys had fist-fights with pupils at the religious school, Ecole des Bons Pères, and with local urchins, boys in their early teens. Some of these were apprentices, naturally hostile to the lycée boys, who were better-dressed. To fight with the boys in the street was a declaration of middle-class identity.[7] One day Anne-Marie came out of a shop to find Poulou rolling on the ground with a strange boy and fighting viciously.[8] Though his size put him at a disadvantage, he enjoyed fighting: the whole body was actively involved – it was the extreme opposite of self-abandonment.

On these boys the war seemed to be having a stronger effect than on Parisian boys. In Paris too a large proportion of the fathers had been called up, but in La Rochelle the boys behaved as though they too were fighting a war. 'We were steeped in the violence of our fathers... One of my school-friends chased his mother with a knife – she had given him potatoes and he didn't like them.'[9]

Feeling challenged by the arrival of a boy from Paris, his classmates tried to impress him, talking boastfully about girls and orgies, while he made out that he was no less of a man than they were. He told them that in Paris he had a girlfriend. Adapting the narrative techniques he had used in his heroic adventure stories, he claimed that he had picked her up after school, gone looking for a hotel with her and made love to her. Needing evidence, he persuaded their maid to pen a letter beginning 'My dearest Jean-Paul'. Admiring and envious, the boys passed the letter around the school, and when he confessed it was a forgery, it only confirmed his reputation as a typical Parisian. Parisians could not be expected to tell the truth.[10]

At the hands of these tough schoolboys, the diminutive, unattractive, squinting Sartre was a natural victim. In his first year he felt that other boys, if not friendly, were at least curious about him, and he did not fail to make an impression. According to one classmate, 'It was exciting to hear him talk. He knew how to get an argument going and keep the ball bouncing for hours.'[11] According to another, he was 'bad-tempered, moody, quarrelsome, unpleasant to the others' and thought himself superior.

He did not work hard. At home he was often slapped for refusing to make more effort;[12] in his second year at the school he felt that no-one wanted what he had to offer. 'I fought constantly with some of them, who in fact were not so highly regarded by the others; there were some more tolerant friends who tried to save me from these battles.'[13] Many of the boys, including most of his friends, were less friendly when others were present than when he was alone with them.[14] None of the boys seemed to like him as much as he liked them and this combined with his misery at home to give him what he called the unhappiest years of his life.

Nearly all the thirteen-year-old boys in the class had girlfriends, even if they exchanged no more than kisses in dark corners, and they went out together on Thursday afternoon, when there was no school. Sartre set his sights on a pretty girl, Gisèle, daughter of a ship's-chandler, who lived by the harbour, but he had no means of making contact with her. Slightly older than he was, she was in great demand, mostly among boys of another school. When he confided in his classmates, he was told not to worry: they would arrange for him to meet her. Turning up, as he was instructed, at the Mall – a park which overlooks the beach – one Thursday afternoon, he saw her cycling along the path and jumped on his bike to follow her. 'Why does he keep pestering me,' she called out, 'this old fool with his big hat?' He had found the hat in the road and thought that it suited him.[15] Possibly she said something about his spectacles or his shortness. In different accounts of the incident he would put different words in her mouth, but fifty years later the snub still rankled. Afterwards the boys tried to persuade him that she must have been trying to hide her feelings, and he was naive enough to let himself go on being humiliated in incidents which reinforced his sense of being ugly, while his unpopularity reminded him constantly of embarrassing moments in the Jardins du Luxembourg when he still had his mother as his champion: 'I can still see myself walking through the Mall ... with my schoolmates in a group while I kept my distance, waiting for them to invite me to come over and join them.'[16]

The French teacher, M. Loosdregt, who had a large, colourful nose, found it particularly hard to keep order, and Sartre, wanting to ingratiate himself with his classmates, joined in the barracking. He received numerous detentions and, three years later, used the teacher as his model for the sententious provincial schoolmaster in *Jésus la Chouette*. 'Your mother has entrusted you to my care, my young friend, I promised her to make a man of you. But promise me in turn always to tread the path of honour. I hope you'll never have to do anything but follow my example.'[17] Sartre's gifts as a mimic extended to his writing.

Equally unhappy at home and at school, he crept into reading as into a refuge. At week-ends and during school holidays, he would often spend the whole day with a book. As books came to matter more, religion, which had never mattered much, mattered still less. One morning, waiting at the bus-stop for two girls, sisters who usually travelled to school with him, he stopped believing as casually as if a new idea had occurred to him: 'You know what? God doesn't exist.'[18] It was not God but literature that conferred immortality.

In November 1917, when the Soviets offered to make peace with Germany, the main worry among the schoolboys was whether France would still be able to win the war.[19] But when Poulou wrote another novel he had no compunction about taking a German hero. Thanks to his grandfather's library his interest in Goetz von Berlichingen (later to be the hero of *Le Diable et le Bon Dieu*) began when he was about eleven. Goetz was no less fascinating to him than Robin Hood is to English children as a man who used evil for good ends.[20] The Goetz novel was written during Poulou's first year at La Rochelle; he did little writing during his next two years at the school, though with his enthusiasm for Roman history, he started libretti for operas about Horatius Cocles and Mucius Scaevola.

Feeling that he was constantly being rebuffed, and putting much of the blame on his face, his shortness, his squint, he became emotionally dependent on two better-looking schoolmates, Pelletier and Boutillier. Together the three of them courted a cinema usherette's pretty daughter, seeing her home from school, and escorting her to the cinema where her mother worked.[21] In her presence the three of them behaved as equals; in her absence Pelletier and Boutillier could treat Poulou like a slave. They exploited him mercilessly and betrayed him ruthlessly, using him as a scapegoat. On their account he received numerous canings. He spent pocket money on buying cakes for them, raising extra money by selling books he stole from his home. It was at this time that he began to daydream about an elite in which he would be king: he pictured a group of elegant, gifted young men and charming girls, all dominated by his wit and charm.[22] His childish charisma had inexplicably vanished; surely he was entitled to more than he was getting from his mother. Hating her dependence on her husband, he needed to think of it as financial and to violate it.

In her handbag, which she kept in a cupboard, was the money she was given for herself and for running the household. She did not notice anything was missing but one night, feeling cold in bed, Poulou put his jacket on top of the blanket, and in the morning, when she shook him by the shoulder, some of the coins fell out. Searching his pockets, she found seventy francs. His explanation was that a boy called Cardino had been so cheeky to him and his friends that they had beaten him up and confiscated his money. He then arranged for Cardino to call at the flat and confirm the story: the deal was that he could keep forty per cent of the money Mme Mancy was going to give him, but must hand over sixty per cent. With his twenty-eight francs Cardino bought a big electric torch, and when his mother found out how he had paid for it, she called on Mme Mancy, who explained why the money had been given to her son.

Belatedly but fiercely, Poulou was rejecting the image of angelic innocence that had been thrust on him in Meudon. 'From their first to their tenth year', he complains in *Saint Genet*, 'children are required to incarnate for the grown-ups the original state of grace.'[23] Sartre lacked only a father while Genet lacked both parents, but what he writes of Genet is true of himself: 'This is a synthetic product ... an artificial creature, it is in sophisms that he will discover the truth ... he will be mineral or spirit but never belong to the intermediate realm: to life. He will never like sport or the physical pleasures, never be greedy or sensual, never have confidence in his body ... His sexuality will be abstract tension and sterility.'[24] Even Sartre's motives for stealing resemble those he imputes to Genet: 'What does he really want? To *be like the others*; nothing more ... The truth is that he is impelled by anxiety ... He steals to relieve the anguish which is attacking him ... For the child who steals and the child who masturbates, to exist is *to be seen by the adults*, and since these secret activities take place in solitude, they *don't exist*.'[25] Genet was ten when he started to steal; Sartre did not feel the need until his mother betrayed him.

Joseph Mancy admonished his step-son severely, but the incident made no apparent change to the basic tenor of their relationship. Without trying to act like a father, Mancy wanted, from a distance, to exert a benevolent but authoritative pressure, helping to prepare Poulou for an academic career in mathematics or physics. Mancy was aware of resistance, but not of its strength. Later Sartre would say: 'I have been anti-authoritarian since knowing my step-father.' It would be hard to overestimate the negative influence of Joseph Mancy. If the whole of Kafka's work was a love-letter to his father, the whole of Sartre's was a declaration of hatred for his step-father: 'He was always the man I was writing against. All through my life; and the fact of writing was against him.'[26] The commitment to literature and philosophy was fortified by revulsion from his step-father's scientific outlook. Poulou was also beginning to associate the bourgeois milieu with reactionary political inclinations: compared with Mancy, Charles Schweitzer was a democrat.

In the disgrace that ensued on the stealing, Schweitzer, who was now seventy-five, was the one man from whom the boy expected sympathy. When he came to La Rochelle, he dropped a coin in a shop; the boy bent to pick it up, only to be pushed aside. He could no longer be trusted. Painfully the arthritic old man stooped to pick up the coin himself.[27]

Coming to depend more than ever on reading, Poulou began to identify in a new way with the law-breaking heroes of stories about duels and sea-voyages, courage and betrayal. Feeling unloved and undersized, he identified with men quite unlike himself. Most enviable of all was their power to overcome resistance, imposing their will with a firm thrust of their glittering sword.[28] These heroes helped the boy: growing like a sturdy plant inside him was a willpower that would soon become formidable.

During three years of living at La Rochelle, Poulou, who never made friends with his step-father, succeeded only briefly in winning back his mother. During the summer of 1921, an abscess in his ear put him in danger of meningitis, and he needed to have an operation. She stayed in the nursing-home with him, sleeping in a bed positioned at right angles to his. When she undressed in the evening, he watched admiringly through half-closed eyelids, thinking of the favourable impression she had been making on his classmates.

Unable to drag her back into the symbiotic paradise, the boy used his intellectual prowess to distinguish himself at school, and during his third year there, he felt more settled.[29] At the prize-giving ceremony on 12 July 1919, he was mentioned on the Tableau d'honneur, receiving first prizes for French composition and Latin translation, second prizes for Latin composition and mathematics, and a prize for Greek translation. He was the first to receive honourable mention in Greek and the fourth in gymnastics.

In October he was moved into the deuxième, where he was the only pupil studying Greek. Though he was writing less, he went on showing stories to his mother, who praised them. 'That's nice, that's a good piece of invention.' Mancy knew the boy was writing, but took no interest in reading his work, so, from the beginning, it was not primarily to males that he looked for encouragement as a writer. But Mancy was making more of an impression than he realized on his step-son when he said: 'He's like me – he'll never know how to talk to women.' He was not intending to be unkind: he wanted the boy to be industrious, reliable, unlikely to fall miserably in love, but Poulou needed to believe that at twenty he would make the girls as mad about him as Mme Lebrun had predicted. Nothing mattered more than to be loved. Writing was a form of seduction: the aim was to peel away the mystery of things and offer them in all their splendour to a girl.[30]

If Poulou now embarked on a series of *actes gratuits* it was not because he had read Gide but because he needed to convince himself that he was not dependent on Mancy. To give himself the feeling of being free, to strengthen his willpower, to submit himself to a distasteful discipline which stemmed only from himself, Poulou forced himself into actions that had no logic or apparent motivation. At the age of fourteen, after coveting a hat for a fortnight and eventually persuading his mother to buy it for him, he threw it under the wheels of a tram. She slapped him twice. Looking back on the event, he saw it as a creative step in his reconstruction of his character: 'I very quickly grew dissatisfied with myself... I'm never straightforward because I always try to adapt, to rebuild.'[31]

At the end of the school year he won first prizes for Latin translation and composition, and second for French composition. But because of the stealing and to protect him, so they said, from 'harmful influences', or to rid themselves of the constant reminder that they had failed to win his goodwill, his mother and Mancy decided that he should complete his schooling in Paris, where Charles Schweitzer arranged for him to be admitted at the Lycée Henri IV. Back in Paris at the age of fifteen, he found himself in the same class as Paul Nizan, who had been at the school since the middle of the previous academic year.

Poulou spent Thursday afternoons and Sundays with his grandparents, who had moved down to the third floor. He slept in their flat on Sunday night, but for the rest of the week he was – for the first time – a boarder. Life was totally different from what it had always been, mainly because relations with the other boys were uninterrupted. Instead of having privacy and long spells of solitude, he slept in a dormitory, which brought out a slight homosexual inclination: he mustered the courage to take other boys' trousers off.[32] Fortunately, Nizan was a boarder, too, and their literary ambition bonded them together even more strongly than a resemblance so pronounced that they were sometimes mistaken for each other. Despite his voracious reading at La Rochelle, Sartre was less advanced than Nizan, who was already steeped in Proust, Gide, Giraudoux and Paul Morand.[33] From the unexacting novels of Jean Farrère, Sartre turned to these writers, who altered his attitude to personal relationships while boarding-school was intensifying his experience of them. Proust's novel became so real for him and Nizan that they talked about the characters as if they were alive: 'What do you think Monsieur de Charlus has done now?'[34]

Having been a Parisian new boy in the school at La Rochelle, he was now a provincial new boy in Paris, and he was so anxious to be accepted that he volunteered to sing in the choir at mass in the school chapel on Sunday. (He would keep silent about this throughout most of his life.)[35] After mass, he went to his grandparents' flat in the rue Le Goff, where he made better use than before of his grandfather's library.

Besides influencing his reading, friendship with Nizan would soon make Sartre feel more at home in his new school, and less provincial.[36] The influence of Nizan merged with that of the French teacher, M. Georgin, who encouraged independent thinking. 'Find your own solution to this problem, your own answer to this question.'[37] Sartre went to the Bibliothèque Sainte-Geneviève and began to feel proud of his mental processes. After two years of producing little, he began to write more often, more seriously and less eclectically,[38] though not escaping the influence of Giraudoux.

The friendship with Nizan became so close that they were known as Nitre and Sarzan:

From 1920 to 1930 especially, at lycée and then university, we were indistinguishable ... He never raised his voice ... merely folded his hands ... letting his fearful remarks drop with a sly, deceptive calmness.

At sixteen he proposed that ... we should be two supermen. He gave us Celtic names... R'ha and Bor'hou ... We walked around Paris for hours, for days. We discovered flora, and fauna, stones, and we were moved to tears when the first neon advertisements were switched on. We thought the world was new because we were in the world ... We walked, we talked, we invented our own language, and intellectual slang ... One night these supermen at large climbed the hill of Sacré Coeur, and saw at their feet a jeweller's shop in disarray. Sticking his cigarette into the left corner of his mouth and grimacing hideously, Nizan said 'Hey, hey, Rastignac!' I repeated 'Hey hey!' as I was intended to, and we walked down, pleased with this discreet revelation of our literary knowledge and the extent of our ambitions.[39]

As in his childhood relationship with his mother, Sartre was sharing values, confidences, giving and receiving support. Nizan, who had established his position since arriving at the school, was incontestably the dominant partner. At sixteen he was something of a poseur, dressing dandyishly; he was enviably successful with the girls, had a close relationship with his father and a precociously extensive vocabulary. 'He could immediately master words he had just picked up... He wrote better than I could, and with his father's mournful eyes, watched himself write.'[40] Nizan's father had been demoted to managing a railway depot. Furious with himself and with his wife for having lived on false promises about a privileged future, he launched into remorseful tirades. One night, bundling his clothes over his arm, he walked out of the house, threatening suicide. His son would later use these incidents in his novel *Antoine Bloyé*.[41] To Sartre this masochistic honesty seemed more admirable than the self-satisfaction of Joseph Mancy.

A strong strain of negativity ran in both boys. 'It had long seemed desirable', Sartre wrote, 'to be and above all to appear very wicked.'[42] This often helped him to overcome his shyness, though he lacked the poise and verbal aggressiveness that made Nizan so attractive. Sartre was possibly using his younger self as his model for the narrator in *Jésus la Chouette*, even if his own shyness was never so extreme. 'I was terrified of going into a shop, especially when I saw the salesgirl in conversation with someone. I was afraid of trespassing on an intimacy... I believed the whole time I stayed in the shop that I could feel their indignant or contemptuous glances weighing down on me. To escape the shame that crimsoned my face and burned my cheeks, I took the hundred paces into some far-off corner and waited for the shop to be empty before going back inside.'[43] But if this represented one side of Sartre's nature it was overruled by the impulses that made him seek the limelight. His ambition was to become a jazz singer and he was extrovert enough for his classmates to appoint him 'S.O.', Satyre Officiel – organizer of celebrations and rags. He also wrote a Ubuesque satire *Vaticiner sans pouvoir* (*Prophesying without Power*), a grotesque description of Rodin's *Penseur*. A classmate remembered it, but Sartre did not,[44] though he did remember writing at about this time the story of an old man who lived in a fifth-floor flat and discovered that he was a Pharaoh.

In 1920 M. Georgin wrote: 'Certainly there's good stuff in him',[45] and in June 1921 he passed the first part of his *baccalauréat*. In France philosophy is taught in the *classe terminale* of lycées, and Sartre now came under the influence of the philosophy teacher, M. Chabrier. He made philosophy seem like a passport to omniscience. 'All the sciences belonged to philosophy ... I thought that if I specialized in philosophy, I'd learn about the whole world I was going to talk about in literature.'[46] M. Chabrier called Sartre an 'excellent pupil: intellect already forceful, adroit in discussing a question but should be a little less self-assured'.[47]

Travelling to Alsace in the summer of 1922 – to Pfaffenhofen and Günsbach – with his grandfather, he had more of the old man's company than at any time since living in the flat. When they visited his disagreeable great-aunt, Caroline Biedermann, Poulou played in the garden with her great-nephew Théo, and played duets with her daughter-in-law. Her hunch-backed daughter Anna made him say 'Ripele' and 'Pipele' to enjoy his

French accent. He remembered the solid Alsatian meals and an expedition to the castle at Lichtenburg in a horse-drawn carriage.[48]

Here in Alsace, nine years ago, he had written 'Pour un papillon', but the seventeen-year-old writer was more extraordinary than the eight-year-old had been. He had turned to realism in the unfinished novel *Jésus la Chouette* (*Jesus the Owl*) about the teacher modelled on M. Loosdregt, and then in the story 'L'Ange du morbide' ('Angel of Morbidity') which securely establishes the distinctive tone of Sartre's early fiction – jaded, disconsolate, acidulous. The twenty-five-year-old central character, a mediocre, pusillanimous university teacher, habitually wears a gaberdine and a sullen expression. 'He had turned all his youthful vitality towards morbidity, out of snobbery and also because his mind was no more than a poor, warped thing, a watch beyond repair, going backwards.'[49] He needs strong ideas, but borrows other people's. Though his schoolfriends had called him a superman and had become his disciples, he had remained a virgin till the age of twenty-two. He becomes the lover of his ugly landlady, who has a goitre. The other tenants are a blind priest and three old women. The story ends with a characteristically caustic sentence: 'He never wrote anything else, and was decorated at the age of fifty-five with the Légion d'honneur, incontestable proof of bourgeois status.' Two of the few constants in Sartre's intellectual development were steadfast hatred of the bourgeoisie and contempt for the rewards it put on offer.

Believing himself, not alternatively but simultaneously, to be brilliant and mediocre, Sartre gives his characters a mixture of the same qualities, writing unforgivingly about the mediocrity: the teacher loves himself 'with all the tenderness, all the goodness, all the infinite solicitude which replaces intellectual values in the second-rate'.[50] Attracted by disease like Thomas Mann, the young Sartre succeeds in giving it a bizarre glamour. All the neighbouring hotels have been made into clinics for the tubercular. After a period of fantasizing about making love to tubercular girls, the character gauchely strikes up an acquaintance with one. Sartre is canny enough to make the relationship stay platonic and to realize the contrast between generalized ideas about tuberculosis, and the messy, embarrassing, painful fits of coughing that the disease entails. There are no explicit references to masturbation, as there are in 'L'Enfance d'un chef', but the soggy actuality of the tubercular cough is contrasted with the vagueness of the erotic daydreams.

Sartre was at once using the morbid affair as a prism to study his own deviations from healthy normality and following in the French tradition of the poète maudit. Baudelaire was neither the first to ennoble suffering nor the last to cultivate literary beauty in filthy soil. It was natural to gravitate towards literature of this kind, which helped to sanction the revulsion he felt from the values his step-father shared with M. Loosdregt. Inevitably Sartre had interiorized many of these values, but he was still quite young – only fourteen or fifteen, he claims – when he came to believe that the best way of arriving at the truth was to argue against himself: '"What? I thought that? But it was idiotic to think that!" You see how it can be said that there was a kind of spontaneity in this but how, at the same time, it always presented itself in the form of a negation ... The discovery (positive or negative) was always made by means of a breach with something from the past. "So this is my principle".'[51] The disadvantage of this strategy is that even if you do arrive at the truth, you depart soon afterwards.

Education in France is a more elaborate, more protracted process than in Britain or the United States: though he did not do any military service until afterwards, Sartre was to go on being a student until he was twenty-four. Like Nizan he was aiming at the Ecole Normale Supérieure, one of the most exclusive of the grandes écoles, where standards are generally higher than in the universities, and the ferociously competitive entrance examinations involved candidates in two years of intensive preparation after the *bac* in special lycée classes. For the *hypokhâgne* and the *khâgne*, the two years of preparing for the Ecole Normale Supérieure, teaching was reputed to be better at the Lycée Louis-le-Grand than at the Henri IV, where Sartre and Nizan were too independent to endear themselves to teachers. After passing the second part of the *bac* in June 22 Sartre is said to have taken leave of the despised headmaster by spitting on his shoes.

THREE · *The Lycée Louis-le-Grand*

Nizan has described the Louis-le-Grand as 'a sort of large, pale-bricked barracks with sun-dials inscribed in gold, where nineteen-year-old boys could not learn much about the world by dint of living among the Greeks, the Romans, the idealist philosophers and the doctrinarians of the July monarchy'.[1] 'We felt an urgent need for action', wrote Sartre. Nothing mattered to him more than his friendship with the more self-confident Nizan, a relationship charged with an emotional intensity Sartre found almost unbearable, though he tried – during the most protracted of their quarrels – to control his feelings by starting an autobiographical novel, *La Semence et le scaphandre* (*Seed and Safeguard*): 'I was hard, jealous, like a maniac lover, without being considerate or tender. Lucelles, independent and sly, found opportunities to deceive me.' He betrays Tailleur, the narrator, by forming new friendships – with an Algerian Jew or a boy from Marseille – 'he avoided me for days, and found me aggressive and morose, though suffocating in my inability to express my tenderness ... But when I'd just left him, I was trembling with joy because I had a friend, and this friend was none other than Lucelles.'[2] Sartre had chosen a feminine-sounding name for the Nizan character, while 'Tailleur' is as close to 'tailor' as Sartre is to 'sartor'. Sartre needed intimacy to replace the lost intimacy with his mother, and after a long estrangement between the friends, lasting from March to October 1923, he would never again become so emotionally dependent on any one man or woman. His promiscuity was partly defensive: more even than the violence of the boys at La Rochelle, which had made brutality seem unavoidable in relationships between men,[3] the quarrel undermined his ability to trust.

Three years his junior, Maurice Merleau-Ponty found that it was 'not easy to be his friend': he did not let fellow students talk to him about their fears or insecurities.[4] But in his habit of holding himself at a distance he was encouraged by the example of Nizan, who confided in no-one: if Sartre failed to understand how much Nizan was suffering, it was because he was not allowed to.

All the boarders in the school wore a loose smock like an artist's, and classmates remember Sartre's as grey and ink-stained.[5] 'We were depressed by our dirty uniforms, our torn smocks ... We were especially overwhelmed by the atmosphere, this unbreathable atmosphere, always the same, emanating from the four walls of the lycée. We use up the time in sterile little disputes and rehearsals of the same old arguments, or in fooling about, spitting, fighting, dragging each other on the ground.' Their favourite game was a variation on hide-and-seek in which the hider had to smoke a pipe.

In the novel the friendship between the two boys flowers when they are allowed out for walks. 'Outside the porter's lodge he adjusted my tie and playfully strangled me for a bit.' Other people are the enemy. 'Each passer-by made us feel strong. Alone, each of us was impressionable, volatile, dependent on public taste. Together we were impervious ... Each outing was a sort of battle against the civilians, and still more than classmates we were brothers in arms.'[6]

At the age of seventeen Sartre lost his virginity to a woman of thirty, a doctor's wife from Thiviers. Informed that he was a boarder she enquired whether he didn't go out on Thursdays and Sundays. She then arranged to meet him at a friend's flat. Without believing that she found him attractive, Sartre understood what was expected of him. Though he made love unenthusiastically, he had the impression she was pleased, but they did not see each other again.[7]

Unchanged by this joyless experience, the pattern of his life changed abruptly after the Delaunay-Belleville company ran into financial trouble with its shipbuilding yards in La Rochelle. Mancy brought his wife to Paris, where they settled at 2 square de Clignancourt, near the Gare de la Chapelle. Sartre, who had been sleeping in the same dormitory as Nizan, now became a day-boarder. Having to cope simultaneously with oppression at the school and domestic oppression in which his mother sided with the domineering Mancy, the seventeen-year-old boy failed to fulfil the promise he had shown at the Lycée Henri IV. His new philosophy teacher, M. Bernes, praising his 'active and alert mind', predicted that he would succeed, but warned him against 'too much facility' and 'excessive elaboration of insufficiently clarified ideas'. For the first year's philosophical dissertation Sartre failed to win either of the two prizes and came only fifth among the runners-up. The first runner-up was a boy who had made friends with Sartre and Nizan, René Maheu, the son of a schoolteacher from near Toulouse: the three of them became almost inseparable.[8]

Apart from philosophy, they studied history, Latin, Greek and French. According to the history teacher, M. Roubaud, Sartre was 'a little confused ... uneven results'. He did better in French. While Nizan won the first of the two prizes, Sartre came second among the runners-up. In Latin composition there were three prizewinners and Sartre tied with another boy in the third place among the runners-up. In Latin translation Nizan won a second prize while Sartre was third of the runners-up.[9]

While the lycée did not encourage intellectual independence, Nizan, who was always inventing theories of his own, spurred Sartre into thinking for himself. They enjoyed disagreeing and arguing; they liked to feel different from other people: many of their moral and aesthetic ideas were formulated when they were among crowds. At moments of discouragement they fell back on the 'theory of the witness', which they had evolved together: they were destined by temperament to be witnesses of 'the vain agitation of the world'. Other people became passionate; their role was to observe, taking notes. The psychological understanding they had acquired was the most desirable quality of all.[10]

In the lycée the approach to philosophy was historical: the main task of the teachers was to summarize the ideas of the great philosophers. But for Sartre, thanks partly to Nizan and partly to Dostoevsky, philosophy and psychology were indistinguishable. His philosophizing was catalysed by his finding an unused alphabetical index on the seat of a *métro* train. Published by Midy Suppositories, with the company's name on the cover, it was intended for free promotional distribution to doctors. Sartre kept it for jottings, grouping them alphabetically and juxtaposing philosophical reflections with aphorisms and fragments of fiction written to define a concept. For 'Soul' the entry is:

He looked into his soul as if looking at himself in a mirror: with the ardent desire to satisfy his longing to be beautiful (as he knew he wasn't) to be intelligent (which he certainly hoped to be) and his fear of finding himself ugly, mean. And he went from mirror to mirror, from introspection to introspection without ever being able to form an opinion based on an idea of the whole.

His definition of 'Love' is ingenious: 'Desire consists of treating a woman as a means, not an end – love consists of treating a woman as an end not a means.' Under 'Art' he notes: 'The secret is to dominate your art.'[11] Dostoevsky seemed to have let him in on a secret. 'I wasn't sure what it was but there was something there which was more than scientific knowledge or ordinary knowledge';[12] he now believed that a writer should be a philosopher, should have a comprehensive view of all knowledge, should unveil 'the truth about the world', should give the reader new insights and ideas.[13] He had found maths and natural science extremely difficult,[14] but he had faith in his own intelligence and in his talent for reporting on the world he observed, though the truths he had to reveal were to be learned not by observing but by writing: 'By combining words, I'd gain real things ... There were groupings of words that yielded a truth.'[15]

Deeply serious in his questing ambition, he was simultaneously driven, if only defensively, towards comedy: aware of his ugliness, he invited laughter in preference to being its victim. When Nizan withdrew into one of his depressions, Sartre was the only one who could make him laugh, and during breaks between lessons the two friends would often put on impromptu performances in the first-floor study. Standing in front of a table covered with a black cloth, Sartre would turn the handle of an imaginary gramophone; Nizan, squatting under the table, would imitate the nasal tones of a crooner. Or they would perform a dialogue consisting of archaic exclamations: 'Si fait.' 'Oui-da.' 'Parbleu.'[16] Together they were exhibitionistic as neither of them would have been alone, though Sartre was using the same mimetic talent that had won him the job of Satyre Officiel so soon after his arrival at the Henri IV. His earliest performances had been given in his grandfather's study to an imaginary audience; at school he consolidated the habit of performing. It would remain central to his thinking: much of his writing has the rhythm of an extempore lecture.

There was no danger now that he would ever be mistaken for Nizan, who was taller and style-conscious, while Sartre dressed carelessly, usually in a black shirt. Nizan had a musical voice and was given to long silences; Sartre had habituated himself to behaving like an extrovert – this too was a performance – and though he could sing well, his speaking voice was hoarse.[17] He had become resigned to the loss of his mother, while Nizan, who suffered from facial neuralgia, was still unbalanced by ardent love for a father who felt himself to be a failure.

In their second and final year at the lycée there were over 70 boys in the class – 79 originally; some dropped out[18] – but Sartre's attitude to philosophy changed, thanks largely to his new teacher, Colonna d'Istria, a small, crippled man whom he at first liked.[19] The first subject set for a long essay was 'Consciousness of Duration', which led Sartre to read Bergson's 'Essai sur les données immédiates de la conscience' (which is translated as 'Time and Free Will'). It was this which made Sartre choose philosophy as his main subject, believing that its concern was with mental processes, and that it would help him to write Dostoevskian fiction. Bergson's reflections on duration and consciousness also prompted him to take a closer interest in 'what went on inside the mind, in the way ideas are formed, how feelings appear, disappear and so on'. His intention was to become not a philosopher but a teacher of philosophy; the subject would also help him towards the psychological understanding he would need as a novelist. The essay he wrote was little more than a résumé of Bergson, and Colonna d'Istria was unimpressed.[20] In the three competitive philosophy examinations held during the year, Sartre was placed 14th, 21st and 14th, while Nizan, who did not sit for the third, came third in the first, and fifth in the second. Maheu came 7th, 16th and 6th.

Sartre did worst of all in French, coming 66th in the first test and 46th in the second, while Nizan came eleventh and fourteenth. The only subject in which Sartre was placed among the top ten was Latin: in composition he came 39th and then 8th; in translation 9th, 26th and 22nd. In Greek translation he came 19th in all three tests. Nor did he win any prizes at the end of the academic year. For philosophical dissertations there were two prizes and eight runners-up. After this, eight other boys were rewarded with a mention, and Sartre was one of these. In Greek translation Nizan was the second runner-up after the two prizewinners, but Sartre failed to distinguish himself in this, in French or in history.[21]

These results assort oddly with the impression he made on his fellow-pupils. Georges Canguilhem wrote: 'He made himself noticeable, certainly, by his capacity for work and his brilliant results, but also by his vivacity and good humour. If he was already capable of discoursing on boredom, he charmed his friends with his humour, loved jokes and wasn't above kicking up a shindy.'[22] Sartre's liveliness was abnormal; he was unable to sleep at night unless he put wax in his ears and a bandage round his eyes.[23] He spoke willingly about his ugliness, but it disappeared, according to Raymond Aron, later a friend at the Ecole Normale, as soon as he started talking. 'His intelligence wiped out the pimples and the bloatedness of his face. For the rest, small, strong-backed, tough, he climbed up ropes, legs at right-angles, with an effortless ease which stupefied us.'[24]

What friends envied most of all was his phenomenal fluency. If he had completed only three hundred pages of a manuscript started three weeks earlier, they would tease him: what had gone wrong?[25] His self-confidence was no less extraordinary. He expected to reach the same level as Hegel. His ambitions, he told Aron, crystallized in two images: wearing an open-necked shirt and white flannel trousers, he was a young man on a beach, sliding, cat-like, from one group of girls to another; or he was at a dinner table, raising his glass in response to a group of men who were standing up to toast him. But generally, though he rarely talked about politics, he despised privilege and the self-importance of employers and bourgeois dignitaries.[26]

Soon after he started to record ideas in the alphabetical index, he began to think about what he called contingency. Going to the cinema (which was still an act he associated with his mother and her defiance of the higher culture championed by his grandfather) he would see films in which narrative necessity linked all the elements together; walking out into the street he would notice a startling absence of necessity. 'People were moving about, they were anybody.'[27]

It was at about this time that the idea of freedom began to excite him. He had already argued with friends at La Rochelle, and already tried to convince Nizan when they were about fifteen that we are as free as we choose to be, but Nizan, more ascetic, was considering whether to become a priest. 'Their morality appeals to me.' Thanks partly to his mother's threats, the idea was dropped. 'I tried to impose my optimism on him', Sartre wrote, 'repeating that we were free. He did not answer, but the faint smile at the corner of his mouth said a good deal about this idea.'[28]

If Sartre failed to win prizes or high marks, it may have been partly to spite his step-father. He absented himself so often from school that he acquired a reputation for being invisible. In 'L'Enfance d'un chef', Berliac, who is modelled partly on Nizan, partly on Sartre, begins to play truant from school. Lucien meets him in a bar on rue des Petits-Champs. They confide in each other, smoke English cigarettes, play records of Sophie Tucker and Al Jolson. They compare notes on feelings towards their mothers, and borrow books by Freud from the Bibliothèque Ste-Geneviève. Lucien starts feeling afraid to kiss his mother good night. 'It was like carrying a volcano inside him.' Having given up masturbation for six months, in order to work harder, he reverts to it.

Residual memories of difficulties at the lycée filter into 'L'Enfance d'un chef', where Lucien tells himself: 'I'm a good student. No, that's a lie. A good student enjoys working – I don't. I get high marks, but I don't enjoy working. Not that I hate working. I don't care. I don't care about anything. I'll never get anywhere.' Questioning himself about what he is, he concludes that he does not exist. His philosophy teacher tries, unsuccessfully, to reassure him with the Cartesian *cogito*. 'If you doubt your existence, you must exist.' Like Sartre, who was intent on denying Mancy any right to feel proud of his step-son, Lucien enjoys the sensation of not having the stuff in him that bourgeois bosses are made of. The idea makes him want to take romantic moonlight walks, but his parents forbid him to go out at night. He closes his eyes, lets himself drift: existence must be an illusion. The world is a comedy without actors. He thinks of writing a treatise on nothingness and imagines that 'people on reading it would disappear like vampires at cockcrow'.[29]

On Thursdays, together with friends from the lycée, Sartre met working-class girls from the St-Michel area in the Jardins du Luxembourg. Most of the girls were glad to flirt and willing to make love. Sartre made a date with a girl of about eighteen who, like the doctor's wife, went to bed with him only once. But the Jardins du Luxembourg, the scene of his early rejection by the other children playing there, went on figuring in his sexual fantasies. Throughout his life he kept an image based on dreams he had when he was about twenty of a pretty blonde dressed in the frock of a little girl and playing with a hoop by the Luxembourg pond. In the dreams he was bare-legged and only a little older than she. Even while he dreamed the sexual symbolism of the stick and the hoop were obvious to him.[30] Perhaps his resistance to Freud was partly a determination not to understand the traumatic aftermath of early rejections.

Sartre was nineteen in August 1924 when he gained seventh place in the entrance examination for the Ecole Normale Supérieure. 'I regained consciousness of myself as a free man, or at least one in the process of liberating himself.'[1] 'Many can say, as I do, that they have had four years of happiness.'[2] In fact he spent five years there, not leaving until the summer of 1929.

The school was at 45 rue d'Ulm, not far from the Sorbonne. Wide stone steps led up to an entrance hall, with the students' pigeon-holes on the right. Beyond the paved courtyard was a garden which had blossoming trees in it and a pool with a fountain and goldfish.

The principal of the school was the literary historian Gustave Lanson, who had taken over in 1919, when he was already sixty-two. Nizan looked down on him as a 'little old man, patriotic, hypocritical and powerful, with a respect for soldiers'. It was assumed that *normaliens* who did military service would be commissioned as officers, but discipline within the school was slack, though students were roused every morning at 7.30 by the breakfast bell and had to sign the register if they came back late at night. They were not compelled to eat any of the meals in the refectory, where the food was so undesirable that most of them patronized the local bistros. Nor was much care taken about hygiene. The dormitory remained un-aired and unswept; the crockery was badly washed and, as if to discourage the boys from keeping themselves clean, the only running water was in a closet used for cleaning shoes and storing dustbins.[3]

Sartre and Nizan shared a study with portraits of Giraudoux and James Joyce on the wall. The two friends were at peace again though Nizan sometimes went for days without speaking to Sartre.[4] Apart from René Maheu and Pierre Guille, their fellow-students included Jean Hyppolite and Raymond Aron. Aron had an extraordinary mixture of humility and pride. One of the most impressive students of his generation, he seemed destined to be a great philosopher. He had a quick, incisive mind, wit, eloquence, a natural authority and such a formidable memory that he never needed to take notes. He was like a brilliant barrister with total mastery over his brief and a capacity for the effortless assimilation of new material. With his thin body, his bony face and his hooded, twinkling eyes, he was at once aloof and available. His devotion to Sartre began at the ENS. Many people would later claim to be more friendly with Sartre than they actually were, but none would suffer more than Aron at not being able to continue a friendship with him, and no-one could have given less provocation for being treated – as Sartre would treat him – like an enemy.

From the beginning Sartre, Nizan and Maheu gravitated into a sub-group consisting mainly of students who had been taught at the Henri IV by Alain (Emile August Chartier). A philosopher and himself a product of the Ecole Normale, he encouraged his pupils to dismantle accepted values and beliefs, to challenge commonplace assumptions. He cultivated a Stendhalian lucidity, hated fanaticism and enjoyed paradox. Even among the radicals, though, Sartre, Nizan, Maheu and Guille stood out as a quartet which was ridiculed by the others, and which accordingly became hostile,[5] but the whole Alain group was fairly brutal in its language, fairly violent in its behaviour. Late at night the boys would hide at the top of the stairs to shout 'Thus pissed Zarathustra' as they threw water bombs at boys who were returning in dinner jackets from an evening out.[6] But Sartre had a gentle side. At twenty, according to Jean Fabre, 'he was the best and most generous companion imaginable ... Underneath the cynicism and self-disgust which he willingly displayed ... his secret was indubitably a great softness which he managed neither to acknowledge nor to disclaim.'[7]

The Ecole Normale had been affiliated to the Sorbonne since 1903. *Normaliens* take the ordinary degree at the university, with complementary instruction at the Ecole, but Sartre scarcely ever went to the Sorbonne. Apart from Sartre and Nizan, there were only three students of philosophy in the first year – Aron, Canguilhem and Lagache – so the five saw a lot of each other.[8] Throughout his five years Sartre gave a good deal of time to psychology and, in his first year, together with Nizan, Aron and Lagache, attended a course in pathological psychology given at the psychiatric hospital of Ste-Anne by Georges Dumas, who was pleased to have four *normaliens* in his class. Sartre and Nizan were even able to earn money by taking part in tests,[9] but Sartre still could not afford the boxing lessons he would have liked to take at a local gymnasium.[10] He worked extremely hard, pitching himself into what was to become a lifelong habit of settling down to his books from nine in the morning till one, and again from five in the evening till nine.

Of the philosophers he read in preparation for his exam, the ones who appealed to him most were Descartes, Spinoza and Rousseau. He liked the rule Descartes had made for himself:

> I have devoted only *very few hours in a day to the thoughts that occupy the imagination*, and very few in a year to those which occupy only the understanding, and I have given all the rest of my time to the relaxation of the senses and the repose of the mind, attempting thus to emulate those who looking at the verdure of a forest or the flight of a bird persuade themselves that they are thinking of nothing.

We can infer from the advice Sartre gave to a friend in 1926 when he quoted these lines that he followed Descartes's rule in a revised form: 'The bird in flight must be *your* bird, the forest *your* forest, and for that to happen you need not to feel it but to transform it slightly.'

It is difficult to assess the part played by the Ecole Normale in shaping a mind that had already matured to the level of sophistication shown in the early fiction. If Sartre was to go on being educated until he was twenty-four, the ideal education would have pulled him away from the tendency that the perceptive M. Bernes had detected during his first year at the Lycée Louis-le-Grand – to write fluently on ideas he had only partially digested. What he badly needed was a close and sustained relationship with a brilliant, sensitive, rigorous teacher who could command his respect. But he was no good at making friends with men in positions of authority; and the Ecole Normale was no good at inculcating the habit of painstaking research into original sources; Sartre was not deflected from his tendency to depend on insufficient facts, insufficiently mastered. But he was already a virtuoso with words, and with his attractive voice he would have the lifelong ability to spellbind an audience of one person, five people or five hundred by speaking as if he were thinking out loud, while the verbal virtuosity already made it dangerously easy for him to write as if he were speaking impromptu.

During his five years at the ENS he learned less from lectures than from reading and conversation. Later in life, except with de Beauvoir, he would seldom match his wits against intellects of a calibre comparable to his own. The company he enjoyed was that of girls, juniors and intellectual inferiors, but at the ENS he was surrounded by brilliant young men of his own age, and, competitive as he already was, he cannot have failed to profit hugely from arguing with Nizan, Aron and other friends, as he did from his voracious reading. Between November 1924 and March 1925, he borrowed about 120 books from the school's library, mixing philosophy with psychology and classics with modern literature. He kept going back to books by Plato, Kant and Schopenhauer, also reading work by Shakespeare, Keats, Cervantes, Goethe, Pascal, Villiers de l'Isle Adam, Mallarmé, Nerval, Chrétien de Troyes, Spinoza, Descartes, Freud, Janet and Hesnard. He took out three books by the psychologist Théodule Ribot, including *La Vie incons-ciente*. In April he read Bergson, Erasmus, Giraudoux, Lucretius and St Augustine's *Confessions*.[11] He was also reading Marx, without taking much in, and Freud, only to be annoyed by the assumption that consciousness was not autonomous. The other students' reactions to Freud are parodied in 'L'Enfance d'un chef' when Lucien and Berliac congratulate themselves on the size of their complexes. More seriously, Lucien feels enlightened about 'this odd feeling of not existing; this protracted blankness in his consciousness, his sleepiness, his confusions, the vain attempts to achieve self-knowledge, attempts that met only a curtain of fog'.[12] The friends get into the habit of interpreting their dreams and their gestures. Lucien throws himself greedily into psycho-analysis: it is a relief to find character situated below the level of consciousness. But whereas Berliac luxuriates in his Oedipus complex, Lucien sees in it 'the sign of a passion for power which later he would like to use for different purposes'.[13]

On Sundays Sartre would lunch with his mother and step-father, seeing his mother on her own once every ten days or so until they moved to St-Etienne, where Mancy was put in charge of the Le Flaive factories.

In his later interviews Sartre would claim that while at the ENS he gave up reading 'classical literature' except for Stendhal. This is belied by the register of books he borrowed from the library. Throughout his five years at the school, the range of his reading is most impressive. During his second year he took out books by Croce, Durkheim, Casanova, James Joyce, Goethe, Hugo, Nietzsche, Bertrand Russell, Strindberg, Wagner, Nerval, Zola, Maupassant, Marcus Aurelius, Epictetus and Georges Sorel, as well as books on Cézanne, van Gogh and Goya. During his third year his reading included Beaumont and Fletcher, Jung, Piaget, Hegel, Croce, Fichte and Hesnard. In his fourth year he borrowed fifteen books by Plato as well as books about Plato and Socrates. He was also reading Descartes, Spinoza and Kant, as well as Piaget, and though he did not have a high opinion of Léon Brunschvicg, the principal philosopher at the ENS, Sartre took out one of his books.[14]

At the same time Sartre came under the spell of the surrealists, who were mostly not much older than the students at the Ecole, and were popular there. He emulated the surrealist indifference to beauty, read Breton and Eluard, trying to imitate the poems in his *L'Immaculée Conception* and doing surrealist exercises in style. He started thinking about madness in relation to surrealism. Having once believed that it was possible to hit on the truth through the arrangement of words, he mimicked the surrealist idiom. In 'L'Enfance d'un chef' Lucien writes a poem with phrases in it like 'The great crabs wrapped in the mantle of fog', and lets himself be seduced by a surrealist, Bergère, after confiding to him that he has tried to commit suicide. Bergère diagnoses the boy's condition as 'disorder' and tells him about Rimbaud's programme for a systematic disordering of all the senses.

The estrangement between the two friends is caused by Berliac's jealousy when Bergère makes Lucien his lover; in actuality the estrangement was caused by Sartre's failure to understand the crisis Nizan was undergoing. Retrospectively Sartre would maintain that Nizan was authentically in rebellion against the school which was 'said to be normal and reputed to be superior' (Nizan's phrase); at the time it looked as though Nizan was a spoilsport, was searching for help no-one could give him. When he confided that he was afraid of dying, Sartre decided that since he gave way so readily to depression, his 'moral health' must be inadequate. At one point Nizan disappeared for three days, to be found, drunk, with some strangers.[15]

In fact he was less self-involved than Sartre, more alert to the political situation, and profoundly troubled – as Sartre would be later – by the need to choose between *la vie intérieure* and political action. Sartre might later have reacted less obdurately against *la vie intérieure* if he had been less devoted to it now – it was his pattern each time he recanted to turn in systematic hatred against the quality he had formerly loved. In *La Semence et le scaphandre* he declared his intention of writing only about his own experience: he equated it with the experience of humanity. The novel contains an account of the dealings he and Nizan had in 1923 with *La Révue sans titre*, in which Sartre, using the pseudonym Jacques Guillemin, published his story 'L'Ange du morbide' and several chapters of *Jésus la Chouette*. Nizan's sense of his isolation was exacerbated by brooding on the disintegration of western civilization. Like many *normaliens* of his generation and young intellectuals – Aragon for instance – he went on flirting with the idea of withdrawing into a religious order, and if in the end he opted (like Aragon) for the PCF (Parti communiste français), the decision was partly provoked by the ineffectuality of the ruling Cartel des Gauches, an alliance of socialists and radicals more determined to fight against inflation than against unemployment and depressed wages.

The leader of the radicals, Edouard Herriot, was characteristic of the provincial bourgeoisie – patriotic and mediocre, the prototypical mayor of Lyons – while his supporters (shopkeepers, smallholders, manufacturers) wanted a policy of *laisser-faire*. The socialists favoured a tougher economic policy, but the party was hopelessly ineffectual. At the Socialist Congress in Tours (December 1920) the party had been split by the vote in favour of affiliation to Moscow, and *Humanité*, founded by Jaurès in 1904, had been taken over by the communist majority. Of the sixty-eight socialists elected in November 1919 only thirteen had joined the Communist Party. Caught between the radicals and the communists, the socialists preserved their identity only by co-operating with neither.

Sartre took little interest in all this, but to many of his contemporaries communism seemed the only socialism that had remained true to itself. Nizan detested half-measures: in his fragmentary novel *Le Gout du définitif*, his *alter ego* is intent on 'rediscovering the truth that had been lost since he started, ten years ago, in the sixth form'.[16]

Nizan was active in the *Groupe d'information internationale*, a student group, led by Georges Friedmann, with the aim of seeing beyond nationalist horizons, but Sartre stayed aloof both from the radical groups and from the reviews they published. The most important of these, *Philosophies*, had been founded 'for the defence of the MIND, MYSTICISM and liberty. Our prime concern is for the renaissance of philosophy and for the creation of epic poetry. For us thought is an action.'[17] The surrealists believed mysticism to be 'the poetic solution of the fundamental problems'.[18] The *Philosophies* group had been founded by Pierre Morhange, who regarded himself as a Rimbaudian visionary. Nizan became one of his five disciples, together with Friedmann, Henri Lefebvre, Norbert Guterman and the aggressive, red-haired Georges Politzer, who formulated slogans such as 'The philosopher will take charge' and 'spiritual dictatorship'.[19] The group's idiom was literary and religious. When Simone de Beauvoir saw the magazine *L'Esprit*, which replaced *Philosophies* in 1926 (after a patron had withdrawn his backing) she recognized that the intellectual young socialists 'were talking about soul, salvation, joy, eternity ... They were interested primarily in spiritual manifestations; for them economics and politics could only be subordinate.' What capitalism had destroyed was 'the sense of being', men must rediscover 'the eternal part of themselves'.[20]

The surrealists were hesitating on the brink of commitment to communism: for Breton, 'one revolution or another, however bloody', was the only way 'to escape, momentarily at least, from this fearful cage in which we go on arguing'.[21] Students were confused by the ideological turbulence, torn between the incompatible insights of Einstein, Freud, Hegel, Marx, Lenin, Valéry and Proust. 'Pell-mell we went back to square one,' wrote Lefebvre, 'but we had access to means of reconstructing the world. The Russian Revolution reduced previous history to a *tabula rasa*, reconstructing society from top to bottom: we were out to emulate it as quickly as possible.'[22] These ideas and pressures were to have a long-term effect on Sartre, but Nizan was more sensitive to the condition of Europe, which had not cured itself of the nationalistic thinking that had led to the world war: 'How can we forgive the generations that were sacrificed for not having removed the need for useless sacrifice?'[23] Perhaps the Communist Party could help mankind to obviate 'an idiotic ending'.

Though no less refractory than his friend, Sartre felt no urge to channel his dissident energy into politics. He needed confrontations to be more direct and personal, needed to find adult correlatives to the childhood pleasure he had taken in the idea of slapping kings in the face. The monarch in the Ecole Normale was Gustave Lanson. If Sartre was to gain enormously in self-confidence during his five years there, it was due less to what he wrote than to what he read, and it was less because he matured psychologically and intellectually than because he competed successfully against brilliant fellow-students, excelling himself not only academically but as an entertainer – mimic, singer, actor, pianist. His most spectacular victory of all was in a battle that no-one would have expected him to win – against the dignified and distinguished Gustave Lanson, who was not going to escape with a slap. He would be made to abdicate.

It was not yet apparent to Lanson that this small student was dangerous, but he was obviously hostile. In March 1925, at the school's annual revue, *A l'ombre de vieilles billes en fleur* – the old faces in flower parodying Proust's young girls – Sartre played M. Lanson, who was seduced by the wife of a rich Brazilian Doña Veraldes, played by Lagache. The allusion was to the international organizations which were recruiting many *normaliens* at this time. In the sketch the school was sent to conquer Brazil. In another sequence Sartre danced in the nude with a semi-nude Nizan. Sartre's skill in mimicking Lanson was formidable. 'The student Sartre', reported *L'Oeuvre*, 'sustained the role of M. Lanson brilliantly', and the review was illustrated by a photograph of Sartre in the impersonation.[24]

His strong streak of exhibitionism made him hanker for a life in which he could appear regularly in front of audiences: still cherishing the idea of becoming a jazz singer, he frequented the College Inn in the rue Vavin. Though he had never been given piano lessons, he not only played competently, but took pupils,[25] as well as teaching philosophy to first-year students who could not otherwise keep up with the work in class. His income from coaching enabled him to eat lunch and dinner in local restaurants, and he readily gave money away to friends, as he did throughout his life.

His ambitions were unbounded; he told a friend: 'I want to be the one who knows the most things.' Meanwhile he wrote a one-act comedy about a man who describes his death-agony, *J'aurai un bel enterrement* (*I'll Have a Nice Funeral*). Instead of joining a political movement, he counted on liberating himself by becoming totally independent of other people. He had – intermittently at least – a clear vision of what he termed moral health, which could be attained only by rejecting all social constraints, starting with those of morality. 'If you are moral, you obey society; if you are immoral, you rebel against it, but on its territory, where you are certain to be defeated. You must be neither one nor the other but superior to all that.'[26] The social aesthetic must be rejected. To covet goods in a shop window is to enslave oneself both to those who make them and those who sell them –

imbeciles who exploit you.[27] In this context Sartre's first *acte gratuit* comes to seem less gratuitous, even if he had not, at the age of fourteen, become aware of why he wanted to destroy the hat that had seemed so desirable. In Paris the rejection of commercial culture was partly a matter of necessity: not being able to afford the goods that were so seductively displayed in the shops, he needed to feel he was rebuffing the seducers. He must not let himself be distracted from what was almost a quest for the absolute.

For most students, male and female, clothes on display in shop-windows are desirable as means of enhancing sex-appeal; Sartre would have been incapable of rejecting the commercial subculture if he had not become more self-confident and more reconciled to his ugliness and his shortness. Until 1925, as he said in 1926, his appearance had made him 'temperamentally very melancholy ... I have absolutely driven that out, because it's a weakness'. He was determined to make himself stronger. By pursuing only objectives that were realistically attainable he could feel more free, stronger and more passionate. It was easier to overcome scruples, and not to be held back by pity. 'I call this state moral health because it's like being physically very well and feeling strong enough to bend a street-lamp with one hand.'[28]

His faith in willpower was reinforced by an energetic but compulsive refusal to recognize himself as a victim of genetic accident. At times he felt jubilantly full of himself, bursting with pride in his future. Looking at self-important senior citizens, he felt vibrantly aware of his hidden powers, as if the spectacles, the squinting eyes, the unprepossessing face, the diminutive body were the disguise he had selected. 'Confronted with men who are intimidating and revered,' he later wrote to a girl, 'you'll be able to think that these are marionettes you can manipulate.'[29] It was his own secret strength he was thinking of. The childhood feeling of play-acting survived in a different form: the student Sartre was the great man of the future pretending to be just a student. This was the Ecole chapter of the autobiography he was living.

Though almost everything in his life was conniving at his feelings of superiority, Nizan, still ahead of him, was the first to win a girl. At the Ecole ball in December 1924 he had met a seventeen-year-old girl who was both beautiful and high-spirited. Descended on her father's side from a composer-conductor at the court of Napoleon III and on her mother's from the Chief Rabbi of Bordeaux, Henriette Alphen lived in a block of flats on the rue Vavin. Rirette, as she was called, would meet Nizan, Sartre and Aron after lectures at the Sorbonne, and they would go into the Jardins du Luxembourg together or back to her flat for tea. She said that if she was not married by the age of twenty, she would take a lover so as to have children.[30]

Both Sartre and Nizan were spending a lot of time with René Maheu, who seems to have taken the lead in evolving a personal mythology out of Cocteau's *Potomak*: the three of them belonged to the Eugènes, the highest caste, that of Socrates and Descartes. All their contemporaries were assigned to inferior orders, mostly among the Marrhanes, who loll about in the infinite, or the Mortimers, who slop about in the blue of the sky. The Catholic philosopher Gabriel Marcel and most contributors to the *Nouvelle Revue française* were classified as belonging to the same species as the Cataboryx, a metaphysical animal that expresses itself in 'borborygmic rumbles'. The Eugène looks down on science, industry and all universal moral systems; he tries to make his life into an original work of art.[31] The three friends could feel isolated, but not alone.

Many of Sartre's paternal relations were still living in Thiviers, and in September 1925 he went there for the funeral of a cousin – the daughter of his aunt Hélène, his father's sister. At the funeral, wearing a dark suit and one of his step-father's hats, he met a beautiful girl of twenty-two. She had long blonde hair and blue eyes.[32] They were both invited to dinner afterwards at his aunt's house but the conversation they wanted to have was interrupted by questions from doctors and lawyers. Leaving early they went for a walk in the fields.[33] Simone-Camille Sans was the daughter of a Toulouse chemist, who had implanted in her a strong taste for reading. Her sexual experiences had been plentiful and eccentric, involving amateur prostitution and orgies in fancy-dress, held in a cellar. The twenty-year-old Sartre reminded her of Mirabeau, and for four days they were inseparable.[34]

Falling into the trick he had used at school in La Rochelle, he pretended there were already two girls in his life, but in his second letter to her, written early in 1926, he admitted that they did not exist. After the meeting in Thiviers, he and Simone-Camille or 'Toulouse' as he called her did not meet for six months, but the relationship continued through correspondence. By the end of 1925 she was writing that she loved him better than her mother, while he regarded himself as her fiancé, though in the surviving letters he uses the term only when he wants to reproach her.[35] Perhaps he would have been equally articulate in conversation, but it is doubtful whether he would have been so aggressive or so self-assured.

This correspondence gave him one of his earliest pretexts for an essay in autobiography. Since childhood, he told her, his main ambition had been to create – create anything, from a philosophical system to a symphony. But he was dissatisfied with everything he did, with each style he used. He was trying to create a new character for himself, devoid of the shaming sentimentalism that made him weep 'like a calf' at plays, films, novels. He was ashamed of being cowardly and soft: 'when a dog barks near me it can make me tremble with fear'.[36] What gave him 'this artificial attitude' she had diagnosed was the determined attempt to check tendencies which persistently reappeared: 'I'm never genuine because I'm always trying to adjust, to recreate; I'll never have the pleasure of being able to act spontaneously.'[37] It almost follows that spontaneity was one of the qualities he admired most in other men. Hankering after sincerity, he was confused by ambivalence towards the feelings that arrived of their own accord, dodging the formidable willpower that was on sentry duty: sometimes he found himself saying nothing or stammeringly saying the opposite of what he had intended or neutralizing the feeling by expressing it in awkward words.

He would have liked to make the 400-mile journey to Toulouse every month, he said, to visit her, but he had been quarrelling with Nizan and had given up hope of earning any money from their collaboration on the translation of Karl Jaspers's *Allgemeine Psychopathologie* (1913). To earn money he was giving lessons in philosophy to a boy, Albert Morel, who was preparing for his *baccalauréat.* He had formerly been tutored by Guille, who had recommended Sartre. Even so, he could only look forward to Easter holidays, he told Toulouse, in which he would 'wander through the streets without spending money – to economize and to be able to visit you – allowing myself twice a week the luxury of a three-franc seat in the cinema'.[38] He was reading Montherlant and warming to the 'gauntleted cavalier' idea of love represented by Alban in *Les Bestiaires.*

After passing the first examination, Sartre found he could do little but 'sit stupefied at my desk'. His friends were dispirited, aimless. 'They go wandering into each other's houses, where they silently eat lumps of sugar and cannot go away ... They would like to talk about their character and say those phoney things one says when one is in this state. Only my presence stops them, for I hate feebleness and tasteless, facile confessions.'[39] He also hated wishy-washy melancholy and reflection about the process of reflecting. He liked Alain's dictum: 'To think is to want.'[40]

Looking at the alphabetical index he had filled with philosophical notes two years previously, he felt ashamed: 'I was so drastic about everything.' He was slowly coming to feel more of a specialist, concentrating, for instance, on solving 'a problem of pure psychology, a problem of detail'.

He was thinking about writing a novel: it would be for her, he said, and he had started reading Charles Andler's six-volume biography of Nietzsche (*Nietzsche: sa vie et pensée*, Paris 1920–31), which developed his ideas about willpower and gave him the basis for a realistic adventure story modelled on the Wagner-Cosima-Nietzsche triangle, with himself in the Nietzschean position and Simone as Cosima. The novel, which he never finished, was to be called *Une Défaite.* In each phase of Frédéric's romantically turbulent life he would write a book, and though he died unknown, glory came afterwards. Unlike Nietzsche, Sartre did not feel unloved, and, luxuriating in André Maurois's *Ariel*, he tried to read Shelley's life as prefiguring the way his own genius would flower.[41] He was thinking of himself when he made the hero of his novel say: 'I'm a genius because I'm alive ... Oh I wish others could experience my life as I do, overflowing, tumultuous ... If only I could express it, tear it out of myself. Then I'd be in reality the genius I'm entitled to be. Only one man is alive for me: myself ... and I cannot believe I am going to die.'[42] This has affinities with the Rimbaudian ecstasy in Brecht's first play, *Baal*. After six months without seeing Toulouse, Sartre raised the money to visit her in the Easter holidays, only to receive a telegram: 'NOT FREE POINTLESS TO COME SUNDAY'. No letter followed, which infuriated him. 'When one is not free, one frees oneself, that's all.' Did he not deserve better treatment than this? 'Who has made you into what you are, who is trying to stop you from turning into a bourgeoise or an aesthete or a great gawk? Who else cares about your intellect?' He gave her an ultimatum: either she must see him in Toulouse on Tuesday 13 April at any time she chose, or she would never hear from him again.[43]

She gave in. They went to a cinema and stayed together until five in the morning. He felt more involved than he had in September, but she talked disturbingly about dances in Toulouse, and he was not sure whether to trust her. What if she had been putting on an act? He sat on a park bench with the pipe he had taken to smoking, and fell asleep with it in one hand and a box of matches in the other. He was awakened by the old park-keeper. 'Mechanically I lit my pipe, thinking it would be pleasant to spend a moment talking to this old man in the state of sad calm sometimes seen in certain heroes of novels after a moving scene (Myshkin for instance chatting with Rogozhin after the murder of Nastasya Filipovna – due allowance being made).'

Sitting afterwards in the Café Regina, waiting for the first train to Paris, he hesitated about whether to declare his love in a letter. He might make a fool of himself, but perhaps there should be a scene in the novel after Wagner's death: Cosima could meet Nietzsche again and show him that 'this brutal female defiance which he was taking for strength was only wildness and weakness'.[44] Towards Toulouse Sartre had been alternating between over-confidence and fear of ridicule. 'I wanted to be not the first but *the only* man you loved.'[45] He had spoken to her in the cinema about his 'sad inner self that plays the fool': perhaps she would understand him better by thinking of what Chaplin wanted to express through the Charlie character.[46] 'I love you with a simplicity worthy of the old park-keeper.'[47] In the train he felt very happy: 'I love a little girl who loves me, who is exactly the little girl I need, I'm determined to come back before July to see her, I trust her, the landscape under the sun is pleasing.'[48] Later letters would be full of promises: 'I want to give you a mental attitude which at the heart of the most mediocre life will ensure that your life is not a failure, that you will not be a Madame Bovary but an artist, without regrets and without sadness.'[49]

When Sartre's aunt Hélène arrived in Paris, she upset his mother by breaking the news of what was going on: Toulouse's mother had been writing to her about it. But when Sartre visited Thiviers to stay with his uncle Joseph, his father's brother, Toulouse made the 130-mile journey to meet him. He noticed, though, that 'love is the thing to be had from you most easily of all ... you are prodigal with little secondary loves'.[50] She should find a woman friend: there must be a woman she could like without loving her.

Back in Paris, Sartre found the spring weather helped him to luxuriate in affectionate possessiveness. 'You're mine, and things are mine, and my love influences the things around me, and the things around me influence my love.'[51] But she irritated him with the logicality of her letters. 'Remember', he admonished, 'that logic is the meal ticket of impotent intellectuals. Try to get ideas in other ways – *without reasoning*.'[52] The five or six great philosophers he was studying, he said, were in no way impeded by self-contradiction. She must not indulge in self-pity or sadness. 'Sadness goes with softness.'[53] It also went with daydreaming, which was dangerous.[54] She should copy Descartes, refusing to spend much time on 'thoughts which occupy the imagination'. Melancholy could always be driven out by willpower. She could saw wood – 'metaphorically, of course' – alter her posture, stop play-acting, work at her novel. 'Always be cheerful. If you really suffer one day, tell me. I've learnt how to console people because so many – without my understanding why – have confided in me.'[55]

At the beginning of 1926 Nizan had been close to joining the Communist Party, but in the summer he was hesitating about whether to leave for Aden, where he had been offered a job as tutor to the son of a businessman. Half ironically he wrote to solicit advice from men of letters, including Georges Duhamel, only to quote their replies mockingly to his friends,[56] who could not judge whether the letters had influenced him. Later Sartre would explain Nizan's decision to leave France by quoting from his novel *Antoine Bloyé*: 'he would have liked to give up this existence ... to become someone else, new, strange, who would be really himself ... lost, like a man who has left no forwarding address but is still active and alive'.[57] In Marxism, according to Sartre, Nizan found a justification for his hatreds and a way of reconciling the conflicting attitudes of his parents.[58]

The gap in Sartre's life was filled by Guille and Maheu, who became his inseparable friends. Secretive and sarcastic, Pierre Guille came from a protestant family with peasant roots.[59] He was the most unambitious of Sartre's friends, and the most empirical. With no desire to write, no interest in formulating theories (though he found Sartre's entertaining) he reserved his enthusiasm for food, wine and the pleasures of the moment. Maheu was fair-haired, with blue eyes and the fresh face of a boy from the country, but he dressed elegantly and spoke with an irony that seemed to affect even the tone of his voice and the twist of his smile. The three of them paid frequent visits to Mme Morel in her flat at the far end of the boulevard Raspail. Born in Argentina of French parents, she was attractive, petite, plump, elegant and vivacious. Her husband was a rich hypochondriac doctor who seldom left his draught-proof room. He encouraged her friendship with Guille, who had accompanied them to Anjou as tutor to their son. According to Simone de Beauvoir's 1960 book, the friendship remained platonic;[60] according to Sartre's letters to Toulouse, Guille became enamoured of Mme Morel, who gradually revealed her sexuality.[61] Guille spent all his spare time at the flat, where he had his own room, and Sartre sometimes spent the night there.[62]

Nizan's absence made it easier for Sartre to believe in his own intellectual prowess. In 1927 he would have to present a thesis for his *diplôme d'études supérieures*: by the end of 1926 he had begun to evolve what he described as 'a complicated theory about the function of the image for the artist' and he was already thinking of evolving a complete system of aesthetics.[63] He had felt, when he first read Bergson, that 'the truth had come down from heaven'; now he needed to 'bring down some other truths'.[64] While the *normaliens* were given a thorough grounding in Aristotelian and mathematical logic, their philosophy teachers tended to assume that physical and mental phenomena could both be analysed in terms of a common underlying reality. From the beginning Sartre disliked idealism, which effectively detached reality from the world, situating it inside consciousness. One pluralistic book which contributed to student resistance against the official philosophy was Jean Wahl's *Vers le concret. (Towards the Concrete)*. The ideas of Alain also helped to lay out an alternative track, and even on the question of images, Alain was refreshingly heterodox. It was puerile, he maintained, to believe that we could keep 'copies of things' in our memory and riffle through them at our convenience.[65] Images did not exist: there were only perceptions and false perceptions.

Certain that images did exist and that they could be equated neither with sensations nor with ideas, Sartre embarked on an ambitious reading programme, which reinforced his conviction that he had hit on an area mapped out inadequately by previous investigators. In Dumas's two-volume *Nouveau traité de psychologie* he found an article by L.Meyerson which defined an image as a perception that is 'reconsidered [*repensée*] and rationalized'.[66] Binet, in his 1903 *Etude experimentelle de l'intelligence*, abandoned the position he had adopted in 1896 (*Psychologie de raisonnement*) but three years before he died in 1911 he was still thinking of images as 'material elements'.[67] Though Bergson had insisted that no solid fragments could enter the flux of consciousness, that inner life presented itself as a constant flow, a 'multiplicity of interpenetration', he consistently thought of the image as an opaque thing that had 'imprinted' itself in the mind. Sartre, who had no difficulty in digesting all this reading, had no hesitation in rejecting it: he would be the one to draw the first accurate map.

By the end of 1926 Sartre had finished the first chapter of his Nietzsche novel, which he was now intending to call *Empédocle*; he promised Toulouse that it would be ready by 1 April next year. In the first chapter the Wagner figure 'plunges the unhappy little fellow into the depths of Contingency and manages to stupefy him by singing him the famous Song'.[68] This was a celebration of contingency in verse. Together with Nizan, Raymond Aron and Daniel Lagache, Sartre had also been planning to write a screenplay based on Jules Renard's 1894 novel *Poil de carotte*, which had been dramatized in 1900. The story is about a sensitive, dreamy boy. Growing up in the country he suffers at the hands of his bullying mother and his neglectful father. Eventually he learns how to protect himself. Sartre could identify with both phases of the boy's experience. 'What we need to place at the centre', he said, 'is the need for tenderness.'

The fiction, the philosophizing, the letters to Toulouse and (no doubt) the conversations with friends were all strongly didactic. Sartre believed in himself as someone who could stiffen the willpower of anyone prepared to take his advice. He claimed to have weaned one of his friends away from homosexuality. 'As the desire did not come from deep inside himself ... he'd have been very unhappy and probably destroyed.'[69] Encouraged by his salvationist success, Sartre wrote dogmatically to Toulouse about the importance of gaining as much power as possible; she must make herself independent of society for the sake of her 'moral health'. He was not asking her to give up emotional pleasures. 'You need to be sentimental (and I too make use of my sentimentality) but for oneself, not other people.'[70]

It was probably in December 1926 that she came to Paris for two weeks. At the ENS ball she made a considerable impact. Henriette Alphen, after marrying Nizan, was to remember the ball as mixing the grand style with informality that smacked of ill-breeding. Some of the students had invited well-born girls whose well-dressed mothers waited for them in the ballroom. She remembers Sartre as being pimply and blonder than he was later. The lampshade on his desk in the study he shared with Nizan was a pink voile undergarment, slightly yellowed, presumably given to him by Toulouse.[71] It was customary in the ENS for students to sport unorthodox lampshades. Though Sartre had borrowed money to entertain her in style, Toulouse was unimpressed by the hotel he had booked and the restaurants he chose.[72] Wanting her to stay on in Paris, he tried to find a job for her at a stationer's, but she had set her sights higher.

It was in April 1927, over eighteen months after he had met her, that he began to use the second person singular in his letters to her. In Paris Maheu had been trying to convince her that Sartre was too complicated ever to be capable of loving simply and straightforwardly, but he found out. 'I will say – and at length – just the opposite at Toulouse.' He was planning to spend four days there at the beginning of May. 'I know that I have a crazy desire to squeeze you in my arms, my dear little girl, and that I am more attached to you than to anyone else in the world.'[73] He believed that when he was with a beautiful girl, her beauty, extending over both of them, became the dominant element. 'I certainly had an appetite for beauty which was not so much sensual as magical. I would have wanted to eat beauty and incorporate it in me.'[74]

More fragile than he wanted to admit, the attachment to Toulouse caused him much anxiety, but in May 1927 he was distracted from it by the unheralded return of Nizan in the middle of the night. 'He came in without knocking. He was pale, grim, rather breathless. He said: "You don't look very cheerful." I answered: "Neither do you." At which we went off drinking and pronouncing judgment on the world, delighted that our friendship had resumed.'[75]

Sartre still felt less oppressed by the educational system, altogether less desperate than Nizan. But, together with three of their friends, they collaborated on organizing the large-scale practical joke which would carry Sartre's protracted duel with Lanson to its triumphant conclusion. During the hullaballoo in May about Lindbergh's solo flight across the Atlantic, the five students telephoned the evening papers to say that the disciplinary council of the ENS had unanimously decided to accolade the pilot by making him an honorary pupil. The papers carried the story, and on 25 May Le Petit Parisien announced: 'Lindbergh will be at the ENS this morning at 9.30'. One of the students bore a slight resemblance to Lindbergh, and when he drove up in a taxi, he was greeted with an ovation from a crowd of about 500 people. As he was carried triumphally on the shoulders of the hoaxers, the crowd followed, and one old man kissed his hands. Reporting the successful impersonation, the newspapers referred scathingly to Gustave Lanson, who promptly resigned.[76]

The joke put a mask of frivolity on a dissatisfaction that was serious. 'The tragic sense of life' – the phrase Miguel de Unamuno had popularized in 1913 – was recurrent in student conversation. It pointed to the unresolved conflicts and problems that were being evaded by the complacent intellectuals in power. There was no question for Sartre of following suit when Nizan joined the Party: that such a close friend could be a revolutionary struck him as 'totally grotesque'. Not even calling himself a socialist, Sartre professed to be glad that the establishment existed. 'I could throw verbal bombs at it.'[77] Before the end of the year he would be summoned in front of the disciplinary council for publishing in the school's magazine a scathing attack on the French army and on the obligation of *normaliens* to do 'special preparatory military service' in it. He helped to organize an ironical petition in which students expressed their desire to give evidence of their patriotism, their respect for work and for institutions. They wished to dissociate themselves from anarchic fellow-students by wearing uniform and submitting to a stricter discipline. Newspaper reports missed the irony.[78] Sartre was nearly always glad to join in practical jokes and frivolous conversations. After supper he would often drink in the Triboulet bar, where serious discussion was prohibited.[79]

The most effective way of protesting against the established philosophy was to evolve an alternative, but this took time. The students were advised to read Marx, 'in order to refute him',[80] but they had no access to the Hegelian dialectic. Lecturers such as Lachelier, author of *Psychologie et métaphysique*, and Brunschvicg, author of *La Conscience occidentale*, were indifferent or hostile to the Hegelian tradition, and there is no mention of Hegel in the extensive bibliography Sartre compiled for his work on 'L'Image dans la vie psychologique: rôle et nature', though it refers to Freud, Jaspers, Piaget and Babinski. Working with Nizan on proof-correcting the translation of Jaspers's *Allgemeine Psychopathologie*, Sartre had been struck by the rejection of scientific aetiology in favour of a studied reliance on intuitive guesses to make connections between discontinuous groups of facts. What emerged for Sartre was the possibility of 'apprehending' an individual character without reference to universal principles or to analytical psychology as taught at the Sorbonne.[81] When he presented his thesis, he was awarded the mark 'très bien'. This was the first serious philosophical essay that would find its way into his mature work. It was to be published in a revised form as part of *L'Imagination* (1936).

Raymond Aron's influence on him at this time has been underrated, partly because Sartre consistently ignored it in interviews, and partly because Simone de Beauvoir played it down in her autobiography. In fact Aron has an important place in the pre-history of existentialism, not only because he later alerted Sartre to phenomenology but because it was Aron, more than any of the teachers at the ENS, who aroused Sartre's interest in the philosophy of history. Aron's doctoral thesis was called *Introduction à la philosophie de l'histoire*, and when Sartre read it, he found himself involved with the question that would eventually be central to his *Critique*: does history have a rational meaning? His feeling after reading Aron's thesis was later confided to a diary: 'I felt encircled and gripped by it, as all my contemporaries did. It made me feel its presence.'[82]

Apart from Guille and Maheu, Aron was closer than anyone else to Sartre and Nizan, and, at the end of the year, when Nizan married Henriette Alphen, it was Sartre and Aron who were the witnesses. Sartre was not less eager, at this stage, to get married, but was less successful. During the summer of 1927 he accepted an invitation from the friendly Alfred Péron, one of Alain's ex-pupils, to stay in Usson-en-Forez in the Massif Central. Sartre's relationship with Toulouse had cooled, and when he met Péron's cousin, the daughter of a grocer, he became unofficially engaged to her,[83] but when he asked his mother and Mancy to approach the girl's parents, he was rejected.

It was in 1927–8 that Sartre wrote *Er l'Arménien*, a hastily composed fiction derived from the story Plato tells at the end of *The Republic* about Er, the son of Armenius. Ten days after his death in battle, Er's body is still fresh, and on the twelfth day, coming back to life, he tells how he has watched judgment being passed on the souls of the dead, the good ascending to heaven, the evil being sent down to hell. Sartre was trying to combine narrative with philosophy in the manner of the Greeks. Er and his sister ascend to heaven, taking petty bourgeois experience with them – Sartre's own, disguised as Greek. The action also involved a large-scale battle with the Titans.[84]

Sartre, Guille and Maheu were spending a lot of time with Mme Morel. Maheu was studying philosophy; Guille was studying literature. Sartre discussed Proust with Guille but their conversation was based more on what they had been doing, and when Sartre showed him and Mme Morel some of what he had written, she laughed at *Une Défaite*, calling Sartre 'misérable Frédéric'.[85] Nizan submitted the novel to Gallimard, but it was rejected.

Preparing for the 1928 *agrégation*, the examination which is decisive in the recruitment of teachers, Sartre wanted to show more originality than he had in either his essay for Colonna d'Istria or in his *diplôme d'études supérieures*. During one of Brunschvicg's seminars, held under the title 'Nietzsche – was he a philosopher?', Sartre tried to explain the ideas he had formulated in his notebook about contingency,[86] and it was on this subject that he wrote in his *agrégation* paper. Students were ranked in order of merit according to the papers they submitted, and Aron was put in the top place, Sartre in the fiftieth. To the astonishment of his fellow-students, he had failed. Returning after the summer holiday to Paris and to the necessity of competing once again in the *agrégation*, he took a room at the

Cité universitaire and asked Aron's advice on the technique of succeeding.[87]

In November 1928 his name features among those of eighty-three *normaliens* who signed a petition against military training, and when *Les Nouvelles littéraires* sent out a questionnaire to university students, Sartre's replies were quoted at length in the issue dated 2 February 1929. Comparing students of his generation to their predecessors, he claimed: 'We are unhappier but more likeable.'[88] More provocative still were the hints of a pessimistically non-conformist philosophy: 'At the root of humanity I see only sadness and boredom.' He attacked 'the determinism which oddly attempts to create a synthesis of existence and being. We are as free as you like, but helpless ... the will to power, action and life are only useless ideologies ... Everything is too feeble; everything carries the seeds of its own death. Above all, adventure – by which I mean that blind faith in haphazard and yet inevitable concatenations of circumstances and events – is a delusion.'[89] The point is the same as the one he had made about the difference between necessity in a fiction and contingency in the street, but he had now found a tone commanding enough to make his seniors listen. He could also formulate incisive slogans against conventional morality. 'Science is the outer surface of a ball', he declared. 'Morality is the hole inside.'[90]

Early in 1929 he received a note from Toulouse suggesting that they should meet again. The previous year she had become the mistress of the famous actor, Charles Dullin, who was in his middle forties. He set her up in a ground-floor flat on the rue Gabrielle and took her on as a pupil at the drama school attached to his theatre, the Atelier. Sartre found her more sophisticated, less provincial, and their relationship resumed. In *La Nausée*, Anny, who is modelled on Toulouse, is an actress being kept by an old man who is no trouble.

Toulouse behaved with a studied outrageousness. In one performance at the Atelier, she came on stage drunk and pulled off the leading actor's wig. Convinced that she was inspired by the devil, she was sketching out a collection of demonic stories,[91] and Sartre witnessed her midnight attempts at conversations with Nietzsche, Albrecht Dürer and Emily Brontë. She claimed to have such an affinity with them that death was no barrier. Their portraits stared out at her from the wall and two enormous dolls called Frederick and Albrecht were propped up in little chairs and dressed as for school: she spoke to them as if they were children. When she took Sartre to the Théâtre de l'Atelier, Dullin, who was playing Volpone, signalled that he was aware of her presence in the auditorium.[92]

In the summer of 1929 the twenty-four-year-old Sartre met a twenty-one-year-old girl who was beautiful, friendly, exceptionally clever, and no taller than he was. A philosophy student at the Sorbonne, she had come second in the June exams of 1927, beaten only by Simone Weil. The daughter of a Paris lawyer, Simone de Beauvoir had attended Léon Brunschvicg's lectures on the history of scientific thought and had responded positively to his idealism. The first left-wing intellectual she had met was Pierre Nodier, a member of the *Philosophies* group;[1] the second to become friendly with her was an ex-pupil of Alain.[2] For a long time before she met Sartre, Nizan and Maheu, she knew them by sight. The first time Sartre was pointed out to her at the Sorbonne, he was wearing a hat and talking to a girl student. De Beauvoir noticed that he was not to be seen in her company for long: she was replaced by a prettier one, who also failed to sustain a relationship. Mostly the three boys went around together. De Beauvoir found Nizan's eyes intimidating; Sartre was reputed to be a drinker. Maheu seemed more accessible, and she struck up an acquaintance by sitting down to eat lunch at his table in the restaurant of the Bibliothèque Nationale: they discussed Hume and Kant. Unlike Nizan and Sartre, he attended Brunschvicg's lectures, and after the Easter holidays, their friendship developed: they told each other they were individualists, lunched regularly together on the first floor of a *salon de thé* and went for walks.[3] But one Sunday, when she saw him in the Jardins du Luxembourg, wandering around the lake with Sartre, Maheu pretended not to see her.[4]

Sartre had already made up his mind to meet her. Thirty-six years later he said: 'I've always thought her beautiful, even though she was wearing a hideous little hat when I first met her. I was dead set on making her acquaintance.'[5] He dedicated a drawing to her – 'Leibniz bathing with the Monads' – and sent it via Maheu, who told her that Sartre and he were both amused by her husky voice.[6] But when Sartre asked to meet her in the evening, she let Maheu persuade her into sending her sister instead.[7]

After having to write an examination paper on 'Liberty and contingency', they had to prepare for the same oral in July, and the four of them arranged to work together on Leibniz at the Cité universitaire:

I felt a bit scared when I went into Sartre's room; books were all over the place, cigarette ends in all the corners and the air was thick with tobacco smoke. Sartre welcomed me like a man of the world; he was smoking a pipe. Silent, a cigarette stuck in the corner of his crooked smile, Nizan scrutinized me through his thick spectacles as if he were thinking about me carefully.[8]

She went back every day. 'Sartre took it upon himself to explain Rousseau's *Le Contrat social* ... he was always the one who knew most about all the writers and every aspect of our syllabus ... I noted: "He's marvellous at training intellects." '[9] They worked all morning; in the afternoon, when Henriette Nizan arrived, they drove round Paris in the Nizans' car or went to the funfair at the Porte d'Orléans. Sartre and Maheu would sing lustily – often songs of their own composition. A motet, for instance, was based on the heading of a chapter in Descartes's *Méditations métaphysiques*. Sartre would sing 'Ole Man River' and the current jazz hits. He liked playing records of Sophie Tucker, Jack Hylton and negro spirituals.[10]

Nizan was living with Henriette and her parents in the rue Vavin. He introduced Sartre, Maheu and de Beauvoir to Irish literature and the new American novelists. 'He was abreast of all the latest fashions in the arts and even ahead of them. He took us to the dreary Café de Flore "to get our own back on the old Deux Magots", he said, gnawing at his fingernails like a mischievous rat.' He was writing a pamphlet against 'the official philosophies', and a book on 'Marxist Wisdom'.[11] The three men had eased themselves further than she had out of the bourgeoisie: they mocked at soulfulness of any kind and at *la vie intérieure*, deflating anything pretentious or precious or idealistic.[12] At first Maheu tried to demand preferential treatment, taking her to the cinema without the other two, and renting a room in a small hotel in the rue Vaneau, where the two of them worked abortively at translating Aristotle's *Nicomachean Ethics*. He explained that he was different from his friends: '*They* always have to find a reason for everything, especially Sartre ... Except when he's asleep, Sartre *thinks* all the time.'[13]

On the evening of 14 July, after eating dinner in an Alsatian restaurant Sartre, Maheu and de Beauvoir watched the fireworks from the lawn of the Cité universitaire. Afterwards Sartre, who had a reputation for munificence, took them in a taxi to the Falstaff in the rue Montparnasse, where they drank cocktails until two in the morning.

On the day of the examination results she met him at the door of the

Sorbonne. 'From now on', he said, 'I'm going to take you under my wing.' He had won first place; she had come second. Nizan had passed; Maheu, who had failed, left the same evening for Bagnoles-de-l'Orne without saying goodbye. He sent Sartre an express letter, conveying his good wishes to 'Castor' – her nickname, the one mark Maheu would leave on her. The French word for 'beaver', it alludes to her industriousness. 'Beavers like company', he told her, 'and they have a constructive bent.' He reappeared a week later, but stayed only for a day. Sartre did not conceal his pleasure at having the beaver to himself, while she soon began to feel time spent without him was time wasted.[14]

At the oral exams he excelled himself, speaking with fearless fluency and enrapturing the jury.[15] She went to the Sorbonne with him, they went out with the Nizans, had drinks at the Balzac with Raymond Aron, who was doing his military service in the Meteorological Corps, and with Politzer, who had joined the Party. At the second-hand bookstalls on the banks of the Seine, Sartre bought her copies of *Pardaillon* and *Fantômas*; in the evening he took her to cowboy films. They sat for hours over coffee in bars and over cocktails at the Falstaff.[16] He conversed like no-one else. His alert mind was abnormally free from prejudice and preconception. When they talked about her he tried, like no-one else, to see her in the perspective of her own values. With other people she normally felt superior both intellectually and by virtue of living more intensely; she was now with someone who had copied into a notebook Hippias's boast: 'I have never met any man who was my equal.'[17] She had thought her desire to write was exceptionally strong, but here was a man who 'lived only in order to write'.[18] Last year he had wanted to marry; his current need was for freedom unrestricted by profession, possessions, family or social roots. He would travel all over the world, collecting experiences to nourish his writing. Believing the work of art to be an end in itself, he spoke of his 'opposition aesthetics'. A book depended on having something to attack.[19]

Though he was still in quest of salvation, hoping to earn immortality through literary merit, he disliked the religious vocabulary that survived from her catholic girlhood, though she was now as materialistic as he was. He appeared to be less interested in fame than in propagating truths that had been revealed to him; when he showed her his notebooks, she soon came to accept his theory of contingency, but she was expecting his commitment to Stendhal and the specific to make generalization difficult for him. She recognized the clumsiness of his myth-making in *Er l'Arménien*, but he had so much determination, vitality, good humour and self-confidence that his work could hardly fail to improve. Her ambition was to tell the whole truth in a novel; it was disconcerting to find that Sartre, Nizan, Aron and Politzer had all evolved more specific ideas for future books.[20]

But now she had a partner. 'He was the double in whom I found all my burning aspiration brought to incandescence.'[21] When the summer holidays separated them at the beginning of August, she was expecting to share her life with him.

Instead of waiting to see her again at the end of the holidays, he travelled to Limousin, where she and her parents were staying in a turreted château that belonged to her uncle and aunt. Her cousin Madeleine was three years her senior. Sartre stayed at a hotel in St-Germain-les-Belles and, to be discreet, they met outside the town. Assuming he would not be content to sit in the grass and talk, de Beauvoir suggested they should bring books, but he refused to read or go for walks. He was allergic to chlorophyll, he said. They met every day. At lunchtime she would go back to the château; Madeleine would conspiratorially leave cheese or gingerbread for Sartre in an abandoned dovecote; in the evening he would dine among commercial travellers at his hotel.[22]

De Beauvoir told her parents he was there to collaborate with her on a critical study of Marxism: they were more likely to approve of an anti-Communist enterprise. But on Sartre's fourth day in Limousin, her father came striding across the field towards them. 'Sartre, who was wearing an aggressively red shirt, jumped to his feet, looking bellicose. My father asked him politely to leave the area: people were gossiping; besides, there were hopes that my cousin would be married, and scandalous behaviour was damaging to her reputation.'[23] Not intimidated, Sartre stayed on for another week, but they met in a chestnut grove some distance away. After he left, the lovers exchanged letters daily.[24]

She returned to Paris in September; he came back in the middle of October, staying with his grandparents in the rue St Jacques. Charles Schweitzer was now eighty-five. Sartre met de Beauvoir every morning in the Jardins du Luxembourg. 'It was late at night before we separated. We walked the streets of Paris, still talking – about ourselves and our relationship, our future life, our still unwritten books.'[25] They were expecting to change the world, but their only weapon would be books; 'public affairs bored us'.[26] Their vague optimism was characteristic of the French left during the autumn of 1929. Misunderstanding the international economic crisis precipitated by the American depression, intellectuals were waiting for capitalism to disintegrate. The national socialists in Germany were not to be taken seriously, while the imminent collapse of colonialism was signalled by the communist agitation in French Indo-China and by Gandhi's popularity in India.[27]

Shortage of money did not obstruct what Sartre and de Beauvoir called their 'radical freedom'.[28] They compared themselves with Kant's dove: instead of holding the bird back, the resistance of the air supported its flight.[29] She was teaching psychology at a girls' school in Neuilly, and paying rent to her grandmother for what had formerly been a drawing-room in the old lady's fifth-floor flat on the rue Denfert-Rochereau. Sartre, who was awaiting call-up, was earning nothing. The shops were full of goods they could not buy, and, unlike the Nizans, they had no car; they went for walks along the Bercy *quais* and by the St-Martin canal. They ate bread and pâté in de Beauvoir's room, had dinner in the Brasserie Demory, drank at the Falstaff, the College Inn, the Vikings' Bar, where mead cocktails were to be had, and the Bec de Gaz on the rue du Montparnasse, where one of the specialities was apricot cocktails.[30] They felt superior to the *beau monde* which lived parasitically on a despicable regime. When de Beauvoir passed Fouquet's or Maxim's, she felt that the real outsiders were the rich, 'cut off from the masses, imprisoned in their luxury and snobbery'.[31]

In Sartre, physical and intellectual energy interpenetrated. He produced an inexhaustible stream of ballads, rhymes, epigrams, madrigals, minifables. Often he would improvise tunes for the verses he made up. He punned shamelessly, playing with assonances and alliterations. Borrowing from Synge and James Stephens, he elaborated a private mythology around the figures of the playboy and the leprechaun who kept misery at bay by cobbling tiny shoes. In the private language that the couple evolved, 'our tiny shoes' meant the books they had not yet written. Neither was immune to depression, but they cheered each other up through caricature and self-parody. Their relationship, they decided, was a morganatic marriage, and when they dressed up for an evening of dancing at La Coupole or for a cinema on the Champs-Elysées, they would be Mr and Mrs Morgan Hattick, an American millionaire and his wife.[32] If Sartre was accused of being a petit bourgeois, he could retort that according to Marx the bourgeois intellectual was capable of rising above the the beliefs of his class.

Freedom was Sartre's ideal, but his immediate future was mortgaged. After eighteen months of compulsory military service, he would have to face the teaching career he dreaded. Hoping to escape from Europe, he applied for a job in Japan as lecturer in French, starting in October 1931, when his military service would be over.

He and de Beauvoir, he insisted, should both feel free to have other lovers; adapting his philosophical terminology to his sexual convenience, he proposed: 'What we have is an *essential* love; but it's good if we both experience *contingent* love affairs too.'[33] On the afternoon of 10 October, after they had watched Pudovkin's new silent film *Storm over Asia* with the Nizans, Sartre suggested that de Beauvoir and he should 'sign a two-year lease'. After two years of living together in the closest possible intimacy, they should separate for two or three years before living together again.

They would never become strangers, but the relationship must not dwindle into a habit. Though she did not relish the prospect of losing him for two or three years, she accepted his proposal, and they promised never to tell each other lies or conceal anything.[34] Ever since the defection of his mother in 1917, Sartre's appetite for symbiotic intimacy had been insatiable. In his friendship with Nizan he had been plagued by jealousy and frustrated by quarrels, separations, ideological differences and above all by Nizan's reluctance or inability to share emotional experience. The closeness with de Beauvoir would be free from all these hindrances. No partner could have done more towards making the non-stop internal monologue (which he loved too much, and therefore detested) into a constantly resumed dialogue. At once creative and highly critical, each of them could provide a constructive daily commentary on the life and work of the other.

For both of them, naturally, there was a certain sacrifice of freedom, but she felt on the whole more liberated. She stopped trying to inhibit tendencies in herself when she noticed the same tendencies in him: he would weep in the cinema, for instance. There were tears on his cheeks when the lights went up at the end of Al Jolson's *The Singing Fool*.[35]

She introduced him to her Polish friend Stépha Avdicovitch and her Spanish friend Fernando Gérassi, an impoverished painter descended from one of the Jewish families driven out of Spain by the Inquisition.[36] Bald, round-faced and intense, he would later appear in *Les Chemins de la liberté* as Gomez. Sartre got on with him well until he left Paris with Stépha to settle in Madrid. Maheu had taken a teaching job in Coutances, and paid only brief visits to Paris. Aron, who was finishing his military service at St-Cyr, sometimes drove Sartre and de Beauvoir out to Versailles for dinner. He had joined the Socialist Party, which they derided as having been infiltrated by the bourgeoisie, but most of Aron's arguments with Sartre were philosophical. Sartre refused to differentiate between the object he was viewing and his view of it. 'I could not enjoy a landscape or a sky except by assuming that it was absolutely the same as what I saw ... Perception, achieved ceremoniously and respectfully, became a sacred act of communication between two absolute substances, the object and my soul.' Essences and universals had been postulated, he maintained, to fend off a reality which other people found frightening.[37] Aron used to go on arguing until his opponent was trapped between two alternatives. '"One thing or the other, *mon petit camarade*", he used to say. "Choose."'[38]

Sartre shared Nizan's enthusiasm for cinema, and using a Pathé-Baby camera they made several home movies. In *Le Vautour de la Sierra* (*The Vulture of the Sierra*) Sartre was a shepherd who used an umbrella to fight against the vulture (Nizan) who also had an umbrella. De Beauvoir and

Henriette were shepherdesses. In another, made on the terrace of the Alphens' house in St-Germain-en-Laye, the two girls were prostitutes. They pulled off Sartre's shirt to reveal that he was wearing a scapular. During a heart-to-heart talk, Christ offered him a cigarette, and, but for technical difficulties, would have taken the Sacred Heart from his bosom to use it as a lighter.[39] The scenarios were modelled on fashionable surrealist films.

According to de Beauvoir, Sartre was being influenced by Guille, who, cheerfully averse to theorizing, maintained that life and ideas always contradicted each other. Thanks to Guille, she says, Sartre learned 'how to collect experiences with an observant concentration unspoiled by after-thought'. Guille made him more alert to nuances. Both men loved to dissect other people's behaviour: 'they could spend hours analysing a gesture or a tone of voice.'[40] Sometimes de Beauvoir, Sartre, Mme Morel and Guille would drive out along the banks of the Marne or into the woods around St-Germain or Fosse-Repose. They would eat in restaurants, drink cocktails in Montparnasse, see the new films, listen to Jack Hylton's band.[41]

After four years of reprieve Sartre started his 18 months of military service in November 1929. Call-up ended a phase of freedom in his life but at twenty-four he was older than most recruits. For at least eight years his commitment to writing had been crucial: the rest of his life could take care of itself. Life, anyway, was a game already lost before you started playing.[42] Besides, his main duty, as a writer destined to be great, was to preserve his freedom. This was explained carefully to any girl who gave signs of incipient fondness.[43]

In the army, together with Guille, he opted for meteorology, and they were both sent to St-Cyr, where Raymond Aron, now a sergeant, was their instructor: they flicked paper darts at him during class.[44] In January 1930 Sartre was transferred to St-Symphorien, near Tours, about 130 miles to the south-west of Paris. For the first time in his life he found that each day was an exact repetition of the previous one. 'Consciousness is attenuated and the body, like that of a swimmer who knows he is caught in seaweed and lets himself go, drifts unresistingly with the current.' Unable to calm his nerves by going out for walks, he wrote to de Beauvoir, trying to describe his state of mind in the first phrases that occurred. 'This terrifying prospect of the empty days ahead of me has given me a sort of nervous excitement which is precisely boredom.'[45]

When his grandmother Schweitzer died at the age of eighty-four, she left him 80,000 old francs – enough to buy him more of such comforts as attracted him. He enjoyed expensive restaurants and travelling in taxis, but physical comfort could be inimical to the exertion he demanded from himself, puritanically determined as he was to exploit his potential to the full. He never read in bed, seldom sat in an armchair: he read in a hard chair with a straight back.[46] Nor would he invest the money. He disliked chequebooks and bank accounts. Now, as later, he carried a large roll of banknotes about with him and spent from it freely. The 80,000 francs lasted only two or three years.

Suddenly a widower at the age of eighty-five, Charles Schweitzer badly needed someone to look after him. Mme Mancy, who went to see him every day, found a housekeeper to run the flat for him, and when his schoolteacher friend came back from Algeria, she spent most of her time with him. He was still potent but, according to the servant, did no sexual favours to the woman who regularly masturbated him.[47]

On Sundays de Beauvoir would sometimes catch the first train from Paris, bringing a supply of books borrowed from Adrienne Monnier's library. Sartre had an insatiable appetite for what he called 'entertaining rubbish'. After cycling to meet her at the station, he would take her to the big brasserie, which had a female orchestra, or to a café, or they would walk in the park or by the Loire. He found it easy to articulate his visual impressions, but they disagreed about whether his feelings were as strong as hers. With his dislike of contingency, he claimed to set more value on what he called 'emotional abstractions' than on disorderly physical reactions – the excessive emotionality that paralyses communication. The writer must preserve a degree of detachment, he argued; while she often felt that 'words have to murder reality before they can imprison it'.[48]

Sometimes he would come to spend Sunday in Paris. When they met on the platform of the railway station, whether at Tours or the Gare d'Austerlitz, his greeting would often be 'I've got a new theory'. Each of his theories was an act of appropriation. The exciting world was not just a world of appearances: it was there to be colonized. 'Looking at the trees and the water, I told myself ecstatically: "There's so much to do."'[49] Usually she would search for the 'underlying sophistry': he was still convinced that phenomena coincided exactly with one's knowledge of them.[50] He obviously gained a great deal from using her as he had previously used Aron to test out newly formed theories in conversation. He would then adjust them.

Though he disliked Freudian psychoanalysis as denying the mind's autonomy, he went on reading psychological books. From introductions to Gestalt psychology, he accepted the premiss that mental process cannot be reduced into elementary units since, from the outset, wholeness and organization are factors. The individual, he believed, was a synthetic totality, and inferences could validly be drawn from studying handwriting and physiognomy. He stared earnestly into the faces of Simone, her sister Hélène (who was known as Poupette) and their friends, trying to analyse what he saw.[51]

Meteorology and soldiering left him with plenty of free time. At St-Cyr he wrote poems. In one of them 'L'Arbre' ('The Tree') he used the proliferation of a tree's branches to symbolize purposeless contingency – an equation he would repeat in *La Nausée*. But when Guille was invited to read Sartre's verse, he laughed.[52]

Sartre started another novel, based on the story of a girl he had never met, a cousin of de Beauvoir's, Zaza Mabille, a lively, sensitive girl who had fallen in love with a *normalien*, Maurice Merleau-Ponty, but been incapable of disobeying her mother, who disapproved. The tension somehow engendered an illness, which eventually killed her. But Guille found it funny when the unhappy hero's glance travelled towards the sea, 'stroking the sunlight against the grain'.[53]

Sartre persevered harder with a philosophical work he started at St-Symphorien. *La Légende de la vérité* (*The Legend of Truth*) had, like *Er l'Arménien*, to be a story, partly because he was imitating Nietzsche, pitching his style somewhere between *Also sprach Zarathustra* and *Zur Genealogie der Moral*. Nor would he allow himself to theorize. Even his distrust of generalizations must not be expressed in generalized terms: everything must be demonstrated. In the new work he tried to correlate variation in the cognitive process with structural differences between social groups. 'Truth is a by-product of commerce', he declared, and commerce was dependent on democracy. Science had emerged as an offshoot of the attitude by which people regarded themselves as interchangeable. In any society the elite rejected this view, producing ideas that were to its own advantage, but the truth was more likely to be found by outsiders who trusted only the evidence of their senses. Sartre saw himself as the writer who could save society from itself, simply by recording his own impressions. The three legends were the legends of certainty (science), the legend of the probable (the abstract philosophy of the aristocracy) and the legend of the solitary man. Once again Nizan acted as middleman, submitting the essay to Editions de l'Europe, but it was rejected.[54]

From St-Symphorien Sartre was sent to the Villa Paulovnia in the neighbourhood of Tours, with two other trained meteorologists – a man from Toulouse who stole and a seminarian with smelly feet.[55] They went out at intervals to check temperature and humidity with instruments kept in a hut.[56] In the summer de Beauvoir came to stay for a month at the small hotel in St-Radegonde, on the banks of the Loire, ten minutes from the Villa Paulovnia. She spent the mornings reading in the open air, and after lunch she would climb the hill to meet him near the meteorological station. 'At intervals of two hours he would go off to take an observation, and I'd see him waving a sort of miniature Eiffel Tower in the air.'[57]

* * *

In February 1931 Sartre learned that he had not been selected for the job in Japan. Disappointment soured the relief of being released from the army at the end of the month. A certificate affirmed that he had 'maintained good conduct throughout his period of service' and that 'he always served honourably and steadfastly'.[58] Annoyance about having to stay in France was mollified when he was invited to deputize during the final term of the university year for a teacher of philosophy at Le Havre. Le Havre is only about 110 miles from Paris, but the teaching job offered to de Beauvoir was at a lycée in Marseille – over 500 miles from Paris and still further from Le Havre. The prospect of separation frightened her so visibly that Sartre offered to marry her: this would qualify them for a joint appointment, and, in the long run, he said, marriage need not seriously affect their way of life. Besides, it was silly to sacrifice oneself to a principle. But she knew him well enough to see that he was already close to panic at the prospect of losing what he cherished most – his freedom. The army had entailed only a temporary loss of the student liberty which he would forfeit permanently when he became a provincial academic.[59] At one stage, when she had intended to marry her cousin, she had pictured herself as a mother, but 'A child would not have strengthened the bonds that united me with Sartre; I did not want Sartre's existence to be extended and prolonged into someone else's.'[60] She also felt so alienated from her parents that the idea of parenthood had been devalued; in any event, childbearing seemed less vital to her than literature, which was 'a way of justifying the world by refashioning it in the pure context of imagination'. But they did revise their pact, agreeing not to have any prolonged separation until they were in their thirties. Though he never felt de Beauvoir (as he had sometimes felt Nizan) to be his intellectual superior, this disadvantage was compensated by the possibility of discussing everything. In argument and in criticizing his work she could be formidable – he called her his 'little judge' – but (unlike Raymond Aron) she never wanted to inflict defeat on him. She was as unreservedly on his side as his mother had once been.

Sartre was extremely lucky. No-one could have been a better replacement for the mother who had been like an elder sister; no other woman could have been more undemanding than de Beauvoir while being so emotionally dependent, so devoted without demanding devotion in return. Something had survived from the devout catholic childhood that had made her think of becoming a nun, but so had something from the ensuing adolescent rebellion. At the age of nineteen she had written in her diary: 'I want my life to obey no other will but my own.' This was aiming too high. She had interiorized too much of what had been taught to her about virtue, chastity and obedience, but she carried something of her defiance into submissiveness to a substitute religion in which Sartre and socialism were the twin gods. She had been bred and groomed for a socially impressive marriage to a respectable catholic; her non-marriage to Sartre was exemplary in a different way. The propriety she retained did not impress her parents but it was impressive. She has led a disciplined, organized, productive life.

Though Sartre once said 'she has the intelligence of a man and the sensitivity of a woman', it was he who launched her on writing *Le Deuxième Sexe*. There was no limit to the amount of help they could give each other. She made excellent use in this and other books of his ideas, his categories, his attitudes, while he benefited from seeing them in both her life and her books. His tendency to live as if he were drafting an autobiography he could tear up and rewrite at any moment was partly encouraged, partly curbed by the knowledge that he had the leading male role in the serial instalments of her widely read autobiography. Her appetite for new experiences was keener than his, but they both needed to validate their experience not only by writing about it but also by having the other react to it verbally and write about it. If, in the long run, she gave him more than he gave her, it was not so much because he got more pleasure out of his infidelities to her than she did out of hers to him, or because she wrote about him (both fictionally and non-fictionally) more than he did about her, but because she translated his theories into her life. Her faith in him was so complete that it was natural for her to change her mind when he changed his, and to emulate his style of living even when she was not sharing his life. She even acquired something of the same indifference to possessions. She did eventually buy a car, and though she was sternly reprimanded by him for this, she could see how useful he found it when she was willing to drive him about.

They also helped each other to keep their childhood alive. In spite of his need for other women, he did most of his travelling with her, and when they were both in Paris, they saw each other almost every day. They never tired of each other's conversation and they liked being separate but together while working, sometimes in the same room, sometimes in different rooms of the same flat, like schoolchildren doing homework. Generally she would play the role of the caring elder sister, making sure that he was not importuned too much by other people, that he did not go to bed too late or drink too much or smoke too much. It was difficult for her to find the right balance between strictness and tolerance, and to many friends and casual acquaintances she seemed over-protective, but however difficult he made it for her, he wanted her to go on playing the role he had given her. He wanted her to look after him.

Friendly Teacher (1931–9)

SIX · *Provincial Schoolmaster*

When Sartre installed himself in Le Havre for the spring term of 1931, staying at the Hôtel Printania, it felt as though he had moved into a greyer climate, shut off from the sun of promise that had illuminated childhood, boyhood and youth. From confidential chats with his doting grandfather to candid conversations with de Beauvoir, from the writing of precocious adventure stories to confident student speculations about imagery, everything had helped him to believe in his future greatness. Encouraged by the game he had played with Nizan, the idea of being a superman had never quite disappeared: everything he did was part of a rehearsal for the golden future; but here he was in Le Havre, a provincial schoolteacher with no option but to let himself be integrated into a disciplinarian system he detested. He had arrived at a phase of life he had dreaded. Though allowing him to feel free, the Ecole Normale had insidiously destined him to be trapped in a provincial intestine of the organism he had hoped to escape by living in Japan.

Social life in Le Havre was strongly coloured by hierarchical snobbery. Controlling the cotton and coffee trade, the protestant bourgeoisie dominated; it was known as 'la côte' because of the villas it had built in more elevated positions. At the lycée the headmaster welcomed parents with a warmth proportionate to their social standing, while teachers who had not passed the *agrégation* were humiliatingly being excluded from the board of examiners for the *baccalauréat* and from the annual outing to Caen. Sartre's position as a teacher distanced him both from the boys and from his own boyhood, but, hating hierarchy and instantly disliking his collegues,[1] he fought his way closer to the boys. 'You saw this little fellow arriving, his hands in his pockets, no hat, which was unusual, smoking a pipe, which was very strange, then he immediately started talking without notes, sitting on his desk. We'd never seen that.' He was liable to appear in his classroom 'wearing a sports jacket, a black shirt and no tie; we understood straight away that this wasn't a teacher like the others'.[2] Psychology featured prominently in his philosophy lessons, and he chatted to the boys without the pomposity and condescension they had come to expect from teachers. When he was teaching philosophy he would often interrupt himself to question them on their own ideas. He was 'vigorous, stimulating, amusing and serious at the same time'. Intellectually he dominated boys irresistibly, leaving an indelible mark. 'He was generous in his marking, but kept his notebooks in a great muddle and wrote down marks at random.'[3] He was 'extraordinarily kind, simple, astonishingly amusing. He took many things seriously, but never his position as a master, or ours as pupils ... We had a relationship with him such as we'd never had with an adult ... a relationship without any of the usual barriers.' He drank with the boys at local bars and cafés, played cards and ping-pong with them, joined them for picnics on the beach, sang them songs from operettas.[4] This unconventional behaviour provoked disapproval from colleagues and complaints from parents, but he cheerfully ignored the headmaster's reprimands, and not only was his non-conformity tolerated, his temporary job became permanent. He gave free extra lessons to pupils who needed them and at the municipal library he persuaded the librarian to be less strict about refusing the boys access to certain books.[5]

In the classroom Sartre would relax, sitting on a table and chatting with equal informality about philosophy and his own habits. He could make the bowl of his pipe shiny, he told them, by rubbing it against the side of his nose, where sweat collected. But some boys felt excluded from the clique he collected around himself. The boys he liked best were the most spirited and spontaneous; some of these would even get treated to meals in local restaurants.[6] He was already beginning to do what he would go on doing throughout his life – surround himself with what was almost a family of young friends who could enjoy a degree of intimacy without ever being quite on an equal footing.

Among the teachers Sartre's three best friends were Alphonse Bonnafé, who taught Latin, French and Greek, the gym-teacher, Rasquin, and the English teacher, Isoré. Bonnafé was a good-looking man who boxed and told amusing stories. Once he and his girl went on a walking tour with Sartre and de Beauvoir. It was Bonnafé's idea to give boxing lessons at a gymnasium in the town. He and Sartre persuaded about eight of the boys to come along, and when Sartre stripped to the waist and boxed with them, his smallness, which had handicapped him as a schoolboy, was advantageous in putting him on the same level as his pupils. But with no spectacles on, he found it hard to defend himself. Mostly the boys took care not to hurt him, but it was tempting for those who were jealous of his favourites to get their own back by delivering a hard blow to the head. When one boy, Albert Palle, did this, Sartre took it in good part, exaggerating his pain in a pantomime of distress.[7]

He loved boxing for the same reason as he had loved schoolboy fighting: it involved the whole body. He also fantasized about being able to fight any man and beat him.[8] At the gymnasium he worked out with a skipping rope and listened intently when Bonnafé gave him tips. Boxing helped him to know the boys better. Like Bonnafé, Rasquin was a good-looking man who told stories about sex and fighting. Though Bonnafé and Sartre made fun of him, Isoré was Sartre's usual companion for lunch at the restaurant which features in *La Nausée*.[9]

With only about sixteen hours of teaching to do each week and needing only about the same amount of time to prepare for it, he had plenty of free time. He spent most of it on trains between Paris and Le Havre, where he cultivated the taste for detective fiction which derived from his boyhood pleasure in adventure stories. He was interested both in the technique of structuring and in the way that dialogue could be charged with tension when loaded with clues to the mystery.[10]

When he finished *La Légende de la vérité*, Nizan submitted it for him to the publisher Rieder, while an extract appeared in the June issue of the periodical *Bifur*. In the notes on contributors, Nizan described Sartre as a young philosopher 'at work on a volume of destructive philosophy'.[11] During July, making a speech at a prize-giving ceremony, he scandalized the conservative parents and teachers by championing cinema as an art, but his private interest was still in distinguishing between the sequentiality of films and the discontinuity of experiences in everyday life.[12]

He and de Beauvoir were planning to go on holiday together in Brittany during the summer, and in June they were briefly reunited with Stépha and Fernando Gérassi, who arrived in high spirits: Stépha was pregnant and a provisional republican government had been formed after King Alfonso had fled from Spain in April. Fernando suggested that they should spend their six-week holiday in Spain instead of Brittany. In Madrid they could stay with him, while the exchange rate was so favourable that inside Spain travelling would be cheap. Neither of them had ever been outside France, and after crossing the frontier, they spent their first evening wandering around Figueroas, where they saw their first *guardia civil* and kept repeating: 'we're in Spain'.[13] Fernando had advised them to buy two first-class *quilometricos* – round-trip tickets valid for any route – and they went on to Barcelona. Instead of merely visiting monuments and museums, they tried to discover the secret of each city by noticing the smells, observing the light, tasting the local dishes, exploring the poorest districts. They spent their evenings in the Barrio Chino, where women signalled their availability by dancing and singing on platforms in the open air.

Sartre did not enjoy walking as much as de Beauvoir did, and he was less voracious for new experiences: he would have been content to sit down after lunch, quietly smoking his pipe; pipe-smoking tended to make him want to settle wherever he was, watching passers-by and talking through clouds of smoke. But when they visited the cathedral at Burgos, his response was so fully engaged that he felt he had never previously looked so attentively at anything.[14]

In October, when *La Légende de la vérité* was rejected by Rieder, Sartre decided against offering it to other publishers. The teaching job left him with enough time to make a serious start on his literary work, and, obligingly, the experience that would be crucial to *La Nausée* occurred soon after the beginning of term. On 7 October he wrote to de Beauvoir about going out to look at a tree:

> To do this, you need only push open the gate of a fine square off the avenue Foch, then choose your victim and a seat. Next comes contemplation. Not far away from me, the young wife of a naval officer was explaining the hardships of a sea-faring career to an aged grandmother, who was nodding her head as if to say: 'That's life.' ... And I looked at the tree. It was beautiful, and I have no hesitation in setting down two facts vital to my biography: it was at Burgos that I understood what a cathedral is, and at Le Havre what a tree is. Unfortunately I'm not sure what kind of tree it was. You'll be able to tell me. You know those toys that turn around in the wind or when they're waved about. There were little green stems everywhere which played the same trick with six or seven leaves they had on top of them. A sketch is enclosed. I await your reply. After twenty minutes, having exhausted the arsenal of comparisons destined, as Mrs Woolf would say, to turn this tree into something different from what it is, I left with a clear conscience.[15]

It was no accident that he had chosen a tree for careful observation. Later on, in *Les Mots*, he recalled his grandfather's advice: 'It isn't enough to have eyes. You must learn to use them. Do you know what Flaubert did when Maupassant was a child? Sat him down in front of a tree and gave him two hours to describe it.'[16] For the most famous sequence in his fiction Sartre would be indebted both to the grandfather he caricatured and to his arch-enemy, Flaubert.

He was intending to use the tree as a symbol of contingency in 'Factum sur la Contingence', which he had just started. (A *factum* is a text published with a polemical purpose.) He wanted to illustrate his argument by describing the district where he lived. 'Naturally everything was contingent there, even the sky, which, according to meteorological probability, should be the same above the whole town of Le Havre, but it isn't.'[17] When he transformed the *factum* into the novel, which was first to be called *Melancholia* (after the Dürer engraving) and was later called *La Nausée*, the Hôtel Printania would be mentioned by name, and the view from the window of Roquentin's room seems to be identical with the view from Sartre's, though the author's mood blurs into the narrator's and into that of people on the railway platform. 'This evening I'm quite relaxed, installed in the bourgeois world. My room faces north-east. Below, the rue des Mutilés and the new railway yard. From my window I see at the corner of the boulevard Victor-Noir the red and white flame of the Rendez-vous des Cheminots. The Paris train has just arrived ... A lot of people are waiting for the last train. They make a sad little group around the lamp-post just under my window.'[18]

De Beauvoir's advice was crucial in making him fictionalize the *factum*, and there is no knowing what balance he would otherwise have achieved in it between generalization and specific detail, though some evidence is provided by an exercise book which probably dates from 1932. Bound in imitation leather, it had originally been used in the classroom. On the opening pages are names of pupils, marks and essay subjects. The thirty-five pages of notes for the *factum* show he was still comparing events in a story with everyday experience. You never feel you're having an adventure; you never know which events will be causally connected to others. The feeling of adventure comes retrospectively.[19] His concern with duration was partly Bergsonian, while he was thinking of his own ugliness in relation to contingency: his features gave the appearance of having been 'thrown together at random'.[20] Other people's features combined harmoniously, but whenever he looked in a mirror he saw the squinting eye first and then features which 'didn't combine to form a definite human face'.[21] In *La Nausée* Roquentin will reflect: 'I understand nothing about this face. Other faces have a meaning. Not mine.'[22] Nothing is more familiar than your own face in the mirror, but scrutinize it at length and it becomes unfamiliar in a way which affects everything else; the price we pay for existential freedom is anguished realization of the world's total strangeness. As Alain Robbe-Grillet has said, some novels confirm the familiarity of the world, others assert its strangeness; *La Nausée* is extraordinary in capturing the transition from one mode of observing to the other.[23] Everything Roquentin sees in the drab provincial town, Bouville, is both nauseatingly unexceptional and nauseatingly inexplicable.

Not that reassurance is to be found in memories of other places, and to discredit complacent bourgeois claims to knowledge based on experience Sartre will make the much-travelled Roquentin question whether the traveller knows any more about humanity than the philosopher who has never left his study.[24] The novel will demonstrate that middle-class professional males – bankers, lawyers, priests, doctors – have no right to make the claims they base on experience. 'In fact experience = resignation ... No unconscious, no experience. Man is what he is in the present tense, and he's alone there.'[25] Nor do historical events lead directly to particular results: the death of a soldier is caused by a set of circumstances, not by the supremacy of Napoleon.[26] Though he could not capitalize yet either in his fiction or in his philosophy on these assumptions, Sartre was beginning to consolidate a strategically advantageous position.

One reason he was attracted to biography was that it seemed to offer a passport to detachment: he could look back from another man's life to steal an overview of his own. He would often forget what he claimed to have learnt in the early thirties and formulated in 1939: 'that one cannot put life into perspective while living it – it steals up on you from behind and you find yourself inside it'. Nevertheless, in 1931, the half-submerged preoccupation with biography and autobiography was helping him to write a good novel.

He was also planning to question 'the metaphysical reality of boredom ... What is boredom? It is where there is simultaneously *too much* and *not enough*.'[27] His notes on contingency differentiate between being and existing. 'What is does not exist. For example an idea.'[28] Most of his reflections at this time revolve around his concept of contingency. If nothing is necessary, it would be possible for everything to be different. 'Nature is in the position of a person who would like to express himself through ideas but has only objects at his disposal.' To this extent he could feel superior to whatever had generated the chestnut tree.

In persuading Sartre to write the book in narrative form, de Beauvoir suggested that it should be charged with the same kind of suspense they both enjoyed in detective fiction.[29] This was how the idea evolved of writing a kind of whodunnit in which contingency would turn out to be the villain.

She went to Paris at every opportunity, sometimes creating extra opportunities by feigning illness, and she spent Christmas there. She had moved out of her grandmother's flat to settle into a cheap hotel on the rue Gay-Lussac.[30] Each time they met, he would show her what he had written. The exercise book contains notes for a diary to be kept by Roquentin, with a summary of entries for every day from 3 to 14 February. Some of the notes are for incidents (e.g. 'walk in the park'), some for reflections ('contingency in me: in my limbs when I walk – incapacity for seeing myself whole').[31]

Since learning how to look at a cathedral or at a tree, and how to avoid being misled by the arsenal of comparisons, Sartre had begun to observe people differently. Roquentin decides at the outset: 'I must say how I see this table, the street, people, my packet of tobacco, because it's that which has changed.'[32] Not that the change in Roquentin tallied with the change in Sartre, who was suffering must less severely from what he calls nausea, and it was easier to catch his *alter ego* in the act of looking than it was to catch himself. Sartre could imagine that he was watching Roquentin's eyes, though, writing in the first person, he could not incorporate his observation of the character's observation: he had to dramatize it, but he could draw dramatic dividends from his inveterate insistence that an object was identical with his perception of it. Underlying some of the narrative is the same preoccupation as in Sartre's work on the image: what is the relationship between the table or the street and the mental pictures we form of them? Sartre's habits of observing were altered by the activity of writing the book: wandering through the provincial streets he would empathize with his character, asking himself how Roquentin would see a pair of braces or a seat in a tram.[33]

Sartre was lucky to have been given his first job in a provincial town: it was easier here than in Paris to regard himself as a solitary individual with no possessions, no roots in bourgeois society and nothing to prevent him from discrediting its ideology. He seldom came in contact with the townspeople except casually in cafés or when he gave one of the lectures financed by the municipality and the library. He discoursed on James Joyce and other modern writers unfamiliar to the townsfolk.[34] The categories of their thinking, he concluded, prevented – or protected – them from coming into close contact with reality. What the bourgeoisie could not do for itself, he would do for it – or against it. At the same time he was writing both for and against himself. He was still a nonentity and he needed to console himself by proving that everyone else was. No-one escapes from muddy mediocrity into glamorous adventures.

Sartre's visits to Paris were frequent enough for him to keep in touch with many of his friends. Apart from de Beauvoir and her sister, Hélène, a painter, he saw Nizan, who was teaching at Bourg, forty miles from Lyon, and jeopardizing his career with publicity attracted by subversive political activities. Guille, who was teaching at Rheims, spent as much time in Paris as Sartre did, while Toulouse, who was now calling herself Simone Jollivet, had strengthened her position in Dullin's company. Staging a play she had written, *L'Ombre* (*The Shade*), Dullin let her star in it, but it was received with booing and hissing. When Sartre went to her flat in rue Gabrielle a couple of days afterwards, the doorbell had been disconnected. A few days later, when he was allowed in, she was swearing vengeance on the public.[35]

For the Easter holidays Sartre went with de Beauvoir to Brittany. Coaxed into a series of sightseeing expeditions, he reacted to Chateaubriand's pretentious tomb by urinating on it.[36] Though the weather was rainy, he agreed to a twenty-five-mile walk around the hill of St-Michel d'Arré, which they climbed.[37]

Though he was coming, generally, to sympathize more with the communists, he did not vote in the election of May 1932. The majority favoured the Cartel des Gauches which had been created in 1924 by Eduard Herriot, grouping together radicals and socialists from the Section française de l'international ouvrière (SFIO). The Cartel favoured rapprochement with Germany, though the nazis were rapidly growing stronger, and as Prime Minister Herriot was inept in his handling of both industry and agriculture. France had weathered the world economic crisis better than most countries, though unemployment was high.

In June, when Sartre had ten free days, he spent them in Marseille with de Beauvoir, who took him happily to the restaurants around the old harbour and the cafés along the Canebière. When the news arrived that she had been appointed to a job in Rouen, they were delighted at the prospect of working only forty-two miles apart. Knowing of their relationship, M. Parodi, the Inspector General, had placed her considerately.[38]

Meanwhile Sartre spent a week with his mother and step-father. Having been invited by Guille and Mme Morel on a car journey through the south of Spain in August, de Beauvoir and Sartre met in Narbonne to make a preliminary trip to the Balearics, going on to Spanish Morocco. On their first morning in Seville, they saw the mayor under military arrest in a black car. The streets were full of soldiers, and rifles were stacked on the pavements. A coup d'état was being attempted by General José Sanjurjo, the man who would be succeeded by Franco four years later as leader of the military junta. A crowd was surging through the streets, singing and bawling; firemen were being deliberately slow to put out fires started in exclusive clubs.[39] But Sanjurjo failed to rally enough support, and the Republic was safe for nearly four more years.

In Cadiz Sartre antagonized Guille by refusing to 'waste time' on paintings by Murillo in the churches: the two couples had to separate. In Ronda Sartre found nothing he wanted to see: 'They're all aristocrats' houses.'[40] His radicalism was vulnerable though: Guille could expose anomalies between the outlook Sartre had borrowed from another class and the bourgeois comforts he was patently enjoying. In Tarifa a boy of about twelve came up to the table where they were eating their fish dinner: 'You're lucky. You can travel. I'll never get away from this place.'[41]

Returning to France, Sartre and de Beauvoir asked to be dropped at Toulouse, where the other Simone showed them around. She was writing a novel about her adolescent sexual experiences, and she worked on the book every night, she said, from twelve to six.[42]

During the autumn term, having no teaching to do on Thursdays, Sartre would often spend the day in Rouen with de Beauvoir. Sometimes she would visit him in Le Havre, and, as before, they went to Paris every week, staying at the Hôtel de Blois. Toulouse introduced them to Dullin, who let them sit in on several rehearsals of *Richard III*. Nizan had spoken to de Beauvoir about another teacher at the school, Colette Audry, a friendly short-haired Trotskyist who knew Simone Weil and took Sartre and de Beauvoir to a film studio where her sister Jacqueline was working as a script-girl.[43]

One Tuesday in Rouen Sartre had an attack of nephritis. He was in such pain and vomited so much that he had to see a doctor. But his resistance to pain was abnormal or (as he preferred to have it put) his philosophical ideas were integral to his relationship with his body, and the doctor was astonished when he insisted that he had not been suffering. In *La Nausée* he gives Anny the same ability to block out awareness of pain. If pain was isolated, he maintained, it was only pain: it could be stopped from taking charge of the body.[44] The idea of self-control appealed to him so strongly that he tried increasingly to programme his mental and physical condition by using stimulants and sedatives; the result was that he became less self-controlled.

He avidly read newspaper reports of crimes and trials, partly because they brought bourgeois morality into question. He sympathized with the Papin sisters, two maids who murdered their mistress (and inspired Genet's play *Les Bonnes*). Crimes, said Sartre, were caused by the social system and avenged by a primitively vindictive judicial system.[45] Fortunately the end of capitalism was imminent: crowds of starving men had marched on Washington, while bankrupt businessmen and financiers were committing suicide.[46] Sartre thought of joining the Communist Party – once, for instance, after a docker, dressed in his blue overall, was ejected from the Café Victor in Rouen after sitting down on the terrace at a neighbouring table. Was it enough to go on supporting the proletariat from the sidelines?[47] Though Sartre had read Marx's *Das Kapital* and *Die Deutsche Ideologie* while a student, he had no contact with the workers – 'an enormous, sombre group which *lived* Marxism'[48] – and it happened only gradually, over the next thirteen years, that Marxism 'put all our acquired culture out of shape'.[49] The next conversion Sartre was to undergo had nothing to do with the oppressed majority.

SEVEN · *A German Credo*

But for Raymond Aron, Sartre's life might have been quite different. If he had not applied to join the meteorological corps, his wartime experiences would not have been what they were, and his early fiction would not have been what it was if Aron had not introduced him to phenomenology.

Since September 1932 Aron had been in Berlin, working at the French Institute there, simultaneously studying Edmund Husserl and writing a thesis. Sartre had not attended the lectures Husserl had given at the Sorbonne in February 1929, but he had subsequently felt attracted to phenomenology, and the turning point came during an evening spent with Aron at the Bec de Gaz in the rue Montparnasse. The two men and de Beauvoir were drinking (apricot cocktails according to de Beauvoir and beer according to Aron) when Aron said: 'You see, mon petit camarade, if you're a phenomenologist, you can talk about this drink and that's philosophy.' Sartre could not hide his excitement.[1] To succeed with the novel he was making out of his *factum* what he needed was a means of blending philosophical reflection with the direct transcription, factual or fictional, of personal experience. Phenomenology, said Aron, by-passed the familiar opposition between realism and idealism, affirming both the supremacy of reason and the reality of the visible world.[2] After buying Emmanuel Lévinas's *La Théorie de l'intuition dans la phénoménologie de Husserl* Sartre leafed hungrily through the uncut pages. He was soon certain that he needed to study phenomenology, and the helpful Aron, who had led him into meteorology, now arranged for him to study at the French Institute in Berlin for the year starting in September.[3]

So far, in his work on the novel, he had been open to influence from a variety of writers including Breton, Michaux, Silone, Moravia, Hemingway, Dos Passos and Céline. De Beauvoir and he both knew passages of *Voyage au bout de la nuit* (*Journey to the End of the Night*) by heart: Céline had evolved a style of writing no less vivid than speech, and Sartre, she says, 'finally gave up the stiff language he had been using in *La Légende de la vérité*'.[4] The influence of Dos Passos and Hemingway was still more important. A French translation of *The 42nd Parallel* had just been published, and Sartre would soon regard Dos Passos as 'the greatest writer of our time'.[5] Here at last was narrative that did not deny contingency: 'Each event is a gleaming and solitary thing, which does not issue out of another – it looms up suddenly, adding itself to other things – something irreducible.' Narrative, for Dos Passos, is adding up.[6] Proust, centring on subjectivity while relating both feelings and actions to past events, implied a causality; Dos Passos, adapting the techniques of American journalism, rejected *la vie intérieure*, crystallizing life into its social components, showing feelings as actions and actions as facts.[7] Dos Passos immediately made inroads into Sartre's conversations. With de Beauvoir he would try to reconstruct incidents as Dos Passos might have described them – the ejection of the docker from the Café Victor, for instance.[8]

Hemingway had an imitable knack of making insignificant-seeming details significant without relying on subjectivism. Objects in his narratives were conspicuously solid, though he offered no more than would have been apparent to the character he was presenting. 'Many of the rules we observed in our novels', says de Beauvoir, 'were inspired by Hemingway.'[9] American culture also filtered into their lives through jazz and Hollywood films. They missed few of the new films starring Greta Garbo, Marlene Dietrich, Joan Crawford or Sylvia Sydney. The script might be poor, but the faces were beautiful.[10] They saw many of Walt Disney's *Silly Symphonies*, and Sartre did imitations of Donald Duck.[11]

They used their Easter holidays to discover London, where they were dismayed by the dreariness of the tea-shops, so unlike continental cafés, but they explored the city and its suburbs, walking for hours through the streets until rain forced them indoors. They were amused by bowler hats, umbrellas and unsophisticated window-dressing, while they liked the docks, the boats, the grimy shop-fronts in the Strand. They visited the National Gallery and the Tate, but Sartre had no desire to see the sights. Buildings, parks, paintings, tapestries had all been meticulously described, he argued, by writers of a previous generation, and, in the process, democratized. They could feel entitled to spend their time on slums. On their next trip to England, he said, he would visit Manchester, Birmingham and other industrial cities.

In the evenings they went to the cinema; Kay Francis's 1932 film *Cynara* gave them Ernest Dowson's line: 'I have been faithful to thee, Cynara! in my fashion', which Sartre was to go on using for years as a sweetener in conversations about infidelity.[12] In Canterbury he was as delighted as de Beauvoir with the cathedral, but in Oxford he baulked at the arrogance of the undergraduates, and refused to go inside the colleges with her.

Often she would resist his endless theorizing. She accepted the connection he made between English cooking and Locke's empiricism – both were founded on the analytical principles of juxtaposition. But when he generalized about London after a mere twelve days there, she insisted that reality defied verbal analysis – only to be told that if you wanted to impose your personal pattern on the world, it was not enough to observe and react.[13]

In March 1933 Henrie Barbusse wrote in *Le Monde* that Hitler would not be able to save the German economy from the collapse which would lead the proletariat to recover its heritage. He was expressing the same naive complacency that was endemic in the German Communist Party. In France, too, the political impotence of left-wingers predisposed them to underestimate the danger. When the Association of Revolutionary Writers, which was formed in July, launched its magazine *Commune*, Nizan was co-editor with Aragon, but in his *Propos*, Alain weakly argued that it was better not to think about the possibility of war: to believe in it was to give one's tacit consent.[14] Sartre, who read the newspapers assiduously, reprimanded de Beauvoir for not taking enough interest in what was going on.[15]

In the classroom, though, he was more willing to discuss his theory of individual freedom than his ambivalence towards communism. He celebrated the end of term by getting drunk with his pupils, finishing up with them in a local brothel. It was his first experience of brothels, but he was too drunk to remember what happened. When he talked about it afterwards, he would claim to have gone 'upstairs on the back of a sturdy whore'.[16]

The summer holiday gave him another chance to go abroad with de Beauvoir and in 1933 they had no compunction about taking advantage of a bargain on offer from Mussolini. Thanks to the Fascist Exhibition, foreign tourists could travel on the Italian railways at a seventy per cent reduction. Sartre and de Beauvoir spent a fortnight in Florence and four days in Rome. But fascism had the country in its grip. Black-shirted party-members had priority on the pavements; on the walls posters endlessly reiterated fascist slogans. At night the streets were deserted. One night, when Sartre and de Beauvoir wanted to stay up till dawn, they were sitting by the fountain on the deserted Piazza Navona when, at about midnight, two blackshirts ordered them back to their hotel. Disobediently they wandered through dark, empty streets for about three hours until they were stopped by a patrol in the Colosseum.[17]

In Berlin though, despite the uniforms, the nazi posters, the abundant evidence of a militarist regime, the occasional glimpse of a communist hiding from the nazis, Sartre could personally enjoy more freedom than he'd had since starting military service four years earlier. At twenty-eight he 'rediscovered the irresponsibility of youth':[18] it was like being a student again. Between his bouts of work – in the morning on Husserl; from about 5.30

in the evening on his novel – he would stroll through the streets, observing the behaviour of uniformed thugs and intimidated Jews, but, unlike Christopher Isherwood, he did not feel this was what he ought to be writing about. Everyday observations need not be accorded priority, though he was responding positively to Husserl's insistence that the philosopher, discarding all preconceptions, must concentrate on phenomenological description. At the Ecole Normale the teaching had been mainly concerned with theories of knowledge, and Sartre had been conditioned to accept 'the illusion which is common to realism and idealism, according to which knowing is eating'. This 'alimentary philosophy' made the mind into a spider which 'drew things into its web, covered them with white spittle and slowly assimilated them, reducing them to its own substance'.[19] Husserl refreshingly insisted that objects could not be dissolved in consciousness, and that consciousness was constituted by its refusal to be substance.[20] It was not self-enclosed and if it tried to coincide with itself, it would only negate itself. Consciousness always needs to be conscious of something else – this is what Husserl meant by intentionality.[21] Phenomenology was a method of disregarding distractingly generalized hypotheses in order to concentrate on phenomena as experienced. Husserl's motto was: 'To the things themselves'. He had taken a good deal – including the term 'intentionality' – from an Austrian philosopher who had exerted a beneficent influence on other novelists, including Kafka and Musil. Franz Brentano maintained that the philosophical task was purely descriptive. Sartre, with his admiration for Hemingway's straightforward accounting of physical action, was well disposed towards this attitude, which was conducive to vivid, ungeneralized writing. Just as an intuition can be empty or full, an account of an incident or thing can be arid, like a catalogue entry, or can be sufficiently well realized to involve the reader in the experience.

It was easier in Berlin that it might have been in Paris to write a philosophical defence of the position he had unsuccessfully defended in arguments with Aron when Sartre had insisted that the landscape he saw was exactly the same as the scenery which was *there*. His aversion to the subject-object dualism was to persist throughout his life: 'So far as I am concerned', he declared in a later interview, 'there is no such thing as subjectivity; there are only internalization and exteriority.'[22] After accepting Husserl's idea of a consciousness which perpetually transcends itself in favour of an object, Sartre went on in *La Transcendance de l'Ego* to argue that instead of being situated inside consciousness, the Ego is out there in the world, an object of consciousness. It is not a concrete structure but a temporary product of reflection. It transcends any individual moment of consciousness; it consists of nothing more than a reflective synthesis of past and present mental impressions. This is to contradict Husserl, who insisted that the

Ego 'is not a piece of the world'.[23] Sartre, who had always disliked the notion of 'inner life', tries to destroy the equation of consciousness with self. The I which is aware, he maintains, is not identical with the me I am aware of. Even when it is conceived abstractly, the I is 'always an infinite contradiction of the material ego'.[24] Not that Sartre is concerned primarily about the self; his book is about consciousness and his intention is to restore its transparency by cleansing it of personal subjectivity. But this encourages a presumption of objectivity. In presenting his variations on Husserl's ideas, Sartre is claiming the right to forget that they are his or Husserl's. He would have us believe that this is simply the way things are. But impersonal consciousness is consciousness without a subject, and this is no less unthinkable than consciousness without an object.

Dividing his day between work and solitary walks, Sartre missed de Beauvoir's company. He ate lunch by himself in the Kurfürstendamm, ate in the evening with five or six of the other students at the French Institute, and sometimes went with them to the movies. He had been relishing the prospect of love affairs with German girls, but soon realized that his German was not good enough. He had to make do with the wife of a French student who was living at the institute, a dreamy, disorganized girl called Marie Girard. She was capable of being passionate, but totally unambitious.[25] He somehow guessed that her father had given her a traumatic experience: had he raped her? Angrily she denied it, but seven years later it would turn out that he had.[26]

Returning to Paris for Christmas was not altogether unlike returning after a term of teaching at Le Havre. Nothing in his life was more continuous than its discontinuity, though the stubborn regularity of his working habits generated a counter-current of continuity. Even on holiday he would work two long shifts each day and, spending his Christmas holiday with de Beauvoir, dividing the time between Paris and Rouen, he sketched out a story based on a teacher who had recently lost her virginity to a married writer; shapely but plain, the girl refused to accept the unmistakable indications that he wanted the affair to be brief. She became increasingly deranged, and when Sartre and de Beauvoir tried to help her out of a suicidal phase, she accused them of being involved in a conspiracy against her. Everything was a sign. After abandoning the story, he later made it into 'La Chambre' ('The Room').

Back in Berlin, he resumed his routine of reading in the mornings and working in the evenings on the novel. Roquentin's narrative depends on the quality of his thinking, which depends on the quality of Sartre's, and this was changing under Husserl's influence, which was more stimulating than Bergson's had been. One crucial element in the phenomenological method was what Husserl called 'Epoche' – a studied withdrawal from the 'natural attitude' to observed objects. Normally we confuse the river we see with the knowledge that water flows downhill; the phenomenologist trains himself to 'step back' from the knowledge of natural or scientific laws and to concentrate wholly on what is perceivable. Roquentin's observations often seem odd because the substructure of familiar assumptions has been deftly removed. The vision is that of a man who habitually steps back, without being aware of doing so, and Sartre uses the Symbolist trick of not naming things until after they have been described. 'From time to time out of the corner of my eye, I see a reddish flash covered with hairs. It's a hand.'[27] The narrative sometimes steps so far back from hands that they become independent animals. Roquentin's hand 'shows me its fat stomach'.[28] In the reading-room, as the Autodidact makes a pass at the schoolboy, Roquentin watches their hands. The boy's 'was resting on its back; slack, gentle and sensual it had the insolent nudity of a girl sunbathing after a swim. A hairy brown object approached hesitantly. It was a big finger, yellowed by tobacco. Next to this hand it was as ungraceful as a male sex organ.'[29] This forces us to visualize sharply.

Sartre was also benefiting (as a novelist) from his knowledge (as a phenomenologist) of the difference between the 'indicative act', which is empty, and the 'intuitive act', which is filled out. Intuition (in this context) is the action by which a consciousness fully confronts an object. It is not enough to have the object in mind. When Sartre learned in Burgos what it meant to look at a cathedral, he had started on the phase of development that led not merely to the experience with the chestnut tree but also to the appreciation of Husserl, who helped him to investigate hands with his consciousness and to describe them as if seeing them for the first time. He was also helped by Heidegger, who said: 'The existent we have to analyse is ourselves. The being of this existent is my own.'[30]

Phenomenology provided a credo that made Sartre confident he could rescue the novel from subjectivism, implicitly refuting Bergson and Proust. Hating the idea of being intellectually in anyone's debt, he always aimed his harshest onslaughts against those who had helped him most. The musical phrase which recurs in Proust's novel, the refrain from Vinteuil's sonata, is parodied in the refrain from 'Some of these days', but, more uneasily, Sartre goes on to use the song as an intimation of what the artist can achieve. Sartre is more effectively ironic in handling Anny's (Proustian) belief in 'privileged moments' and he scores in his variation on one of Proust's favourite themes, the irreversibility of time, while Proust, himself a consummate parodist, is consummately parodied in the visions that place-names induce in Roquentin. On the whole, Sartre's aggressive competitiveness is more a help than a hindrance: he is egged on to his best prose by an arrogant conviction that he can outflank Proust. Looking at the hawthorn bushes, Proust's narrator is convinced that if only he can recapture the impact they first made on him, he will solve the secret of life. Sartre, trying to convey what the stuff of life consists of, filters his own understanding of chestnut trees through Roquentin's jaundiced consciousness.

Though everything comes through this filter, the narrative makes authoritative statements about the nature of consciousness, the nature of existence, the nature of time, and the nature of emotion, simultaneously focusing on outward appearances, and vividly characterizing social life in a provincial town. The tedium of Sunday, the regular customers in the restaurant, the people in the reading-room are all brought powerfully to life. Husserl had led Sartre to a new way of uniting the subject with the object. Consciousness can define itself not by looking inwards but by looking outwards. Sartre would have been less successful if he had been less vindictive. In the middle of his essay on Husserl he pauses to gloat: 'At last we have got rid of Proust.' Temporarily at least, help could be accepted in killing off one of the father-figures who had been dominant for too long. Later it would be Husserl's turn, and later still Heidegger's, to be dismissed with a parting insult.

In 1931, when he sat down in Le Havre to look at the chestnut tree, Sartre had not yet studied either Husserl or Heidegger, but when he wrote the crucial episode in *La Nausée*, he was under the influence of both. For Heidegger, the most important question was what Being is. Ever since Socrates and Plato had pushed philosophy towards analysis and rationality, thinkers had failed, he complained, to concentrate on the fundamental question: what is it that *is* in everything there is? Normally Being is hidden: we see only individual beings and objects, attaching names to them without asking the right questions. 'We do not see the tree for the trees.' Studied properly, anything 'can become a clearing in which Being declares itself'. Sartre, who had already looked quite hard at a tree, now did his best to make Being declare itself through one. 'Normally', Roquentin is made to reflect, 'existence hides itself. It's there, around us, inside us, it is *us*, you can't say two words without talking about it ... but ... if I'd been asked what existence was, I'd have said it was nothing.'[31] Now, suddenly, it is to become something, but this something is different from the Being that had revealed itself to Heidegger, who believed that the best approach was one of radical astonishment, and that the world was neither hostile nor nauseating. Sartre's stomach was more easily upset. In praising Husserl for saving philosophy from subjectivism, he insisted on the validity of emotion as a means of perceiving:

Knowledge or pure 'representation' is only one of the possible forms of my consciousness 'of' this tree – I can also love it, fear it, hate it, and this intentionality –

consciousness overtaking itself – is rediscovered in the fear, hate and love ... All of a sudden these famous 'subjective' reactions ... are only ways of discovering the world ... It's a *quality* of this Japanese mask to be frightening ... not the sum of our subjective reactions to a piece of sculpted wood. Husserl has restored to things their charm and their terror.[32]

The analogy is misleading: a tree is not a piece of sculpted wood, but in *La Nausée* Roquentin is upset by Sartre's old anxiety about contingency. In a geometric form or in a work of art each part is (or should be) necessary in relation to all the other parts, but a real landscape (unlike a painted landscape) oozes with superfluity. Nothing is indispensable. 'We were a heap of existing entities, embarrassed, unsure of ourselves, we hadn't the least reason to be there, none of us, each existing entity, awkward, vaguely uneasy, felt superfluous in relation to the others.' Sartre hated nothing more than not being needed and Roquentin even thinks of doing away with himself in order to get rid of at least one superfluous existence.[33] In spite of being so miscellaneous, though, the entities all have Being in common. 'It had lost the inoffensive aspect of an abstract category: it was the actual glue of things, this root was moulded in existence ... the diversity of things, their individuality was only an illusion, a coating. This coating had melted, leaving moist solids, monstrous and chaotic – nude, fearfully and obscenely nude.'[34]

There may be a subterranean connection between Roquentin's attitude to the tree and Sartre's to the nude female body, threatening him with glutinous or at least moist orifices and with contingent fertility. The root of the chestnut tree leads Sartre to the word that became so important to Camus: 'Absurdity was neither an idea in my head nor a spoken word but this long serpent, dead at my feet, this wooden serpent ... I realized that I'd found the key to existence, the key to my nausea, to my whole life ... I'd experienced the absolute: the absolute or the absurd ... In front of this great rugged paw, neither ignorance nor knowledge mattered: the world of explanations and reasons is not that of existence.'[35] No less articulate than Heidegger, Sartre is less objective but more impassioned, and here he launches himself excitingly into the space between things and explanations. Though the originality of the novel pivots on its philosophical eclecticism, Sartre was not merely popularizing the ideas of Heidegger, he was dramatizing them.

In discovering Husserl he had undercut the conflict between idealism and realism by concentrating on description. Heidegger learned from Husserl, but made the phenomenological enquiry into a more passive process, in which the philosopher allows the phenomenon to speak for itself. In Greek, *phenomenon* means 'that which will reveal itself', but it will reveal itself only if we listen attentively after freeing ourselves from preconceptions. While Husserl had not attempted to uproot Cartesian thinking, Heidegger insists that the central fact of human experience is Being-in-the-world. The observing ego is not separate from the observed world of objects and landscapes. Existence means standing outside oneself: being is not encapsulated within the skin, but spreads over the field of vision, which is a field of being – *Dasein* (literally: being there). In Sartre's phrase, phenomena can interrogate emotions. Eager to refute the alimentary philosophy which made consciousness draw objects into its maw, Sartre pushed emotion outside subjectivity into description.

> This blackness there, against my foot, it didn't look black, but more like a confused effort to imagine blackness made by someone who'd never seen it and couldn't stop himself, who'd imagined an ambiguous being on the far side of colour. It *looked like* a colour but also a bruise, or rather a secretion, a greasiness – and to something else, a smell for example, it based itself on the smell of moist earth, of moist, lukewarm wood, a black smell spread like a varnish on this nervous wood, an aroma of chewed fibre, sweetish.[36]

As a novelist he could let his disgust goad his description into greater vividness, but what was valid as a method of working was not valid as a philosophical axiom.

Roquentin's nausea is obviously connected with adult commitments – with a fear, akin to Sartre's, of responsibilities that will drag him away from his boyhood freedom – and with sexual dissatisfaction. Though he is not sexually frustrated – the restaurateur's wife never says no – Roquentin seems unconcerned about what she looks like, and lets his mind wander while making love,[37] but the novel does not explain his deficient emotionality as a result of past experience. Sartre wants to deny the past any power, but the book profits from the urgency of its fixation on the present. The narrative modulates skilfully between past tense and present tense, but the diary method helps to keep the camera aimed at the very recent past, while the movement from one moment of consciousness to the next generates an intensity which helps us to forget the relationship between one decade and the next. Almost nothing is said about Roquentin's parents or his childhood, while his decision to abandon his biography of de Rollebon functions as an assertion that no meaningful patterns are to be extrapolated from analysis of the past. There are no causal connections. One accident ensues on another. While Sartre appears to be more concerned with consciousness than Hemingway or Dos Passos, and his narrative tone could scarcely be more different from theirs, his premiss is much the same: 'things

are exactly what they appear to be – and *behind them* ... there was nothing'.[38]
If everything is exhaustively described, nothing needs to be explained in
terms of process. Looking at his face in the mirror, Roquentin sees something no longer human. 'Brown wrinkles on either side of the feverish
swelling of the lips, crevasses, molehills.'[39] Features have become a landscape. Sartre's narrative, like Proust's, is carrying philosophical and psychological ideas in suspension, but Roquentin sets his face against the possibility
of searching for lost time: 'I will never find either this woman or that
night. I lean over each second, I try to use it up; nothing goes by without
my snatching at it, fixing it for ever in myself – nothing, neither the fleeting
tenderness of those lovely eyes nor the noises of the street, nor the false
brightness of early morning; yet the moment passes and I cannot hold
it. I'm glad it passes.'[40] This is both anti-Proustian and anti-Faustian. At
the same time, Sartre anticipates the synchronic analyses of structuralism
by insisting that nothing needs to be explained diachronically.

The presence of Heidegger in the novel is so strong that Sartre understand-
ably wanted to deny it: we need to be suspicious of the chronology he
has put on record. He was to complete the second draft of the novel before
he left Berlin in July, but according to evidence planted in interviews and
in the *Carnets* he had made little headway with Heidegger by then. He
had bought *Sein und Zeit* before Christmas, intending to switch after Easter
from Husserl to Heidegger. But 'I had been taken by Husserl. I was looking
at everything in the light of his philosophy, which, besides, was more accessible to me because it looked Cartesian. I was "Husserlian" and ... I could
not come to Heidegger till I'd used up Husserl. And, for me, to use up
a philosophy is to reflect in its perspectives, to evolve personal ideas at
its expense until I get into a cul-de-sac. I needed four years to use up
Husserl.'[41] In April, he says, he had attempted to read *Sein und Zeit* but
had given up after fifty pages, partly because of the difficult vocabulary,
and partly because commitment to Husserl was making Heidegger indigest-
ible.[42] But Roquentin's reflections on existence suggest that Sartre had
digested Heidegger rather well. Later on in life he was to claim that he
did not read Kafka until after *La Nausée* was written.

This obsessive care in covering his tracks belongs to his complex about
self-generation: in literature, as in life, he wanted to believe he had no
progenitors, though he would later applaud Mallarmé for insisting that
all the ideas in our consciousness are old ideas, and already, in *La Nausée*,
Sartre makes the Autodidact disappointed when Roquentin pretends to
be impressed with the originality of an entry in his notebook. Surely the
idea can't be valid unless someone has already thought of it?

The strength of Sartre's negative feelings towards other novelists (Balzac,
Flaubert, Proust) helps him to a scorchingly new tone, while the language

is fresh and vigorous – neither rhetorical, like that of his plays, nor abstract, like that of his philosophical works. This abstractness is prefigured in *La Nausée* when Roquentin warns himself against flowery writing – 'I need to clean myself up with abstract thoughts as transparent as water'[43] – and later, during the chestnut tree episode, when he complains that things exist too strongly. If only they could be drier, more abstract. Here a surprisingly strong nostalgia for a unified system, sanctioned by divine planning, combines with Sartre's horrified recoil from abundance, viscosity, fertility, pullulation, suggestively serpentine roots. Like a star actor, who expects his prominence to be guaranteed by the script, Sartre wanted no part in crowd scenes. If Nature is teeming with life, one small intellectual is unlikely to be missed (Someone's missing – it's Sartre!). An inveterate townsman, uneasy in the country, he even projects his resentment onto the landscape. Things don't want to exist, Roquentin tells us. 'Weary and old, they went on existing with bad grace, simply because they were too weak to die, because death could reach them only from outside; it's only melodies that carry their own death proudly inside them like an internal necessity.'[44] The tension and the resonance come from direct confrontation with a mode of existence Sartre finds uncongenial; subjectively but concretely he is dramatizing man's relationship with the planet, and he is writing better than he will later when he withdraws too far from landscape and townscape into hygienic abstraction.

In the confrontation with the tree, no alien eyes stare back, but in the municipal gallery Roquentin feels challenged by the faces in the portraits. Looking at Olivier Blévigne, the merchant, he can find no fault in the handsome, unwrinkled features but the gaze is implacably accusing. 'His judgment transfixed me like a sword and raised doubts about my right to exist.'[45] Later Sartre will make Genet, Mallarmé and Flaubert feel as children that they have been put in the dock by the challenging stare of bourgeois seniors. Like Roquentin they have rejected the values their elders incarnate. Nor is Roquentin prepared to learn the lesson that another painted dignitary, Rémy Parottin, is prepared to teach – about the admirable role of the elite. Roquentin's decision to abandon the biography comes immediately after his visit to the gallery, as if the complacent portraits have convinced him that the virtues necessary to fulfil his task are virtues he despises.

Sartre was now doing exactly what Raymond Aron had light-heartedly predicted – philosophizing while talking about an apricot cocktail. As Roquentin is staring at the chestnut tree or at the portraits, the philosophical points emerge casually but forcefully. We not only share the man's vision – we will never be able to shake it off. We are free to disagree with his redefinition of existence, but not to forget it.

Sartre was better able to identify with Roquentin because he was writing out of isolation, separated in Berlin, as he had been in Le Havre, from the group that had surrounded him for so many years in Paris, and though his moods cannot be inferred directly from his character's, there is an obvious affinity, while Sartre's walks through Berlin contributed to Roquentin's through Bouville. Like James Joyce, writing in Paris about Dublin, or Günter Grass, recollecting Danzig in Paris, Sartre was reconstructing streets and scenes quite different from the ones in view, but unlike Joyce and Grass he was pushed by distance towards abstraction, though carefully selected details evoke a distinctive atmosphere.

In February 1934 de Beauvoir arrived in Berlin: she had persuaded a doctor to certify that she needed two weeks of rest.[46] Sartre took her to the Romanisches Café and to 'some debauched nightspots by the Alexanderplatz'[47] where she saw the inevitable transvestites. She also had her first taste of an ordeal that would be recurrent in her life: she had to meet Sartre's mistress and to give no sign of jealousy. When she was introduced to Marie Girard, de Beauvoir knew that her own relationship with Sartre was not in danger,[48] but it cannot have been easy to remain unemotional.

When her term ended in July he went to meet her in Hamburg, so that they could tour Germany together before he settled back in France. German anti-nazis were still expecting Hitler's regime to prove unstable, but all over the country there was evidence that it was establishing itself. In Hamburg the nazis had demolished part of the red-light district, leaving only a few streets. In Lübeck battalions of brown-shirted nazis were parading through the quiet streets. Sartre and de Beauvoir had planned to visit Vienna, but after the news that Dollfuss had been assassinated, they opted instead for Munich, Nuremberg (which was festooned with swastika flags), Rothenburg and the Königssee. Following Dullin's advice they went to Oberammergau for the Passion Play. It was the 300th anniversary of its first performance there, and the village was so crowded that they had to sleep on straw mattresses in a shed. Twenty thousand people watched the performance, which lasted for ten hours, with a two-hour interval. Dullin would have approved of the 'truthfulness that had nothing to do with realism'.[49] Sartre liked the way Judas, on being given the silver coins, counted out loud from one to thirty.[50]

In Strasbourg they saw one of the first colour films – *The Mystery of the Wax Museum*, with Fay Wray, and they were so pleased with the Alsace scenery that for three days they walked. They had no more luggage than could be carried in their pockets. Sartre sang songs he made up as he went along.

He and de Beauvoir were quite dissimilar in their reactions to tiredness:

'she accepts her exhaustion and immerses herself in it, so that it becomes an agreeable and desired state, while I find the same fatigue disagreeable, because I do not consent to it, until I definitely feel I *can't* go on. There's a way of cleaving to oneself, which I don't understand. This has advantages and disadvantages.'[51] It was a tremendous advantage to him when writing that he fought so stubbornly against fatigue, but on holiday with her he had to fight himself simultaneously on a number of levels. His tastes and instincts conflicted with hers. She was never happier then when tramping along difficult footpaths, filling her lungs with bracing air and enjoying magnificent scenery, while he was subject to what he called 'pre-fatigue, a disagreeable feeling of something that's going to descend on you'.[52] Tiredness also afflicted him with physical symptoms – pimples, boils, blisters, raw skin.[53] Nor did he like the country. As she said, 'he abhors – the word isn't too strong – the seething life of insects and the profusion of plants ... he feels at home only in towns, at the heart of an artificial universe consisting of man-made objects. He likes neither raw vegetables nor milk which has come straight from the cow. Nor oysters – nothing but cooked food, and he always asks for bottled fruit rather than the natural product.'[54] In the chestnut tree episode of *La Nausée* he would make good use of the hatred he felt towards the profusion of animal and vegetable life; in *Les Séquestrés d'Altona* he would draw on his aversion to shellfish. But in his friendship with de Beauvoir he was wrestling with his impulses in almost the same way as he fought against fatigue. His own tastes must not be allowed to obtrude. The word 'love' is inadequate to explain the sacrifices Sartre was making. Like Flaubert, he was simultaneously proud and ashamed of his own sensitivity. Flaubert distanced himself from it by dramatizing it in the character of a woman, Emmy Bovary, who was unlike him, not only in her sex. More aggressive than Flaubert and more desperate, Sartre was a refugee from *la vie intérieure*. Having tried to abolish privacy with his group of friends, he found that it was easier with de Beauvoir. Both consciousnesses could enjoy symbiotic transparency. Later on, in *Le Diable et le Bon Dieu* Goetz will have a similar urge to be fused with a woman: without ceasing to be himself he would like to *become* her.

Sartre and de Beauvoir separated at Mulhouse. Before returning to Le Havre he went to spend two weeks with his mother and step-father, who had been having a great deal of trouble with Charles Schweitzer. Now ninety, he had been installed in the ground floor of their house. After he had twice tried to throw himself out of a window and had defecated in a cupboard at his eldest son's house, the family had decided that he would be less troublesome if he were separated from his woman-friend who was masturbating him (according to the servant) until the blood came.

Accordingly, the eldest son kidnapped him, and when he had been installed with the Mancys, he made only half-hearted attempts to see her, but once, whether from genuine confusion or senile malice, he made a pass at his daughter.[55]

EIGHT · *Back to Bouville*

Settling down again during the autumn of 1934 into the routine of teaching at Le Havre, where Raymond Aron had replaced him for the last academic year, Sartre found it more enjoyable than before.[1] One of his liveliest new pupils was Jacques-Laurent Bost, the youngest son of the lycée's protestant chaplain, who had nine children. The eldest, the novelist Pierre Bost, was fifteen years older than Jacques-Laurent, who testifies that the boys never felt their philosophy teacher was bored. Twelve of the seventeen pupils, he says, were genuinely interested, and they felt free to interrupt or ask questions. During the year of Sartre's absence, favourable reports on him and his teaching had been circulating, together with rumours about the incident in the brothel.

It was pleasant not to see nazis in the street, but the French economic crisis was deepening: while unemployment rose to two million, rightists whipped up resentment against the foreign students who would soon be competing for jobs. In January 1935, ninety per cent of the Saarlanders voted for reunion with Germany. Though Moscow was in favour of forming a common front, it was not easy for the PCF to change tack after years of rebuffing socialist attempts at rapprochement; but as Laval's right-wing government showed its ineffectuality, communists, socialists and radicals gradually began to co-operate.

Accepting the consensus of friends that the novel was overwritten, Sartre went on pruning his prose until he was sidetracked by an opportunity to develop his ideas on imagery in response to a commission from Henri Delacroix, who was now editing a series for Alcan called *Nouvelle Encyclopédie philosophique*. Eager to revise his thesis in a Husserlian perspective, Sartre started a book to be titled *L'Image* or *Les Mondes imaginaires*. Summarizing theories about imagination evolved by Descartes, Spinoza, Leibniz, Hume, Taine, Bergson and the Würzburg psychologists, only to dismiss them because they had all believed thoughts could be imageless, Sartre claimed that Husserl had made the first major contribution to a psychology of the imagination. He had understood that a remembered image, unlike a pickle which can be lifted out of the jar intact, is reshaped in the process, and feeling is always integral to the reshaping.

Husserl did not establish any clear-cut opposition between perceiving and imagining: you are perceiving a Dürer engraving whether you see it as black lines on white paper or as a knight, Death and the Devil. But for Sartre perception is merely passive; interpreting belongs to imagination. From this premiss he could go on to question the motivation behind the decision whether to form visual data into a perception or an image, and to deny that the difference between the two could derive merely from intentionality. What was needed, he concluded was a phenomenological psychology, and the conclusion was, of course, a beginning. He must write one.

He worked hard at *L'Image* but his routine did not preclude frequent meetings with de Beauvoir in Le Havre and Rouen. In Le Havre they wandered around the old docks, ate in a brasserie, talked in the Café Guillaume Tell, where Sartre did much of his writing. After the first few weeks of enjoying teaching after the year of solitude and freedom, he had begun to feel ambivalent about the restrictions of having a job. In the café they talked about their prospects. Nothing new was ever going to happen. They would go on seeing the same friends, go on conducting the same scrupulously self-critical conversation.[2]

Much as he enjoyed writing, he was coming to depend on stimulants to screw himself into optimum productivity. At eight or nine o'clock in the morning he would start swallowing pep pills, which made it impossible for him to sleep at night without a sedative. He started taking four or five tablets of Belladénal at night, and went on needing sleeping pills for the rest of his life. He also used them to lower his blood pressure when it became too high. It was no accident that he dreamed little – or usually forgot his dreams – from this time onwards.[3] In one of his short stories, 'Erostrate', he used a dream told to him by Bost, and he liked girls to tell him their dreams, but he had few of his own.

In Rouen he played Russian billiards with de Beauvoir at the October fair, and began to patronize the café-restaurant that would feature in *La Nausée*. 'A half-dozen marble-topped tables bathed, summer and winter alike, in an aquarium light; the *patron*, bald and melancholy, did the serving; the menu consisted of little but eggs and tinned cassoulet.'[4]

For the Christmas holidays de Beauvoir persuaded him to make an attempt at skiing with her. For ten days they stayed at a small *pension* in Montroc, above the Chamonix valley. A ten-year-old boy showed them how to turn, and, unconcerned with other people's reactions, they persisted, trying to teach themselves on the beginners' slope.

Back in Le Havre, teaching, working at *L'Image* and thinking about the novel, he became subject to fits of depression. In class, according to Bost, he would sometimes 'turn icy; it did not last long – no more than about fifteen minutes. He would bite his nails and every so often he'd stare at the class, and, after a silence of perhaps forty-five seconds, he'd say: "On all those faces not one gleam of intelligence."[5] Thinking about Roquentin's depressions could work therapeutically against his own, but these overlapped with those of the character. Bost once saw him despondently observing seaweed slapping against a rock, with the same expression on his face as he had in the classroom when things were going badly or he was particularly disgruntled.[6]

In February 1935 he had his first experiences with mescalin. Knowing of his concern with images and anomalies of perception, his old friend Daniel Lagache, now an intern in psychiatry at St Anne, suggested that he could have an injection in the hospital to see what hallucinations it induced. They met at a bistro near the hospital and Lagache introduced him to another intern who was working with the drug.[7] It was not dangerous, he promised Sartre: at worst one might behave rather oddly for a few days afterwards.

In the hospital Sartre had to lie down in a dimly lit room. Objects began to change unspeakably in shape and size. When a doctor approached, his hand and his foot grew bigger; smaller as he went away. An umbrella hanging on the coat-rack looked like a vulture, with its handle as neck and beak. Attacked by devil-fish, Sartre was trying unsuccessfully to fight them off when he was called to the telephone. It was de Beauvoir. To her his voice sounded thick and blurred. Travelling with her in the train back to Le Havre he stared at the acorn-like ornaments on her shoes, waiting for them to turn into giant dung-beetles.[8]

In the morning the effects seemed to have worn off,[9] but for several days he was deeply depressed and unable to rely on his vision. A black spot danced constantly in front of his eyes. Houses seemed to have eyes and jaws; clockfaces had the features of an owl. The symptoms, he assumed, would get worse: he believed himself to be suffering from 'chronic hallucinatory psychosis', which, according to current belief, meant that within ten years he would be insane. One Sunday, when de Beauvoir and Colette Audry visited him in Le Havre, he made little effort to be agreeable or even to talk. Confiding in de Beauvoir about the symptoms, he rejected her assurance that he was not having psychotic hallucinations.[10] Working at his book and still insisting that consciousness could always differentiate between an image and an external object, he forced himself to look for what he could see, becoming distraught when he could not find it.[11]

Nor could he garner reassurance from doctors, who insisted that mescalin could not be causing the trouble. During the Easter holiday at the Italian Lakes with de Beauvoir he was in high spirits for much of the time, but on their return to Paris, he relapsed. Fernando Gérassi had an exhibition at the Galérie Bonjean, but Sartre stayed morosely in a corner throughout the *vernissage*. Sitting in cafés with de Beauvoir, or walking with her in the street, he sank into long silences. A doctor prescribed belladonna, but advised him to continue working.[12] He was worst when alone, and he spent more time than usual in Rouen to be with de Beauvoir when she was not teaching, and she provided a pupil to keep him company when she was.[13]

Known as 'la petite Russe', Olga Kosakiewicz was the daughter of a Russian nobleman and a Frenchwoman. Pale, blonde, temperamental, tempestuously unpredictable, Olga sometimes won high marks, sometimes turned in poor work. A flood of tears in the classroom had prompted de Beauvoir to invite her out for a walk, and after finding that she could talk more openly to the girl than to any of her older friends, she had started taking her out to lunch once a week at a brasserie, where Olga, who disliked eating and talking at the same time, would do neither. She and Sartre seemed to enjoy being with each other. She had in common with Toulouse something which de Beauvoir lacked – a combination of imperiousness and impetuosity. Probably Sartre had been unaware of missing it, but when he found it again he responded, and in *La Nausée* he pays tribute to it through his characterization of Anny. When she meets Roquentin again after not seeing him for four years, her first words are: 'Come in and sit down anywhere you like except in the armchair by the window.'

Sartre's passion for Olga would last for two years, coinciding with an instability that seemed to 'push out the limits of the probable'. 'I entered a world that was darker but less pale. As for Olga, my passion for her burnt away my normal impurities like the flame of a Bunsen burner.'[14] He even began to worry about his waistline. During the year in Germany he had put on weight and he had only laughed, after his return to France, when Guille had 'taken my stomach in his hands, through my sweater, to show Mme Morel that I had a big one'.[15] At intervals he inspected his stomach in the looking-glass, weighed himself on machines outside chemists' shops and tried to diet. One day Mme Morel observed: 'You like forcing yourself to do what you don't like doing.' This was a constant in his behaviour: it gave him the sense of being free. But he never persevered, never wanted badly enough to give up eating bread.[16]

One cause of his *malaise* was reluctance to grow up into what he called 'l'âge de raison'. No longer protected by a group of friends, he had to fend for himself in a society he hated, to be involved with headmaster, senior staff, colleagues, parents for whom he felt the contempt he made Roquentin feel towards the *salauds* of the bourgeoisie.[17] The novel provided an outlet for his spleen, but his childhood confidence about his future greatness had boomeranged back on him. Nizan's books were being published – *Cheval de Troie* (*Trojan Horse*) came out in 1935 – but Sartre had not found a publisher even for *La Transcendance de l'Ego.*

On 21 March 1935 Charles Schweitzer died at the age of 91. Five days earlier, Hitler, repudiating the disarmament clause in the Versailles Treaty, had introduced compulsory military service, causing panic in France. At the beginning of May, a Franco-Soviet pact of mutual assistance was signed, which accelerated the rapprochement between the three left-wing parties. In July the three leaders, Daladier, Blum and Thorez, addressed a joint meeting of their parties, and on Bastille Day, 14 July, socialists, radicals and communists marched through the streets, waving tricolour flags, shouting slogans and singing songs. Sartre and de Beauvoir watched, but without wanting to join in.[18]

At the beginning of the summer holidays Sartre went on a Norwegian cruise with his mother and step-father. At a fancy-dress ball on the boat he appeared in a black velvet dress of his mother's, wearing a blonde wig with long pigtails. He met an ageing American Jewess who was dressed as a man and found him charming. They talked in German and when she wanted to dance, he used the style he had picked up from Olga.[19] The following morning, seeing him undisguised, the lady lost interest.[20]

His experiences on the Norwegian cruise led him to write a short story 'Soleil de minuit' ('Midnight Sun'). It was about a thirteen-year-old girl on a cruise with her parents – she had imagined that the midnight sun was only a red ball with no power to illuminate, but at midnight the boat passes an island and the sunlight is strong enough for her to see the birds on it.[21] He also started a story based on the all-women orchestra they had seen at the café in St-Symphorien, but he tore it up after thirty pages.[22]

Returning from Norway he joined de Beauvoir for a hiking holiday. There was no possibility that the four of them could go on holiday together: de Beauvoir was never even to meet Mancy, but, without telling him, Sartre's mother often invited her out to tea. Sartre and de Beauvoir hiked through the middle of France, where he lost his only manuscript of the Norwegian story. He was always careless with manuscripts. Once he had written something, it belonged to the past; what he cared about was what he would write next. They followed the river Tarn through mountainous countryside, climbed the Aigoual, walked for hours over rough upland plateaux. They lunched on hard-boiled eggs and sausages in the open air. At Le Rozier they met Guille, who was also on a walking holiday, together with his attractive cousin, Thérèse. The four of them climbed rocks together, ate trout and écrevisse, paddled in the Tarn. As always, Sartre and de Beauvoir had planned their itinerary in careful detail. He preferred buildings to woods, and they visited châteaux, abbeys and villages.

All this time he still felt convinced that a lobster was pursuing him until one evening, in a crowded bus, which was taking them to Castelnau-de-Montmirail, he announced that he was tired of being mad. After this he was consistently cheerful.[23]

He was happy to be back with Olga, who put him into a state of almost permanent excitement. 'For the first time in my life, someone could make me feel humble and disarmed. I wanted to learn from her.'[24] Her consciousness seemed 'naked and spontaneous, capable only of feeling, with violence and purity'. She had more power than anyone had previously had to change his behaviour patterns. With her he often stayed awake all night, going without sleep for forty hours. 'At the same time and precisely because of this passion, I began to lose faith in salvation through art. Art seemed useless in comparison with this cruel, violent and naked purity.'[25] One conversation with de Beauvoir was enough to convince him that he was overstating the case against art, but a strong hostility to it was latent in him, and she was sucked by the force of his admiration into a deeper involvement with the impetuous young girl. Despite the nine-year age gap, the two women saw more of each other in Rouen during term-time than either of them did of Sartre. Like him, de Beauvoir admired Olga's refusal to hide her feelings. She valued emotions above ideas, 'life values' above spiritual values. Sometimes she would go on dancing till she passed out from exhaustion. In 1935 she twice failed her medical exams, and the parents, who throughout her childhood had seemed liberal and enlightened, now seemed treacherously authoritarian. At home in Beuzeville she was forbidden to smoke or stay up late, and they had decided to send her to a girls' boarding-school in Caen. Without Sartre's encouragement de Beauvoir would not have tried to intervene, but he had started an honours course in philosophy at Le Havre for male and female students, and by visiting Olga's parents in Beuzeville de Beauvoir persuaded them to let her coach their daughter for her diploma. De Beauvoir had moved out of her hotel in Rouen to rent a room in an old three-storey building Olga had recommended, Le Petit Mouton, in an alley off the rue de la République. Now Olga rented a room there herself.

Ivich, the girl in Sartre's *L'Age de raison* who is based on Olga, is the most vivid character in the novel. Mathieu, Sartre's *alter ego*, is not sure what he wants from her. Her face, largely hidden by fair curls, is broad, pale, girlish and sensual. Other people think her pretty; Mathieu knows she is plain. 'Mathieu stood at her side, ugly, importunate, forgotten. Yet he wouldn't have wished to be handsome: she was never more alone than when confronted with beauty ... he could call her by her name or touch her shoulder, but she was out of reach, with her frail figure and her lovely hard throat; she looked painted and varnished, like a Tahitian girl on a Gauguin canvas – not usable.'[26]

Olga could not concentrate on philosophy: when de Beauvoir asked her to précis a chapter of Bergson, she ate a pound of sweets and wrote none of the essay.[27] After two fruitless years of studying medicine she was so scared of failing that she preferred not to compete; recrimination only increased her indolence. Sartre gave up trying to teach her, and by Christmas de Beauvoir followed suit. Both believed they could learn from her: living for the present, she could throw herself uninhibitedly into any experience – dancing, listening to a gipsy violinist or to her own heartbeats. When de Beauvoir recommended Stendhal, Proust, Conrad, Olga reacted to the characters as if they were real people. In de Beauvoir's room they played chess, drinking cherry brandy in inordinate quantities.[28]

Back in Rouen during 1936, after a Christmas skiing holiday with de Beauvoir in Switzerland, Sartre tried to monopolize Olga, clowning for her, making up songs and stories like a father half in love with his nubile daughter, and he grew jealous when she appeared to prefer the company of a good-looking young teacher. De Beauvoir tried to keep jealousy at bay while Sartre apprehensively watched Olga's changes of expression; no-one must matter more to her than he did. Despising routine, braving lack of food or sleep, and questing in her immature, rebellious, capricious way after the absolute, Olga became so important to both of them that it irked their friends. Though they had no desire for a baby, they had once thought, momentarily, of adopting a distraught, half-drunk, charming girl they met in Montparnasse; now it was Olga who provided a passport back into adolescence. Singing, making up plays, intently analysing the exact flavour of cassis,[29] Sartre was escaping from the age of reason; once again, he was a member of a trio, and this time, as the only male in it, he could usually dominate the triangular relationship, partly because he, like Olga, was less interested than de Beauvoir was in the triangle as such. She was at a point which frequently disappeared from Sartre's field of vision, while the girl, amazed and happy to have so much power over both adults, found it easier to manipulate them separately.

As a writer Sartre had another setback when Alcan rejected the second half of *L'Image*. Only the first half, which interested him less, having less original thinking in it, would be published in 1936 under the title *L'Imagination*. The second half was not to appear until 1940, and then in a revised form *L'Imaginaire*.

For their Easter holidays Sartre and de Beauvoir took Olga to Paris, where they sat through two consecutive performances of Chaplin's first talkie, *Modern Times*. Sartre would later borrow its French title for his monthly, *Les Temps modernes*.

Ivich's brother in the novel, Boris, was modelled on the nineteen-year-old Jacques Bost. Sartre, who was coaching him for a teacher's diploma in philosophy, befriended him and brought him to Rouen. To distinguish him from his brother Pierre, they called him Little Bost. 'To us', writes de Beauvoir, 'he was an incarnation of youth. He had youthful grace, so casual it was almost insolent, and also a narcissistic fragility ... Needing security, he sought adult company.'[30] He was unambitious and unoriginal, but lively, quick-witted, naturally stylish, droll and rather charming. His party piece was striking matches with his toes.[31] Like Olga, Bost was to some extent a surrogate child – not a girl to be protected and cherished but a male, gratifyingly unlike the surrogate father physically, but with personality traits which appeared to have less connection with heredity than with Sartre's teaching. In the novel Boris has constructed his life around the ideal of liberty expounded by Mathieu in the classroom. Since the individual should be accountable to no-one but himself, Boris conscientiously defies bourgeois morality by stealing. He challenges the assumptions of everyone but Mathieu and Ivich, who are above criticism.

Apart from 'Soleil de minuit', Sartre's first story was 'Erostrate', which he wrote during 1936, basing it partly on another student, Didelot, who was brilliant, illegitimate, depressive and fascistic. One morning he drank coffee, wrote a letter to his grandmother, another to a girlfriend, went into the bathroom and cut his throat with two razor blades. Still alive, he went onto the roof, shouted to warn passers-by not to get in the way, and jumped.[32] The story is about a man who plans to kill people with his revolver, using the last bullet on himself. The narrative picks up Sartre's childhood pleasure at looking down on passers-by from a vantage point high in a building; the story also prefigures the interest he would take in Jean Genet. Some sentences read like undiscovered Genet juvenilia, especially when the narrative alludes to the Papin sisters. The character lusts for the transformation that crime can bring, but what is most revealing is his ease in identifying with the anti-humanistic viewpoint. As to Roquentin, fellow-citizens are innately repulsive. There is something unpleasant about the way the human body is jointed, with 'legs which open and close at will'. (Sartre describes them as if they were shellfish.) The humanist loves 'human flesh, people's appearance of being gravely wounded by education, and the way they seem to reinvent walking at every pace'. Like *La Nausée*, the story exudes contempt for the values and activities of stolid middle-class citizens.

In contrast to the bourgeoisie Olga behaved like the exiled aristocrat she was. De Beauvoir wrote: 'Together we hated Sunday crowds, conformist ladies and gentlemen, the provinces, families, children and all the humanisms. We liked exotic music, the *quais* of the Seine, barges, loafers, little bars with a doubtful reputation, the emptiness of night time.'[33] Under the influence of phenomenology, Sartre tried to put the world in brackets, to jerk himself out of taking normal behaviour for granted. One stratagem was to visit a mental hospital outside Rouen. Taking de Beauvoir, Olga and Bost with him, he went to look at the blue-uniformed inmates, who were mostly stupefied with boredom.[34] Alternately flirtatious and withdrawn, Olga provoked Sartre by refusing to tether herself. This prerogative was meant to be his. They quarrelled frequently and one day, two hours after he had put her on the train to Rouen, she was told over the telephone that on the railway platform an angry little man had picked a fight with a much bigger man, who had blinded him in one eye. Now in hospital, the little man had asked for her to be informed. In panic, Olga rushed to tell de Beauvoir, but it had been Sartre on the telephone, disguising his voice.[35]

Olga was like a sexy child trying to win the alliance of one parent against the other. About their relationships with Olga, Sartre and de Beauvoir argued endlessly, using phenomenological jargon. Olga often became violent while Sartre, who prided himself on being stoical, lapsed into protracted gloom. During the Easter holidays, when they visited 'Toulouse', Olga pressed a lighted cigarette ferociously into her hand.[36] De Beauvoir used the episode in her first novel, *L'Invitée*; in *L'Age de raison*, Sartre builds a nightclub scene to a climax in which Ivich slashes with a sharp knife at the palm of her left hand, opening the flesh from the ball of the thumb to the root of the little finger, and Mathieu outbids her by pushing the blade right through the palm of his hand.[37]

Dividing himself between the woman and the girl, Sartre felt safer with de Beauvoir, but the young blonde could arouse him to fury, ecstasy or alarm. The first serious rift in his alliance with de Beauvoir resulted not from intimacy with Olga but from a quarrel with her, and from the rapprochement between her and de Beauvoir which predictably ensued. While they were confiding in each other, he could confide in neither.[38] His partnership with de Beauvoir remained unsteady until July, when Olga rejoined her parents in Beuzeville. For the coming academic year he could choose between a job in Lyon, teaching a *khâgne*, and one in Laon, teaching for the *baccalauréat*. The Mancys pressured him to accept the Lyon offer, but he opted for Laon, which is much closer to Paris, where de Beauvoir had been offered a teaching job. Another reason was that since the Lyon job involved a promotion, he would have been expected to stay in it for several years; since the Laon job did not, he might well be moved to Paris at the next reshuffle.

NINE · *Intimacy*

In Laon, as at Le Havre, Sartre kept his distance from the other teachers. The most hostile was a M.Jollivet, master of the sixth form, who explained, threateningly, that he was 'the leader of a group, Monsieur'. At a ceremony held to celebrate the fiftieth anniversary of the lycée, one of the teachers would have to make a speech, and, to ensure that Sartre did not stay aloof from school affairs, all eleven members of Jollivet's group voted for him. The likeliest of the other candidates was a literature teacher who also received eleven votes, but because Sartre, who had been forewarned of the danger, helped the headmaster's secretary to count the votes, it was announced that the literature teacher had received thirteen votes to Sartre's nine.[1] He was no less adamant than he had been at Le Havre in refusing to attend boring meetings and one day in the common room he came to blows with a teacher who told him off for his absence from a *tableau d'honneur* meeting. The man was about his own age and, going round and round the room, they went on fighting until another teacher came in.[2]

While his indifference to school affairs remained stable, his interest in politics went on growing. When the electoral victory of the Popular Front was followed by strikes in the aircraft factories around Paris, he and de Beauvoir contributed to the strikers' collection, infuriating Guille, who said they were helping to endanger the Blum experiment. In June they were pleased with the Matignon Agreement, which gave the workers collective contracts, wage increases, a forty-hour week and paid holidays.[3]

Having decided to spend their summer vacation in Italy, Sartre and de Beauvoir were feeling elated despite the news of civil war in Spain. If the majority of the people wanted a republic, the minority of rebels must soon be defeated. On their way southwards, the lovers stopped at Grenoble, met Guille and his family at Guillestre, and took him on a bus to Marseille. In Rome Sartre and de Beauvoir stayed at the Albergo del Sole for ten days. In Naples they booked rooms at a hotel near the station, in the centre of the working-class district.[4] On holiday they took it in turns to be 'leader of the expedition'. It was now Sartre's turn: they started off by exploring the prosperous-looking main streets. When they found the narrow alleyways off the Via Roma, he was outraged by the evidence of starvation so close to the expensive, sumptuous food available for elegant ladies and gentlemen in silk clothes, and he started a story called 'Dépaysement' ('Bewilderment'). A ragged child picks up a piece of rotting water-melon from a fly-infested drain and starts eating it. In a cave-like room, open to the street, a woman is ill in bed.

> I could no longer see anything but flesh, wretched flowers of flesh floating in a blue darkness, flesh to squash, suck, eat, moist flesh drenched with sweat, urine, milk. All of a sudden a man knelt down next to a little girl and looked at her, laughing. She laughed too. She said: 'Papa, my papa.' Then, raising the child's dress a little, the man bit into her grey thighs as if they were bread. I smiled. No movement has ever seemed so natural, so *necessary*.[5]

The act of incestuous cannibalism represents his attempt to invent an action correlative to the squalid vista of poverty. Like 'Soleil de Minuit', 'Dépaysement' was written out of the feeling that objects, streets, landscapes contained secrets which could never be translated into words, but that there must be a way of evoking three-dimensional reality without trying to detach a two-dimensional meaning from it. What was a garden like when no-one was looking at it? He wanted to present glimpses of solid objects, combining a heterogeneous mixture of them in a brief action, rather in the manner of Katherine Mansfield.[6]

Unable to afford the funicular railway which carried tourists to the top of Vesuvius, he and de Beauvoir took a train to the nearest station on the Circumvesuvia and walked the rest of the way, despite the lava, slag and ashes which made the going difficult. After visiting Capri, Pompeii and Paestum they separated for two days while she went to Amalfi and he returned to Naples. Two sailors he met in a bar took him to a brothel where, in a circular room with mirrored walls, two naked women, neither of them young, performed *tableaux vivants* based on the frescoes in the Villa of the Mysteries at Pompeii. The women feature in 'Dépaysement'.[7]

On the boat to Palermo, Sartre and de Beauvoir slept on deck; in the city they travelled in horse-drawn cabs to visit churches and palazzi. At Selina Sartre tried to charm the lizards by whistling. On the ferry back to the mainland de Beauvoir was annoyed to see him reading newspapers instead of looking at the sunset. In Rome he was worrying about Spain, Hitler and Olga; ending up in Venice, they decided to save money by not going to bed on their last night. After the cafés closed, they sat on the steps of the Piazza San Marco, strolled beside the canals, watched the early morning barges, saw the market arcades being reopened. Afterwards Sartre announced that he had again been pursued by a lobster.

They arrived back in Paris on 14 September, so short of money that, shoeless, he had to wear his white espadrilles in the rain.[8]

In Laon, he settled into an ancient hotel, comfortable but with a distinctive fusty smell.[9] Involved in teaching again he forgot about lobsters, and he could escape to Paris twice a week. De Beauvoir, who was teaching at the Lycée Molière in Passy, was living in a small room at the Hôtel Royal Bretagne in the rue de la Gaîté. They met at the Gare du Nord and usually had a drink at a café near the station before going to Montparnasse, where they based themselves at the Café du Dôme.

When she was not teaching, she breakfasted there and stayed on to write, surrounded by German refugees and other foreigners reading papers or playing chess. The painter Ossip Zadkine and the writer Ilya Ehrenburg were among the regulars, while Giacometti was to be seen every evening wandering along the pavement, alone or with an attractive girl. De Beauvoir, like Sartre, found women more interesting to watch than men – models, artists' girlfriends, minor actresses, bizarre women who talked to themselves.[10]

When Olga ran away from her parents, booking herself a room in the Royal Bretagne, she resumed her unsteady relationship with Sartre, but not her pretence of studying philosophy. She got herself a job as a waitress in the boulevard St-Michel, and the pointlessness of her work enervated her. When Sartre found he had decisively lost her to Jacques Bost, he took the defeat well, vengefully consoling himself by starting a friendship with her younger sister, Wanda, who was subject to the same temperamental unpredictability, whether through genetic inheritance or through a habit of copying her sister. Their intimacy and their commitment to each other soon developed, but stopped short of lovemaking.

The defeat he did not take well was the rejection of his novel, which had been submitted by Nizan to one of Gallimard's readers. 'I had put the whole of myself into this book and spent a long time working on it. To reject it was to reject me.'[11] When he went with de Beauvoir to spend his Christmas in Chamonix, he could not hold his tears back. 'I had staked a great deal on the novel.'[12]

As 1937 began, his relationship with Olga resumed, though he would never again be so important to her as Bost. It was now that Bost's novelist brother Pierre became helpful, going to see Gaston Gallimard, asking him to read Sartre's novel himself. Still more effective was the intervention of Dullin, who was an old friend of Gallimard's. Sartre's spirits were boosted sufficiently for him to continue work on 'Dépaysement'.

But Sartre's growing interest in politics did not help him to feel at peace. Puzzled by the Moscow trials, he questioned Nizan, who answered guardedly, not concealing his anxiety. In France a group organized by right-wing extremists was sending arms to Franco, who was also receiving help from Hitler and Mussolini, while Blum's socialist government, like Stanley Baldwin's conservative government, did nothing to help the republicans. When Fernando Gérassi came back on leave from fighting in Spain, he reported that the People's Army was under-equipped, disorganized and short of trained men. The individuals who joined the International Brigades were mostly useless; Simone Weil had crossed the frontier and asked for a gun, but had been sent to work in the kitchens, where she spilled boiling oil over her feet.[13]

Sartre felt uneasy about not wanting to join the volunteers, and ambivalent when Bost did want to: wasn't he too immature to fight? But shouldn't he have the right to decide for himself? Sartre spoke to Nizan, who put Bost in touch with André Malraux. Anxiety about Bost's future in Spain gave Sartre the idea for a short story, 'Le Mur' ('The Wall'). Captured by the fascists, and sentenced to death, a boy and two men are in a cell waiting for daylight and trying to prepare themselves for the moment of facing the firing squad. A Belgian doctor, who spends the night with them, is unsympathetically interested in their physiological reactions. The boy, Juan, is the most hysterical – emotion as evasion; the narrator, Pablo, is the most clear-sighted, trying to use his imagination truthfully. Concern for Bost helped Sartre to project himself convincingly into the death cell, but Malraux was discouraging: only trained soldiers would be useful, he said.

Sartre's story 'Intimité' ('Intimacy') was probably written at about this time. It seems to have been developed from overheard fragments of café conversations which afford glimpses into other people's lives, as do the fragments Roquentin overhears in Le Rendez-vous des Cheminots. But identifying with the two girls and naming one of them, Rirette, after Rirette Nizan, Sartre is more sympathetic than he was in the novel. The basic situation is absurd: in spite of Rirette's encouragement, Lulu cannot bring herself to leave her impotent husband, Henri, for her lover, Pierre. The commonplace self-satisfaction and the vulgar sensuality of the two girls is brought ironically into focus, but the mimicry is so delicately accurate as to seem almost tender.

Before the winter was over, de Beauvoir collapsed during a dinner party. She was taken home in a taxi, and, two days later, driven in an ambulance to a nursing home at St-Cloud recommended by Mme Morel.[14] The doctors diagnosed pulmonary congestion, but no doubt the tension with Sartre and Olga had helped to weaken her. Every day he took the train to St-Cloud and suddenly his passion for Olga evaporated: his need was for de Beauvoir. 'I was nervous, unsettled. I looked forward each day to the moment of seeing her, and beyond that moment to I don't know what impossible rapprochement.'[15] When she was discharged from the nursing home Sartre arranged for her to be moved into a more comfortable hotel, where she was still bedridden during the Easter holidays. He looked after her, fetching her lunch from the Coupole and sitting at her bedside for hours.[16]

In her absence he had fun with Bost. They improvised games; one was to complete the *Paris-Soir* crossword without looking at any of the 'down' clues. In April 1937 they shook hands on the oath that in September they would buy ragged clothes from a second-hand shop, dress like tramps and set out with only ten francs each in their pockets to live for a week by begging and stealing. Sartre felt secretly flattered whenever they planned such juvenile escapades. Bost said 'we' and 'us'.[17] His charm was at its greatest when he put on performances just for Sartre, singing songs in English or improvising the role of a barman ejecting a drunken Sartre. Bost also elaborated on his baroque fantasies – in one of them he had twenty-seven girls, including de Beauvoir, her sister Poupette, Wanda and their friend de Roulet's girl. After buying the Hôtel du Théâtre, he would install his mistresses there, one in each room. De Beauvoir would be allowed out to change her library books, but the others would all be confined to the hotel.[18]

In April, while de Beauvoir was recuperating in the Midi, Sartre suddenly found that thanks to Dullin and Pierre Bost, success was no longer out of reach. The novel, Sartre was told, had previously been rejected on the assumption that it had been submitted for the monthly *Nouvelle Revue française* which was published by Gallimard and edited by Jean Paulhan. Sartre was summoned to the Gallimard offices, where Paulhan asked: 'Do you know Kafka? In spite of the differences I can think of no other modern literature for comparison with your book.' He went on to ask for stories he could print in the NRF. In any case Sartre could be quite confident about the novel: 'Gallimard *can't* not take it.' Sartre was then introduced to the philosopher Brice Parain, who was working for Gallimard and said the novel had at first reminded him of Dostoevsky, but he found some of the sequences too protracted and disliked the diary form. Meeting Bost afterwards in a café, Sartre put on an air of extreme dejection, throwing the typescript down on the table. Bost seemed shattered, until Sartre told him it had been accepted.

When Gaston Gallimard read the book, his only objection was to the title *Melancholia*; his suggestion was *La Nausée*. De Beauvoir demurred, not wanting it to sound like a naturalistic novel. In any case it would be published in 1938. Meanwhile 'Le Mur' would appear in the July issue of the NRF, and he resumed work on the story 'La Chambre', which derived not only from the experience with Louise Perron, the psychotic school-teacher, but also from the visits to the asylum in Rouen, and from the delusions he had suffered after the mescalin injections. Pierre, who never leaves his room, is persecuted by flying statues, which make a noise like an aeroplane. The story is told from the viewpoint of three other characters – his mother-in-law, his father-in-law and his wife, Eve, who goes on making love to him, but intends to kill him before mental illness has reduced him to dementia. Accusing her of wanting to live solely by imagination, her father tells her it is wrong to enter into the delusions of the mad.

Happy that fame was at last on the horizon, Sartre did not intend to spend less time on writing letters, taking out girls, enjoying himself with friends. A long April letter to the convalescent de Beauvoir complains about the pressure on his time: 'I love you very much but I absolutely no longer have time for being soulful (*les états d'âme*).'[19] Constantly hungry for the gossip integral to close friendship, he was spending a lot of time with Bost and Olga, seeing them separately more than he saw them together – Olga talked to him about Bost; he talked to her about Wanda. He talked to Bost about de Beauvoir, sometimes – and the joke may have been only an exaggeration of the truth – describing her as 'a woman of steel', who scared him.[20] He was also seeing Poupette, writing to Wanda, trying to write every day to de Beauvoir. He was anxious about her: 'You walk too much. You take risks ... you're going to put too much strain on your heart.'[21] The story would have to wait until he could spare time for it.

In any event her absence catalysed a contingent affair with a friend of Poupette's who had also become a friend of de Beauvoir's. Towards the end of April, Sartre took her for a long walk through the streets of Paris. She was wearing make-up for the first time. When he took her up to his room and kissed her on the cheek, she kissed him on the mouth. After they had made love, she said: 'I almost enjoyed it.' He presented her with a copy of 'Erostrate' and took her back to her husband.[22]

If the affair – which he described in full detail to de Beauvoir – had any effect on his relationship with her, it was to strengthen it. His letters to her became more detailed and reminiscent of Kafka's letters to Felice in the diary-like reporting of day-to-day trivia. Reading a letter of hers which described how tears had come to her eyes, he found that tears came to his.[23] On 11 May he wrote that he was hurrying to finish the novel – he still called it his *factum* – to have it ready for her return.[24]

In July, when 'Le Mur' appeared in the NRF it caused a furore. Sartre received a great many letters, and he was no less pleased with the offer of a teaching job at the Lycée Pasteur in Neuilly. After six years as a schoolmaster, six years of being exiled from Paris during term-time, he could at least work where he wanted to.

For the summer holidays he and de Beauvoir went to Greece with Bost. One day, when they were strolling through the slums near the Acropolis, urchins threw stones at them. They consoled themselves by thinking they were not really tourists of the kind the children took them for. Piraeus was full of beggars, who sat scratching their scabs, while a surprising proportion of the children were crippled, blind or mutilated. Even the middle-class Athenians looked unhappy in comparison with the Italians.

They stayed at a hotel off Omonia Square. Bost was allowed to sleep on the roof without paying. They breakfasted on the pavement terrace outside a patisserie, explored the streets, the markets and the port, but gave most of their time to the Acropolis. After visiting the tiered amphitheatre at Epidaurus, they spent the night in the open air at the foot of the slope. Waking up there with de Beauvoir next to him was a memory Sartre would treasure.[25] Travelling on ageing steamers and sleeping on deck, they visited Mykonos, Delos and Syra, where they all slept on the roof of the hotel. After a long walk on Santorini to the ruins of Thera and the sanctuary of Stavrós they arrived hot, exhausted and bad-tempered at Emborio, urgently needing food and drink, but the streets were deserted, and the only woman they saw fled in fear. Eventually they lighted on a decrepit café, where they were served with a tomato salad decorated with dead flies. The description of Argos in the first act of Sartre's play *Les Mouches* (*The Flies*) derives from this experience.[26]

After leaving Bost to sail from Piraeus back to France, Sartre and de Beauvoir went on to Delphi, and spent three days on the terraced slopes of Mount Olympus, sleeping under a blanket in the open air. Relying on the itinerary de Beauvoir had prepared from the *Guide Bleu*, they had thought it would be easier to cross the mountains. Sartre, who was scared of dogs, had to fight off a fierce mongrel with a stick.

They went by bus to Sparta, and slept on the floor of a ruined palace in Mistra, where Sartre stole a skull from an ossuary. De Beauvoir wanted to climb Mount Taygetus (nine and a half hours up, five and a half hours down) but Sartre refused. They spent two days at a hotel in Mycenae; he would remember being alone there with her 'under a beautiful staring sky, surrounded by these strange tombs and these rocks'. Though their money was running out, they went north to Macedonia and waited in Salonika until Bost telegraphed their September salaries. They bought too little food for the journey back and on the mailboat they were hungry in spite of the cakes and fruit given to them by the cooks. After two days together in Marseille, Sartre left for Paris, while de Beauvoir toured Alsace with Olga. As so often before, a holiday with de Beauvoir had renewed their solidarity. 'I haven't stopped feeling that there's an internal link between us', he wrote. 'Whatever I thought, it seemed as though I was saying it to you or rather that you were thinking it with me ... I had the feeling of two consciousnesses melted into one.'[27] Olga was jealous.[28] The Mancys were also being possessive: they wanted him to work in their flat and have lunch there.[29] Everything was reported to de Beauvoir in detail, with extensive quotations from conversations; though the letters were not intended as rehearsals for writing fiction, Sartre was training himself to select the most revealing phrases from what people said. For de Beauvoir, though she would have preferred not to share him with so many people, there was consolation both in reading the letters and in knowing that he needed to share the experiences with her.

The Lycée Pasteur was a huge, red-brick building, which reminded Sartre's mother of the palace at Versailles. From Montparnasse he would be able to get there in twenty-seven minutes on the bus. When de Beauvoir came back from Alsace they moved into the Hôtel Mistral in the rue Cels between the Montparnasse cemetery and the Avenue du Maine, but he took a room on the floor above hers. 'So we had all the advantages of sharing our lives, but none of the inconveniences.'[30]

If Sartre had forgotten during the summer holiday how rapidly life was changing for him, Paris soon reminded him. He had been alive for thirty-two years without achieving any conspicuous success, but he could not fail to realize that he was on the threshold of fame. 'I felt suddenly inundated with a formidable and profound youthfulness. I was happy and I found my life beautiful. Not that it had anything in it of "the life of a great man", but it was *my* life.'[1] He was not playing a role, and he was no longer straining to keep pace with a flamboyantly passionate young girl.

Settling in Paris did not change his attitude to home or to possessions. He was not interested in owning or even renting a flat with furniture, a library and ornaments in it. 'I would always be ill at ease in a flat, quickly transforming it into a stable. And I have never kept anything for as long as ten years except a pipe and a pen.' He would buy a new suit once a year and wear it all the time. Other possessions, including books, would sooner or later get lost, damaged or given away.[2] He was always rather embarrassed by presents, feeling there ought to be some better way of accepting them, but he enjoyed giving to Wanda: though she never expressed thanks, the object visibly became precious to her – he could enjoy possessiveness vicariously.[3] In the same way he could enjoy other people's homes – he especially liked being in Mme Morel's rue Vavin flat and in Toulouse's at Montmartre – he enjoyed their domestic pride.[4] But he liked to write in cafés, and claimed that no-one would suffer less if private property were abolished.[5]

Instead of starting another novel he settled down to a book on phenomenological psychology, intending to call it *La Psyché*, but the only fragment which was later published – in December 1939 – was then titled *Esquisse d'une théorie des émotions* (*Sketch for a Theory of the Emotions*). Taking an oddly narrow view of emotion, he equates it with responding unrealistically to external pressures. All emotions, he maintains, are reducible to 'the creation of a magical world, the use of our bodies as instruments of incantation'. By magic he means self-delusion: unable to rearrange circumstances as we'd like to, we distort our apprehension of them; incantation distracts us into believing that what we desire is within reach.

Though masturbation is never mentioned, it seems to be his model for the way in which emotion pressures the imagination. He describes the object as if it were an absent lover: the image which is formed by the *acte magique* of imagination gives us the illusion of totally possessing something which, in reality, would yield itself only gradually to perception, and then seldom in accordance with the perceiver's desires. If we succumb to the illusion, we are in a vortex which sucks us into crediting the imagination with a power it does not possess to change external reality; the image always produces confusion between desire and knowledge: 'It may happen that we try vainly by our treatment of the object to give birth within ourselves to the belief that it really exists: we can temporarily camouflage but we cannot destroy the immediate awareness of its nothingness.'

This is cautionary writing, addressed more to himself than to the reader, and in his distrust of the image we find the roots of Sartre's lifelong hostility towards *l'imaginaire*. Later he will refuse to discriminate between escapist writers and those who exercise self-discipline in the use of the imagination (Shakespeare and Stendhal, for instance). He will want the whole of literature to stand condemned, and he is already firing a broadside at all emotion: we fall back on emotion when we feel incapable of taking effective action. Fear works 'to negate something in the external world by means of magical behaviour'; at worst we faint, blotting out all awareness. He describes joy as 'characterized by a certain impatience'. We disport ourselves as if the object of our desires is already within reach. A man, told that a woman loves him, may start dancing and singing, 'forgetting the judicious and energetic exertions that will be requisite if he is to deserve this love and develop it, to earn it through innumerable details (smiles, little attentions, etc)'. This quaint account of a lover's obligations is not what we would have expected from the author of *La Nausée*. In the characterization of Anny, who laughs unpredictably, gives peremptory orders and capricious answers, putting herself totally at the disposal of her moods, Sartre had seemed to be championing an engagingly feminine assertion of the vitality Roquentin would always lack. But the *Esquisse* might have been written by a Roquentin who had never met her: nothing in it accounts either for the emotionality which animates her or for the equally irrational emotionality which prompted Sartre both in his reactions to Toulouse or to Olga and in his arbitrary dismissal of emotion. His fastidious distaste for it is inseparable from a distaste for the body, which he does not want to represent as something passive, the involuntary victim of invasion by adrenalin. It is this extremist anti-determinism which, joining forces with Sartre's unacknowledged emotionality, makes him insist that the nausea is not inside

Roquentin; when he sees it on the walls of the café, on the braces of the men, he is inside it. The *Esquisse* reminds us of this when Sartre argues that to see an object as horrible is to achieve a passage to the infinite. 'The horribleness is now in the object, in the heart of it. It is its emotive texture. It constitutes it. So, while the emotion lasts, an irresistible and definitive quality of the thing emerges ... Horribleness ... is a revelation of the meaning of the world.'[6] As philosophy this is nonsense; as a writer's credo it is useful.

At the end of October 1937 the Spanish government retreated to Barcelona, and at the end of November Franco began his naval blockade of the Spanish coast. Though newspapers carried photographs of corpses heaped on pavements after air raids on Madrid, Barcelona, Valencia and Lerida, France and England nervously preserved their neutrality, while Hitler and Mussolini went on helping Franco. When Fernando Gérassi arrived on leave in Paris, he did not exempt Sartre or de Beauvoir from his scathing contempt: 'Salauds de Français'.[7]

In December Italy withdrew from the League of Nations, and war had come to seem unavoidable by the time Sartre and de Beauvoir left to spend their Christmas holidays in the Mégève with Bost, who was expecting to be called up and to be killed at the front. In between skiing lessons, Sartre and de Beauvoir read Pepys and Swift in translation.[8]

When Sartre gave up *La Psyché* after working at it for three months and writing four hundred pages, it was largely because it had been stopping him from writing enough fiction. De Beauvoir was convinced that this was where his main talent lay. 'Yes, you can execute little philosophical arabesques, but you'll never be a philosopher.'[9] He channelled his energy into his book, *Le Mur*, which consisted of four short stories and one long one. 'L'Enfance d'un chef' is more like a novel than any of his other stories, but implicitly it contradicts *La Nausée* by exposing causal connections between childhood events and adult personality in the biography of a hypothetical counter-self influenced by the extremists of the right, by anti-semitism, by surrealism and by psycho-analysis, though the events of 1924–5, when Sartre was twenty, are confused (as Michael Rybalka points out) with those of 1935–8.[10] Sartre had once enjoyed his step-father's unhappy awareness that Poulou would never grow into a captain of industry or a businessman with a large staff. Like a character-actor specializing in roles remote from his own personality, Sartre moved from his affectionate empathizing (in 'Intimité') with two almost mindless girls to a more studied identification with a male who is physically dissimilar – above average height – and who is learning to take sadistic pleasure in exerting his authority.

As Michel Contat discovered, one of the models for Lucien Fleurier was a literary young man Sartre had known in about 1924: he 'stuffed himself with pub poetry when it was fashionable, showed off a mistress, then, when his father died, leaving him the family factory, resumed the straight and narrow path'. He told Sartre: 'It's better to do what everybody does than to be like nobody.'[11] The story intertwines strands from Sartre's past with strands of experience that might lead to the assumption of boss-status in business or industry.

He had intended to visit Algeria with de Beauvoir in the spring, but just before the end of term, she had a relapse, and when she recovered, there was time only for a short holiday in the Basque country. At Bozouls near Rodez she noticed how much of his hair was falling out. For him this was a 'symbolical disaster'. He had not been thinking about ageing or the approach of death, but now, at thirty-two, he suddenly felt 'as old as the world'. He went on massaging his scalp vigorously in front of mirrors, afraid of premature baldness and of the ageing process. At the age of twenty-two he had noted a saying by the early-nineteenth-century Swiss writer Rodolphe Töpffer: 'He who has not achieved fame by the age of twenty-eight must give up the idea of glory.' At twenty-two this had excited him, but at twenty-eight he was still unknown and unpublished. On their way back to Paris they stopped at Saintes and La Rochelle, where they walked around the harbour fortifications discussing 'l'Enfance d'un chef'. She wanted him to carry the story further, but his own instinct, which he followed, was to break off at Lucien's emergence into manhood.[12]

From 21 March 1938 *La Nausée* had been on sale in the bookshops,[13] and the reviews began to appear in May. In *Vendredi* A.-M.Petitjean saluted a novel 'in which an enormous talent bursts out, in which everything evinces one of our greatest novelists'.[14] Paul Nizan reviewed the book in *Ce Soir*: 'M. Sartre could have been a French Kafka by virtue of his gift for expressing the horror of certain intellectual situations, were it not that his thinking ... is entirely foreign to moral problems ... There is no doubt that in M. Sartre we possess a philosophical novelist of the first order.'[15] In the *Journal-Echo de Paris* Edmond Jaloux predicted that the novel 'might well make a durable mark on the literary evolution of our epoch',[16] and a longer review by Jaloux in *Les Nouvelles littéraires* helped to establish Sartre's reputation: 'It seems to me that no book has poured out for its reader such a quantity of disgust ... We get the impression of witnessing a visionary's walks through a world that is being created: everything is gluey, viscous, unshaped.'[17] The twenty-five-year-old Albert Camus, writing in *Alger républicain*, declared that: 'Infinite talent is revealed by a flexibility natural enough to hold its own at the extremities of conscious thought and by a doleful lucidity. That is enough to make us love *La Nausée* as the first declaration of a singular and vigorous mind. We wait with impatience for future works and lessons from it.'[18] The novel was in the running to win the prestigious Prix Interallié, and Sartre and de Beauvoir were excited at the prospect of being rich enough to fly from Paris to London.[19] The Interallié was finally awarded to Nizan for his novel *La Conspiration*, in which the name Sartre is given to a policeman. Reviewing it, Sartre asked: 'Can a communist write a novel?' and answered: 'I am not convinced that he can: he does not have the right to make himself the accomplice of his characters.'[20]

'Le Mur' had appeared in the July 1937 issue of the NRF which had begun to publish Sartre's critical work in February 1938, starting with a review of *Sartoris* which helped to establish Faulkner's reputation in France. 'Here actions (putting boots on, climbing stairs, jumping on a horse) are not intended to characterize but to conceal ... From time to time, laconically, he reveals a consciousness. But it is like a conjuror who displays the box when it is empty.'[21]

At the same time Sartre was planning his next novel, and in July, after de Beauvoir had left for a preliminary holiday in the Alps before the holiday they were to share in Morocco, he wrote to tell her: 'I have all at once found the subject of my novel, its proportions and its title. Just as you wished: the subject is freedom.' The title was to be *Lucifer*. The book was to be in two parts called 'La Révolte' and 'Le Serment' ('The Oath').[22] The idea would grow into *Les Chemins de la liberté*.

Though unwilling to risk embroiling himself in anything that might become like 'l'affaire Olga',[23] he began to flirt with an Atelier drama student, whose aunt, intending to make the girl less vulnerable, had made her more vulnerable by warning her that he was said to be irresistible. Their first kiss was violent. She 'sucked my tongue with the strength of an electric suction fan, so that it still hurts, and glued herself to me sinuously with her whole body. She seems very pleased with the way things are developing.'[24] She might not have been so pleased if she had known de Beauvoir was receiving detailed bulletins, with the reassurance: 'No vows are being exchanged.'[25] He told the girl that he didn't know what to do with her: 'You've arrived in my life like a dog on a putting green; I wanted to take you without having the least *need* of you, which is much more flattering. I've got three days to give you: let's take them and try to make the most of them.'[26] She brought him back into contact with Maurice Merleau-Ponty, whom he had not seen since leaving the ENS. Merleau-Ponty, who was in love with the girl, called Sartre a *salaud*. Sartre's response was that he too loved her but, because of de Beauvoir and Wanda, had no space for her in his life.[27] They spent the night in bed together without making love but without going to sleep either. She was 'Provençale as the Devil, full of odours and curiously hairy, with a little black fur at the small of the back, and a body that's quite white, whiter than mine. At first I was a bit surprised, almost disgusted by this rather violent sensuality and these legs which prick like an unshaven chin ... Her thighs are shaped like a drop of water, wider at the bottom than the top ... Very beautiful legs, a muscular stomach, absolutely flat, not the least shadow of a breast.' In the morning she told him that she was jealous of de Beauvoir but not of Wanda. Sartre's bulletin ended with the assurance: 'I am extricating myself from all these storms to remain united with you.'[28]

After two nights with the girl he reported that she had begun to love him passionately and that he was uncertain whether he had taken her virginity. 'In any case that appeared to be a profoundly difficult and disagreeable job. You understand that I didn't sleep with her because you'd forbidden me to do that, saying: "Don't get yourself into trouble."' The jealous Merleau-Ponty now reprimanded Sartre for not sleeping with her, but she was saying that she loved him too much. One night she gave him 'more than a very intimate kiss', explaining that normally the male sex organ horrified her, but not his.[29] He didn't mind talking to her in the second person singular, he told de Beauvoir, because the girl was 'Provençale and it goes well with her prune-like looks'.[30] During their last night together he did take her virginity. She told him he wasn't hurting her but, a moment later, asked him to withdraw.[31]

De Beauvoir was not his only confidante. Meeting Mme Morel at eleven one Saturday evening, he entertained her with an account of what had just gone on between him and another girl, an actress he had taken out to dinner at the Bouteille d'Or. She had wanted him to caress her arm while eating his cassoulet. Afterwards she invited him to rub her stomach and her bosom. He could render her this service, he said, only between ten-thirty and eleven. Though she did not want to make love, she lay down on a divan, pulling him down on top of her. 'Hug me. I want to feel very small, very small, very small.' He soon got bored, and said so, but they kissed before parting, and, despite his verbal betrayal, they became lovers the next day: 'Of all those who have honoured me in recent months with their love, none has been so agreeable physically nor so touching in transports of passion.'[32] But he went on seeing the drama student and wrote to tell de Beauvoir: 'Only you can give me the impression of living in a new present, oh charmer of my heart and my eyes, bulwark of my life, my consciousness, my reason.'[33]

His success with both girls was making him more demanding in his relationship with Wanda. Though he belittled her as having 'the mental faculties of a dragonfly', he was no longer content with kissing her on the mouth and being half-heartedly reprimanded. She had a horror, she said, of kissing without making contact. Sitting on her sister's unmade bed in the room the girls shared in the rue Delambre, she explained that she didn't know what sensuality was. This was a matter of great regret to her because it meant she could never have a complete relationship with him and never be an artist: without sensuality one could not hope to succeed in the arts. He comforted her and eventually kissed her, holding her down on the bed and climbing on top. She disengaged herself, and angrily he hurried away, but not quickly enough: he could hear her vomiting in the lavatory. She had been drinking white rum and sherry.

One evening, at a café near the Palais-Royal, where he had often taken Olga, he delivered an ultimatum to Wanda: the relationship would end unless they became lovers. She immediately promised to do everything he wanted but explained that she took no great physical pleasure in anything but contact and certain kisses, with him and with one other man.[34] When he and de Beauvoir left for Morocco, her virginity was still intact.

They had booked third-class tickets from Marseille to Casablanca, but they were switched to second-class accommodation by a friend who worked for the shipping company. From the depressing slums of Casablanca they went on to Bous-bir, where they met a heavily tatooed Arab woman, who took them to her room, removed her flowing robes, rippled her stomach muscles and smoked a cigarette through her vagina.[35] In Fez they lost their way in the back streets and accepted help from a young man just as the sun was setting. When an old Muslim shouted a warning to them, their guide took to his heels.[36] They quickly retreated as the first lamps were being lit and chains were being secured to close the narrow streets on either side of them.[37]

Determined to eat the native food, they sat on the floor of a restaurant and used their fingers to eat pastilla, chicken with lemon, mechoui, couscous and the marrow of gazelles' horns. Sartre was afterwards ill for two days.

In Meknès, where they were the only Europeans, Sartre smoked kief in a Moorish café. In Marrakesh they watched snake-charmers and sword-swallowers, and they went for a three-day walking tour in the Atlas Mountains, sleeping in rest-huts below the Berber villages and bargaining with peasants for unleavened loaves. Sartre entertained her with stories he improvised about a sergeant who hated flies and an Arab who could piss upwards.

Travelling to the south by long-distance bus, they saw evidence of drought and famine. Starving villagers had tried to migrate northwards, only to find the authorities had blocked the roads. In Ouarzazate the baggy-trousered hotel proprietor, coughing incessantly, described the typhus epidemic that had ravaged the country. Every day he distributed free boiled rice to local children. Some were blind or one-eyed; many were deformed. They squatted in the courtyard, dipping rhythmically with their hands into the large bowls – the point of the rhythm being that all should get an equal share.[38]

When Sartre and de Beauvoir arrived back in Marseille, Europe appeared to be on the brink of war. She decided to leave, as planned, for a walking-tour of the Alps with Olga, but only after he had promised to wire her *poste restante* if the situation deteriorated. And at Gap, on 25 September, she found a telegram telling her to come immediately. Hitler had demanded the surrender of Prague within six days. While she was one of the many who argued that any injustice was preferable to war, Sartre, who could have been called up at any moment, questioned the wisdom of appeasing Hitler. Restless, they went a great deal to the cinema and read each edition of the newspapers,[39] until on 29 September, at Munich, Daladier and Chamberlain signed a pact with Hitler and Mussolini: Germany was to have the Sudetenland, but Czechoslovakia's remaining frontiers were to be kept intact.

Far from being unable to work, Sartre started on his novel and resumed *La Psyché*. He would have preferred to express all his ideas through fiction, he told an interviewer, but 'there are things which are too technical, demanding a purely philosophical vocabulary. So I see myself obliged, so to speak, to duplicate each novel with an essay.'[40] He was also consolidating and formulating his ideas about the novel in critical essays and reviews, such as the one about François Mauriac, which begins by asking how the novel can create a world which stands up when its only material is words – *signifiés*. Saussure had used the word *signifié* in a different sense, referring to the thing indicated, the meaning of the word, as opposed to its form, the *signifiant*. 'How does it happen that Stavrogin comes to life? I don't imagine Stavrogin, I wait for him. I wait for his actions, for the end of his adventures. This opaque matter which I stir when I read *The Possessed* is my own expectation. It is my time.'[41] Sartre was reminding both his readers and himself of what he had learned from reading and writing fiction – that movement in a novel is the movement of the reader's eye over motionless words. 'For the duration of my impatience and ignorance to be trapped, shaped and given back to me as the flesh of these invented figures' the novelist must know how to produce

a time similar to mine, in which the future is not formed. I must not be allowed to suspect that the future actions of the characters have been fixed in advance by heredity, social pressures or any other force. Psychological analysis is fatal; the novelist must present only emotions and unpredictable actions. He has no right to judge his characters except from the viewpoint of other characters. Mauriac's mistake is to instruct the reader instead of arousing his impatience.[42]

Sartre could channel most of his didactic impulses into his non-fiction, though his fiction was programmatic. He thought of it as a three-phase enterprise and went on to the end of his life talking about '*La Nausée*, the stories, the novels'.[43] The object of *La Nausée* had been the same when it had been conceived as a work of non-fiction: to expose the stuff of existence. The stories displayed the handling of that stuff by various individuals, who all had less affinity to Sartre than Roquentin had, while the novel was a more ambitious project. Thomas Mann had shown in *Buddenbrooks* that a huge fresco could be filled with contrasting characters, and this made Sartre think initially of a vast space with no predetermination in the narrative that would fill it.[44] He was now regarding himself as primarily a novelist. His intention was that the new novel should be a 'continuation' of *La Nausée*. Roquentin would discover his liberty only on losing it – through enlistment – and on being demobilized he would be ripe for the pleasure of the *acte gratuit* in line with Gide's Lafcadio in *Les Caves du Vatican* and the surrealists. But whereas his hero's predecessors had had difficulty in screwing themselves up for the *acte gratuit*, Roquentin had no alternative. He would rape and murder a woman. Nevertheless it was Sartre's aim, he said, to counterbalance the pessimism of *La Nausée*: 'You will see existence rehabilitated, and my hero will act, will taste what action is like.'[45]

After catching Dullin's attention accidentally at an audition when she was reading in cues for a friend, Olga discovered that she had talent as an actress, and she began taking lessons in mime from Jean-Louis Barrault. St-Germain-des-Prés was one of her haunts and it was probably she who got Sartre and de Beauvoir into the habit of patronizing the Café de Flore, which had served as the headquarters of the right-wing Action Française at the beginning of the century. Sartre could concentrate better in a café than at home. 'It's a milieu of indifference, where other people exist without troubling about me while I don't worry about them. Anonymous drinkers who argue noisily at the next table disturb me less than a wife and children who would walk about on tiptoe so as not to disturb me.' If a pretty girl came into the café, he'd watch her sit down and go on working: 'She's passed like a movement of consciousness, no more.'[46] By the time Sartre, de Beauvoir and Olga formed the habit of spending their evening at the Flore, it had become a rendezvous for film people, but they sometimes returned to the Dôme, where the clientele was slightly shabbier.[47]

In February 1939 *Le Mur* was published. Sartre had discarded 'Dépaysement', though Paulhan liked it, but in addition to the title story the volume contained 'La Chambre', 'Intimité', 'Erostrate' and 'L'Enfance d'un chef'. Sartre had been wondering whether to explain in a preface that he took no pleasure in degradation, and that the book had its place in a scheme. While *La Nausée* defined existence, each of the five stories enacted a misguided attempt at escape.[48] No preface was included but in the 1967 edition he explained what he'd had in mind. In 'Le Mur' Pablo tries unsuccessfully to imagine his own existence after death. In 'La Chambre' Eve tries unsuccessfully to penetrate into her husband's madness. In 'Erostrate', Paul Hilbert (an anti-type of Roquentin, and Sartre's most fanatical anti-humanist) tried to reject the human condition by means of a monstrous *acte gratuit*. In 'Intimité' Lola tries to throw a smokescreen between herself and the gaze she fixes on herself. Lucien Fleurier almost escapes from existence into contemplation of his rights, but the attempt fails because the rights do not exist. Each of the five escape routes is blocked by a wall: 'to run away from existence is still to exist'.[49] The resultant force of the stories might be negative, but Sartre intended to be positive in the fiction that would follow.

He sent a copy to his step-father, who returned it with a note of the point at which he had stopped reading. Reviews were mixed. The playwright Gabriel Marcel found the stories 'distinctly superior to *La Nausée*'. André Rousseaux wrote an unfriendly review in *Le Figaro*, and in *Le Temps* André Thérive condemned 'a crudity so relentless that it smacks of the obsessive'.[50] One of the most complimentary reviews came from Camus in *Alger républicain*: 'A great writer always brings with him his world and his sermon. That of M. Sartre wins converts for nihilism but also for lucidity.'[51]

Since returning from Germany four years ago, Sartre had read Heidegger's *Was ist Metaphysik?* in Corbin's new French translation. It was no coincidence that Corbin translated it at this time: there was now a potential public for it. It was not only that Heidegger's notion of the 'pathetic' made an impact, with his use of words such as Death, Destiny and Nothing: many readers needed tools for understanding history and destiny. Writing after the 1914–18 war – a period which brought despair to those who had taken it for granted that it was 'natural' to be German – he advocated voluntary assumption of one's period.

At this, the most creative phase of Sartre's development, reading and writing were almost inseparable activities. Just as consciousness (in his view of it) spontaneously reached out to passive objects, his creativity reached out to books. Hemingway and Heidegger had both been waiting patiently for his mind to alight on them, to draw them into his evolving system. He did not at first talk about Heidegger to de Beauvoir, but during the Easter holidays, while they were travelling through Provence, going by train and bus from one village to the next, they found themselves sitting on a stone bench at Sisteron, and here he told her about Heidegger's description of man as a 'creature of distances', and about the way that the world revealed itself to 'maladjusted instruments'.[52] The phrase 'creature of distances' seemed to confirm the idea of a fissure in the heart of consciousness. A man would not be what he is if there were no space between what he is and his awareness of it.

Though Sartre still took intense pleasure in de Beauvoir's companionship and still benefited from having her as his resident critic, success was changing the quality of his partnership with her. At first they had both been beginners, outsiders planning a raid on the citadel. There were no limits to their generosity in helping each other, but there were limits to their intimacy, even as lovers. They continued throughout their lives to address each other in the second person plural, and as success made him busier, he tried less to keep her in touch with everything he was reading, writing, thinking, doing. Apprehensive that he was not giving her fulfilment as a woman, he found it easier to channel this anxiety into fiction than to keep the promise he had made to discuss everything with her openly. He was confused about his feelings towards Olga and uncertain whether de Beauvoir might be ambivalent about having a baby, even if she had assured him she did not want one.

To Mme Morel it was by no means out of the question that they should have a child. 'She is very much insisting', wrote Sartre in July 1938, 'that I give you a baby. "To see what he'd be like," she said. She will bring him up.'[53] Here were two dangerous areas of ambivalence that he could neither afford to explore in reality nor afford not to explore in fiction. In *L'Age de raison* Mathieu and Marcelle have made the same pledge Sartre and de Beauvoir had made to discuss everything frankly. 'When Mathieu had committed himself to Marcelle, he had permanently renounced all thoughts of solitude – the cool thoughts shy and shadowy which sometimes slipped into him with the furtive vivacity of fish. He could only love Marcelle openly: she *was* his openness, his companion, his witness, his adviser, his judge.'[54] In *L'Invitée* de Beauvoir makes her heroine feel as if nothing that happens to her is real until she has told her lover about it. 'When he gives the moments back to her, they are clearer, more polished, more complete.' Each of them enjoyed giving moments back to the other, and though de Beauvoir was upset by Sartre's infidelities, she was glad to know he could not enjoy them fully without confiding in her. How much she gave back was up to her; usually she seems to have been generous. In *L'Invitée*, Françoise, de Beauvoir's *alter ego*, becomes so jealous of Xavière, the fictional Olga, that the action culminates in murder, but the fiction functioned as a safety-valve, and at the end of her life de Beauvoir spoke of her life of Olga as if the girl had been more her friend than Sartre's.[55]

Sartre, like Mathieu, was liable to feel 'impregnated with humble gratitude'[56] when a friend held back from judging him, and Marcelle is doubly threatening because she could produce a child which would have another pair of judging eyes. Like Sartre, Mathieu feels uneasy in the presence of children. 'He had the sense of being engulfed by the child's eyes. "Children are greedy creatures," he thought, "all their senses are mouths." Pablo's expression wasn't human yet, but this was already more than life. It wasn't long since the child had come out of a stomach, and it looked like it: he was there, unsettled, quite small, he still had the velvety unwholesomeness of something vomited.'[57] The nausea in the consciousness of the observer is fear of being observed. It is essential to prevent Marcelle's baby from being born; 'there was the whole of a little being, thoughtful and weasel-faced, devious and glum, with a white skin, big ears and moles, with a handful of distinguishing features you enter in passports, a little fellow who would never run through the streets with one foot on the kerb and one in the gutter ...'.[58] The curious mixture of affection and disgust is symptomatic. It is partly disgust with life, though Mathieu also enjoys it, but marriage is a sacrifice of freedom, so the foetus is sometimes a tumour and sometimes an inflammation, as if Marcelle has been stung at the bottom of her stomach.[59]

There was no autobiographical basis for the pregnancy, and the unflattering portrayal was probably part of the design to distance Marcelle from de Beauvoir, but Sartre, addressing her through the fiction, may have been aiming to discourage any lingering inclination towards maternity. He also shared Mathieu's fear that even without marrying he had been trapped into a relationship no better than a bourgeois marriage. The pact of openness, he tells himself, works mainly in her favour: 'He especially liked talking about himself, displaying his little crises of conscience, his moral scruples.'[60] She intensely enjoys listening to all this, but he secretly fears that the arrangement is working to her disadvantage, though he tells himself not to worry about her. If anything were troubling her, she would tell him. But would she?

Sartre was obviously uneasy about the growing imbalance in his relationship with de Beauvoir. Her love for him was so strong and so durable that there were no limits to her tolerance. He learned that he could afford to be less scrupulous about keeping the pact, and less considerate in his behaviour. This helped to make the relationship less exciting for him. She had not learnt what Proust could have taught her about love: that it cannot survive without the pain of anxiety and the need to conquer new territory. We love only what we do not entirely possess. De Beauvoir made it obvious to Sartre that he entirely possessed her. His need for her would continue throughout his life, but he needed her more as a mirror than as a lover, and if she now started to go on holidays without him, it was because his craving for her physical presence was dwindling. He had never felt the same urge as she did to escape into the country at every opportunity, and he accompanied her neither on her Whitsun walking tour in the Morvan area nor on her June climbing holiday in the Jura. Not that their relationship was harmed by disagreement about appeasement. It was already known that the nazis were killing Jews in concentration camps, but she still maintained that war should be avoided at all costs: even if France was in danger of being engulfed like Austria, it would be absurd to condemn a million Frenchmen to dying. No, said Sartre, appeasement was making everyone into accomplices of Hitler. War would not be worse than nazi occupation of France. 'I don't want Nizan's eyes to be gouged out with a coffeespoon.'[61]

When Colette Audry's communist friends grumbled at her for wasting time with Sartre and de Beauvoir, she had usually answered brightly: 'I'm getting the man of tomorrow ready.'[62] They had retained some of their unrealistic youthful optimism about moulding the cultural future, while their friends, emulating their fluctuating enthusiasms, helped them to believe they were setting trends. Having been so largely deprived of family life during childhood, Sartre would need, throughout the rest of his life, to be surrounded by an ersatz 'family' of friends. Invariably it was younger people who were recruited, with Sartre and de Beauvoir in the quasi-parental roles, though he had more say than she did over who was enlisted and who was expelled. 'It's exhausting,' complained Bost, 'having to hold your opinions at the same moment as you do.'[63] Awareness of being imitated encouraged Sartre to change positions even faster than he might otherwise have done. But if war came, everything would change.

In May 1939 he took part in the international anti-fascist conference. One of the writers he met there was Ilya Ehrenburg, who had returned to Russia and become more Stalinist since his days of frequenting Left Bank cafés. In March the German army had occupied Czechoslovakia, Daladier had been empowered by the Assembly to accelerate rearmament, Madrid had surrendered to Franco, and Poland had received a joint pledge of support from Britain and France. Sartre and de Beauvoir had hoped to visit Russia in the summer, but they decided instead on a holiday in Portugal, if the peace held. But when an invitation came from Mme Morel to stay at her villa in Juan-les-Pins, they decided to venture no further. With her rucksack on her back, de Beauvoir set off alone on 15 July to hike southwards; she would meet Sartre in Marseille.

With the Wanda relationship neither consummated nor abandoned, he was beginning a passionate relationship with a Polish girl, Bianca Bienenfeld, another friend of de Beauvoir's whom he found attractive. She wrote to him in July, enclosing her first letter in one de Beauvoir was writing to him: in his reply he declared his love and promised to show her part of his unfinished novel.[64] He wanted to share his future with her, he said: '*our* future is your future, there's no difference'. De Beauvoir, he wrote, lived 'in a world where you are ubiquitous at the same time' and loved Bianca more than she realized.[65] Bianca had suggested that she and Sartre should tell each other everything, immediately, and he accepted the idea enthusiastically. He loved her and thought about her all the time.[66] Writing to her from St-Sauveur, where he was staying with his mother, he described his boredom. Until lunchtime he wandered from café to café. 'I drink black coffees, but with dead flies floating in them, and I write my novel.'[67] Having lost his suitcase on the way, he had nothing to read, and time seemed to pass very slowly. His mother couldn't enjoy his company in the presence of her husband, but wanted Sartre to be there because Mancy wanted him to be there.[68] Dutifully he helped Mancy to wash the car, but it had been stupid to think he'd be able to concentrate on writing.[69]

Wanda had agreed to go on holiday with him before he left for Marseille, and he took her to Avignon and then to Aigues-Mortes. Short of money, he had calculated carefully how much he could afford to spend, but train-fares were higher than he'd realized, and he had to balance his budget by economizing drastically. Instead of going to restaurants they lived on fruit and sandwiches, sharing a bedroom to save money. In the evening she took forty-five minutes to get herself ready for bed, insisting on being alone in the bedroom all this while. At both Avignon and Aigues-Mortes they were staying at cheap hotels which closed at eleven, so he was reduced to taking prolonged walks around the corridors. At Aigues-Mortes he aroused the suspicion of the night-porter, who followed him, calling out: 'Who's there?' He locked himself into the lavatory and read Nietzsche. But in the morning Wanda finally surrendered her virginity. Afterwards she said she hated him and felt totally exhausted. All these details were reported to de Beauvoir in the bulletin he wrote later the same day.[70] But the relationship with Wanda developed pleasantly. They made love morning and evening. She seemed to enjoy it greatly, but lay supine for fifteen minutes afterwards, and, to feel fully alive, they both needed to quarrel violently as a build-up to reconciliation.[71]

Knowing that he concealed nothing from de Beauvoir, Wanda entreated him to make an exception of what she had told him about Olga. He gave his promise, with no intention of keeping it. 'You will benefit,' he told de Beauvoir, 'and so will I. I get the impression she's out to destroy the "friendship" I have for you bit by bit. It's quite amusing.'[72] Believing in a healthy diet, Wanda was trying to wean him off coffee and croissants. She would get up early and go out, naked under her overcoat, to buy fruit from the market, but after breakfast she would settle back to sleep. At about eleven he would furtively get up, wash, enjoy coffee and croissants in a café before calling at the post office to collect the letter from de Beauvoir that was usually waiting.[73] After reading her letters he tore up even the ones she wanted him to keep; once Wanda came into the room while he was finishing a letter to de Beauvoir: 'You know my feelings but I daren't write them down because it's possible to read upside down.'[74]

Elation at his literary articulacy (with de Beauvoir as his audience) was in competition with triumph as a seducer (with Bianca and Wanda as victims). Though he had a strong need, now as later, to be on intimate terms with women, he did not much enjoy making love. 'I was more a masturbator of women than a copulator ... For me what mattered most in a sexual relationship was embracing, caressing, moving my lips over a body ... I came erect quickly, easily; I made love often, but without very much pleasure. Just a little pleasure at the end, but fairly second-rate. I preferred being in contact with the whole body, caressing the body, in short being active with my hands, with my legs, touching the other person.'[75] Even in bed freedom had to be experienced actively; an erection felt too much like something that happened to him. The indifference to lovemaking was partly incredulity that a woman could be enjoying his body. During his first important affair, the one with Toulouse, he was repeatedly told that he was ugly, and it seemed to him that in the act of love the woman's beauty was being enjoyed by both lovers. 'Reciprocity was the thing I felt least; the fact that the other person could equally take pleasure in feeling my body.'[76]

Throughout his life he was enormously reluctant to relax, to let go. Though he had a strong constitution, he felt at ease with his body only when it was in action, doing something for him. What remained from his childhood was not only his fantasy of himself as a man of action but the illusion of having – so long as he was doing something – a body quite different from the one he would have seen in the mirror: 'The truth is that I saw myself as if I were the same size as anyone else.'[77] He habituated himself to speaking loudly, addressing people taller than he was. 'My imaginary body was the body of a strong military captain, of a Pardaillon in fact, that is to say a cloak-and-dagger hero ... And I've never stopped thinking that: it's been some sort of compensation for my shortness ... which I've felt only abstractly.'[78] The imaginary body, abstract at first, became more real: 'I imputed great value to the activity I felt in my hands, more strength, more power to activity in my body. If I pushed at a rock, my action was more violent and the rock heavier in the imaginary dimension than in reality.'[79]

He stayed with Bianca in La Clusaz before joining de Beauvoir in Marseille, where they took a room in a hotel overlooking the old harbour. In the evening, eating at a restaurant by the sea, they gave money to beggars without interrupting their conversation. In the morning, after breakfast, they went on to read newspapers and write letters in the Café Riche, where they saw the Nizans, who were due to sail that evening with their children to Corsica. After the parents had bought their children a rubber boat from one of the big shops, they all ate a bouillabaisse together in a small restaurant by the harbour. According to Nizan, the tripartite agreement was being ratified, and Germany would soon be on her knees.

Afterwards, walking along the quay with the children, they met Bost, who was now a second-class infantryman on leave after being stationed in the Ardennes. He'd been in Marseille since the morning, sitting in a brasserie, confident he would spot them sooner or later. They all had a drink at the Cintra before the Nizans left.[80] Sartre and de Beauvoir did not know they would never see Nizan again.

They went with Bost to Martigues, where they ate another bouillabaisse while rain pattered against the canopy above their heads. Watching gaily painted boats bobbing up and down, they discussed the future. The Germans were moving into Danzig and Sartre would soon be called up. Was it better to return from the front blinded or limbless? When the rain stopped, they went for a walk.[81] De Beauvoir was never to forget what Sartre looked like, unable to relax, talking to Bost while sitting uncomfortably on blocks of stone with sharp ridges.[82]

They were waiting for news from Mme Morel, who was coming from Cavallo. When she arrived, she took Sartre and de Beauvoir to stay at the villa which had been built by her father. Sartre wrote in the mornings, while de Beauvoir read. In the middle of the day, they would go down to the sea, where he gave her swimming lessons. Though he was a good swimmer, he could not help believing that one day he would be dragged down by a sea monster with twenty-four legs and huge crab-like pincers. Sometimes he would strike out for the shore in a panic.

After reading in the newspapers that the Supreme Soviet was about to make a non-aggression pact with nazi Germany, Sartre and de Beauvoir, less certain than ever of the future and wanting a few days together, made an excursion into the Pyrenees. In the train from Juan-les-Pins to Carcassonne soldiers recalled from leave annexed the reserved seats. 'We're the ones who're going to get killed first.'[83] At Foix, eating cassoulet and foie-gras in a hotel, Sartre said that in the fourth volume of his novel, after hearing about the nazi–Soviet pact, the Gérassi character would resign from the Party and ask Mathieu for help, counterbalancing the episode in volume one where he offers help.

In Paris, with the theatres, many shops and many restaurants closed for the August recess, the contrast between the *quartiers* had disappeared.

'There was nothing but a totality which was Paris. A totality which for me belonged to the past.' Making telephone calls, wandering through the streets, going to the cinema, he found 'there was this unpleasant feeling which is hope'.[84] On 31 August, the day before the nazi army marched into Poland, he was still hoping: 'With the state of mind the German people is in, it's impossible that Hitler's intending to start a war. It's bluff.'[85]

On the day Poland was invaded de Beauvoir travelled with Sartre to Passy and waited for him in the café by the viaduct while he visited the Mancys, who had been living in the avenue de Lamballe since 1933. Learning that mobilization would start the next day, he went back to search for his kitbag and his army boots in the cellar of the hotel, and then took a taxi to the assembly centre, where he was told to report in Nancy the next day. At the Café de Flore a tough-looking woman was quietly weeping, but most people seemed cheerful.[86]

Early the next morning, sitting with de Beauvoir outside a café in the deserted Gare de l'Est, waiting for the 7.50 train to Nancy, he did his best to convince her that as a meteorologist he would be in no danger.[87]

In the train he tried for the first time to make contact with soldiers. 'I'd promised myself that I'd fraternize, but I can't ... I lack both fluency of speech and an agreeable manner.'[88] On the train he finished Kafka's *Der Prozess*, which made him feel more like a creature of distances. It was his body which felt impatient to arrive, his legs which wanted to be stretched, his gullet which was thirsty. 'But I *myself*, finally, will never be in a better state than on this train.'[89]

PART THREE
War (1939–45)

'The war has really divided my life in two',[1] Sartre said, quoting Jules Romains: '... as if the whole of his personality had abruptly been transported from one environment to another ... Nothing internal or external could be perceived in the same way as before.'[2] For eighteen months his normal life was to be held in abeyance as he served first as a soldier and then as a prisoner-of-war. He was posted to the meteorological unit attached to an artillery division in Sector 108, just behind the front in Alsace. The unit was to be shuttled between several small towns near Strasbourg. He would be sent to Ceintrey, Marmontier, Brumath, Morsbrunn, Bouxwiller and then back to Brumath.

At three o'clock in the morning of Sunday 3 September, he arrived at the reception camp of Essey-les-Nancy, where he was told: 'You're with ZII, but ZII has already left.' He was issued with denims and a helmet, which were both too big for him. He wandered aimlessly about; no-one could tell him anything about ZII. He slept on a straw mattress.[3] He was not happy to find himself at such close quarters with so many men, 'coarse types who shit, wash, snore, exude maleness'.[4]

After lunch, when he heard that war had been declared, he felt as if he were going to start his national service all over again. Depressed, he stretched out on his bed until a small, spectacled corporal appeared at the door. 'Is there someone called Sartre here?' The corporal, Jean Pierre, had two other private soldiers in his meteorological unit – a fat, lazy-looking man of about forty, Müller, and a shrewd-looking, curly-haired Jew, Pieterkowski, who, to conceal his Jewishness, called himself Pieter. That night, Sartre slept in their barrack-room. In the morning a lorry took them to Ceintrey, a village sixteen miles away. Thanks to Pieter, who was good at asking for what he wanted, they were billeted with one of the locals, an eighty-nine-year-old clergyman. The spectacled corporal, a nervous, guilt-ridden maths teacher, allowed Pieter, who ran a hat-shop, to take the lead. He arranged for the four of them to have their meals at the house of a retired cook. It looked as though they would have nothing to do except make a couple of meteorological observations every day, and Sartre wasted no time in settling down to work on his novel; by Tuesday he had drafted twelve pages.

A man addicted to physical comfort might have found it impossible to concentrate while living the life of a soldier, but Sartre was enjoying his new life so much that he looked back with quizzical incredulity at the dread he had felt towards military service.[5]

The four soldiers were given two mattresses to put on the floor; Sartre shared with Jean Pierre, who neither snored as loudly as Müller nor roared like an animal, as Pieter sometimes did in his sleep. But Jean Pierre was a somnambulist. For years he'd been having a recurrent dream about being trapped under the debris of a house that had collapsed. 'You get woken up ten times (I've never wanted to urinate so much) and in pitch darkness you grope your way ten times to the window, push the shutters aside and piss into the street.'[6] It was not easy to live at such close quarters with the other three, but once it had struck him that Müller, the most irritating, was rather like a sea-elephant, it was easier to put up with him. Sartre was so habituated to working in cafés that chatter and noises did not disrupt his concentration; by Friday he had finished his draft of chapter II and started a fair copy. He could spend more time working than he had in Paris.[7] In letters to de Beauvoir he was apologetic about not feeling more depressed by their separation: 'it's because the war *interests me*. It's like being in a foreign country I'm going to explore gradually.'

On Thursday he learned that on Monday 11 September the four of them would be posted to join the artillery in Marmontier and not, as they had expected, the air force. Their work would consist of taking meteorological observations by sending up balloons about two feet in diameter and watching them through a theodolite. In the air force they would have had to follow the balloon for six kilometres; in the artillery it was only one kilometre. Calculations for gauging the 'ballistic wind' were quite complicated, but he would still have plenty of time for his novel.

At a quarter to two on Monday morning the men were roused from their sleep. Wearing a tin helmet and carrying a rifle, a gas mask and four packs, 'fifty or so men crept across the village in the black night like conspirators'. They had a long wait for the train and after watching 'the greyness of dawn spreading over all these somnolent men', Sartre decided to keep a diary.[8] They arrived at Marmontier, a charming old village with green and pink cottages surrounded by orchards overflowing with fruit. They were put into a boys' school, where they slept on straw.

The village was cold, dark, and less than thirteen miles from the front. The next day they were given a room in the house of a woman who let them eat the greengages in her garden. There were no beds in the room, only two rather narrow mattresses; sharing with Pierre and using a rucksack as a pillow, Sartre often toppled onto the floor. Nor was there any furniture: he wrote his first letters sitting on a crate of equipment and resting his paper on a taller crate.[9] But they ate well. Though Müller, who was mean, would have preferred to eat at the mobile canteen, Pieter persuaded him that the four of them should have their meals at a restaurant.

On Thursday 14 September Sartre began his diary, and by Saturday he was thinking it could be published posthumously.[10] 'It provides me with quite a little secret life on top of the other one, with pleasures, anxieties and regrets. I wouldn't have got to know even half of them without this little black leather object.'[11] It was at risk, though, like the novel. If he tried to keep his writing with him, they might get lost or damaged; if he posted them to de Beauvoir they might go astray or arouse the suspicions of the censor. Probably it would be safer to post the novel to her, fifty pages at a time.[12] Uncertain whether army life would go on affording him so much leisure, he did more writing than reading.

On average he was producing five pages of the novel, four pages of diary and three letters every day. More stringently even than before, he rebuffed fatigue like a puritan resisting temptation. The feeling of exhaustion presented you with a choice – you could overcome it. In working, as when hiking on holiday with de Beauvoir, he needed to prove that his strength contradicted his size. He argues in *L'Etre et le Néant* that weariness does not depend on the difficulty of the journey or how much sleep you had the night before. Although stubborn resistance to fatigue can, he admits, by symptomatic of an inferiority complex, the complex is itself a way of choosing yourself and choosing whether to succeed or to fail. To tell yourself that you are ugly, he maintains, is not an objective judgment but a prediction that women will reject you.[13] He had no intention of achieving too little, either in his literary output or as a seducer.

One of his three daily letters was to de Beauvoir and it was for her, he said, that he was keeping the diary. 'You are on the horizon of all my thoughts. Everything I think or write or feel is for you.'[14] This could not possibly be true. Obsessed though he was by the ideal of freedom, he voluntarily imposed a censorship on his diary, bizarrely handicapping himself in the area which mattered most, in the core of his existence as a writer: as he would later admit to Pierre, he could confide nothing to the diary that he did not want de Beauvoir to read.[15] But, campaigning consciously and semi-consciously against the idea of the self, he had always inclined to deprive himself of privacy, as if to keep his ego permanently on a weight-reducing diet.

Since the age of sixteen, intimacy had never implied privacy. With Nizan, Guille and de Beauvoir, he had had 'a life in which I constantly felt the whole tension of another presence, and hardened myself to support it. Living in a couple made me hard and transparent as a diamond; otherwise I couldn't have stood it. This is no doubt one of the main reasons my life has been so "public".' Feeling as if his friends could see into his innermost thoughts, he felt constantly constrained to explain himself. It was more important to share ideas and feelings than to let them develop; in the diaries he was not so much conducting a self-analysis as forcing feelings and memories to the surface, while treating both like ideas he could manipulate. At the same time the notion of confessional solidarity with de Beauvoir was a satisfying refuge from conversation with unstimulating fellow-soldiers. The camaraderie of army life was inimical to egalitarianism. One entry in his diary reads: 'I am now cured of socialism, if I needed to be cured of it.'[16]

According to the diary it was thanks to de Beauvoir that Paris still existed for him, and having a stronger sense than he did of what the war was, she was making it real for him. If he got six days of leave he would spend them all with her; if he got eight days, he would devote two to Wanda, who was sometimes writing every day, sometimes lapsing from regularity.[17] Later he modified this plan: if it was eight days, three would be allocated to Wanda, but by pretending that he had to see his mother and step-father, he could give de Beauvoir two hours at lunchtime on each of the Wanda days.[18]

After the four men had been sleeping on the floor for fifteen days, Pierre managed to raise their standard of living, arranging for them to pay only six francs a night for a room on the first floor of the best hotel in the village. It might be possible for de Beauvoir to visit him, Sartre suggested, if she could obtain a pass and a safe-conduct, but he was not allowed to tell her where he was, and he did not know how much longer he would be there. On Tuesday 3 October the order was given that they were to move. It looked as though they would be marched to Brumath, a training school twelve miles away, but Pieter complained of a hernia, and finally a lorry arrived to fetch them. They were lodged in a barn with three order-lies, who had to sleep on the straw while the four meteorologists took the four beds. Their only job was to make meteorological observations and to telephone the artillery officers about the direction and force of the wind. According to Sartre their balloons were liable to get lost behind chimneys, and the men, burdened with the theodolite, would have to run in pursuit, but as Pierre has objected, there was never more than one balloon and they could not have run while carrying a theodolite, which, as Sartre had previously written, took an hour to set up.[19]

There was no shooting in progress, and though he had to spend the day in the school hall the army had taken over, he was free to work on his novel or write letters.

It was now ten years since he had agreed with de Beauvoir on their 'two-year lease' after watching *Storm over Asia*. To celebrate the tenth anniversary of their 'morganatic marriage', he had been intending to enclose a petal in his letter of 6 October to symbolize a bouquet, 'but there are no flowers here, just manure'. The anniversary fell on the tenth. 'My love, you've given me ten years of happiness ... My dear, dear love, I immediately renew the lease for a further ten years.'[20] In later letters he would promise that the relationship with Wanda would not go on after the war;[21] he equated de Beauvoir with 'all the tenderness and the poetic sense of life'.[22]

The men moved out of the barn when they were billeted at the home of a warder in a lunatic asylum, but every morning there were rumours that the unit would be moved later in the day; every evening they were still there. In spite of the uncertainty Sartre produced seventy-three pages of the novel in thirteen days,[23] and when Paulhan accepted his proposal for *Réflexions sur la mort*, he started work on it. He was also writing an article on Gide and planning a volume of stories called *Histoires pour l'oncle Jules*, based on the stories he had improvised for de Beauvoir in Marrakesh.

His pre-war life had vanished, but he was more than content with the opportunity war had brought for intensive literary activity. Expecting peace within a year or two,[24] and not wanting to waste something so precious as war, he organized his time with a mixture of puritanic rigour and greed for the sensual pleasure of writing. He got out of bed at six or six-thirty, though reveille was not until eight. He breakfasted at the inn, starting at about seven to write his diary. He worked on his novel from seven-thirty to eleven, returning to the inn for a seven-franc lunch, during which he would read. He had to be on parade in the courtyard of the town hall at one-thirty. Returning to the schoolroom, he would start writing again, distracted by impatience for the mail to be delivered at three. At about four he would start replying to letters, often going on till seven. Instead of eating dinner, he would drink a little red wine in his barrack-room, working till about eight-thirty, when he would either sleep or go on guard duty, snatching spells of sleep on the straw.[25] Working fast on his first draft of the novel, he did not stop to make a fair copy.[26] He had to vary his routine according to observation duties, but these never took up much of the day, and sometimes he would volunteer for extra guard duty to gain additional writing time at night.[27] On 24 October, a day he received no letters, he worked at the novel from eight a.m. till half past eleven, and philosophized into his diary from twenty past one till twenty past five. By five he was feeling exhausted.[28]

In the same way that he had written in Berlin about Le Havre, he could write in Brumath about Paris, letting the distance help him towards a studied

Husserlian withdrawal from the natural attitude. Uprooted from his Parisian routine, he made creative use of his self-criticism, projecting it into his characterization of Mathieu, who blames himself for not taking enough physical exercise, for not being politically committed, for indecisively letting time slip by. 'He had never been able to sink himself completely into any love-affair, any pleasure, never been really unhappy; it always seemed to him that he was somewhere else, hadn't yet quite been born. He was waiting. And all this time, gently, slyly, the years had come, they had seized him from behind. Thirty-four years.'[29] Twenty-four years later, when Sartre accuses himself in *Les Mots* of being unable to throw himself wholeheartedly into any task or passion or friendship, he appears to have forgotten levelling this accusation against Mathieu.

If Mathieu, at this stage of his development, feels inferior to Brunet, who has made full use of his freedom by sacrificing it to the Party, the feeling derives from the more ambivalent attitude of the student Sartre to his card-carrying friend Nizan. For Brunet every action is relevant to an overall design. 'Nothing can now deprive my life of its meaning, nothing can stop it from being a destiny.'[30] The contrast between the two men parallels the contrast Sartre had drawn between events in a story and contingent events in actuality: his novel is about a man whose life lacks necessity. Mathieu incarnates 'that total lack of attachment which Hegel calls terrorist and which is really the opposite of freedom ... Brunet incarnates "the spirit of seriousness"'.[31] From the age of twenty-five he has been committed, whereas Mathieu has lapsed into what is virtually a bourgeois marriage. 'You are married, Mathieu,' says Daniel, 'you live like a bourgeois.'[32] Sartre, in the army, was writing fiction from an extraordinary vantage point. He felt closer to de Beauvoir than when they were together: 'There is only one of us', he wrote, and 'My dear little one, today I'd willingly give a finger to see you for five minutes and *tell* you that I love you.'[33] But in her absence he was completely free – even free to accuse himself via the novel of being involved in a bourgeois relationship with her. By temperament Sartre was a mixture of bon viveur and ascetic, with no great sexual appetite. In one letter he spoke happily of his 'monastic life with comfort, central heating and running water'.[34]

The accusation derives partly from the banter he provoked by using his money to enjoy bourgeois comforts. While most of the men were sleeping on straw mattresses, Pieter used his influence to find a room Sartre could share with Pierre in a private house where the landlady even provided eiderdowns.[35] Needing the companionship of a partner, Sartre used Pierre to fill part of the gap created by de Beauvoir's absence. Though he did not share Sartre's passion for breakfasting, Pierre was seduced into a routine of setting the alarm clock for six instead of seven and cycling out into the cold for the sake of two fat sandwiches and a glass of chicory juice at the Rose.[36]

The companionship of Pierre and Pieter was unlike any Sartre had known. He entered energetically into protracted conversations with both men, wrote about them at length in his diaries and used them in *La Mort dans l'âme*, where Charlot Wroclaw is modelled on Pieter and Sergeant Pierné on Pierre. When the three of them were sharing sleeping quarters with Müller, it had been Müller, not Sartre, who had been the odd man out. Because Müller smelt so bad, none of them wanted to share a mattress with him,[37] and his habits were particularly offensive. He failed to wash out pots and mess-tins; after telling him off for this, Sartre suspected that Müller was taking his revenge by stealing letters.[38] Generally Sartre enjoyed a feeling of solidarity with Pieter and Pierre against Müller, who was shamelessly greedy. When others offered him their unwanted meat, he would eat up to seven portions a day.[39]

Conversations with Pieter and Pierre had their effect on the philosophical thinking in which Sartre's existentialism was beginning to take shape. When Pieter gently reminded him that he must 'take people as they are', his impatient reaction was: 'Yes, but I know in my bones that people aren't; they do.'[40] This thinking had one of its deepest roots in an obstinate rejection of fatality and passivity. Wanting to believe in a maximum of autonomy he had no relish for the accidental *données* of existence: spontaneity of consciousness and strength of will had to compensate for everything that was determined, including face and body. He even wanted to believe that he had chosen to be alive at this time. No-one could have predicted that the years 1918–39 would acquire a new meaning from the war, but 'I should take it as my destiny, should understand that in *choosing* this period for myself, I was choosing myself for this war'. He had chosen even the time he was born – concretely, not in the metaphysical sense of choosing a character.[41]

In Brumath he was well placed to analyse the feeling Mathieu has in Paris – 'that he was somewhere else'. None of Sartre's intentions had led him here, and he looked back ironically at his last ideas of the future: 'Où sont les avenirs d'antan?' Where are the futures of yesteryear? In the novel Mathieu is made to remember crucial moments in his past – smashing a valuable vase at the age of seventeen, fighting with another boy at the age of sixteen, and, after forcing him to eat sand, dedicating himself to freedom: 'he had made a bet that his entire life would resemble this extraordinary moment'. The novel would have been quite different if Sartre had written it as a civilian. Caught up in his peacetime routine, he had been anything but introspective, and there is some autobiography but little self-portraiture in his previous fiction, if we discount juvenilia.

His interest in himself was still geared to his future, and if he was now going all out to characterize himself in detail, it was with an eye on what he wanted to become. The war had pushed him into the wings; when he went back on stage, it would be in a different role. The image he used in the diary was of a snake sloughing its skin, and he felt entitled 'to look at this dead skin, this brittle image of the snake that will be left behind, and to take stock'.[42]

Thinking about his life as if he were constantly revising an autobiography, he felt that his earliest self had been shaped by childhood decisions. Mathieu remembers early moments 'with their private future, like a little personal heaven, quite round, above them, and this future, it was himself, just as he was at the moment, slack and maturing, they had rights over him, bridging all this time that had elapsed, they sustained their demands, and he often felt a desolating remorse because his unconcerned and cynical present was the old future of those past days'.[43] Like the leisureliness of childhood, the leisureliness of army life was conducive to living autobiographically: notes for the unpublished chapters could be drastically revised.

Combined with the disruption of his normal routine, the diary-writing encouraged his tendency to think with his eyes, spying on himself to catch inclination unawares. But he did not intend to go on watching himself when the war ended: 'I will no longer keep these diaries, or if I do, I will not talk about myself.'[44] All the more intensive for having a time-limit imposed on it, the experiment in self-observation led him to new ideas about what he came to call 'authenticity'. It also deepened his habit of philosophizing, his technique of translating introspection into ontological generalization. Philosophy gave him an alternative to Proustian subjectivity.

In the same way that the seventeen-year-old philosopher had been encouraged by having the alphabetical index as a receptacle for insights, his diary worked like a midwife on his existentialism: the 'little, black, leather-bound object' was bringing the ideas to birth. He had masses of ideas, he wrote on 26 October, and Pieter was calling him a 'war-profiteer' because he capitalized so much on the leisure of military life.[45]

The leisure was being shared – imaginatively – with de Beauvoir. Separation was making their literary relationship more intense: quite apart from the long, regular letters he was writing, her presence was behind the diary, which she would read, and the novel, on which she would be more than an editor if less than a collaborator. He was more independent of her in his philosophizing, but he was beginning to hunger for her presence. In her absence he could no longer take her love for granted. If her collapse with pulmonary congestion had suddenly reduced his need for Olga, separation was gradually increasing his desire for de Beauvoir.

By the middle of October he was impatiently puzzling about how to tell her what to do and where to come. He must not arouse the suspicions of the censor, who had obliterated several passages in one of his letters to his mother.[46] 'By the way', he wrote to de Beauvoir on 15 October, 'you don't tell me how Emma received Bernard and René Ulmann when they rang her bell; I hope she didn't play the same trick as last month when Maurice Adrien and Thérèse Héricourt, who had gone there specially, couldn't get in.'[47] Emma was a character he had just invented: her mother, he suggested, would probably have no objection if de Beauvoir took her to the Midi on 1 November; the capital initials of the other invented names spell Brumath: de Beauvoir would understand that he wanted her to come there on 1 November. On 21 October he explained that he had just received a letter from Emma, who could probably receive de Beauvoir in November. 'You'll be able to see quite a lot of her although she has her work: in the morning at eleven and till about one and then in the evening at about five, when she comes out of the office ... She tells me she'll be pleased to see you.'[48] Four days later he was again urging her to visit Emma. 'The war hadn't started when you last saw each other, which means you've never shared thoughts and feelings about this war. I want the war to belong equally to both of you.'[49] In another letter he promised that Emma would give de Beauvoir 130 pages of his novel and the first of the black notebooks, which he had entrusted to her.[50] Just before the end of the month he sent her a sketch map of Brumath saying it was a map of Quimper, and instructions about how to find Emma.[51] After meeting de Beauvoir in the turban she had taken to wearing, Wanda had described her looking 'beautiful, like a young Hindu in a turban';[52] Sartre now asked her to wear the turban when she went to see Emma.[53]

Arriving in Brumath too late in the evening to make contact, de Beauvoir booked into an uncomfortable hotel, set her alarm for seven and went to the Taverne du Cerf, expecting to find him eating his breakfast. He was not there, but she wrote him a note and, outside the headquarters, found a soldier who promised to deliver it. A few minutes later, Sartre appeared in air force uniform with 'a horrible mossy beard which does not suit him'.[54] The cafés were out of bounds, so they went to her room in the hotel for an hour. He then had to report for duty, but reappeared at eleven, clean-shaven. He tried to arrange for her to stay at his lodgings by telling the landlady that his wife had arrived. The woman knew he was not married, but the word 'fiancée' persuaded her to provide a separate room. They had dinner in the crowded Lion d'Or, which smelled of sauerkraut. In the morning, before going off to make meteorological observations, he gave her a hundred pages of *L'Age de raison*, which she read approvingly, noting down her reservations about Marcelle. At lunchtime he went off with two soldiers to find a room he could share with her. His theory about the war was that it would be modern, with no real fighting in it, just as modern painting had no real subject-matter. Before she left on 5 November for Paris, they had read and discussed each other's diaries: literature was giving them at least an approximation to sharing each other's lives.

He wrote to her the next day, saying he'd been 'profoundly and peacefully happy'.[55] He was astonished at how much she had given him, but above all, 'your presence, quite alone and quite naked and your little face and your tender smiles and your little arms around my neck ... I'd be able to live with you no matter where'.[56] He resumed writing to her every day, and the letter of 8 November ends: 'Your little husband loves you.'[57] Wanda, jealous when he wrote to her about de Beauvoir's visit, wanted to visit him too,[58] but rumours were circulating that they would soon be moving from Brumath.

De Beauvoir had made him see that Marcelle was the least convincing character. In her he had departed further than with any of the other characters from the real-life model but, impressively objective, de Beauvoir's criticisms had nothing to do with herself or their relationship. It was for the novel's sake that he set about remodelling Marcelle, a task which was disappointingly time-taking.[59] He knew too that he must not say too much about liberty in the first volume, and he was worried that a chapter full of action might make readers intolerant of 'poetic mud' in the next.[60] Eager to write a play, he was impatient to have the novel out of the way.[61] He also wanted to write more philosophy, especially after being awakened so often in the night by the need to urinate: by thinking philosophically to distract himself from his discomfort, he had arrived at a new idea about the will. As he had explained to de Beauvoir, the will needed passive resistance; this insight could be combined with Spinoza's idea that consciousness and will were identical. Using his diary to take stock of moral ideas he had propounded since the age of seventeen, he started to sketch out a morality. Nietzsche had understood that the death of God created an urgent need for a new system of values; Sartre, who felt able to provide one, knew his outlook had changed radically since he wrote *La Transcendance de l'Ego*. His stoicism had collapsed, and he had been propelled towards his new position by the war, by Arthur Koestler's *Spanish Testament*, an account of experiences in a death cell during the civil war, by Antoine de Saint-Exupéry's novel *Terre des Hommes* (1939, translated as *Wind, Sand and Stars*) and by *Verdun*, the sixteenth volume in Jules Romains's twenty-seven-volume cycle *Les Hommes de bonne volonté* (1932–47, *Men of Good Will*). Sartre called his new ethic a 'morality of complaisance'. 'We have come some way since the time we were rationalist, Cartesian and anti-existentialist.'[62] What should be the aim of human activity? It should aim at itself, he answered, 'human reality can and should be its own end because it is always on the side of the future – it is its own reprieve'.[63] He did not mean to equate morality with social utilitarianism or with the individualism which mistakes the individual for an end. For Husserl reality is neither a fact nor a value but a relationship between a fact and a value. Consisting primarily of consciousness, it is nothing if not consciousness of being. It is free, but total freedom exists only for the man who takes responsibility for the existence of human reality. Consciousness does not have an origin outside itself, and it projects itself into the future to be its own foundation there. This possibility of being one's own foundation is the source of all values.[64]

To *accept* everything that happens is both excessive and inadequate, but we should understand that nothing can happen to us except through ourselves, and we must take responsibility for everything exactly as if we had willed it. We must always move forwards from the event as if it had been given to us by decree and as if the object were to find out what progress we could then make.[65] This is an exciting idea, and his new philosophy made an impact when he explained it to friends; a clerk called Selzer[66] said he had changed completely, thanks to Sartre. Leaving home, three months ago, he had been desperate, but he now felt almost serene: he had accepted the war as an event in his own life. 'He is nervous, and in thanking me, he stammers. I'm nervous too and drink milk ... Always this strange impression that none of this is meant for me, that I'm playing a part, that I'm basically a wretched charlatan who's deceiving everybody.'[67] He was worried that the novel, belonging partly to an earlier phase of his thinking, muddled Husserlian and existentialist ideas of liberty.[68]

He had little difficulty in getting up at about half past six. After a leisurely breakfast at the Rose and the first meteorological observation of the day, he was free to work from about nine. He had lunch with Pieter at the Ecrevisse and after the second observation he was free to work again.[69] At the Ecrevisse the radio would sometimes be switched on in the room adjoining the dining-room and towards the end of November he caught the strains of jazz mixed with the clatter of plates and the buzz of conversation: 'That suddenly made a poetic and cruel Paris loom up before me in exactly the way a jealous, exiled lover might think of it as surrounding his mistress.'[70] The feeling was only momentary, but he made use of it in a letter to Wanda, and then confided to de Beauvoir: 'I pretended it was of her that I was jealous.'[71] In fact the only pretence seems to have been in making out that the jealousy was faked. He was afraid that Wanda might be having an affair, possibly with the actor Roger Blin,[72] though even if she was, Sartre felt confident she was 'caught up in my destiny, like a louse in a head of hair'.[73] He spent less than twenty per cent of the day, he said, worrying about her; the rest of the time was devoted to thinking happily about de Beauvoir and to working.[74]

When the division was moved to Morsbronn, twelve miles away, Sartre was expecting to be there about seven weeks. They left at four in the morning of 5 December, on a lorry which, three hours later, pulled up outside a rather dilapidated hotel on a hill less than half a mile outside the village. Inside, crammed with soldiers' packs, haversacks and military parapher-nalia, the hotel looked more like a headquarters than the peaceful school at Brumath had, and the bedrooms smelled of mushrooms. The flowered wallpaper was dirty and torn.[75] Sartre had been hoping for a room of his own, but he had to share with Jean Pierre. He was immediately given a job as a telephone operator, working in a large room bustling with officers, some leaving, some arriving. At first he felt proud to be in charge of the imposing apparatus, which had little black shutters and about twenty plugs on cables, but after twelve hours of non-stop work his head was aching, and he still had to spend the night on a divan next to the switchboard. He wrote his diary in the pauses between operating it and overhearing conversations about the war, which still looked as though it might fail to develop. He started, between interruptions, to read Flaubert's *Education sentimentale*, but hated the gallantry and refinement of the period; he also complained that the book was stupid and badly written.[76]

His routine at Morsbronn gave him less time for the novel. He found an isolated café he could use as a sanctuary between seven and half-past-eight, reading, drinking coffee, eating bread and butter.[77] He should have made three meteorological observations every day, taking responsibility for the telephone one day in every four and for sweeping out the rooms and making up the fires one day in eight.[78] But, to give him more time for writing, Pierre took over all his duties every third day for a month.[79] He wrote to de Beauvoir: 'I'm quite absorbed by the atmosphere of this place and by my morality; nothing outside matters more than you do.'[80] In another letter he wrote: 'I'm quite alone with you.'[81] Her visit had worked on him like a time-bomb, and the move to Morsbronn, he told her, had killed his passion for Wanda; it was exactly as if she no longer existed.[82] He signed the letter: 'Your little husband',[83] and in another letter to de Beauvoir he claimed to dislike writing hypocritically to Wanda about how much he loved her.

By the middle of December he had resumed work on the novel, starting on the final chapter, which consisted mainly of dialogue.[84] He was expecting to have it finished before he went on leave early in the new year. He would bring the diaries to Paris, so that de Beauvoir could read about his new conception of nothingness, which had occurred to him while he was reading Kierkegaard;[85] he also had new theories about violence and bad faith.[86]

At the party on Christmas Eve he sang the Toreador's Song from *Carmen*, making the other soldiers join in the chorus,[87] and before the year was over he finished the novel, but after writing the word 'Fin', he tore up the three final pages and threw them into the coal bucket. His dislike of writing endings never expressed itself more clearly. He had to rummage for the fragments of paper and stick them carefully together.[88] His intention was to call the second volume *Septembre* and to make a start on it within a couple of days. Instead he started on the short stories, *Histoires pour l'oncle Jules* and on a bloodthirsty play, *Prométhée*, full of rape and massacre. He felt so pleased with this that he sang 'The Man I Love' during a meteorological observation, making the theodolite shake.[89] But he soon tore up both the stories and the play.[90] He was writing even more prolifically than at Brumath, where he had produced 150 pages of the novel in September and October. The capsules of ink in his fountain pen were lasting only a day and a half,[91] and within two days he filled 81 pages of his diary.[92] Knowing that the evening was the best time for writing, he lived on bread and chocolate for three days to save the time he would have spent on going out to a restaurant.[93] He was too absorbed in his work to waste time on washing or shaving. He let his beard grow,[94] and acquired a reputation for being dirty. Pierre was told 'Your chum's famous in the division.'[95] He felt he had appropriated more freedom than ever before and he made experiments which struck his companions as silly: 'Today I won't smoke. I'm going to prove that I'm free.'[96] But he was pleased with his progress: 'it seems to me that I'm on the way, as biographers say round about page 150 of their book, "towards finding myself"'.[97] But he did not try to live in accordance with his new philosophy; the only role it had in his life was to cheer him up when he was feeling depressed,[98] and it was gratifying to believe he had explained the singleness of the world for the plurality of consciousnesses and had conclusively overcome the dichotomy between realism and idealism.[99] Contingency was favouring him: having none of his philosophical books with him, he had to rediscover Husserl and Heidegger by thinking the problems out without consulting them. In this way he liberated himself from them, using the techniques of phenomenology and existentialism, to develop his own ideas about perception and existence. 'The war and the sense of being, in spite of everything, a bit "lost", have given me courage.'[100] But how could he keep the novel abreast of his thinking? It worried him that many of the best ideas in it had been elaborated out of Heidegger's ten succinct pages on historicity.[101]

Impatient to go on leave, Sartre was especially looking forward to eating omelettes again and to being with de Beauvoir. He had promised to divide his time between her and Wanda, but he had also been writing regularly to another girl – probably Bianca – and he did not want her to know he was going to be in Paris. To continue his correspondence with her he gave Pierre carefully numbered letters, one of which was to be mailed each day. On the eighth day Pierre was to send her a telegram.[102]

Not wanting to be seen in the streets of Paris wearing uniform and 'looking like Punch', he arranged for de Beauvoir to collect some of his civilian clothes from his mother's flat so that he could change as soon as he arrived.[103] When his eleven days of leave started on 4 February, he felt highly privileged to resume the life he had once taken for granted.

Scarcely any men were to be seen in the streets, except for the old and the infirm.[104] Night-life had fizzled out; nightclubs looked moribund. 'Let's not go to the Chantilly,' Wanda said, 'it's too cold there.'[105] In peacetime he felt distanced from other people by the way they were all looking forward to events from which he was excluded; now everyone's life seemed to have been adjourned. One evening, waiting for de Beauvoir outside a café in the Champs-Elysées, he felt all the more alive for having been uprooted from this dead city, where 'this new, felt-lined discretion had given the cafés in the evening the secretive look of brothels'.[106] At Le Jockey, with Wanda, it seemed to him that they were no less in love than other couples who were dancing, but that he was not available: he could not stay. But 'it's much easier to live decently and authentically in war than in peace'.[107] He had been more authentic in camp, he believed, than he was being in Paris.[108]

Wanda's reactions to his diaries could hardly have been more different from de Beauvoir's. Though in many ways an extremely private person, de Beauvoir had a strong drive to publish nearly all her documentation of her own existence and of his. She was more proprietorial literarily than sexually. The ontological insecurity of both Kosakiewicz sisters took a different form. Olga was so averse to being written about that de Beauvoir gave her less space in the autobiography than she would have liked to. Less histrionic offstage than Olga, Wanda was more exhibitionistic, but when Sartre told her that he was intending to publish his diaries, she was incredulous and disapproving. How could he expose something so intimate? In fact they were published only posthumously, and their authenticity has been impugned by Jean Pierre, who maintains that Sartre's diaries were confiscated in the stalag by a German officer, and that the published volumes were written after his return to Paris. This is unlikely. Some of the later volumes may have been confiscated and irretrievably lost, but after going on leave to Paris Sartre is unlikely to have taken the early volumes back to the camp, and it would have been out of character for him to spend so much time on faking something that was not even intended for immediate publication.

Early in the morning of 15 February he changed back into uniform.

But in Paris he had employed a civilian tailor to remake his uniform, and putting it on, together with his new pair of puttees, he felt cleaner than he had been since the beginning of the war.[109] As he boarded the train, which was filled with soldiers returning from leave, de Beauvoir joined the queue of wives and girlfriends waiting for a final kiss on the high step outside the carriage door. She was the first woman to leave, walking away fast.[110] Sartre was not returning to Morsbrunn: the unit had moved to Bouxwiller, but his immediate anxiety was due to the other soldiers on the train. They were terrified of a spring offensive.

At Bouxwiller Sartre could work during the morning and evening in the Hôtel du Soleil, a large, ill-named café where he always felt cold. On the first floor was a big room which had been used in peacetime as a cinema. It had a lot of chairs in it, a ping-pong table and about fifteen tables with patterned tablecloths and vases of flowers on them. Fifty or so soldiers would be sitting around, reading, writing and playing cards, while a wireless set relayed music.[111] Looking around him, he felt no desire for personal contact. 'Collectively they touch me somewhat, but if I consider them individually, most of them shock me either by their attitude or their way of speaking ... I don't like men – I mean the male of the species ... In short, for me there is a half of the human race which scarcely exists.'[112]

Though he had felt, when he was with Wanda at Le Jockey, that he was in love with her, his memories of her evaporated quickly; he told de Beauvoir that memories of her stayed more vivid.[113] He felt guilty about giving Wanda a little knife de Beauvoir had given him,[114] and he was suspicious that Wanda was involved with another man,[115] but when she found out about the letters he had written in 1938 to the drama student, he was frantic with anxiety. The girl showed the letters to a friend of Olga's, Marcel Mouloudji, a scruffy writer of Berber origin, who spent much of his time at the Flore, and occasionally acted in films; he told Wanda about them, letting her form the impression that Sartre's affair with the girl was not over when his affair with her began, and that to impress the girl he had told her Wanda was in love with him. To pacify Wanda, Sartre sent her a vicious letter he had just written to the girl: Wanda was invited to read it before posting it to the girl in the unsealed envelope he sent her.

I never loved you. I found you physically pleasing, though rather vulgar, but I have a certain sadism which your vulgarity actually attracted ... In your romantic brain you staged a beautiful comedy about love which was reciprocated but frustrated by a vow taken previously, and I didn't interfere, because I thought separation would be easier for you to bear ... I wasn't enjoying myself much with you. My letters, which were an exercise in impassioned writing that afforded a good deal of laughter to the Beaver and me, did not entirely deceive you at the time.[116]

At first Sartre was pleased with his stratagem, calling it a 'stroke of genius' and explaining to de Beauvoir: 'I'm becoming tougher with people.'[117] In his strenuous efforts to reassure Wanda, he wrote: 'You know quite well that I'd trample on the whole world (including the Beaver) ... in order to stay on good terms with you.'[118] Confessing this betrayal to de Beauvoir, he apologized, saying he had never known how to lead his sexual life or his emotional life: 'I quite profoundly and sincerely consider myself to be a *salaud* ... a sickening sort of academic sadist, a wage-earning Don Juan.' He promised to have no more casual affairs,[119] but he did not plan to give up the practice of deceiving; during his next leave Wanda would be made to believe that he was in Paris for five days less than he was actually there: this would give him more time with de Beauvoir.[120] 'My little one, my charming Beaver, I swear to you I'm absolutely honest with you. If I weren't, there'd be nothing left in the world in face of which I'm not a liar – I would lose myself.'[121] At the beginning of the affair with Wanda, he had decided to sacrifice her at the slightest sign that de Beauvoir wanted him to, and meanwhile to sacrifice the others to her.[122] 'I promise you there will be no more affairs for a long time (a long time after the war, of course, or it would be too easy) ... All that was always a matter of seducing, I can see that clearly now I'm writing it down, and once the good woman was seduced, I was quite astonished to have her on my hands.'[123] All this was over. 'Not only you but my *relations* with you are precious to me. And so far as any sort of "conjugal" seduction is concerned', Wanda would be 'amply sufficient'.[124]

These were not the only plans he was making for his post-war life: he would apply his new morality and would involve himself in politics. To conform to his idea of 'authenticity', he must take responsibility for his situation in life. He could not have known how fashionable his ideas would become but, in an unposted letter, he declared his intentions: 'As for politics ... I shall go alone into this soufflé, I shall follow no-one, and those who want to follow me can follow me.' It was important, he went on, to protect the younger generation from coming out of the war with guilty consciences, and no-one was better equipped to protect them than their seniors, who had fought at their side.

On 15 March the unit was moved from Bouxwiller back to Brumath. Again he was to work in the school building, but this time on the first floor. The next day, Saturday, he went back to the Rose. The two barmaids were still there, the sleepy redhead, Jeannette, and the fat promiscuous brown-haired Alice, who was now married to a soldier.[125] Most of the soldiers were received by the civilians in Brumath with open arms, 'but I play no part in the game: no-one recognizes me ... except the large old woman at the Rose, who squeezes my hand cordially'.[126]

The day before the move, he had received from de Beauvoir's sister Poupette the first third of his novel in typescript. Re-reading, he found the theme did not emerge clearly enough. Mathieu was lacking in unity and the chapters were insufficiently connected. What worried Sartre most was that too little of the past was visible behind the present of each character. The reader should know, he decided, where Mathieu came from, where he had taught, how he met Boris and Ivich.[127] One solution, would be to write a prologue set in 1928, ten years before the main story begins. The reader would meet Ivich, Mathieu and Marcelle long before they meet each other: 'That will give roots to my characters and this will enable me to lighten the rest of the text.'[128] By the middle of March he was devoting ten hours of each day to the prologue.[129] He was now expecting the novel to be ready by October and to be 600 pages long. 'I've always considered abundance a virtue.'[130]

After just over two weeks in Brumath he had to leave again. In Paris, when he showed de Beauvoir his new prologue, she had no difficulty in persuading him to scrap it. He talked at length about the philosophy he was evolving. She was to remember a damp evening when they were strolling around the Gare du Nord: 'I had an impression of incurable desolation; I had wished too fervently for the absolute and suffered its absence too much not to recognize in myself this useless reaching towards Being.'[131]

Chatting with her about his philosophical theories, he netted ideas for developing them, and some of her reactions gave him ideas for Mathieu. Revising the novel when he was back in Brumath, he profited from the criticisms of his 'little judge'. 'It's for you I write when I revise, much more than when I invent.'[132] Before the book went to the printer, she would be given carte blanche to make cuts.[133]

Wanting to write an essay on Malraux, Sartre read or re-read his novels, noticing how eager he was to show characters trying to absorb into the bloodstream of their willpower the circumstances they could not control.[134] 'He irritates me because he is too much like me: he's like John the Baptist to my Jesus.'[135] They were both writing on the assumption that 'The age of fundamentals is being resumed ... Reason needs to be founded all over again.' This is how a character puts it in *L'Espoir*; to Sartre it seemed that people were finally understanding what Nietzsche had said about the need for new principles in a world without God.[136]

Sartre's main relaxation was playing chess. In Brumath on average he'd play six or seven games a day, sometimes nine. When he played in the afternoon, he could plead that it was better to write in the morning when his mind was more lucid. At the end of April, when he played two games simultaneously, he claimed to have won both.[137] But he never admits to being beaten by Pierre, while Pierre claims to have won an average of one game in three.[138]

After eight months of not having a room of his own, Sartre acquired one on the 30th, when he was installed in the Hôtel Bellevue. 'It's a dainty little room with marbled wallpaper, a bed, a little table, a jug of water and washbowl, a bedside table and a flower-vase. I'm ecstatic.'[139] The more imposing hotel the officers had taken was infested with bedbugs, so the men, hoping to avoid a swap, went around scratching themselves.[140]

Sartre's relationship with Wanda came plunging towards a new crisis when she wrote that she was ill and alone, with some kind of lesion. 'My God,' she wrote, 'how I want you to come, to come at all costs.' Without knowing how serious the illness was, Sartre responded by offering to marry her. He would then get three days of leave; apart from deserting, there was no other way he could come. De Beauvoir must have been astounded by his letter of 12 May. Less than six months ago he had signed himself 'Your little husband', and only three months ago had assured her that, from the beginning of the Wanda affair, his intention had been to break it off 'at the slightest sign' that de Beauvoir wanted him to. He now explained that the marriage would be 'purely symbolical', meaning that he was committed to Wanda and that from now on he would do all he could for her. It would be a nuisance, though, having to conceal the marriage from his mother and step-father, who were bound to find out eventually, and it would not be pleasant for de Beauvoir. To compensate, he would spend a whole day with her, telling Wanda that since Germany had just invaded Holland, soldiers were being allowed only two days of compassionate leave instead of three. Or perhaps de Beauvoir would prefer not to be in Paris, this time, while he was there: it might be more sensible to stay with Mme Morel at La Pouèze, a village near Angers where she had settled.[141] This superficial considerateness must have been extremely hurtful. While telling de Beauvoir that he was about to marry another woman, he was implying that he had never stopped taking her point of view into account. He obviously assumed that even when he was married to Wanda, de Beauvoir would be no less available than she had always been, except during these three days when she might prefer not to be in Paris.

He was soon regretting the offer of marriage. Even if Wanda was already better, she was quite capable of responding: 'Marry me all the same – at least we'll have three days together.' After instructing de Beauvoir to find out about the illness,[142] Sartre received two letters from Wanda, who was not seriously ill. 'In these circumstances I think it is pointless to marry her; I shall write to tell her that it would serve no purpose.' His letter to de Beauvoir ends: 'We are *inseparable*.' After his act of betrayal, his confidence was strikingly arrogant, but he was not miscalculating.

On 12 May 1940 the Germans invaded Holland and Belgium, but Sartre's unrealistic optimism was unchecked: 'they will overstrain their resources in defending such a vast front'.[143] He told Pierre off for being pessimistic.[144] But though the 'phoney' war was becoming real, the texture of their lives was not changing. Meteorological observations four times a day and, for Sartre, agitation over the novel. Was it lacking in vitality? Refusing to be thrown off balance by the Wanda episode, his 'little judge' was asking for a new scene between Mathieu and Daniel; he gave himself a month to finish the book, and, working on it now, had no feeling of manipulating puppet-strings,[145] but he was impatient to start a philosophical book about nothingness.[146] Even when he heard that some of his diaries, which de Beauvoir had loaned to Bost, might have been lost, it scarcely worried him: what counted was that they had led him to the idea of nothingness, which was still alive in his head.[147]

'Somewhere in the North', he wrote to de Beauvoir, 'not only the country's destiny is being decided, but mine and yours.'[148] But he was still in no danger. 'I am not serving any purpose.'[149] The war was helping him to ruminate and regroup memories. 'It's true that one becomes more profound.'[150] The sound of gunfire was audible almost constantly, and defeatist rumours were circulating. What if the Germans were to win? 'Oh but in any case they won't treat France the same as Poland. Life would still be livable.'[151]

By 19 May Sartre learned that the Germans had taken Laon. He instructed de Beauvoir to leave Paris for La Pouèze, and to send the Kosakiewicz sisters to Laigle. 'Think how atrocious it would be for me to know Paris was being bombarded, besieged or surrounded and to know you were inside it...'[152] How were they going to celebrate the end of the war 'if one of your little legs is missing or perhaps the whole head?'[153] He felt completely free and completely helpless. He went on working at the novel, but he was losing momentum. He played chess, read thrillers. 'There are moments when, like you, I feel it's maniacal and obstinate to write while men are dying like flies in the North and while the whole of Europe's fate is at stake, but what can I do?'[154] On 14 May the Dutch army surrendered, and the advancing Germans broke through French defences near Sedan. Except for two days when Sartre was too depressed to write, he went on with the novel, though it was impossible to think about publication or to believe that people would eventually read the book.[155] He had been purged of the vanity that had ensued on the success of *La Nausée*: he felt as 'pure' as when he was writing it; 'and besides it's *against* the breakdown of democracy and liberty, against the defeat of the Allies – symbolically – that I'm performing the act of writing.'[156] Though he went on planning the rest of the novel – the entire action of the final volume could take place when Mathieu was on leave[157] – he felt cut off from any future, especially any literary future.[158] While the German army advanced, Sartre played chess.[159]

France could no longer be expected to win the war; 'neither do I think we'll lose it: I think nothing, the future remains closed'.[160] On 10 June, the day Italy declared war on France and Britain, the radio reported that a battle was raging to the north of Paris. 'All the same I worked well today, the Mathieu-Marcelle chapter is finished.' He was expecting an armistice and the return of peace.[161] With enough goodwill they would find that life could be lived without cowardice, though not without humiliations. At least they would see each other again soon, 'and that gives me, in spite of myself, a kind of joy'.[162] The Germans had reached St-Dizier, on the Marne, and the French army was retreating, to avoid being cut off. The radio gave the impression that an armistice was imminent, that America was certain to stay neutral. Pieter tried not to show that he was terrified.[163]

During ten chaotic days of retreating, they stopped at Haguenau, in the extreme north-east of France. When they arrived there on 10 June, the evacuated town had been empty for a month. In the classroom of a catholic girls' school Sartre found exercise books which stopped at 10 May. For the last five days the men had seen no newspapers, heard no news on the radio, received no letters. They did not know when they would leave or where they would go. It was Wednesday but the closed shops made it look like Sunday, except that flour-like dust was accumulating on goods in the windows. The streets were deserted.[164] In 1942 when Sartre reproduced the experience for the Geneva-based review *Messages*, he used the title 'La Mort dans l'âme' but it is not merely the phrase that links the episode to the third novel in his series, it is the necessity of coming to terms with a reality that felt like fantasy or fiction.

They were moved back to Breschwillers and then to Padoux, in Lorraine. With the German army approaching, French soldiers were drawn into arguments with pro-German Alsatians. Sartre's unit was moved from village to village until the men were abandoned by their officers, who walked off into a forest, carrying a white flag. Of the 200 officers from the headquarters, only the commandant and two others stayed with the men, the commandant's reason being that he was too drunk to run away.[165] The sergeants also stayed. When Sartre was taken prisoner on the morning of his thirty-fifth birthday, 21 June 1940, he felt as if he were acting in a film. He had slept in a peasant's house on the village square. He dressed quickly. A gun was firing at a church, where a few French soldiers were holding out. He found himself among a large group that was being marched by armed

Germans to a gendarmerie barracks. He was shut up in the attic with a lot of men he knew. They had to sleep on the floor. They were left there for several days without enough to eat; he was sometimes dizzy with hunger.[166]

The next day the eighty-four-year-old Marshal Pétain, who for six days had been in control of the French administration, concluded an armistice with Germany. It was agreed that French troops captured in Germany would stay there till the end of the war. Sartre was sent to Baccarat, between Strasbourg and Nancy. Four days before the armistice was signed, Charles de Gaulle, a tank expert who had been serving as Under-Secretary of State for War, flew to England and broadcast an appeal: all Frenchmen who wanted to fight on should contact him. The British government recognized him (in August) as leader of the Free French movement, but by then the armistice had been ratified by the French National Assembly, which met at Vichy in July. Plenary powers were given to Pétain, but in his Vichy regime, which was to survive until 1944, the real power was wielded by the astute Pierre Laval, an opportunist who, convinced that the Allies would lose, made no effort to help them, though he did secure more independence for France than was allowed to any other defeated country. Only the northern and western half of France was occupied by the Germans, and the Vichy government was allowed to keep an 'armistice army' of 100,000 men.

'My captivity', Sartre wrote on 8 July, 'is limited to camping.' The prisoners were sleeping in tents. He was with Pieter and Pierre still, and they were still being kept so short of food that, physically enfeebled, Sartre felt stupefied and somnolent. Time slipped past as if he were dreaming. Even when the supply of food improved, he was depressed by the extreme cold and by his fellow prisoners – 'stupidity, meanness, jealousy, idiotic tricks, coprophilia etc. I've assumed some authority over the men around me, but one loses all desire to laugh.'[167] For five weeks he let his beard grow and despite the danger of lice – hundreds of men had them – he scarcely ever washed, becoming even dirtier than he had been at Brumath. He walked around with much the same expression on his face as when he was with his step-father. The ersatz coffee they were given at six in the morning was made from roasted barley. They were fed at eleven in the morning and five in the afternoon with bread and soup made from barley, cabbage or pork. At six in the evening they had to parade in columns. Otherwise they were free to do what they liked. On sunny days men would sunbathe, stark naked on blankets in the courtyard. 'The paradox of our situation is that it's both impossible and easy to live in it.'[168]

Sartre was hoping to be liberated before the end of August, but by 22 July he had resumed work on the novel, had started to write *L'Etre et le Néant*,[169] and was soon feeling so involved in the momentum that at night, as in the camp at Morsbronn, he felt impatient to resume work in the morning.[170] But he was reminded of his identity when a spectacled habitué of the Café Flore asked him whether he was related to Sartre the author. He now began to wash and shave again.[171]

None of de Beauvoir's letters appeared to have been censored but he could write to her only on postcards or by smuggling a letter to be mailed outside the camp through the civilian post. He promised that as soon as they were reunited, they would start living together.[172] He was anxious about Bost; he also asked for news of Nizan, Guille, Maheu and Aron, who, as a Jew, might be in danger. Pieter, who was not expecting to survive, had become almost unapproachable.[173] Without trying to spend much time with him, Sartre forged ahead with his work. He had been moved into a big unfurnished room with fourteen other men. Incessant rain confined them indoors, where everything had to be done on the floor – sleeping, reading, writing[174] – but Sartre had completed seventy-six pages of *L'Etre et le Néant* by 12 August.

TWELVE · *Stalag*

In the middle of the month he was transferred to a prisoner-of-war camp, Stalag XIID, which was on a hilltop at Trier, near the Luxembourg border. For ten months he had worn a uniform without once catching sight of the enemy until the day he was captured. Though he had sometimes tried to picture German soldiers in Left Bank cafés,[1] he had been unable to, but now, in daily contact with the Germans, he felt an exhilarating solidarity with the French prisoners. They were all at risk together, though the only immediate danger was of being kicked or slapped. Infuriated by their indolent disobedience, the adjutant, who was nicknamed Pilchard, dealt out slaps galore, while other Germans followed his example; far from feeling humiliated, Sartre was oddly excited by the daily violence. One evening, trying to creep into his hut after curfew, he found a torch shining in his face. 'The sentry began to shout, threatening me with his bayonet. I knew he had no intention of bayoneting me in the stomach but he was thinking about stabbing my thighs: he was waiting for me to turn my back on him. I turned slowly, never had I been so vividly and clearly aware of all this impotent meat collected at the base of my back. In the end I received a hard kick which threw me against the door. I was still laughing as I went into the hut.' When he told the others why he was laughing, they joined in.

Among the prisoners were Poles and Czechs, who made fun of the retreating French army. The Czechs had not forgiven France for watching passively in March 1939 when Hitler's armies occupied Czechoslovakia; the Poles were equally contemptuous, and according to a Russian deserter, the French were all rabbits.[2]

Pierre and Pieter were among the prisoners but Sartre preferred the companionship of a more intellectual group clustered around an officer, Captain Bourdin, who had effective control over the infirmary, where he arranged for Sartre to be used as an interpreter. He was quartered in a room with two other prisoners. As at Baccarat, he was free to move about inside the camp. Some of the priests and chaplains knew his work or at least his name, and he offered, if they could gather an audience for him, to give a lecture. About twenty prisoners assembled and, talking without notes, he discoursed on the treatment of death in the work of Rilke, Malraux and Heidegger. The prisoners were more attentive when he raised the question of whether the women of France would now prefer German soldiers, who had proved their courage, to Frenchmen, who had not.[3]

After about three months he lost his job in the infirmary, but, not wanting to work in the fields, managed to get himself classified as an artist. The 'artists' included professional and amateur musicians, actors, boxers and wrestlers. They were paid a salary by the Germans, and they had a hut of their own. To keep fit he joined the boxers and wrestlers in their regular morning work-outs – first for thirty minutes, later for forty-five.[4] Hanging up on the wall of the hut were guitars, banjos, flutes and trumpets provided by the Germans for the 'artists' to keep up the morale of the prisoners by giving concerts, and there was a piano, on which the Belgians played swing, rather in the style of the College Inn.

There was also a little theatre where, twice a month, on Sundays, a performance was staged for the 1,500 prisoners in the camp. The man who had been put in charge of the actors, Chaumis, thought he could remember seeing a play by Sartre, who did not contradict him and was then commissioned to write scripts for the troupe. None of these was staged,[5] and Sartre spent most of his time in conversation with the priests, who all came from the bourgeoisie. Now, with easier opportunities than ever before or after for fraternizing with working-class men, he chose not to. He had a genuine love for the tough vulgarisms of working-class speech, but his liking for the people was generalized and theoretical. Except when eating or sleeping, he scarcely spent any time in the hut. He sat at a long table, writing or reading, and when he was with the priests, they discussed such questions as the virgin birth. He made friends with a Jesuit called Paul Feller, the abbé Henri Leroy, Marius Perrin, the Basque abbé Etchegoyen, and a Dominican, père Boisselot. Perrin was interested in phenomenology, and Sartre began to tutor him, patiently translating, sentence by sentence, from a copy of Heidegger's *Sein und Zeit* which had been procured from a Benedictine in a monastery at Trier. After finding a copy of Claudel's *Le Soulier de satin* in the artists' hut, Sartre asked the priests to help him find a cast without drawing on the troupe of actors. Feller had a good voice, as did Marc Bénard, a journalist and painter from Le Havre. Though the enterprise was abortive, it prepared the ground for one which was not.

When the priests were planning Christmas celebrations, Sartre not only offered to join the choir which would sing hymns, carols and the Pilgrims' Chorus from *Tannhäuser*,[6] he suggested they should return to the old custom of complementing midnight mass with a mystery play. By writing scripts for the troupe, he had convinced himself that he had talent as a playwright. Would the priests let him create a play which would not, strictly speaking, be Christian but would be suitable for Christmas performance? They were easily persuaded – partly because, underrating his toughness, they scented an opportunity of converting him.

Abandoning the Heidegger sessions with Perrin, Sartre set to work on a script, bearing his actors in mind. He would use Feller, abbé Leroy and Marc Bénard, as well as actors from the troupe, and he would play a part himself. By introducing a chorus, he would involve a large number of prisoners. Three weeks before Christmas, the script was still unfinished, but the play was already in rehearsal; the best way for the actors to learn their lines was by rehearsing them.

Bariona, ou le Fils du tonnerre (*Bariona or the Thunder's Son*) is set on 24 December in a village twenty-five leagues from Bethlehem. Sartre situated the action on the edge of the Nativity story: a man would set out to kill the Christ child, a well-meaning man, prompted by concern to avert delusion and submissiveness. His plot would be abandoned, but the change of plan would itself constitute a climax in the play. Directing the actors himself, Sartre copied what he'd watched Dullin doing in rehearsal, but without being so rude. The priests assumed that he'd had professional experience as a director,[7] and from the way the actors responded to the script, he could see he had not overestimated his talent as a playwright.[8] He could create tension, even in scenes between minor characters whose only function was to retail information about offstage events. He could translate philosophical ideas into impressive theatrical rhetoric, could make the audience sympathize with the characters while structuring his story-telling so that the climaxes made considerable impact.

As in *L'Age de raison*, he introduced many of his own preoccupations – both philosophical and private. Bariona, the village chief, is, like Mathieu, an *alter ego*, a man with strong feelings about liberty and with no wish for offspring. The German occupation of France is reflected in the situation of the village, which is being squeezed by the fiscal ruthlessness of the Romans; rebellion would be suicidal, but why not inaugurate a defiant religion that will eventually depopulate the Roman empire, leaving it without soldiers and slaves? 'We shall set an example throughout Judaea and I hope it is the origin of a new religion, the religion of nothingness, and that the Romans stay masters of our deserted towns ... by the God of Vengeance and Anger, by Jehovah, I swear never to have a child.'[9] Bariona will be unable to keep this oath – his wife is already pregnant – but Sartre kept it.

Influenced by Giraudoux and by Cocteau's adaptations of Sophocles' *Antigone* (1922) and *Oedipus Rex* (1922–5), Sartre introduced an ironical

narrator, a chorus that used contemporary language, and a series of anach-
ronisms. One of the shepherds plays a mouth-organ; characters talk about
factories and capitalism. But this was not whimsicality: Sartre was using
the Nativity to camouflage a message about the possibilities of resistance
in occupied France. To the words 'Peace on earth to men of goodwill',
Bariona replies defiantly: 'I shall not ask for grace or express gratitude.
I shall bend my knee to no-one, I shall put my dignity into my hatred,
I shall keep an exact record of everything suffered by me and by others.'
He tells the villagers that God himself 'can do nothing against this pillar
of granite, against this irresistible column, man's freedom'. Before it could
be performed, the script was censored by the Germans, but no objec-
tions were raised. This is not so odd as it seems. With the success
Sartre had achieved before the war and with the interest the German
commanders were taking in French intellectuals, they are unlikely to have
been ignorant of his identity. But their policy was to clamp down only
on pro-Jewish and anti-German sentiment: if the intellectuals were
gagged they would appear to be hostile and dangerous; to let them
speak out was to blur the difference between co-existence and collaboration.

Pilate was played by Marc Bénard, who also designed the set. Sartre
appeared as one of the three kings, Balthazar, who protests when Bariona
tries to stop the villagers from going to worship the new-born Messiah.
'Look your misfortune in the face,' Bariona exhorts, 'for the dignity of
man lies in his despair ... For man, you see, is always more than he is
... Wherever a man is, he is always elsewhere ... To the man who hopes,
everything is smiles and the world is given like a present.'

Sartre was clever enough to make *Bariona* neither too much like nor
too much unlike a religious play. The climax is a conversion, not to Christianity but to optimism in a situation no less dispiriting than that of occupied
France. Sartre made his point obliquely. Bariona plans to strangle the
Christ-child in order to save his villagers from a creed of submissiveness.
In the manger he again meets Balthazar, who again argues with him.
Skilfully, Sartre divides his message between the two characters. Though
the baby is now surrounded by worshippers, says Balthazar, they would
all abandon him if they knew he was going neither to drive out the Romans
nor put a stop to human suffering. But Bariona existentializes Christianity:
'Christ is here to teach you that you are responsible for yourself and your
suffering.'

Playing Balthazar, Sartre acted so persuasively that one member of the
audience, misunderstanding the play's meaning, was subsequently con-
verted. The applause of the prisoners, which was enthusiastic and sustained,
gave Sartre his first taste of direct contact with a big audience. He had

found a way of preaching in his own style, of rousing the prisoners with a pungent mixture of hope and existentialist pessimism. You are alone, he was saying, you have only yourself to rely on. He had hit on a way of carrying his teaching beyond the classroom, and of using words to share – not just with de Beauvoir but with a public – his own pride in being alone and alive.

At the end of the performance he joined in the celebration of the mass, singing canticles and responses with the choir.[10] To Perrin this seemed to bode well for his salvation, but the communion Sartre was enjoying was not religious. At the Stalag he had rediscovered collective life, satisfying a need which had been starved since he left the Ecole Normale. 'What I liked at the camp was the feeling of belonging to a crowd. Uninterrupted contact, night and day, talking directly to equals.'[11]

Since being captured, he had not been able to keep up the flow of daily correspondence with de Beauvoir, but they went on exchanging letters. It was worrying that no news had come from Nizan – the priests noticed that he talked more about his friend than about his mother – and eventually he learned that Nizan had been killed at the front on 6 May. Sartre stopped talking about him but gave no indication of what he felt. He resumed his readings of Heidegger with Perrin, appearing punctually every morning at ten. Discussing the sixth chapter, 'Die Sorge als Sein des Daseins' ('Care as Being of Existence'), Sartre confided his intention of writing a book on the subject. Sometimes Perrin would let his attention wander to the lice on Sartre's pullover. He noticed that Sartre never killed them, though he often said he had no respect for what was called 'life'.[12]

The idea of escaping from the camp had been in his mind for a long time. Before Christmas, wanting to tell de Beauvoir that she could expect to see him in Paris soon, he wrote that Poulou would shortly arrive there. Prisoners did escape, and postcards arrived containing coded messages to say they were safely home or had made contact with de Gaulle.[13] Some escaped with help from postal workers, who smuggled them with the mail to a garage on the edge of Paris but charged several thousand francs for the service.[14] A cheaper means of escape offered itself when the Germans began to release civilians imprisoned because they had been mistaken for servicemen. They could prove their civilian status by showing their reservist's pay-book, while others could fake civilian status: a group of prisoners was forging reservists' pay-books. Perrin, who was involved with this group, produced a document certifying that Sartre suffered from 'partial blindness of the right eye, causing difficulties in orientation'.[15] Convinced by Perrin that he could pass himself off as a man who would have been rejected at the medical, Sartre offered to coach the priest in how to simulate the symptoms of epilepsy, so that they could escape together.[16] Eventually, though, Perrin decided to stay on in the camp; Sartre would escape alone.

But the freedom Sartre wanted was not the freedom he had enjoyed before the war. Mathieu had been under pressure from Brunet and from his brother to prove himself free to surrender his freedom – whether to the PCF or to an unwanted marriage; Sartre would commit himself to neither, but he was determined to take action against the nazis: for too long people who valued freedom had left the initiative to others who did not. 'One can't belong to a party: they're all rotten including the Communist Party.'[17] 'If I joined a party, it would be out of a generosity that was too self-conscious to be moral. The C.P. is right to distrust intellectuals.'[18] What was needed was a new party, the Party of Liberty, open to everyone who would commit himself to the ideal of freedom for all.[19]

Growing impatient to live a more political life, Sartre seized at the opportunity of escape offered by a wizened little man known as Braco – short for *braconnier*, poacher. He claimed to have killed his wife after finding her in bed with a lover; he now lived mainly by stealing jackets from the store and selling them to prisoners who had been captured with money on them.[20] One day in March he brought Sartre and Perrin a piece of headed writing paper, undated, with a message in German to the guard: 'Please allow bearer and two accompanying prisoners to pass.' It had not been forged but had been picked up by Braco after a farmer had used it and thrown it into a ditch without even crumpling it up. Every day local farmers came into the camp to sell their produce. With the aid of a man, half Luxemburger, half Alsatian, who had trading relationships with the Germans and sometimes dealt in clothes, civilian outfits were acquired for Sartre and the two men who would accompany him. They would wear their Stalag uniform until they were outside the camp, with a change of clothes inside the bags they would carry, following Sartre who would be dressed as a farmer. Perrin watched them leave the camp: 'The "civilian" walked in front, his gait relaxed and heavy, a briefcase in his hand, like every self-respecting German. From the distance he looked like rather a prosperous farmer ... The prisoners followed, side by side, stooping under their luggage. I don't think they raised their eyes once ... I presume that the "farmer" preserved the appearance of a bad-tempered animal and that he made the right impression, for the barrier was raised almost at once.'[21]

Subsequently the communists would try to discredit Sartre by alleging that the escape had been staged: the Germans had made a bargain to release him because he had promised to work for them. Though this slur can be dismissed, one problem remains. After *Bariona* they could hardly have failed to realize he was the Sartre who had written *La Nausée*, and if they had wanted to recapture him in Paris after his escape, it would not have been difficult for them. But it would be more advantageous to have him at liberty. If he was one of the intellectuals who could function freely under their regime, he would be helping to demonstrate that it was not oppressive.

As soon as he arrived in Paris, he went into a café, where it was daunting to see how far apart the customers were sitting. 'Suddenly I was afraid – or nearly – I couldn't understand how these squat, bulging buildings could contain such deserts; I was lost: the scattered drinkers seemed further away than the stars.'[1] Habituated by the Stalag to close physical proximity with fellow-prisoners, he no longer had the right to put his hand on a man's leg or greet him with friendly abuse.[2]

He was reunited with de Beauvoir towards the end of March. He left a note at the Hôtel Mistral, where she was living: he would be at the Café des Trois Mousquetaires. He waited there two hours, and then went for a walk, leaving a note with a waiter who knew her. When he came back she was waiting for him.

It was not easy to resume their relationship. He was a stranger to the *modus vivendi* that had been evolved between Parisians and the German occupiers. Dubbed 'King Otto I' by Céline, the German ambassador, Otto Abetz, an attractive, cultured, urbane Francophile, used his position to construct a nexus of friendly relations with distinguished French socialites, intellectuals and artists, as well as intimate relationships with French actresses. At the German Institute thousands of people enrolled for the German language courses, while many of the best-known actors and writers (including Barrault, Cocteau and Céline) were often to be seen in the building.[3] A German victory seemed inevitable. Wanting a maximum of collaboration and a minimum of resistance – in both senses of both words – the Germans set out to be tolerant. Writers and artists would have been reluctant to stop working, even if they had not needed to earn money; the Germans aimed for a maximum of cultural continuity: the risk of anti-nazi propaganda was balanced by the advantage of involving French intellectuals in complicity. Though paper was in short supply, Abetz ensured that Paris publishers received generous allocations, while the literary censor, Gerhard Heller, rarely used his powers of veto.[4]

Sartre was disturbed to hear that de Beauvoir had signed a declaration that she was neither Jewish nor a freemason. Questioned about goods sold on the black market, she confessed to buying tea from it.[5] Sartre had arrived in Paris with a purpose: he was going to organize a movement of resistance.[6] He was planning to form a group which would find grassroots support all over France;[7] it had not occurred to him that a number of resistance groups might already be in existence.

He moved into the Hôtel Mistral, but, as before, took a room of his own, a squalid room with a lavatory in the corner. Without troubling to get himself demobilized – he would have had to report at Bourg (Ain), in the free zone – he was able to resume teaching at the Lycée Pasteur in Neuilly when the summer term began and the Inspector General, Davy, promised that in September he could teach the *khâgne* at the Lycée Condorcet.

As a teacher Sartre now tried to be unobtrusive, and this was disappointing for the boys: rumours had reached the Lycée Pasteur about the friendly pre-war Sartre who had sat tie-less on a table as he chatted entertainingly, sometimes letting the boys sit on the steps of a staircase instead of at their desks in a classroom. He was still a good teacher, positive and clear, but he never talked about the war or about his experiences in the Stalag, and he would round off each lesson by dictating a summary of what he had just said.[8]

In September 1939 he had written that he was 'cured of socialism', but the name he now chose for his group was 'Socialisme et liberté'. To recruit members he sought out former pupils, and met Merleau-Ponty, who had served as an infantry officer.[9] Merleau-Ponty had also come under the influence of Husserl, and was already at work on the book which would be published ten years later, *La Phénoménologie de la perception*. He immediately joined Sartre's group, as did Bost, who had recovered from the wound and was able, even under these austere conditions, to enjoy civilian life in Paris. The first meeting of the group was held in de Beauvoir's room at the Hôtel Mistral. Merleau-Ponty and Bost attended, as did the anthropologist Jean Pouillon, two *normaliens* called Jean Cuzin and Jean Desanti, Desanti's wife Dominique, and a few of their friends. Desanti was in favour of attacking prominent collaborators, including Marcel Déat, formerly a socialist minister but now leader of the pro-nazi Rassemblement nationale populaire, but the consensus was in favour of moving more slowly: they would recruit more supporters by forming cells of five people, each member having the responsibility of finding five new members. They would also collect information, which would be publicized by circulating pamphlets and a news bulletin, to be edited alternately by a Marxist and a non-Marxist.[10]

For Sartre there was nothing that could not be summed up with an epigram, and in the first bulletin, he argued that if Germany won the war, it would be the function of the Resistance to make sure that she lost the peace. Many other groups had been formed, but in the spring of 1941 there was little organized resistance, partly because the PCF had been following the Comintern directive to support Stalin's policy towards Hitler. By 1940 numerous communist students were already rebelling against the Party line and many of them took part in the demonstration on 11 November at the Arc de Triomphe, but in the spring of 1941 there would not have been more than fifty men in Paris capable of using weapons against the Germans. Georges Politzer was one of the few intellectuals who took initiatives that helped an effective resistance to emerge. Another was Charles Tillon, who contacted veterans from Spain who could train men to become instructors in the use of weapons.[11]

There were also right-wing groups, and Sartre made contact with one of these, the Pentagon. He also met Jean Cavaillès, a philosophy teacher who had started a resistance movement at Clermont. Members of Sartre's group were extravagantly incautious: Bost carried a duplicating machine through the streets; Pouillon regularly carried pamphlets in his briefcase.[12] But in one way they were less at risk than other groups: since they had all known each other for some time, it was unlikely that an insider would denounce them to the Germans.

The most quixotic of all Sartre's activities for 'Socialisme et liberté' was to write a draft of about a hundred pages for a French postwar constitution. Assuming that current actions could make sense only in the perspective of a plan for the future, he used Proudhon and Marx as his models in formulating proposals for a utopian France in which objects would be valued according to the quantity of work that went into making them, while each group of workers and tradesmen would be represented in a democratic parliament. The document was destroyed when the woman who was smuggling it to the free zone in the south, nervous of being discovered with it on the train, flushed it down a lavatory.[13]

London was being blitzed, and in May the House of Commons had been hit by a bomb. In North Africa Rommel's army was advancing, and the Vichy government promised naval help to Germany. In June the nazis invaded Russia, and although this provoked an Anglo-Soviet alliance, the German army had little trouble in piercing the Stalin Line and taking Smolensk, making it look as though Hitler's invasion of Russia would be more successful than Napoleon's. In France persecution of the Jews was stepped up. They were forbidden to carry on any business activities, schools were limited to a quota of Jewish pupils, foreign Jews were interned and deported, while anti-semitic propaganda was intensified, though most Parisians stayed away from cinemas showing German films such as *Jud Süss* (Jew Süss).[14] The communists had already been under attack in the press; after Russia entered the war, they were liable to be arrested as public enemies.

Resistance intellectuals mostly refused to write for the press, which came under nazi scrutiny, but Sartre, acting against de Beauvoir's advice, accepted the offer of a regular column in the weekly *Comoedia*, which was being revived under the editorship of a journalist, René Delange, who claimed that the paper would be independent and unaffected by censorship. Sartre was eager to write about *Moby Dick*, and his piece appeared in the issue dated 2 January 1941, but once he had seen the paper, he refused to go on writing for it.[15]

Theatrical activity continued in Paris. Barrault staged Aeschylus' *Suppliant Women* at the Roland-Garros Stadium with music by Honegger. Olga played a small part, which gave Sartre the idea of writing a play with a good part for her. This time he would have a bigger audience than in the Stalag. He would again be writing as a victim to fellow-victims, using history and myth as a code for smuggling inflammatory ideas across the frontier of censorship.

There was nothing to stop him from taking a summer holiday with de Beauvoir: provided that you went without luggage, it was easy to cross into the free zone, and while they were there, he could get himself demobilized. But his main object was to make contacts for 'Socialisme et liberté'. De Beauvoir already had a bicycle; Sartre was given one by her friend and former pupil Nathalie Sorokine, who stole bicycles. Jacques Bost lent them a tent and camping equipment. Parcels could be sent into the free zone, so they forwarded the bicycles and luggage to a priest who had escaped from the Stalag to Roanne. They booked railway tickets to Montceau-les-Mines: at a café there the patron could put them in touch with someone who would smuggle them across the border. They sat waiting in suspense all afternoon, until a woman of about forty, dressed in black, sat down with them and offered, for a fairly small fee, to take them across. She would be in greater danger than they would. When it was dark, they followed her in silence across fields and through woods. Sometimes she would signal them to stop moving. Eventually they were in the free zone. They spent the rest of the night at an inn where they were given mattresses in a room they shared with six other refugees and a baby. In the morning they caught the train to Roanne.

They collected their bicycles and pedalled about twenty-five miles before booking into a hotel. They rode on and spent the next night in a field outside Macon. They soon became expert at pitching and striking the tent, but as Sartre was less enamoured than de Beauvoir of the open-air life, they usually camped near a town or village so that they could breakfast in a bistro.[16]

At Bourg on 23 August Sartre was issued with a certificate of demobilization, though not without being reprimanded by the French officer for faking entries in his service book. With de Beauvoir he went for walks over the hills around Lyon, and saw American films in the cinemas. At St-Etienne he showed her the house that had belonged to his family. He preferred bicycling to walking, but sometimes pedalled so slowly that he fell off. 'I was thinking about something else', he explained.[17] It seemed odd that in the middle of a war they should be cycling peacefully along hill roads in the Cévennes, but Cavaillès had given him some addresses and he made contact with one member of the Resistance, a *normalien* called Kahn.

They cycled down to Marseille, found a room near the old harbour and repeated walks they had taken on previous visits. At a café in Porquerolles, Sartre began to work on the opening scene of his play *Les Mouches* (*The Flies*). After his classical education he was more at home with Greek myth than with biblical history, and the first theatrical experience he remembered was seeing Mounet-Sully as Oedipus.[18] After searching for Gide at his home in Chabris, Sartre was directed by his daughter Catherine to look for him at a hotel in Grasse, but when Sartre asked for advice, Gide, misunderstanding his intentions, told him the story of a married Dutchman who had discovered homosexual inclinations and had come to ask for an address.[19] The conversation with André Malraux was no more productive. At his villa in St-Jean-Cap-Ferrat he fed Sartre with Chicken Maryland and advised him that no action could usefully be taken.[20]

In Grenoble Colette Audry told them about a village near Chalons where it was easy to make arrangements for crossing back over the border. About twenty people, all with bicycles, followed a guide along narrow woodland tracks to a road with barbed-wire fencing all along it: they had to wriggle under the wire. Sartre and de Beauvoir had spent all their money. A draft was waiting for them at Auxerre, but travelling through Burgundy they were tormented by hunger. From Auxerre they returned to Paris by train, but left again to stay with Mme Morel. They returned to Paris in time for the start of Sartre's first term at the Lycée Condorcet, where he was to go on teaching until 1944.[21]

During the summer, relations between the Germans and French had deteriorated. The communists had organized a riot near the Porte St-Denis, and two demonstrators had been shot. A German soldier had been killed, and a Frenchman had tried to assassinate Laval and Déat. There had been sabotage on the railways, and the Germans were operating a reprisal system, shooting several hostages – usually communists or Jews – when any member of the Wehrmacht was killed: in October the death of two

German officers was avenged by shooting ninety-eight Frenchmen and imprisoning twenty-seven in concentration camps.

German armies had occupied most of western Russia and the Ukraine, but the retreating Russians burned the land they were surrendering. After the attack on Pearl Harbor, America had entered the war, but in the Pacific the Japanese had been winning a series of significant victories. In this perspective, it was hard for Sartre to go on believing, as he had in the Stalag, that he had a historical function as an organizer of resistance. Other groups were disintegrating. The communists were better organized, while the non-communist left was no longer so critical of the Stalin–Hitler pact; to Sartre the advantages of a common front were obvious, but Party members distrusted 'petty-bourgeois intellectuals', and even some of Sartre's friends believed the rumour that his release from the Stalag must mean he had agreed to work for the Germans as an *agent provocateur*. In his group morale plummeted as some members defected, and a young woman, a former student of de Beauvoir's, was deported after joining a similar group. In the end Sartre and Merleau-Ponty decided to dissolve the group, which had accomplished nothing. Sartre would concentrate on his play.[22]

During the hard winter, though they were by no means well off, Sartre and de Beauvoir helped to support Olga, Wanda, Bost and Nathalie Sorokine, who was living in a small hotel on the rue Delambre. Even the cheapest restaurants were now too expensive for them and at the age of thirty-three de Beauvoir finally resigned herself to cooking regular meals – an effort she would have to sustain for three years. At the Hôtel Mistral she moved into a room with kitchen attached to it, borrowing saucepans, casseroles and crockery from her sister's studio. She made careful use of the coupons in their ration books, and searched diligently for unrationed foods such as cabbage, beetroot, pasta and dried vegetables. But there was little in the shops, and they were often hungry. Even this did not interfere with Sartre's obsessiveness as a writer; de Beauvoir found it harder than he did to work with an empty stomach, but easier to give up smoking. He would search in the gutters and under the seats of cafés for dog-ends he could use to fill his pipe.

Their pride was sapped, and though some comfort was to be had from the sense of solidarity with the thirty-five million people who could no longer feel that their country was their own, he also experienced, more shamingly, an involuntary solidarity with the Germans who were sharing 'the unanimous life of a big city'.[23] The uniformed foreigners in the streets did not seem hostile. Clutching briefcases and hurrying to their office, or getting lost and asking help in imperfect French, or sitting in cafés sipping lemonade, they caused embarrassment without provoking hatred. At night it was different. Just before midnight, running footsteps on the pavements belonged to Frenchmen hurrying to observe the curfew; after midnight the footsteps were all German. Frightened yells were sometimes to be heard. 'There was no-one in Paris without a relation or a friend who had been arrested or deported or shot.' As Sartre said, it seemed as though there were hidden holes in the city, and that it was gradually being emptied through these holes, as if seized by an internal haemorrhage that had not revealed itself.[24]

Together with goods that had disappeared from the shops, laughter had dwindled in everyday conversation. There were no tourists in the streets and few cars. Many shops, cafés and bars had closed: the proprietor had disappeared or been deported. Hotels and cinemas had been requisitioned by the Germans. There were plinths without statues, unilluminated advertisements, public gardens disfigured by zig-zag trenches and reinforced concrete pillboxes.[25] There were no pictures in the Louvre, no English or American books in the bookshops, no wine from the free zone – the shops displayed only dummy bottles of Meursault and St-Emilion.[26]

No apparent attempt was made to monitor what Sartre taught to his pupils in the lycée, but the boys could not be sure whether they would ever take their examination. His job was to prepare them for the future; no-one could know what the future would be like.

Orders had been issued that everyone was to take shelter when the air-raid siren sounded, closing shops and offices. In Paris these orders were ignored. English and American bombs were being dropped elsewhere in France, but not here. Like his compatriots, Sartre felt ambivalent towards the damage, destruction and death: these had to be welcome in so far as they were weakening the Germans.[27] Since coupons were needed for shoe-repairs, de Beauvoir, who was permanently wearing her turban and troubling less about her appearance, took to wearing wooden-soled clogs. She and Sartre saw little of their former friends except the four who had become almost members of their family – Wanda, Olga, Bost and Nathalie. Nor did the six see each other at the same time. De Beauvoir testifies: 'When I was chatting at the Flore with Olga (or Nathalie), when Sartre went out with Wanda, when Nathalie and Wanda were talking together, none of us would ever have sat down at their table ... We always had and would always keep a predilection for conversation *à deux*.'[28] Sartre and she had abandoned Montparnasse. Usually they would breakfast at the Café des Trois Mousquetaires, where the radio was always turned on loudly, and in the evening meet at the Flore, where nothing was to be had except ersatz beer and coffee.

Sartre would spend a good deal of the day at either the Flore or the Coupole, packing a subversive message into the story of Orestes. 'The drama I'd have liked to write was about a terrorist who, by ambushing Germans, becomes the pretext for the execution of fifty hostages.'[29] After an ambush, Resistance fighters could save the hostages' lives only by giving themselves up; the play argues that they should neither do this nor feel guilty about causing the deaths of innocent people. Sartre also wanted to show how absurd it was to accept defeat as a punishment which France deserved. Pétain was preaching submissiveness. 'You are suffering,' he told the French people on 17 June 1941, 'and you will still go on suffering for a long time, because we have not yet expiated all our faults.'[30] The press was echoing this dismal message; no counter-argument could have been published openly, but Sartre could reiterate in his play the point he had made in *Bariona*: even the gods are powerless to interfere with human freedom.

Giraudoux had already retold the story in his 1937 play, *Electre*. When he brought the gods into the action, he usually deprived them of dignity and power; Sartre followed suit. The way Jupiter befriends Aegisthus, the usurper, parallels the way history has favoured Hitler, while Thebes, infested with flies, represents Paris under German occupation. As in *Bariona* the social situation is one in which the oppressed citizens appear to have little freedom, but a hero can show them how to preserve their integrity by rejecting the role of helpless victim and accepting responsibility for their situation.

In Aeschylus' *Oresteia* only superhuman powers can rescue Orestes from his guilt. But Sartre's Orestes follows Heidegger in believing conscience is the will to accept the guilt that is inescapable. While the occupying army makes it impossible to fight for the future except by putting other people's lives at risk, Orestes is exemplary because he can ignore the Pétainiste arguments of Jupiter and Aegisthus, the proto-fascist god and king who try to scare him away from Thebes or bully him into acceptance of the *status quo*.

Like Mathieu, and like Sartre, Orestes at first finds freedom a burden. He feels no urge to avenge the death of his father. What can these people have to do with him? A king should share the memories of his people, and after growing up in exile, Orestes has different memories. Electra's attitude is more rebellious. Reviling the god who has allowed the people to condone the murder and accept the rule of the usurper, she is waiting impatiently for her brother, while Clytemnestra feels scared. The queen represents the docile conformism of occupied France: 'For fifteen years we have kept silent, and only our eyes betray us.'

The usurper, Aegisthus, has little appetite left for living: 'Almighty God, who am I unless it is the fear that other people have of me?' Orestes is uniquely dangerous because he knows that he is free, and, as Jupiter admits,

'Once freedom explodes in a human soul, the gods can do nothing against that man.' Aegisthus is killed on stage; Clytemnestra offstage, but the killer Orestes has chosen to become is quite different from his sister in his reaction to the dog-like Eumenides. Though she has taken no part in the killing, she is so overwhelmed with remorse that she cannot stand up to them. While Gide had often dramatized the challenge of individualism to religious authority, and in *Amphitryon 38* (1929) Giraudoux's Alcmena had taught Jupiter that the gods could not manipulate human relationships, Sartre generates greater theatrical electricity out of Orestes' defiance:

> I *am* my liberty. You had scarcely created me when I stopped belonging to you ... Suddenly liberty burst on men and went through me. Nature jumped backwards. I was ageless and felt quite alone in the middle of your well-meaning little world, like a man who has lost his shadow; there was nothing left in heaven, neither good nor evil. Nor anyone to give me orders ... For I, Jupiter, am a man, and each man must find his own way. Nature hates men, and so, god of the gods, do you ... As for me, I don't hate you. What have I got to do with you or you with me? We'll pass each other, like boats in a stream, without touching.

Before leaving Argos he displays his pride in the crime which is his *raison d'être*. 'You can neither punish me nor reprimand me, and that's why I make you afraid. Yet I love you, my people, and it's for you that I killed.' This is very much a Resistance Orestes, a destroyer who does not see it as his duty to stay with his people as their ruler.

At Christmas Sartre and de Beauvoir travelled to stay with Mme Morel in La Pouèze, taking their bicycles in the train to Angers, and cycling the final fourteen miles. They were given more meat than they'd had in Paris, but dinner invariably consisted of apple fritters.[31] Mostly they stayed indoors, enjoying the luxurious log fires, chatting with Mme Morel, who no longer came to Paris, and reading, though bookshops were no longer full of exciting new publications.

Back in Paris, de Beauvoir stayed on in the Hôtel Mistral, but Sartre moved several times. His longest stays were all in hotels close to the Jardins du Luxembourg – the Hôtel Welcome in the rue de Seine, the Grand Hôtel de Paris in the rue Bonaparte and the Hôtel Chaplain in the rue Jules-Chaplin. But de Beauvoir was not left alone in the Mistral. Nathalie moved there from the rue Delambre, and when the sirens sounded, hammered on de Beauvoir's door, begging her to shelter in the Métro station. But de Beauvoir was confident the Allies would never bomb the centre of Paris.[32]

The Mancys still had the flat in Passy, where Sartre visited them a good deal. His relationship with his step-father had been improved by the war and the hostility they shared towards collaborators.

Before Easter Marc Bénard was released from the Stalag. He was living at Le Havre, in a big house belonging to his father-in-law, a successful lawyer; Sartre and de Beauvoir were invited there for the Easter holidays. The old port of Rouen and the suburbs of Le Havre had been badly damaged, and when they arrived at the house, which was on high ground near the port, Bénard's father-in-law told them what a good view he had of RAF raids, and how exciting it was when a bomb hit a petrol refinery. Later on, walking with Bénard to the old quartier St-François, Sartre and de Beauvoir found nothing left of the sailors' dives or of the slate-fronted houses they had liked so much.

Served in handsome dishes, the dinner consisted of swedes. Afterwards, while they were sitting around the wireless, listening to the BBC news, the hum of British bombers became audible.[33] Without moving from their chairs, they listened to both the broadcast and the sound of dropping bombs – a whistle followed by a loud explosion close by. The radio voice sounded closer than the bombs, though only a few hundred yards away houses were being pulverized, and in the morning they saw shrapnel in the garden.

Leaving Le Havre, Sartre and de Beauvoir crossed the Seine by ferry. The rest of their holidays was spent in La Pouèze. They returned to Paris by train, carrying eggs with them, and from now on the indefatigable Mme Morel sent them two or three food parcels every month. But the post was slow, and the roast pork in the first parcel had maggots in it. De Beauvoir did not throw it away, and each time a stinking parcel arrived, she cooked as much as she could of the meat, using herbs to disguise the taste.[34]

Since the beginning of February, Jews in the occupied zone had been forbidden to change their address or to go out after eight in the evening. From June they were ordered to wear a yellow star of David. There were few survivors among those who obeyed, but many disobeyed, especially in Montparnasse and St-Germain-des-Prés. Even after the decree of 15 July, which forbade Jews to enter restaurants, cinemas or any public buildings, they were still to be seen in the cafés. Rumours were circulating about Gestapo round-ups. French Jews were being interned in a camp at Drancy; thousands were deported to Germany. Many went into hiding in the free zone; many were caught while trying to escape. At the end of May Sartre learned that the red-haired Politzer had been tortured and shot.

Sartre has been criticized for not joining the Resistance and neither protesting against what was happening to the Jews nor helping individual

Jews in danger. True to his pattern of discontinuity, he had swung from organizing his own underground resistance movement to the generalized hymn about liberty that could be sung safely through a play. Jean Wahl was disappointed that he remained silent when all Jewish teachers in France were sacked;[35] Vladimir Jankélévitch suggested that all Sartre's post-war political activity was 'a kind of unhealthy compensation, a remorse, a quest for the danger he did not want to run during the war'.[36] It would have been easy to put himself at risk in 1942; for him, as for others, the question of how to balance the danger against the usefulness of the contribution he could make was a delicate moral question which changed its centre of gravity as it gradually became apparent that the Germans were not going to win the war: optimism was reinforced by ulterior considerations – the masters of the future would be impressed unfavourably by good conduct marks awarded during the Occupation.

Resistance to the Germans gathered momentum slowly. Inside France the most important leader was Jean Moulin. After escaping from the Vichy zone into Portugal, he made his way to England, where he met de Gaulle, who had him parachuted back into France at the beginning of 1942. He made contact with leaders of underground networks, and many intellectuals were now involving themselves in sabotage work. Sartre took minimal risks in 1942, even managing to keep his job at the lycée when other teachers, suspected of anti-nazism, were dismissed, but in 1943 he swung to the opposite extreme. At the end of May Moulin organized the first meeting of the Conseil national de la Résistance, aiming to co-ordinate militant and intellectual movements. Sartre's name was not mentioned at this meeting, but, eager to become more involved, he volunteered for action when he met the secretary of the committee, Pierre Kaan. Committee members though, were suspicious of him as a writer whose work had been published and staged during the Occupation.[37] He now put himself at risk again by contributing to underground papers, *Combat* and *Les Lettres françaises*, but it is doubtful whether he did much more than this after the disbandment of 'Socialisme et liberté' in the autumn of 1941.

Basically the Vichy government was anti-republican and authoritarian, blaming the defeat of France on the decadence that had ensued on the 1789 revolution. Pierre Laval, who had emerged in the autumn of 1940 as the main spokesman for Vichy France, was eclipsed by the anglophobe Admiral Darlan, who acted as chief minister from February 1941 to April 1942, but his policy of military collaboration with the Germans failed to win him their trust, and it was on Hitler's orders that Laval was reinstated as chief minister in April 1942. By shrewd manoeuvring, he managed to stop France's commitment to Germany from going any deeper, while sabotage continued, regardless of the admonitory notices on the tiled walls of Métro stations, reminding the French people about the savage reprisals. The closest male relations of offenders would be shot, their wives deported, their children interned. As part of a drive to drum up support among intellectuals, a collaborationist bookshop was opened in the Quartier Latin, but it was wrecked by a grenade. Students staged anti-German demonstrations, and one group of youngsters wore zoot suits and long hair, carrying umbrellas and taking an exorbitant interest in swing music.

Sartre made no attempt to publish his novel, but he was keen for his play to be staged. Jean-Louis Barrault, who had been playing Hamlet at the Comédie Française, rejected it, but Dullin was sympathetic, though he had been losing money at the Théâtre de la Cité – the new name for what had been the Théâtre Sarah-Bernhardt. (A theatre could not bear the name of a Jewish actress.) With the crowd of extras it entailed, *Les Mouches* would be an expensive play to mount, and when Dullin thought he had found a rich backer, the man turned out to be a penniless confidence trickster.[38]

With no prospect of a production until the new season began in the autumn, Sartre had no reason to stay in Paris through the summer, and he left with de Beauvoir and Bost for a cycling holiday in the free zone. Once again it was easy to cross the border illegally: they had been given an address in Sauveterre, near Avignon, and after a guide had arrived on his bicycle to lead the way down a country lane, they had lunch in Navarreux, where the inn was crowded with refugees, mostly Jewish. Sartre, de Beauvoir and Bost went on to tour the Pyrenees together, but one advantage of having Bost was that Sartre could stay behind, writing, while the other two went out on expeditions. They went to Lourdes, and when the two of them walked from the Col du Tourmalet to the top of the Midi de Bigorre, they left Sartre sitting in a field with a writing pad on his knees. Despite the strong wind, a great many pages had been filled by the time they got back.[39]

It was an exhausting and uncomfortable holiday. Unable to find hotels, the three of them often had to sleep in barns, and when they tried to cycle uphill they could feel how undernourished they were. For lunch they could usually buy fruit and tomatoes in a village, but meat was scarce, and they mostly dined on soup and some unattractive vegetable dish. At Foix Sartre and de Beauvoir parted company with Bost, who wanted to visit friends in Lyon before returning to Paris, but after being caught while trying to cross the border, he spent a fortnight in the prison at Chalons.

Sartre and de Beauvoir made their way through Provence to Marseille, sometimes stealing grapes from vineyards they passed. In the Marseille cinemas American films were to be seen, and they stayed in the town for several days, despite the food shortage. The expensive restaurants were still open, but only rationed food was on sale in the shops. Hunger reduced Sartre and de Beauvoir to eating mouldy bread spread with a ferociously garlicky ersatz aïoli made without eggs. Afterwards they would suck tasteless red or green water-ices.[40]

After cycling across the Larzac plateau, they went on to Pau by train, but then had to waste a day, waiting for their bicycles to arrive. They cycled on to Navarreux, where they found nothing to eat. A friend of de Beauvoir's family was living about twelve miles away, but Sartre refused to go with her. She was given a loan and a generous lunch, but when they arrived at Dax, he was weak with hunger. The only food they could buy was a plate of lentils. They bought tickets for Angers so that they could go on to La Pouèze, but they had to spend a night in Bordeaux, where they slept in the station waiting-room. Before cycling from Angers to La Pouèze they tried to revive themselves by taking a shower, but in the dining-room, after eating a few spoonfuls of soup, Sartre collapsed. He stayed in bed for three days. De Beauvoir had lost sixteen pounds in weight and she was covered with spots.[41]

They stayed for a month in Mme Morel's eccentric household, which consisted almost entirely of old woman. Dr Morel had been in bed since the beginning of the war. His room was illuminated only dimly, by a night-light. He would lie motionless for days, and he was liable to attacks, which brought him out in a sweat. An elderly maid, Joséphine, looked after him. There were also a bald, octogenarian housekeeper, Nanette, who had worked for the Morels in Paris, and an eighty-two-year-old hunchbacked woman, who lived on the first floor of the house. On the ground floor was an elderly Russian princess. She was stone-deaf and never left her room, which she shared with a small long-haired white dog. Mme Morel's Briard collie bitch was kept on a chain because she was dangerous to children and small animals, but while Sartre and de Beauvoir were there she broke free and disembowelled the white dog. The ancient princess sobbed for hours.

Sartre could not easily be persuaded to go out for a walk or a bicycle ride; his inclination was to stay indoors reading and writing. He was working simultaneously on the sequel to *L'Age de raison* and on *L'Etre et le Néant*, the gigantic philosophical treatise which had been growing out of the ideas assembled in his army diaries. Each of the new books profited from being evolved alongside the other; *L'Etre et le Néant* was written fast, on the basis of thinking he had already done. Neither book would have been what it was but for the Occupation, which gave a new edge and a new resonance to Sartre's passion for liberty. In *Les Mouches* he had highlighted the freedom inalienably available to the man who refused to view himself as a criminal or a sinner; *L'Etre et le Néant* centres on the freedom of the individual to choose – and especially to choose himself – within a historical situation that appears to enslave him. 'My birth makes me a worker, a Frenchman, a hereditary syphilitic or a tubercular';[42] but I must 'obey Nature in order to command Nature'; Sartre endorses Descartes's advice: we should 'try to conquer ourselves, rather than fortune'. While our freedom of action may be restricted by various obstacles, we are free to form the perspective in which they reveal themselves as limitations. Or in Sartre's terms, 'a free For-itself can exist only in a resistant world ... Success is not important to liberty.'[43] But there are no accidents in life. 'If I am enlisted in a war, this war is *my* war; it is in my image, and I deserve it.'[44] Unless I opt out by deserting or committing suicide, 'everything happens as if I carried the entire responsibility for this war ... To live this war is to choose myself through it, and to choose it through my choice of myself ... So *I am* this war which concludes and limits and explains the period which preceded it.'[45]

Similarly in the new novel, *Le Sursis* (*The Reprieve*), Boris is made to reflect that he is lucky in comparison with young men killed in street accidents or dying of cholera. He had known that war was coming and his parents 'had put him into the world for this war: they had brought him up for it, had sent him to the lycée, to the Sorbonne, they had given him culture ... they had spared no expense to make sure he would be a fine corpse, fresh and healthy ... It's my war. It's what made me, and I made it: we're inseparable. I can't even imagine what I'd be like if it hadn't been due to break out.'[46]

Sartre's characters have to be heroic in their willingness to shoulder responsibility for contemporary history, and later on his existentialism would win popularity by implicitly promising to raise its adherents to the same level of heroism by making them fully accountable; choosing themselves, they were volunteering to take responsibility for their epoch. Each decision would have a cosmic dimension: abandoned by God, humanity depended on each individual.

In his January 1939 essay on Husserl, Sartre had written rhetorically about the horror and charm of the world phenomenology had restored – the world of artists and prophets, 'frightening, hostile, dangerous, with havens of grace and love'. It is not through any Proustian immersion in subjectivity that we can find ourselves: 'it is on the road, in the town, in the middle of the crowd, a thing among things, a man among men'.[47] This panache continues into *L'Etre et le Néant*, which equates consciousness with choice, choice with action and freedom with passion, without ignoring frustration and suffering. Human reality, writes Sartre, is 'by nature an unhappy consciousness with no chance of escaping its unhappy state'.[48]

It is constantly hungry for the physical existence it can never achieve. This is dramatized in the novel when Mathieu, leaning over the parapet of a bridge, feels envious of the stone. 'It was there enormous and solid, enclosing in itself the squashed silence and the compressed darkness which are the interior of things. It was there; a plenitude. He would have liked to grapple on to this stone, melt into it, fill himself with its opacity and repose. But it could be of no help to him: it was outside, permanently.'[49] Consciousness is equated with lack and with nothingness. The For-itself is always in flight from the In-itself and always in pursuit of it. Neither could exist without the other, but they are structurally incompatible. Here the influence of Husserl and Heidegger had not so much displaced as reinforced that of Bergson who had characterized human reality as something which can be defined only as movement into the future. We are free when our actions emanate from our whole personality and when we take off into the future, but spontaneity is inhibited when consciousness feels like a thing.[50] Sartre is indebted to Bergson for this crucial equation of consciousness with flight into the future. The assumption is that, like movement, it has no corporal existence, no physical constituents.

In his fundamental division of Being into two orders, the For-itself and the In-itself, Sartre ignores the problem of animal consciousness (and animal elements in human consciousness); while assuming, as in *La Transcendance de l'Ego*, that consciousness is independent of self, he feels entitled to disregard the question of how consciousness is rooted in the brain. 'Nothing of what I see comes from me,' he declares, 'there is *nothing* outside what I see or what I could see.' In *L'Etre et le Néant*, as in *La Transcendance de l'Ego*, consciousness is transcendance, a project in which the For-itself goes beyond itself, but in the new book, Hegel is accused of letting epistemological and ontological optimism hush up 'the scandal of the plurality of consciousness'.[51] Sartre, like Marx, is substantially indebted to Hegel's analysis of the relationship between the Master and the Slave, but Iris Murdoch is as unfair to dismiss *L'Etre et le Néant* as 'a lengthy footnote to *The Phenomenology of Mind*'[52] as George Steiner is to dismiss it as a footnote to Heidegger's *Sein und Zeit*.[53] Unlike Hegel, Sartre recognizes that there is no reciprocity between Master and Slave, no common measure 'between what I am for him, what he is for me, what I am for myself, what he is for himself'.[54] The relationship between the self and the other is quadrilateral, and Sartre is at his best in characterizing it. He had always felt abnormally vulnerable to the gaze of other people – a weakness which is the source of great strength in his writing – and in the army, having to survive without privacy, he became even more concerned with our awareness of the way other people are aware of us. It feels as though the other person has stolen my being from me, and this is welcome in so far as it tends to stabilize me in objective existence, but I have no control over the image he forms of me. If I look at someone who is looking at me, I see only his eyes, not his look. Forming an image of him, I make him into an object which I possess. Since I build my subjectivity on the collapse of his, conflict is inevitable, involving both sadism and masochism. I am a slave in so far as I need someone else to constitute me as a body but I turn his aggression against him when I make him into an object.[55]

Many of Sartre's key-terms (including Being, Nothingness, Transcendance, For-itself, In-itself and Facticity) derive from Heidegger, but this is not to say that Sartre uses them in the same sense. His Nothingness is different from Heidegger's concept of an active or nihilating nothingness (*das nichtende Nichts*), while *Sein und Zeit* characterizes Being as something impersonal which is simultaneously close to use and remote from us, simultaneously hidden and revealed. Heidegger identifies phenomenological truth with revelation of Being, maintaining that every philosophical question pivots on the question of existence, but, as he explains when he dissociates himself from Sartrian existentialism in his 'Brief über den Humanismus' ('Letter on Humanism', 1946–7) he never equated existence with 'the actuality of the *ego cogito*'. He had not been referring to 'the actuality of subjects who act with and for each other' but to 'ecstatic dwelling in the nearness of Being'. What Sartre means by Being is closer to what Heidegger means by *Dasein*, the conscious being of the questioner who has power to organize his impressions of the world. When Roquentin confronted the chestnut tree, he was grappling with what Heidegger calls the truth of Being, but Sartre's wartime experiences tended to make him think of the individual as surrounded only by other adults and things – a world without children, animals or plants.

He criticizes the asexuality of Heidegger's *Dasein*, but his own explanation of sexuality ignores animal impulses, and presents sexual appetite as independent of physiological structure. Since our organs do not derive from the ontology of consciousness, he insists, the same must be true of sexual desire:[56] what I want to possess is the subjectivity of the other. I need her to make herself into an object on which I can act. I try to strip her body not only of clothing but also of movements, making it – and making myself – into flesh, as my consciousness slides towards consenting passivity.

> Suddenly the one who desires turns into a heavy tranquillity, which is frightening, his eyes stare and seem half-closed, his movements are clogged with a heavy, sticky sweetness ... and when one fights against this desire, it is this languor one is fighting. If the resistance succeeds, the desire, before vanishing, becomes distinct and clear, like hunger ... One will feel lucid, but with heavy head and a pounding heart.[57]

Desire is a lack of being,[58] a feeling which arises from the For-itself's need to rediscover its being, which has been estranged by the other.[59] Sartre's obsessive voluntarism has generated a puritanic animosity against sexual abandon: Thou shalt be free but Thou shalt never let go.

In his view all human appetites and activities are tributaries of the stream towards being. Even the acquisitive impulse derives from this source. Ownership is primarily a symbolical or magical relationship. What I secretly want is the world – I want to be it and to possess it; the object I desire is merely representative.[60] I am the objects which belong to me. Without them I am nothing but a nothingness which possesses. Through ownership I rediscover a form of being which tallies with the being I have in the eyes of other people, and property serves as a defence against them. 'What is mine is myself in non-subjective form in so far as I am the free foundation of it.'[61] Destroying and consuming are variant forms of possessing. In destroying an object I establish my appropriation of it, at the same time as stopping it from brandishing its impenetrability at me; this is what Charles does in *Le Sursis* when he smashes the mug which the nurse has given him as a souvenir. She is not as kind as she seems. In *L'Etre et le Néant* Sartre argues that underneath all generosity is an urge to destroy, which is basically an urge to possess. To give is to enslave. The beneficiary is obliged to preserve this part of myself which I no longer want.[62]

Even smoking can be analysed similarly as an acquisitive and destructive activity. Rhythmically annihilated as I breathe, tobacco represents the world, which, symbolically, I am destroying and incorporating. The argument has circled back to nothingness. What I am is a lack of being, and what I lack is the being that exists all round me. This is what I want. 'So my freedom is choosing to be God – a choice which is translated and reflected in all my activities.'[63]

Every human reality is a passion in that it tries to lose itself in order to become a foundation for being and at the same time to form the In-itself which escapes contingency by being its own foundation, the *Ens causa sui*, which religions call God. The passion of man, therefore, inverts that of Christ, for man loses himself as man so that God may be born. But the idea of God contradicts itself, and we lose ourselves in vain. Man is a useless passion.[64]

This is his conclusion in *L'Etre et le Néant*.

Throughout the book philosophy is bordering on psychology. For nearly twenty years – from his study of psychological books while at the Ecole Normale to his study of his fellow-soldiers' behaviour – nothing had interested Sartre more than the functioning of human consciousness. The vitality of both his fiction and his philosophy is nourished by insights that come from the same stockpot of observations and reflections. Neither of the new books could have been written without Husserl and Heidegger, but eclectic though he was, Sartre was also stubbornly critical, and in L'Etre et le Néant it soon becomes obvious that he had been unable to forgive Heidegger for not taking consciousness as his starting point. In the Introduction, gravitating away from Husserl towards Heidegger, Sartre seems to be penetrating to a deeper ontological level, but he makes only a perfunctory case for 'fulness of being'. For consciousness to operate, he argues, something must be there for it to focus on – and he subsequently concerns himself less with the nature of being than with the contrast between what he defines as its two modes – the For-itself and the In-itself. Everything devoid of consciousness belongs to the In-itself, while the For-itself is equated with nihilation. Underneath Sartre's radicalism is a bedrock of Cartesian conservatism. Conditioned by his philosophical training, he goes on taking the cogito as the starting point, while for Heidegger the central truth is the truth of Being.

No less than Bariona, L'Etre et le Néant is the product of a period in which France was occupied by the enemy; one of Sartre's needs was to console himself and his readers by emphasizing the freedom available in an anthropocentric universe. For Sartre, man is the only god in a godless world; for Heidegger we are not 'in a situation where there are only human beings' but in one 'where principally there is Being'.[65] Though Heidegger's periphrastic and repetitious glorification of Being may appear to lack philosophical sophistication, he is cogent in his attacks on Sartre's simplistic adherence to the Cartesian cogito, his humanism in which man is the sole source of meaning, and his uncritical use of such terms as 'man', 'existence' and 'essence'. More cautious in its use of language, Heidegger's philosophy is more durable, less obviously a product of its period.

Temperamentally, Heidegger is more individualistic. Language is the key to understanding and after analysing the etymology of 'existence' he reminds us that man should stand out into the truth of Being. Dasein should not let itself be held down by the chatter and mediocrity of public life, by mass existence which levels off genuine possibilities. Nevertheless, Heidegger is closer to Marx, for whom 'social man' is 'natural man', than is the Sartre of L'Etre et le Néant. Involving himself with the problem of alienation, Marx, according to Heidegger, 'recognizes the essential importance of the historical in Being'.[66] In 1947, when Heidegger wrote his 'Brief über den Humanismus', Sartre had not yet proved himself capable of a fruitful dialogue with Marxism.[67]

He was still more involved in a dialogue with theology. Like the ending of L'Etre et le Néant, which affirms the futility of 'choosing to be God',

Le Sursis demonstrates that we can neither possess the world as a totality of being nor look at it from any extra-terrestrial viewpoint:

> If you tried to stand face to face with the planet, it would crumble into fragments, nothing would be left except consciousness, a hundred million free consciousnesses, each of which would see walls, the glowing end of a cigar, familiar faces. Each would construct its destiny on its own responsibility. But if you *were* one of these consciousnesses, you'd be reminded by scarcely perceptible prompting and modifications of your place in the colony of polyps. The war: everybody is free but the chips are down. It's there, it's everywhere, it's the totality of all my thoughts, all Hitler's words, all Gomez's actions, but nobody is there to do the adding up. It exists only for God. But God doesn't exist. Yet the war exists.

In September 1938 it looks as though war is unavoidable. The politicians sidestep it by sacrificing Czechoslovakia to the nazis, but the evasion of the crisis has little bearing on the ontological issues, which are the issues that matter. The mirage of war forces the characters to confront themselves, confront each other, confront their environment. What they discover is not a mirage and it is only the most myopic who are happy about the cowardly compromise made in Munich.

The novel also clarifies the contrast between Mathieu and Daniel in terms of Mathieu's recognition that he is nothing and Daniel's stubborn belief that he is something. In *L'Age de raison* Mathieu had been made to say: 'I am not... one is never anything.' This reminds us of Sartre's 1939 expostulation to Pieter: 'I know in my bones that people aren't; they do.' At this level Sartre's thinking is anti-Heideggerian and his emphasis on action accords with his insistence on the insubstantiality of consciousness, which he defines in *L'Etre et le Néant* as 'the being which has in its being consciousness of the nothingness of its being'.[68] The characters in *Les Chemins de la liberté* are trying – most of them in what Sartre calls bad faith – to catch up with their own being, to coincide with themselves in a solid, thing-like existence. Daniel wants 'to be a pederast in the same way that an oak tree is an oak tree'. In *L'Age de raison* he had assumed that freedom was to be found in doing the opposite of what he wanted. After trying and failing to drown his beloved cats he had tried and failed to edge Mathieu into freely sacrificing his freedom by marrying the pregnant Marcelle. When Daniel marries her himself he fails to make himself as unhappy as he had expected to be. In desperation – but without realizing how desperate he is – he turns to religion, inverting the Cartesian *cogito* into 'I am seen, therefore I am', and luxuriating in the belief that God is watching him. 'I no longer have to bear the responsibility for the clammy proceedings of my body: he who sees me brought me into existence; I am as he sees me. I turn my nocturnal, eternal face towards the night, I stand up straight, like a challenge.'[69] Though Georges Bataille was not a theist, Daniel's arrogant abjection was modelled partly on the addled mysticism of Bataille's book *L'Expérience intérieure*, which Sartre reviewed at length in *Cahiers du Sud*.[70]

Daniel is guilty of 'bad faith', which, for Sartre, is primarily a matter of hiding the truth from oneself. He analyses a variety of stratagems for doing this, developing his attack on psycho-analysis by arguing that the idea of the unconscious mind is a justification for telling lies without feeling like a liar: one postulates involuntary self-deception.[71] Daniel confesses he is evil: the apparent sincerity is only a camouflage for escaping responsibility by denying freedom. Sartre's hostility to Freud is above all a refusal to admit any limitation on individual freedom.

In his attack on François Mauriac, Sartre had criticized him for acting as Thérèse's accomplice by sharing her freedom, while relaying her thoughts at the same time as pronouncing judgment on her, taking a god-like viewpoint and assuming divine power in prescribing her destiny. If novels were entirely fictional, the novelist would unavoidably be giving his characters their destiny, but in *Le Sursis* Sartre does his best to make history take responsibility. With the action set in 1938 history can be shown to reprieve all those called up for military service. The impending war touches them, but history cannot quite be persuaded to take over the role of omniscient narrator, though it does help Sartre to move on to a more experimental technique derived partly from Dos Passos, partly from Virginia Woolf. Instead of being interconnected through personal relationships, the narrative threads remain separate, the object being to show contrasted individuals all caught up in the same historical situation. In *L'Age de raison* most of the action consists of thoughts developing, moment-by-moment, in the consciousnesses of Mathieu, Daniel, Boris and Ivich, while there are only six other important characters – Marcelle, Lola, Brunet and his wife Sarah, Jacques and his wife Odette. In *Le Sursis* the cast of characters is bigger. Much depends on simultaneity, and within eight days, Friday 23 September 1938 to the following Friday, we move – often unaware of the transition until after we have made it – from one character to another, one place to another. Central Europe is in turmoil. The narrative jumps like a film from incident to incident – the heads of state meeting at Munich and privately preoccupied with trivialities; an illiterate shepherd unable to defend himself against con-men who want his money and non-commissioned officers who want to humiliate him; a rich Jewish businessman trying to forget his Jewishness; a Czech schoolmaster looking at the swastika flags on the balcony opposite. Another character, Philippe, is based on Baudelaire, whose step-father became a general. Like the poet in Sartre's biography of him, Philippe is immature, self-destructive, emotionally fixated on his step-father. To convince himself that he isn't a coward the boy protests against the war by shouting in public places. Some of the sequences involving Mathieu, Daniel and Boris are quite long; other sequences are succinct, with situations developed no more elaborately than in a short story. Though the construction is actually careful, the structure gives the appearance of being determined only by the calendar progression from one day to the next in a frightening European crisis.

D.H. Lawrence believed that form in the novel pushed the writer towards telling the truth; Sartre believed it helped to fend the truth off. In *La Nausée* Roquentin was, as a biographer, exploiting the power narrative has to give us an illusion of freedom from contingency, while Sartre worked hard to stop the form of the book from neutralizing all the nauseating odours exuded by his images of formlessness. In *L'Age de raison* the problem was different because it was the first volume in a series: the narrative could remain open-ended, and in *Le Sursis*, which is formally less conventional than any of his other fictions or plays, he develops an idea latent in the essay he wrote in 1938 about Dos Passos's simulation of historical time in 1914: 'Big disturbances – war, love, a political movement, a strike – disappear, crumble into an infinity of little odds and ends which one can just line up, side by side.' The example Sartre quotes is Dos Passos's dramatization of the armistice: at the beginning of November rumours begin to circulate, and then, one afternoon, Major Wood, bursting into the office Evelyn shares with Eleanor, kisses both girls.

In *Le Sursis*, when the shepherd is ejected from a fashionable restaurant, Sartre appears to be remembering the incident in 1932, when an overalled worker was ejected from a Rouen café. Afterwards he and de Beauvoir had speculated about the way Dos Passos might have described the incident, and in the 1938 essay on Dos Passos, Sartre introduces a brief parody in which two friends express their passionate hatred of war: 'Paul declared that he'd rather do anything than fight and Jean said that he agreed and they both got excited and said they were happy to be in agreement. When he got home, Paul decided to see Jean more often.'[72] Already, one of the seeds for *Le Sursis* had been planted.

Well written and well constructed, the novel is consistently impressive – while *L'Etre et le Néant* is more uneven. In many of its best passages, the prose tends to be rhetorical and loosely metaphorical; in the worst, it is abstract, repetitive and disfigured with sub-Heideggerian jargon. But the best parts could have been achieved neither without an unscientific imprecision nor without the co-presence of the worst parts. *L'Etre et le*

Néant is not a footnote to *Sein und Zeit*, but an answer to it – an alternative attempt at a twentieth-century metaphysic, a comprehensive explanation of existence. Searching for a feeling which could reveal something essential about existence, Heidegger, prompted by Kierkegaard, had singled out anxiety. 'What gives rise to anxiety', writes Heidegger, 'is being-in-the-world as such.'[73] Pitched headlong into life, we find ourselves face to face with the absurdity of the human condition, or, as Heidegger prefers to put it, '*Dasein* finds itself face-to-face with the nothingness of the possible impossibility of its own existence'.[74] The anxiety this produces is the anxiety Sartre had tried to translate into the nausea that is not inside Roquentin: he is inside it. Glutinously, the world is vomiting its plenitude at him as it overflows with contingent existence.

Sartre's allergy to the glutinous sap of *Natura naturans* also has its effect on *L'Etre et le Néant*. Insisting on the need for a psycho-analysis of *things*, he argues that the world consists of potentialities which do not belong to the In-itself.[75] Inspired by Jacques Audiberti's phrase 'the secret blackness of milk', Sartre suggests that if there is a secret meaning in snow, it will turn out to be an ontological meaning.[76] If we are disgusted by what is glutinous, this can be explained only by its combination of physical and moral qualities.[77] In relation to the In-itself, stickiness has a symbolic value which is identical with its psychic meaning. It appears as 'the outline of a fusion of the world with myself'. 'It is like a leech sucking me.'[78] *La Nausée* left us free to keep Roquentin's vision at arm's length as that of a neurotic; here the personal allergy is integral to the philosophy.

The underlying fear seems to be one of being devoured, as in his fear of shellfish with claws. His nervousness, when swimming, that an octopus might attack him is indicative of the same phobia. One day he might get sucked under. The anxiety may have extended – in a milder form – to the fluids encountered in the orifices of the female body. Though he preferred women's company to that of men, he seems to have assumed a polarity between consciousness (which he pictured as active, alert, male) and flesh (inert, flabby, clinging, female.) If consciousness is to preserve its freedom and its capacity for penetration, it must express itself in prose as beautiful and hard as steel; at the end of *La Nausée* it is clear that Roquentin is better off without Anny if he is going to write a novel. In *Le Sursis*, Boris's escape from the clinging Lola echoes Mathieu's escape in *L'Age de raison* from the pregnant Marcelle. When he finally beds the less feminine and more sympathetic Ivich in *Le Sursis* – almost a rape, coinciding with that of Czechoslovakia – the usual Sartrean polarity is preserved but reversed: the viscosity is male while a female consciousness holds on to its independence. 'A glutinous perturbation like blood invaded Ivich's thighs and stomach, it slid into her blood, I'm not a girl who gets raped, she opened, let herself be stabbed, but while shivers of ice and fire rose up to her chest, her head stayed cool, she had saved her head and she yelled at him in her head: "I hate you".'[79]

Camus's first novel *L'Etranger* (*The Outsider*) had been published in the middle of June 1942 and by September, when Sartre reviewed it, had already been hailed as 'the best book since the armistice'. Camus's essays, *Le Mythe de Sisyphe*, intended for simultaneous publication with the novel, had been delayed, mainly because the German censor vetoed the chapter about Kafka, and the book was not published until mid-October, but copies were ready earlier, and Sartre had read it before he wrote his essay in September.

If Camus had been influenced by *La Nausée*, the influence worked negatively: thinking Sartre placed too much faith in language and lucidity, Camus veered towards silence. 'A man is more of a man', he wrote in *Sisyphe*, 'by virtue of what he keeps silent about than of what he says.' In *L'Etranger*, Meursault cannot, as narrator, be made to keep silent, but he does not understand the story he tells, while his girlfriend, Marie, when she gives evidence in court, feels that she is being compelled to say the opposite of what she thinks. For Camus, knowledge could be attained not by reasoning but only by means of a leap to faith. Temperamentally he was more religious than Sartre and more optimistic, believing man could assert his innocence against the absurdity of his condition. Sartre was quick to recognize Meursault as an innocent, and to understand that what Camus meant by absurdity was disconnection between human yearnings for unity and the insuperable heterogeneity of the environment. 'If I were a tree among trees', says Camus, perhaps remembering Sartre's chestnut tree, 'this life would mean something, or rather this problem wouldn't, because I'd be part of the world. I'd *be* the world which, at the moment, I'm opposing with my whole consciousness.'[80] Without mentioning Sartre by name he says that 'this "nausea" as a contemporary writer calls it is also the absurd'. People secrete the inhuman. When you see a man telephoning inside a glass booth, his incomprehensible dumb show makes you wonder why he is alive. For Sartre absurdity was contingency raised to the power of the absolute: the key to Roquentin's nausea was the wooden serpent, the root of the tree, the purposeless abundance of natural fecundity. Camus's absurdity is closer to alienation. He did not share Sartre's aversion to viscosity or to the moist areas of the human body; he took more pleasure in sex and in the sensation of being alive. He hated the limitations of human intelligence, but he also hated emotional pretentiousness. If Meursault incarnates the 'grace of the absurd' (to use Sartre's phrase) it is partly a matter of rejecting all pious pretences, emotional and traditional.

Like Sartre, Camus had studied philosophy, but he was less of a philosopher, and while Sartre portrayed a consciousness that was restlessly moving outwards towards the world, Camus cultivated a prose style that implied passive receptivity. Events are recorded, never in the past tense, always in the perfect or the present, as if there is no connection between them, no causality. Sartre noticed the indebtedness to the laconic prose of Hemingway, who never used long sentences. In Camus's novel, as in Hemingway's stories and novels, each of the short sentences refuses to profit from the momentum generated by the previous sentence. Each one is a new beginning.[81] But whereas Hemingway always wrote in this style, Camus was affecting it. He had another, more poetic style. The trick he was playing in *L'Etranger*, complained Sartre, was to introduce a glass wall between the reader and the characters: the wall was transparent to events but opaque to their meaning.[82] The discontinuity between the sentences implied a discontinuity between actions which were not really discontinuous. In a novel, insisted Sartre, it must be obvious that time is irreversible; *L'Etranger* was not so much a novel as a moral fable, reminiscent of Voltaire.[83]

FOURTEEN · *The Future Reappears*

In the autumn of 1942 it began to seem possible that Germany would be defeated. In Africa the British Eighth Army, under its new commander, General Montgomery, was forcing Rommel's army to retreat, and on 8 November the Allies landed in French North Africa under the leadership of General Eisenhower. France lost its free zone when the Germans hurriedly occupied it in order to defend the Mediterranean coast, but from now on it was exciting to read the newspapers. Each day could bring news that meant the Third Reich was closer to collapse; meanwhile the Vichy government became more vindictive towards Jews, foreigners and those suspected of helping the Resistance. Trainloads of victims were deported.

Once again it was possible to believe in the future, but when Sartre and de Beauvoir arrived back in Paris for the autumn term, they could not settle down into a comfortable routine. Her hotel room had been let to someone else. After several days of searching in Montparnasse and St-Germain-des-Prés for another hotel room with a kitchen, she found a dilapidated room with peeling walls in the rue Dauphine. She hired a handcart to shift her possessions, and Nathalie helped her to push it through the streets of Paris to her sordid new home. The kitchen had a lavatory in it; the bedroom had an iron bedstead, a wardrobe, a table, two wooden chairs. The prostitute who lived on the same floor left her four-year-old son to sob on the landing whenever she had a man with her. Mice would soon gnaw through a wooden partition to get at the lentils and dried peas in de Beauvoir's cupboard; rumour had it that large rats were breeding all over Paris. When Marc Bénard and his wife came to dinner, they were unable to hide their dismay at the squalor. The meal consisted of potato pie and carrots.[1]

It was an uncomfortable winter, with coal shortages and power cuts. Candles were scarce too, and when they were not teaching, Sartre and de Beauvoir spent most of their time at the Flore, which was illuminated by acetylene lamps whenever the electricity failed. In order to get the warmest table, next to a stove-pipe, de Beauvoir would arrive soon after the café opened at eight in the morning. Picasso was a regular customer, as was Jacques Prévert. As soon as the air-raid sirens sounded, the café had to close. Most of the customers were hustled out into the street, but a few of the regulars, including Sartre and de Beauvoir, were allowed to wait for the all-clear in a room on the first floor.[2]

For the Christmas holidays they went back to La Pouèze, where they listened excitedly to BBC news programmes. On 29 December the German thrust towards Stalingrad was defeated at Kotelnikovo, and the good news continued after Sartre and de Beauvoir returned to Paris for the beginning of term. At the Casablanca conference, held during the second half of January 1943, President Roosevelt demanded unconditional surrender. Towards the end of the month Berlin was bombed by daylight for the first time, and at the beginning of February the last German troops in Stalingrad surrendered. A couple of weeks later, Laval, who had for some time been recruiting work-parties for Germany, issued a new decree: all the young men who reached call-up age between 1940 and 1942 must serve for two years with the Service du Travail. Many escaped to join the Maquis.

A number of anti-nazi committees were being organized by the communists who were recruiting prominent non-communists for them, and early in the year Sartre was invited through François Billoux, a communist he had known in the Stalag, to join the Comité national des écrivains (CNE) which had the poet Paul Eluard as its President. Members included Mauriac, Paulhan, Claude Morgan and Jean Guéhenno. At the meetings Sartre, according to Morgan, would try to avoid making divisive proposals.

In the spring Dullin started rehearsing *Les Mouches*, directing, as well as playing the part of Jupiter, with Jean Lannier as Orestes, Olga (calling herself Olga Dominique) as Electra and with Wanda in a small part. A newcomer to professional theatre at the age of thirty-seven, Sartre learned a great deal from watching rehearsals. Without asking for cuts or revisions Dullin could make dialogue less rhetorical by telling the actors: 'Don't play the words, play the situation.' Later Sartre would tell himself: 'Don't write the words, write the situation.'[3] Dullin, who had worked with Jacques Copeau, maintained that Dionysian violence should be presented with Apollonian restraint. As Sartre testifies, 'intangible richness arose out of poverty; violence and bloodshed were suggested with serenity, and, evolved with patience, the union of these opposites... contributed an astonishing *tension* which had been missing from my play'.[4] Not that the course of rehearsals ran smoothly. As a producer Dullin was taking a risk in staging a potentially controversial play in such a big theatre, while as a director he was not at ease on such a large stage. Jean Lannier was inexperienced, as was Olga, who would burst into tears when Dullin lost his temper.[5]

The dress rehearsal was held in the afternoon, when the electricity was less likely to be cut off than it was in the evening. While Sartre was standing in the foyer, Albert Camus came up to introduce himself.[6] Attractive and well built, he looked athletic; in his native Algeria he had been a football star.

When the play opened on 3 June, it was impossible for the audience to miss the political meaning of Orestes' speeches about liberty, but most of the critics prudently ignored it. In *Paris-Soir* Jacques Berland complained that Sartre was more of an essayist than a playwright,[7] while another reviewer accused him of 'flogging a humanity he detests'.[8] In *Les Lettres françaises* Michel Leiris wrote an unsigned panegyric, remarking on the play's political implications,[9] but, as Dullin wrote later, 'It rapidly became a complete flop; the box-office was pathetic.'[10] Undeterred, he put the production back into his repertoire when the theatre reopened in October after the summer recess. The play was given about forty performances.

By staging *Les Mouches* Dullin was helping Sartre almost as much as when he urged Gallimard to publish *La Nausée*. As he showed in *L'Etre et le Néant*, Sartre was abnormally conscious of the interplay between the image we have of ourselves and the image other people have of us. Using all the means at their disposal – newspapers, radio, cinema, public placards – nazis and collaborationists were projecting a humiliating image of the French people; had it not been for Dullin, the only platform for Sartre's defiant ideas on human freedom would have been *L'Être et le Néant*, which attracted little attention when it was published in the summer. At the theatre, even if audiences were small, the play was upholding the option of freeing oneself from a historical trap by committing an atrocious act and taking full responsibility for it. Zola had said that the novelist must 'kill the hero' in order to show 'the ordinary course of average lives'; Sartre's slogan was: 'No more characters; the heroes are freedoms caught in a trap like all of us.' His paradoxical assumption is that we have no freedom except to be free.

Like the theatre, French cinema had been lamed but not paralysed by the Occupation. In December 1940 the Germans had established the Comité d'organisation de l'industrie cinématographique (COIC), which had expelled all Jews from the industry and banned trade unions. Many films were clogged with collaborationist propaganda, but myth, symbolism and historical drama were still viable modes. Though Cocteau and Jacques Prévert went on working in the cinema, most of the scenarios submitted to the studios were mediocre, but the director, Jean Delannoy, who in 1943 had directed Cocteau's *L'Eternel Retour*, a reworking of the Tristan and Isolde story, arranged for Sartre to be signed up by Pathé. When he left Paris for his summer holidays, he was already being paid a retainer, and it seemed he might soon be earning enough to give up teaching.[11]

De Beauvoir had left earlier for three weeks of solo cycling in the country. He travelled by train to meet her in Uzerche, thirty-five miles from Limoges. With the manuscript of *Le Sursis* in his saddlebag they cycled together in a leisurely way, putting on yellow plastic capes when it rained. At Beaulieu a storm blew up while they were eating in a hotel, and they came out to find the cycles had been blown over and the saddlebags carried off in a stream of yellowish water. The manuscript was floating in the gutter. It was easy to dry it out; not so easy to restore the passages where the ink had smudged.[12]

Even the best hotels were serving only vegetarian meals, and real coffee was scarce. Eggs, which were sometimes to be had from farms, could be taken to restaurants, so that the meal could be fortified with an omelette. Sometimes they slept in barns, and at Conques they slept in a school-room on palliasses. At Vaour, spending the night in a stable, they were attacked by bugs. After cycling to Toulouse, they adjourned to stay for the last part of August and the whole of September with Mme Morel at La Pouèze, where the main pleasure was listening to BBC news pro-grammes. Mussolini had been overthrown in July, and on 8 September General Eisenhower announced that Italy had signed an armistice. On 9 September the Allies landed at Salerno, while in the east, the Red Army was advancing steadily.

Sartre worked on *Le Sursis* at La Pouèze, but after they returned to Paris put it aside in favour of a new play. The initiative came from the owner of a pharmaceutical factory near Lyon, Marc Barbezat, who at his own expense published an elegant literary periodical, *L'Arbalète*, which he printed on a hand press. It appeared twice a year. He had just married Olga Perret, the young actress who had played Clytemnestra in *Les Mouches*, and the idea was that Sartre's script would contain parts for her and Wanda, who was now attending Dullin's classes. Barbezat, who offered to finance the production, wanted a play that could tour the country.[13]

Sartre set out to write a short play with a single set and only two or three characters. To obviate complaints about the relative size of the roles, he decided that none of the three principal characters, a man and two women, would ever leave the stage. After playing with the idea of keeping them in a cellar throughout a prolonged bombardment, he decided to put them in hell. He called the play *Les Autres* (*The Others*), and it was published under this title in *L'Arbalète* (No. 8, Spring 1944). The title was later changed to *Huis clos*. A legal term for 'behind closed doors', this is usually translated as *In Camera* or *No Exit*.

The script was written in a fortnight, and the absence of rhetoric shows how much he had learned from watching Dullin rehearse. *Huis clos* is Sartre's first play in which the statement is made through the actors and the situation. Again his basic concern was freedom. Hell would have been of little interest to him unless he had found a way of using it to imply the opposite of imprisonment. Though the dead can do nothing to change their lives, Sartre wanted, as in *Le Sursis*, to attack the bad faith of men like Daniel who live as if they have no control over their behaviour. Such people are 'encrusted in a series of habits, of customs ... This is a living death.'[14]

One of the play's roots was in Sartre's wartime experience of being unable to escape from the hellishly intrusive gaze of other people. The play is a three-dimensional metaphor exploring this deprivation while fleshing out points Sartre had made in *L'Etre et le Néant* about Being-for-others. Hegel had treated this as a necessary stage in the growth of self-consciousness: (as Sartre put it in *L'Etre et le Néant*) 'I need the other as a mediator between myself and me'.[15] In hell (as he portrays it in the play) there are no mirrors: each of the three main characters depends on the other two to reflect an image. Had there been only two people in the room, they might have become lovers, but the gaze of an excluded third person is bound to be less flattering.[16] In a triangular situation – as Sartre had found with de Beauvoir and Olga – each is tortured by the other two: hell consists of other people.

Without knowing much about Camus, Sartre invited him to direct the play and to act the only important male part. Their second meeting took place at the Flore. According to de Beauvoir, who was with them, Camus had charm and a boyish sense of humour; he would address Pascal, one of the waiters, as Descartes.[17] After a slow start, the conversation gathered momentum when they talked about Francis Ponge, and ex-surrealist and a communist, who was now active (unlike Sartre and Camus) in the intellectual Resistance. The conversation went on to theatre. As a student in Algiers, Camus had formed a theatrical group, Le Théâtre du Travail, and from 1936 onwards had worked as adapter, producer, director and actor. After baulking when Sartre came out with his offer, Camus let himself be persuaded. Soon the production was under way. An ex-pupil of Sartre's, R.J.Chauffard, who was working for Dullin, was cast in the small part of the waiter, and Camus started rehearsing in de Beauvoir's hotel room with Wanda, Olga Perret and Chauffard.

Camus had not yet settled in Paris though he had worked there for a couple of months in 1940 for *Paris-Soir* and had spent a fortnight there in January 1943, returning on 1 June, the day before Sartre met him at the theatre. De Beauvoir describes him as a simple, cheerful man, nonchalant but enthusiastic. The idea of editing a monthly review emerged out of Sartre's impatience for the future to begin. This had never been stronger than it was during the final years of the war. At cafés, restaurants, dinner parties, conversation bristled with plans for the future.

Sartre's main friendships were with Camus, Michel Leiris and Raymond Queneau. Formerly, as a surrealist, Leiris had powdered his face white and painted landscapes on his bare scalp. With his shaven head and the formality he affected in dress and manner, he had always seemed intimidating at meetings of the CNE, but he and his wife Zette turned out to be friendly. Soon Zette was helping de Beauvoir to buy meat and at dinner parties the Leirises were frequent guests, as were Queneau – another ex-surrealist – and his wife Jeanine. Queneau had not yet started to write for the cinema, but he had been playing since the thirties with the dichotomy between spoken French and the literary language. Sartre wanted to have a review of his own with his friends on the editorial board, while another project was that together with de Beauvoir, Camus and Merleau-Ponty he would take over the section on ethics in the philosophical volume Gallimard was planning for his *Encyclopédie*.

Rehearsals of the play stopped when Olga Perret was arrested, suspected of working for the Resistance. Frustrated, worried, restless, Sartre made himself concentrate on the first of his scripts for Pathé, *Les Jeux sont faits* (translated as *The Chips Are Down*). Once again he tried to float a Resistance message in a bottle that would drift past the censor, but the screenplay was rejected by Pathé. The film was not made until 1947, when Delannoy directed it with Micheline Presle as Eve. In *Huis clos* the three characters can' watch what is happening on earth, while the space they occupy has no terrestrial location, though it looks just like a drawing-room furnished in a Second Empire style. In Sartre's screenplay the Paris occupied by the dead overlaps with the Paris occupied by the living, and he writes some effective sequences in which living and dead characters are simultaneously visible to the audience, though the dead are invisible to the living. Those who have just died find it hard to remember that they can't intervene.

As a screenwriter Sartre is energetic and inventive, with the same flair he showed in the theatre for engaging the audience's sympathy for the characters, but this film is marred by melodrama and by the obligation he felt to put a love story in the centre of the action, though it was clever not to let Eve and Pierre meet until they are dead. She has been a rich woman, married to André Charlier, secretary of the militia; Pierre was the leader of a revolutionary movement trying to overthrow the vicious military regime of the Regent. She has been poisoned by André, who married her for her dowry and now has designs on her younger sister; he has been shot by a traitor. Though dead, they are sufficiently in love to qualify for a twenty-four-hour resurrection. If they can prove themselves capable of staying together as lovers, they will be allowed to stay alive. Like Brecht (in *Puntila*) Sartre shows how social barriers make it hard for a rich middle-class girl to settle down with a proletarian lover, but in the screenplay the barriers are not insuperable. The main obstacle to love is revolutionary commitment to freedom. Knowing of the Regent's plan to liquidate the resistance movement, Pierre cannot abandon his comrades, and he gets himself shot for the second time.

When the script was rejected, Sartre knew that he would have to go on teaching his *baccalauréat* classes at the Lycée Condorcet. So short of money he was nearly always hungry, he was glad to earn by lecturing to Dullin's students on the history of theatre, but *L'Etre et le Néant* would bring in only negligible royalties. De Beauvoir had been accused by her collaborationist headmistress of corrupting a minor and had lost her teaching job, but she got work on the national radio network. To steer herself into non-political territory, she proposed a series about traditional festivals from the Middle Ages onwards. With help from Bost, she pieced old ballads together with material she found in the Bibliothèque Nationale.[18]

By the beginning of 1944, when she went off with Bost but without Sartre to ski in Morzine, it looked as though the war would soon be over. The Russians had recaptured two-thirds of the territory taken by the Germans, and on 20 January the RAF dropped 2,300 tons of bombs on Berlin. Cologne, Hamburg and other German cities had been attacked no less ruthlessly, while, in France, it was not only factories, ports and railway junctions that were bombed. Nantes was devastated, and even the suburbs of Paris were under attack. The Resistance had become more active and rumours were circulating about German reprisals. Sometimes it was said that the entire male population of a village had been shot. On 4 March, twenty-two 'foreign terrorists' were killed. They had been condemned to death on 18 February, and photographs of the young faces were posted up on the walls of Métro stations.

Sartre was now a member not only of the CNE but also of the Comité national du théâtre, and he was averaging three meetings a week. Many of the writers involved saw each other frequently, and when a panel was formed to award the Prix de la Pléiade, which had just been founded by Gallimard, Sartre's fellow-judges were Eluard, Malraux, Camus, Paulhan, Blanchot, Queneau, Raymond Tual, the novelist Marcel Arland, with Jacques Lemarchand, the novelist and drama critic, in the chair. The prize of 100,000 francs was awarded to Mouloudji for his novel *Enrico*. For Sartre, possibly, literary merit was not the only criterion: he liked to champion emergent proletarian culture-heroes. Mouloudji, who was not so well qualified for this role as Camus, would soon be dropped, and Genet, whose potential was greater, would be picked up.

A celebration lunch for Mouloudji was organized at the Hoggar, where de Beauvoir's lamb chop consisted entirely of bone and gristle. Hunger was such a familiar feeling and food such an overriding preoccupation that Picasso made it the theme of his play *Le Désir attrapé par la queue* (*Desire Caught by the Tail*). When Michel Leiris arranged to give a public reading of the play, Camus rehearsed the actors. Leiris, who had done the casting, had appropriated the main part, Big Foot, for himself. Sartre was Round End and de Beauvoir the Cousin. Picasso's mistress, Dora Marr, played Fat Misery.

Picasso was in the audience, as was the young Spanish actress Maria Casarès, who fell under Camus's spell as he read the stage directions with calculated monotony,[19] rapping on the floor with a walking stick to indicate each change of locale. The readers stood up each time they had to speak. The Leirises' drawing-room was too small to accommodate the audience, which included Georges Braque, Jean-Louis Barrault, Armand Salacrou, Georges Bataille and Jacques Lacan. De Beauvoir was complimented by Picasso on her appearance, which was enhanced by Olga's red angora sweater and Wanda's big blue pearls.[20] Those who stayed after midnight had, because of the curfew, to stay till dawn; Mouloudji sang 'Les Petits pavés', Sartre sang 'Les Papillons de nuit' and 'J'ai vendu mon âme au diable'.

Eager to continue the mood of celebration, some of the friends went on to organize a series of 'fiestas', as Leiris called them. The first was held in March at Georges Bataille's flat, where the musician René Leibowitz was in hiding; for the second fiesta Bost's mother lent them her villa in Taverny.[21] They drank and they clowned. Queneau and Bataille duelled with bottles; Camus and Lemarchand played tunes on saucepan lids; Sartre conducted an imaginary orchestra from the bottom of a cupboard.

Over Easter, while Sartre and de Beauvoir were in La Pouèze, Paris was bombed: the RAF had started attacking railway stations. When they arrived from La Pouèze, the Gare du Nord, the Gare de l'Est and the Gare de Lyon were out of action.[22] Life became more chaotic, with food still scarcer. In the evening the Métro stopped at ten; at theatres and cinemas fewer performances were given.[23] In April the Allies dropped 81,000 tons of bombs, mainly on Germany; in Italy the German army was retreating rapidly throughout May. But Jews were being packed off to Germany in sealed trains, and Nathalie lost her lover, a 19-year-old Spanish Jew, Jean-Pierre Bourla. Sartre tried to console de Beauvoir with an *ad hoc* theory: every life is complete at its end and death is no less absurd at the age of eighty than at the age of nineteen.[24]

* * *

Throughout his life Sartre was to strike up remarkably few friendships with men of his own age. Bost had graduated from being a pupil to being a member of the family, but it was never a relationship between equals, whereas with Camus Sartre could have a great deal of fun. Though less subversive than Sartre, Camus was in some ways still like a tough Algerian street urchin and they could tell each other obscene stories while de Beauvoir and Maria Casarès or Camus's wife Francine tried to look shocked. Later Sartre would describe him as 'probably the last good friend I had'.[25] The friendship was to be short-lived, but it was highly enjoyable while it lasted, not only for both men but for their other friends. Bost, for instance, bene-fited. His ambition was to be a journalist, and after reading his book on his experiences in the infantry, *Le Dernier des métiers*, Camus published it in the collection he was editing for Gallimard and sent Bost to the front line as a war correspondent. He willingly gave jobs to other protégés of Sartre, and de Beauvoir attests that when they opened *Combat* in the morning, 'it was almost like reading through our personal mail'.[26] It was Camus who involved him in writing for the underground paper *Combat* from the spring of 1944.[27] Part of Camus's appeal was that he did not belong to the bourgeoisie, but, as a proletarian culture-hero he was soon be be eclipsed.

One afternoon in May he was with Sartre and de Beauvoir at the Flore when a man with close-cropped hair and thin lips came across to introduce himself. 'You Sartre?' he asked. He looked like a boxer, a lightweight. He was Jean Genet. Cocteau, who had discovered him in prison, was claim-ing him to be the greatest writer of the age, and Barbezat had published a section of *Notre-Dame des fleurs* in *L'Arbalète*. De Beauvoir describes him as a good listener, but Sartre, five years later, complained that he could not remember discussing anything with Genet except Genet. 'My passion is to understand people and his to remain in ignorance about them.'[28] Genet had charm and boldness of judgment but he was intolerant of anec-dotes and small-talk. When de Beauvoir took him up to admire the view from the penthouse terrace of her hotel, his response was: 'What the devil am I expected to make of *that*?'[29] Nor was he a man they could invite to one of their fiestas.[30]

Sartre would not begin to write about Genet until the beginning of 1950, but it was in 1944 that he wrote *Baudelaire*, the first of his three biographies. 'If we don't regress continually', he said later, about Flaubert, 'to the auth-or's desires and objectives, back to the total enterprise ... we'd just be making the book into a fetish ... like a piece of merchandise, considering it as a thing and not as the reality of a man, objectified by his work.'[31] The key question – 'How much can we know about a man?' – had to be answered in terms of the individual. By 1971 Sartre would assert: 'every man is utterly knowable'[32] and in his study of Baudelaire he claims: 'each event reflects back the irreducible totality that he was from the first day to the last'.[33] Long before he started to use the word 'totalize', Sartre committed himself to a biographical accountancy in which each fact is a figure in a column which can be added up. Though Roquentin had given up hope of understanding the Marquis de Rollebon, Sartre was to devote a major part of his working life to biography, but none of his biographies is conventional in approach. His strong tendency towards the synchronic looks forward to the structuralists and backward to Bergson, who had insisted on the unity of the personality, which must be apprehended intuitively or empathically. Instead of detailing the succession of events, Sartre refuses to concern himself with the way Baudelaire developed. His eccentric assumption is that the only crucial decision in Baudelaire's life was made at the age of seven, when his mother remarried, and the child chose his destiny. According to Bergson, we exist in space more than we do in time, and we live more for the external world than we do for ourselves. Sartre writes of Baudelaire's personality as though it had, throughout his adult life, a consistency determined by this childhood decision. Trying to construct a detailed portrait of the man, Sartre cantilevers speculatively out from the writings and the known biographical facts. He makes the ungrounded suggestion that Baudelaire would have preferred meat cooked in sauces to grills, and preserves to fresh fruit.[34] Sartre does not mention that these are his own preferences.

The book is important as an attempt to repudiate what might have struck Sartre as part of his own psychological destiny. Like Lucien in 'L'Enfance d'un chef' and like Flaubert, Baudelaire was an anti-type. Traumatized by his mother's second marriage, Baudelaire took refuge in *la vie imaginaire*. Writing with a ferocity aimed partly at conventional literary values but mainly at the part of himself he was determined to slough off, Sartre castigates Baudelaire for being immature, morbidly narcissistic, masochistic, dishonest, obsessive, onanistic and exhibitionistic. The charges are all the more serious for Sartre's assumption that we can choose what we want to be. Baudelaire is therefore held to be 'fully and lucidly responsible' even for his syphilis, for his failure to achieve financial independence and for his emotional dependence on his mother. Instead of evaluating the poetry, Sartre condemns the man for his defective manliness. Like the unforgivable Flaubert, Baudelaire had chosen to be an effeminate artist rather than a man of action; as if reminding himself to avoid that pitfall, Sartre condemns Baudelaire's literary achievements as useless, treating the poems as if they were no more than an appendage of his dandyism, pieces of literary self-indulgence, written not to help humanity but to reflect his own image. Instead of trying to change the world or even to change himself,

Baudelaire merely tries to see himself as if he were someone else and, because this is impossible, depends, like an addict, on the disapproval of his step-father and his mother. Their judgment makes him into an object. In Baudelaire self-hatred and narcissism coalesce as he chooses to live in bad faith. This is Sartre's Baudelaire; not only was the real Baudelaire quite affectionate towards his step-father, he was also active on the barricades and championed social reform.

Sartre had brainwashed himself into believing that poetry was altogether undesirable – only prose could be useful – but four years previously his attitude to poetry had been different: 'I'm furious not to be a poet', he wrote in 1940, 'to be so heavily fettered to prose.'[35] This was his reaction a fortnight after composing a twenty-three-line poem, only to feel that it should be reduced to five lines.[36] Pleased that his prose sometimes approximated to the poetic, he ruefully tried to analyse why poetry was beyond his range:

> There's something tangled in me, a secret shame, a cynicism learnt too slowly, and then also a lack of charm; my feelings haven't found their language, I feel them, I reach out a timid finger, and the moment I touch them, I change them into prose. The choice of words betrays me. If I start, if I find a poetic phrase, it's subverted by a word that slips in, a word that's too pointed, too plain; the movement of the phrase is rhetorical...[37]

Even while writing this, he was hoping that when he re-read it, he would 'discover in stupefied amazement that I'd just created with my prose the beautiful object, the ship in the bottle, I was vainly asking of poetry'.[38] Hopes of this kind would linger long after he started to denounce poetry as useless.

The third fiesta was held at Toulouse's flat, where the huge circular drawing-room opened on to a garden. The hall and the rooms had been decorated with flowers, ribbons, garlands, knick-knacks, but Toulouse had drunk too much during her preparations, and the guests were welcomed by a nervous Dullin. Camus arrived with Maria Casarès, who was rehearsing his play *La Malentendu*. The others included the Salacrous, the Queneaus, Olga Kosakiewicz, Bost, the Leirises and students from Dullin's drama school. When Dullin recited some of Villon's ballades, Jeanine Queneau responded by barking like a dog until Olga tapped her reprovingly on the nose. At three in the morning, Toulouse made her appearance, wearing rouge on her eyelids and blue eye-shadow on her cheeks. Unsteadily she danced a *paso doble* with Camus. The party lasted till daylight, and when Sartre and de Beauvoir, together with Olga and Bost, were walking through the deserted Place de Rennes, they saw placards on the station wall: no trains would run until further notice. Later on in the day it was announced over the radio that English and American troops had landed in Normandy.

Sartre and de Beauvoir drank ersatz gin outside the Flore, celebrating the future.[39]

By the time Olga Perret was released, plans were under way for a production of *Huis clos* at the Vieux-Colombier, and Camus, who felt unqualified to direct stars, had withdrawn. The production was entrusted to the actor-director Raymond Rouleau, who cast his wife, Gaby Sylvia, as Estelle, with Michel Vitold as Garcin, Tania Balachova as Inès and R.-J.Chauffard still in the part he had started to rehearse, the waiter. For Sartre these interpretations of the four roles were definitive.[40] The first night was scheduled for 10 June. The performance went well, and the audience was amused at the idea that in this hellish hotel the lights would stay on all the time: 'We have unlimited electricity.' The play was presented as part of a double bill: what followed was a comedy which was so boring that not all the audience stayed. It was understandable that the theatrical manager, Anet Badel, should decide to reverse the order of the two plays. But he failed to alter the programmes or the posters. Claude Morgan was one of those under the impression that Sartre had written the comedy.[41]

Soon afterwards, Jean Vilar, who, as co-director of a touring company, La Roulotte, had been staging plays by Strindberg, and had been organizing a series of lectures on theatre, invited Sartre to give one of them. The audience included Cocteau, Camus and Barrault, who all asked questions; fashionably dressed ladies afterwards approached Sartre for his autograph.[42] When Cocteau came to *Huis clos* with Genet, Sartre and de Beauvoir met them after the performance. Cocteau dominated the conversation, complimenting Sartre on the play before expatiating on his own theatrical experiences. Afterwards they walked down the rue Bonaparte to the *quais*. Watching searchlight beams in the sky and flares flashing, Cocteau maintained that the poet should hold aloof from the follies of war and politics.[43]

It was hard to hold aloof from the nazis' final acts of vengeance. At Oradour-sur-Glane thirteen hundred people were burned alive, in their homes or in the church. Rumour had it that in the Midi children had been seen dangling from butcher's hooks, which had been pushed through their throats. Because of his involvement with *Combat*, Sartre was in danger after a member of the network confessed names to the authorities. Camus advised him to go into hiding, and after staying for a few days at the Leirises' flat, he went to Neuilly-sur-Clermont, together with de Beauvoir. They stayed for three weeks in the village *auberge-épicerie*, eating and working in the public bar to the sound of billiard balls clicking and villagers chatting as they drank and played cards.

On 11 August, hearing that the Americans had reached the outskirts of Chartres, Sartre and de Beauvoir set off on their bicycles for Paris, determined not to miss the Liberation. Told that the Germans were retreating along the main road, they took a side road to Chantilly, where they boarded a train, which came to a halt after a few miles as it was machine-gunned from the air by an RAF plane. Sartre and de Beauvoir were among the passengers who, as the plane zoomed away, rushed for shelter to the nearest ditch. From the front carriages ambulance attendants carried out bodies on improvised stretchers. Some of the passengers refused to go back on the train, but Sartre and de Beauvoir resumed their journey. Finding the Métro was closed, they cycled to book in at the Hôtel Welcome. At the Flore they met Camus, who had taken over as editor of *Combat*, and was preparing for its first public issue. He said the leaders of the Resistance had agreed that Paris should liberate itself. It was clear that this would cost lives, but nothing else was clear. What was happening, in fact, was that the American Third Army had begun to surround the city, but with the intention of isolating it in order to avoid the destruction and bloodshed of a siege. Inside the city an uncoordinated insurrection had already begun, with communist partisans working at cross purposes with de Gaulle's FFI (Forces françaises de l'intérieur). Camus commissioned Sartre to write a detailed account of the Liberation for serial publication in the paper.

The electricity had been cut off, and there was no food on sale. The police had disappeared from the streets, and on 16 August the gas was cut off. At the Hôtel Chaplain Bost had built square tins into a stove that could be fuelled with newspapers, but it was hard to cook spaghetti on it, and the room filled with smoke. Rumours were circulating. Shooting had been heard inside the prisons; arrests and deportations were still going on. The worst fear was that the whole of Paris would be blown up when the Germans left: people were saying that mines had been laid under the whole area surrounding the Palais du Luxembourg. In fact Hitler had ordered that Paris should be destroyed but the Francophile Abetz disobeyed.

In the afternoon of 18 August German army trucks packed with troops and boxes drove northwards up the boulevard St-Michel, but in the morning the swastika flag was still flying from the Palais du Luxembourg. De Beauvoir saw a platoon of German soldiers emerging from the building to march down the boulevard St-Germain. Before they turned the corner, the Germans loosed a parting volley of machine-gun fire at pedestrians. People were carried away on stretchers; a concierge came out to scrub the blood off the steps. After Sartre had left for a committee meeting at the Comédie Française, de Beauvoir walked to the Leirises' flat, and from there she saw the French flag flying from the Préfecture. Progressively, resistance was being mobilized inside the city. Parisians were recapturing their own public buildings, and the FFI had been firing on the Germans, who often took revenge on innocuous civilians. Friends kept ringing Sartre up excitedly with news and rumours. In the evening, he was at the Hôtel Chaplain with de Beauvoir and the Leirises when some boys rode by on bicycles, shouting that the Germans had asked for a cease-fire.

In the morning it was being said that the Third Army was only three or four miles from Paris. Tricolours and flags had appeared in windows. In the Carrefour Buci shoppers were picked off by gunmen on the roof of a hotel. After storming into the building, FFI soldiers emerged with a dozen Japanese prisoners. Laughing savagely at them, the crowd pounced. Some of the Japanese had their trousers pulled off and their bottoms spanked before they were driven away in a police car.[44]

Sartre spent the day wandering around the streets of the *quartier*. It would have been safer to stay indoors, but the best way to write the articles for *Combat* was from first-hand experience. 'I describe only what I've seen... It begins like a holiday and, today still, the boulevard St-Germain, deserted and intermittently swept by machine gunfire, keeps an appearance of tragic solemnity.'[45] In the afternoon loudspeaker trucks drove around with the announcement that all fighting had stopped, but shots were still to be heard, and alarmist rumours were circulating. One woman said that if a single shot was fired, the Germans would bombard Paris: their guns were already trained on the city.[46]

More men were joining the Resistance fighters; women were cooking for them in improvised canteens. German army trucks were ambushed openly in the streets; while men sat fishing on the Seine, freedom fighters were sheltering behind balustrades along the *quais*. But German trucks and armoured cars were still driving about, and according to one rumour German tanks were approaching to shell the buildings along the *quais*. Columns of German armoured cars were still firing at pedestrians, and at the corner of the rue St-André-des-Arts de Beauvoir saw a pool of blood. FFI fighters were shouting 'Stop' and 'Go' to tell pedestrians when it was safe to cross the road.

On 21 August the Comité Parisien de la Libération issued fighting orders. Citizens of Paris must use methods of all kinds to stop the enemy from moving: 'Cut down trees, dig anti-tank pits, set up barricades.' The idea was to force the remaining soldiers into surrender, though the Germans, who still had large forces in the area, could have quashed the insurrection savagely. As soon as Eisenhower, who was in command, learned of this call to the barricades, he changed his plans, sending General Leclerc's army to advance on the centre of the city.

In the first public issue of *Combat*, which was distributed in the streets the same day, Camus's editorial supported the call to arms: 'It's by fighting the invaders and traitors that the FFI are re-establishing the Republic in our country'. An unsigned text on the same page was titled 'From Resistance to Revolution', and this slogan would appear daily under the masthead of the newspaper. 'We know what our orders are', wrote Sartre in one of his articles. 'Hit a German over the head and take his revolver, get hold of a gun, with the gun get hold of a car, with the car take an armoured car and a tank. This has raised more than one smile among the cynics of the Resistance, and yet the programme is being realized, point by point, under my eyes.'[47]

Barricades had been erected in the Place St-Germain-des-Prés and along the boulevard. Liaison officers cycled up and down the boulevard Montparnasse, telling citizens to help with the barricades. Fewer German tanks and armoured cars were to be seen in the streets, but snipers were shooting from rooftops, and while Sartre and de Beauvoir were listening in the Salacrous' flat to the BBC announcement that Paris had been liberated, gunshots were still to be heard. In the evening, when de Beauvoir was on her way to dinner at the Hôtel Chaplain, a passing cyclist shouted that General Leclerc had reached the Place de l'Hôtel-de-Ville. As Sartre and de Beauvoir arrived at the Carrefour Montparnasse, bells began to peal all over Paris. A bonfire was lit in the middle of the road, and, joining hands, they all danced around it, singing until an approaching German tank dispersed the crowd.

At six o'clock in the morning of 24 August Leclerc's troops marched in columns to the avenue d'Orléans, with crowds cheering on the pavements, the excitement surviving the snipers' shots that still rang out. A few collapsed bodies would be carried away, but the crowd would go on cheering. The streets were draped with flags; girls threw their arms around soldiers' necks. The next day Sartre, together with other members of the Comité National de Théâtre, watched from a balcony in the Hôtel du Louvre as de Gaulle marched down the Champs-Elysées, followed by police officers, soldiers and freedom fighters. When shooting started, the FFI mistook the committee members for militiamen and opened fire. They retreated inside, unhurt.

Sartre and de Beauvoir were having dinner with Genet, the Leirises and a uniformed American friend of theirs when a solitary German plane began to drop bombs: the Halle aux Vins was destroyed, as was a house in the rue Monge. And that was not the end of it. Sniping continued, rocket bombs fell on the suburbs, but the uniforms in the streets were American. These were soldiers who chewed gum and parted their fingers in the V-sign.

But the excited mob dealt out only a rough justice. Had the shaven-headed old woman been any more of a collaborationist than those who had insulted her?[48] So long as the occupying forces had been there, moral issues had been clear-cut, but with liberation came inhibiting ambivalences. In the first public issue of *Les Lettres françaises* Sartre wrote: 'We have never been more free than under the German occupation.'[49] What had created a feeling of community was the need for silence. Faced with the possibility of betraying members of the Resistance to the nazis, each Frenchman had been responsible to the community and to himself. 'And the choice each man made of himself was authentic, because it was made in the presence of death, since it could always have been made in the form "Rather death than..."...So the question of liberty itself was posed and we were at the edge of the deepest knowledge man can have of himself.'[50]

A pamphlet had been printed – probably in 1943, when the communists were campaigning for unity of action – denouncing Sartre, Montherlant and the novelist Alphonse de Chateaubriant as collaborationists. For Sartre, as for Henri in de Beauvoir's 1954 novel *Les Mandarins*, the choice appeared to be between siding actively with the working class and becoming an object of hatred. 'Unless he could prove it was not so, he was an enemy for hundreds of millions of men, an enemy of humanity. He didn't want that at any price.'[51] Sartre had no intention of joining the Party; he wanted to be a useful – if critical – ally.[52] After refusing an invitation to write for the communist weekly *Action*, partly because it had attacked Malraux unfairly, he was surprised to come under attack himself. Though his existentialism had made little impression, as yet, on the public, the communists were quick to see that it might emerge, dangerously, as an alternative to communism. Sartre's response to the attack was an article published in *Action* at the end of December under the title 'A propos de l'existentialisme: Mise au point' ('definition of terms'). Though he was trying to be conciliatory, this did not improve his relationship with the communists.

Huis clos was translated into several foreign languages. In London it was banned from the stage by the Lord Chamberlain, but broadcast four times by the BBC. In Paris it was due for revival at the Vieux-Colombier in September, and Sartre went on writing for the cinema, taking the idea for *Typhus* from the epidemic which had broken out in Morocco shortly before he and de Beauvoir went there in 1938. Though his scenario remained unused until 1953, when Yves Allegret directed *Les Orgueilleux* (*The Proud Ones*), Sartre could now count on earning enough from cinema and theatre to give up teaching. When he applied to the university for leave of absence, he was within six months of his fortieth birthday. A writer of his talent, versatility and energy might have expected to turn professional sooner, especially after discovering in the army how prolific he could be. But *L'Age de raison* and *Le Sursis* were still unpublished, and unlike Brecht, who was able, during his wartime exile, to stockpile unproduced plays, Sartre was not temperamentally suited to writing for his desk drawer. Instead of turning back to fiction, though, immediately after the Liberation, he worked on the essay he had intended to call 'La Situation des juifs en France'; the title was changed to *Réflexions sur la question juive*, but the main thrust was against the anti-semites rather than in favour of the Jews. During the Occupation it had been embarrassing to see Jews wearing yellow stars: it was obvious that well-meaning non-Jews who took off their hats to them were humiliating them no less than people who ignored them. After the Liberation, Jewish survivors were coming back to their homes, but, as if nervous of offending the anti-semites, French newspapers kept almost silent about the gas chambers.

Angered by this cowardly discretion, Sartre made up his mind to speak out, though he did not yet know when or where he would publish his polemic. The black American writer Richard Wright had told him: 'There is no negro problem in the United States, there is only a white problem.' In France, Sartre declared, there was no Jewish problem, only a problem of anti-semitism. It is the anti-semite who *makes* the Jew; the question to ask was not 'What is a Jew?' but 'What have you made the Jews into?'[53] Though Sartre's polemic is well-intentioned, his thinking is superficial. Thirty-five years later he will admit to Benny Lévy: 'I wrote without any documentation, without reading one Jewish book ... I wrote what I thought.'[54]

More important, his premises are more anti-semitic than he realizes. One commentator has noticed that the word 'aryan', which occurs seventeen times in the essay, is in inverted commas only five times.[55] Sartre has not dissociated himself from the racialism implicit in this nazi word. He has no quarrel with the assumption that the Jew is congenitally different from the non-Jew. For the Jew, he maintains, authenticity is to live out fully his condition as a Jew. Refusing to feel ashamed of his 'own kind', he must accept the obligation to live in a situation that is unlivable; he must take pride in his humiliation. Though Sartre is dutifully condemning anti-semitism as an irrational passion, a lower-middle-class snobbery, he is doing nothing to contradict the grossly prejudiced remark he had made about the Jewish soldier he befriended: 'Rationalist Jews like Pieter are inauthentic in so far as they consider themselves to be men first of all, not Jews.'[56] The satire on the Jewish businessman in *Le Sursis* is acceptable; he is going out of his way to deny his Jewishness. But how did Sartre require Pieter to behave? How should he show that he was living out his condition as a Jew before living out his condition as a man?

It was not until November that Sartre submitted his two novels to Gallimard, using the title *Les Chemins de la liberté* for what he was then planning as a trilogy. He dedicated it to Wanda. The foreword tells us that the three volumes will cover the years 1938–44, bringing the characters to the Liberation of Paris 'but perhaps not to their own liberation'. He explained the stylistic difference between the first two novels: in 1937–8 individual existence had seemed feasible in a watertight compartment; in September 1938 'the partitions melt'. But he was trying to write a 'heroic novel', he said, promising that the characters who seemed most cowardly would prove themselves in the third volume to be capable of acting heroically.[57]

Searching for a Third Way (1945–57)

What Sartre did not know was that thanks to the melting of the partitions he was going to let four years go by before he worked on the third novel. He was swept away from his literary moorings by the vast tide of euphoria which surged out of the Liberation and was swelled by the PCF's need to secure intellectuals as allies. Damaged cities could be reconstructed but there could be no resurgence of national self-confidence until a new foundation was built for moral, cultural and intellectual life. 'The ambition of our Party', said a member of the Central Committee, Roger Garaudy, at the tenth congress, 'is to be the animator of France's intellectual and moral renaissance.'[1] This did not seem unrealistic. The right had been discredited by its opportunistic collaboration with the nazis; the Party had gained prestige from being identified with the cause of resistance. In co-ordinating anti-nazi militancy it had genuinely played an important role; its objective now was to dominate progressive forces by co-ordinating them without waving its political banner. Front organizations with non-communist names (such as the CNE) were given non-communist presidents as figureheads but were kept under careful control, while the youth organization, Jeunesses communistes, was dissolved in 1945 to be replaced by the Union de la jeunesse républicaine de la France.[2] Intellectuals were at first easy prey because the Resistance had encouraged the feeling that the sword was mightier than the pen, and their appetite for action was still keen: private creativity could stay in abeyance till the writers had played their part in shaping the future of France.

Like other left-wingers inside and outside the Party, Sartre had no notion in 1945 of how envenomed the struggle for dominance was to become. What seemed important was that work should be done collectively: he was happy to invest time and energy in a monthly review that would involve him and de Beauvoir in collaborating with a group of friends to wield an influence that was simultaneously political and literary. An obvious space for the new review was created by the disappearance of the *Nouvelle Revue française*, which had continued during the Occupation and was therefore banned. One sign of Sartre's over-optimism about the possibility of editorial co-operation between politically opposed writers was his idea of inviting both Malraux and Camus to join his editorial committee; not wanting to work under his leadership, both refused.

Camus's refusal must have been disappointing for Sartre. Reading *La Peste* (*The Plague*), which was not yet published, he had concluded that 'the principal characteristics of French literature of the future can probably be discerned in the sombre and pure work of Camus'.[3] Dr Rieux was particularly appealing as a man fighting with severely limited resources against an irresistible natural force, a rebel against the vicious intractability of the natural world. He was modestly asserting the pre-eminence of the human spirit, said Sartre, while Camus, modestly, but more effectively than any other writer, was carrying the heroic spirit of the Resistance into post-war literature. 'It is this belief in action which is austere, modest and useful that distinguishes the generation of Camus from the generation of Malraux.'[4]

When the editorial committee was formed in September, political standpoints were hardly less heterogeneous than they would have been if Malraux and Camus had accepted the invitations. Those who joined Sartre were de Beauvoir, Leiris, Merleau-Ponty, Jean Paulhan, Camus's associate Albert Ollivier and Raymond Aron. Paulhan had helped to found the clandestine *Lettres françaises*; Aron had come back after living since 1940 in London, where he had co-edited a review, *La France libre*, which had not found favour with the Gaullists. Briefly Sartre's friendship with Aron flickered back into life. Aron's daughter Dominique had the impression that he was her family's 'best friend', and it was taken for granted that she would go on holiday with de Beauvoir.[5]

Sartre, as he said, rose above his disgust only when he could 'rally support for a solid organization'; what he was trying to do with *Les Temps modernes* was what he had failed to do during the war with 'Socialisme et liberté', but it was no longer realistic to believe that strong anti-fascist feelings would be enough to unite those he wanted to fight under his new banner. In the discussions about a title, Leiris, still surrealistic in his inclinations, proposed *Grabuge* (*Squabble*) but they settled on the more neutral name *Les Temps modernes*, partly because of Chaplin's film, partly because it stressed the commitment to the present.

Almost a year was to elapse before the first issue appeared, though it had been under discussion since the middle of 1943. Paper was in short supply and Jacques Soustelle, the Minister of Information, who was in charge of allocating quotas, was not impressed by the editorial committee: hadn't Aron been an anti-Gaullist? Resigned to the prospect of a long delay, Sartre was not reluctant to absent himself from Paris when an opportunity arose to visit the USA. Wanting to publicize the American war effort in France, the Office of War Information in Washington arranged for a group of French journalists to be invited. 'I have never seen Sartre so elated', writes de Beauvoir, 'as the day Camus offered him the job of representing *Combat*.'[6] Here was his first chance to make contact with the culture that had produced jazz, Chaplin, Dos Passos and Hemingway. Afterwards it was arranged that he would also represent *Le Figaro*.

Hemingway was now in Paris, and it was through Nathalie Sorokine that Sartre met him. A blonde popular among GIs, she had formed a relationship with Hemingway's younger brother. When Ernest Hemingway came to Paris as a war correspondent, he stayed at the Ritz, and invited his brother, who suggested that Nathalie, Sartre and de Beauvoir should go along with him. They were shown into a big ugly bedroom with two brass bedsteads in it. On one of these was the large body of Hemingway, who was wearing pyjamas and a green eyeshade. He had influenza. On a table within reach was a collection of empty and half-empty whisky bottles. Hemingway levered himself up to clasp Sartre in a bear-hug. 'You're a general', he enthused. 'Me, I'm only a captain. You're a general.' The subsequent conversation was fuelled by a great deal of drinking. Sartre left, exhausted, at about three in the morning; de Beauvoir stayed till dawn.[7]

She was disappointed not to accompany him to the States and in *Les Mandarins* Flora knows what it means when Henri pretends to be sorry that she is not going with him to Portugal. Had he really wanted her to go with him, he could have arranged it, and he knows she knows he no longer loves her, though they still make love and still exchange loving declarations. She accommodates herself gladly to his needs. 'You wouldn't be yourself', she says, forgivingly, 'if you weren't wishing for new horizons, new nourishment ... It's enough for me to be necessary to you.' She knows that this eager subordination of her needs to his is itself a source of irritation to him, but there is nothing she can do. What de Beauvoir could do was keep her unhappiness under control by using it in her fiction.[8]

It was a cold December, in which physical discomfort was exacerbated for both of them by his anxiety about whether he could get the papers he needed for the American trip. In the middle of the month the Germans began their offensive in the Ardennes, and Sartre was worrying about Bost, who was at the front. By Christmas Eve the attack had been halted, but it was hard to feel festive. Sartre and de Beauvoir spent New Year's Eve with Camus, who was living with Francine in Gide's flat on the rue Vaneau. Pointing to one of the least talkative guests, Camus said he was the model for Meursault in *L'Etranger*. According to Herbert Lottman, this was most likely Pierre Galindo, a phlegmatic, heavy-set, tough-looking man who had probably been in a fight with Arabs on a beach and had befriended Camus in Algiers.[9]

On 12 January 1945 when Sartre and seven other journalists left for America on a military plane, he was flying for the first time. It was midnight when they arrived at La Guardia airport, and no-one was there to meet them or to warn the customs men not to be rude.[10] Eventually he was driven to the Plaza Hotel.[11] The next day, a Sunday, he wandered through the streets of New York, trying to discover the character of the unfamiliar city, but it seemed to have no character. 'What I was looking for, no doubt, was a European city.'[12] He had been expecting boulevards with cafés like the Flore. Skyscrapers had once seemed to symbolize America's fabulous wealth, and to represent the architecture of the future,[13] but they looked bewilderingly unlike buildings for people to live in,[14] while 'the numerical anonymity of the streets and avenues' made him feel there was no reason to be in one place rather than another.[15]

Though his lumber-jacket caused some embarrassment to his hosts,[16] his first despatch, cabled on 22 January to *Le Figaro*, described the warmth of his reception. Feeling little gratitude to Camus, Sartre had no scruples about sending all the best articles to *Le Figaro* and only the second best to *Combat*. He went on, deliberately undiplomatic, to report conflicts between French supporters of Pétain and de Gaulle in America, alleging that money had been provided either by the State Department or by tycoons for a newspaper that had harmed the interests of France. On 25 January the *New York Times* published a despatch from its Paris correspondent, accusing him of wanting to undermine Franco-American friendship, and six days later it published a letter attacking him and naming the paper as *Pour la Victoire*. He replied in the issue of 1 February, accusing the Paris correspondent of plucking quotations out of context.[17] This was not the kind of publicity the Office of War Information had wanted, and for a while it seemed that Sartre might be sent ignominiously back to France,[18] but the scandal was soon forgotten.

The French journalists were flown from one big city to another, guided around factories, supplied with statistics, taken to look at bridges, buildings, dams. 'We'll have seen more steel and aluminium', Sartre complained, 'than human beings.'[19] In New York he found Stépha and Fernando Gérassi, who introduced him to the sculptor Alexander Calder. Among the French refugees he met were André Masson, Fernand Léger, Yves Tanguy, Claude Lévi-Strauss and the former leader of the surrealist movement, André Breton. In Hollywood Sartre found Henriette Nizan, who was earning her living by writing sub-titles for French films. She told him about the PCF's campaign of vilification against her dead husband. In the South Sartre discovered that ninety per cent of the coloured population still had no vote.

Soon he was involved in a relationship that became surprisingly important. Dolorès Vanetti had worked as an actress in Paris. She was intense, vivacious, clever, with a striking resemblance to de Beauvoir. She had been working for the Office of War Information since it started broadcasting in French, and when the eight journalists arrived for a series of interviews, Sartre was the last in the line as they filed into the recording studio. He stumbled against something, accidentally or deliberately dropped his pipe and got into conversation with her as he picked it up. Constantly amazed at how lively and entertaining he was when he concentrated his entire, formidable energy on pleasing her, she became his guide to New York, translating newspaper articles for him, pointing out famous faces – Stravinsky, Garbo – in the Russian Tea Room.[20] Later he would say that she had 'given America' to him.

Writing to de Beauvoir at the beginning of the forties he had promised not to have any more casual affairs for a long time after the war. The war was not yet over, but he was deeply involved in an amour that would jeopardize his relationship with her more seriously than his love for either of the Kosakiewicz sisters had. However badly hurt de Beauvoir had been by his offer to marry Wanda, it had made little if any difference to their subsequent intimacy. He still wanted to talk or write to de Beauvoir about more or less everything that happened, still confided in her about his feelings towards other women. But Dolorès was a more formidable challenger, and though the proprietorial challenge was ultimately to be defeated, the affair was a turning point in the relationship with de Beauvoir. Without fully honouring their pact, he had usually respected it; it was now that he stopped giving her even a literary participation in his emotional life, and his dependence on her would never be the same. From now on letters to her would be shorter, more infrequent and less informative.

On 10 March President Roosevelt received the French journalists. 'What is immediately striking', Sartre wrote, 'is the deeply human charm of this long face, at once delicate and hard, the eyes gleaming with intelligence. A kind of generous warmth is apparent: something open and communicative, which assorts curiously with the slightly ferocious sharpness of the jaw.'[21] Five weeks later the President died at the age of sixty-three. He was succeeded by Harry Truman.

Sartre was not accustomed to cities in which the streets are not primarily places for walking, and sometimes he felt like a parcel being collected and delivered.[22] One reason for the anti-Americanism he developed was that he witnessed the pressure put on Americans to conform before he witnessed the pressure put on Russians. Education, both in colleges and extramurally, struck him as being directed at teaching Americans how to be more American,[23] and New York looked like 'the most conformist city in the world'.[24]

Sartre was to stay in the States for about four months.

Only nine days after he had left France, his step-father had died, at the age of seventy, but, not wanting her son to sacrifice his opportunity of seeing America, the widow had not told him the news. She was now sixty-three. In the summer Sartre took her on holiday with him in the country. By then the Allies were in control of Germany, which had been divided into four zones, and during the second half of July, Stalin, Truman and Churchill were demanding the unconditional surrender of Japan. But the peace began to turn sour before it had even begun. On 6 August an atomic bomb was dropped on Hiroshima and, three days later, another on Nagasaki.

Before the second slaughter Sartre had rejoined de Beauvoir to spend a month at La Pouèze, where, overcoming his outrage, he settled down to work on his play *Les Vainqueurs* (*The Victors*), later retitled *Morts sans sépulture* (which is translated as *Men without Shadows*). Though his plays did more than any of his other writings to win him success, fame and money, he never invested as much emotional energy in them as in his philosophy or his novels. A major motive was to provide roles for the women who were emotionally and financially dependent on him. *Les Vainqueurs* gave Wanda her first big opportunity as an actress: she established herself professionally under the name Marie-Olivier.

In his essay on occupied Paris he had equated the limits of individual freedom with powers of resistance to torture and death; in the play he shows men and one woman defining themselves in terms of their ability to resist pressure. The torturers and the victims are all French. The situation is straightforward and potentially melodramatic: Vichy militia are trying to extract from freedom fighters information about the whereabouts of their leader, Jean. He turns up during the action in the school attic which is being used as a prison, but his captors are still ignorant of his identity. The woman, Lucie, is his lover, and the youngest of the freedom fighters, François, is her 15-year-old brother. The boy is so likely to crack under torture, betraying Jean and other comrades, that she consents when the others decide to strangle him, while one of the older men, Sorbier, commits suicide because he does not trust himself to keep silent under torture. Lucie is raped by her captors, the others are not only tortured but humiliated, demoralized, crippled by guilt feelings. Sartre shows how the militiamen are motivated less by the wish to extract information than by the need to humiliate the patriots, depriving them of their right to feel superior. Later, in *Qu'est-ce que c'est que la littérature?* Sartre will describe explicitly the quasi-sexual intimacy in which the torturer is symbolically gratifying his hatred of all mankind, while the victim, by pushing himself to his limits, comes to terms both with his torturer and with his self-hatred. Torture is communion in which two freedoms meet in the destruction of the human.[25]

Sartre's continuing preoccupation with torture depends partly on his understanding that, in forcing himself to work the way he did, he was both torturer and victim. He was coming to terms with his self-hatred by pushing himself to his limits. Left with little interest in living, the freedom fighters in the play are not yet free to die. Not only are they physically imprisoned, they are imprisoned by their own liberty, which forces them to go on taking decisions. In a sense they are, as the title suggests, already dead. They have no chance of escaping or of being released, but so long as there is life in them, they have to go on using their freedom.

After spending a month at La Pouèze, Sartre and de Beauvoir could enjoy their first postwar summer holiday: they visited Bruges, Antwerp and Ghent. They did not know that in returning to Paris they would be returning to fame, but the fashion for existentialism surged up suddenly. Sartre's article 'A propos de l'existentialisme: Mise au point' had been published in *Action* on 29 December 1944, and in the issue dated 8 June 1945 he had been attacked by the Marxist sociologist Henri Lefebvre, who condemned him as an idealistic subjectivist manufacturer of weapons against communism. Sartre did not want to be associated with a body of ideas that would seem like an alternative to Marxism. In his 'Mise au point' he had written: 'Class struggle is a fact: I accept it unreservedly', and after Lefebvre's article appeared, he tried to repudiate existentialism. At a colloquium organized by the publishers Editions du Cerf – a firm controlled by the Dominicans – Gabriel Marcel described him as an existentialist, but Sartre retorted: 'My philosophy is a philosophy of existence; existentialism – I don't know what it is.'[1]

In the early autumn he stopped trying to reject the label. In September, *L'Age de raison* and *Le Sursis* made their long-delayed appearance. Though the earlier novel reached back to the beginning of the war, it belonged, so far as the public was concerned, to the latest phase of Sartre's existentialism, which seemed to offer a possibility of moral and cultural rehabilitation.

Together with the material damage inflicted on France by the German occupation, the Allied bombing, the fighting and sabotage as Hitler's armies retreated, the people had suffered a profound loss of self-confidence. For more than four years they had been divided, but not cleanly into two halves; between the Resistance fighters at one extreme and the collaborators – uniformed and un-uniformed – at the other, there had been a wide spectrum of attitudes. Everyone had made compromises, sometimes by remaining passive – failing to help Jews or failing to stop a neighbour from denouncing a Resistance network. Everyone had taken risks, but criteria were quantitative – how much risk, how much to be gained? For the unstable majority it had been impossible even to hope wholeheartedly and consistently. When a German victory seemed inevitable, many wanted it to come quickly; once it became obvious that Germany was going to be defeated, people started to destroy evidence of their co-operation with the nazi authorities. The same people were demonstrative in celebrating the victory of the Allies.

The one commodity in plentiful supply when the war ended was guilt feelings. Hungry, cold, impoverished, disoriented, people were uneasy about the past, apprehensive about the future. Cultural and educational continuities had been broken by the book-burning nazis with their rabid anti-semitism and their bigotry about decadence. It was obvious that in France pre-war values would never be reinstated in their old form, and morale would have to be boosted before the people could be rallied into the task of clearing away debris and reconstructing. Of all the French intellectuals the diminutive Sartre might superficially have looked least like the one capable of becoming a leader, but in fact he was well equipped for the role. Nothing could have qualified him for it better than the private disposition which had generated his ideas. What people wanted to believe was that they could afford to forget the past and make a fresh start. Sartre had been inclined all his life to disregard the past and let the present take its tinge from his appetite for the future. In *Les Mouches* he had already hit out against the pessimistic Pétainist view that the defeat of France had been divine retribution for moral degeneracy. Sartrean existentialism mingled optimism with responsibility: each of us chooses the historical context in which he lives. If this idea had been formulated cynically to secure a maximum of popularity for Sartre, it could not have been more effective. What he was offering the French people was a chance to accept a share of the blame for the immediate past at the same time as affirming their willingness to take charge of the immediate future. They must commit themselves morally and politically. Those who had not taken part in the Resistance could feel solidarity with those who had; those who could not believe in God could believe, religiously, in man. The Occupation had shown that morality and politics could not be kept apart; Sartre was a political moralist with no allegiance to any party or any church. He would force his followers to be free.

His popularity is partly explained by de Beauvoir's description in *Les Mandarins* of the impact Robert makes as a public speaker.

Behind the words he spoke, this friendship he offered us was a certainty: men are not condemned to hatred, to warfare ... Day after day I saw him bent over his desk, eyes bloodshot, back hunched, alone and doubting himself: it was this same man five thousand people were applauding. What exactly was he to them? At once a great writer and the man of the vigilance committees and the anti-fascist meetings; an intellectual committed to the revolution without denying his nature as an intellectual ... he did not offer a programme, he gave us tasks. And they were so urgent we couldn't fail to perform them: victory was assured by its very necessity.[2]

Sartre was neither unaware of his power over audiences nor unexcited by it. Reality was at last confirming both his childhood fantasies and the semi-adolescent fantasies of impassioned conversations with de Beauvoir about their future as cultural reformers. If Sartre was capable of being a leader, a shaper of public opinion, a shaper of France's future, he must stop thinking of himself as just a writer. A review would provide a channel of communication through which influence could be exerted, and in sharing editorial decisions with colleagues he would be sharing his thinking. If consciousness and the self were not identical, why shouldn't experiments be made in non-individual thinking? The symbiotic relationship with de Beauvoir had succeeded, at least partially, in breaking down barriers of privacy. Only intellectual intimacy would be involved in exchanging editorial ideas with a committee but, unlike writing a book, editing *Les Temps modernes* would depend on collective thinking. Or so it seemed.

But it was hard to think clearly in the euphoria induced by sudden fame. De Beauvoir too was floated into prominence. *L'Invitée*, her novel about the triangular relationship with Olga, had been accepted by Gallimard in the summer of 1942 and published in the spring of 1943. Her second, *Le Sang des autres* (*The Blood of Others*), a story about the Resistance, came out in September 1945, just before Sartre's two novels. But it was the huge vogue for existentialism that made her famous as her name and her face kept appearing alongside Sartre's in the newspapers. Publicity established them as a couple and it made no difference when the first issue of *Les Temps modernes* appeared with Sartre's 'Présentation' dedicated to Dolorès.

Written with formidable evangelistic cogency, it made the case for *la littérature engagée*. If the Commune of 1871 had been followed by repression, Flaubert and the Goncourts were to blame 'because they did not write one line to prevent it'.[3] But 'we' – and the word invited his readers to feel at one with him – will take responsibility for the future: 'we make it ours, we want no other future'.[4] Looking back critically at his childhood ambitions, he condemned the authors who wooed posterity; his concerns would be with the present and the immediate future: 'it is our task as a writer to expose the eternal values implicit in these social or political debates ... What is absolute, what a thousand years of history cannot destroy, is *this* irreplaceable, incomparable decision which [a man] takes at this moment about these circumstances. To sum up, our intention is to unite and to produce certain changes in the society that surrounds us.'[5]

The jibes at Proust are cheap and unfair: 'A pederast, Proust thought he could use his homosexual experience to describe Swann's love for Odette; a bourgeois, he presents this feeling of a rich, idle bourgeois for a kept woman as the prototype of love.' Proust is denounced as an 'intellectualist' and an 'accomplice of bourgeois propaganda' who had helped to spread 'the myth of human nature'. Sartre's target was the fallacy that emotions can be independent of their social context, and in his polemical excitement he did not care if he coarsened subtler arguments he had advanced in calmer moments, or if he made pronouncements his editorial colleagues would not have backed. His anti-literary extremism was at odds with the appointment of René Etiemble as the review's literary critic, but after starting his monthly articles for *Les Temps modernes* in October 1946 Etiemble continued them until 1952. He was a serious littérateur who only later became famous as the author of *Parlez-vous Franglais?*

Sartre in his opening manifesto promised that the new review would not serve any of the political parties, though it would take up a position in relation to political and social events, helping literature to recover its social function. In another article, 'La Fin de la guerre' ('The End of the War') Sartre again invited the reader to join in taking responsibility for the future: the atomic bomb, by giving humanity the chance to exterminate itself, has brought us new freedom and new responsibility. Each day we will have to decide that we want to survive.[6] The issue contained an article by an ex-pupil who had joined the PCF, Jean Kanapa, and one by Jean Pouillon, who sneered at the reforms that could be effected constitutionally; he condemned 'revolution by law' as an attempt 'to prolong what it pretends to abolish'. It was clear that the review was committed to the ideal of democracy; it was not clear how its relationship with communism would develop.

On 24 October Sartre lectured on existentialism in Brussels, and, four days later, speaking to the Club Maintenant in Paris, he took as his title 'L'Existentialisme est-il un humanisme?' Women fainted – partly, perhaps because of oxygen shortage in the overcrowded room – and he could scarcely make himself heard. In the lecture he described T.E. Lawrence as an existentialist, but this passage is suppressed in the published text, which, dropping the interrogative, he called 'L'Existentialisme est un humanisme'.[7] The next day, interviewed for the magazine *Paru*, he claimed to want no disciples,[8] but in the coming months he would be fêted, quoted, emulated, discussed, attacked. The short-lived weekly *Terre des hommes* published a response by Gide to the 'Présentation' in *Les Temps modernes*. Other prominent intellectuals joined in the controversy: Gabriel Marcel condemned Sartre's existentialism as negative;[9] the Christian essayist Pierre Emmanuel denounced it as 'une maladie de l'esprit'. Many communists attacked it. Henri Lefebvre called it 'a phenomenon of rottenness altogether in line with the decomposition of bourgeois culture', but Francis Ponge was ready to pay tribute to a philosophy which has not yet expressed a morality. In the streets Sartre was endlessly photographed, endlessly followed, endlessly accosted by strangers. When he walked into a café, people would welcome him, wave, shout.[10] Communists attacked him for keeping young people away from Marxism; gossip columnists denounced him for preaching despair.

Camus battled to stop himself from being bracketed with the existentialists, while Sartre dissociated himself from Camus's 'philosophy of the absurd': what Camus meant by absurdity was the disjunction between man's reasonable expectations and the irrationality of the world, whereas Sartre, when he spoke of the absurd, meant contingency.[11]

The vogue for existentialism promoted *Les Temps modernes*. Though the review may have been read only superficially by most of the existentialists who bought it, it went on ticking loudly as the politico-literary conscience of the new movement; it was also a public dressing-room in which Sartre could be seen struggling to adjust his priorities. At editorial meetings the discussion ranged freely, like a conversation, over heterogeneous subjects, and his main function was to pick out which ones ought to be treated in the review.[12] He left others to sift articles submitted and do routine editorial work, but his decisions shaped the contents, while the review was to exert a strong influence – not always an obvious one – on his decisions about how to divide his time. What should his priorities be? His philosophy was pulled away from ontology and psychology towards sociology and what he began to call anthropology. Though he denied there was any such thing as 'human nature', he often expressed belief in the possibility of defining 'the essence of man', while his interest in politics had been gaining ground steadily, but alongside the opportunity for collective thinking, the review offered him power he could never have exerted as a private individual. The objectives he stated in his 'Présentation' are ambitious: 'to change man's social condition and the conception he has of himself'.[13] Redefining and reshaping should be inseparable parts of the same process: the researcher was not so much a scientist as a catalyst; bourgeois analysts might posit the possibility of scientific detachment in research on human affairs, but the humane researcher got caught up in the chemistry. The anthropologist should not try to remain uninvolved in the society he was observing. Maintaining that while men have in common their 'metaphysical condition', they consist of 'irreducible totalities'. Sartre pledged that the new review would contribute 'to the constitution of a synthetic anthropology'.[14] The question he had not faced squarely was whether he wanted papal authority over the new anthropology or whether he was prepared to settle altruistically for a modest editorial role, holding the balance between philosophers, psychologists and trained anthropologists who could be commissioned to contribute essays.

Though Marcel Mauss, the author of *Essai sur le don*, had introduced the term 'social anthropology' in France during 1938,[15] 'ethnography' had been the word generally in use. At the Collège de France, where Mauss held a chair from 1931 to 1942, his subject was called Sociology. His 1925 book, *Essai sur le don*, which focused on systems of exchanging gifts in pre-industrial societies, was seminal: Lévi-Strauss, Sartre, Merleau-Ponty and Michel Leiris all came under its sway. For *Les Temps modernes* Leiris was a key figure. It was natural that he should be: he was not only closer to Sartre than Merleau-Ponty was, he was closer to anthropology than Sartre. His book, *L'Afrique fantôme*, had been based on a 1931 expedition led by Marcel Griaule, a professor at the Sorbonne, to French West Africa. Perched between anthropology and literature, Leiris's writing was exemplary and progressive. Dissociating himself from the patronizing ethnographers who tried to remain detached from the primitive societies they studied, Leiris insisted that there must be give and take between investigator and society. He also anticipated Lévi-Strauss's thesis that linguistic models can be employed in studying the unconscious processes behind the symbolic systems a society uses. Lévi-Strauss credits Leiris with initiating in his literary work the study of unconscious structuring in vocabulary; but linguistics was going to be kept out of the new review, although Merleau-Ponty lectured on Saussure at the Ecole Normale in 1948–9.[16] According to Lévi-Strauss linguistics was the key to positive knowledge of social facts, but Sartre never accepted this. Without naming Saussure in his *Esquisse pour une theorie des émotions* he had spoken of the 'signifier' and the 'signified', but he had little interest in the study of language, and he was not open to influence from Merleau-Ponty on this subject, though politically Sartre accepted him as mentor.

Merleau-Ponty's political influence was soon to drag Sartre away from his promise of non-alignment. In the fourth issue (January 1946) Merleau-Ponty proclaimed that their intention was to 'rediscover Marxism on the road of contemporary truth and in the analysis of our times'. 'In short', he wrote, 'we must carry out the policy of the Communist Party.'[17] Not yet trusting his own political judgment, Sartre uncritically accepted Merleau-Ponty's. 'He showed me what my own thoughts were.' The two men were vastly different – by temperament Merleau-Ponty was more withdrawn, more academic. They never became friendly, seldom ate meals together, though Merleau-Ponty relayed to the readers of *Les Temps modernes* ideas which were taken to be Sartre's. Articles which were signed T.M. were written by Merleau-Ponty. He always wanted Sartre to read them before they were published, but Sartre gave his approval in advance,[18] under pretext of involving both himself and the readers in thinking that was done more collectively than individually. The journalist, he would write later, 'does not create thoughts in his readers – this might disunite them – he *uncovers* their thoughts for them: but not the thought of each one in each one – the thought of all in each one'.[19] Sartre was trusting Merleau-Ponty to uncover the thought of all in him. The ideal is transparent collectivity: the barriers of individuality are to be knocked aside.

All this is unrealistic but the euphoria helped Sartre to achieve one of his greatest successes: he popularized the concept of *la littérature engagée.* The phrase did not catch on in England until the middle fifties, but in France there were many who shared Sartre's quasi-nostalgic attitude to the Occupation, when the one luxury generally available had been the simplicity of political decisions. Writing in clandestine papers at the risk of his life, the writer had been in a comparable position to that of Osip Mandelstam and Anna Akhmatova in Russia after the revolution, or as dissident writers in communist countries today. Commitment is automatic when the writer is risking his life or his liberty. To Sartre French and English literature of 1918–39 seemed inflationary: words had been thrown around like paper money unbacked by hard currency.[20] The writer should be fully immersed in each statement he made; writing was an action that could have and should have practical consequences.

He believed in the power of *Les Temps modernes* to alter the *Zeitgeist* by reflecting it. 'An anecdote reflects an entire era as much as the contents of a political constitution. We would track down meaning, we would tell the truth about the world and our own lives.'[21] It was easier to campaign idealistically for consensus among 'us' than to preserve harmony among the editorial committee, but the review's success was assured: it had become fashionable, and no sooner had the third issue arrived in the bookshops than, confidently, he absented himself from Paris for four months.

To get himself invited back to America he had been in touch with universities there. He was missing Dolorès. On 12 December he embarked on a Liberty ship, a military cargo boat which would take eighteen days to cross the ocean. Under the aegis of the Rélations culturelles françaises, he made star appearances at Harvard, Princeton, Yale, New York and in Canada. During the first half of 1946 he lectured a lot on the situation of French literature, but did surprisingly little writing, except for a screenplay which was nourished by his antipathy to the United States. It approximates in several ways to an apologia for Stalinism – he even drags concentration camps into the plot, though the action is set in a small country based partly on Cuba. Its capitalist neighbour, by threatening invasion, makes it impossible for the revolutionary leader to nationalize the oil industry. Sartre's original title for the screenplay was *Les Mains sales* (*Dirty Hands*), the title he used later for a play on the same theme. The 1946 screenplay pivots on the friendship between two members of the central committee: Lucien is an almost saintly journalist, who refuses to have any traffic with violence, while Jean, after leading the revolution, shoulders responsibility for governing the country. Once it had looked as though Lucien could act as Jean's conscience, restraining him from violence, but Lucien dies in one of Jean's concentration camps. Sartre's point is that violence cannot be dismissed as unnecessary. In one sense Lucien is a parasite. In an almost credible showdown Jean tells him: 'Yes, I've got blood on my hands. But I saved you from having it on yours ... You think I wouldn't have preferred to keep mine clean?' Jean is not just a tyrant: genuine love of the people makes him detest poverty even more than the violence he uses to get rid of it, but as he grows to detest himself, he falls back on heavy drinking. Sartre eventually settled on the title *L'Engrenage* (*In the Mesh*) – an allusion to the trap that catches not only Jean but the new revolutionary leader who condemns him to death and starts simultaneously on the slide that will tumble him into the same oppressive violence.

Since 1938 Sartre had never let so much time go by with so little literary activity. During January he described his daily routine in a letter. He would rise at nine, linger over his toilet and breakfast till eleven, lunch with Dolorès or with admirers, wander till six in the streets of New York, 'which I now know as well as Paris', meet Dolorès again, and drink with her in a bar till two in the morning. From Friday afternoon till Sunday afternoon he would stay inside her flat to avoid being seen by the porters: she had not yet entirely separated from her husband. Sartre was short of money, spending at least a day on writing each lecture, which brought in only $50, while he was at first earning nothing from journalism.[22] But he was soon to receive an advance of 300,000 francs on the Broadway production of *Huis clos*.

He had intended to return by boat, leaving at the end of February, but he was offered some lucrative lectures in Toronto, Ottawa and Montreal during the second week of March, and he did not want to leave Dolorès. He had never departed so far from his working routine for the sake of Toulouse, de Beauvoir, Olga or Wanda, and by February he was describing Dolorès as the woman he knew best after de Beauvoir. Though timid, she was capable of becoming so passionate that it scared him, 'but when she's happy, she can be as open and innocent as a child'.[23] When Columbia University offered him a job, he told her he wanted to marry her and to stay there for two years. Even if she had been free to marry, she would have been sceptical about whether it would be wise for him to settle there for so long without intending to learn the language.[24] They compromised by agreeing to spend two or three months together each year. He stayed until April, giving a course of lectures on existentialism in Switzerland during late May and early June, and leaving Paris again, later in the month, to lecture in Italy. After returning to Paris in April, he told de Beauvoir that Dolorès was deeply in harmony with him. When they went out together they always had the same instincts, he said, about when to stop, when to go on. Disconcerted, de Beauvoir asked explicitly whether Dolorès was more important to him than she was. His answer was non-committal: 'She's enormously important to me, but you're the one I'm with.'[25]

He had missed some dramatic political developments. In January 1946, when de Gaulle had resigned as the head of the provisional government, a coalition was formed, and a decision had to be taken about the constitution. In the elections held in October 1945 for a Constituent Assembly, the Communist Party and the SFIO had won an overall majority, and, unlike the christian socialists of the MRP (Mouvement républicain populaire), they favoured a single-chamber system. A second chamber might act as a curb on radical legislation. It was decided to hold a referendum.

While posters were going up on the hoardings, exhorting voters to say 'Yes' or 'No' – de Gaulle emerged from retirement to recommend a 'No' vote, while the communists campaigned vigorously for a 'Yes' – Sartre succumbed to mumps. The doctor painted his face and neck with a black ointment, and soon he was well enough to receive visitors in bed; his room was always full of people willing to risk infection. Wearing a pointed nightcap over the helmet of bandages on his swollen face, he looked bizarre; by the beginning of May he could discard these, but the face was still swollen, with a pimple on the nose. Sartre had no desire to vote: what mattered, according to him, was to know which side one supported: it would be best to vote communist and to vote 'No'. In Les Temps modernes, Aron and Ollivier had both written articles in favour of voting 'No': this caused a furore at Combat, where most journalists were voting 'Yes'.[26]

In May Sartre took de Beauvoir with him on the Swiss lecture tour, which was organized by the publisher Skira. Articles about atheist existentialism proliferated in Swiss newspapers and magazines, many of them attacking Sartre as a corrupting influence, an apostle of conscienceless freedom. In Geneva he had an audience of over a thousand. He went on to Zürich, where Huis clos was being staged.

In Lausanne, after lecturing in a large, packed cinema, he was taken by the organizers to drink in a bar, where the man who sat down next to him was a young Austrian historian, André Gorz, who had read all his books. Fascinated by the 'novelty and complexity of his thought',[27] Gorz had adopted his terminology and had formed the impression that Sartre had an answer to every possible question. But in the bar, brushing cigarette ash off his waistcoat or spilling wine on someone else's sleeve, the diminutive philosopher seemed more human than any of his surrounding admirers. An air of generosity was suggested by the expansiveness of his gestures. 'Cigarette in hand, he raised his whole arm to the shoulder, so that to approach him was to risk a blow from his elbow.'[28] He seemed to have a huge appetite for living and a horror of abstract ideas; his philosophy corresponded to a strong personal need.

Sartre and de Beauvoir frequently had meals with the sculptor Giacometti and his wife Annette. He talked, often obscurely, about his progress from his first thick statue to his later attenuated figures, and he talked, more entertainingly, about women, especially when Annette was not with him. He would describe his adventures in brothels, looking for women who were slightly ungainly, slightly ugly.[29] One evening, drinking in a small group on the terrace of la Pergola, Giacometti, after staring admiringly at Sartre for some time, brought the conversation to an astonished silence by saying: 'Sartre, you're beautiful.'

With a friendly laugh Sartre answered: 'I think there are quite a few things you can say about me but that I'm beautiful – sincerely – I don't think so.'

Giacometti insisted: 'You're beautiful.'

'Okay, fine. I'm beautiful.'

'You're like Hamlet. Yes. You always think Hamlet was a tall, thin guy, and so on, eh? No, me, I'm sure he was a little fellow who drank beer, eh? A fat little man with hair like yours and eyes like yours. Very beautiful.'[30]

In Paris, during June, Sartre met another young man, Jean Cau, who had written to him earlier, asking for help in finding a job. Sartre now decided to offer him one – as his secretary. At first there was little for Cau to do except fend off admirers, but it was not yet clear whether Sartre's workload would increase after the dissolution of the editorial committee at *Les Temps modernes*. Aron and Ollivier had resigned in June 1946, and nearly eight years were to elapse before a new editorial committee was named on the cover. At first Sartre's name appeared there alone as editor: Merleau-Ponty, who in practice was not only political editor but *gérant* or editor-in-chief, stolidly refused to accept any front-page credit. With him at the helm politics was certain to be given prominence, but Sartre did not try to bring the literary policy into line. He was content for Leiris to be poetry editor and for René Etiemble to have freedom of expression, though his literary values were anything but Sartrean. The literature that appeared in *Les Temps modernes* during its first six years was oddly heterogeneous – poetry by Beckett, Char, Ponge, Queneau and several black poets, including Aimé Césaire, prose by Kafka, Faulkner, Ignazio Silone, Michel de Ghelderode, Nathalie Sarraute, Maurice Blanchot, Jean Genet, Leiris, Violette Leduc, Marguerite Duras, Boris Vian, Robert Merle and Nelson Algren. Sartre was palpably undecided about both literary values and the value of literature. During the next twelve months, when he wrote *Qu'est-ce que c'est que la littérature?* partly to make his mind up, he still let the literary pages of the review float free from the conclusions he reached.

Lecturing in Italy, he found it was possible to make a better relationship with the Italian communists than with the French: in Milan the self-educated novelist Elio Vittorini was friendly – he was editor of *Il Politecnico*, which had published a translation of Sartre's 'Présentation' – but Sartre's Italian publisher, Bompiani, who belonged to the extreme right, found his author's speech-making so embarrassing that he reneged on the agreement. Vittorini arranged a meeting with Arnoldo Mondadori, who was glad to take Sartre over, and arranged for him to stay with de Beauvoir at luxurious hotels in Venice and in Rome. There they made friends with Silone and Carlo Levi, who had written *Cristo si è fermato a Eboli* (*Christ Stopped at Eboli*).

Returning to Paris Sartre had finally to confront the problem he had sidestepped by absenting himself in America and Italy. His political navigator, Merleau-Ponty, was using a map drawn according to principles that contradicted those of *L'Etre et le Néant*. Since writing it, Sartre had edged towards envisaging a society without masters or slaves: instead of exploiting each other, men would unite to exploit the natural world. But he could give up neither his faith in freedom nor his belief that consciousness had no material foundation. He therefore baulked at Stalin's *Dialectical and Historical Materialism* – still, apparently, his main source. He quotes from it three times in 'Matérialisme et révolution', while the references to Marx appear mainly in the footnotes, which were not added until 1949, but it was already apparent in 1946 that he was more in sympathy with what Marx wrote before he came under the influence of Engels, who maintained that nature proceeded dialectically. The idea was anathema to Sartre: if a determining pattern was built ineluctably into the processes of nature and history, and if all the activities of consciousness were conditioned by social and economic circumstances, men were not free.

Sartre regarded dialectical materialism as a mythology: it was understandable that communists should be nervous of a philosophy founded on human freedom. Their need was for discipline, and to insist that man was already free was to imply that revolution was unnecessary. Nevertheless, Sartre argued, his own philosophy, centring as it did on action, was more suitable for revolutionaries. Action was resistance against the stubborn impenetrability of the universe; the revolutionary act was the free act *par excellence.* A new ideology would protect the communists from the danger that the myth of materialism would suffocate the revolutionary project. He was thinking of his own future philosophical projects when he prescribed what the 'business of the philosopher' should be – 'to make the truths contained in materialism hold together and to construct, gradually, a philosophy which suits the needs of the revolution as closely as the myth does'.[31] After the publication of 'Matérialisme et révolution' in the June and July issues of the review, his relations with the Communist Party deteriorated still further.

The wartime arrangements about dividing his leave between de Beauvoir and Wanda had heralded a pattern of scheduled promiscuity. In December 1945 he had started an affair with Boris Vian's wife Michelle, who had long silky blonde hair and a happy smile. She was vivacious, warm, open, and behind the effervescent enthusiasm was a deep knowledge of books and music. Her taste in both was more catholic than Sartre's, and she loved poetry. The affair was kept secret, and when Sartre was away from Paris he wrote to her care of Cau, who handed the letters to her. Sartre now had at least three other women, Dolorès, the tolerant de Beauvoir and the jealous Wanda,[32] but with Dolorès on the far side of the Atlantic he could divide most of his leisure and holidays between Michelle and the other two.

In his summer writing he expressed his feelings about racism in America. A new play was needed to make up a double bill with *Morts sans sépulture*, which was going to be revived during the autumn at the Théâtre Antoine. Skilfully and rapidly Sartre constructed *La Putain respectueuse* (*The Respectful Prostitute*), a play in two scenes, set in the American South, and based on a well-known Alabama case, the Scottsboro Case of 1931. In the play a well-meaning prostitute agrees to give false evidence against an innocuous black in order to protect a well-born white who has drunkenly shot another black. The girl, Lizzie, is unable to resist the rhetoric of a distinguished-looking senator, the boy's uncle, who convinces her that his nephew's life is worth more to America than that of the black. In the climactic scene Lizzie, who has a revolver, tries to take vengeance on Fred, the senator's son, who, after sleeping with her, has tried, insultingly, to bully her into saving his cousin's life, and, no less insultingly, blames her for the lust he felt while, as a member of a lynch mob, he shot another innocent black. The characters are all stereotypes, and to any Americans in the audience it would be as obvious as it was to the *New Yorker's* correspondent, Janet Flanner, that Sartre had not met many authentic Southern-gentleman lynchers during his tours of America.[33] But when Lizzie, unable to shoot Fred, accepts his offer to set her up as his mistress, the audience is trapped into wanting an act of violence which the play withholds.

* * *

Ignoring the recommendations of the communist and socialist majority, the voters rejected its constitution, but in the elections of 10 November, the communists won 186 seats, the MRP 166 and the socialists 103, which caused a political deadlock. Camus's position was still a long way from de Gaulle's, while Merleau-Ponty, who had earlier been troubled by the pre-war Moscow trials, was provoked into defending them. In answer to Arthur Koestler's book *The Yogi and the Commissar*, Merleau-Ponty started in October 1946 on a series of articles, 'Le Yogi et le prolétarien' ('The Yogi and the Proletarian'), arguing – more or less as Sartre had in *L'Engrenage* – that politics was inevitably immoral: no regime was innocent of violence. The important question was whether communist violence could help to humanize humanity. Generally Merleau-Ponty tended to equate morality with bourgeois moralism; for Sartre, who felt no qualms in supporting him, the basic dichotomy was between ideas and actions. Traditional morality belonged to the cerebral world of his grandfather; to be effective, any political leader must deny himself the luxury of keeping his hands clean.

Sartre was now so secure in his intellectual and emotional independence that he could afford to share a home, once again, with his mother, and he seems to have taken the decision without any rigorous self-questioning about motivation. Was he trying, twenty-nine years later, to compensate himself for the defeat he had sustained when she became Mme Mancy? It was she who suggested they should live together again: she had sustained a loss almost as great as his when marriage put an end to their close relationship.

For five years, since escaping from the Stalag, he had been living in hotels and working in cafés, owning no furniture or ornaments; now he settled into the small flat she bought at 42 rue Bonaparte on the fourth floor with a view of the place St-Germain-des-Prés. The best room in the flat became his, but it had to serve as both study and bedroom: for sixteen years a narrow divan became his bed at night. The only other furniture was a leather armchair and two chairs. On the wall between the two windows he put a reproduction of Dürer's *Melancholia*, and facing the desk was a picture Fernand Léger had given him. Having accumulated no possessions while living in hotels, he now began to buy books from the shops in the rue Bonaparte and the rue Mazarine; he grew possessive about his Bibliothèque de la Pléiade classics. The shelves were soon thickly lined. From his window he could see the church and the Café des Deux Magots. Mme Mancy kept the drawing-room and a small bedroom for herself. Eugénie, the old housekeeper, slept in the bedroom at the back. Mme Mancy enjoyed saying 'this is my third marriage',[34] and she confused visitors by calling Sartre Poulou.[35] The flat changed the rhythm of his life: he was on the move less, and he would play the piano almost every evening before his final stint of writing.

When Jean Cau (who was never given a key to the flat) rang the bell in the morning, he would sometimes hear piano duets being played, but the music stopped and Mme Mancy withdrew to her room. Cau worked on a folding table which became the dining-table whenever Sartre and 'ma petite maman' had lunch together. Cau, who was never asked to do any research, answered the telephone, made out the cheques, ran errands, filtered demands on Sartre's time. Some of these were rejected by Cau, some were passed on to Sartre, who rejected most of them himself. 'I haven't got time to talk to that idiot.' 'I'm not going to let those fools bore my arse off.' 'Why should I waste time on that clot?'[36] The language was no more violent than the desperation to defend precious working time. In the 1953 play *Kean*, the actor's relationship with his secretary, Solomon, is closely modelled on Sartre's relationship with Cau.[37] The secretary's main functions are to protect the actor from unwanted visitors, including creditors, to restrain his financial fecklessness, discouraging him from acts of reckless generosity, to make practical suggestions about how to drum up credit for the needs of the moment, and, not least important, to be available as raisonneur and confidant when no-one else is around. Though less exhibitionistic than a star actor, Sartre disliked being alone, even when writing, and it was more fun to behave unreasonably in the presence of a secretarial stooge who reliably argued from a commonsensical standpoint.

Cau's daily stint of work for Sartre ended at lunchtime; in the afternoon de Beauvoir came to the flat and worked at the other table in the same room.[38] Because they were habituated to working in cafés, neither of them was much distracted by the other's presence.

At the end of October Sartre attended a meeting convened by Koestler at André Malraux's flat in Boulogne-Billancourt. Koestler's proposal was that since the French League for Human Rights was dominated by the communists, intellectuals should take the lead in creating a new organization. The chief spokesman for the project was Manès Sperber, a former emissary of the Comintern, who had defected during the trials. Camus supported the project, but Malraux was so sceptical and Sartre so hostile that the idea was dropped.

Sartre had first met Koestler on the Pont-Royal during October when the small, dark, intense, thick-haired, French-speaking Hungarian had come up to introduce himself. Later, at the flat in rue Bonaparte, Koestler told him: 'You're a better novelist than I am, but not such a good philosopher.'[39] Sartre nonetheless took to him and made a formal offer of friendship. It was Koestler who at first demurred, and they quarrelled during a drunken evening at Camus's flat when Sartre abused an American journalist as being an enemy of freedom and Koestler in turn denounced Sartre as an apologist for Stalin's terrorism. Koestler afterwards wrote an apologetic letter to Sartre who replied warmly and at great length.[40]

One evening Sartre, de Beauvoir, Camus, Francine, Koestler and his pretty English wife, Mamaine, had dinner together, went on to a little dance hall in the rue des Gravilliers and then to a nightclub, the Schéhérezade. Lugubriously maintaining that friendship was incompatible with differences of political opinion, Koestler accused Sartre and Camus of trying to compromise with the Soviets, but conceded that for Camus, as for him, friendship mattered more than politics. Although Sartre was due to lecture the next afternoon at the Sorbonne, they went on at four in the morning to a bistro in Les Halles, where they drank a great deal. Koestler threw a crust of bread which hit his wife in the eye. Sartre was sometimes giggling, sometimes weeping. De Beauvoir, in a state of drunken depression, suggested as they walked back across a bridge that they might just as well throw themselves into the Seine. After a couple of hours' sleep Sartre drugged himself with orthedrine to prepare his lecture, which was on the responsibility of the writer.[41] He spoke about violence, saying that in the modern world nothing could be done without it: what the writer must condemn was useless or excessive violence.[42]

A week later, when *Morts sans sépulture* and *La Putain respectueuse* opened at the Antoine, Sartre was giving subtler support to violence with a case-history which suggested that nothing else could clean off the racism that was corroding the American system of justice. Mainly because of a municipal councillor who was campaigning to have the play banned, its title was censored by the Métro authorities. On posters in underground stations it had to be announced as *La P. . . . . respectueuse*. But, at the first night, it was the torture sequences in *Morts sans sépulture* which caused a scandal. One woman stood up and shouted 'disgraceful'; in the stalls people even came to blows. Aron's wife, who had almost fainted, left in the interval, followed by her husband.[43] The torture scene was toned down: instead of having his nails pulled out on stage, Sorbier was merely beaten with truncheons.[44] Press reactions were generally unfavourable: Sartre was accused of writing Grand Guignol and of reviving old hatreds, but after a hundred performances the double bill was still playing to enthusiastic audiences.[45] The communists mostly supported *Morts sans sépulture*, but condemned *La Putain respectueuse* for showing a black man trembling with fear.[46]

Later on in the month de Beauvoir left for a lecture tour of Holland, where, after a week, Sartre joined her. Together they looked at paintings by Rembrandt and Vermeer. What moved Sartre most was a beautiful red-brick wall on one of the canvases. On the train to Utrecht he was still speculating about *why* it was so beautiful, and the experience led to the analysis of art he put forward in *Qu'est-ce que c'est que la littérature?* which he began to write a few weeks later,[47] taking a more favourable view of the aesthetic experience than he had in *L'Etre et le Néant.*

His own involvement was more complex than ever before. With his novel held in suspense, he was open to the influence of all the writing he was publishing in *Les Temps modernes*, literary, political, psychological, anthropological. In February and March 1946 the review had published extracts from Leiris's *Biffures* (*Crossings Out*), a volume in his autobiographical sequence. Leiris's interest in the exchange that occurs between writer and reader derived from Mauss's *Essai sur le don*; and Sartre, looking at Dutch paintings, became acutely aware that, like the reader, the viewer is making a collaborative contribution. Studying van Gogh's painting of a red path, you follow it further than the painter took it; in Dostoevsky's *Crime and Punishment* you have to create your own Raskolnikov. Through art, Sartre now suggests, it is possible to achieve a fusion of subjectivity and objectivity, a reconciliation between the Self and the Other. The goal of art is to recover the world as it is, but as if the willpower of the reader were bringing it into existence.

Qu'est-ce que c'est que la littérature? was prompted by Sartre's need to test how his thinking about literature was being affected by pressure from current events, from editorial experience, from his anthropological programme. His tendency was always to blur the question 'How much can we know about a man?' with 'How much can we know about man?' but the blurring took different forms. The activity of writing was, for Sartre, a natural movement towards answering both questions, but the activity had become different from what it was when, as a schoolteacher in Le Havre, he tried to redefine the quality of existence in *La Nausée*, or when as a soldier and then as a prisoner-of-war, he had almost unlimited leisure for making notes and for redrafting chapters. Now that he was so busy, what had emerged, alongside his devaluation of poetry, was an aversion to polished prose. Prose should be serviceable, lucid, workmanlike, but not crafted too painstakingly. Time should not be wasted on rewriting the same sentence to make it more beautiful. This principle was in conflict both with his early realization that truth could emerge from an arrangement of words and with his habit of making epigrams for all occasions. But he was always attracted to principles that went painfully against the grain. From now on his practice as a writer was inconsistent: the work he regarded as literary was constructed in a different way from the more hurried philosophical or political or journalistic work. For this he would often take drugs to accelerate the process of translating facts and ideas into written words; for the 'literary' work he would never drug himself, though he kept a thermos of strong tea on his desk and consumed about a litre each morning.[48]

The review provided an immediate outlet for anything he wrote, but contributing to it was not so much a matter of taking a fresh initiative as of answering criticism, modifying statements already made, responding to challenges that came in different forms and at different angles – from Merleau-Ponty, from communist attackers, from friends who were less radical. Quarrels exploded around him almost daily, sometimes arising from political differences, sometimes from aggressively boyish competitiveness. On one drunken evening Camus and Koestler agreed to race on all fours across the place St-Michel. Koestler arrived first on the far side but Camus accused him of cheating. In the fight that ensued Koestler gave Camus a black eye.[49]

In December, Sartre went with de Beauvoir to a party given by the Vians. Merleau-Ponty and Bost were among the guests. When Camus arrived he accused Merleau-Ponty of trying to justify the Moscow trials in 'Le Yogi et le prolétarien'. After Sartre joined in, supporting Merleau-Ponty, Camus walked out, slamming the door. Sartre and Bost pursued him into the street, but he refused to come back.[50]

Hanging over Sartre all this time was the shadow of his unfinished novel sequence. In America, during February 1946, he had been intending to complete it on his return to France,[51] but other demands on his time proved irresistible. The day after the party, he lectured on oppressed minorities in America. Before the end of the month he had joined the French League for a Free Palestine, an organization associated with Zionist terrorist groups. In *Qu'est-ce que c'est que la littérature?* he condemned British policy in Palestine and attacked Flaubert (who claimed to use the term *bourgeois* for 'anyone who thought basely') for failing to notice that the bourgeoisie was a class of oppressors. Flaubert's prose turned its back on reality, said Sartre, while the destructiveness of the surrealists was only the culmination of a negativism that had permeated literature since the eighteenth century. Not that Sartre, who had equated consciousness with nothingness, was hostile to negativity. What literature should be, he maintained, was a synthesis of negation and movement towards a future order. 'In short literature is essentially the subjectivity of a society in permanent revolution.'[52]

Qu'est-ce que c'est que la littérature? was to be published in *Les Temps modernes* between February and July 1947. He dedicated it to Dolorès, who was due to arrive in Paris during January, while de Beauvoir was giving a lecture tour in the United States. When she arrived there, she met Dolorès, who had not yet left, and was, de Beauvoir writes, no less charming than Sartre made her out to be. Before embarking, Dolorès wrote to declare her intention of trying to procure from him an invitation to settle in France. She knew Camus and, in March, managed to make peace between the two men. Sartre did not invite her to stay permanently, but at the beginning of May he asked de Beauvoir to stay on in the United States for an extra ten days because Dolorès was extending her stay in Paris; de Beauvoir spent the ten days with the novelist Nelson Algren, first in Chicago, then in New York. The affair has its counterpart in *Les Mandarins*.[53]

In the spring of 1947 General de Gaulle decisively re-entered French politics. When, twelve months earlier, his admirers had formed the Gaullist Union, he had ostentatiously had nothing to do with it, but on 7 April 1947, he called for the formation of a Rassemblement du peuple français. This was to be a party against parties, or, in effect, a union of non-communists. Though the RPF rapidly gained support, the PCF, which had won over many supporters from the socialist party, had not given up hope of taking control; but it found itself in difficulties as inflation led to agitation for wage increases, and to strikes, which it ambivalently supported although it was part of the government. In May, the socialist Prime Minister, Paul Ramadier, reacted by dismissing the communist ministers, effectively creating an alliance of socialists and MRP against the communists. In June the situation was further complicated when General Marshall made his crucial speech on American economic aid to Europe. 'The generosity of an ogre', Merleau-Ponty called it. Few other non-communists opposed it but Sartre sided with Merleau-Ponty.

It was in this tense situation that Sartre published 'La Situation de l'écrivain en 1947', the hundred-page final section of *Qu'est-ce que c'est que la littérature?* Like Brecht, he was assuming that only frivolous writers want to spend time on an unpolitical love story. Unlike Brecht, Sartre had an extremely subtle and philosophical mind, which he intermittently subordinated to the need for hard-hitting polemic. The success of *Les Temps modernes* encouraged him to feel as confident of holding his audience's attention as he had in the classroom, and no less liable to chat while writing, to rake stimulating insights together in a random way, often repeating himself, and scarcely troubling about structure.

Merleau-Ponty's influence was pulling him towards Marxism, while the tendency to think anthropologically encouraged him to view literature in its social context, focusing particularly on reciprocity between writer and reader. *Qu'est-ce que c'est que la littérature?* claims that literature can realize its full essence only in a classless society. Flaubert, Baudelaire and the Symbolist poets had been content to ignore the oppressed masses who did not read their work; to function fully, the writer must align himself with the majority. The surrealists, having no readers among the proletariat, had been parasites on the class they had insulted: 'their revolt remains on the margin of the revolution'.[54] The Resistance had given Sartre a glimpse into the possibility of addressing himself to the whole community; more damagingly, it had addicted him to for-or-against partisanship. What the writer should do, he now argued, was use the mass media to convert the reader's goodwill into an active ambition to change the world.[55]

But he went on to repeat the question he had asked ten years earlier about Nizan's novel: is it possible to be a communist and remain a writer? Sartre's answer was unequivocal: 'the politics of Stalinist communism are incompatible with the honest practice of the literary profession'.[56] The Party was currently trying to impose on its intellectuals 'two contradictory conservatisms: materialist scholasticism and Christian moralism'.[57] Like nazism, Gaullism and catholicism, French communism was mystifying its adherents; the duty of the writer was not to deplore the inadequacy of language but to use language in a campaign to liberate the victims of mystification.[58] The end does not justify the means – in L'Engrenage he had suggested that it did – and the Party must not be allowed to go on 'lying to its own troops'.[59] By now he knew there was no chance of taking effective political action as an ally of the PCF – hence his emphasis on the practical value of the action that the writer could take in 'demystifying'.

But it was difficult to use Les Temps modernes as a space to explore tensions between his ontological thinking and his political stance. If the review was to be effective, it must build a consensus among readers, but Sartre, who went on giving Merleau-Ponty a free rein, could not always achieve consensus in himself: there was too much dissension between what he called 'the myself I am for the Other' and 'the myself I am for me'.[60] In 1939 his diary had given him 'quite a little secret life on top of the other one'; now, starting to write notes, for his book on ethics, he found himself communing mainly with the 'self he was for him'. His public self was more exposed than when he had promised, at the end of L'Etre et le Néant, an ethical sequel. If he broke the promise, it was not through shortage of time. The notebooks he filled during 1947–9 contain more words than L'Etre et le Néant, but in their scrupulousness and in their criticism of dialectical materialism, they have more of an affinity with his diaries than with either his published journalism or his published philosophy.

In spite of having Les Temps modernes and a large following of young 'existentialists', Sartre felt isolated. He was under constant attack from the communists. Pravda had denounced existentialism, and in his book L'Existentialisme n'est pas un humanisme Jean Kanapa condemned the self-styled existentialists as fascists and enemies of mankind, while anti-communists and non-communists were alienated by Sartre's support for the Party and his continued opposition to Marshall Aid. It was under these pressures that he wrote his notes on ethics, struggling not only with the conflict between his existentialist ontology and his political inclinations but with the still greater problem of how to reconcile politics with morality. In 1944 he had told an interviewer that morality was his 'dominant preoccupation';[61] the notebooks show that until 1949 he kept returning to the problem of goodness in a world where God had 'fallen into time'.[62] In ostensibly putting God at the centre of the universe, man had put himself there – eternity was seen as a perpetuation of judgments about virtue and vice, whereas modern ideologies tended to subordinate man to historical movements.[63] But historical processes were far more complex than dialectical materialism made them out to be.[64] There were periods in which history was destiny for a nation or a class;[65] in the feudal period no dialectic had been at work: disunity had constantly been suppressed.[66] Sartre could see how God had often been manipulated into working for the preservation of the *status quo*,[67] but it was absurd to argue, as Lenin did, that anything which helps the revolution is morally good.[68] Far from being justified by the end, the means can destroy the end,[69] while violence, though often perpetrated in the name of freedom, destroys the freedom of other people,[70] and lying, though it is the inverse of physical violence, is also destructive. The impossible ideal of violence is to force the liberty of the other person into wanting what I want him to want.[71]

Acquired when he was a schoolteacher, the habit of taking long summer holidays was to persist. He would usually leave Paris in July, as if the term had just ended, returning in October, as if a new academic year were about to begin.[72]

In July he and de Beauvoir were invited to London for the production of *Men without Shadows* and *The Respectable* (sic) *Prostitute* at the Lyric Theatre, Hammersmith, directed by the 22-year-old Peter Brook, who self-confidently told Sartre: 'You've got a surprise coming.' The surprise was that a scene had been cut. He and de Beauvoir stayed only four days but took time to wander through the blitz-scarred streets.[73]

In August they flew to Copenhagen, where they visited the Tivoli and the sailors' dives, drinking aquavit into the small hours. They went on to Sweden, disembarking in Helsingborg, and spending three days looking at canals and lakes before they went on to Stockholm. They visited the Drottningsholm Theatre, and, one night, saw the aurora borealis. From Stockholm they went northwards, travelling alternately by boat and train in Lapland, staying for several days at Abisko in a hotel surrounded by a forest full of reindeer.[74]

SEVENTEEN · *Democratic Revolutionist*

An individual fighting to end the Cold War was almost like Camus's Dr Rieux fighting the plague, and any political action, whatever its intentions, was liable to increase the tension instead of reducing it,[1] but in October 1947 while de Beauvoir was in Chicago with Nelson Algren, Sartre started a series of programmes for radio. Alphonse Bonnafé, his old friend from the school at Le Havre, took the initiative through his father, a close friend of President Ramadier. The series, which was called *La Tribune des Temps modernes*, was to go out with contributions from Sartre's colleagues on the review.

The first broadcast was transmitted on 6 October and the second followed after a gap of a fortnight, with contributions from de Beauvoir, Merleau-Ponty, Pontalis and Bonnafé, with R.-J.Chauffard playing the part of a typical Gaullist. Sartre derided the idea that war was inevitable, arguing that there was little to choose between the two great powers, and comparing the Rassemblement's posters with those of the nazis. Pontalis complained about the General's contempt for the masses, while Bonnafé compared him to Hitler.[2] The broadcast provoked furious reactions. To a comment by Sartre on the General's physique Paul Claudel riposted: 'Is he satisfied with his own?'[3] Condemned by right-wing newspapers for his disrespect towards the great liberator of France, Sartre was attacked on the radio by two well-known Gaullists, General Guillain de Bénouville and Henri Torrès, who challenged him to a radio debate. In the studio, before the broadcast, they attacked him insultingly, while the embarrassed Raymond Aron, who had been invited to take part, remained silent, unable to support either the enraged Gaullists or the comparison of de Gaulle with Hitler.[4] Sartre remained silent too. Listeners must have been puzzled: the only voice to be heard was that of Torrès, who said Sartre's attack on de Gaulle deserved nothing but public contempt. Aron's silence, which Sartre took for betrayal, precipitated the rupture that had long been inevitable between the two old friends.

Conservative newspapers became less hostile after Sartre's attack on the communists in the broadcast of 27 October. Three more programmes followed in November but on 3 December Ramadier was displaced by the MRP leader Robert Schuman, who immediately suppressed the broadcasts scheduled for December.[5] Later on, after hearing rumours about his 'quarrel' with Sartre, Aron, together with Manès Sperber, called at Sartre's flat, hoping to make peace. 'Fine', said Sartre, 'we'll have lunch together one of these days.' But they never did.[6]

In November and December the PCF encouraged a new wave of strikes, but these failed, in spite of the Party's hold on the trade union movement and on the majority of industrial workers. After so many communist ministers had been dismissed, the new defeat made the Party look ineffectual, intensifying the feeling of many malcontents on the left that what was needed was a new socialist movement. In November Sartre was one of those who signed an appeal addressed to 'all the world's democratic and social forces'. The main concern was for peace. A divided Europe was dangerous because Russia and America were each nervous of the other's influence; a united Europe would be more reassuring to both.[7] The other signatories included André Breton, Camus and David Rousset. A fat ex-Trotskyite with several missing teeth and a black patch over one eye, Rousset had written *L'Univers concentrationnaire*, an impressive book about surviving in nazi camps. Koestler, who was not involved in the appeal, was prophesying that the communists would seize power in France, and Europe would fall into Stalin's hands. Sartre, de Beauvoir and Camus were with him and Mamaine one night at a Russian nightclub when they all got very drunk on vodka and champagne. Koestler, suddenly furious at Sartre, who was flirting, deliberately outrageous, with Mamaine, threw a glass at his head. Outside on the pavement, Koestler hit Camus, who had affably put a hand on his shoulder. Leaving Mamaine to take care of her husband, Sartre and de Beauvoir climbed into a car with the bewildered Camus, who, drunkenly lamenting the destruction of a friendship, sent them into frightening lurches as he drove along, weeping.[8]

Koestler considered Gaullism to be the least of the available evils. He was in a bar one day with a Gaullist journalist who teased de Beauvoir by pretending that Sartre had promised to support the Rassemblement after being offered substantial incentives. Koestler merely laughed but she failed to see the joke, and later, when Koestler, meeting her with Sartre in the street, tried to arrange a meeting, Sartre, after hesitating, refused: 'With opinions that diverge so widely, people can't even see a film together.'[9] This ended the friendship that had begun with Sartre's formal initiative.

Once again Sartre and de Beauvoir spent Christmas with Mme Morel at La Pouèze, where he settled down to write *Les Mains sales*. As in the screenplay *L'Engrenage*, the central conflict is between a man who believes he can keep his hands clean and a leader who knows he can't; less eager than he had been in 1946 to justify Stalinism, Sartre can empathize better with both men. Hugo is a young bourgeois intellectual, intent on proving himself as a man of action. But he finds that commitment to the Party is incompatible with honesty. Hugo is sufficiently self-obsessed to go around with photographs of himself as a child. If he represents the self Sartre was trying to reject, Hoederer represents his fantasy of what he might have been – a man of working-class origin, ignorant of literature, with a warm love of mankind and a mature political wisdom, a man of action motivated by genuine concern for the welfare of the majority. In contrast the other leaders of the PCF are unimaginative, cold and misanthropically ruthless in carrying out the orders that come from Moscow.

In an article published in November 1947 Sartre had condemned psychological drama for its blindness to 'the willpower, the oath and the *hubris* which form the virtues and vices of tragedy'. What theatre should show is 'a character creating himself, the moment of choosing, of the voluntary decision that commits him to a moral code and a way of living'. To 'bring the whole man into play' the dramatist should build situations which force the characters to choose between alternatives one of which can lead to death. Freedom is 'revealed in its highest form' when it consents to lose itself so that it can affirm itself. 'The most dramatic situations leave men with only two ways out, and the play is good if in choosing the way out they choose themselves.'[10] It is in this sense that Sartre's plays are heroic. The freedom fighters in *Morts sans sépulture* do not choose to die, but do choose themselves, which exposes the bad faith of the fascist collaborators who kill them. In the final climax of *Les Mains sales*, Hugo must either accept personal responsibility for obeying the order to kill Hoederer or continue as an uncritical servant of the Party which has recently shifted to the policies for which Hoederer died. Hugo's life has been cowardly: but for sexual jealousy, he would never have found the courage to shoot the older man, but in his heroic death he assumes full responsibility both for his unheroic life and for the ill-judged orders he was belatedly obeying.

Unfortunately Sartre's dramaturgical principles join forces with his predilection for melodrama. The final sequence, which culminates in Hugo's decision that he is 'not fit for salvage', is theatrically cruder than the earlier development of the relationship between the two men. Sartre's sources for the characterization of Hugo were not exclusively autobiographical: he was also thinking of former students on the rebound from middle-class families towards the Party and of a story de Beauvoir had told him after meeting one of Trotsky's former secretaries in New York. Trotsky's murderer, when taken on as another secretary, had lived for some time in the well-guarded house at close quarters with the man he was going to kill.

While Sartre was in Holland with de Beauvoir during November 1946, his handwriting had been analysed by a graphologist; the character of Hoederer is developed in his absence when Hugo and his wife, Jessica, are in his room, looking at various objects and studying his handwriting. The role of Jessica was one of Sartre's most generous gifts to Wanda but the character's pert waywardness makes her reminiscent of Ivich; the writing derives more from Olga than from her sister, while the slangy style of the dialogue generally derives from the way Sartre had always carried on conversations with friends.

The case against moral purity is the same case that was made in *L'Engrenage*, but Hoederer makes it more forcefully: 'It's not by refusing to lie we'll get rid of falsehood; it's by going all out to get rid of class barriers. Purity! That's an ideal for fakirs and monks. You intellectuals, you middleclass anarchists use it as an excuse for doing nothing ... Me, I've got dirty hands. Right up to the elbow. They've gone deep into shit and blood. So what? Think anyone can rule without hurting?' He is more tolerant, more humane and more realistic than either the orthodox communist bosses or the renegade bourgeois intellectuals, and he is vindicated by the central irony of the play, which shows how the Party swings round to his ideas after killing him for them. This is more resonant than the point Sartre had made in *L'Engrenage* when he showed that François, caught, as Jean was, between the revolutionary demands of the people and the military power of the neighbouring capitalist country, had no option but to make compromises. Sartre had not intended to engineer a powerful anti-communist weapon, but one of the themes in *Les Mains sales* is that actions, once committed, can boomerang into consequences at odds with the original intentions. The play turned out to be a boomerang.

Existentialism was at the height of its fashion and Sartre was hardly less attractive to sightseers than the Eiffel Tower. Coaches would drive slowly past les Deux Magots in the hope of offering a passing glimpse.[11] But the vogue had little to do with his ideas. There was even an existentialist way of dressing – black shirts, black pullovers, black trousers – derived, absurdly, from the fascist style,[12] though the popularity of jazz had been swelled by the removal of the nazi embargo on black American culture. 'Le swing' had secretly been enjoyed during the Occupation in cellar bars, and as the need for secrecy vanished the appetite grew. During April 1947 a cellar nightclub called the Tabou opened in the rue Dauphine, with Boris Vian playing the trumpet, a young red-haired prizewinnng poetess called Anne-Marie Cazalis receiving the customers, and, later on, a beautiful young actress with long black hair, Juliette Greco, as chanteuse. Greco had never considered herself to be a singer and Sartre encouraged her to make the transition, helping her to choose lyrics and giving her one he had written for *Huis clos* and eventually cut. To provide new music for it he introduced her to the composer Joseph Kosma, who went on to collaborate with her successfully.[13] The newspapers gossiped a great deal about the Tabou, especially about the brawling which went on, their implication being that Sartre's philosophy encouraged orgies. Far from being regulars at the Tabou, he and de Beauvoir went there only twice.[14]

When he took her to Berlin in February for the opening of *Les Mouches* he was courted by the Americans, but he kept his distance.[15] Back in Paris, knowing he had power to make himself useful, he gave evidence at the trial of a former student, Robert Misrahi, a member of the Stern Gang Zionist terrorist group. He had been found in possession of arms. Thanks partly to Sartre, who said he had been a good student, Misrahi was let off with a fine. 'The duty of non-Jews', said Sartre, 'is to help the Jews.'[16]

In *Les Mains sales* Hoederer advises Hugo that instead of trying to prove himself as a man of action he should do the work for which he is best qualified: 'Your talent is for writing ... A good journalist is more valuable than a bad assassin.' Sartre was arguing against his own deep-seated compulsion to prove himself as a man while equating masculinity with action and femininity with art. But instead of listening to his own advice he began to involve himself in practical politics. Though he had attended many of the meetings which led to the manifesto of November 1947, he had not sat on the organizing committee, which consisted of David Rousset, Jean Rous and Georges Altman, editor of *Franc-tireur*, which had about 300,000 readers, mainly in the working class. Rousset was the prime mover. The Rassemblement démocratique révolutionnaire was founded at the beginning of 1948, and when Sartre joined in February, many people expected his presence to be decisive in rallying support. But he no longer had as much pull on public opinion as in the early days of existentialism. The intention was to create a genuinely democratic alternative to a party which was democratic in neither structure nor procedure: the PCF made no attempt to find out whether its policies coincided with what its members wanted. Stalinism, said Rousset, had nothing to do with socialism.

In February 1948 the committee of the RDR published an appeal in the papers attacking both capitalist democracy and Stalinism. 'For us, means are no less important than ends ... We will have nothing to do with this double dealing that consists of practising, in the present, unworthy means which are known as such, for the sake of securing, in the future, a noble end.'[17] At a press conference held on 10 March with Sartre and Rousset among the speakers, the RDR offered itself as a rallying point for the militants

'Poulou' with Anne-Marie. 'It was easy to win praise from his mother.... He was fair and rosy-complexioned, with plump cheeks and curls. Endless photographs of him were taken; his mother retouched them with crayons.' See page 21.

Sartre started at the Ecole Normale Supérieure in August 1924 and left in 1929, when he was twenty-four. 'Many can say, as I do, that they have had four years of happiness there.' See page 52.

Sartre as a private soldier looking through a theodolite at a meteorological balloon held by his corporal, Jean Pierre, somewhere in Alsace during the first nine months of the war.

Sartre at the age of thirty-seven working as a schoolteacher at the Lycée Condorcet (1942).

Paul Nizan (1905–40). 'That such a close friend should be a revolutionary struck me as totally grotesque.'

Sartre in 1939. 'He had never been able to sink himself completely into any love-affair, any pleasure, never been really unhappy; it always seemed to him that he was somewhere else, hadn't yet been quite born. He was waiting. And all this time, gently, slyly, the years had come, they had seized him from behind. Thirty-four years.'
See page 148.

Simone de Beauvoir in 1955. Thirty-six years after he met her in 1928 Sartre said: 'I have always thought her beautiful'.

Left: Wanda Kosakiewicz, who used Marie-Olivier as her stage name. 'You know quite well that I would trample on the whole world (including de Beauvoir) . . . in order to stay on good terms with you.' See page 158.

Below: Sartre and de Beauvoir with Boris and Michelle Vian, who were still married when Michelle's affair with Sartre began in December 1945. She remained a close friend until he died in 1980. But when they went on holiday together she was left on her own most of the day while Sartre worked to the same routine as in Paris. See page 277.

Right: Albert Camus (1913–60). 'With Camus Sartre could have a great deal of fun ... in some ways he was still like a tough Algerian street urchin and they could tell each other obscene stories while de Beauvoir and Maria Casarès or Francine Camus would appear to be shocked. Later Sartre would describe him as "probably the last good friend I had".' See page 204.

Below: Sartre at the Pont-Royal with (left to right) Dolorès Vanetti – 'She's enormously important to me' (p. 232) – Jacques-Laurent Bost, an ex-pupil who was the model for Boris in *Les Chemins de la liberté,* Jean Cau, who was Sartre's secretary for twelve years, and Jean Genet (1907–86).

Left: Sartre and de Beauvoir with Claude Lanzmann, who joined the editorial committee of *Les Temps modernes* in 1952 and became her lover but remained on good terms with Sartre.

Below: Sartre in June 1957 with François Mauriac (1885–1970). 'God is not an artist and neither is M. Mauriac.'

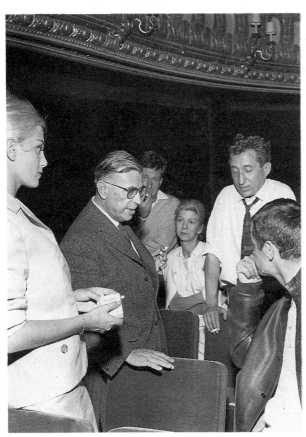

Left: At the Théâtre de la Renaissance during rehearsals of *Les Séquestrés d'Altona* during September 1959. Serge Reggiani, who played Frantz, is on the right at the front; Evelyne Rey (Johanna) is on the left. 'Sartre was to become one of the most important men in her life, while she was to become – until her suicide – one of the most important women in his, a mistress, like Wanda, for whom he wrote plays.' See page 294.

Below: Sartre with Arlette Elkaïm in January 1965 after adopting her as his daughter. She was nineteen when they met in March 1956, and she soon became his mistress. When he died intestate, Arlette was left with full copyright control over everything he had written, including his letters to de Beauvoir, which were published illegally.
See page 441.

Sartre with Tito in Yugoslavia during 1960.

Sartre in March 1968 addressing a meeting held to protest against the war in Vietnam.

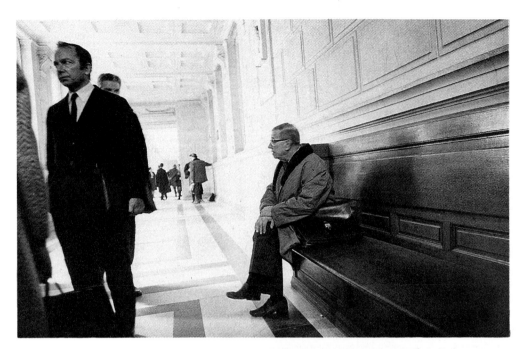

Above: Sartre in court during February 1970 waiting to appear as a witness at the trial of Roland Castro. See page 405.

Right: Sartre outside the Renault works at Billancourt in October 1970, speaking out against the suppression of *La Cause du peuple* and the Geismar trial. 'The intellectuals should be the allies of the people. . . . Geismar, the man on trial, he is the people himself.' See page 410.

Above: Daniel Cohn-Bendit (right), who became friendly with Sartre during the 1968 student rebellion, acts as his interpreter at a Stuttgart press conference in December 1974 after they have visited Andreas Baader of the Baader-Meinhof gang in Stammheim prison. Sartre is already almost blind. Sitting on the other side of him is Klaus Croissant, Baader's lawyer. See page 427.

Left: Accompanied by André Glucksmann (left) and Raymond Aron (centre) Sartre is leaving the Elysée, where they have been received by the President, Giscard d'Estaing, together with other delegates from the committee organizing relief for the Vietnamese 'boat people'. See page 435.

Above: The crowd surrounding Sartre's hearse on 19 April 1980 as the cortège moves towards the cemetery in Montparnasse. Eight days later the coffin will be disinterred for cremation at Père-Lachaise.

Right: A chair has been brought for Simone de Beauvoir's graveside farewell to Sartre.

of leftist parties. The object was to 'organize democracy', putting Europe 'in the forefront of the struggle for freedom'. When the RDR's first public meeting was held, nine days later, about a thousand people crowded into the Salle Wagram. Sartre took issue with those who attacked the workers' 'sordid materialism'. Hunger was a sign of solidarity. 'You are never hungry alone. When a man's hungry, he's hungry with all the comrades of his class, with people who receive the same wages.'[18] Since the RDR was not a party, members of other parties could not be stopped from joining, though leading communists were quick to denounce Sartre and Rousset as agents of the government and Wall Street, while the SFIO threatened to excommunicate any member who joined the RDR. But when the left wing of the SFIO split, nearly twenty per cent of its socialist separatists, Action socialiste révolutionnaire (ASR), did join the new movement.

In the first issue of *La Gauche*, the RDR's paper (published fortnightly and later monthly), Sartre wrote that their prime objective was to link 'revolutionary claims' with 'the idea of freedom'.[19] In an interview he explained that he did not want reforms but a bloodless revolution, retaining the freedom which capitalism claimed as its *raison d'être*, but extending it to everybody.[20] Camus contributed to *La Gauche*, pleading for 'democracy without catechism';[21] Merleau-Ponty also gave his allegiance to the RDR, though half-heartedly, not believing in force of numbers as a means of putting pressure on the PCF. Though he was a founding member of the executive committee, he never attended meetings.[22]

Sartre's involvement with the new movement did not prevent him from seeing a good deal of Jean Cocteau, who agreed to take a hand in the staging of *Les Mains sales* when it was in rehearsal at the Théâtre Antoine. According to rumours that were circulating, the play would have the effect of restoring Sartre's popularity.[23] The production was by Pierre Valdé, 'amicalement supervisée' (as the programme has it) by Cocteau. François Périer played Hugo, with André Luguet as Hoederer. Sartre was absent from the first performance, lecturing at a masonic lodge in the hope of enlisting members for the RDR.

The communist papers attacked the play viciously: *Humanité* called Sartre a 'nauseous writer', a 'Third Force demagogue' and an 'understudy for Koestler', while Marguerite Duras wrote a spiteful review in *Action*. Later on Ilya Ehrenburg would complain in *Les Lettres françaises* that during a witch-hunt against the communists Sartre had 'joined his fate with the fate of Jules Moch [a Gaullist minister], with the fate of Mr Dulles [the US secretary of state], of Mr Churchill and the others who have inspired the crusade'.[24] But the force of the play was irresistible. In Paris the original production ran for nearly eighteen months. As a printed text it became Sartre's most popular fiction in France: by the end of 1978, 1,892,000 copies had been sold, compared with 1,670,000 of *La Nausée*.[25]

The new novel, *La Mort dans l'âme* – the third in Sartre's sequence and the last he was to complete – reflects a situation and an attitude which had changed since he completed *L'Age de raison*. In 1945 he had promised that Mathieu would finally liberate himself from his past. 'He will find love and get himself on the right track. He'll commit himself freely, which will give the world a meaning for him.'[26] In the 1948 novel Mathieu's final scene coincides with the defeat of France. The soldiers have been abandoned by their officers; the country is on the point of capitulating. For the routed, disorganized, dispirited men, the question of whether to fight on is not a question of honour or patriotism. It is a moral choice, but not one that can be made rationally. If they go on shooting from inside buildings, the Germans may decide to burn down the village, killing women and children. If Mathieu joins the small group of soldiers who intend to fire on the advancing Germans from the tower of the church, he is probably condemning himself to die for no good reason – an absurdity which makes him feel exultant. 'I'm deciding that death was the secret meaning of my life, that I have been living to die. I'm dying to prove that it's impossible to live. My eyes will close the world, put it permanently out.'[27] Mathieu sees what looks like a toad crawling towards the town hall – a German with a grenade in his hand. Mathieu kills the man. 'For years he'd been trying to act. In vain. His actions had been stolen from him, one by one; he had been soft as butter. This time nothing had been taken away. He'd squeezed the trigger, and for once something had happened.'[28]

Though he does not dissociate himself from Mathieu's attitude – which is in line with the feeling Boris had in *Le Sursis*: that he'd been put into the world for *his* war – Sartre is not content to end the novel on this note: as the Germans advance, bombarding the church tower with a cannon, Mathieu is left shooting from the parapet. The image has roots in Sartre's childhood feelings on looking down from a high window; at his vantage point with a rifle in his hand, Mathieu is also in the same position as Erostrate in Sartre's short story. The reader assumes that Mathieu cannot survive, and in the last section of *La Mort dans l'âme* he does not reappear. The sequence is set in a Stalag, where we see that Brunet, the dedicated communist, still has a greater sense of purpose than any of the other prisoners: even here he can work energetically for the Party, and soon, finding that some prisoners are already comrades, while others can be indoctrinated, he is creating a cell. But whereas Sartre in 1940 had felt a compassionate and sometimes passionate solidarity with fellow-prisoners in the Stalag, Brunet is interested only in the ones he can use, despising the others as a bunch of *salauds*.

Sartre introduces a new *alter ego*, Schneider. (This, the German word for 'tailor', is reminiscent of the name 'Tailleur' Sartre had used in *La Semence et le scaphandre*, playing on the Latin word *sartor*.) Schneider voices misgivings about communists who are machine-like in obeying orders. It is here that Sartre introduces the phrase *la mort dans l'âme*. When Brunet blames the French soldiers for their defeat, Schneider loses his temper: it is the leaders who are to blame both for the defeat and for the ensuing demoralization. 'He's stuck there, he's fallen out of the world, out of history, with dead ideas. He's trying to fight back, to rethink the situation. But with what? He's only got old-fashioned tools for thinking with. You've put death into his soul.'[29] *La Mort dans l'âme* is Sartre's title for the novel but the English translation is called *Iron in the Soul*.

Sartre was working simultaneously on the novel and on his notes about morality, which reflect the same disenchantment with communist orthodoxy. Leaders, he complains, who lie to achieve unity are like the priest, the oppressor or the psycho-analyst who claims to understand his patients better than they understand themselves.[30] Brunet is doing his duty as a good Party member, but 'duty', like 'goodness', needs critical redefinition. Following Nietzsche, Sartre sees duty as 'the violence of other people, but interiorized'.[31] When I obey the call of duty, I am submitting to the voice of someone else who refuses to take account of the current situation, other people's intentions, temporality, means. 'Someone else is incessantly repeating: "I don't want to know".' Duty is alienated liberty, depersonalized.[32] Enslaving himself to the PCF, Brunet is enslaving his followers to him and enjoying his power. Sartre's attitude has changed substantially since Mathieu felt envious of the purposeful Brunet.

As in *Les Mains sales* Sartre is incensed less by Moscow than by the PCF. 'The Party will re-establish itself without you', Schneider tells Brunet, 'and on principles you know nothing about. You could escape and you don't dare, because you're afraid of what you'll find down there. You, you've got death in your soul.'[33]

From Sartre's belief in existentialist freedom of choice, it followed that the French soldiers had chosen to be defeated, and he shared their humiliation. Writing in 1948 about his experiences of eight years earlier, he found it easier to be compassionate. The bewilderment, boredom and frustration of the men is vividly dramatized, and he extends a retrospective literary sympathy to his Jewish friend, Pieter. When Pieter gave up hope, Sartre found little to say, but Mathieu tries to console Charlot, who retorts: 'You'd have to be a Jew ... Otherwise you can't understand ... It's not me that's scared, it's my race inside me.'[34]

The critic Geneviève Idt has noticed how Sartre uses the novel to continue an argument with Malraux and Camus.[35] In *L'Espoir* Malraux's faith in revolutionary art is asserted through a conversation between a Spanish painter and an American journalist; visiting an art gallery with an American journalist, Sartre's Gomez realizes that he is no longer a painter: 'I've gone blind ... It would be necessary not to have shot human beings.'[36] Calling Sartre's novel 'a reply to *La Peste*', Geneviève Idt compares the two sermons of Camus's Father Paneloux with the sermon of the Pétainist priest in Sartre's stalag, a sermon based not on the attitude of the priests Sartre knew in Trier but on proclamations by the Vichy government. While Camus focuses on a change of attitude in an individual priest, Sartre is generalizing as he had in *Les Mouches*, about collaborationist defeatism, but whereas Camus's sympathy for the ordinary people was vague, Sartre is admirably specific in dramatizing the feelings of defeated soldiers.

Some of his ironies rest on the absurdities of squabbles in which private trivialities upstage major political events. On the day the German army enters Paris Ivich grumbles furiously to a waiter about ersatz coffee; a French soldier fastidiously washes his shirts in the river. During May 1948 events in Paris were full of anomalies not much less absurd: as Sartre complained in a letter, the newspapers were paying more attention to the British Princess Elizabeth, who was there on a visit, than to the hardships of Jewish survivors, who were being stopped by the British from settling in Palestine. (As early as May 1948, Sartre favoured the creation of a Jewish state.) To make it easier for himself to bring the past alive, he often transposed experiences from the present. The novel opens with a heatwave in New York during June 1940; in May 1948 Paris was as hot as it normally is in July: 'We're living in our shirt-sleeves; we're sleeping naked.'[37]

During the spring, holidaying with de Beauvoir at Ramatuelle, near St-Tropez, he'd been able to write undisturbed; back in Paris, working at the novel, the ethics and a book on Mallarmé, which was lost after several hundred pages had been written,[38] he wrote as usual in two shifts – from nine in the morning till two and from five till nine – but it was seldom without interruptions. Twice a week he had meetings with the regular contributors to *Les Temps modernes*, and while de Beauvoir was with Nelson Algren in the United States, Guatemala and Mexico, Sartre enjoyed an affair with a young American reporter whose current task was to write bulletins on Princess Elizabeth's doings in Paris. Far from being repelled, Sartre liked the journalist's involvement in her job. It was obvious that 'la petite', as he called her, would never matter to him as much as Dolorès did, but she came regularly to the flat in rue Bonaparte at about five, so exhausted after a day of pursuing the princess that she flopped down on his bed and slept deeply for a couple of hours. She could play the violin, and he enjoyed accompanying her on the piano. They played Schubert. They would spend the night together, either in her flat or in his – his mother liked her – and it would be painful to end the affair, but for de Beauvoir, he promised, there would be no upsets when she returned in June. On the contrary, he was looking forward to telling her all about the affair and to taking her on holiday in August.[39]

They went to Algeria, spending the first two weeks in Algiers, but they slept in separate hotel bedrooms. They could now afford to explore coast roads in taxis,[40] but it was no longer so easy for them to enjoy togetherness in a foreign country.

They returned to find pessimistic Parisians predicting war between America and Russia. In June the Russians had blockaded Berlin and supplies were still being air-lifted in; Yugoslavia had been expelled from the Cominform for hostility to the USSR: on 1 September the creation of the North China People's Republic had been announced by the communists. Would the US intervene to support Chiang Kai-shek against Mao Tse-tung, concentrating American troops in the East, and leaving Europe to be overrun by the Russians? In March France had joined with Britain and the Benelux countries in a treaty of mutual assistance, but the Atlantic Pact had not yet been signed, and Sartre would go on fighting to keep Europe neutral. The world, he believed, would be cut permanently in two if Robert Schuman aligned France with the US.

On 12 September a courageous American eccentric, a former bomber pilot, Gary Davis, proclaimed himself a citizen of the world, renounced his US citizenship and started a sit-in at the headquarters of the United Nations in the Palais de Chaillot. In October, after he had been evicted by the police, he was supported by a 'council of solidarity' which included Camus, the philosopher Emanuel Mounier, André Breton and Richard Wright, who had settled in Paris. There were press conferences and rallies; in December one of these drew 20,000 people, but Sartre refused to join in. All his energy for political agitation went into campaigning for a neutral Europe and against colonialism. On 18 November he told a Moroccan audience: 'Those who oppress you oppress us for the same reasons.'

He was in no mood to get rich on Broadway royalties. Under the title *Red Gloves* an unauthorized adaptation of *Les Mains sales* had opened during November at New Haven with Charles Boyer as Hoederer. When Sartre protested he was told by his publisher, Nagel, that he had already made five million francs. The advance booking so far amounted to $280,000. But Sartre vetoed the production.

The play's success in Paris did help to reinstate Sartre's reputation, but relatively few of his admirers wanted to follow him into the RDR. In Paris the movement had only 830 members by the end of 1948, though about 4,000 people crowded into the hall when a 'day of studies' was held on 13 December in the Salle Pleyel, while, according to the *Franc-tireur*, another 2,000 were turned away. With 'internationalism of the spirit' as their main theme, the speakers included Sartre, Camus, Rousset, Breton, Carlo Levi and Richard Wright. The speakers might have recruited more support if they had not seemed so disunited, but Sartre, more pro-Russian and anti-American than Rousset or Camus, was maintaining that the Soviet camps had no major political or social importance.[41] The meeting failed to reverse the trend which would continue throughout 1949: thousands of people flocked to hear the star speakers at the rallies, but membership remained low.

In January 1949 the principal battle of words was fought after Victor Kravchenko, a former Russian government official who had defected, published a book, *I Chose Freedom*, which drew attention to the existence of Soviet labour camps. He sued *Les Lettres françaises* for suggesting that the text must have been written by agents of the American government. Sartre and de Beauvoir attended a session of the trial, at which pro-communist witnesses sent from Moscow confronted anti-communist witnesses sponsored by the Americans. The trial was important mainly for its revelations about the labour camps. It would no longer be possible to deny their existence; the choice was between affirming it and remaining evasively silent. This, for Sartre, was to be a long-term problem; the immediate problem at the beginning of 1949 was how to respond to Georg Lukács, who was in Paris for the publication of his book *Existentialisme ou marxisme?* At his lectures and press conferences he called existentialism an 'indirect apologia for capitalism'.[42] Sartre retorted that Lukács was himself a 'crypto-existentialist'.[43] The two writers never met.

Sartre's more serious formulations were being made in the notebooks. Wanting to work on ethics and on the final novel of his tetralogy, he left Paris with de Beauvoir for the south of France. She had picked an isolated hotel on the Esterel coast, but feeling unsettled there, they moved on to Le Cagnard, high up in Cagnes. As usual they had separate rooms; they stayed for three weeks.

He was going to call the novel *La Dernière Chance* but he completed only about seventy pages. Mathieu reappears in a stalag after two months in hospital; Sartre loops back to his memories of prison-camp during the winter of 1940-1. Eight years later, this experience still seemed crucial: 'Listen', says Mathieu, in one draft of the fragment, '... once I was an individual, and then I learnt that truth chased after me, and in the end I experienced something extraordinary. The comradeship of defeat ... In defeat you get the impression that men can find their own salvation.'[44] Emerging from the hospital, Mathieu feels like a new man: 'Mathieu was not yet a prisoner, he had just been born.'[45] This places a gauche emphasis on the feeling of renaissance. Solidarity with his fellow-prisoners had given Sartre the sense of having a new self, and nostalgia for this feeling was to haunt all his efforts to compromise with the one political party that could claim to represent the working majority. The isolation of Schneider corresponds both to the isolation of Paul Nizan after he left the Party, and to the postwar isolation of Sartre, who could never bring himself to join it. In wanting to help Brunet when, like a sheepdog, he is herding like-minded lambs together, Schneider is motivated less by conviction than by need for comradeship, but Brunet, like Hugo in *Les Mains sales*, finds that during his imprisonment the party line has changed, making nonsense of everything he had dutifully done. When Chalais, one of the PCF bosses, arrives in the Stalag, Brunet is reprimanded: the men he has indoctrinated may turn to Gaullism; he should have denounced de Gaulle and Pétain, together with the imperialism of the bourgeois democracies, and he should have praised the love of peace in the working masses.[46]

Sartre felt ambivalent towards men who, unable to think for themselves, succumbed to indoctrination. One of the soldiers tells Mathieu: 'In the camp you're never alone, not even for a shit.' The sentence refers back to the disappearance of privacy which Sartre had first hated, and then begun to love as he came to feel at one with the men. While he cannot forgive the leaders who manipulate the defeated soldiers, making them feel ashamed and inadequate, he cannot forgive the men for being duped so easily. In the fragmentary fourth volume, Brunet furiously intervenes when two of his loyal followers are beating up Schneider, who, according to Chalais, is liable to denounce them.[47] Sartre had been told how Nizan suffered at the hands of former comrades when he left the Party; even his wife was ordered to denounce him.[48]

Writing in his notebooks about stupidity Sartre refers mainly to the mindlessness that puts people at the mercy of political charlatans. Fools give up their human reality and their liberty to the deceiver who offers to take responsibility for their decisions. This man is transformed into a god.[49] Brunet and Chalais acquire godlike powers over their devotees. The fool lets other people steal the world from him, building his future out of their past, thinking slowly what they have already thought quickly.[50]

On the other hand, cohesive pressure is indispensable if solidarity is to be mustered against oppression. Sartre tries hard in the notebooks to analyse what oppression is. As in *L'Etre et le Néant*, he uses Hegel's model of the master and the slave, but he goes beyond it, dividing the oppressed into four groups – children, the ignorant, the stupid, women – and he finds that oppression can exist in three situations: when a society excludes some of its members from a culture or system of values it has created; when a class or group, put into an almost intolerable position, cannot count on the free will of other people to rescue it; when there is forced labour.[51] The oppressor makes himself into destiny, as the parent does for the child.[52] Usually oppression is viewed in a political, social and economic perspective, but Sartre's standpoint is ontological: 'It is precisely the character of en-slavement that Hegel failed to see: all you enslave is a freedom; you enslave it because it is freedom ... the purpose of the enslavement is not the utiliz-ation of a labour force but the diminution and appropriation of a freedom by the other.'[53]

Huis clos had illustrated the argument advanced in *L'Etre et le Néant* about rivalry between the freedoms of two individuals. Friendship is an exchange of favours; in a business or professional relationship the customer or client pays, but the slave, having nothing to offer, pays with his person.[54] His work reflects not his own image, but only his master's, so the purpose of his work is stolen from him.[55] In the morality of slavery, as in the morality of duty or devotion, I choose the other as preferable to myself.[56]

These reflections on oppression lead Sartre to ideas about revolution and violence, irreconcilable with what he had written earlier in the note-books, when he had argued that revolutionaries always have a bad con-science because they are fighting not just against a *status quo* but against themselves and against an established right.[57] He had also maintained that all violence is in bad faith. To refute Trotsky's argument about the justifica-tion of the means by the end, he had argued that the means can be wrong, not because it is immoral but because it can destroy the end.[58] Violence often conceals a desire for the destruction of the end by the means.[59] Violence is invariably grounded on the assumption that a latent order will emerge when the ill-will, which masks it, has been destroyed. Sexual desire involves violence to the extent that the desired person is transformed into an object,[60] while the rapist is using violence in the conviction that there will be no future: the violent triumph of desire will freeze the end for ever in the absolute.[61]

We cannot be sure of when Sartre's later notes on violence and revolution were written; what seems crucial is that in the interim he had come under the influence of Genet and the books he published between 1944 and 1948, especially the autobiographical novels, *Notre Dame de fleurs* and *Querelle de Brest*, and the directly autobiographical *Journal du voleur*. These books suggest that a glamorously unglamorous counterworld is constructed by criminals. 'What I call violence', writes Genet, 'is passive courage infatuated by danger.' In pursuit of evil he has embarked on adventures which lead to prison, where he feels as secure as a monarch in his palace. 'My talent consists of the love I feel towards the state of imprisonment ... My courage consists in annihilating all the usual reasons for living, and then making up new ones.' In this perverse panache and apocalyptic bravado, as in this style of living and writing, the rhythms and attitudes of Rimbaud are un-mistakably echoed.

Not that Sartre was a reader who would easily let himself be overcome by intoxicating prose rhythms. The main appeal of Genet was that he showed Sartre the way out of the ethical maze. After five years of making notes without deciding how to use them, Sartre had almost arrived at the moment of asserting his freedom deliciously by deciding to leave the book unwritten. As a writer Genet was not logically convincing but as a man he had allowed himself to be taken over by the idea other people had of him, and the story of his life taught Sartre a new way of chasing goodness out of evil. Genet had chosen to let himself be possessed. Unlike the dutiful slave, the pious worshipper and the loyal Party member, all victims of the manip-ulator who steals their humanity, making them prefer the other to the self, Genet reverses the negative into a way of living. Caught by the community in an impossible system of values, he restructures his derelict life as an abrasive celebration of its impossibility. Instead of becoming an object, the slave discovers his subjectivity in what the masters call evil. He chooses to be in the wrong, and, erecting no alternative system of values, submits to self-loathing. He feels murderous, not just towards others but towards the other that he has interiorized. The project is suicidal. Since the future is controlled by the master, the slave recognizes himself only in the passing moment of rebellion. He dismisses the future and all the retribution it holds for his present assertiveness. By accompanying Genet this far along a non-Marxian road towards abjection, Sartre has made himself a partisan of rebellion. The *status quo* is intolerable, and no ethics can be established until after a revolution more public and positive than Genet's.

After three weeks in the South of France, Sartre and de Beauvoir returned to a Paris torn by disagreement about Marshall Aid and the Atlantic Pact, which was to be signed on 4 April. To emphasize its aggressive implications, the communists launched a 'Peace movement', and Picasso's white dove was conceived as a symbol for the rally to be held at the Salle Pleyel on 30 April. The RDR announced a counter-attraction on the same date – an 'International Day of Resistance to Dictatorship and War'. On the 16th the leaders of the two movements held a meeting, but compromise was impossible. Visiting the United States to make contact with American trade unions and raise funds, Rousset should have anticipated that left-wingers would accuse him of accepting money from the CIA. He exacerbated the split in the RDR by writing an article conceding that the Atlantic Pact was 'not a measure of war' and denouncing the Soviet government as represent-ing 'the fiercest social reaction since the disappearance of nazism'.[62] On 30 April the morning meeting was held at the Sorbonne, where the big lecture hall was filled, and in the evening about ten thousand people packed into the Vélodrome d'Hiver, but Sartre was absent from the speakers' platform. Together with Merleau-Ponty and Richard Wright, Sartre sent a message: he wanted nothing to do with an event that would encourage anti-communism. Implacably hostile to the Atlantic Pact, he held that Europe should remain neutral, and that it would not even keep its cultural autonomy if it accepted economic help from America. It did not matter whether French culture survived: what he wanted was a united socialist Europe, economically and culturally dependent on neither the United States nor Soviet Russia.[63] Instead of campaigning for this the RDR was being betrayed by Rousset and by Altman, who was defending American policy in the *Franc-tireur*. When Sartre demanded a national conference, so that members from all over France could state their views, Rousset objected that it would cost too much. Eventually, when Sartre subsidized it personally, an extraordinary conference was announced for 30 June. He then spoke out against the April rally, and the majority supported him, but this meant that there was no future for the movement. 'Breakdown of the RDR. Serious blow. New and definitive apprenticeship to realism. You can't create a movement.'[64]

Earlier in 1948 Sartre had been persuading Dolorès not to settle in Paris, but he was glad to spend his summer holiday with her, while de Beauvoir shared hers with Nelson Algren. Sartre and Dolorès went to Guatemala, Panama, Curaçao, Haiti and Cuba, where they spent an evening in Havana with Ernest Hemingway and his wife, who was disappointed that the two writers 'talked like businessmen'.[1] In Haiti Sartre was intrigued by the voodoo ceremony he witnessed,[2] but appalled by the poverty. 'Haiti throws itself passionately on everything that evokes French culture ... and among the rich Antilles, this black republic is the only one to be dying of hunger.'[3] Throughout the trip his relationship with Dolorès was deteriorating: he was finding her company less enjoyable while she was finding him depressive, remote, grumpy.[4]

In August, staying at La Pouèze with Mme Morel, he worked for twelve hours every day, alternating between his notes on ethics and a preface for the Gallimard collection of Genet's works. After writing about 360,000 words on ethics, he had arrived at an impasse. 'All I know', he wrote in a letter, 'is that I'd like to create a morality in which evil is an integral part of good.'[5] He had not yet abandoned the book on ethics; when he did, much of the accumulated material would be shifted into the work on Genet. Such transpositions are typical of Sartre: the whole of his work can be read as an inconsequential series of instalments in one enormous unfinishable book. Ostensibly a biography, *Saint Genet* is largely a discourse on the nature of good and evil. Genet is more than a pretext, but less than the whole subject. The Sartrean monologue is like a dialogue between the philosopher who generalizes about Being and the biographer who instead of chronicling events tries to give a comprehensive account of how a mind works. The universe, Sartre complained, 'has the derisory fate of manifesting itself *through* a particular consciousness and above all *to* a particular consciousness. All its "there is" is suspended in my finitude.'[6] Focusing on Genet's finitude, he presents an anthology of insights into good and evil.

The crucial point is that in a world debased by alienation no ethical principle can be validated. From condemning violence as a means which contaminates the end, he has come to accept Marx's contention that war is good if it serves the interests of the proletariat and bad if it does not. There can be no morality without freedom, and freedom has been cut in two. True morality is not a prohibition of evil but a concrete totality which synthesizes evil with good. Sartre was above all a moralist and if he was shifting towards a more dialectical mode of thinking, the tendency began from a need to think dialectically about ethics. But his reflexes were Kantian. His habit, as Raymond Aron had noticed, was to judge other people less according to their actions than their intentions, 'and he ended up with an irrevocable judgment, good or bad, based on the ulterior motive he imputed to the person'.[7]

While working on Mallarmé in 1948-9 he produced about 2,000 pages of notes and 500 pages of a book. Though both were subsequently lost, except for fragments, he gave Mallarmé more attention than any other poet: 'Mallarmé and Genet ... both of them consciously engaged ... Mallarmé is our greatest poet. Passionate, wild ... His commitment seems as complete as possible: social as well as poetic.'[8] On the surface Mallarmé could hardly have been less passionate or wild. He was a diffident, polite schoolteacher, who concealed his feelings and kept people at a distance, but his thinking was subversive.

According to Nietzsche, the desire to create, like the desire to destroy, can spring either from overflowing Dionysian vigour or from *ressentiment*, the malice of the underprivileged, outraged by the wellbeing of others. The man of *ressentiment* revenges himself on reality by burning his image into it. The poets dominant during the second half of the nineteenth century all, according to Sartre, made themselves into agents of the counter-revolution by cultivating incomprehensibility and contemplating nothingness. It was easier to abolish the universe than to touch the established order.[9] From the Parnassians to the Symbolists, French poets did nothing but flatter the bourgeoisie by holding up to it a mirror which threw back only an aristocratic image.[10] The values of a defunct nobility informed the preciosity of the poets, who refined the negative image that the property-owning class needed to have of itself. But there was no reciprocity between readers and poets, whose ideal was to annihilate the world and recreate it through words.[11] 'The terrorism of politeness', Sartre called it. An extremist, Mallarmé was chosen by the negative poetry of his period as its means of committing suicide.[12] In the biography of Flaubert, which he would start in 1954, Sartre would impute to him the same diabolical project of trying to make the world unreal, tossing it into the void of *l'imaginaire*.

In writing about Mallarmé like this Sartre pays little attention either to his development or to what differentiates him from other poets. Nihilism is presented as all-embracing. Sartre's objective in this abandoned book is to write in the perspective of his synthetic anthropology, combining Freudian and Marxian insights, without forgetting Marcel Mauss. Trying to visualize the relationship between poets and public as a single series of transactions, Sartre perceives the bourgeoisie emulating aristocratic orgies in ritual destruction of worldly goods, while the poets belong to a secret fraternity whose initiation rites involve suicide and rebirth.[13] Anthropology's archetypal patterns dominate the imagery. Though some of Sartre's insights are valid, the generalizations dull the critical acumen, while the biography (in so far as we can judge it from the fragments) fails to bring its subject to life. As in *Saint Genet* Sartre's basic question is how does a man make himself into a writer; as in *Saint Genet* and *L'Idiot de la famille*, the facts are tailored to fit the new myth Sartre is creating. When he asserts 'From the first day Mallarmé saw in his wife the image of his own desolation' or that his grandmother 'loved him with a phoney lucidity, snivelling and grumpy',[14] we are given no evidence and no sources. Sartre's method in *L'Idiot de la famille* will be the same. No substantiation, no footnotes. He has done the thinking for us; here are his conclusions. The myth is very much the same myth as in *Saint Genet*; we will meet it again in both *Les Mots* and *L'Idiot de la famille*: the decision that will shape the writer is taken by adults during the victim's childhood. The boy is withered by a glance:

> The child knows that they are his truth. 'You will be a civil servant [*administrateur*] like your father.' This time he embraces his janitor destiny with a glance ... Under his eyes his future personality, unfolded, acts out his future career in dumbshow, parades its dull vicissitudes in front of him. These tics will be his. What am I saying? They are there already. Family life is a gallery of mirrors; the child, the man, the dotard are reflections which change places. In them he sees his future, in other words the family's past, incessantly repeated.[15]

This is the leitmotif of Sartrean biography.

Once again a peaceful period of writing outside Paris was followed, when Sartre returned, by a busy period, full of interruptions and political decisions. No longer believing that anything could be achieved through the RDR, he had come closer to Merleau-Ponty's view of the role they should play.[16] If they entered the political arena, they would appear as either allies or rivals of the PCF; instead they should limit themselves to exerting influence through *Les Temps modernes*.[17] When he resigned from the RDR on 12 October, Sartre was inflicting a fatal wound on a movement which could not in any case have survived for long. His departure, reported *Le Monde*, evidenced the RDR's failure to resolve its internal quarrels.[18]

In the controversy which exploded at the end of the year about Soviet labour camps Sartre wholeheartedly supported Merleau-Ponty against Rousset, whose expostulations against the camps were serialized in *Le Figaro littéraire* during November. The defence of the Soviet Union which appeared in the January 1950 issue of *Les Temps modernes* was written by Merleau-Ponty but signed jointly. While some apologists for the Soviet regime were denying the existence of the camps, Merleau-Ponty admitted it and tried to explain why Russian workers did not find them intolerable. Many 'young heroes' and 'gifted bureaucrats' no doubt assumed that the prisoners were 'lunatics, anti-social people, men of ill will'. And whereas German concentration camps had not been part of a movement towards classlessness, the USSR was 'broadly on the side of the forces that are fighting against the familiar forms of exploitation'. This was the great commonplace of pro-Soviet apologias: the repulsive present is justified by the happy future. Merleau-Ponty went on to affirm: 'we have the same values as a communist', and Sartre, no longer believing that the means can undermine the end, agreed that the Soviet Union should not be compared critically with capitalist countries; if there were anomalies in the Soviet system, the Russian proletariat could be trusted to get rid of them at the right moment.

Though his intellect was no less subtle than André Gide's, Sartre was less scrupulous in stamping on doubts about the Soviet Union. Gide, his senior by thirty-six years, had already been through the whole gamut of disillusionment with the West, optimism about the Soviet alternative, disillusionment with it. Appalled during his long African expedition (1925–6) by the white exploitation of the blacks, he returned to become a champion of victims and underdogs all over the world. Having started, like Sartre, as an impassioned advocate of individual liberty, he changed his mind. 'The triumph of the individual is the renunciation of individualism.' Communism seemed to promise 'a new and better form of civilization'. Like Sartre, he felt ashamed of his bourgeois privileges, guilty at having a place in the lifeboat while most people were left to swim or drown; in 1932 he wrote that he would gladly sacrifice his life for the success of the Soviet Union. But when he visited the country in 1936, he saw a dictatorial state ruthlessly imposing uniformity of style and uniformity of opionion on a helpless people. The workers were being exploited, but so deviously that they did not know whom to blame. Gide's conclusion was that the spirit of communism was no longer different from the spirit of fascism. In his 1936 pamphlet *Retour de l'URSS* he ridiculed the argument that deportations, exploitation and undemocratic government were provisional measures, indispensable if the gains of 1917 were to be preserved. Essentially this was the argument Sartre and Merleau-Ponty were using, fourteen years later.

Contemporary history, though, was throwing up criticism of the Soviet system. After Marshal Tito's defiance of his Russian overlords, Yugoslavia had been expelled in June 1948 from the Cominform, but in July Tito had received a vote of confidence from the Yugoslav Communist Party, which was subsequently purged of its Cominform supporters.

The PCF was hostile to Tito, but Sartre, writing a preface for a book by Louis Dalmas, *Le Communisme yougoslave depuis le rupture avec Moscou*, comes out strongly in support of Yugoslav dissidence. Soviet policy could be defended as corresponding to 'the objective requirements of the situation' in Russia, but Lenin had promised that the Soviet Union would give disinterested aid to states on the road to socialism, so that their economic unity could be re-established without domination. Was there any reason to think Tito had been more despotic or terroristic than the Politburo?

In June Sartre met Koestler and Mamaine who were in the neighbouring compartment on a night train to Berlin, where they were attending a congress for cultural freedom. When Koestler invited him to share the food and drink Mamaine had brought in a basket – the train had no restaurant car – Sartre accepted gladly, though Koestler felt sure he would have refused if de Beauvoir had been travelling with him: 'minus her he behaved like a schoolboy on holiday'.[19]

But she was the holiday companion he liked best of all: having spent his last summer holiday with Dolorès, he was planning to take a spring holiday with de Beauvoir in Italy or Egypt.[20] Michel Leiris suggested that instead they should visit black Africa to investigate what was happening, especially on the Ivory Coast, where the RDA (Révolution démocratique africaine) had been brutally repressed. De Beauvoir was eager to see the Sahara, so they planned to start in Algiers, going on to Hoggar, Gao, Timbuktu, Bobo-Dioulasso and Bamako.

They stayed for several days in Ghardaia, where Sartre agreed to give a lecture, and then drove in trucks across the Sahara, stopping sometimes for twenty-four hours, sometimes just for a night. They spent over a week at Tamanrasset,[21] in spite of a hotel-keeper who let himself into de Beauvoir's bedroom and tried to seduce her.[22] They flew over the Niger to Gao, a town built of mud, where, following the sound of tom-toms, they found a wedding being celebrated with dancing in a courtyard.[23] Two days later Sartre succumbed to fever. With a temperature of 104, he took so much quinine that he lost his sense of balance, and, unable to see or to hear, stayed in bed for two days before flying on to Bobo-Dioulasso.

One of the native districts was controlled by the RDA, but although their arrival had been reported in the local newspaper, none of the rebels made contact, probably because the PCF had been trying to discourage them from meeting him.

In the evening they flew to Bamako, where they again failed to make contact with the RDA, though they stayed for several days before moving on to Dakar. Exhausted they spent two weeks recuperating in Morocco before going back to Paris, where Sartre found Dolorès had installed herself. His attempts to dissuade her had not been forceful enough. But he was no longer emotionally involved, and he knew she would be more demandingly proprietorial than Michelle. The moment had come for partial withdrawal and negotiation. Wanda, who was having little success as an actress, had been glad to accept his offer of a regular income, parts in all his plays and meetings at regular intervals. But to Dolorès it seemed insulting when he offered a flat, an income and scheduled times for togetherness. The relationship, which had lasted for five years, ended in a clean break.

After this his partnership with de Beauvoir was never again to be seriously threatened by any of his affairs. The relationship with Michelle would continue to the end of his life; some of his future mistresses would be beautiful, some of his intimacies extremely intense, but no other woman would ever bring him so close as Dolorès had to sacrificing de Beauvoir, who would go on being his resident critic and his chief partner in conversation. Above all she would go on looking after him. Dolorès had tried persistently, as other women would try later, to expropriate him from de Beauvoir, but the partnership, which had lasted since 1929, would last till shortly before his death. He and de Beauvoir even gave the impression of thinking jointly. They could complete each other's sentences.[24] In company he talked much more than she did, but she always looked as if her ideas were in complete harmony with his. Nevertheless they went on addressing each other as 'vous'.

In September 1950 the Korean War broke out. Korea had been split in 1945 into two halves, with the Russians occupying the northern half and the Americans the southern half. In August 1948 a republic had been proclaimed in the south, with Syngman Rhee as its president; four weeks later a republic was proclaimed in the north, and it claimed sovereignty over the whole country. The danger of civil war was obvious, especially after the American occupying forces were withdrawn in June 1949, and after a number of provocations around the border, the communist forces invaded the south on 25 June, capturing Seoul, the capital, within three days.

It was being said that China would detonate a world war by attacking Formosa. People queued outside grocers' shops to stockpile tinned food. Some of Sartre's friends, including Francine Camus, spoke of killing themselves when the Red Army entered France, and her husband tried to persuade Sartre not to stay.[25] Merleau-Ponty joked about working as a lift-man in New York.[26] For *Les Temps modernes*, he insisted, the only possibility was to keep silent about politics. It was obvious that Russia had encouraged the invasion of South Korea: Stalin was no less of an imperialist than the Western leaders.[27] Sartre did not see the need for silence, but he did not try to overrule Merleau-Ponty after accepting his political judgment for so long. 'I was swimming in uncertainty.'[28]

At the beginning of 1951, finding it harder than ever to make headway with his ethics, he started a new play, constructing it around the same moral point he now considered crucial: that good and evil are not opposites. *Le Diable et le Bon Dieu* (*The Devil and the Good Lord*) carries its central character to the conclusion: 'On this earth at this time, good and evil are inseparable.' Götz von Berlichingen (1480–1562) was a warrior knight who reluctantly fought on the side of the peasants during the rebellion of 1525. He wrote an autobiography which was not published until 1731,[29] and Goethe's play *Götz von Berlichingen mit der eisernen Hand* (published 1773, produced 1774) portrays him as a champion of freedom. Sartre had been only twelve when he started to write a novel about Goetz, but the new impulse came from a conversation with Jean-Louis Barrault, who summed up the plot of Cervantes's 1615 play *El rufián dichoso* (*The Blessed Scoundrel*) about a bandit from Seville who throws dice to decide whether he should go on doing evil. He ends up as a saintly friar in Mexico.

The argument for canonizing Genet in the biography is that a man can approximate to saintliness by embracing all the evil projected on him by ostensibly virtuous people. Sartre compares Genet to Marcel Jouhandeau, who, in novels published in the twenties and thirties, had made a cult of abjection: 'Only passion or vice throw you into the same destitution as saintliness. I believe that it's only when man is at this point of finding himself abandoned by everything and by himself that he is closest to grace – I mean to being worthy of it.'[30] This is the pattern Sartre imposes on Goetz, who makes his appearance in the play as a bastard outsider (like the young Genet) and swings perversely into a piety motivated not by reverence for God but by rage at his unforgivable absence.

Though Sartre was not intending to allegorize Genet's options in the play, its main issues relate closely to the issues in the book, while Sartre's Goetz is caught as helplessly as his Genet in the trap contrived by traditional morality. Because the sixteenth century is more theocentric than the twentieth, the warrior knight can be shown (more clearly than the modern criminal can) to be taking up positions determined by attitudes to God. A professional soldier, Goetz is a killer, and the peasants suffer from his ruthlessness; Sartre makes the Brechtian point that when war grows out of a quarrel between the rich, it is the poor who get killed.

Also at the back of Sartre's mind was Luther's reactions to the peasants during the wars of 1524–5.[31] The repression was ferocious and the peasants ended up worse off than before. Sartre was trying to write a 'play of crowds', in which the main characters could be understood and judged through their effects on the crowds they galvanize.[32] But, evolved for heroic drama, Sartre's dramatic technique was inadequate. He was facing many of the same problems as Brecht in *Mutter Courage*. Both plays differ from Shakespeare's history plays in containing no on-stage battle scenes; both try to graft a moral and political argument into a historical situation; both try to convey the illusion that armies are fighting, towns being besieged, citizens being massacred. But Brecht is more successful that Sartre in suggesting the background of collective violence and in splicing action tightly into dialogue. Remembering what he had learnt from Dullin – to write the situations, not the words – Sartre does his best to avoid static arguments, but he makes his points verbally, in rhetorical harangues, sometimes in analytical discussions, and in aphorisms which are occasionally reminiscent of Oscar Wilde. 'What's boring about evil', complains Goetz, 'is that you get used to it. To invent you have to be a genius. Tonight I hardly feel inspired!'

Like Sartre's Genet, this Goetz is driven to extremism in good and evil but not by passion or sadism or masochism. Goetz is activated by the nonstop argument he carries on with himself and with the absolute. God, he says, is the only enemy worth fighting. Like one of the Marquis de Sade's characters, he perpetrates outrages in order to submit the human condition to a laboratory test: is it possible that wholesale cruelty will go unpunished? Once it is clear that no retribution is forthcoming, the only remaining hope is that God will be embarrassed: 'I am the man who makes the Almighty uncomfortable. In me God feels horrified at himself.'

Told by Heinrich, an ex-priest, that it is impossible for anyone on earth to do good, Goetz finds the challenge irresistible, and, drawing more directly on Cervantes's play, Sartre writes a dice-throwing sequence in which Goetz cheats in order to lose. He wants to pay the forfeit, which is to live altruistically. As he forces himself to act lovingly towards his fellow-creatures, the play becomes more than ever like a dramatized debate. Comedy is uneasily balanced against sentimental melodrama when he embraces a leper, though the action swings ironically against Goetz when the leper shows more interest in being presented with an indulgence.

The two women in the play, Catherine (the role created for Wanda) and Hilda, are little more than foils to Goetz, while Heinrich and the peasant leader Nasty are incarnations of opposing viewpoints, Nasty representing approximately the attitudes of the Communist Party, while Heinrich exemplifies Sartre's habit of contradicting former principles. He is intended to embody a refutation of the idea that people are always free to choose. Heinrich 'cannot choose either the Church, which has abandoned the poor, or the poor, who have abandoned the Church ... He is *totally conditioned* by his situation.'[33] This tendency to argue through a play makes for bad drama while increasing the biographical interest of the text. Sartre was also projecting his own problems on his hero, writing almost enviously about a man who never experienced any difficulty in moving forward from ideas to actions. Sartre could be described exactly as he described Goetz – 'an adventurer whose failure will never make him into a militant, though he will form alliances with militants throughout the rest of his life ... Goetz's failure is to some extent that of anarchism; also that of paternalism, the anarchism of the masters'.[34]

Until the outbreak of the Korean War and the dissolution of the RDR, Sartre had not been politically impotent, but he now felt he was in an impossible situation. What would happen if the Russians occupied France? If he stayed it would be dangerous not to collaborate, but he could not picture himself living in South America with other rich refugees from France.[35] In the meantime he was free to write about freedom, but his writing was of no interest to the enslaved majority: if it was not intelligible to 'the Hindu dying of starvation' it was worthless.[36] No longer a hunger artist of nausea and alienation, Sartre was frustrated in his lust for solidarity with the rest of humanity. Though Goetz gives away his estates to found a community based on love and brotherhood, he is jealous of Hilda, who has the knack of making people love her, while he, lacking her simplicity, feels uncertain whether he genuinely loves the people or merely wants them to love him. The secret subject of the play is Sartre's sense of being isolated and of lacking warmth. The whole of his quest for power was ambivalent: he wanted it for his own sake but also because he believed empirically that good was separate from evil and that he could use power to do good. One reason he admired spontaneity so much in others was that he had tried unsuccessfully to cultivate it himself. According to Cau, 'All his generosities are in his head: they don't correspond to anything but moral signals, codes worked out cerebrally. His friendship is not warm but dry, like his voice, like his laugh.'[37] The generosity was partly aggressive – a means of dominating; the detachment was partly defensive and partly necessitated by the isolation. 'I killed God', says Goetz, 'because he separated me from men, and now his death is isolating me still more effectively.' When he throws in his lot with the rebels, Nasty will not accept him as a common soldier, a man among men, but only as a leader. Like the heroes of Sartre's childhood reading, Goetz is an adventurer; he ends up wanting to fight on the side of the peasants, but needing both to conceal his atheism from them and to terrorize them; Sartre was an intellectual adventurer who would never succeed in making himself as indispensable to the Party leaders as Goetz was to Nasty, but, like Goetz, he was caught between the impossibility of cultivating his own garden, indifferent to historical movements, and the impossibility of being honest in public.

When he started writing *Le Diable et le Bon Dieu*, Sartre, who had been reading extensively about the French Revolution, wanted to incorporate in the play a comprehensive view of society, and he evolved a character called Dosia to represent the aristocracy.[38] Eventually he scrapped Dosia, introducing a banker who could put forward some of the same arguments, but because there is no rival figure of temporal authority (while the figures of spiritual authority are so feeble and the women mere foils) Goetz's only real conflict is with himself, while the offstage battles fail to function as an objective correlative to it.

Sartre seems envious of the way violence comes naturally to the man of action. Goetz kills with no more compunction that a writer has in crossing out a word. But Goetz is most destructive when he tries not to be: giving his land to the peasants he is making slaughter inevitable, and in the final moment of the play, when he kills a peasant to establish his authority over the others, he is reflecting the latest phase in Sartre's thinking about violence. It is indispensable.

By the time he left La Pouèze, Sartre had finished the first act, and after his return to Paris, Simone Berriau, who was still running the Théâtre Antoine, arranged for him to read his script to Louis Jouvet. The first act is extremely long, and, at the reading, her husband kept dozing off, as did their friend Yves Mirande, while Jouvet, who knew he did not have long to live – he was suffering from a heart condition – listened impassively, making no comment even at the end. He found the play blasphemous, but asked his confessor for permission to direct it.[39] This granted, they began to discuss casting. The obvious choice for Goetz was Pierre Brasseur, the heavyweight actor who had done so well in Barrault's film *Les Enfants du Paradis* (1945) and on stage in the 1948 revival of Claudel's *Partage de Midi*. Hilda would be played by Maria Casarès with Jean Vilar as Heinrich.

The production was scheduled to open in May. To escape from interruptions while finishing the script, Sartre decided to leave Paris. De Beauvoir wanted to go skiing, so, together with Bost, they left for Auron, in the Alpes Maritimes, where Sartre stayed in his room, writing, while the other two skied. Sartre and de Beauvoir went on to St-Tropez, and from there back to Ramatuelle, where Brasseur visited them to discuss the character.[40]

When rehearsals started, the final scenes were still unwritten, and Sartre did not try to conceal his contempt for Brasseur and Jouvet, while they were frustrated by his uncooperativeness and infuriated by his high-handedness. To everyone but him it was obvious that the play was too long, but instead of cutting he added to the text and instead of attending rehearsals he sent Cau as his emissary with the new dialogue. Brasseur was provoked into writing drunkenly abusive letters: 'I'm fed up with you, Sartre, you're a cunt. I'm fed up to the teeth. I shit on your play with my piles. With a great bunch of piles I shit on your stupidity.' Sartre read only part of the letter. 'He repeats himself too much when he's raving.'[41]

Brasseur refused to learn Goetz's soliloquy in scene nine, which incorporates material from St John of the Cross. Never averse to eclecticism, Sartre also borrowed a remark of Savonarola's ('The Church is a harlot'), repartee taken from Clement VII ('You are a bastard.' 'Yes, like Jesus Christ.') and a paraphrase of a statement by a Cluniac monk quoted in Huizinga's *The Waning of the Middle Ages*. Odo of Cluny makes the point that if men were endowed with vision like the lynx of Boeotia, penetrating to the entrails, they would never want to embrace the mucus, bile, gall and excrement that lies hidden under the skin of a lovely woman.[42]

When Camus came to collect Casarès from rehearsals, they would sometimes have a drink with Sartre,[43] but little was left of the friendship between the two men. The ailing Jouvet, who had been fairly passive during rehearsals, left for the country without even waiting to watch the first performance, but the play was a success. The run, which began on 7 June 1951, continued until March 1952, though critics and apparently audiences were confused, misinterpreting the final moment when Goetz knifes the peasant soldier who refuses to fight under his leadership. He is not returning to the gratuitous pursuit of evil; all it means is that he has recognized the impossibility of suiting his actions to his ideals. As Francis Jeanson put it, 'Goetz's itinerary has seemed to exhaust all possible forms of idealism'.[44] The blind forces of history always dragoon the individual into betraying his conscience as he chooses between turning his back on the current situation and trying to control it.

The royalty income removed Sartre's financial anxieties but he was ill at ease, worrying that the Korean War might develop into a world war. Nor could he even commit *Les Temps modernes* to an unequivocal position: he described the review during 'the interregnum of 1950–2' as 'a ship without a captain'.[45] The war had isolated the PCF from the rest of the left, and if the review was drifting, it was drifting towards the isolated position occupied by the Party. Merleau-Ponty would have preferred to repudiate the Party, but for Sartre this was out of the question. 'It's impossible to take an anti-communist position without being against the proletariat.' On the other hand it would be impossible to take a pro-communist position without reneging on the promise he had made in his Présentation that the editors should belong to no party and no church: the idea had been to investigate problems without any predetermined commitment to their solution. Merleau-Ponty, when he had forced political silence on the review, had been honouring this principle; Sartre was willing to jettison it. But from the beginning he had never wanted to keep the editorial reins in his hands. To do that he would have had to spend much more time in Paris.

In the middle of July he left again with de Beauvoir. First they flew to Norway. From Oslo they crossed the Telemark; then, cruising in a ship, Sartre showed her the scenery he had enjoyed sixteen years earlier with his mother and Mancy, and from the deck they watched the midnight brightness of the sky, which had inspired his story 'Soleil de Minuit'. Next they spent ten days in Iceland, went on to Edinburgh, and visited the Hebrides. Travelling across Scotland they were oppressed by inhospitable hotel-keepers who refused to provide a table for writing in the bedroom. ('If you want to write, go into the writing-room.')

After a fortnight in London,[46] they returned to Paris, where Sartre resumed meetings at his flat on alternate Sunday afternoons for contributors to Les Temps modernes. The closer orientation towards the Party was confirmed by the enlistment of new collaborators, Guy de Chambure, Bernard Dort, and two journalists with a philosophical background, Claude Lanzmann and Marcel Péju. Both had jobs on newspapers, rewriting other people's articles. Lanzmann was an attractive man from a provincial Jewish bourgeois family. Olivier Todd describes him as a mixture of Malraux, Proust and the novelist Roger Vailland.[47] Péju had interviewed Sartre about Le Diable et le Bon Dieu for Samedi Soir,[48] and Sartre was pleased with what he wrote. A degree of unanimity began to emerge, but the new orientation meant that a breach with Camus could not be forestalled much longer. Before he had completed L'Homme révolté (The Rebel) in July 1952, it was arranged that a chapter – the one on Nietzsche and nihilism – would be excerpted in Les Temps modernes. It appeared in the August issue with no indication that the book was out to attack the communists. Comparing the idea of revolution with the actions it had triggered, Camus argued that the utopian end could not justify the violent means. Hegel is condemned for equating reason with fate, Marx trounced for assuming that the class struggle is powered by the force of reason, while the PCF is found guilty of ruthless deference to Moscow and ruthless indifference to the individual. Camus makes the point Sartre had already made in Les Mains sales about the slaughter of those who are out of step with Party policy, whether they are slightly ahead or slightly behind, but he attacks Sartre for failing to produce a moral philosophy that could transform existentialist *Angst* into a positive rebelliousness. Sartre is accused – not quite fairly – of jumping into an uncritical acceptance of historical determinism as interpreted by the Party. But behind Camus's book was something even more deeply inimical to Sartre's present position. Both writers had been changed by the sense of crisis during the Occupation; in Sartre the change was permanent and he no longer wanted to relax into a literary career. Camus, who did want to, intended *L'Homme révolté* as his final statement about political philosophy.

It was published in October, and generally acclaimed. *Le Figaro littéraire* called it Camus's most important work, while *Le Monde* pronounced it to be the most valuable book to have appeared since the war.[49] Even if he was displeased to receive praise from the extreme right, Camus was more disconcerted by the protracted silence of *Les Temps modernes*. What was happening at the fortnightly editorial meetings was that de Beauvoir was regularly reminding the others, who had all read the book, that it had to be reviewed, but none of them liked it and the general feeling was that Camus, instead of studying Marx and Engels, had relied on résumés of their work and had failed to understand it.[50] When Sartre asked for a volunteer to review the book, no-one spoke up, and eventually the job was given to the twenty-nine-year-old Francis Jeanson, who had fought with the FFI in North Africa and Germany, and had written a book about Sartre, *Le Problème morale et la penseé de Sartre*, to which Sartre had contributed a preface.

To write *Le Diable et le Bon Dieu*, he had put aside his biography of Genet, but in thinking about Goetz he had never stopped thinking about Genet, though Sartre was less interested in writing objectively about either man than in using him as an exemplar for an intricate system of generalizations: the extremes of good and evil meet, while for the hero, as for the saint, the only way to earn social esteem is by self-destruction. It is easy to move from soldiering to saintliness: you internalize the process of dying, and slow it down. Refusing to explore or enjoy the environment, you sacrifice everything to God. Sartre could see close parallels between the career of his Goetz, the strategy of Genet and the strategy of anyone who, instead of venturing out into an active relationship with the world, tries to transubstantiate it into language. Sartre is fascinated by the way Genet uses words onanistically to destroy and transfigure. His books consists of 'words which clash, which burn themselves up', becoming 'an index of the rigorously impractical operations to which he has devoted his life. Thanks to language, Genet can lend a being to nothingness and remain restlessly in the domain of shadow, that's to say of evil.'[51] The landscape is dissolved, while the characters are, as Genet says, 'pretexts for my iridescence, then for my transparency, finally for my absence; these boys I describe evaporate. Nothing remains of them except what remains of me ... I exist only through them, while they are nothing, existing only through me.'[52]

Sartre keeps comparing Genet with Mallarmé, who recognized the '"universal determinability" and the "absolute negativity" of consciousness. He too was going to pass this "blanket condemnation on everything which is perceptible".'[53] Sartre was still concerned with the problem of mental digestion: the individual consciousness cannot stomach the glutinous proliferations of external reality. In the 1939 essay on Husserl he used the spider image to attack the illusion that made consciousness devour objects.[54] This analogy makes the process of perceiving seem more repulsive than the object perceived, but in the chestnut tree episode the ugliness is in the object, and Sartre, who has never felt entirely at ease with the physical environment, welcomes Genet as an ally, equally allergic to it: 'He hates matter. Excluded, he looks at the goods of this world through a pane of glass, like poor children looking at cakes through a shop-window ... Matter is the unintelligible, the unforgivable outrage; it represents his impotence and the reality of his exile.'[55] It is as a refugee that he settles in literature. He dislikes things, but relishes the words that represent them; hates flowers, but loves their names.[56] Again and again, Sartre comes back to characterizing language as something that dissolves reality in order to reconstitute it, destroys the world in order to reproduce it. Quoting Maurice Blanchot, he equates language with 'the flight of being into significations, the evaporation of the significations, in short, annihilation', but at the same time it inscribes nothingness in being. Like the surrealists, Genet operates a war-machine which recuperates non-being while dissolving reality – we get many repetitions of this phrase, and many variations on it.[57]

In *Qu'est-ce que c'est que la littérature?* Sartre had castigated the surrealists for their lack of social commitment; he condones that of Genet, who is judged by a new set of criteria. Mauriac had been roundly condemned for manipulating characters like puppets instead of giving them leeway to make decisions of their own; Genet once said to Sartre: 'My books aren't novels because none of my characters takes a decision on his own.'[58] Instead of recognizing this as a limitation, Sartre praises the desert-like desolation of *Notre-Dame des fleurs*: 'all his characters are inert, tossed about by fate; the author is a savage god who gets drunk on human sacrifice'.[59]

Does this god allow himself to be seen? His words not only burn themselves but burn him, and the Genet phoenix which emerges is a fantasy, no less factitious than his seductive murderers and brutish pimps. 'To compose', writes Sartre, 'is, for him, to recreate himself.'[60] Less critical than he seems, and always attracted to self-generation or regeneration, Sartre raises no objection; in fact he carries the process one stage further, burning the phoenix to conjure up a new one. Like Sartre's studies of Baudelaire and Flaubert, *Saint Genet* is not so much a biography as an elaborate, brilliant, inaccurate display of how another consciousness functions. Not content with leaving out most of the biographical facts, Sartre distorts the ones he introduces: 'Between his years at the Mettray reformatory (he was fifteen) and his first burglary (he was twenty-five) ten years pass without marking him.'[61] Later we are told that these ten years were 'astonishingly full: he becomes an apprentice, runs away, gets caught; placed in a bourgeois household, he steals, he's sent to Mettray, he escapes again, he begs, travels round France, joins the Foreign Legion, deserts, escapes to Barcelona, lives by begging and prostituting himself in the Barrio Chino, steals again, leaves Spain and goes everywhere, Italy, Poland, Czechoslovakia, Germany, stealing and crossing frontiers illegally'.[62] No-one could be unmarked by all this, but Sartre, still fixated on the notion that a single choice, made in childhood, determines the future, distances himself scornfully from the biographers who would have built several colourful chapters out of these adventures.

Genet describes himself as having been homosexual before he started stealing; Sartre contradicts him without adducing any evidence: the primary disorientation was due to oppression, he says. Genet must have identified himself as homosexual after being bullied into identifying himself as a thief. 'This first violation was the gaze of the other person, which took him by surprise, penetrated him, transformed him permanently into an object ... An actual rape can register in our moral conscience as an iniquitous yet irrevocable condemnation, and, inversely, a condemnation can be experienced as a rape.'[63] Here, as Douglas Collins has pointed out, Sartre was following Angelo Hesnard's 1957 book *L'Univers morbide*, which condemns the 'moral rape' that forces children into an alien discipline.[64] Sartre had started reading Hesnard at the Ecole Normale, borrowing the books *Relativité* and *L'Inconscience* in his first year and taking both out again in his third. He was excited by the idea of the homosexualizing gaze of the Other: he had already written, in 'L'Enfance d'un chef', about the intrusive adult gaze that can take the boy from behind, as in buggery. 'Lucien invented a new game: in the morning, when he took his bath alone in the bathroom like a grown-up, he pretended that someone was watching him through the keyhole ... Then he turned his back to the door and squatted on all fours to make his bottom stick out ridiculously.'[65] It is almost as if Sartre had been waiting since 1937 for a subject like Genet, whose life was arguably changed by a single traumatic moment of 'moral rape'.

Sartre may have been unaware of how much he was identifying with Genet, though, in an awkwardly defensive footnote, he attacks the assumption that a critic is likely to be revealing more about himself than about his subject.[66] Sartre tries to keep himself out of the picture, not even confessing that he too was caught stealing in childhood. But the affinity goes deeper. Like Baudelaire, Genet had been rejected by his mother, and he revenges himself in fantasy: he imagines vomiting on her hands.[67] In the novel *Pompes funèbres* the burial of the illegitimate child may represent 'the perpetual funeral of the child Genet'.[68] Sartre could be describing himself – or anyone – when he says: 'Genet is so made that all his feelings have double and triple depth. The liveliest, the freshest passion is at the same time a pretext for reliving the decisive moment of this childhood.'[69] In *Les Mots* Sartre will alienate his childhood: in many ways he comes closer to himself when writing about Genet – not least when he discusses Genet's technique of coming to terms with disaster by persuading himself that he willed it.[70] More philosophically minded and less overtly self-involved than his subject, Sartre generalizes this compulsion, contending not that he wanted everything which happened to him, but that we are all responsible for our situation. Sartre's doctrines about choice have neurotic roots.

Even when he describes Genet's technique of writing while in prison, Sartre is inadvertently describing his own while at liberty: 'When the masturbator changes into the artist, it is still to act on himself; let's remember that he throws himself into writing as if into stealing or making love – frenziedly, doped by orthodrine tablets, and he doesn't put his pen down until he's finished ... He hurries towards the moment when he will write "The End" at the foot of the final page, and when he'll have *nothing else to say* because he will have *said everything*.' I don't know whether Sartre used orthodrine while writing *Saint Genet*, but, like *L'Etre et le Néant* and the notes on morality, the book was obviously written in a headlong rush, with a strong urge to leave nothing unsaid. Sartre's 573-page book can be described by applying his own description of Genet's fictions: systematically it develops in the realm of the imaginary all the possibilities latent in the actual situation – especially those which have not been realized.[71] *Saint Genet* is an analytical work, but it also belongs to the 'realm of the imaginary', even if the experience of writing it helped to dissuade Sartre from devoting time to imaginative literature. To him Genet incarnated 'solitude pushed into passion'.[72] If we want to reconcile the object and the subject, Sartre concludes – and no-one has wanted this more urgently than he did – we must, if only once, 'realize this latent solitude which eats into our acts and thoughts'.[73] In warning the reader Sartre was revealing his own fear.

The interaction between Sartre and Genet was far-reaching, but there was no reciprocity, no exchange of gifts equal in value. Genet was the loser: writing, for the first time, the biography of a living writer, Sartre stopped him in mid-career, crushing the artist under a massive and premature monument. Genet wrote no more books and only three more plays. After reading the typescript he expressed his reaction by trying to throw it into the fire. The relationship between the two men deteriorated sharply and it is hard to believe that Genet's abdication from literature was due more to the suicide of Abdullah, a boy who loved him, than to Sartre's book. To Cocteau Genet complained: 'You and Sartre have made me into a statue ... I'm another person and this other person has to find something to say.' Cocteau's verdict was: 'Jean has changed since Sartre's book. He seems at the same time to be conforming to it and running away from it.'[74]

Where Sartre was most unlike Genet was in his evangelism: his task, he believed, was to construct an ideology which would help people to understand the world and how to behave in it.[75] He read voraciously, recommending books to de Beauvoir, but his priorities were changing: work had come to matter more, and friendship less. Fantasies about fame had once been a source of excitement; the reality of fame brought more power than pleasure. He was determined to stay in the public eye and to make full use of the power, but the quality of his writing was deteriorating because, mixing with people less, he was observing less and theorizing more, while, busier than ever, he had less time for research, for reading books, for seeing films, and for sitting in cafés. This had been one of his main pleasures but now tiresome strangers would accost him.

He was spending less time with de Beauvoir; Olga and Bost were not in Paris; since Dullin's death Toulouse had been living an isolated life.[76] At home he chained himself to a heavy working routine.[77] Jean Cau, the man who regularly saw him at work, describes him in non-human images – bullock, monster, mule, machine – while the people around him are 'satellites'.[78]

Sartre was involving himself more deeply in an alliance with the PCF, but it was not he who took the initiative. The Party had consistently opposed the war in Vietnam, which had been in progress since 1946. France was unmistakably losing: by now much of the country was controlled by the Vietminh. A French sailor, Henri Martin, had volunteered at the end of 1945 for the campaign in Indo-China against the Japanese who had gone on fighting when their country surrendered. He was sent to Vietnam, where he found himself pitted against the Vietnamese. Three times he applied unsuccessfully for a transfer. After being sent back to France at the end of 1947, he was posted in 1948 to Toulon, and in 1949 he began to stick up leaflets, which he wrote himself, protesting against the war in Indo-China. Arrested in May 1950, he was condemned by a court-martial to five years of imprisonment.

When a committee was formed to campaign for his liberation, Sartre joined it after being approached by Claude Roy, a communist who had never been unfriendly, and by Jean Chaintron, an old working-class militant. When Sartre was received by President Auriol, after signing an appeal addressed to him, the president agreed that the sentence was excessive, but said he could offer no remission so long as the communists went on campaigning for it.[1] Sartre then undertook to collaborate on editing a book about the affair.[2]

It was not until later that Camus was invited to join the campaign, but in February, when the French League for the Rights of Man arranged a meeting to protest against the death sentence passed in Spain on a group of labour leaders, he selected the speakers, and Sartre was one of them.[3] But, refusing to join the Henri Martin campaign, Camus said that 'the values of liberty would only be compromised and confused with other values if defended in *Les Temps modernes* and associated with those who approve of it'. The review's silence about *L'Homme révolté* was still unbroken, and in April, at a café on the place St-Sulpice, when Camus talked derisively about hostile reviewers, Sartre was too embarrassed to reply.[4] Jeanson was already at work on his critique. 'He'll be the harshest,' Sartre had said, 'but at least he'll be polite.'[5] Meeting Camus in the street, Sartre warned him that the review would be unfavourable; he seemed so perturbed that Sartre invited him to write a reply.[6] The review turned out to be even harsher than Sartre had expected, and he persuaded Jeanson to tone it down,[7] but it was still unequivocally hostile. Published in the May issue under the punning title 'Albert Camus ou l'âme révoltée' ('or the revolted soul'), it accused Camus of rejecting history in favour of ineffectual moralizing; the book was described as a 'pseudo-philosophy of a pseudo-history of "revolutions"'.[8] Deeply depressed – he had lost all appetite for life, he said – Camus went on hesitating about whether to exercise his right of reply.[9]

Now that Michelle Vian had separated from her husband, her affair with Sartre came out into the open, and in May they drove to the south of France together with de Beauvoir and Bost, who shared the driving. They were at St-Tropez when Merleau-Ponty arrived there with his wife. The two men argued, but with no hope of reaching any agreement: Merleau-Ponty was moving decisively away from the left as Sartre was becoming more radical. Not that he would ever cease to be preoccupied with literature. He continued his work on Mallarmé before returning by train to Paris for some meetings.[10] He soon left again for three weeks in Italy with Michelle, but for most of the time she was left on her own: Sartre worked no less hard on holiday than he did in Paris.[11]

They were in Rome when he heard about the demonstration of 28 May in Paris. In April General Eisenhower had resigned as Supreme Allied Commander in Europe, and had been succeeded by General Matthew Ridgway, who in Korea had taken over from General MacArthur when he became critical of American policy. In August 1951 Ridgway had broken off armistice talks, accusing the communists of violating the agreements on demilitarization. When he visited Paris in May 1952, the PCF organized a demonstration, which became violent, and the police pitched in brutally. The next day several leading communists were arrested, including Jacques Duclos, an ex-pastrycook and leader of the Party in the National Assembly. Two pigeons were found in his car, and he was accused of espionage on the assumption that they were carrier-pigeons; in fact he had been intending to eat them. At the same time the Party's newspapers were seized. A protest strike was organized for 2 June, and after it failed, Sartre was furious when the right-wing press reacted in the way anyone would have expected it to react, claiming that the working-class had lost faith in the Party. 'The last connections were broken,' wrote Sartre, 'my vision was transformed: an anti-communist is a swine, I can see no way out of that, and I never will ... After ten years of brooding about it, I had reached breaking point, and I needed only a gentle push. In the language of the church, this was a conversion ... I swore against the bourgeoisie a hatred which will die only when I do.'[12] If the workers had failed to support the strike, he argued, their motives must be personal : their inaction did not amount to a criticism of the Party. He was also under the influence of Henri Guillemin's *Le Coup du 2 Décembre*. 'It's a book which mattered to me : the documentation Guillemin provides showed me how much shit there can be in a bourgeois heart.'[13] Besides telling the story of Louis Napoleon's 1851 coup d'état, which changed the French constitution, Guillemin marshals extracts from letters, diaries, newspapers and magazines as evidence that, after the easy defeat of the communist riots in June 1849, what the rightists wanted was not a republic but a dictatorship.

Sartre's explosion of hatred was partly against himself : he spoke of wanting to break the bones in his head.[14] He was too angry to stay in Italy. 'I had to write or suffocate.'[15] Returning to Paris, he worked feverishly at *Les Communistes et la paix* (*The Communists and Peace*). 'In two weeks', de Beauvoir told her sister, 'he's gone for five nights with no sleep, and during the other nights slept only four or five hours.'[16]

Of all the turning points in his life this was probably the most important : if commitment as defined in *Qu'est-ce que c'est que la littérature?* had already been making him into a different kind of writer, he now passed the point of no return. The creative momentum gained from writing three novels and seven short stories had petered out before his fourth novel, *La Mort dans l'âme*, was written. Though the outbreak of war had boosted his creativity, it had been impossible to publish either *L'Age de raison* or *Le Sursis* during the Occupation, and there is no knowing how his career might have developed if they had not been delayed until 1945. Though both novels made international impact, they had lost most of their relevance to current politics and to his current thinking. But even if he had not lost so much of his creative momentum, he would probably have been floated into a different kind of activity by the surge of popularity brought to him by the vogue for existentialism.

Fame meant power, and for about seven years after the end of the war it was by no means absurd to believe that he might have a key role to play in saving the world from a new war. He was convinced that everything depended on keeping Europe neutral. Later it would be apparent that he had overrated both his own influence and the militancy of the two great powers, but it is easy to see why he could not have settled down to cultivate his fictional garden. Even after he had failed both in his opposition to the Atlantic Pact and in his efforts to create inside France a democratic, revolutionary alternative to communism, it was clear that for a man so capable of public-spirited hatred, there would be plenty of other battles to fight. He always had more to do than could possibly be done in the time available to him, and though he did not succeed fully in any of the major political or philosophical or literary tasks he set himself, the sum total of his achievements was to be enormous.

The paradox is rooted in the most fundamental of his personal problems – what was he? What should he be doing? He was permanently uncertain about whether he should be taking the advice he made Hoederer give Hugo – 'Your talent is for writing' – or whether he was justified in leaving his desk littered with unfinished work while setting out on another journey to see socialism on the advance or colonialism being exposed for the evil it was or while accepting yet another invitation to let his name and his face be used in publicizing another political cause of obvious importance. People were really suffering. He could give real help in fighting oppression. If he enjoyed the publicity and the popularity, did that detract from the value of his contribution? Or was he still fixated on the notion of earning his salvation through good works? Or on the deep-seated anxieties about not being a man of action and not being needed? Or was he deliberately overcrowding his life to give himself an excuse for not finishing the work which in any case he would have been unable to finish adequately, however much time he had at his disposal?

Did he even ask himself these questions as he plunged into over-commitment? The more hectic the activity, the less danger there would be of having time to brood about motivations. From 1952 till his death in 1980 he never tried (as Camus did) to reduce his political commitments and his output as a writer of politically loaded books in order to leave more space for self-examination, creativity and literature. Sartre's only major literary objective would be in line with that of *Qu'est-ce que c'est que la littérature?* – to condemn nineteenth-century writers, especially Flaubert and Mallarmé, for failing to help the working class.

The man who says there is shit in the bourgeois heart is too angry to care about style or logic. Sartre's rage, which gave him a violent urgency, also carried him close to Lenin's unsentimental belief in the Party as more reliable than the proletariat. Marx had maintained that the proletariat – because its sufferings are universal – is the universal class which will lead the world to revolution; though Lenin proclaimed faith in 'the spontaneous awakening of the masses', he wanted the Party to take the lead by making the proletariat conscious of itself. In *Les Communistes et la paix* Sartre will equate the Party with the movement which unites the workers by carrying them towards revolution. Without the Party they remain amorphous, impotent.

In the first of the three long essays he published under this title, he denounced his former ally Georges Altman, and ridiculed the ideal of the RDR – a democratic alternative to Stalinist communism. 'Where is the political team that will implement the programme? Where is the majority that will carry it into power?'[17] Having joined in attacks on the Party as being democratic in neither structure nor procedure, Sartre now turned all his polemical artillery against its critics. Abandoning his principle of preserving a neutral position between the two power blocs, he gave his allegiance to the Soviet Union, which 'wants peace and proves it every day'.[18]

When the first essay appeared in the July issue of *Les Temps modernes*, it was obvious that he was steering the review to the left. If he remembered his initial promise of non-alignment, he would not have worried. He was at one of the many crises in which he believed with all the fervency of the convert that until now he had been totally wrong but now he was totally right. For Sartre nothing was more thrilling, more enjoyable, than the moment when a project or a system of belief collapses to reveal, amid the ruins, the basis on which a new one can be built. In May 1949 *Les Temps modernes* had protested against the Soviet system by proclaiming : 'There is no socialism when one citizen out of twenty is in a camp.' In 1952 the system was unchanged but Sartre, no less than the PCF, was now supporting it. In *Drôle d'amitié* he condemned the bullying PCF militant he had admired in *L'Age de raison* but he never turned his critical artillery against Soviet Party henchmen. The communists welcomed his support ; Kanapa applauded his courage and generosity,[19] but René Etiemble disliked the new line and Sartre's new friends, especially Claude Roy, whom Etiemble called 'a Stalinist nazi'.[20]

When Camus finally wrote his reply, in a letter dated 30 June, he addressed himself to Sartre, calling him 'Monsieur le Directeur'. He was weary, he said, of receiving 'lessons in effectiveness from critics who have never pointed anything but their armchairs in the direction of history'.[21] Complaining about the feebleness of Jeanson's review, Camus called him 'a bourgeois Marxist' who wanted 'a revolt against everything except the Communist Party and the communist state'. Sartre was furious. 'I'm going to answer him in any case', he told Jeanson. 'You can if you want to.'[22]

Sartre did not know, when he wrote his letter, that he'd never see Camus again, but he did know that their friendship was dead. 'Many things brought us together, few divided us. But these few were still too many.'[23] The letter begins angrily, accusing Camus of 'dull self-importance' and of carrying a 'portable altar' around with him as if the value of his book had been divinely guaranteed.[24] Later on the polemic becomes more guarded. Claiming that he is not a Marxist – a claim which by now is highly equivocal – Sartre admits to being bourgeois, just like Camus and Jeanson,[25] but Camus, wanting to destroy the Party without having anything to offer in its place,[26] is guilty of a 'quietism' which refuses to distinguish between the oppressors.[27] The heat of Sartre's argument remains intense, but the language becomes flat. 'The iron curtain is only a mirror, and each half of the world reflects the other half. Each turn of the screw here corresponds to a turn of the screw there, and finally, here and there, we are the screwers and the screwed.'[28]

He goes on to write generously about Camus's achievements in *L'Etranger* and in the Resistance. 'You personified the conflicts of the era, and you subsumed them through your ardour for living them. You were a *person*, the most complex and the richest : the last and most welcome of Chateaubriand's heirs, and the zealous defender of a social cause.'[29] Since then Camus had detached himself from contemporary history : 'Only half of you is still living among us ... You are no more than an abstraction of revolt.'[30] Sartre ends by inviting Camus to write back, but if he does, there will be no answer to this answer. 'I refuse to fight you.'[31]

Sales of *Les Temps modernes* had never been higher. Since *Les Communistes et la paix* each edition had been selling out within a few days, and selling out again when reprinted. Agog at the quarrel between the two star writers, readers were hoping Camus would reply, but he did not. In his diary he wrote : 'They admit sin but refuse grace ... Something in them, ultimately, aspires to servitude.'[32]

At the end of July Sartre travelled by train to Milan where de Beauvoir was waiting for him, and together they drove in her car through Cremona, Ferrara, Ravenna, Urbino and Bari. In Sicily they visited Agrigento and Syracuse. They drove back to Rome, drove on to explore Italy. She wanted to see as much as possible; he wanted to write the second part of *Les Communistes et la paix*. They compromised, but not without quarrelling.

In this second part he tries to substantiate his contention that the Party is the exact expression of the working classes. 'What it represents in their eyes is their aspirations, their inclinations, their wishes', carrying these to the highest level of efficacy.[33] The isolated worker is a sub-man; he achieves humanity only by refusing to be what he is, by rebelling against his situation, by acting in unison with fellow-workers. Indispensable to this is the organization the Party provides; it is only through collective struggle that the proletariat can come into existence as a proletariat.[34] It must therefore be regarded not only as interdependent with the Party but as inseparable from it. There can be no question of working-class spontaneity: 'it's a matter of an Order which makes order prevail and issues orders'.[35] Though Sartre has come around to an unequivocally Leninist position, the rapport between leaders and led is described, in the manner of *L'Etre et le Néant*, as if it were a one-to-one relationship. Diffuse sovereignty is concentrated in the leader and reflected to each member of the group, who, in obeying, functions as a repository of sovereignty. Acting in unison through the collective dimension, everyone is a leader. Like Trotsky, who once wrote 'Our "truth" of course is not absolute',[36] Sartre did not always quite believe in his own arguments.

It was inevitable that the quarrel with Camus would soon be followed by a quarrel with Merleau-Ponty. Though he had resigned in 1950 as political editor, he was still editor-in-chief, and he found it hard to work with the extremists such as Claude Roy whom Sartre was using as his adjutants. Though they were not named as members of the editorial board, Sartre, as he later admitted, was letting himself be prodded by them into moving further leftwards.[37] Merleau-Ponty, who had been meticulous in submitting all his contributions to Sartre, was annoyed when Sartre failed to show him the second instalment of *Les Communistes et la paix* until it was in proof. Sartre was feeling guilty about his past deference to Merleau-Ponty's political leadership and about the silence they had preserved since the outbreak of the Korean War in 1950. With the enthusiasm of the convert, Sartre was determined to speak out decisively, and, upset though he was, Merleau-Ponty neither provoked a quarrel nor stated his views in an article. He regularly attended the fortnightly editorial meetings but arrived late, left early and kept his opinions to himself. Had he been more outspoken, Pouillon and Pontalis, already uneasy at Sartre's new radicalism, might have rallied to Merleau-Ponty's support.[38]

Intellectual life in France tends to be schismatic, and even if Merleau-Ponty, who was a colleague of Lévi-Strauss at the Collège de France, had remained on better terms with Sartre, it is unlikely that he would have been able to cement an alliance between the two men, though a good deal of Lévi-Strauss's work was published in *Les Temps modernes* during the early fifties. Listing 'books which have advanced knowledge' in 'Le Réformisme et les fétiches', a contribution to the February 1956 issue of the review, Sartre pays tribute to the 'ethnographic works' of Lévi-Strauss, together with books by Henri Guillemin, the historians Georges Lefebvre and Marc Bloch, and the art criticism of Pierre Francastel, but in calling Lévi-Strauss an ethnographer, Sartre was implicitly laying claim to anthropology as his own territory as well as resisting Lévi-Strauss's attempts to differentiate his anthropology from traditionalist ethnography. Like Leiris and Sartre, Lévi-Strauss was hostile to both colonialism and the non-interventionist anthropology that had grown up under the old system. The anthropologist is naturally drawn to territories where an old culture has been defeated though not extirpated, but he is professionally predisposed to being more of a cultural conservationist than the anti-conservative Sartre. As imperialism ran into one crisis after another during the fifties, Sartre gave more time – and more space in the review – to the injustices of the old system and the brutality of the colonial oppressors. In 1946 the French use of torture in Madagascar had already been exposed in Roger Stéphane's reports.[39] During the fifties the allocation of space in *Les Temps modernes* reflected not only Sartre's shift of interest from literature to politics but his lack of interest in language. Merleau-Ponty, as he concerned himself less with left-wing politics and more with linguistics, flirted with structuralism, accepting the view that all cultural phenomena belong to a single order, that language is not transparent and that political action needs to be based on accurate understanding of the symbolic systems a society is using. But Sartre, after his brief flicker of interest in the Saussurian terminology, turned his back on the structuralists, recognizing them as rivals and believing that he could fight them more effectively by ignoring them than by confronting them directly. He would make indirect assaults on positions held by Lévi-Strauss and Roland Barthes but mostly without mentioning them or structuralism by name.

In the autumn, Sartre supported several political protests. In the middle of October, after Alain Le Léap, secretary general of the communist-dominated union, the CGT (Confédération générale du travail) had been arrested for 'demoralization of the nation', Sartre protested in *Libération* and *Ce Soir*.[40] In the middle of November he signed the 'Manifesto against the Cold War' prepared by the CNE. Four days later, no longer wanting to seem critical of the Party, he banned a production of *Les Mains sales* in Vienna. He had been involved since the summer with the Peace Movement, and in December when it was announced that a World Congress for Peace was to be held in Vienna he decided – either on his own initiative or at the suggestion of Aragon – to attend, dismissing the arguments of the editorial board, who tried to dissuade him.[41] Nearly all the delegates from the West were communists. Making a speech on 2 December Sartre said that the only way to campaign for peace was to campaign with the communists; anti-communism was a no-man's land obstructing collaboration between all those who sincerely wanted peace.[42] He was given a standing ovation, and on 23 December, when a meeting was held at the Vélodrome d'Hiver to report on the congress, two of the speakers were Sartre and Jacques Duclos, who sat next to each other.[43] Sartre was at his most naive. Since he had come of age, he said, three events had suddenly given him hope – the Popular Front of 1936, the Liberation of France, and the Vienna Congress.[44]

Just before the year ended, after lecturing at the university of Freiburg, he went to visit Heidegger, but spent only half an hour with him,[45] and described him as looking like a retired colonel. 'The old man of the mountain, that's what he is.' Afterwards, climbing into his reserved railway carriage, Sartre found it was full of roses sent by Heidegger. As soon as the train had pulled out of the station, he threw them out of the window.[46] Sartre's debt to Heidegger was immeasurable and therefore intolerable. Since the critique of his existentialism in Heidegger's 1947 'Brief über den Humanismus', Sartre had moved in the direction it had prescribed, exploring the historical dimension of Being and entering into a more fruitful dialogue with Marxism. Had he wanted or managed to enter into a dialogue with Heidegger, it could have been profitable, but he could tolerate only dead masters, and in *Questions de méthode* Jaspers is absurdly taken as the representative of existentialism, the case of Heidegger being implausibly dismissed as 'too complex for treatment'. Without *Sein und Zeit*, Sartre could have written neither *La Nausée* nor *L'Etre et le Néant*, but the Sartre who met Heidegger wanted to turn his back on the Sartre of the thirties and forties.

Nor was he the same Sartre who had once read Marx, Lenin and Rosa Luxemburg. The experience of re-reading them after his 'conversion' was quite different, and he felt bolstered in his new-found faith. As Merleau-Ponty preserved his silence, refusing to challenge this faith, it seemed inevitable that one of the other moderates would soon throw down a gauntlet, but none did. It was Sartre himself who provoked a confrontation. After a number of spirited discussions with Claude Lefort, a former Trotskyite, a friend of Merleau-Ponty's, and a regular contributor to the review, Sartre invited him to formulate his arguments in an article. The article, which focused on Sartre's equation of the Party with the working class, accused him of 'counter-revolutionary Stalinism'. In reply Sartre reiterated the points he had made in *Les Communistes et la paix*. 'The Party is distinct from the masses only in so far as it is the union of the masses. Through this union they create their identity.' Though he had never been in the Party himself, Sartre accused Lefort of bad faith in not showing his solidarity with the proletariat by joining; instead he was trying to 'anchor himself in the intellectual bourgeoisie'.

Either Sartre was angry or, more probably, the acrimonious tone was calculated to make it impossible for Merleau-Ponty to preserve a neutral silence. He threatened to resign unless a particularly offensive paragraph was cut.[47] Lefort's thirty-page article and Sartre's fifty-nine-page reply appeared together in the April issue;[48] Merleau-Ponty's resignation followed in May after a further piece of provocation. Above an article by Pierre Naville about the 'contradictions of capitalism' Merleau-Ponty wrote a caption pointing to Naville's silence about the 'contradictions of socialism'. Sartre removed this caption. In an impassioned argument over the telephone, the two editors charged each other with abuse of power, and Merleau-Ponty never again had anything to do with the review.[49] Péju was invited to take over from Merleau-Ponty, but, modestly, he called himself general secretary of the review. He was more anti-Stalinist than Sartre and more resistant to pressure from the PCF, which was frequently proposing writers and articles. Sartre, who gave Péju a free hand to say No, seemed glad not to be the one who was refusing. Nor did he try to stop Péju from publishing in the review an article he had written about Slansky (Rudolf Salzmann) the Secretary General of the Czech Communist Party who had been tried for treason in November 1952 and executed.[50] (He would be rehabilitated in 1963.)

In June Sartre was in Venice with Michelle Vian when the Americans executed Julius and Ethel Rosenberg, two scientists accused of atomic spying. It was two years since they had been condemned to death, but the evidence was so unconvincing that even the Pope had joined in the international clamour for their reprieve. On the day their execution was announced Sartre and Michelle were due to meet de Beauvoir and Claude Lanzmann, who were holidaying together. Lanzmann arranged for *Libération* to publish an article by Sartre, who shut himself up in his hotel room and gave vent to his anger by writing as if innocent people had never been executed in the Soviet Union. In January nine doctors (seven of them Jewish) had been accused of plotting to murder Zhdanov and had been tortured; their innocence had been revealed later. In Stalin's persecution of the Jews hundreds of innocent people were vanishing, and Sartre's silence on the subject was so audible that François Mauriac took him publicly to task for it, but the killing of the Rosenbergs made him angry enough to work all day on his article. In the evening he read it to de Beauvoir, Lanzmann and Michelle Vian, afterwards rewriting it in the light of their comments.

> This is a legal lynching which covers a whole people with blood and glaringly exposes once and for all the bankruptcy of the Atlantic Pact and your incapacity to assume the leadership of the Western world ... You've allowed the United States to become the cradle of a new fascism ... fascism is defined not by the number of its victims but its way of killing them ... you have quite simply tried to stop the progress of science by a human sacrifice ... your country is sick with fear.[51]

Aron's comment was that this text belongs to the literature of hyper-Stalinism.[52]

It was in 1953 that Sartre began spending his summers in Rome, and it was there in July that he made his adaptation of *Kean ou Désordre et génie*

(*Kean or Chaos and Genius*), a play written for the nineteenth-century actor Frédérick Lemaître. It dates from 1836 and it was credited to Alexandre Dumas *père*, though most of the writing appears to have been done by a journeyman playwright, de Courcy, in collaboration with Lemaître. In 1951, during rehearsals of *Le Diable et le Bon Dieu* Sartre had talked about *Kean*, and in March 1953, while he was at St-Tropez, Pierre Brasseur had asked him to rewrite it. Had the play been staged in its original form, it might have made the audience laugh, like a recent production of Hugo's *Ernani* which Sartre had seen. Both *Ernani* and *Kean* are good examples of heroic melodrama, a form which attracted him, but he especially liked *Kean*: its hero belongs (as Francis Jeanson has noticed) to Sartre's line of affectionately portrayed bastards – Orestes, Hugo, Genet and Goetz.[53] He could identify with bastards, as he could with the actor 'who never stops "acting the part of himself"'. A great actor can, as Sartre put it in his programme note, 'talk to the audience about his art, his private life, his difficulties and his misfortunes, but according to the rules of his profession: discreetly, modestly, that's to say by slipping into someone else's skin'.[54] This is exactly what the creative writer does. 'It's simultaneously a marvellous gift and a curse: he is his own victim, never knowing who he really is, whether he's acting or not.' In his complicated sex life, Sartre had often during conversations with willing women and suspicious men stepped into the no-man's-land between sincerity and deception; though he claimed, in an interview, that conversations with Brasseur had taught him how 'the actor sometimes puts on an act to deceive himself',[55] the conversation must have reminded Sartre of himself. He could also project his hatred of the bourgeoisie into Kean, who had 'become an actor in order to escape from his resentment against society, and brought it to a kind of revolutionary force'.[56] In Sartre's private behaviour there were occasional manic outbreaks of rebelliousness, but a great actor more often looks like a man of action than a writer can.

Sartre liked the optimistic ending of the original play,[57] and preserved all the scenes in the last act. He made extensive changes to the consumptive heroine, Anna, who in the original play finds her cure in theatre, and he made her rival, the countess, more coquettish. He tightened and deepened Kean's speeches about the glory and abjection of being an actor, and he pruned the sentimental rhetoric, but *Kean* is by no means an original play. It was to open on 14 November at the Sarah-Bernhardt, with Brasseur directing as well as playing Kean. Wanda appeared as Anna with Claude Gensac as the countess. Audiences were enthusiastic.

Sartre was still intending to finish his novel, but his intentions were compromised by his restlessness. Dislike of the political status quo sharpened his need to keep escaping from Paris. After a brief return he left again, this time with de Beauvoir, for a summer holiday using an Amsterdam hotel as base. They visited museums, drove out to explore the banks of the Rhine and the Moselle, went to see what was left of the Stalag on the hill above Trier were he had been a prisoner thirteen years earlier. All they found was rusty barbed wire and a few huts.[58] Alarmed to hear that Lanzmann had been in a car crash outside Cahors, they left to visit him in hospital there, but he was not badly hurt, and as soon as he recovered, the three of them went driving together, first around the Lot and the Limousin, later around Toulouse and the forest of Gresigne. Both men were tolerant of de Beauvoir's relationship with the other. Finally, alone with Sartre, she toured Brittany.[59]

As usual Sartre worked hard while on holiday, and when the book he had edited on Henri Martin was published at the end of October – by then Martin had been released – he said that his working time was being divided between his work on ethics and an autobiography.[60] The ethical book had been abandoned in 1949, and though he subsequently worked on it spasmodically, it is unlikely that he was intending to publish it. The autobiographical project was more serious. *Les Mots* was not published until ten years later but most of it, Sartre says, was written in 1953.[61] His original title for it, *Jean-sans-terre* ('John Lackland', the nickname for the English King John), puns challengingly on the title of Proust's autobiographical novel *Jean Santeuil*, which was not published until 1952. 'Sans-terre', said Sartre, 'meant: without inheritance, without possessions. That meant what I was.'[62] Though it was to be abandoned later, this title points to a characteristic that was crucial. Like Genet, who swallowed the label other people had stuck on him when he became the 'thief' they anathematized, Sartre made it a virtue to own nothing. In childhood he had never suffered deprivation but never felt he was in his own home with his own possessions around him; in adult life he defiantly went on in the same track. His pipe was indisputably his, but living first in hotels and then in his mother's flat, he owned neither the building nor the furniture he used. His bed was not his, and he was keeping only a few of the books he read. A private joke was involved in choosing the title *Jeans-sans-terre* and after developing a negative relationship with Proust in so many of the motifs of *La Nausée* Sartre must have been amused to read in *Jean Santeuil* that the creative writer, B, thinks it would have been pleasant to live as a philosophy teacher in a small provincial town, playing cards every evening at the café and drinking bock.[63]

Sartre's conversion had led him to a new crisis in his ambivalence towards the written word. No-one can ever have taken a more sensuous pleasure in the act of penning words on paper; no-one can have agonized more over indulging himself by retreating into *l'imaginaire*. Sartre felt he was preserving the present moment in the aspic of literature instead of fusing his consciousness generously with that of the group. Even when writing an activist article about a current political situation, he was not doing what he felt he should be doing: taking direct action. But to someone so fond of the phrase 'Loser wins', every defeat was potentially a victory; couldn't a retreat into autobiography be an advance? He could show that as a child he had been 'completely mistaken about the meaning of life', show himself to have been 'the plaything of circumstances', explain why it had seemed so important to become a writer.[64] Or as he put it in a later interview, 'I grew up in a period when the greatest teachers of thinking were, after all, Gide and Proust, a period in fact of subjectivism and aestheticism'.[65] What he intended to show in *Jean-sans-terre* was that he had been 'constantly in a hurry to change, uncomfortable inside my own skin, uneasy with other people'.[66] The book was not going to be limited to an account of his childhood: 'I wanted to write my whole life from a political viewpoint, that's to say my childhood, my youth and middle age, giving it a political meaning in terms of my arrival at communism.'[67] The book was going to be quite long – possibly two volumes, or at least one thick one.[68] But after drafting the childhood section, 'I haven't at all written the childhood I wanted to write'.[69] 'It struck me as unbalanced. There's no reason to drag an unfortunate creature through the mud, just because he writes.'[70]

Since the death of Stalin (5 March 1953) and the appointment of Khrushchev in September as first secretary of the Central Committee, it had been hard to predict how the Cold War would develop. A fortnight after Stalin's death, the West German Bundestag had approved the agreements about establishing a European Defence Community, but it was not yet in existence, and at the beginning of 1954, Sartre was taking every opportunity to denounce the idea. At the end of February he went to Knokke-le-Zoute in Belgium for a conference between Eastern and Western writers organized by the Russian-born novelist Elsa Triolet, Aragon's wife. Brecht, Anna Seghers and Carlo Levi were there, together with several Russian writers, who invited Sartre to Moscow in May. After the conference had agreed on the text of an appeal to prepare the way for a much larger meeting, Brecht caused consternation by proposing they should incorporate in the appeal a protest against the American atomic test (1 March) at Bikini in the Marshall Islands. Instead, the signatories pledged themselves to make their works consistent with their 'will to peace' and to 'combat war' in their writing.

Sartre's contribution was to go on with *Les Communistes et la paix* in *Les Temps modernes*. The third instalment has its roots in the intuitive judgment that had made Sartre link the events of December 1851, as Guillemin described them, with the arrest of Jacques Duclos. Sartre draws interestingly on reading he had done during the last few years about the French Revolution and French nineteenth-century history, buying books of memoirs and books on agriculture. Had the mentality of the rightists changed since 1851? If the strike of June 1953 had failed, there must be a historical explanation for the workers' apathy, and, stimulated by Guillemin, Sartre began to search for it.

In writing social and economic history, he is polemical and unscholarly. Before the rising of 1848, he says, there had been only two classes in France – the bourgeoisie and the animals: the humanity of the workers had been denied. During the June days, when General Cavaignac led troops against the Paris workmen, fifteen hundred people were shot; in 1871, during the week of the Commune's defeat, twenty thousand people were shot. 'Everywhere else the working class is starved; only in France has it been bled. The proletarian of 1886 sells his labour to the men who have killed his father or his elder brothers.'[71] Sartre musters evidence to show that class-war has been waged literally. 'The secret of the working class is that it holds the French bourgeoisie to be a gang of criminals.'[72]

He writes about the bourgeoisie as if it had a collective consciousness and as if its collective will had consistently been articulated in the government's economic policy. Successive governments, he says, concerned less to enrich France than to weaken the proletariat, have deliberately depressed the economy. 'Economic Malthusianism' is his name for the under-production designed to demoralize and impoverish the workers. The unskilled are especially vulnerable, being interchangeable. Strike action is therefore ineffectual unless organized on a big scale, while the division of the proletariat between skilled and unskilled workers makes it easier for the bourgeoisie to retain control. If the proletariat (unlike the bourgeoisie) has no collective consciousness, working-class unity can be achieved only when imposed from outside.[73] The masses have no defence except through mass action: they must be organized into one movement, into obeying one word of command.[74] 'When everything is linked, Malthusianism and misery, inflation of prices, rearmament and Marshallization, to reject the Communist Party's policy is to carry out that of the government.'[75]

There is no space in *Les Communistes et la paix* for the sympathy Sartre had shown in *La Dernière Chance* towards men too 'stupid' to resist indoctrination. His sympathy for the abused soldiers in his novel derived from experience; his sympathy for factory workers is more perfunctory and theoretical. 'Each man perceives the existence of his neighbours in the form of the collective rhythm to which he must adapt himself ... the semi-automatic machine is the instrument *par excellence* for massification'.[76]

'Massification' involves dehumanization. 'To the extent that massification engenders at once isolation and interchangeability, it gives birth to imitation as a mechanical relationship between the molecules.'[77] Though the values of the working class are valid for the whole of humanity – the only valid viewpoint is that of the most deprived – the masses are the object of history.[78] The militant works to transform the 'masses object' into the 'proletariat subject'. His aim is 'to liquidate their granular structure in favour of an organic unity'.[79] Here Sartre is laying himself open to a charge that was to be levelled against him two years later by Merleau-Ponty: 'if the workers are nothing, not even proletarians, until they create the Party, the Party rests on nothing which has been established – not even the history they have in common.'[80] Sartre, says Merleau-Ponty, was falling back on the model he had evolved for *L'Etre et le Néant*, equating the activist with the active For-itself and the masses with the inert In-itself.

The essay, which occupied eighty-eight pages in the April 1954 issue of the review, appears to have been written in less of a hurry than the first two essays: it is carefully thought out and it has more research behind it than most of his political writing. Though he seldom mentions his sources, Sartre quotes a great many statistics, and he had delved deeply into the history of the French working-class movement. Generally he had been doing too much, and his blood pressure was too high. The doctor recommended a long rest in the country,[81] but Sartre habitually ignored doctors, and, until leaving for the Soviet Union at the end of May, kept himself extremely busy, hitting out energetically at government policy. An editorial note published in the May issue renewed his attack on the atrocities perpetrated in the Indo-Chinese War. 'If it is forbidden to call Bidault [the Foreign Minister] a criminal, we shall call him a very guilty man; if we are prevented from speaking of the blood on his hands, we shall speak of the scales over his eyes.'[82] Sartre also wrote prefaces for the catalogue of a Giacometti exhibition and for Cartier-Bresson's book of photographs taken in China. He wrote a protest in *Libération* about the banning of the Soviet ballet ('Next year, M. Lamiel, Ulanova will still be dancing, but you will no longer be President of the Council').[83] He attended a meeting organized by the CNE in a suburban Renault factory, where he spoke to the workers about torture as described by Julius Fucik in his book about communist militants in a Czech prison during 1942–3.[84] Working on the Cartier-Bresson preface, Sartre had to stay up for several nights, and on the way to Moscow he stopped in Berlin to make a speech at a meeting held by the Peace Movement.[85]

From the window of his Moscow hotel bedroom Sartre watched the parade in Red Square celebrating the anniversary of the Ukraine's integration into Russia in May 1923. The programme arranged for him was strenuous.

The sightseeing included visits to the university and to factories. At the dacha of the writer Konstantin Simonov he had to survive a four-hour banquet with wine from Armenia and Georgia as well as twenty toasts in vodka. He travelled by train to Leningrad, where he was driven around the city for four hours, and after an hour's rest, he had to spend four hours in the Palace of Culture. The next day, which was no less full, ended in an evening at the ballet. After returning to Moscow, he was flown to Uzbekistan. He was scheduled to travel with Ilya Ehrenburg to Stockholm for a meeting of the Peace Movement, but instead he was taken to a hospital,[86] and, detained for ten days, treated for hypertension, high blood pressure and an excessive intake of alcohol.

After he returned to Paris on 24 June, still exhausted, he gave *Libération* an enthusiastic report of his impressions. The interview was published in five instalments under such captions as 'Freedom of criticism is complete in the USSR and the Soviet citizen is continually improving his condition in the bosom of a society making non-stop progress.'[87] 'I met a new breed of men.' It was impossible 'not to think of them as friends'. In Russia, he reported, man was 'conscious of the incessant and harmonious progress in both his own life and social life. Individual and collective interests coincide.' Except for some reservations about Soviet architecture, he was blandly uncritical about the USSR, and when the journalists Pierre and Hélène Lazareff, who had been in Russia at roughly the same time, reacted less enthusiastically in *France-Soir*, Sartre tried in one of the *Libération* interviews to discredit them,[88] while at some level, perhaps, he was trying to refute André Gide. Sartre was aware that there was as much oppression and deviousness in the Soviet Union, as little justice and democracy as in 1936, but the truth mattered less than the commitment to befriend the communists. Twenty years later Sartre would claim that what had been printed as a series of interviews with him had actually been written by Jean Cau; 'I gave him a certain number of main points.' Sartre now conceded that what he had seen in the USSR 'did not fill me with enthusiasm ... I had a lot of reservations'.[89]

Recuperating in Italy with Michelle, he tried to work on his autobiography, but made little headway.[90] An event, though, which vastly strengthened his positive feelings towards Italy was a meeting with the veteran leader of the Communist Party, Palmiro Togliatti, who had worked with Gramsci. They had started the weekly *Ordine nuovo* together in 1919 and then founded the national Communist Party in 1921. Unlike Maurice Thorez, the French leader, Togliatti was not stolidly submissive to Stalinism. It was also said in France that the PCF was less highly regarded in Moscow than the Italian party, which was larger, more useful, more militant, with a more intelligent leader. For the next ten years Togliatti's ideas would be filtered sympathetically to French leftists through *Les Temps modernes*, especially after 1956, when he formulated the principle of 'polycentrism'. Instead of having a single centre, international communism should have several – Moscow, Peking, Havana and so on. The idea was anathema to Thorez, who in any case would not have wanted Rome to be seen as the centre of European communism.

One meeting was enough to make Sartre think of Togliatti as his friend, but he did not stay long in Rome. Repeating the pattern of the previous summer, he returned to Paris, only to leave again in de Beauvoir's car for a second holiday with her. In the Strasbourg hotel where they spent their first night he still seemed exhausted. 'For a long time he stayed sitting in his chair, hands on his knees, back slumped, eyes blank'; over dinner he told her that literature was shit.[91]

They drove through Alsace and the Black Forest to Munich and Salzburg. By now he was feeling energetic enough to start working again. After a week of excursions to the surrounding countryside, revisiting the lakes and mountains, they went on to Vienna, where he had banned the production of *Les Mains sales*. The contract had been signed without consulting him and to explain his veto, he told a press conference how the play had been exploited by the anti-communists.

In December he accepted the vice-chairmanship of the Franco-Soviet Association, which was closely linked to the Comintern, and in February 1955 spoke at a meeting commemorating the victory at Stalingrad. The British and the Americans, he declared, had been given too much credit for winning the war: it was the Soviet victory at Stalingrad that had made the Normandy landing possible and necessary. One lesson to be learned from it was that 'it would be dangerous to differentiate between the Russian people and its leaders'. Their popularity was demonstrated by the courage and goodwill of the soldiers. 'The people have created their regime and they are inseparable from it.' A second lesson was that France needed to go on being Russia's ally: it would be absurd to rearm Germany against the country that had been their ally in both world wars.[92]

Though Sartre was unstinting in the time he lavished on left-wing causes, he had no intention of abandoning biography, and he was launched on the biggest of all his projects by a conversation with Roger Garaudy, who had been on the PCF's central committee since 1945. Garaudy maintained that, to understand an individual or a group, the Marxist perspective was indispensable.[93] Why had no-one written a Marxist biography? Sartre became very excited. Why shouldn't Marxism take over psycho-analysis? After all, an individual's upbringing could condemn him to repeat the history of his family or the history of society.[94] In *Saint Genet* Sartre had already attempted a comprehensive statement about one man, dovetailing Freudian and Marxian insights, but Flaubert, the writer who filled Sartre with the most stimulating mixture of love and hatred, would provide a better focus for investigating the damage inflicted by a characteristic bourgeois family. It had long been inevitable that sooner or later Sartre would start a biography of Flaubert; the interesting question is whether it was inevitable that he would leave it unfinished. During the spring he did some research, quickly completing a first draft.

Early in 1955 he took another working holiday, motoring down to Marseille with de Beauvoir and Lanzmann. A summit conference of Britain, France, the US and the USSR was to be held at Geneva in the early summer, and in the climate of *détente* Sartre felt anxious about the influence of the right-wing press. In the play *Nekrassov* his object was to undermine anti-communist propaganda. He was remembering his pledge at the Vienna Congress, to 'combat war' in his writing; he may also have been remembering the practical joke at the ENS in 1927, when a student's impersonation of Lindbergh forced Lanson to resign. In the play a confidence trickster impersonates Nekrassov, a Soviet minister, making it seem that he has defected, and in their mindless crusade against communism the directors of a Paris evening newspaper lap up the information he feeds them. This is the most Shavian of Sartre's plays, with no semblance of free will in the characters, who are mostly caricatures, brusquely manipulated according to the needs of the far-fetched plot. Like *Le Diable et le Bon Dieu*, *Nekrassov* is designed to express an attitude towards society, but Sartre's dramatic technique derived from the bourgeois theatre he wanted to reject. As a theatrical storyteller he was far from incompetent, but, wisely, he had never attempted comedy or farce. A good satire could have been written about the relationships between management and journalists in the right-wing papers, but not by Sartre. He was uncertain about how to divide the focus between the confidence trickster and the newspapers, while anger made him heavy-handed.

Again he gave his play to Simone Berriau for production at the Théâtre Antoine; again the script was unfinished when rehearsals began. The director was Jean Meyer, who had worked mainly in the Comédie Française. Michel Vitold played the confidence trickster, with Chauffard as a police inspector. Wanda had a role as the communist daughter of an anti-communist journalist. The atmosphere at rehearsals was overcast by political disagreement as well as by the usual arguments about the exorbitant length of Sartre's script. Several of the actors withdrew. The date of the opening had to be postponed more than once, and public controversy broke before the premiere on 8 June: on that evening a hostile tract was distributed by a group calling itself the Free Circle of Russian Studies. Though the communist papers supported the play, most of the reviewers were hostile, and the production ran for only sixty performances.

In one way Sartre benefited from the short run. Michel Vitold, who had played Garcin both in the 1944 premiere of *Huis clos* and in the 1946 revival, as well as directing *Morts sans sépulture* and *La Putain respectueuse* in 1946, had an insatiable appetite for Sartrean drama. Whetted again, it made him want a third go at Garcin, though the play had been revived only two years previously at the Comédie Caumartin with Gaby Sylvia. For the 1955 revival Vitold had Judith Magre as Inès, while Claude Lanzmann's beautiful sister, Evelyne Rey, was Estelle. She was living with Rezvani, a Persian writer and musician, and her other lover was Claude Roy; together with these two, Sartre was to become one of the most important men in her life, while she was to become – until her suicide – one of the most important women in his, a mistress, like Wanda, for whom he wrote plays. She never ceased to be touched and surprised by his combination of humility and gratitude on receiving sexual favours.[95]

At the end of June he travelled with de Beauvoir to Helsinki for an eight-day congress of the Peace Movement. There were representatives from all over the world. During one of the lunch breaks Georg Lukács started a discussion about liberty, telling Sartre, who listened politely, about the historical conditioning of the individual.[96] But the writer who behaved most like a cultural commissar was Ilya Ehrenburg, who instructed Sartre not to be too militant about the US when making his speech: the Kremlin wanted conciliation.[97] Speaking on the 26th, the fifth day of the conference, Sartre obediently appealed for co-operation between the US and the USSR and for economic aid to underdeveloped countries. Peace and liberty were synonymous; nations must respect each other's independence.[98]

Cartier-Bresson's photographs of China had served as an introduction to the country; in the early summer Sartre and de Beauvoir received an invitation and finally went in September, arriving on the 6th, to spend two months there. In Russia the name Sartre was not completely unknown; in China, after reports in the newspapers that he had written a life of Nekrassov, people assumed he was the biographer of the nineteenth-century Russian poet.[99] The People's Republic of China had been proclaimed on 1 October 1949; on 1 October 1955, nearly four weeks after his arrival, Sartre watched the anniversary parade in Peking; he was presented to Mao Tsetung, but with no chance of having a conversation.

The population of China was 600 million, and even to the visitor from the West, the country's poverty was immediately apparent, though the predominant impression was one of cleanliness and health. If until recently conditions had encouraged vermin and the spread of disease, while the majority of people had been undernourished and inadequately dressed, the revolution had established hygiene and stability. Sartre was impressed by the prevailing calm and the moderation of the army, which appeared to be totally in control. The revolution, he concluded, had 'begun by ridding China of inflation, misery and rising prices, insecurity, anarchy and local despotism'.[100] But the stability was not stasis: 'the present reality of China is its future ... One of us was saying: "In China you feel already dead." This is often true, because the most tangible reality is a future which the young will see, and we certainly shan't.'[101]

Having spent a day in Moscow on the way out, he and de Beauvoir spent a week there on the way back. Compared with the socialist reconstruction in China, the rebuilding in Russia looked highly mechanized.[102] They visited monasteries, churches, schools and theatres, seeing Gorki's *The Lower Depths* and Mayakovsky's *The Bed-Bug*.[103] At Simonov's suggestion, Sartre addressed a conference of Soviet critics about the critic's role.[104]

France's Algerian troubles had begun in November 1954, when the nationalist FLN (Front de libération nationale) launched an armed insurrection. Algeria was legally integral to France – under the interior minister's jurisdiction. Only about ten per cent of the nine million people in the country were white, but, as in South Africa, the minority dominated. The Arabs had few legal rights and little economic power. The injustice of the situation was obvious, but in France not even the communists advocated Algerian independence. The left favoured reforms, but government policy was to crush the rebellion by military force.

Les Temps modernes had been critical of French colonialism in North Africa before the rebellion, and in October 1955 the editorial sided with the rebels: the Algerians associated French rule with repression, racism and torture. Sartre warned Péju not to go too far in supporting the FLN,[105] but the November issue came out explicitly in favour of Algerian independence; by then a group of intellectuals had started an information centre, which published evidence that rebels were being tortured, while thousands of Arabs had been interned in camps.

At the beginning of 1956 it did not look as though the war would drag on for over six years. In the elections of 2 January 1956 the left-wing Front Républicain gained a majority, and making his inaugural speech on 31 January, the new socialist premier, Guy Mollet, called the war 'cruel and insane'. Four days earlier, at a protest meeting in the Salle Wagram, Sartre condemned France for using the nineteenth-century economic machinery of colonial exploitation; the only possible line of action was to support the Algerian fight against tyranny.[106]

When a young friend of his, doing his military service, had been drafted to Morocco, Sartre advised him not to desert. 'You must go there and work. Do agitprop amongst your soldier comrades.'[107] But in Algeria Sartre favoured desertion. Camus took the opposite line: he supported the French presence in his native country. This damaged his prestige among progressive intellectuals and posthumously damaged his worldwide reputation. In the United States, for instance, his stock was to sink in the sixties as Sartre's rose. Sartre was least popular there when aligning himself with the PCF, as he was doing in 1956. The distance he had travelled, ideologically, since his involvement with the RDR was apparent when Pierre Hervé, a leading communist intellectual, published a short book, *La Révolution et les fétiches*, attacking the Party bureaucracy and making points similar to those Sartre had made during 1948 in *Entretiens sur la politique*, condemning the Party's dogmatism and its undemocratic procedures. As if to demonstrate its intolerance of internal criticism, the PCF expelled Hervé on 14 February 1956. Sartre's article, which is dated four days earlier, makes the point that Hervé was exposing himself to the risk of expulsion in 'addressing himself to a Popular Front of the future', and it maintains that if Hervé is making a mistake, he is making it in good faith. His expulsion 'would be deplorable'.[108] 'He's an idealist? A reformist? Undeniably. But we all hope his opponents will discuss it [the book].'[109] Marxism does not need to be on the defensive now that the bourgeoisie is on the retreat: 'faced with Marxism, its ideas die without the Marxists' having to raise a little finger'.[110] This was the moment for Marxism to expand, outflank the last bourgeois philosophies, interpret them, smash their shell and incorporate their substance.'[111] 'Since the very interesting studies by Politzer, psychology has been stagnant.'[112] Georges Politzer had formulated a Marxist critique of psychoanalysis, proposing an alternative 'concrete psychology' based on economic determinism. One of the most masterly self-publicists, Sartre took the opportunity of mentioning that he was at work on a biography which would bring psycho-analysis inside a Marxist framework.

But the painstaking intellectuality of his approach did not stop him from betraying intellectuals during his love affair with the Party. To his readers it must have looked as though he was on the point of joining: 'Transported by history, the Communist Party manifests an extraordinarily objective intelligence. It makes few mistakes; it does what it must do; but this intelligence – which gets confused with *praxis* – is not often embodied in its intellectuals.'[113] What was needed was a living Marxism, free from the dogmatism that inhibits movement; it should have been possible for philosophers, economists, 'ethnographers', psychologists to undertake specific research and then contribute their findings to the Party. As it was, Marxism, instead of developing, was repeating itself; 'Marxism has stopped'.[114]

In retrospect the PCF's expulsion of Hervé looks all the sillier for coinciding with Khrushchev's astonishingly explicit condemnation of Stalin's 'bloody crimes' at the twentieth Party Congress. By now the Kremlin's slow movement towards tolerance seemed to have gathered momentum and suddenly, three years after the dictator's death, the word Stalinism could be used, like a dustbin, for collecting everything that did not match the new decor. Stalin could be blamed for the 'cult of personality' and for the assumption that armed conflict was inevitable. It was not. Imperialism could wither peacefully away; each nation had the right to find its own route to socialism.

It is possible that Sartre actually wrote his article after the expulsion and after Khrushchev's speech but retrospectively dated it 10 February to make it look as if he had anticipated both. Sartre's plea for an expansionist Marxism is oddly in tune with Khrushchev's attitude, and even if the article followed the speech, Sartre was much faster than the PCF to pick up Moscow's cue. At the end of March *Humanité* reprinted a *Pravda* attack on Stalin, but there was nothing conciliatory in the speeches at the PCF's national Party Congress in Le Havre, and, speaking in Grenoble, Duclos defended Stalin,[115] as did Courtade in *Humanité*, putting the blame on Beria. When the Trotskyite Pierre Naville attacked Sartre in March, he seemed to be expressing the views of the Party. His articles, which appeared in *France-Observateur*, denied that Marxism had stopped, and condemned Sartre's equation of it with the Party. Sartre replied in *Les Temps modernes* (March–April), and Naville wrote a second piece in *France-Observateur* (19 April). In July, speaking at the fourteenth Party Congress, Garaudy mentioned Sartre's article, but denied that Hervé's deviancy had been provoked by Party dogmatism.[116] Hervé quickly wrote a new book, *Lettre à Sartre*, claiming Khrushchev as an ally.

Dividing himself between political controversy and journeyman writing, Sartre was working between November 1955 and May 1956 on a screen version of Arthur Miller's play *The Crucible*, which linked McCarthyite 'witch-hunting' in the US with witch-hunting in seventeenth-century Salem. Marcel Aymé's adaptation, which had been produced in the theatre under the title *Les Sorcières de Salem*, irritated Sartre. Not content with making the social and political issues more explicit, he introduced a strong element of class-conflict, building up the role of the deputy governor, Danforth. Raymond Rouleau, who had directed the play, also directed the film, playing Danforth himself, and using the same actors who had played the leading parts – most effectively – on stage: Yves Montand (John Proctor), Simone Signoret (Elizabeth) and Mylène Demongeot, who had taken over from Nicole Courcel as Abigail. For the screenplay Sartre received 6,000 francs from the producer, Bernard Borderie.[117]

In March he met a nineteen-year-old Jewish Algerian girl, Arlette El Kaïm, who had written to him from Versailles, where she had been studying *L'Etre et le Néant*. She was writing a thesis on injustice for the competitive entrance examination to the Ecole Normale Supérieure in Sèvres. Although his affair with Evelyne Rey had begun only recently, Arlette was soon to become sexually involved with him.

At the end of the month he went to Venice for a colloquium organized by the Société européenne de culture, an organization founded six years earlier to establish rapport between intellectuals from Eastern and Western European countries. Britain was represented by Stephen Spender, J.D. Bernal and Alan Pryce-Jones. When Sartre took his seat, he noticed on the empty chair next to him a card with the name Merleau-Ponty on it. When Merleau-Ponty arrived, late, during a speech, he tiptoed behind Sartre, touching him lightly on the shoulder and then smiling.[118] One of the English speakers was so naive that Sartre and Merleau-Ponty were equally exasperated, and they spent some of the evenings together, though never alone, and not without a certain awkwardness.[119] During the session on 26 March, when Merleau-Ponty spoke about the 'thaw', Sartre insisted that the communist half of the world was no more frozen than the Western half. We too should be asking ourselves how we were going to unfreeze, and we had no right to ask 'people in possession of a cultural ideology such as Marxism to accept a truth belonging to another ideological system without trying to see how that truth can be integrated into Marxism.'[120] It was too easy for us to forget that all our ideas were conditioned by bourgeois ideology.[121] The two men argued at some length: while Merleau-Ponty favoured coexistence and mutual tolerance, Sartre maintained that 'coexistence can only be a dynamic movement of integration'.[122] Discussing psycho-analysis, Sartre argued that in Marxist hands it could become 'a discipline allied to sociology and economics'. Merleau-Ponty retorted that first the Marxist would have to take psycho-analysis seriously, without devaluing it or calling it a bourgeois ideology. Sartre maintained that it was a bourgeois ideology, and could cease to be one only if released from its limits and negations by being absorbed into a totality.[123]

Throughout the spring and early summer the thaw seemed to be proceeding. In April Khrushchev dissolved the Cominform and, together with Marshal Bulganin, the Russian premier, paid a ten-day visit to Britain. In June Marshal Tito's visit to Moscow was followed by a Soviet–Pakistani trade pact, but by the end of the month the caution of the PCF seemed to be vindicated. The rising of 17 June 1953 in East Berlin had occurred just over three months after Stalin's death, when the thaw had hardly begun; it led to the June 1956 risings in Poland and Hungary, and they led to the end of the thaw.

In Budapest Mátyás Rákosi, who had served Stalin loyally, had remained as first secretary during the liberalizing regime of Imre Nagy (1953–5) and had regained control of the country in 1955. Criticism of Rákosi culminated towards the end of June, when journalists who had been branded as 'bourgeois' were being rehabilitated, while intellectuals were clamouring for freedom of expression and the return of Nagy. In Poland the shortage of food led to disturbances. On 28 June thousands of metalworkers in Poznan went on strike, demanding bread. When the police fired on the crowds, forty-eight workers were killed. According to the PCF, the riot had been provoked by foreign agents.

Sartre made no public comment before leaving Paris for his summer holiday with Michelle, de Beauvoir and Lanzmann. Setting off in two cars, they drove to Venice, where they spent two days, and went on to Belgrade. In Yugoslavia collectivization had caused widespread hardship, which was obvious even when driving along country roads between Belgrade and Skopje.[124] After crossing the frontier into Greece, Sartre and Michelle stayed in Salonika, while de Beauvoir and Lanzmann drove to Athens. Michelle drove Sartre to Rome, where the others eventually joined them. The four of them passed a few days together in Naples, Amalfi and Paestum, and when Lanzmann took the train back to Paris, the others stayed in Rome, remaining there till the end of October, reading in Italian newspapers about events in Poland. In September the Poznan trial began, accompanied by riots and demonstrations. Sentences were lenient, but the people, no longer unable to hope for democracy and independence, went on pressing for the withdrawal of Soviet troops, for workers' management in industry, for the slowing down of collectivization. Wladyslaw Gomulka, who had been forced to resign as leader of the Polish Communist Party in 1948, and had been released from prison in 1955, regained a place on the central committee, where he demanded the dismissal of all pro-Soviet leaders. Khrushchev was in Warsaw as Russian tanks began to bear down on the city; Gomulka was arming workers and preparing Polish troops to fight against the Russians when Khrushchev abruptly decided against violent confrontation, leaving Gomulka in control of the country.

In Hungary violence was not avoided. Rákosi had been dismissed in July, but when Andras Hegedüs, who had replaced Nagy as premier, was offered the job of first secretary, he declined: it would have required a 'ruthlessness and militancy I did not possess'.[125] Lenin said that the precondition for a successful revolution is present when popular discontent coincides with a failure of confidence in the ruling class. This was true of Budapest. In October, hungry for the freedom that was within reach if only the Soviet overlords behaved as they had in Poland, students began to demonstrate. Soon they were joined by armed factory workers, and so many Hungarian soldiers sided with the rebels that the Soviet commanders, unable to control the rising, signed an armistice. Hegedüs, who had been living in dread of a popular uprising, was flown to safety in Moscow, while Nagy, who was reinstated, asked for Hungary to be given the same neutral status as Austria. If only the West had supported him, the Kremlin might have given in, but a presidential election campaign was under way in the United States, while Britain and France were preoccupied with the Suez Canal, which had been seized in July by the uncompromising Colonel Nasser, just over a month after he had been elected president of Egypt. At the end of October, while Soviet troops were invading north-east Hungary, French and British planes were dropping bombs on Egyptian airfields. On 2 November the Hungarian government renounced the Warsaw treaty and appealed to the United Nations, but two days later, when Soviet forces attacked Budapest, Nagy had to take refuge in the Yugoslav Embassy.

Sartre's loyalty to the Soviet Union did not evaporate overnight. 'If the USSR is worth no more and no less than capitalist England, then there is really nothing for us to do except cultivate our garden.'[126] On his return from Italy, Sartre was appalled by the reaction of the PCF, which had congratulated the Soviet Union on its action, while Party newspapers used such phrases as 'dogs of the fallen classes' and 'Versaillais' to describe the Hungarians who had attempted a 'fascist putsch'.[127] Sartre finally committed himself on 4 November. In an interview with *L'Express* he condemned the Soviet aggression as 'a crime', which 'had been made possible and perhaps necessary (from the Soviet viewpoint) by twelve years of terror and imbecility ... What the Hungarian people is teaching us with its blood is the complete failure of socialism as merchandise imported from the USSR.' America should not have tried to interfere with the construction of socialism in the 'satellite' countries, but the main culprit was Khrushchev. Without being able to raise Soviet living standards, he had catalogued in detail the misdeeds of 'a holy personality who has represented the regime for so long'. The Kremlin was now being run by 'a group (army "hawks", old Stalinists?) which is outdoing Stalinism after denouncing it'. Sartre was breaking off his relationships with the Soviet writers who didn't (or couldn't) denounce the aggression against Hungary, and with the present leaders of the PCF. 'All their comments, all their actions are the outcome of thirty years of lying and sclerosis,' while the reports in *Humanité* were 'repugnant lies'. For Sartre it would never again be possible to have relations with the leaders of the PCF, though he had no quarrel with 'all the sincere and honest men of the left, even those who stay in the Party'.[128] He resigned from the Franco-Soviet Association, but stayed in the Peace Movement and in the CNE, though he was not satisfied with the wording of the protest produced by the communist president, Aragon.[129]

Sartre was now released from the hidden embarrassment involved in giving unqualified support to the PCF, as he had for nearly five years. Instead of completing *Les Communistes et la paix*, which had appeared in *Les Temps modernes* with 'à suivre' ('to be continued') at the end of the third essay, he published 'Le Fantôme de Staline', which is the best piece of political journalism he had written. Disciplining himself into voicing no public disapproval of the USSR, he had battened down a great deal of energy, which was now released in a vigorous attempt to understand the causes of the Hungarian rising and the Soviet reaction. Confronting truths he had evaded, Sartre struggled openly with the difficulties of taking a position. The tension is apparent in his prose, which is less flabby and less rhetorical than in *Les Communistes et la paix*. He is still writing too quickly, but he approximates more closely to reproducing the flow of his thinking.

For help in reconstructing what had happened in Hungary he was indebted to François Fejtö, author of *La Tragédie hongroise ou la Révolution socialiste antisoviétique*, which came out before the end of the year, with a preface by Sartre praising Fejtö's objectivity in the book and in his many articles about Hungary. Ignoring the will of the Hungarian people, the Soviet Union had 'criminally over-industrialized' the country, while collectivizing agriculture.[130] In Russia the revolutionaries had understood that socialism was inseparable from economic planning: a balance had to be struck between the long-term interests of socialist construction and the working class's natural appetite for a higher standard of living.[131] But it had been a mistake, characteristic of Stalinism, to impose homologous economies on all the 'people's democracies' of central Europe, and in Hungary the Soviet intervention had been followed by a general strike, which showed the world that the Red Army was the enemy of the Hungarian workers.[132]

Hungary was still in ferment while Sartre was writing – in the resistance, which continued till mid-December, between twenty and fifty thousand Hungarians were killed – and before the essay was published in January 1957, Sartre added a footnote to challenge the decision by the new premier, János Kádár, to quash the workers' councils: 'What is this socialism which is bent on destroying organs of control elected by the proletariat?'[133] Writing about the worker in bourgeois society, Marx had argued that his revolutionary force came from 'the contradiction between his human *nature* and his actual life, which is the manifest, decisive and total rejection of that nature'.[134] In Hungary over-industrialization and enforced collectivization had produced a contradiction which was no less ferocious. The Kremlin had loosened its undemocratic grip on Poland; why not allow Budapest a 'Hungarian Gomulkism'?[135]

Though he knew how simplistic it was to hold Stalin personally responsible for everything that had gone wrong with the Soviet system, Sartre was quick to exploit the new words 'Stalinism' and 'de-Stalinization'. Dictatorship, he argued, might have been unavoidable while the Soviet Union was in danger of being destroyed by Western nuclear bombs, but not now that the Kremlin could negotiate from a position of strength.[136] The Hungarian rising could have been avoided if Nagy had been recalled in 1955 or even at the beginning of October 1956; what had made it inevitable was the 'explosive mixture in the bosom of the Party itself of a Stalinism that is still aggressive with partisans of de-Stalinization'.[137] Temporarily the neo-Stalinist faction had gained control.[138] What angered Sartre most was the damage that had been done to the cause. Instead of exploiting the opportunity to win popularity, Nagy and the Kremlin had made the Red Army look oppressive.[139]

On 7 November Sartre and de Beauvoir signed a letter affirming friendship for the USSR and for socialism but condemning the use of guns and tanks in Hungary. Socialism could never be achieved at bayonet point. The letter was also signed by Vercors as well as by leading French communist intellectuals – Claude Roy, Roger Vailland, J.-F. Rolland and Claude Morgan.[140] On the following day, the directing committee of the CNE (including Sartre and Aragon) issued an open appeal to Kádár for the protection of Hungarian writers. But in the Soviet Union intellectuals were supporting the regime. Thirty-five Russian writers publicly condemned the French writers' protest. When the National Council of the Peace Movement met in December, Sartre and other non-communists managed to pass a resolution calling for the Russian troops to withdraw.[141] But he was still as hostile as ever towards the anti-communists. What should the French *gauchistes* do? Unity without the PCF was impotence; unity against it could lead to fascism; unity with it was impossible. Unless a new popular front could be formed, there would be no way of saving France from its 'colonial cancers', its Malthusian economy and its involvement in NATO.[142] In the meantime, the way to work constructively was to work for the de-Stalinization of the PCF.[143]

On 21 November Rolland was expelled from the PCF, while the other three members who had signed the letter were publicly censured and subsequently kept under close surveillance. In March 1957 Roy's membership was suspended. *Humanité* welcomed the Kádár government: 'Popular power is re-established solidly.'[144]

PART FIVE

Towards Revolution
(1957–68)

TWENTY · *Back to Philosophy*

Since the beginning of 1952, when he had taken his oath of lifelong hatred against the bourgeoisie and had agreed to work with the PCF on the Henri Martin affair, Sartre had written little except *Les Communistes et la paix*, *Nekrassov* and a quick first draft of the Flaubert biography. In his confrontations with Camus, Lefort and Hervé he had expressed himself through long essays in *Les Temps modernes*, but never before had his motivations been so unliterary. His priority had been to protest, to campaign, to denounce, supporting the FLN and the ideal of world peace as presented at international conferences organized by the communists, while denouncing NATO and the European Defence Community.

Now, after condemning the repressive Soviet action in Hungary, he became more tolerant neither towards colonial repression nor towards the United States. His support for the FLN was to continue, but for nearly six years he paid no visit to the Soviet Union. He was no less concerned with Marxism, but, never unambitious, he was intending to change it. Between the 1954 conversation with Roger Garaudy and the March 1956 confrontation with Merleau-Ponty at the Vienna congress Sartre had gone on thinking and talking about a Marxist take-over bid for psycho-analysis and this intention underlies the two major books he was yet to write, his *Critique de la raison dialectique* and his Flaubert biography. He was not exactly retreating into writing. He was still campaigning, but on different ground.

Strongly in sympathy with the opposition inside the communist world, he often encountered Polish intellectuals in Paris, and during November he was invited to the Polish embassy, where he met the editor of the review *Twórczość*, Jerzy Lisowski, who was planning a French issue. He invited Sartre to write about the situation of existentialism in 1957. Henri Lefebvre had been invited to discuss developments in French Marxism. Sartre had been feeling inclined to associate the word existentialism with 'a past, peripheral cultural fashion, not unlike a particular brand of soap',[1] but he agreed to write an essay, which he called 'Marxism and Existentialism'.

His play *Les Mouches* was currently being rehearsed in Poland, and he attended the premiere in January 1957. The February–March issue of *Les Temps modernes* was a Polish issue, collecting articles, reports and verse published in Polish papers since 1954: 'Here we finally see what should exist, what can exist today and will exist tomorrow – a communism freed from Stalinism.'[2]

In France the government was hardly troubling to deny that Algerians were being tortured, raped, plundered. There were executions without a trial, ruthless and arbitrary reprisals against the civilian population. Over a year had passed since the abbé Gau, an MRP deputy, had made a speech in the Assembly, denouncing police methods as 'worthy of the Gestapo'. In 1956, when the FLN leader Ahmed Ben Bella had been kidnapped in a Moroccan plane by the French secret services, Mollet had retrospectively given his approval. By 1957 about 400,000 French servicemen were being deployed in Algeria to maintain the peace, venting on the unfortunate Algerians the spleen that had accumulated out of frustration and defeat in Vietnam. The French government made only perfunctory attempts to discipline the army: the real power was in the hands of the settlers' leaders and their administration, controlled by the unscrupulous minister-resident Robert Lacoste. In the second week of April Sartre described French methods of 'pacification' in 'Une entreprise de démoralisation', an article commissioned by *Le Monde*. He seized the opportunity of reaching a wide public, cogently accusing the French people of complicity. When the article was rejected, he published it in *Les Temps modernes*.[3] Though he had always been anti-colonialist, he was not so closely in touch with the Algerians as Francis Jeanson, who had distanced himself from Sartre after 'Le Fantôme de Staline', considering it to be too anti-Soviet. Jeanson had worked in Algeria during the war, and had many Moslem friends.[4] Siding wholeheartedly with the FLN, he started a clandestine paper, *Vérités pour...*

Sartre was in the process of trying to make himself into a humanist. Fifteen years later he would say: 'Today the new style of intellectual must give everything to the people.'[5] Sixteen years earlier he had admitted: 'I don't like men – I mean the male of the species ... For me there is a half of the human race which scarcely exists.'[6] Now, at the age of fifty-one, he was always ready – at once self-denying and indulgent towards his appetite for self-denial – to leave his desk for a demonstration or a political meeting. He was less ready to leave it for long sessions of gossip with friends in cafés. To the end of his life he would go on spending a great deal of time with the female of the species, but he had no interest in writing novels or short stories about personal relationships. In biography and even in autobiography, his aim was to look beyond the individual to the social pressure. Talking in June 1957 about the book which was to become *Les*

Mots, he claimed that he was trying to view himself as a member of a group. 'My own experience can be significant to the extent that it can be that of a crowd of people who resemble me ... intellectuals of the Third and Fourth Republics ... In what you see as something rich and original I am constrained no longer to see anything more than one manifestation among others of a certain intellectual of a certain type.'[7] It is hard to picture a crowd of people who resemble Sartre, but he was trying to escape from self-involvement, at the same time as indulging a drive he had in common with Tintoretto: 'that diligent and almost sadistic violence I call the full employment of oneself'. With his phenomenal energy and his greedy, sensual enjoyment of writing he produced what he knew to be an abnormal number of written words almost every day, but the love of writing was coupled with a hatred of artistically remodelled sentences. Prose should just communicate the ideas that were in the head. Like Tintoretto, Sartre was imprisoned by his greed to exploit his talents, but while Tintoretto '*always*' finished everything, with the terrifying application of a man bent on completing his sentence, no matter what else he does',[8] Sartre would assert his freedom by leaving work unfinished.

In Sartre, as in Brecht, the writings of Marx and Engels encouraged the spread of self-dislike into passionate campaigning for an escape from the self, together with a generalized revulsion against the idea of individuality. In 'Le Fantôme de Staline' Sartre attacked bourgeois individualism: what bourgeois man respects in himself and claims to respect in other people is the value of the individual personality, whereas Soviet man subordinates his identity to the group, avoiding the 'vices of bourgeois personilization'. Tintoretto is praised in Sartre's 1957 essay for being competent to paint in a variety of styles, those of Veronese or Titian for instance, and for training assistants and members of his family to collaborate with him. Some of the pictures which bear his name are the work of 'a strong collective personality'.[9] In the summer, writing a preface for André Gorz's *Le Traitre*, Sartre compares the book with an experiment to determine whether 'I did it' can accurately be said of any action. Who is speaking? Who has acted? Rimbaud insisted: 'Je est un autre'; in Gorz's book language appears to be speaking by itself, and when the word 'I' is pronounced, the glimpse of a speaker is no more than a mirage.[10] Like Genet, Gorz appears to himself as someone else.[11]

Growing as it had from Sartre's abandoned notes for an ethic, his book on Genet is more philosophical than sociological, but the massive biography of Flaubert begun in 1954 pulls the social and intellectual background into the foreground. The contrast between Flaubert's mother-fixation and the father-fixation of Baudelaire (who was born during the same year, 1821) is attributed to the difference between their environments. With her aristocratic connections, Flaubert's mother represented a class of ownership verging on liquidation, while his father, who had roots in the peasantry and the countryside, used wealth to buy land; Baudelaire came from an urban family of shareholders.[12] This may fail to prove Sartre's point but he argues convincingly that the Marxist biographer cannot afford to reject psycho-analysis when it helps 'to establish how a child lives his family relations inside a given society'.[13] Psycho-analysis also provides a means of moving from generalization and abstraction to individual particularities. Engels had tried to dismiss these as irrelevant to the course of history, which would have been no different, he said, if Napoleon had never been born, but Sartre's intellect is seen at its formidable best in the intellectual acrobatics he performs on the tightrope stretching between the biographical fact and the totalizing movement.

The world 'totalize' recurs frequently in his work from 1957 onwards, but the idea goes back to 1942. In *Le Sursis* he was already asking what would happen if you tried 'to stand face to face with the planet'. During a world war the war is 'the totality of all my thoughts, all Hitler's words, all Gomez's actions, but nobody is there to do the adding up'. The paradox is that the whole war has a tangible existence though none of us can come into contact with more than a fragment of it. In the absence of God there is no witness. When Sartre started to use the word 'totalize' he gave it a number of overlapping meanings. To totalize is to synthesize a plurality into a unity, but sometimes he makes 'totalization' synonymous with *praxis* (activity directed at an object), treating all work as an attempt to make a new synthesis out of existing elements. Detotalization follows when the synthesis proves to be unfinished.

In *Le Sursis* the totalizer was contemporary history and Sartre tried to make it take over the narrative function; in a biography the writer must concern himself with the 'total individual': between the individual and his background, conditioning is reciprocal. Each statement of Robespierre's, each habit, each circumstance will yield its full meaning only if viewed in the context of his political attitude and his social position. But the relationship between circumstance and behaviour does not emerge clearly in a biography based on a linear narrative of actions: 'a life develops in spirals constantly passing the same points at different levels of integration and complexity'.

Sartre makes a good case in favour of reclaiming psycho-analysis for Marxism in spite of the blurring between the two questions 'How much can we know about a man?' and 'Is there any such thing as a truth about man?' Used like this, the words 'thing' and 'truth' are almost meaningless, while the word 'man' is a vague synthesis spanning neanderthal man, medieval beggars, African pygmies and French intellectuals. But Sartre was driven by the urge to reduce human history to a single, explainable entity; this is the motive behind *Questions de méthode*, which he evolved from the essay for *Twórczość* on Marxism and existentialism. Expanding it and adapting it under the new title for French readers, he published it in *Les Temps modernes*,[14] where it took its natural place, as a battle in his campaign to found a synthetic anthropology independent of Lévi-Strauss's structural anthropology.

Since publishing his essay 'L'Analyse structurale en linguistique et anthropologie' in August 1945,[15] Lévi-Strauss had made frequent use of the words 'structure' and 'structural' in titles of essays and papers. The collection of these in *L'Anthropologie structurale* did not appear until 1958, but Jean Pouillon had supported Lévi-Strauss in *Les Temps modernes*, writing in 1956 that although he was not the first to emphasize the structural character of social phenomena, his originality lay in taking it seriously and 'calmly deriving all the consequences from it'. Without being explicitly anti-structuralist in *Questions de méthode* or in *Critique de la raison dialectique* Sartre declared his intention of founding an 'anthropologie structurelle', the difference in spelling pointing to its difference from Lévi-Strauss's. The only question Sartre wants to raise, he says, is whether we are in a position to construct a theory 'of man as he structures himself historically'. To formulate the question like this is arguably to beg it by putting 'man' and 'himself' in the singular, but Sartre's combative object was to annex the word *structure* for chronological progression, when the method of the structuralists was to sidestep historical change, looking only at resultant structures. While Sartre was drafting *Questions de méthode*, he realized it was going to lead into a much bigger work, and a few weeks before publishing the first volume of his *Critique de la raison dialectique*, he said that he had been struggling for fifteen years to 'lay the political foundations of anthropology'.

As a Marxist he wanted to believe that dialectical materialism offered a complete interpretation of history – that all the contradictions, conflicts, heterogeneities, anomalies could be subsumed in a single totalization. Sartre is simultaneously concerned to provide Marxism with an adequate theory of knowledge – both Marx and Lenin had worked without one – and to combat Heideggerian existentialism which consistently makes Being its point of departure. Sartre insists that history is the history of human initiatives. What emerges as the crucial problem is how to map the jungle of obscure interconnections between historical movements and individual actions.

The philosophical concern with history is less academic than political. If there is no God to face the planet, history has either to make itself or to be made. Writing about the future in which the 'universal class', the proletariat, will lead the world to revolution, Marx said: 'Its goal and its historical action are irrevocable and visibly traced out for it in the very circumstances of its life.' This implies either determinism or scientism: the future of the class is either predestined or predictable from objective analysis of evidence already available. Sartre had consistently rejected determinism, but how are we to define the space in which choices are made? As Merleau-Ponty noticed, Sartre had always been reluctant to acknowledge a middle ground between subject and object, whether between men and things, or between men and others, and the new phase of Sartrean thinking seems to be indebted both to Merleau-Ponty and to the early thinking of Georg Lukács. In his 1923 book *History and Class Consciousness*, which he later repudiated under pressure from Stalinist orthodoxy, Lukács made an abortive but courageous attempt at what Merleau-Ponty and Sartre attempted much later – to rescue Marx from the rigidities of the Marxists by analysing the complexity of reciprocal relationships. In Merleau-Ponty's restatement of the argument in his 1955 book *Les Aventures de la dialectique* the viewpoint is phenomenological. To regard consciousness as a centrifugal movement without opacity, he says, is to relegate history and the social to a series of instantaneous observations. If there is an interworld of human relationships, a residue of history, between men and things, the individual can no longer be held responsible, as in early Sartrean existentialism, for choosing the whole contemporary environment, and it is easier to recognize that all action is partly symbolic, reaching not only for a practical result but for the meaning it has as gesture.

In the *Critique* Sartre would make a large-scale raid on the historical interworld; his immediate concern in *Questions de méthode* is to separate the basic truths of Marxism from the dogmatic superstructure, while curing himself of habits formed after his 'conversion' of 1952. He had to disentangle his thinking from compromises he had made for the Party's sake. 'I considered that true Marxism had been completely twisted, falsified by the communists.'[16] Marxism, he said, 'possesses theoretical bases', but 'no longer *knows* anything'.[17] (Sartre likes to follow an abstract collective subject with a personalizing predicate.) 'For the majority of Marxists, thinking is pretending to totalize, which provides a pretext for substituting the universal for the specific.'[18] 'The method is identical with Terror in its inflexible refusal to *differentiate*.'[19] These are ferocious criticisms, but Sartre, who only five years ago has declared: 'I am not a Marxist', now maintains that no anti-Marxist idea can be anything more than the revival of a pre-Marxist idea. Marxism is the only valid philosophy for our time. He quotes approvingly Garaudy's claim: 'Today Marxism forms the only system of co-ordinates which makes it possible to situate and to define a thought in any area – from political economy to physics, from history to ethics.' A philosophy is 'first of all a particular way in which the rising class becomes conscious of itself', and there have been few real philosophies since the seventeenth century, if philosophy is to be 'simultaneously a totalization of knowledge, a method, a regulative Idea, an offensive weapon, and a community of language, if this "vision of the world" is also an instrument which ferments decaying societies, if this particular conception of man and society becomes the culture and sometimes the nature of the whole class'.[20] According to Sartre there have been only three philosophies in this period: 'that of Descartes and Locke; that of Kant versus Hegel; and Marxism.' 'It is impossible to go beyond them until man has gone beyond the historical moment they express.'[21]

So what about existentialism? It should be ranked not as a philosophy but as an ideology. 'It is a parasitical system living on the margin of knowledge which at first it opposed but into which today it seeks to be integrated.'[22] The appearance of self-critical modesty is specious; behind it is an arrogant appropriation of work done by precursors. Sartre is personifying existentialism as if Kierkegaard, Heidegger, Jaspers and Gabriel Marcel had all been generals with him as commander-in-chief. The allegation that existentialism at first opposed knowledge is characteristically loose – Kierkegaard set himself up against Hegel, but so did Marx, and Sartre now wants to lead the deserting existentialists back to the headquarters of Marxist knowledge. Encapsulating the history of Western philosophy in shamelessly inaccurate generalization, Sartre is simultaneously proposing that the new role of existentialism should be to counteract abstract generalization: 'Marxism has reabsorbed man into the idea, and existentialism seeks him everywhere *where he is*, at his work, in his home, in the street.'[23] This echoes the exciting rhetoric that had been inspired by Sartre's early infatuation with Husserl.

That Sartre wants to outflank structuralism is clear when he claims that the 'progressive-regressive method' can 'integrate sociology and history in the perspective of a materialist dialectic'.[24] He claims to be deriving the method from a study by Henri Lefebvre of a rural community.[25] The first step is to see what Lefebvre called the 'horizontal complexity' of a society: we describe what is currently visible: habitat, family structure, agricultural and mechanical techniques, etc. Each of these has its history, and this is what comes under observation in the second phase. Nervous that things might sound too simple, Lefebvre calls this the analytico-regressive phase and tells us that we are now concerned with 'vertical complexity'. We then proceed to synthesis. With the understanding we have acquired of the past, we return to the present in what Lefebvre calls the 'historical-genetic' phase. This appproach is what Sartre calls the 'regressive-progressive method'. No less expert than Lefebvre in introducing terminology which obfuscates a simple procedure, he explains that we move backwards into the determining set of political, ideological, social and economic circumstances, and then forwards into analysing the project by which man internalizes these forces and then externalizes them while producing himself in the world as an organized totality. Misled by the marriage between his own jargon and Lefebvre's, Sartre seems to be forgetting that he has already used the terms regressive and progressive when discussing Freudian psychoanalysis in *L'Etre et le Néant*; 'by a regressive psycho-analysis one climbs back from the considered action to my ultimate potentiality; and by a synthetic progression one goes down again from this ultimate potentiality to the considered action, grasping its integration in the total form'.[26]

In the forties Sartre had complained that 'the dimension of the future does not exist for psycho-analysis'.[27] He was less unfriendly now to Freudianism, but hostile to structuralism. His anthropology has a wider range, he claims, dealing not just with structures that have already been evolved but with the process of evolution. In 1949 Lévi-Strauss had already formulated his own definition of history and anthropology in terms of progressive and retrogressive movement: 'The anthropologist goes forwards, striving to attain, through the conscious, which he never forgets, more and more of the unconscious; whereas the historian advances, as it were, backwards, keeping his eyes fixed on concrete and specific activities from which he withdraws only to review them in a fuller and richer perspective.'[28] For Lévi-Strauss 'the solidarity of the two disciplines is a true two-faced Janus', but for Sartre the historian is the dominant partner. But he now writes with a certain awkwardness, which reflects itself in the use of language that is significantly more jargon-ridden than the language of *L'Etre et le Néant*.

The postwar popularity of existentialism had grown out of its dramatic and challenging redefinition of freedom: instead of being hemmed in by contemporary history we are responsible for it. In relegating existentialism to a subordinate position in the Marxist system, Sartre is also reducing human freedom to a mere gleam on the horizon. He quotes *Das Kapital*: 'This reign of freedom cannot begin until there is an end to the work imposed by necessity and external finality.'[29] Sartre goes on: 'As soon as there is a margin of *real* freedom *for everyone* beyond the production of a livelihood, Marxism will have lived out its span; a philosophy of freedom will replace it. But we have no means, no intellectual instrument, no concrete experience to enable us to conceive of this freedom or this philosophy.'[30] This is a violent volte-face, which allies Sartre with Marx's assumption that oppression has nothing to do with human aggression and that under a different social structure injustice could be eliminated. But Sartre no longer seems to want a revolution. Progressing on a spiral like the one he describes, Sartre's thinking has arrived at a new level without moving away from its stubborn core of disbelief in evil human impulses. In *Saint Genet* and in *Le Diable et le Bon Dieu* he had brought good and evil close together; in abandoning his notes towards an ethic he had denied the validity of moral standards in our oppressive society. In *Questions de méthode* he was assuming that we do have access to a truth about man, but he made no serious attempt to erect a distinction between philosophical truth and truth in reporting on impressions. Whereas Gide had been scrupulously honest after his return from the USSR, Sartre, after his first visit to Moscow, had told expedient lies, and even now, after unbuckling the straitjacket, he was dangerously close to writing a philosophy for the rising class in which truth is equated with what serves the cause.

All through 1957 *Les Temps modernes* was keeping up its campaign against the failure of the feeble French government to enforce justice in Algeria. Women were being raped; people were disappearing; others were being arbitrarily arrested. Suspects were being tortured with electric goads, having their bones broken, having their nails torn out. The French army and the French settlers, the *colons*, were directly responsible for these outrages; the government was indirectly responsible in failing to keep its forces under control. But there was no stability at the centre. Intent on staying in power, Guy Mollet, who was squandering half a million troops on the Algerian war, came increasingly under attack from the moderates while increasingly trying to stop French papers from publishing the facts. Between 11 April and 2 May *France-Observateur* was twice suppressed, but Mollet's government collapsed in May, and in June *Les Temps modernes* reprinted the articles that had provoked the seizure of *France-Observateur*.[31] Mollet was succeeded by Maurice Bourgès-Manoury, a radical, who formed a ministry during the second week of June, but it survived for only ten weeks. During the year *Les Temps modernes* was impounded four times in Algeria, but not in France until November.[32]

In the July–August issue, reviewing Albert Memmi's double volume *Portrait du colonisateur* and *Portrait du colonisé*, Sartre argued that colonialism depended on a system of production which divided humanity into two classes. 'For some people privilege and humanity are inseparable: they make themselves men by the free exercise of their rights; for the others the lack of rights sanctions their misery, their chronic hunger, their ignorance, in short their sub-human status.'[33] The dehumanization of the oppressed recoils on the oppressor, who has to overcome all compassionate impulses for the sake of the system. 'In short he "dehumanizes" himself in turn.'[34] The system was not even economically advantageous to the colonial power: France would eventually be forced to abandon the Algerian War as too expensive.[35] Sartre's forecast, of course, was accurate.

In December he was one of the left-wing intellectuals to testify at the trial of Ben Saddok, who had assassinated the former vice-president of the Algerian assembly. Ben Saddok's lawyer, Pierre Stibbe, wanted Camus, who had just won the Nobel Prize, to read a passage from one of his essays at the trial, but his mother was still in Algiers and he refused to involve himself. Jacques Soustelle, who had been governor-general of Algeria since the beginning of 1955, appeared as a witness for the prosecution. Sartre, who was one of the last to speak, argued that the young man's action was not a terrorist attack but a political murder: during the Resistance similar killings had been applauded as heroic.[36] At dinner with de Beauvoir and Lanzmann, Sartre, who for some time had been allowed no alcohol, succumbed to the need for whisky and soon became agitated: to please the right-wingers on the jury he had spoken as if he disapproved of terrorism.[37] The next day Ben Saddok was sentenced to life imprisonment.

The fall of Bourgès-Manoury in October had been followed by thirty-five days of chaos. In November a new government – the twentieth of the Fourth Republic – was formed by Félix Gaillard, a young radical who had been finance minister. Struggling energetically against the economic crisis, he raised taxes, devalued the franc by twenty per cent, and borrowed heavily. But the Tunisian President Bourguiba refused to co-operate with him against the FLN, who were operating successfully from bases inside Tunisia, and on 16 January 1958 sixteen French soldiers were killed on the Algerian side of the border near the small Tunisian village of Sakhiet. A French bomber then attacked the village, killing sixty-nine people, including twenty children. Not daring to antagonize the army by condemning the raid, Gaillard merely offered to pay compensation to the Tunisians. 'He has made us all into accomplices', Sartre declared in 'Nous sommes tous des assassins', published in the March issue of *Les Temps modernes*.[38]

In February there was a huge demand in French bookshops for a first-hand account of torture in Algeria – *La Question* by Henri Alleg, communist editor of the newspaper *Alger républicain*, which had been suppressed in September 1955. In November 1956 he had begun to publish it illegally. Arrested by French parachutists in June 1957, he had been imprisoned for a month. Still fascinated by the rapport between torturer and victim, Sartre reviewed Alleg's book for *L'Express*, pointing to the anomalies which were exposed: thugs could enjoy the convulsions of a man being electrocuted but couldn't bear the sound of his screaming; torture was being used to destroy in the Arabs the qualities that Europeans most admire – courage, willpower, intelligence, loyalty.[39] *L'Express* was seized by the police and when Sartre's review was printed as a pamphlet it was immediately impounded.

The violence infected Paris. Policemen were being shot in reprisal by Algerians, and on 13 March the police demonstrated in front of the Chambre de Députés. De Beauvoir found she was recoiling from French military uniforms as she once had from swastikas, while Sartre's work on *Critique de la raison dialectique* was activated partly by the need to distract himself from what was going on.

> He did not work in his usual way, pausing, crossing words out, tearing up pages, starting them all over again; for hours at a stretch he rushed from one sheet of paper to the next without re-reading them, as if possessed by words his pen couldn't catch, even at this gallop. I would hear him crunching corydrane capsules to maintain the impetus ... by the end of the afternoon he was exhausted, his concentration shattered. His gestures were uncertain and he would often say one word instead of another.[40]

Corydrane was a mixture of aspirin and amphetamines. Until it was prohibited in 1971, it was on sale at pharmacies. Advertised as a tonic, analgesic and anti-pyretic, it was effective as a stimulant and was popular among students and intellectuals, who found it increased their productivity. The recommended dose was one or two tablets in the morning and again at midday; Sartre was taking ten at a time and, before the book was finished, twenty. As he put it, he 'abused drugs a great deal' for twenty years, but most of all while writing the *Critique*. Besides corydrane he was taking orthodrine – a tube would last him a day. 'As soon as one passed a certain point', he told de Beauvoir 'one began to be destroyed, and the risk was a reality ... One liked destruction as such, one liked having blurred ideas which were vaguely interrogative and which then disintegrated ... It also meant that one could drop dead, but there was no knowing when.' He needed to test how far he could push both body and mind. He reached the stage of having no skin left on his tongue. For a time he was partially deaf.

There is a case, of course, to be made for narcotic inflation of the mental marketplace. Imaginative writers from Coleridge and de Quincey to Rimbaud and the surrealists had provided a distinguished precedent. What is odd about the case of Sartre is that though he wrote philosophy while stoned, he took care to keep his mental faculties intact while writing fiction. 'I felt that in a novel the way one chose and juxtaposed words and formed phrases – in short the style – and then the way one analysed emotions made it a prerequisite that one should be absolutely normal.' While he was writing the *Critique* (or so he said sixteen years later) 'I thought I had in my head ... all the ideas I was putting down on paper ... A tube of corydrane meant: these ideas will be analysed in the next two days.'[41]

When Sartre indulges in the painful pleasure of recriminating against an earlier self, he is liable to exaggerate, but here the internal evidence supports the self-accusation. From any point of view the *Critique* (with or without the second half he left unpublished) forms the climax of his philosophical writing. His object was to restructure the entire foundation of Marxist philosophy, to demonstrate the dialectical unity in both external reality and knowledge. Had he succeeded, history would have been shown to have a single meaning, while analytical reason would have been discredited as conducive to atomistic thinking that advanced the interests of the bourgeoisie. Nothing could have mattered to Sartre more than to accomplish this vastly ambitious enterprise, but he was bizarrely determined not to use his full powers as a mental athlete. Instead of keeping himself in a fit state to look up passages in the Marxist philosophers and in his own earlier writings, to check facts, sources, quotations, statistics, he was content to rely on his drugged memory and to take evasive refuge in the kind of abstraction which infuriated Engels when Marx resorted to it. Like *Die Heilige Familie*, the *Critique* would be of no interest to the general public.

The writing, especially in the published volume, is muddled, long-winded, repetitious and jargon-ridden, the jargon being used inconsistently, while the philosophy rubs up indigestibly against long sections which are more political, historical, economic, sociological and polemical. Sartre also transposes material from his draft for the Flaubert biography. During his fifteen-year struggle 'to lay the political foundations of anthropology', the project, he said, had grown 'like a generalized cancer'. Not knowing what to do with the ideas that presented themselves, he had put them down in whatever book he was working on, but they were 'all in place now', or so he claimed a few weeks before the first volume was published. The second, he said, would be out within a year.[42]

In so far as the *Critique* bases itself on the 'progressive-regressive method', the first volume is regressive; the second was scheduled to deal progressively with the history of humanity, proving that it had a single meaning. The first task he sets himself is to survey the historical interworld by sketching out a general theory about the evolution of groups and the relationships between them. Relationships between individuals are ignored, though he promises in the Introduction that he will carefully 'follow the threads of Ariadne' from individual *praxis* to collective action. In the second volume he will analyse Stalin's regime as an example of individual leadership in relation to collective need, but in the volume he published the individual disappears from historical categories. A man's understanding of his own life, Sartre argues, must reach the point of denying its distinctiveness to find its dialectical intelligibility in the history of humanity.[43] After concealing itself in the accumulating facts of what is happening, the dialectic reveals itself in making them comprehensible.[44]

To cope with the historical interworld the concept Sartre introduces is reciprocity. He is following Lukács and Merleau-Ponty, but he follows half-heartedly: he has not shaken off the conviction that between one consciousness and another the relationship must be one of struggle for subject-object domination. His emphasis is not on consciousness but on *praxis*, and *praxis* brings men into relationship either with other men or with things. Sartre portrays both kinds of relationship as taking place in a world of scarcity. Because materials are in short supply we compete instead of collaborating. Ignoring sexual rivalry and the shortage of physical beauty, he assumes that life could be less competitive and qualitatively better if material supplies were more abundant. As it is, there can be no social justice, only a vicious cycle of oppression. 'Everyone struggles against an order which crushes his body really and materially, while he sustains and strengthens the order by resisting it.'[45]

Nor can any form of social contract provide a basis of justice. Like Marx he takes the state to be a product of the class system, while reciprocity is possible, he says, only when rebellion brings a group together. In an oppressive society there can be no freedom without violence. Sartre contrasts seriality (exemplified by people in a bus queue, bored, passive, indifferent to each other) with the group-in-fusion, which is collectively active. When the Bastille was being stormed, everyone in the crowd was behaving in a new way, not as alienated, not as an individual, but as an individual incarnation of 'the common person'. In *Les Communistes et la paix* he had written unrealistically as if this kind of cohesiveness existed between the Party and the proletariat. Everyone, he said, is a leader. As a description of the crowd which marched on the Bastille this phrase would be less inaccurate – people were united by a common purpose which led to immediate action – but it is revealing that Sartre should have come to believe in collective violence as the only available form of human freedom. The man who had once admitted to disliking the male half of the human race and who in the Stalag had shunned the company of working-class soldiers was now glorifying the common people when herded together in righteous lust for vengeance.

After launching himself in impassioned championship of individual freedom, Sartre had already made his most extraordinary volte-face when he allied himself in *Questions de méthode* with Marx's contention that no freedom can be available until 'there is an end to the work imposed by necessity and external finality'. In an oppressive society there can be no liberty without violence, no hope without terror: 'the structures of freedom and reciprocity' take on their full meaning only when they appear in the 'practical material movement of terror'. Though the idea of a social contract is inadmissible, the individual who pledges himself to the group has 'freely consented to the liquidation of [his] person as free constituent *praxis*'. Those who betray the group deserve to be lynched. 'I am a brother in violence to my neighbours ... Violence is the actual power of this lateral reciprocity of love.'[46] This contradicts Sartre's entries in his wartime diaries about the pointlessness of trying to sacrifice future freedom: an oath was an 'empty incantation', 'an avowal of distress ... I cannot choose my subsequent choices'. On the other hand the equation of violence with the 'lateral reciprocity of love' is reminiscent of the freedom fighters in *Morts sans sépulture* when they kill the fifteen-year-old François, who might have cracked under torture and betrayed their beloved leader. Though Sartre was already thirty-five when the German army marched into France, the Occupation had been intellectually formative: the Resistance had tended to sanctify violence. But to offer the group this much power over the individual in peacetime is to reject liberalism no less contemptuously than Brecht in *Die Massnahme* (*The Remedial Measure*). In this 1930 play the agitators renounce their name and their personal identity, becoming 'blank leaves for the Revolution to write its orders on'. When one of them follows his own impulses instead of obeying orders, he is shot by his comrades, but they shoot him lovingly.

Like Brecht, Sartre was committed to an all-out battle against the individual ego. The *Critique* often refers to 'the common person' and makes frequent use of Marx's phrase 'the accidental individual'. During the spring and summer of 1958 Sartre's political conviction had been hardening around the core of ambivalence which was already merging discomfort with himself into hatred of the self. Pascal had said: 'Le moi est haïssable.' Sartre had questioned whether 'I did it' can ever be said accurately. Nor was he by any means the only anti-individualist among progressive French intellectuals. Lévi-Strauss claimed to be 'nothing but the place where my work is done'; Sartre, who had been more creative, was at his worst in writing based, uncreatively, on the implicit denial that his knowledge centred on his experience.

Writing about Lucien, Mathieu or Goetz, he was writing about himself; in the *Critique* he was trying to view himself as a member of a class and to view the class with the detachment that might come from taking a wide-angle view of its conflicts. One of the books most important to him during the war was Jean-Léon Jaurès's four-volume history of the French Revolution, and if Sartre keeps coming back to this subject, it was mainly because the revolution had crystallized the French bourgeoisie while sweeping the individual into successive tides of collective movement. Dissatisfied with the human condition, Sartre had once yearned for the unambiguous existence of a thing – Mathieu wishing he could be a stone; another stratagem for escaping from the self had been to view consciousness as impersonal, with individuality as its object, not its subject. The new alternative was to believe that the individual disappears as soon as he understands his connection with the 'cultural field' which consists of a 'synthetic bond between everyone'.[47] With the Tennis Court Oath as his model, Sartre thinks of swearing as 'a regulatory and totalizing praxis'.[48] But the effort to think anonymously in the plural leads to jargon-ridden writing about activity in which the subject is collective and the action singular. 'Common *praxis* is *dialectical*' he asserts. 'It totalizes the object, pursues some total aim, unifies the practico-inert field and dissolves it in the synthesis of the *common practical field*.'[49]

Together with 'scarcity', 'the practico-inert' is one of the key concepts in his explanation of why freedom is available only to the insurrectionary group. The practico-inert is the area which contains the residue of past *praxis*. As Sartre sees it – taking, as so often, a literary model – work consists of 'imprinting' one's image on inorganic materiality, or, to put it less clearly, the worker is realizing himself by externalizing interiority. This leads Sartre back to Hegel, who believed that alienation inevitably accompanied object-ification. During the process of objectifying himself in his work, the subject becomes something other than himself. He loses out in both his involvement with things and his involvement with other people, who appropriate his product, thievishly adapting it to their own use. So just as there is no existing without *praxis*, and no *praxis* without objectification, there is no objectification without alienation. The worker who leaves one factory job for another is merely defining the limits that confine him, while confirming his destiny, which is to be exploited. 'All men are slaves in so far as their life unfolds in the practico-inert field and in so far as this field is always conditioned by scarcity ... The alienation of the exploited is inseparable from that of the exploiters.'[50]

Undeniably, Sartre's attitude is complicated by his emotional hostility to things. Like the chestnut tree, objects are unforgivable. Though the *Critique* is never rhetorical in the manner of *L'Etre et le Néant* it uses highly charged emotional language to denounce them. We are victims of 'violence, shadows and witchcraft'; we have to fight against 'the evil actions of material which has been worked on'. But this time he has no Roquentin to pick up the bill: it is Sartre himself who is telling us that objects persecute us.

If it had not been for the corydrane, his emotionality would be all the more surprising in a manifesto for a new rationality. Marx would never have maintained that dialectical reason and analytical reason were mutually exclusive, but in *Questions de méthode* Sartre had already made a highly unreasonable demand for an alternative rationality. 'Because no-one has

been prepared to establish this rationality in experience, I state factually:
nobody in the East or West writes or utters a sentence about us or our
contemporaries which is not a flagrant error ... Our present ideas are
false because they have died before us. Some stink of carrion, while others
are clean little skeletons; it's all the same thing.'[51] This is to carry the
hyperbole of platform rhetoric into serious philosophizing, and in setting
out to invalidate analytical reason he was once again undertaking a Hercu-
lean task he would have to abandon. He is, as Lévi-Strauss complains,
undecided about whether analytical reason is sometimes admissible as a
necessary component of dialectical reason. Totalization, claims Lévi-
Strauss, has been taken for granted by anthropologists since Malinowski,
but for them it is only a point of departure. Once the philosopher, using
dialectical reason, has constituted a totality, it is for the scientist to do
the serious work of analysing it.[52] The penultimate chapter of Lévi-Strauss's
1962 book *La Pensée sauvage* made its first appearance in *Les Temps modernes*
and the final chapter, an attack on Sartre's *Critique*, derived from seminars
in which Jean Pouillon participated.[53] Before launching his attack Lévi-
Strauss admits that he has been using Sartrean terminology with the ulterior
purpose of leading the reader to this point; none of the criticisms he makes
in the chapter is more damaging than the incidental reminder of how the
terminology, like the concepts, has failed to pass into general usage, even
among philosophers or sociologists. But Lévi-Strauss surrenders the word
'anthropology' to Sartre, reverting to 'ethnology' for his own work.

Their rivalry is a fight between two champions who each have the same
ambition – to update Marxism. Lévi-Strauss agrees that *praxis* 'constitutes
the fundamental totality for the sciences of man'.[54] But while both were
influenced by Mauss's *Essai sur le don*, Lévi-Strauss believed that Sartre
had misunderstood Mauss and that between *praxis* and practices there is
always a conceptual scheme. What Lévi-Strauss wanted to contribute was
a theory of superstructures, an explanation of the way matter and form
come together in structures. The problem of infrastructures could be rele-
gated to the historian.[55] Unfortunately the two leaders of the two rival anthropologies were each content to score debating points off the other without
direct confrontation. Even if collaboration was out of the question, discussion was not. *Les Temps modernes* could have made a more important contribution to French intellectual life. So averse to the idea of leadership that
he was incapable of being a good editor, Sartre was also too busy, absent
from Paris for too much of the year, and insufficiently committed to the
editorial function. Altogether, in thirty-five years of directing the review,
he scarcely did any editing; he took full control over only one issue. Merleau-Ponty had given his services generously and self-effacingly; perhaps
to protect himself against the after-effects of generosity, Sartre would later

make the gesture and the effort of editing the issue dedicated to his former colleague's memory.

The review might have developed differently if Merleau-Ponty had been more aggressive and preferred confrontation to withdrawal. Of the others the one intellectually best qualified to arbitrate was Pouillon, but he was neither strong enough personally nor in a position of sufficient strength. The core of the problem that Sartre and Lévi-Strauss should have confronted has been summarized by Howard Davies: 'Sartre can tolerate the concept of structure only as a configuration of praxis and practico-inert within the group, while Lévi-Strauss fails to explicate the relationship of praxis and structure.'[56] Davies also makes the point that *Les Temps modernes* missed a good opportunity to test out the theory of ensembles Sartre had advanced in the *Critique*: the review could have investigated political developments in primitive societies.[57] Much later – in 1966 – Pouillon would edit an issue devoted to structuralism, contending in his own essay that co-ordination between the two anthropologies is feasible: *structural* refers to structure as syntax while *structurelle* refers to structure as reality. But neither Sartre nor Lévi-Strauss contributed to the issue. Oddly enough, friendship continued between Lévi-Strauss and de Beauvoir, who accepted his advice not only on *Le Deuxième sexe* (1949) but on *La Vieillesse* (1970).[58]

Not that events in France were conducive to healthy intellectual controversy while the political crisis continued. In February 1958 after the bombing of Sakhiet, Gaillard, the ineffectual premier, resigned, and for five weeks none of the candidates for the succession was able to form a government. Trying to steep himself in work, Sartre dosed himself recklessly with corydrane, which exacerbated his restlessness. He had always tended to move a great deal, swinging his arms so much as he walked that his shoulders seemed to be rolling, but during his fifties he was becoming more fidgety. In de Beauvoir's flat he paced about so much that she had an extra piece of carpet put down to conceal the threadbare patch he had made.[59]

By 5 May President Coty was making overtures to de Gaulle, who seemed willing enough to take over, but on 8 May Coty approached Pierre Pflimlin, a liberal. The *colons* were outraged, while the generals warned the president that the anxieties of the army could be allayed only by a government firmly committed to keeping Algeria French. In spite of this, Pflimlin managed to form a government on 13 May. This triggered an insurrection in Algiers. With de Gaulle's supporters active among them, demonstrators occupied the government building. The army, which could have stopped them, assumed control. Pflimlin's government nervously ordered General Salan to take charge in Algiers, but it seemed possible that he would be strong enough to take charge in Paris too. People were terrified of the parachute regiments: at any moment the sky might be full of parachutes, meaning civil war had begun. But the mood of the army was unpredictable: if the generals had attempted a coup, would their men have supported them?

We do not know how much de Gaulle did to precipitate the demand for him in Algiers. There were limits to his popularity in the army: officers who had supported the Vichy government did not regard him as their friend, but they had no alternative leader, and when Guy Mollet's Section française de l'internationale ouvrière opted for him in preference to an alliance with the communists, his return became inevitable, though it was still possible to throw obstacles in his way. Sartre's article 'Le Prétendant' was published in *L'Express* on 22 May. 'The solitude of this man, shut up in his lofty grandeur, prevents him in any case from becoming head of state in a republic. Or – in other words – prevents the state he will control from remaining a republic'.[60]

On the evening of 27 May de Gaulle said that if he was not given power within forty-eight hours, he would seize it. It was not an idle threat: the army was behind him. The next day Sartre and de Beauvoir joined a massive anti-Gaullist demonstration from the place de la Nation to the place de la République. When the *Marseillaise* and the *Chant du Départ* were sung, Sartre joined in lustily, glad to be part of a group-in-fusion.

Even now the mental shutters could be adjusted for writing, but, putting the *Critique* aside, he worked at the play he had promised Simone Berriau for the autumn season at the Antoine.[61] In February, during a public discussion with Arthur Adamov and Michel Butor, he had spoken up for topicality: theatre could be revitalized only by plays dealing with current political events.[62] His next play, he said, would be about a Frenchman who had tortured Algerians. Three years earlier, after *Nekrassov*, he had intended never to give the bourgeois public another play, but now, provoked into writing about torture, he wanted to reach the biggest possible audience.

After four days of rumours that the parachutists had landed, fears of civil war were unallayed. There were demonstrations and counter-demonstrations, shouts of 'Vive de Gaulle' and of 'No fascists in France', processions and counter-processions with placards and flags. But the sixty-nine socialist deputies had been cowed into supporting de Gaulle, while President Coty threatened to resign unless de Gaulle were put in office. Sartre's protracted campaign against him had been like an adult repetition of his campaigning at the Ecole Normale against Gustave Lanson, but this time the unacceptable father-figure, the embodiment of authoritarianism, was invincible.

Despondent though he was, Sartre was not too depressed to have a meeting on 31 May 1958 with the American film director John Huston, who in 1946 had scored a big success with a stage production of *Huis clos* on Broadway. He had later flirted with the idea of basing a film on *Le Diable et le Bon Dieu* and he now invited Sartre to script a Hollywood film about Freud. Ever since 1945, when he had directed *Let There Be Light*, a sixty-minute documentary film for the US Army Pictorial Service about battle neurosis, Huston had wanted to make a Freud film, and now that Ernest Jones had completed his biography – the three volumes appeared in 1953, 1955 and 1957 – it seemed to be the right moment. Huston's idea was to centre the film on the earlier part of Freud's career, building a thriller-like suspense around the discovery of psycho-analysis.

It was not just financial need that made Sartre accept the commission. Certainly he needed money: he had just borrowed twelve million old francs from his mother to pay taxes. His outgoings were in the region of 1,800,000 francs a month, though of this only about 300,000 francs were spent on himself, the rest going to his clan of dependants, including his mother, Michelle and Wanda. The film would bring in £25,000, but like the exorbitantly generous Kean of the play he would not have been prepared to atone for his munificence by accepting jobs he considered unworthy. His reaction to Huston's offer meant that at last he felt ready for a serious confrontation with Freud. Even at the Ecole Normale, where he had read widely in psychology, he had opted mostly for disciples, Freudians and anti-Freudians, reading little by the man himself. The motive, no doubt, was the same as Freud's for refusing to read Nietzsche – fear of being influenced. But Sartre's attempt to sidestep Freud had been unsuccessful. The biographies of Baudelaire and Genet are nothing if not Freudian in their approach, and now, after proclaiming psycho-analysis to be compatible with Marxism, Sartre welcomed the paid opportunity to study the great man's life and work. Nor was the idea of a film unattractive; if we discount the adaptation of *Kean*, Sartre had never written fiction based on biographical fact, but he would not have undertaken to write about Freud in any other way.

He was also glad to have an assignment that would distract him from the uncontrollable political situation. After a brief period without corydrane he was taking it again. 'I'm not sad,' he told de Beauvoir, 'but I'm asleep. It's like a morgue.'[1]

On the day after he met Huston the death sentence was passed on the Fourth Republic when the national assembly elected de Gaulle as prime minister. Sartre took part in another hostile demonstration the same day, but nothing could stop the sixty-eight-year-old general from consolidating his power, though he had no formula for solving the Algerian problem. He was quick to visit Algiers, and on 4 June he assured the rebels he had understood them. His main concern was to make himself acceptable.

Sartre reacted in accordance with his usual pattern. He would have achieved nothing by staying in Paris; on 16 June he left for three months in Italy. De Beauvoir had left Paris two days earlier for Milan, where he joined her. Dining in the Piazza del Duomo he told her it was a long time since he had felt so calm.[2] They moved on to Venice, where they stayed for a fortnight, visiting Ravenna and Spoleto before settling in Rome on 4 July. Simone Berriau was planning to stage his new play in October and he tried to work at it in the hotel, but made little headway, even after breaking his rule about not using corydrane when writing creatively. The only result was that he sometimes scribbled illegibly, sometimes produced sentences that were either meaningless or irrelevant.[3] To make himself concentrate he was using the air conditioner to keep his room extremely cold, though outside the heat was a hundred degrees.

His idea was to show how an ex-soldier, by refusing to talk about his Algerian experiences, caused the disintegration of his family;[4] Sartre completed a draft of the first act, but when he showed it to de Beauvoir she told him it was like a sentimental drama by Sudermann.[5] In her diary she wrote: 'He's in no mood to write "fiction" these days. He's doing it only because he's contracted to.'[6] Anxiety that he might have difficulties over censorship was another deterrent, and he failed to finish the play.

But he did start studying Freud. He was never reluctant to jettison premises basic to earlier work, but it was not clear at the outset how flagrantly he would contradict his anti-Freudian writing. Sketching out the scenario that would consist of ninety-five typed pages and would be ready by the middle of December, he found himself telling a story in a way that accorded neither with the assumptions of the *Critique*, which reduces the individual to an air-bubble caught between social pressures, nor with those of his early fiction, which represents the self as incessantly being recreated by ongoing consciousness as if the past can have no causal hold over the present.

On the other hand he was not turning his back on Marx, who had struck an oddly Freudian note in a passage Sartre loved to quote from *Der 18. Brumaire des Louis-Napoleon* (1852):

Men make their own history, but not in any way they please; they make it under circumstances not chosen by themselves but directly encountered, given and transmitted from the past. The tradition of the dead generations weighs like a nightmare on the brain of the living. Just when they seem to be revolutionizing themselves and things, creating something unprecedented ... they nervously conjure up the spirits of the past.

Freud, who discovered that it was possible to exorcize the spirits of the past by analysing the nightmares, used to derive general principles from self-analysis and from case-histories. For Sartre too, or at least for the Sartre of 1958, singular experience can lead to universal conclusions, even if the individual is only a singularized universal. In the first paragraph of his synopsis he sums up what the film is to be about: 'A man undertakes to understand other people because this seems the only way to understand himself, and he realizes that his researches on other people and on himself can be conducted simultaneously.'[7] The film would show how Freud, like a detective, collected from patients clues which helped to solve the problem of his own fixation; this theme had a special appeal to the author of the *Critique*. Rejecting the idea of objectivity based on scientific detachment, Sartre held that the dialectic reveals itself only to an observer situated in interiority, to an investigator whose enquiries are integral to his personal experience as well as being a project aimed at modifying the universe. Analysing his own dreams alongside his patients' neuroses, Freud changed the history of human thought by discovering the truth about himself.

In Rome Sartre did his preliminary reading and his preliminary thinking. Only the first volume of Jones's biography had appeared in a French translation, but this is the one which deals with the period Huston wanted to cover, ending with the breakthrough that ensued on the death of Freud's father in 1896. Jones's book had an immediate effect on Sartre's attitude, making it much easier for him to identify with Freud, who turned out to be diffident, obstinate and fractious. He refused to advance his own career by kowtowing to orthodox medical opinion. His hostility to the establishment even had certain affinities with Sartre's. A Jew in an unmistakably (if patchily) anti-semitic city, Freud was torn between the dream of passing unnoticed among gentiles and the drive to revenge himself by subverting their whole system of thinking. In Sartre, as in Freud, a secret wish to be someone else, or at least to be more like other people, had developed into a violent compulsion to make the others more like him by imposing his ideas on them. Both men were driven by painfully irreconcilable feelings of love and hatred towards the culture that had grown up out of Western civilization. Though Freud was more bourgeois than Sartre in his style of living and less outspoken in his criticism of the bourgeois family, he built in psycho-analysis a weapon that was to disrupt its stability more than anything Sartre wrote.

Sartre soon found that his reading of Freud brought him uncomfortably close to his own experience. He would have no choice but to be an observer situated in interiority. For Freud the weakness of his father had been problematic; for Sartre the early loss of his father had not been the boon he made it out to be, and Freud's immature reliance on father-substitutes was easily comprehensible to a man who had grown up in the home of an autocratic grandfather. There is an unmistakable resemblance between Charles Schweitzer and Sartre's version of the authoritarian Dr Meynert, who after accepting the young Freud as his protégé, ferociously rejects him as soon as he begins to make decisions for himself.

Sartre decided early on that the film would be structured around the relationship with the father and the surrogate fathers. Unable to model himself on the feeble Jakob Freud, Sigmund becomes inordinately dependent on doctors who are paternally supportive and sometimes bullying. One, Breuer, gives him financial help; one, Fliess, is Freud's junior, but he is sufficiently dominant and charismatic for this not to matter. The patriarchal Meynert is the first to encounter resistance, but to arrive at maturity Freud has to achieve independence from them all. This he can do only after the death of Jakob. The synopsis suggests two possible beginnings for the film, and in one of these Freud's offscreen voice is heard saying: 'It all began with the death of my father.' At the end of the film the voice would say: 'I knew very well that it was all over. I was on my own ... I was forty-one. It was my turn to play the role of father.'

This theme is skilfully interwoven with that of Freud's reactions to his female patients. It is unconscious aggression against Jakob that makes him willing to believe that thirteen of his patients have been victims of paternal rape. He wants to degrade the image of paternity; eventually he realizes that he has been listening to fantasies which tell the truth not about what happened but about the desires these women kept secret from themselves. This is how Freud discovered infantile sexuality.

After spending nearly a month with de Beauvoir, Sartre travelled with her to Pisa, where he met Michelle Vian and took her to Rome, where, line by line, she gave him an oral translation of the second and third volumes in Jones's biography of Freud. Before the end of August, though, he promised Jean-Jacques Servan-Schreiber, who had founded the weekly *L'Express*, to put the screenplay aside for long enough to write three articles about the referendum to be held in France on the new constitution, which had been drafted by de Gaulle's legal adviser, Michel Debré. The object was to strengthen the executive, separating it from the legislature, while maintaining an independent judiciary. The draft was amended by a parliamentary committee chaired by Paul Reynaud, who in 1940 had succeeded Daladier as premier. It was published on 4 September, and then submitted to the referendum, which was to be held on 28 September. Sartre's first article for *L'Express* was written in Rome and shortened in Paris by de Beauvoir and Servan-Schreiber. It appeared in the newspaper on 11 September under the title 'La Constitution du mépris' ('The Constitution of Contempt'). Attacking de Gaulle for blackmailing his country, Sartre called on the French to reject the constitution.

He arrived back in Paris on 16 September, but on the 20th, about to start on his second article, he succumbed to a liver infection. He had been feeling exhausted even before the train journey from Rome, and in the afternoon he looked too feverish and weak to write, but he worked for twenty-eight hours with little interruption, and when de Beauvoir left him at eleven on Monday evening, he started another twelve-hour stint. By Monday afternoon he gave the impression of being deaf and blind, but he went on to make a speech at an anti-Gaullist meeting.[8] The article was called 'Les Grenouilles qui demandent un roi' ('The Frogs Who Want a King'). Sartre analysed the failure of the Fourth Republic, which had survived for less than thirteen years. It was already apparent, he argued, that far from introducing the necessary reforms, de Gaulle was continuing the abuses which had been rightly denounced. But three days later, when the referendum was held, seventy-nine per cent of the voters supported the constitution.

'It's rather awful', de Beauvoir wrote in her diary, 'to be against a whole country, your own country; you feel as though you're already an exile.'[9] No longer needing to brace himself for fighting, Sartre had to recognize that he was ill. He kept losing his sense of balance, had attacks of giddiness and non-stop headaches, but instead of consulting a doctor, he dosed himself with optalidon, belladénal and corydrane. On 2 October, putting down a wine glass while lunching with Simone Berriau, he missed the edge of the table by several inches. She immediately telephoned a doctor, Professor Moreau, who diagnosed fatigue in the left ventricle of the heart, and recommended complete rest. He prescribed certain drugs, and promised the apathetic patient that he would soon be more animated. But he must not drink or smoke. He did not entirely ignore the doctor's instructions but refused to rest. Sometimes he felt better but sometimes, as on 13 October, he had difficulty in both walking and talking, while his handwriting and spelling had deteriorated alarmingly. The headaches persisted, and, in comparison with his old self, he was still lethargic, stiff-necked, wooden in his movements, uncertain in his speech and puffy in the face. His moods were unpredictable, fits of violent irascibility punctuating an ominous tranquillity.[10]

De Beauvoir knew she must intervene but did not know how often or how firmly. When she found him at his desk, fighting off exhaustion to keep the pen travelling across the page, she was risking an explosion of anger each time she entreated him to rest. Sometimes he would answer: 'All right, five minutes', and then sleep for two or three hours. Once she persuaded him to cancel an appointment with a girlfriend, who was reduced to tears when she saw how badly he had jumbled the words together on the scribbled message. When de Beauvoir spoke to Professor Moreau, he warned her that though Sartre was only fifty-three, he could be dead within six months if he went on 'racing against the clock'. She then approached Simone Berriau, who agreed to postpone the play until the following autumn. Sartre received the news with an apathetic smile more worrying to de Beauvoir than a fit of temper. But he did begin to work less.[11]

The first parliament of the Fifth Republic was to be elected towards the end of November 1958. In the campaign even Guy Mollet supported de Gaulle, who shrewdly maintained that he was not to be seen as the leader of a particular party. But the new Gaullist party, the Union for the New Republic (UNR), won 206 of the 549 seats, while the christian democrats and independents had won 249, so he was not going to need any help from the socialists.

Of Sartre's earlier books the one contradicted most blatantly by the Freud synopsis is *L'Etre et le Néant*, in which Sartre had denounced the error of picturing consciousness as a territory in which barriers could be erected: in the 1917 *General Introduction to Psycho-Analysis*, Freud compares the unconscious to an ante-room with a door-keeper who decides which visitors will be admitted to the adjoining reception-room. Inaccurately, Sartre had taken this spatial differentiation between conscious and unconscious to be no different from the distinction Freud later introduced between ego and id. The pro-Freudian position Sartre adopts in the synopsis is all the more remarkable for being based on the early stages of Freud's development. Sartre's philosophy of liberty had seemed incompatible with the idea that consciousness could be betrayed from within by forces which remained unknown. He had admitted the existence of self-deception but attributed it to *mauvaise foi*. Now, at the opposite extreme, he was to complain about Huston: 'What's tiresome is that he doesn't believe in the unconscious.'

In the synopsis Sartre makes the reactionary Dr Meynert contend that consciousness is always transparent: 'Besides I don't waste time spying on myself. I'm as transparent as spring water.'[12] But Sartre sides with Freud, who notices that Meynert keeps pulling at his moustache and chewing it while tapping at the left side of his nose with his forefinger. The body speaks in a code unintelligible to Meynert's consciousness.

In both the ninety-five-page scenario and the 800-page screenplay Sartre was to construct from it, fact and fiction are judiciously fused. The patient who features most prominently is the beautiful Cecily Körtner, who has spells of paralysis in which her fists are clenched and her arms held as if she is about to lift something. Freud will eventually decode this: she would like her mother to go away so that she can be the one to save her father from falling. She is also punishing herself for desiring her father and to distract herself from guilt-feelings over her mother's suicide attempt. Cecily is based mainly on a patient of Breuer's, 'Anna O.' or Bertha Pappen-heim, whom Freud never treated and probably never even met. When she developed a hysterical pregnancy in 1892 Breuer broke off his treatment, and much of Sartre's action is based on hypothesizing what might have happened if Freud had taken over the case. He also interpolates an affair between Cecily's father and a pretty governess: this is borrowed from Freud's case-history about 'Dora', which was written up in 1901.

It was in 1896, the year of his father's death, that Freud introduced the term 'psycho-analysis', but to tell the story Huston wanted him to tell Sartre needed to conflate events which spread over ten years. Breuer started to treat Bertha Pappenheim in 1890, and though Freud began to analyse his own dreams in 1895, it was not until 1897 that he embarked on the self-analysis which was to last three years, culminating in the discovery of infantile sexuality and the Oedipus complex, though both were prefigured in the correspondence with Wilhelm Fliess. Some of these letters had been published in *The Origins of Psycho-Analysis*, and the relationship between the two men is dramatized in the screenplay, which hints tellingly at the erotic element in Freud's feelings for the domineering young doctor. As Freud saw, if only belatedly, the female side of his personality had responded to Fliess's flamboyant masculinity. But it was not only because of writing for Hollywood that Sartre held back from looking closely at Freud's way of dealing with his femininity. Though there was a lot of transference in his long friendship with Fliess – the correspondence continued from 1887 to 1904 – Freud's failure in the 'Dora' case was primarily a failure of transference. Still inexperienced as an analyst, he was rigid and aggressive in resisting the emotional pressures of the eighteen-year-old girl. With Fliess he was relaxed enough to let his female side come into play; with 'Dora' he was not. In contrast Sartre could relax completely with young girls – even if the therapeutic benefits were one-sided – but he was incapable of sustaining an affectionate friendship with a man.

In the screenplay the death of Jakob Freud coincides with Sigmund's breakthrough in curing Cecily and he is finally able to acknowledge his aggressiveness towards the inoffensive old father: 'His sweetness disarmed me. I'd have liked Moses to be my father. The Law!' Sartre could have made a parallel statement starting with 'His absence disarmed me'. He makes Freud tell Breuer: 'I took all these fathers to protect me against myself, and I gave myself no respite because I hadn't destroyed them. You all fascinated me, and I wanted to kill my father in you.' Sartre would not have wanted to understand why he found it so easy to identify with a man who had a self-effacing father or to recognize anything Oedipal in his refusal to forgive his step-father for taking possession of the mother who had once been like a cuddly sister. Though Sartre had never needed counterparts in his life to such tyrants as Meynert, Breuer and Fliess, he had quickly learned to use his writing as a weapon against men in stronger positions. With fiction such as 'L'Ange du morbide' he attacked teachers, using philosophy to demolish the formidable Brunschvicg. Sartre had also surrounded himself with a 'family' of younger friends, had played a semi-paternal role to a long line of loving younger women from Olga to Michelle Vian and Arlette El Kaïm, while fictionally killing off parents and father figures in *Les Mouches* and *Les Mains sales.* Freud had needed bullying surrogate fathers. 'You see Fliess', he says in the screenplay, 'people like me need to be tyrannized. I don't know why.'

Sartre had reacted in the opposite way to the paternal vacuum. He had been able, even as a student, not only to manage without paternal guidance but to profit from his contempt towards authorities, and though he needed, like Freud, to cram an abnormal amount of work into each day, he needed no prodding from outside. The tyrant had been securely internalized. And while Freud had been devaluing his father by believing the stories of his hysterical patients, Sartre, who had acquired an equally strong grudge against his mother, was devaluing the parent-child relationship, not only denouncing the family but committing sacrilege against it by seducing all his surrogate daughters. Soon he will even go to the extreme of adopting a young mistress as his daughter.

Sartre's declaration of war on the father-figure meant that he had to live permanently under siege. He was in constant fear of being influenced, and when he was, he had to deny it, even to himself. The fear of influence was so anguishing, the defence system so overdeveloped, the belief in making fresh starts so compulsive that he refused to learn anything even from what he wrote himself. In the screenplay he could exploit the understanding he had acquired of his own self-destructiveness by exposing the self-destructiveness of Freud, who goes on smoking in spite of his cough. But Sartre went on making ashtrays overflow with the stub ends of Boyards, and gave complete freedom to his other self-destructive tendencies, including the compulsion to go on overworking throughout the autumn and winter.

After completing the synopsis on 15 December 1958, he resumed work on the *Critique*. In the same way that he had once been obsessed by the contrast between lived experience and adventure stories, he was now struggling to explain the relationship between the individual moment of experience and the history in which moments have at most a symbolical value: each particularity is representative of the total reality. Dialectical reason was attractive because it seemed to offer him a means of uniting each moment, as experienced, with the historical totalization: a relationship must be established between each of history's component events and its overall meaning.

His assumption is that human activity always sets up a tension between itself and everything in the past which has gone into making the *status quo*. Hunger is a need which forces me to rearrange the universe, however slightly: an apple, which grew, is absorbed into a digestive system. In orienting ourselves towards the future, we disturb the past. As a writer Sartre had discovered that the reality of the mountain can be conveyed by a story about a pilot flying over it, the desert realized in an account of the traveller whose life it threatens, though neither the mountain nor the desert take any action. In the same way, history is an adversary which goes on absorbing and negating human initiative. This idea should have educed vivid writing, but, hamstrung with abstractions, Sartre mostly fails to bring his subject-matter alive, except when writing about the French Revolution. His trite remarks about factory workers obviously derive from hearsay: in Husserlian terms these are 'empty' intuitions.

Superficially it might seem odd that, dividing his time between screenplay and book, he was content to put so much good writing into dialogue destined for Hollywood and so much bad writing into what should have become his greatest philosophical work. Though there are sentimental and melo-dramatic lapses in the screenplay, the general level of the writing is high. Sartre, defying his principles, is allowing himself to write well. In the *Critique* he was conscious of writing badly. He would later say that the book could have been better written had he taken time to make cuts and revisions. But the narrow escape from a heart attack had warned him to be careful how he allocated time, and this sharpened his ambivalence towards good writing. If he was helping to jerk contemporary Marxism out of its somnolence, he was doing something important, but to write imaginative literature or to spend time on polishing his prose was to shut himself off from other people in the present, to abdicate from the possibility of putting pressure on the future.

It was only recently that he had given up all his lingering hopes of completing *La Dernière Chance.* He said in 1959 that one of his main reasons for writing *Les Séquestrés d'Altona* was frustration at being unable to finish his novel: 'I can't express the ambiguities of our period in this story, which is set in 1943. On the other hand, this unfinished work weighs down on me: I find it hard to start another novel without having completed this one.'[13] He had little incentive, anyway, to start a new one, believing that he had outgrown his literary ambitions: 'I had transposed religious needs into literary longings ... writing is an escape, a sign of weakness.'[14] But the play would present both Wanda and Evelyne with a bouquet of opportunities.

Looking back on the writing he had done before he was forty, he associated it with his childhood fear of death. Just as a Christian could use his life to prove himself worthy of immortality, a writer could merit posthumous glory. But Sartre, while looking sceptically backwards at his attempts to achieve immortality by writing creatively, could exploit his insight in the screenplay. Freud is compulsive about arriving early whenever he has to catch a train. The phobia has roots in early childhood. His first train journey took him from happiness in Freiberg to poverty in Vienna. After trains had come to represent death and misery, his fear of death was transposed into fear of missing trains. In Sartre's synopsis the phobia is established in an early sequence and cured on the final page. The instincts of the artist were still functioning long after he had decided to stop functioning as an artist.

Without explicitly repudiating *L'Etre et le Néant*, he was indicating that he now believed desires and memories could be pushed down into the unconscious. Much of the plot turns on this. One male patient has suppressed his patricidal impulses. Cecily Körtner's strabism – it must have amused Sartre to inflict his own ailment on a beautiful woman – derives from an experience she did not want to remember with her father's corpse, and she has repressed memories of how he died in a brothel, together with details of a quarrel about the pretty governess who was sacked by his jealous wife. When Sartre accepted the commission, he had not known how deeply it would involve him. Though the screenplay was never to be made into a film – it was too long for Huston and television companies have so far ignored it – it deserves to be taken as a piece of writing no less serious than Sartre's biography of Baudelaire. It is no less thoughtful, while the texture of the writing is no less rich. Considered alongside Sartre's three biographical books, it emerges as more straightforwardly biographical than any of them, and though Freud is not canonized, he is treated no less respectfully than Genet. He is not given quite the heroic treatment that Huston probably wanted, but in contrast to the other doctors, who are doctrinaire, self-involved, pompous, reactionary and prejudiced, Freud has the courage to look open-mindedly at the clues which present themselves in clinical practice. Initially a weak man, he is redeemed by his determination to find out the truth: through this he grows strong.

Like Freud's, Sartre's life was full of quarrels, and for two years he had not been on speaking terms with Francis Jeanson, who had disapproved of his reaction to the Soviet intervention in Hungary during 1956. Since the beginning of 1958 Jeanson had been campaigning for the Algerian rebels by editing the clandestine monthly *Vérités pour* ... One of the women in his network was a friend of Evelyne Rey, who had no difficulty in persuading Sartre to resume contact with Jeanson, and as soon as the two men saw each other again, Sartre was pledging full support. 'You know I'm one hundred per cent in agreement with the action you're taking. Use me in any way you can.' He immediately gave Jeanson an interview for the June issue. The French people, he said, 'have no other defence in this country which is turning fascist and ruining itself bit by bit, than to acknowledge frankly their new but profound solidarity with the Algerian fighters'.[15] Jeanson also involved Sartre's *Temps modernes* colleagues in pro-Algerian activity. De Beauvoir agreed that her car and her flat could be used; Péju and Lanzmann offered to shelter Algerians; Leiris gave money.[16]

It was in Rome, when Sartre again spent the summer there, that he settled down to finish his play, transferring the action to Altona, a district of Hamburg, and transforming the Frenchman who had tortured Algerians into a German who had tortured partisans during the war. Sartre also developed a motif he had introduced in the screenplay: Freud is called in to see Charles von Schroeh, a man who for six years has never stepped outside his room. He sits on a kitchen stool with thin red tape around his legs. He believes that he is evil and that the tape is holding him back from going into the street and killing someone. But when Freud hypnotizes him, it emerges that the fantasy of killing a stranger is only a disguise for his impulse to kill the father he despises.

In the screenplay, despite numerous references to anti-semitism, Sartre makes little effort to show that individuality is, as he had contended in the *Critique*, an unimportant by-product of social forces. Though the new play follows the filmscript in centring on the father-son relationship, it follows the *Critique* in trying to look at contemporary history as it might be viewed by a future historian, and in demonstrating that choices stem not from the willpower of a private individual but from the economy. The father, head of a protestant family ennobled by Wilhelm II, is a leading Hamburg shipbuilder who has tried to remain politically uncommitted. Without supporting the Nazi Party he has had dealings with its leaders, selling them land which has been used as a concentration camp. Frantz, like Goetz, is a man caught between two traditions. Educated to be imperious, he has resented the superior manipulative power of the father who can extricate him from any difficulty. Even when Frantz tries to rescue a Polish rabbi who has escaped from the concentration camp, the father can still protect him, but not the rabbi. The experience of seeing the Jew beaten to death is crucial: 'Two leaders – either one must kill the other or become his wife. I was Hitler's wife. The rabbi was bleeding, and I discovered at the heart of my impotence I don't know what acquiescence. I have supreme power. Hitler has made me an Other, implacable and holy, made me himself.'

Once again de Beauvoir came to spend a month in Rome with Sartre. Again he showed her what he had written of the play, and again the 'little judge' found that her advice had helped him greatly. He went on working at it while she was there, and when he gave her his draft of the final act, in which a family council sat in judgment on Frantz, she was again reminded of Sudermann. Sartre's original idea, he told her, had been for a confrontation between father and son. As soon as he reverted to this they were both satisfied with the result.[17] The scene shows that Frantz is what he has been made – not so much by his father (who, like the father in 'L'Enfance d'un chef', has groomed his son to be a leader) as by the shipbuilding business. 'My poor child! I wanted you to run the firm after me. It does the running. It chooses its men. Me, I'm not needed any more. I own it, but I'm no longer in command. As for you, little prince; it rejected you from the first moment. Why should it need a prince? It trains and recruits its own managers.' Imbued with his father's talents, passions and appetite for power, Frantz has been prepared for a life which existed only in the pre-war world. Impersonal forces gave birth to the frustration behind the personal need for violence, the need to torture.

Sartre is building his play towards a powerful final climax in which father and son, like lovers, commit suicide together. When Frantz was eight the Father used to say: 'We must get you ready for the war. We're going to drive really fast.' And they drove, at speed, over the Devil's Bridge. This is how they will die, while the two women who are devoted to Frantz – his incestuous sister (played by Wanda) and his brother's wife (played by Evelyne Rey) – listen to one of the tape-recordings he has made during thirteen years of self-imposed solitary confinement in his room, defending his century against the crabs who, for him, represent posterity and sit in judgment on Germany. They are the totalizers; they also incarnate the old shellfish phobia. *Huis clos* had centred on a man caught in limbo between two women and needing to be judged; Frantz has created his own limbo, but his need is not dissimilar – to have judgment passed on him. This was Sartre's need and in what was his last serious attempt to offer himself as a creative artist to the judgment of critics and theatregoers, his underlying motives were bizarrely muddled. He was helping two mistresses who were both beautiful, both desperate for success, both unable to sell themselves in the theatre except when he wrote parts for them. He needed money. He wanted to give himself a final chance to rework motifs which had always been important to him – the loving attempt of the sister, Léni, to enter a man's madness echoes the futile attempt of the wife in 'La Chambre'; in *Morts sans sépulture* he had already made an imaginative effort to probe the motivations of the torturer.

The new play's title, *Les Séquestrés d'Altona*, echoes Sartre's title for his 1957 essay on Tintoretto, 'Le Séquestré de Vénise'. Like the painter who used his sons as apprentices, von Gerlach produces a dynasty of shipbuilders, while both families incarnate bourgeois puritanism during the decline of a formerly aristocratic republic. This subject-matter seemed to promise an opportunity of combining Marxian with Freudian insights. As in the Freud screenplay, he no longer denies the possibility of defining or understanding a personality by digging up memories from the past. In his over-anxiety to show how behaviour is conditioned by memories of the past he went to the lengths of introducing gauchely filmic flashbacks, using part of the stage for a straightforward re-enactment of past events. The effect in the theatre is clumsy, and, throughout most of the action, the treatment of mental imbalance is less convincing than in the screenplay, partly because Frantz's abnormal behaviour seems contrived. Too much depends on argument, and Sartre fails to splice the Marxian and the Freudian together. The screenplay had been authentically Freudian, taking its shape, like Freud's case-histories, from a progressive movement towards enlightenment, maturity and health; the play is informed with a non-Marxist pessimism, and its movement is towards death and defeat. Frantz's apologia for the twentieth century is founded on self-deception, and in the final monologue Sartre comes closer than ever before to affirming that there is such a thing as human nature and that it is evil:

The century would have been good if man had not been kept under surveillance by his merciless age-old enemy, by the carnivorous species sworn to his destruction, by the malignant, hairless beast, by man. One and one make one, that's our riddle. The beast was hiding, we saw his look suddenly, in the naked eyes of our neighbours. Then we struck, preventively, in legitimate self-defence.

I took the beast by surprise, I struck, a man fell, in his dying eyes, I saw the beast, still alive, myself.

This is fine theatrical rhetoric but it is only through statement, not action, that Sartre could clarify what he wanted to say about violence; the resonance of this prose derives from a combination of strong feelings about Algeria with deep fears about the next world war.

After the month with de Beauvoir in Rome Sartre had moved on to stay for a few weeks with Arlette El Kaïm in Venice. Starting the holiday in one of the grandest hotels, they ran short of money and moved to a noisy pensione near the station. It was here that he worked on the final sequence. When he performed Frantz's monologue for her she thought it too melodramatic for the rest of the play, but she was misled by his declamatory performance.[18]

He told an interviewer that he wanted the audience to condemn the characters as being the same sort of people who worked during the Occupation at the Gestapo headquarters in the rue de Saussaies;[19] in fact he generates considerable sympathy for all but one of the characters – the younger brother, who is cowardly and calculating. Wanting Frantz to appear as 'a victim in so far as one is ready to excuse him and a criminal in so far as one is ready to condemn him',[20] Sartre delays until the fourth act the revelation that he has been a torturer.

He was still revising Frantz's final speech when the play went into rehearsal with François Darbon directing a cast headed by Serge Reggiani as Frantz and Fernand Ledoux as the Father. As usual there was trouble during rehearsals; as usual the main sticking point was Sartre's obstinacy over cuts; as usual de Beauvoir attended rehearsals, and acted as intermediary, not only encouraging him to cut but helping him to make the cuts, though, as usual, she was in a difficult position, understanding the extent to which his plays had their roots in his relationships with other women. The actors were having difficulty with their lines, and the opening had to be postponed until 23 September, but the play was still far too long when it opened. It was only after the first night that Sartre submitted, agreeing to drastic cuts which took nearly half an hour off the running time. Even now his motivation was suspect. Pressure from the theatre manager, Véra Korène, no doubt played a part, but he was in a hurry to leave Paris with Arlette and he did not even wait for the reviews.

He had been invited to Ireland by Huston, who had read the screenplay and been corresponding with him about it. To escape from American taxation the fifty-three-year-old film director had rented an enormous Georgian house in County Kildare, 60 miles south-west of Dublin. He had been there since 1952.

From his bedroom Sartre could see a seemingly endless expanse of fields with cows and horses in them. The producer of the film was to be Max Reinhardt's son Wolfgang, who was staying at the house and helped Sartre to make cuts. The other guests were a random mixture. After inviting people he hardly knew, Huston would pay little attention to them. Reinhardt's mistress, Mrs Phillips, did more than their host to put the guests at their ease. Huston, who enjoyed doing the opposite, once left Sartre and Arlette alone with a major who spoke no French. Hoping to start a conversation in English, he said: 'Churchill is funny when he speaks French.' The only response Sartre managed was 'Ha, ha!' The three of them waited in embarrassed silence until they were called for dinner.[21]

De Beauvoir wrote to Sartre, enclosing reviews of the play, which were much more favourable than he had expected. Reggiani's performance was singled out for praise, while production and decor came under attack. Huston, who was with Sartre when the bulky envelope was delivered, noticed that he seemed in no hurry to open it. When he finally did, the good reviews gave him no apparent pleasure.

Huston talked a great deal about *Let There Be Light*, his 1945 film about shellshocked soldiers. He had seen men coming off boats in large groups, some mute, some amnesiac, some paralysed, some shaking. He often said that shooting this film had been like a religious experience, and one evening he showed it to his houseguests, together with his 1944 film *The Battle of San Pietro*. Sartre found both films mediocre and propagandist, but when the lights came up afterwards, Huston's eyes were wet with tears. In *Let There Be Light* he had filmed army psychiatrists hypnotizing victims of combat neurosis, and Huston, who enjoyed showing the prowess he had acquired as a hypnotist, offered to demonstrate on 'the Arab girl'. He had formed the impression that Arlette was there as Sartre's secretary. Her English was good and after each working session she typed out a translation of Sartre's notes and suggestions. Huston had no difficulty in hypnotizing her, but after seeing her succumb, Sartre offered himself as a subject, and this time Huston had to admit failure.

Sartre was equally resistant in other ways to this tall, tough, equable man who usually found it so easy to charm and to dominate. Sartre had no personal experience of Hollywood directors. Hollywood films had been a major source of pleasure throughout his life – he went to the cinema, on average, once a week with Michelle, in addition to his cinema-going with de Beauvoir and with other girlfriends – but trying to work with Huston was quite unlike working in the Paris theatre with directors who were impressed by his intellectual standing and respectfully tolerant towards long monologues. Huston, who liked action, simplicity and having his own way, soon aroused Sartre's antipathy. Writing to de Beauvoir, Sartre

reported that Huston had used himself up. 'The man has emigrated. I
don't know where. He's not even sad: he's *empty*, except in moments of
childish vanity, when he puts on a red dinner jacket or rides a horse (not
very well) or counts his paintings or tells workmen what to do. Impossible
to hold his attention five minutes: he can no longer work, he runs away
from thinking.'[22]

Huston had written successful screenplays of his own and had often
worked collaboratively with other screenwriters, but he had never encountered anyone like this Frenchman, who, while he talked, made notes
on his own ideas, and who got up so early that he had usually written
about twenty-five pages of dialogue by the time Huston appeared, around
10.30.

He noticed how heavily Sartre was relying on pills, and generally formed
a most unfavourable impression: Sartre was

> a little barrel of a man and as ugly as a human being can be. His face was
> both bloated and pitted, his teeth were yellowed and he was wall-eyed. He wore
> a gray suit, black shoes, white shirt, tie and vest. His appearance never changed.
> He would come down in the morning in this suit, and he would still be wearing
> it last thing at night. The suit always appeared to be clean and the shirt was
> clean, but I never knew if he owned one gray suit or several identical gray
> suits.

The routine of work was interrupted when Huston came down one morning to find Sartre with a swollen cheek. He had an abscessed tooth, but
when Huston suggested driving to a dentist in Dublin, Sartre opted for
a local Galway dentist and made no fuss when the man pulled out the
tooth.

Sartre stayed in the house, St Clerans, for ten days, but the only point
on which the two men were agreed was that Marilyn Monroe would be
the ideal Cecily. According to Huston, Sartre judged her to be the finest
actress alive. But neither man acquired any respect for the other. Sartre
was not amused when Huston claimed that in his unconscious there was
nothing,[23] while Huston found Sartre totally unwilling to be flexible. 'I've
never worked with anyone so obstinate and categorical. Impossible to have
a conversation with him. Impossible to interrupt him. You'd wait for him
to catch his breath but he wouldn't. The words came out in an absolute
torrent. It happened once that, exhausted by the strain, I walked out of
the room. The buzzing of his voice followed me a moment, and when
I came back, he hadn't even noticed I'd gone out.' Sartre's version of
the story is different: several of them had been in a smoking-room, talking,
when Huston abruptly walked out. Sartre struggled valiantly to keep the
conversation going.[24]

The most obvious of the problems was the length of the script, which would have run, according to Huston, for five hours. Sartre was not unwilling to rewrite, and after returning to Paris he went on working at it, making substantial changes. In several of the new sequences Viennese anti-semitism came into sharper focus, but instead of shortening the screenplay he made it longer, rather as if he were writing for the Paris theatre.

The film was eventually shot with a hybrid script. In 1947, two years after he had scripted *Let There Be Light* for Huston, Charles Kaufman had drafted a screenplay about Freud. Wolfgang Reinhardt collaborated with him on revising this, and they incorporated some of Sartre's material. But he did not allow his name to be used and during shooting still more changes were made to the text as Huston introduced dialogue of his own, adding to the confusion of Montgomery Clift, who played Freud, with the nineteen-year-old Susannah York as Cecily. According to Huston, 'Much of what Sartre had done was in our version – in fact it was the backbone of it. In some scenes his dialogue was left intact.'[25]

TWENTY-TWO · *Unofficial Ambassador*

The sixties began with the death of Camus. On 4 January 1960 he was in a car with Michel Gallimard (Gaston's nephew), Michel's wife, Janine, and her eighteen-year-old daughter, Anne. They were on their way back to Paris from the south of France. Michel was driving the Facel-Vega, not going fast. They were on the route nationale, just outside the village of Villeblevin, sixty-eight miles from Paris, when the car swerved off the damp road, hit one of the roadside plane trees and crashed against another. Camus was thrown backwards and killed instantly, as his head hit the rear window, skull fractured, neck broken. The cause of the accident is still unknown. Perhaps an axle broke, perhaps the steering went out of control. The two women survived, but Gallimard died six days later from a brain haemorrhage.[1]

As soon as Claude Lanzmann heard the news he telephoned Sartre but it was de Beauvoir, alone in the flat, who answered the telephone. When she put down the receiver, throat tight, lips trembling, she ordered herself not to cry. 'He no longer meant anything to me.' But throughout the evening she, Sartre and Bost spoke of almost nothing but Camus. Sartre's homage to him appeared in *France-Observateur* on the 7th.

> We had quarrelled, he and I, but a quarrel is nothing, even if you never see each other again. It's simply another way of living together, without losing sight of each other in this narrow little world which is given to us ... In this century and against history he was the representative and the present heir of that long line of moralists whose work perhaps constitutes what is most original in French literature ... Camus would always go on being one of the main forces in our cultural realm and representing, in his own way, the history of France and of this century.[2]

Sartre was obviously trying not to contradict what he had written in his angry reply to Camus's *Temps modernes* letter, but quite apart from the immediate illogicality ('never see each other ... without losing sight of each other') there is a contradiction between 'Only half of you lives among us and you are tempted to withdraw altogether' (August 1952) and this funereal tribute to Camus for always putting 'the political act in question'. Whereas Sartre's letter had charged Camus with letting his morality turn into moralism – 'Today it is only literature, perhaps it will be immorality tomorrow' – the *France-Observateur* article makes the opposite point. However much you disagree with Camus, he is a moral force you have to reckon with. For Sartre the contradiction was unavoidable, but there was no dialectical escape route.

When Sartre was invited to Cuba, he was not at first keen to go, though he knew it would not be the Cuba he had seen in 1949 with Dolorès. It was in April 1958 that Fidel Castro had declared total war against Fulgencio Batista's government, and in January 1959 the President had fled to Dominica. Manuel Urrutia had been appointed provisional governor, but Castro had strengthened his position by purges and by postponing the elections. Sartre and de Beauvoir were invited by Carlos Francqui, editor of the biggest Cuban newspaper, *Revolución.* Eventually, persuaded, they left in February 1960, wanting first-hand experience of a revolution that was still in progress.

Unlike China, Cuba was small enough for direct and frequent contact between leaders and people. In a luxurious, air-conditioned hotel, the Nacional, Sartre had a bedroom larger than his Paris flat.[3] The Havana Hilton had been renamed the Havana Libre, but the twenty or so expensive hotels were all thriving. He strolled with de Beauvoir for hours in the streets. In the working-class districts the poor seemed neither better nor worse off than formerly; other areas looked more prosperous. There were plenty of de luxe restaurants, and the brothels, which had been closed after the revolution, had reopened.[4] But the country was visibly in the hands of the rebels. 'Beards and long hair are still the insignia of the 3,000 pioneers of the revolution.'[5] The average age of government ministers was twenty-nine.[6]

They met Ché Guevara, who received them at midnight to give them coffee in his office at the National Bank. 'I'm first of all a doctor,' he said, 'then something of a soldier, and finally, as you can see, a banker.'[7] He had exerted himself to acquire the technical knowledge a state banker needs.[8] The revolutionary leaders seemed to be managing on little sleep. When Castro arranged to pick up Sartre and de Beauvoir from their hotel, he arrived punctually at a quarter to eight in the morning, and had to wait ten minutes for them. He then announced that he would take them to see several beaches, including Varadero, the best known, sixty-two miles from Havana. This was a tour of inspection Castro had been planning to make anyway, needing to resurrect the island's tourism.

Several times the car was halted by groups of peasants clamouring for Castro to look at villages under co-operative construction. Like a tired but loving father, he seemed unable to refuse any demand for his presence and attention. Eventually Sartre asked whether people had the right to anything they demanded. Castro's answer was: 'A man's needs give him his fundamental right over other people.' 'And if he asks for the moon?' 'If someone asked me for the moon it would be because someone needed it.' Humanism, Sartre pursued, should be founded on need. 'That's the only humanism there is', Castro agreed. 'We have to demand from each man everything he can give, but I'll never sacrifice this generation to the next. That would be abstract.'[9]

Finally invited to Castro's home, Sartre and de Beauvoir were driven to the marshes of Cienaga de Zapata. A motor-boat took them across a canal that was being dredged. They slept in a long hut with a corrugated iron roof and reinforced concrete walls. On either side of the central corridor were about twenty mattresses on double-decker bunks. Castro, his brother, his family and his guests would sleep in the same space. Before supper Castro went outside with a shotgun, took aim, fired into a muddy pond. A large fish floated to the surface, stomach upwards.[10] Generally Castro was friendly and warm, though anxious about the way Sartre would report on his impressions in France. It would be better, Castro suggested, to avoid the word 'socialism'.[11]

Almost every day the newspapers published photographs of Sartre and de Beauvoir with Castro and Ché. Ché came out with one sentence Sartre would often quote: 'It's not my fault if reality is Marxist.'[12] Introducing a talk by Sartre on Cuban television, Castro told viewers he was their friend. After this people stopped him in the street, and passing taxi-drivers shouted: 'Sartre, it's Sartre!'[13] But what pleased him most was the endemic gaiety. 'It's the honeymoon of the revolution', he said.[14]

Having promised to write a preface for a new edition of Paul Nizan's book *Aden-Arabie*, he worked on it in the mornings after breakfasting with de Beauvoir on strong black coffee and pineapple. Addressing himself to the younger generation, he incorporated such phrases as 'In a society which reserves its women for the old and the rich ...'.[15] Although Sartre could not have predicted the 1968 rebellion, he was starting to sow seeds for it: explicitly blaming himself for having failed to rebel, as Nizan did, at the Ecole Normale, Sartre was implying that anything less than rebellion was ineffectual. In January he had given two interviews, one to the seventeen-year-old Patrice Cournot, editor of a review for the young, *Le Semeur*,[16] and the other for the first issue of *Les Cahiers libres de la jeunesse*.[17] In this he told the interviewer that the idea of justice was neither indispensable nor useful. No-one could be free unless the whole world was, and life would not be human until everyone had enough to eat. The preface to *Aden-Arabie* is more self-accusing. Belonging, as he did, to a generation that had betrayed its youthful ideals, how could he give advice to the young? How could he say 'Be Cubans, be Russians, be Chinese, or if you prefer, be Africans'?[18] Men of his age had no advice to give, but Nizan could still speak to the young: 'Yesterday he was our contemporary; today he is theirs.'[19] Speculating on what Nizan might have told them, Sartre echoed the conversation with Castro: 'You are dying of modesty. Dare to desire. Be insatiable ... Don't be shamed to want the moon. You should have it.'[20] In leaving for Aden, Nizan had rejected everything he had been given in France, where he had felt constrained and manipulated. He had gone to inspect the damage done by imperialism.

In blaming himself for not following Nizan into political commitment while at the Ecole Normale, Sartre was blaming himself for not having already reached conclusions he was to reach much later. 'Before Sartre', as Merleau-Ponty sums it up, 'Nizan lived this pan-tragism, this flooding anguish which is the flux of history.'[21] Where Nizan saw an unhappy human intermingling, a reciprocity of suffering, Sartre had then seen only the mutual estrangement of subject-object relationships. But Merleau-Ponty is right to be suspicious of the mature Sartre who blames his immature self for not knowing better. What he does not admit now is that he did know something then which he has since chosen to forget: that beneath its objectivity, communist thought is 'secretly flabby and humid', that 'the communist negation, being positively inverted, is not what is says it is'.[22] Sartre had suspected from the beginning what Nizan did not discover until the nazi-Soviet pact – that it takes courage to join the Party and cowardice to remain a member. Sartre is surely wrong to assume that if Nizan had survived, the Resistance would have brought him back into the communist ranks.

On the return journey, Sartre and de Beauvoir spent eight hours in New York, where the Cuban attaché had organized a press conference at the Waldorf so that the Sartrean truth about Cuba could immediately be disseminated.[23] After arriving in Paris Sartre turned down the opportunity of a conversation with Khrushchev at a meeting of writers and journalists, but took de Beauvoir to a reception held for the Soviet leader at the embassy. In her simple black dress the placid Nina Khrushchev contrasted sharply with the overdressed Gaullist ladies in their elaborate hats.[24]

The incongruity between Sartre's personal popularity and popular indifference to his major work was never more apparent than during the spring of 1960. In March, when he lectured on theatre at the Sorbonne, speaking for over two hours without a break, the students gave him a huge ovation and surged around him as he walked to his taxi.[25] But while his preface helped *Aden-Arabie* to make a big impact on students and the general reading public, the *Critique*, which was published in May, attracted little excitement, except from the communists and from the right-wing reviewers, who savaged it. The drive to work on the second part had only the most exiguous connection with any image of how readers might react.

Most of the 781 typed pages were probably written between Sartre's return from Cuba in March and his departure for Brazil in September, but he was no further than page 20 when he slipped into his old habit of rashly promising a separate work to cover ground he would not be able to cover in the present one. He would write another book about conflict, demonstrating the full truth of dialectical materialism.[26] Prepared though he always was to write at enormous length, Sartre was already half-aware that he would reach no conclusion, and despite the number of unredeemed promises he already had on his conscience, he went on making them, like a gambler asking for credit.

He starts the second part of the *Critique* with a new effort to keep a promise he had made in the first. The dialectic, he had said, must 'proceed *from individuals* and not from some sort of supra-individual ensemble'.[27] He had soon afterwards lost sight of the individual, doing what he condemns Hegel for doing – arguing aprioristically that both individuals and collectives are part of a totalization which produces them and goes beyond them. While a battle is being fought, thousands of consciousnesses are active, but history ignores them. When Sartre now tries to identify imaginatively with the individual soldier, the writing is briefly reminiscent of *Les Chemins de la liberté*, but the concrete is soon displaced by the abstract as he reiterates the question he still sees as crucial – is totalization possible without an extraterrestrial totalizer or does history disintegrate into 'a plurality of individual histories'?[28]

Boxing is then made to serve as an analogy for social conflict: are the two boxers collaborating on a common project while lashing out at each other? They are gathering up the aggressions of the audience, he argues, and '*boxing as a whole*' is present in each blow they exchange; both men belong to 'the world of boxing', which has conventions, as well as rules. But he writes about this 'world' as if he has not seen much of it, and his attempt to portray two boxers is half-hearted because his interest in them is half abstract. They are not individuals; they are manifestations of the concrete universal which is incessantly producing itself as the animation and temporalization of individual contingency.[29] Conflict, which is unity fighting against itself, pits *common individuals* against each other. When he concludes that one 'enveloping totalization' has been present throughout the boxing-match, this seems to have little bearing on the separate consciousnesses of soldiers on a battlefield. It is not enough to explain that competing sub-groups always express the workings of a wider dialectic.

Nor does he ever look critically at Marx's contention that the history of every society is the history of class-conflict. Even boxing is explained in terms of class. Capitalism domesticates violence by coercing the under-privileged into releasing their aggressions against each other. The historian, like the policeman, needs witnesses, but in violence there are only partic-ipants, so the evidence is suspect.[30] Many good points, like this one, emerge sporadically, but the argument is hopelessly unstructured, partly because Sartre's political objectives are at odds with his philosophical objectives. He needs to believe that his thinking can contribute to contemporary social-ism; it may be helpful, in the future, to leaders of progressive movements if he can explain how the Bolshevik revolution led to Stalinism. Also wanting to clarify his own ideas on this question, he devotes 400 pages to it, with his misgivings about the Soviet bureaucracy visibly sharpened by his exhilar-ating experiences of the close relationship between leaders and led in Cuba. In the Russian Revolution, as in the French, the cause of Terror had been loss of contact with the people.

Was it conceivable, he asked, that Soviet society could be controlled by 'a group of impecunious, unprivileged revolutionaries who refuse all titles'?[31] The question, he suggests, may be connected with the question of whether divergent pressures and interests inside revolutionary Russia had coagulated into a single, comprehensible history. He analyses Soviet history from the conflict between Stalin and Trotsky during the twenties to the revival of anti-semitism in the early fifties. First he argues that the conflict between the two leaders was not the result of personal incompatibility but the totalization of a 'contradiction in the Party's common *praxis*'.[32] Trotsky's urge to revolutionize Europe was defeated by Stalin's more realis-tic concentration on building socialism in one country. For this he needed a united workforce, even if he had to 'destroy the workers as free practical organisms and as common individuals'.[33] Elites were created in both the proletariat and the bureaucracy; the oppression extirpated by the revolution was replaced by new oppression, necessary to unify the workforce; forced collectivization and terror reduced the peasantry to resentful impotence.

The new generation of Soviet peasants has interiorized the terror.[34] In Soviet society, each local *praxis*, each singular destiny is an incarnation of the totalizing *praxis*.[35] Discussing collectivization, Sartre shows himself to be aware of the misery it caused, but unsympathetic. Human suffering vanishes in his abstract summary of 'this irreversible temporalization which in history will take the name of Stalinism'.[36] Sometimes his use of jargon is in what he would once have called bad faith.

Stalin is described as 'not just an individual': he incarnates and singular-izes the practical totalization which constitutes this moment of Russian history.[37] An inflexible leader was needed, but could someone else with a different temperament and a different past have avoided the purges, the show trials, the labour camps? Though Stalin's brutality is condemned, together with the 'absurd cultural isolation' into which he led the Soviet Union, and the 'endless lies about the condition of the European worker',[38] Sartre argues that Stalin's personal aggressiveness is inseparable from aggressions necessary to the historical situation: 'if the process of planned growth could be directed by an angel, *praxis* would combine the maximum objectivity. The angel would never be blind, spiteful or brutal: it would always be what it has to be.' But a fallible human being is liable to do too little or too much, and then go too far in the opposite direction. Stalin's policies did not tally with the 'objectives and demands of socialization', but they were inevitable 'in so far as this society in its first phase demanded to be controlled by one individual'.[39] Though Sartre rejects Plekhanov's doctrine that the function forms the man, he also rejects the psychological explanation of historical events. In the French Revolution Robespierre's inferiority complex did not cause the Terror, which was necessary because he and his colleagues had to invent a practical exteriorization of the dangers they had interiorized.[40] But Sartre had not set out to contradict Marx's assumption that the mode of production is always the decisive factor, and the amalgam of evidence and argument was pulling the book away from its objective – to show that history was intelligible as a totalization without a totalizer. Nor could Sartre resolve the difficulty with the formulaic assertion that history integrates accidents and contingencies, that each event, however private, should be considered as an incarnation.[41]

It is understandable, of course, that he should have chosen to re-examine the Bolshevik and French revolutions without asking himself whether they provide the most useful illustrations of the way history moves. Was it necessary or unnecessary for slaughter and totalitarian bureaucracy to displace revolutionary idealism? He believed that *praxis* is invariably deformed because the men behind it invariably 'become other men involved in achieving other objectives by other means'.[42] Human activity is helplessly absorbed into the *practico-inert*. Men 'realize themselves in the process of objectifying themselves, and this changes them'.[43] The new phrase Sartre introduces for this process is 'totalization of envelopment', and he maintains, neither lucidly nor convincingly, that 'all individual behaviour represents the reproduction of the social totalization of envelopment under the forms of an enveloped totalization'.[44]

When he goes on to speak about the 'circularity of counter-finalities', he virtually invents a historical unconscious. Our autonomy is undermined by 'totalization of envelopment', which produces an environment that deflects the course of our actions.[45] All the elements in the practical field, including the agents, are conditioned by the totalization of envelopment.[46] Though Sartre is now writing, in his characteristic jargon, no less deterministically than Hegel, he is at least penetrating more deeply than in Part One into the questions he had raised at the outset as crucial. 'If the dialectic is possible', he had said, *praxis* must be explained as an experience of freedom and of necessity, while swarms of individual destinies must appear in history as subject to a totalizing movement.[47] When Part One patently failed to fulfil these conditions, how could he have been content to leave Part Two unpublished, even if it succeeds only partially?

The decision not to publish must mean that he was aware of the extent to which he had fallen short of his objectives, but he could not have fulfilled them just by writing about revolutionary conflict and the conflict that follows revolution. He would have had to deal with power conflicts in bourgeois society and to demonstrate that the history of the world was a single history, not a proliferation of separate histories. He might also have been forced to question the extent to which he had been misled by a tendency he shared with other French intellectuals – to treat the history of France as if it were coextensive with the history of Western civilization. He had set himself an impossible task; he was addicted to the impossible. Since 1948 he had stood no more chance of changing the PCF from outside than of keeping Europe out of the Atlantic Pact or creating a new alliance between Marx and Freud. Without completing any of his major projects he was making ever-increasing demands on his phenomenal stamina. His style of living was precariously balanced between contradictory demands. He was travelling dutifully around the world in response to invitations prompted by the publicity he could bring, while, in the time that remained, he went on living the half-life of a writer. He was fond of saying: 'You have to choose: live or tell stories.'[48] He no longer wanted to tell stories but refused to choose. During the last twenty years of his life he was going to give at least as much time to travel, political journalism and agitprop as to philosophy, literature and biography, but when he was in Paris he spent most of the day in his untidy study. A young writer who visited him for the first time in March 1961 observed: 'Literature had overrun the room. The bookshelves could not accommodate the books: there were piles on his desk, on chairs, on the floor, together with files, typescripts, notebooks, as well as pipes, packets of Boyard cigarettes, overflowing ashtrays, boxes of matches. Scarcely anywhere could you see an inch of the wood of the furniture.'[49]

When he abandoned the *Critique* it was in order to concentrate on *L'Idiot de la famille*.[50] His addiction to the impossible was so helpless that even after abandoning a book, he would still go on for years, as he had with his ethics and his novel tetralogy, half-believing that he might bring himself to do more work on it. Eight years later he would still be hoping that the second part of the *Critique* would eventually appear, though he spoke of what he had intended as if the intention belonged to the past: 'I was going to end by studying the unity of objects in a society completely rent asunder by class struggle, and considering several classes and their actions to show how these objects were completely frustrated.'[51]

During the second week in May 1960, he accepted another pretext for pushing work aside by reverting to his role as unofficial ambassador. He went to Yugoslavia, accepting an invitation from the writers' union. Two of his plays, *Huis clos* and *Les Séquestrés d'Altona*, were being performed in Belgrade, and he went to see both productions: he was received by Marshal Tito and he lectured to students at Belgrade University.

In the middle of June he appeared as a witness at the trial of Georges Arnaud, a journalist who had been arrested in April for 'failing to denounce a malefactor'. The malefactor was Francis Jeanson, who had invited correspondents of all the main foreign newspapers to a meeting about Algeria. Held by a military tribunal, the trial had a large audience of left-wing intellectuals; giving evidence, Sartre denounced the Algerian War and the repression in France: 'Now we have no platform except the courts.'[52] The overcrowded room was so hot that he left with de Beauvoir almost as soon as he had given his evidence. Arnaud was convicted with a suspended sentence.[53]

Before his visit to Cuba Sartre had been invited to visit Brazil, the likeliest candidate for revolution among the Latin American countries. He now felt more inclined to accept the Brazilian invitation: according to progressive Brazilians, it would be helpful not only to the Cubans – for the fate of Cuba depended on Latin America – but also to the French left and the Algerians if an authoritative French voice were raised in Brazil to promote Castroism and to contradict pronouncements of de Gaulle's Minister of Cultural Affairs, André Malraux.[54] Sartre and de Beauvoir decided to spend three months in Brazil, but before they left in mid-August, he had begun to formulate reasons for feeling hostile to almost everyone in France except the young. Writing the Nizan preface and reflecting on the men of his own age who had settled down into amoral materialism, he had felt a strong desire to distance himself both from them and from the *gauchistes* who had been so ineffectual in protesting against the war in Algeria. The younger generation, he told an interviewer, was not going to be content with 'verbal action'. 'It is only the young who have responded to mystification in the right way – that's to say with violence. For me the only true men of the left in France today are twenty years old.'[55] After this it was natural for Sartre to join forces with the signatories who pledged themselves to civil disobedience in the 'Manifesto of the 121'. 'Their fates are linked too. The victory of the FLN will be the victory of the left.' The other 120 dissidents included Marguerite Duras, Simone Signoret, Pierre Boulez, André Masson, Claude Lanzmann and Claude Roy.

By the time he left for Brazil, Sartre, who had recklessly gone on over-working, was suffering from a deep-seated depression and from shingles.[56] He and de Beauvoir were met at the airport by the forty-eight-year-old Jorge Amado, the pioneer of the politically committed novel in Brazil. He introduced them to many of his hospitable friends, and took them to Bahia, where he had grown up. Seventy per cent of the population there was black. In the covered market place he bought Sartre and de Beauvoir neck-laces and bracelets made from coloured seeds, pottery, earthenware figur-ines, black-faced dolls, musical instruments, knick-knacks. Sartre was nervous of the native cooking, but de Beauvoir sampled some of it.[57] At Recife an entertainment was laid on for them with blacks disguised as Indians dancing sophisticated ballets;[58] they attended two voodoo ceremon-ies,[59] and a *candomble*, a religious ceremony amalgamating Haitian voodoo with African ritual and Catholic liturgy, combining incense with the sacrifice of chickens. In the streets at night, young foot-boxers fought with razor-blades attached to their ankles.[60]

Sartre and de Beauvoir visited Copacabana and Rio, where they saw the work of young Brazilian architects, pupils of Le Corbusier. Of the three million inhabitants, nearly a quarter were living in huts made of planks, iron sheeting and cardboard on derelict land which was marshy or rocky. In the religious rituals of this depressed and under-nourished sub-proletariat, drugs were used to induce delirium, and in their trances initiates would inflict burns and wounds on themselves.[61]

De Beauvoir had read in Freyre's *Maîtres et esclaves* (*Masters and Slaves*) that in north-east Brazil girls used to marry at thirteen while at the height of their beauty, which had already begun to fade at fifteen; to his embarrass-ment Sartre sometimes found himself exchanging provocative glances with well-developed girls, forgetting quite how young they were.[62]

At his lectures audiences were responsive, especially when he talked about Cuba.[63] In Recife and Bahia he discussed Algeria without openly attacking the French government, but in a press conference at the university in Rio he replied candidly to questions about de Gaulle and Malraux. From then on the press paid attention to him, and when his book on Cuba *Huracán sobre el azucar* (*Hurricane on the Sugar*) appeared in translation, a mass of people turned up at the autographing session in a brightly decor-ated hall.[64] He had authorized Spanish, Portuguese and English translations of the book, which was based on his articles in *France-Soir*, but he did not want it to appear in French.

When he and de Beauvoir flew to São Paolo, they were met by a crowd at the airport and found that a Sartre Society had been formed at the university; in Rio they were given the rank of honorary citizens.

In France Jeanson was due to be tried by a military tribunal. Sartre had promised Jeanson's lawyers to make a surprise appearance as a witness, but the date of the hearing had been postponed to 7 September, while he was still in Brazil, and when Lanzmann telephoned him there, he said that all he could do was send a message to be read out. He despatched a three-line telegram confirming his 'total solidarity' with Jeanson's network, but even when the disappointed lawyers managed to offer him a free return flight, he refused to come, resisting the pleas of Lanzmann and Péju over the telephone. He told them that he still had shingles, but consented when Péju asked to write a letter in his name. What Péju then wrote was strongly worded: 'During the Resistance, teachers at the Sorbonne did not hesitate to relay messages and make contacts. If Jeanson had asked me to carry suitcases or hide Algerian militants, and if I could have done it without endangering them, I would have done it without hesitation.' The accused were in the dock 'as our delegates. What they represent is the future of France. And the ephemeral power which is preparing to judge them no longer represents anything.' Péju's draft was retouched by Lanzmann and typed. A forged signature was added and, since there was no authenticating envelope, the letter was presented to the tribunal together with Sartre's telegram.[65]

To the defendants Sartre's absence looked like a cowardly betrayal but the letter caused a scandal. In *Le Figaro* Thierry Maulnier wrote that the only logical step for Sartre to take now was to join the ranks of the FLN with a gun or a bomb in his hand.[66] One deputy asked for legal action to be taken against him.[67] The Minister of Information accused him of representing 'an anarchic and suicidal dictatorship wanting to force itself on a perplexed and decadent intelligentsia'.[68]

Meanwhile Sartre and de Beauvoir went on touring Brazil. In Brasilia they met the architect responsible for it, Oscar Niemeyer, who used them as his audience for a conversation with himself: 'Is it possible to create socialist architecture in a non-socialist country? Obviously not.'[69] With Niemeyer and Amado, they met the president, Kubitschek, who considered Brasilia to be his personal achievement.[70]

The end of their Brazilian trip was nightmarish. Ill with what was diagnosed as typhoid, de Beauvoir was taken to a hospital for tropical diseases in Recife. Depressed in his hotel, Sartre was drinking Scotch and taking phenol-barbitone to avoid sleepless nights. Rumours reached them that Sartre would be arrested as soon as he arrived in France. He could buy no French newspapers but finally a long-delayed letter from Lanzmann brought him up to date with events. The 121 signatories of the Manifesto had been banned from broadcasting on radio or television. On 1 October police had seized the new issue of *Les Temps modernes*. Five thousand war veterans had marched down the Champs-Elysées shouting: 'Kill Sartre'. Lanzmann's advice was that instead of returning to Paris they should stay in Barcelona.[71]

Wanting to spend a few days in Havana on the way to Europe, they first had to make the thousand-mile journey back to Rio. In Cuba the honeymoon of the revolution was already over: they had the impression of less gaiety, less freedom.[72] In an interview he gave later to a Hungarian journalist Sartre complained: 'I have the impression that in Cuba there is now interference with diverse literary tendencies.'[73] But his misgivings would have no effect on the help he had already given to Castro by acting as his spokesman both in Brazil and in the West.

TWENTY-THREE · *'Kill Sartre'*

They flew to Madrid and then Barcelona, where Bost and Jean Pouillon met them at a hotel near the cathedral. Thanks to the letter Sartre had encouraged Péju to forge, but had not yet read, he had been much vilified in the press; over the telephone, Lanzmann now advised him and de Beauvoir to drive home: if they flew, it might cause brawling at the airport, and possibly they would be arrested.

When they arrived at the frontier, the official told them he was under orders to advise Paris. Some of the 121 signatories were in prison; others had deliberately inculpated themselves for the sake of publicity. Eager to get themselves officially charged, too, Sartre and de Beauvoir were surprised to encounter procrastination. An examining magistrate reported sick; after a new date had been fixed, a pretext was found for postponing it. Sartre had been condemned to stay at liberty. 'You don't arrest Voltaire', said de Gaulle, who may have been forgetting that Voltaire had spent nearly a year in the Bastille.

But Sartre and de Beauvoir did not escape with impunity. At restaurants other customers made them feel like public enemies, and Sartre received so many insulting and threatening telephone calls that he stopped picking up the receiver, except when friends went through the routine of letting the telephone ring once, hanging up, letting it ring once again, hanging up again, and then letting it ring till he answered.[1] In the evenings when he was with de Beauvoir they dined frugally in her studio, eating ham and listening to the gramophone.[2] For both of them social life depended mainly on the small surviving 'family' of friends, including Bost and Olga, and on the *Temps modernes* team, which met in the morning twice a month at de Beauvoir's flat.[3] But Sartre, though he had given permission for a statement to be written in his name, was unable to forgive the man who had made him so unpopular. Péju was sacked.

The review went on reporting truthfully about events in Algeria and acts of vengeance against Muslims in Paris. An article by Lanzmann revealed what he had learned from a secret file about psychological and physical torture involving electrodes, burning, broken bottles, hanging, strangling.[4] Though de Gaulle was well aware that the FLN was unbeatable and that none of the European countries could hold on to their African colonies much longer, he could not be sure that the French people would think him indispensable once the war was over, and he was nervous of provoking the powerful reactionaries who insisted on keeping Algeria French. In handling the generals he was cautious, conciliatory, but in November 1960 he had finally announced that without waiting for peace with the FLN, he wanted to give Algeria its own laws, institutions and foreign policy. A referendum was to be held in both France and Algeria at the beginning of 1961. For the *colons* the end was in sight, and, like the Germans during the last weeks of the Occupation, they reacted viciously. The Organisation de l'armée secrète (OAS) started assassinating Muslims and European sympathizers first in Algeria and then in France, counting on terrorism to delay settlement in Algeria. One of their main weapons was the plastic bomb. Not that the FLN held back from terrorist attacks. Both sides were fairly arbitrary in choosing targets.

Like other writers in *Les Temps modernes* and other members of the '121', Sartre campaigned for a 'No' vote in the referendum. As he told *L'Express*, 'the question posed links self-determination with the establishment of provisional institutions in Algeria, aimed at giving power to a hypothetical third force between "ultras" and the FLN ... To vote "yes" is to refuse to wake up, to go on dreaming.'[5] But de Gaulle won a massive majority.

In April Sartre left Paris again, travelling with de Beauvoir and Bost to Antibes, where they heard about Castro's 'Bay of Pigs' victory over an ill-judged attempt, backed, apparently, by the Americans, to invade Cuba. Sartre and de Beauvoir visited what had once been Mme Morel's villa: it had been made into a clinic and was surrounded by tall buildings. On 21 April, four days after the abortive invasion of Cuba, there was a rising in Algiers, led by four retired generals (Salan, Challe, Zeller and Jouhared). Paratroopers of the Foreign Legion took over most of the public buildings, government representatives were arrested, and a state of siege was proclaimed. What the rebels wanted was a guarantee that Algeria would stay French. De Gaulle, who had made himself president, announced a state of emergency, and his Prime Minister, Debré, broadcast a panicky appeal to the nation, asking people to go to the nearest aerodrome and reason with any paratroopers who landed. In the meantime, all the bridges of Paris had been blocked with buses. In the morning twelve million French workers were on strike, but on 23 April de Gaulle addressed the army, asking the men to disobey their leaders. Consisting largely of national servicemen who were scared their demobilization might be delayed, the army obeyed the president, and within five days the rebellion had collapsed.

But to be sure of keeping Algerian affairs under close personal control, de Gaulle continued the state of emergency until the end of September.

Sartre and de Beauvoir were still in Antibes on 4 May when Merleau-Ponty died suddenly of a heart attack. Sartre threw himself into work. Without even troubling to re-read his earlier essay on Tintoretto, he settled down to write on the painting 'St George and the Dragon', which he had often seen in London. As before, he emphasized the sense Tintoretto gave him of feeling imprisoned. The volatile Venetian firmament could be depicted, but must be placed firmly out of reach. Humanity must prove itself innocent or be found guilty 'under the bituminous lid of a leaden sky'.[6]

The Nizan preface had displayed the pleasure Sartre took in condemning himself; already at risk as the most famous of the '121', he gambled against himself more dangerously in the provocative interview he gave *France-Observateur* in the middle of May. The 'terrorism of the rich' was counter-productive, he said. The strategy was to make it look as though a breakdown in negotiations would lead straight to civil war, but since the assassinations were increasing people's impatience for peace, the terrorists were helping France to wake up out of her lethargy.[7] After this, he began to receive threatening letters. Anticipating a bomb attack on his flat, he settled his mother in a hotel, moving in temporarily with de Beauvoir. He was working – rather too frenetically and using too much corydrane – on an essay about Merleau-Ponty, who, although his junior by three years, had been a father figure politically, and in his book *Signes* had defended Sartre against his morbid tendency to condemn himself. But he went on attacking himself both in the essay and in the overdoses of corydrane, which were affecting his hearing. Sometimes he was so deaf by the afternoon that he could not hear when the doorbell rang.[8] Feeling more than usually in need of the therapeutic Roman summer, he was planning to leave with de Beauvoir on 19 July. At seven-thirty in the morning they were packing the last of their suitcases when the telephone rang. A plastic bomb had exploded in the entrance hall of 42 rue Bonaparte but had done little damage.

In Rome they gave themselves a less arduous routine than usual, sleeping in communicating rooms, rising late, listening to music on de Beauvoir's transistor before going down for coffee and newspapers. The morning stint of work would be followed by a car-ride into the centre of Rome and a walk; the afternoon stint by dinner in the Piazza Santa Maria in Trastevere or at one of their other favourite restaurants, and finally a drink on a terrace with a view of the campagna.[9] But the news was conducive to neither relaxation nor work: clashes between French and Tunisians; slaughter in Bizerta, followed by de Gaulle's refusal to evacuate it; the building of the Berlin Wall.

Since the first proposals for a compromise peace between France and Algeria, one of the loudest voices raised against the idea was that of Frantz Fanon, a Martiniquan doctor, great-grandson of a slave, author of *Peaux noirs, masques blancs* (*Black Skins, White Masks*) and *L'An v de la révolution algérienne* (*Year 5 of the Algerian Revolution*) and a member of the provisional revolutionary government of Algeria. He had been influenced by Sartre's *Critique* – especially by the discussion of Terror – and after he had invited Sartre to write a preface for his new book, *Les Damnés de la terre* (*The Wretched of the Earth*), the first chapter, 'De la violence', had been published in the June issue of *Les Temps modernes*. Fanon was convinced that since colonialism depended on violence, counter-violence was the only possible answer. After Sartre had agreed to write a preface, Fanon came to Rome, although, two years earlier, when he was in hospital there, he had escaped only just in time when an assassin found the way to his room. After he and Sartre had lunch together, the conversation went on until two in the morning, and when de Beauvoir pleaded that Sartre needed sleep, Fanon's reaction was: 'I don't like men who hoard their resources.' He told Lanzmann: 'I'd give 20,000 francs a day if I could talk to Sartre from morning till night for two weeks.' As it was they talked almost non-stop for three days. In the Algerian war Fanon, who had been supplying the guerrillas with drugs, had trained terrorists in how to resist torture and how to keep calm when planting bombs or throwing grenades.[10] According to de Beauvoir Fanon's face would express less anguish when he described the 'counter-violence' of the blacks and the vengeance of the Algerians than when he spoke of Congolese mutilated by Belgians or Angolans by Portuguese – faces battered to flatness, lips pierced and padlocked.[11] He accused Sartre of not doing enough to expiate the crime of being French: how could he go on trying to live normally? The two men talked again when Fanon came back to Rome, ten days later, on his way to Tunis, but this was to be their last meeting. Already ill with leukaemia, Fanon would be dead before the end of the year. As soon as he left Rome, Sartre started on the preface, writing less feverishly than during the early summer in Paris. 'I am recomposing myself', he said.[12]

In 1947 he had been unambiguously hostile to violence: perpetrated in the name of liberty, it deprived people of their liberty.[13] In the 1951 play *Le Diable et le Bon Dieu*, he showed that his attitude had changed, and in *Saint Genet* he was taking the view that without violent resistance and militancy the oppressed majority could never come fully alive. In 1959 he had written the *Critique*, with its apologia for terrorism, which had influenced Fanon, and now, in his preface to *Les Damnés de la terre*, his most outspoken defence of violence is couched in an impassioned declaration of solidarity with the Algerian rebels. Violence must come as the Third World throws off the yoke imposed by the violence of imperialism. 'Our victims know us by their wounds and their fetters ... You, so liberal, so human, who love culture to the point of preciosity, you pretend to forget you have colonies and that massacres are carried out in your name.'[14]

Fanon was no more than a catalyst but the Algerian experience had produced a chemical change in Sartre's thinking. His political horizon had broadened. The urge to show that the PCF had left the French proletariat in the lurch was displaced by the urge to show that the oppressed peasantry of the Third World was being left in the lurch not only by the bourgeois imperialists but by the Western proletariat. What he had seen in Cuba and Brazil changed his perspective on what he knew about Algeria. The true revolutionaries of the sixties were to be found in Asia and Africa, where the dividing-line between working class and middle class had not been obscured. The wretched of the earth had nothing to lose by rebelling, and in France, where neither the Party official nor the *embourgeoisé* proletarian was ready to see himself as a comrade of the dark-skinned victim, university students were less complacently self-involved. When *Les Damnés de la terre* was published they read in Sartre's preface that violence was the only cure for 'colonial neurosis'. The native would discover his lost innocence when his rage boiled over. By shooting a European he could destroy both the oppressor and the part of himself that had been oppressed. Even in France culture was being reconstituted according to the image that the *colon* had of it. The outbreaks of violence in Paris showed that 'the time of wizards and fetishes' would continue until common sense was fighting on the same side as the rebels, whose 'counter-violence' was a reassertion of human values.

Since 1940, when the diary-writing Sartre had found a tension between the secret self and the self other people saw, he had given himself a long and necessary training in resistance to internal tension. He was willing to collaborate with such disparate men as John Huston and Frantz Fanon. Comfortably distanced from the violence that had spread from Algeria to OAS bombings in Paris, he and de Beauvoir were enjoying the Italian summer while, articulated between the covers of one book, the alliance between Sartre and Fanon helped to encourage violence and to create '*tiers-mondisme*' (orientation towards the Third World) in the French revolutionary young. On them his influence was to continue with only minor fluctuations until the 1968 rebellion, but his standing as an intellectual was to be seriously damaged by the success of the structuralists. Distracted by his activism and complacently aware that Lévi-Strauss, Barthes, Foucault, Derrida, Lacan and the writers, such as Jean Ricardou, associated with the review *Tel Quel*, had all been influenced by his strong opposition to essentialist

determinism and by his insistence on the disunity of the self, Sartre under-
estimated these writers, attempting neither to keep abreast of their work,
nor to use *Les Temps modernes* as a forum for debate. Generally his tendency
was to avoid one-to-one confrontations – written or oral – with intellectual
equals, and he failed to learn, except superficially, from what ought to
have been a cautionary experience at the beginning of the sixties when,
for once, accepting an invitation to lecture at the Ecole Normale, he committed himself to a confrontation with Louis Althusser. An Algerian and a
Party member, Althusser taught at the Ecole Normale and wanted his structuralist Marxism to have a scientifically anti-humanist basis. He had not
yet published *Pour Marx* but his ideas already had great appeal for the
students. According to Régis Debray, then a student at the Ecole, Althusser
emerged as the more dialectical of the two thinkers: 'he said that the Sartrean
cogito was difficult to sustain inside a Marxist problematic of history'.[15]
Though the experience strengthened Sartre's inclination to avoid such
debates, he was not prompted to make his position less vulnerable by using
structuralist Marxism as a perspective for updating the ideas he had
advanced in his *Critique*.

In Italy he was equally remote from OAS violence and French intellectual
debate. In the sea at Anzio he saw an ancient Egyptian galley floating on
the waves: *Cleopatra* was being filmed with Elizabeth Taylor. Sitting next
to Sartre in the ruins of the little theatre at Tusculum, de Beauvoir felt
nostalgic for the tranquillity of their early holidays: 'If we've got another
twenty years to live, let's try to enjoy them.' But they had to confront open
violence in Paris on their return. In September, after de Gaulle had entered
into serious negotiations with the FLN, the OAS tried to assassinate him,
and in both France and Algeria plastic bombs were becoming almost commonplace. By the end of 1961 there had been six hundred explosions and
an arrested OAS agent was found to be carrying a list of three thousand
addresses due to be bombed during 1962.[16] In Paris the police had been
clubbing Algerians to death in the streets in full view of the public; corpses
were said to have been found hanging in the Bois de Boulogne; others,
mutilated, in the Seine. Ten thousand Algerians had been herded into
the Vélodrome d'Hiver as if it were a camp.[17] On 17 October an Algerian
demonstration was murderously suppressed, and on 1 November Algerian
rallies were banned; in response Sartre was one of those who organized
a silent demonstration by French intellectuals in the place Maubert. In
jails throughout France Algerian prisoners and French sympathizers had
just begun a hunger strike. Sartre made a speech; a plastic bomb was thrown
but no-one was seriously hurt; people started a sit-down on the pavement
and some were arrested; the demonstration was given good coverage on
the radio.

* * *

In *Les Temps modernes* much of the space, actually, was given to exposure of what was going on, but the October issue was devoted to Merleau-Ponty. In the first version of his own essay on Merleau-Ponty, written during July 1961 in Rome,[18] Sartre comments on the references in *Signes* to him and Nizan, but in the published version, which is quite different, no mention is made of what Merleau-Ponty had said about them. While Lacan contributed to the memorial number of the review, Lévi-Strauss was left to pay his tribute independently. He did this by dedicating *La Pensée sauvage* to his dead friend.

After the failure of the RDR in 1949 Sartre had intended to play no further part in organizing political groups, but he now decided to join forces with the mathematician Laurent Schwartz and Jean-Pierre Vigier to form a 'League for Anti-Fascist Movements'. Vigier, a communist who was advocating rapprochement with the non-communist left, had taken the initiative, asking Sartre and other prominent intellectuals to sign a pamphlet denouncing the OAS and racism; Sartre wanted to go much further – taking action in support of the Algerian rebels, and condemning what seemed virtually to be an alliance between the government and the OAS.

Knowing he was likely to be on the hit-list of the OAS assassins, who were active again, he tried to take a room in a hotel, only to be rejected by the nervous manager. In the end Sartre's new secretary, Claude Faux, rented a furnished flat in his own name; Sartre and de Beauvoir both moved in. The flat was in an unfinished building on the boulevard St-Germain, with rubble on the staircase. Noisy builders worked all day, and so little light came in from the narrow rue St-Guillaume that they always needed electric lights on.[19]

On 18 November a demonstration against fascism and racism was organized, mainly by the young communists. A crowd of about 8,000 turned out in support, and with de Beauvoir, Sartre paraded behind a placard proclaiming 'Peace in Algeria'. By faking breakdowns, car-drivers at first stopped the police-cars from reaching the demonstrators, but when the procession reached the boulevard Haussmann, the police, savagely using outsize truncheons, caused a stampede. Faux, who was trapped in the police charge, saw one demonstrator with the flesh hanging away from his face.[20]

During another anti-OAS demonstration on 19 December, the police charged at the leaders of the procession, beating up those who were carrying placards. Many people were seriously hurt.[21] Sartre tried to immerse himself in work on Flaubert.

In January 1962, hearing a nearby explosion at about two in the morning, he took it to mean that the OAS had discovered where he was living. Smoke was drifting from the rue St-Guillaume, broken glass was falling onto the pavement, planks had been blown out into the road. Police cars and a fire engine arrived. The shirt shop on the corner had been demolished by a plastic bomb, but it turned out that the target had been the shop owner, an Algerian-born Frenchman who had refused to collect funds for the OAS. Only three days later another plastic bomb exploded at 42 rue Bonaparte on the floor above Sartre's flat. It had destroyed both flats as well as the bedrooms of the floor above. Sartre's front door had been blown off, and his Norman cupboard smashed. From the third floor upwards, the staircase was hanging out through a vast hole in the wall. Inside the flat the floors were littered with papers, doors had been blown off their hinges, walls and ceilings covered in soot.[22] Many of Sartre's unpublished manuscripts disappeared.

Shortly afterwards, his mother received a telephone call from Mme Morel, who had not been in touch for a long time. She said nothing about the bomb. 'Of course, you know, I'm in favour of Algeria staying French.'[23] On the other side of the balance, Sartre received a warmly sympathetic letter from his uncle, Albert Schweitzer. He wrote back: 'Each time I see your name among those who are campaigning against atomic war, I feel how close I am to you.'[24]

The police protection Sartre was given after the bomb could not fail to put him in greater danger. Two policemen stood outside the house during the day and went off duty in the evening; the bombers worked at night, and few nights passed without the noise of explosions.[25] Sartre and de Beauvoir moved into a large block of flats overlooking the Seine on the quai Louis-Blériot, not knowing that two OAS killers were hiding there. The danger increased when *Djamula Boupacha* was published – a book, co-authored by de Beauvoir and an Algerian lawyer, Gisèle Halimi, about an Algerian girl who had been viciously tortured. This immediately provoked threatening telephone calls.[26]

On 8 February, during another anti-OAS demonstration, the police charged the crowd. When some of the demonstrators tried to escape into the Charonne Métro station, the police tore up metal tree guards to throw at them. Five adults were killed and a boy of sixteen. The official explanation was that the crowd had 'crushed itself'. The trade unions arranged to make the funeral into a mass demonstration. All the workers in Paris went on strike, and with no public transport running the traffic was immobilized by jams while a crowd of about 700,000 demonstrators converged on the cemetry at Père Lachaise.

But it was no easier to collaborate with the communists than it had been in the forties. Strongly opposed to what it ought to have wanted – radical action among the masses – the PCF insisted that there should be no opposition to the government, only to the OAS, and that membership of the league should be limited to intellectuals. Sartre had to let them change its name to 'Front for Action and Co-ordination among University Teachers and Intellectuals for an Anti-Fascist Movement' (FAC). In March, when Sartre gave a lecture about Algeria in Brussels, he had an audience of 6,000,[27] but, as before, his popularity made the communists nervous that he might be instrumental in creating a rival political force. When he was to address a meeting of the FAC at the Mutualité, a bomb warning was issued, which reduced the size of the audience to about 2,000.[28]

'Collaboration with the Communist Party is both necessary and imposs-ible', he told *La Voie communiste*; 'The Party wants to shut the sympathetic intellectuals up into a ghetto.' In effect the PCF had steered the working class away from politics: 'Steam is let off on the social level, but the political conflict is no longer discussed.'[29]

At the beginning of March a conference opened at Evian to negotiate peace with the FLN, and on the 19th both sides ordered a cease-fire. Special privileges were to be accorded to the Europeans in Algeria, but about 750,000 of them decided to emigrate. A referendum was held in France on 7 April, but before the July referendum in Algeria there was a recrudescence of violence. European women drove their cars into Muslim children; public buildings were blown up; the OAS fired on people queuing for tickets to leave the country. Muslim districts were bombarded; unemployed Arabs were machine-gunned in front of labour exchanges. Two dozen deaths on average were reported daily in the newspapers. Torturers escaped with impunity, while deserters were ferociously punished.[30]

Since the Liberation it had never been more unpleasant to live in Paris, and Sartre was impatient to resume his travelling. It was eight years since he and de Beauvoir had been in Russia, and when they arrived on 1 June, accepting an invitation from the Union of Soviet Writers, there was plentiful evidence of higher living standards. The women were dressed more brightly, displays in shop-windows were more appealing. But the labour camps were still in existence.[31] The interpreter assigned to Sartre and de Beauvoir was Lena Zonina, secretary of the Union's French section. She was a beautiful thirty-nine-year-old woman with dark eyes in an oval face. She was of Jewish descent, highly intelligent, and, as Sartre was soon to discover, passionate. He was to return eight times to the Soviet Union within just over four years; she was not the least important of his reasons.

With de Beauvoir he met Vosnesensky, attended one of his poetry read-ings, and saw Andrei Tarkovsky's film *The Childhood of Ivan*, which Sartre ranked alongside Truffaut's *Les 400 coups* as one of the best postwar films. In Leningrad they saw a production of Brecht's *Der Gute Mensch von Sezuan* in the style of Stanislavsky.[32] With Dorosh, a writer, and his wife, a physics professor, they spent two days in Rostov.[33] In Leningrad they saw

Dostoevsky's house and drank vodka to the memory of Pushkin on the spot where he had fought a duel.[34] In Moscow they accepted invitations to the houses of writers and intellectuals, and Sartre met Khrushchev. On the way back to France, they stayed in Poland. In Warsaw they were driven around the town by their friend Jerzy Lisowski; they met the writer Kazimierz Brandys and Professor Jan Kott, who had translated Sartre's plays into Polish; in Cracow they saw the university, the cathedral and the castle.[35]

Within little more than a fortnight Sartre was back in Russia to take part in a world congress for peace and general disarmament. He gave a speech under the title 'The Demilitarization of Culture'. Even Kafka, he said, had been exploited during the Cold War: banned in Russia, he was championed in the West as an enemy of the bureaucracy characteristic of the Eastern bloc.[36] What Krushchev had said about peaceful competition between the two blocs should also apply to culture. Some of the more liberal Soviet intellectuals responded enthusiastically to these arguments; encouraged, Sartre would go on working like a diplomat with no state behind him but with *détente* as his objective.

Deviating from his normal routine, Sartre made an autumn trip to Rome where he began to sketch out a new play based on Euripides' *Alcestis*, the queen who offered to die in place of the king, Admetus, when he claimed that he was too busy to die, having to rule his country and to win a war. Sartre wanted to imply in his version the story of female emancipation. When Alcestis returns, spared by Death, her husband is held in contempt as the man who let a woman die for him. The French for Alcestis is Alceste, which led to a confusion in *Le Figaro*. On 20 November it was announced that Sartre's next play would be about a 'neo-misanthropist', a character who would remind audiences of Molière's Alceste.[37]

At the end of December he went back to Russia with de Beauvoir – the third visit within six months. He wanted to explore the possibility of setting up an international community of writers. Ilya Ehrenburg was friendly, as were Vosnesensky and other intellectuals, while the cultural thaw appeared to be progressing. Solzhenitsyn's novel about the camps, *A Day in the Life of Ivan Denisovich*, had been published by *Novy Mir*: Pravda had printed Yevtushenko's poem 'Stalin's Heirs', which asked for extra guards around the tomb of the former leader to make sure there was no resurrection. Sartre and de Beauvoir went to see the large exhibition of modern painting and sculpture at the Manège, but after Khrushchev's visit to it the cultural atmosphere began to change. He ferociously denounced formalism and abstraction; in an ominously anti-semitic speech his propaganda chief Ilyichev attacked 'ideological coexistence'.[38]

After returning from Russia with de Beauvoir on 13 January 1963 Sartre settled down to work on *Les Mots*. Of all his books this is the one which can most easily be read quickly, but it is also the most devious; a superficial reading yields only a fraction of what went into the making of it. Though he wants it to look as though he has written down everything he can remember about his childhood, he has none of the passion most autobiographers have for resurrecting their past. He could have questioned his mother and his uncles about what they remembered; he could have searched for old photographs and tracked down what he had written himself about childhood when his memories were fresher – in letters to Toulouse, for instance, and in his 1940 diaries. But the autobiographical commitment failed to galvanize him either out of his usual habit of writing as if all the necessary facts were already in his head or out of his indifference to his past writings, which he tended to dismiss as if they were unreal, like past events. At the beginning of 1962 while moving out of his flat, he had forgotten to take the manuscripts from the big cupboard on the landing – a memory lapse which was highly profitable for the landlord – and when he had the chance to retrieve two volumes of the war diaries de Beauvoir had lent to Bost (who had lost them when wounded and unconscious) Sartre refused. A second-hand bookseller was offering them for the same price as a collector was willing to give. But why should he pay for what he had written himself?[39] And why should he exert himself to research his own childhood? Was it not his – a possession to manipulate in any way he wished? His instinct was not so much to repair the damage time had inflicted on his memories as to complete the demolition; if he was still haunted by ghosts from the past, perhaps they could be exorcized by the book.

TWENTY-FOUR · *Writing is Neurosis*

Sartre's motives for writing an autobiography were mixed, if not confused. The need for money bulked quite large. To invest so much time as he had since 1954 in travelling, unremunerative political activity and such unremunerative books as the *Critique* he had borrowed money from Gallimard as an advance on his next book, but without agreeing what the next book was to be. An English publisher was now trying to commission a new work from him, but after letting himself be persuaded that his obligation was to Gallimard, he went back to the autobiography abandoned in 1953, shortly after his 'conversion' to communism, when he had been 'close to regretting' his commitment to literature.[1] 'Madness' and 'neurosis' were the words he now used for what was generally called 'vocation', but in the new version of the book he tried to be less severe with his young self: 'Action too has its problems and one can be led to it by neurosis ... Salvation is no more to be achieved through politics than through literature.'[2]

During his friendship with Nizan they had gone on planning despite their atheism how to earn their salvation; Sartre is still doing this now, and he never freed himself from the fear he had dramatized in *Les Séquestrés d'Altona* about being judged in the unpredictable future. But though he is unguarded in his use of such words as 'neurosis' and 'salvation', the autobiography is motivated partly by the need to defend himself against the danger of being seduced by the idea of posterity – he plants the addiction among childhood fantasies – and partly by the fear of having gone too far towards Freudianism.

First of all, though, he tried to go even further, inviting Pontalis to psycho-analyse him. How was this to be taken? A surrender to what he had recently called a bourgeois ideology? A dangerous stratagem, like that of a boxer feigning weakness? He was prompted, he said, more by curiosity about psycho-analytic method than by a need for analysis. Pontalis was too canny to fall into the trap. After knowing Sartre for twenty years he valued the friendship too highly to jeopardize it by accepting him as a patient. Nor was he entirely clear about Sartre's motives. Perhaps he felt challenged in a new way by the Jewish doctor who had fought so hard against father-figures before becoming a patriarchal archetype. Perhaps he relished the prospect of psycho-analytical sessions in which the golden brain duelled against Freudian insights. Sartre did not look for another analyst when Pontalis refused but he did conduct a kind of self-analysis in *Les Mots*, as if he could manage no less easily without an analyst than without a father. Pontalis construed his original title, *Jean-sans-terre*, to mean 'Jean-sans-père'.

Les Mots is a monologue which makes gestures towards duologue. The voice we hear is always that of the well-known fifty-eight-year-old writer, sitting in a room which overlooks a cemetery. Ostensibly the main character in the narrative is Poulou, but no young boy, however precocious, would be capable of the ideas imputed to him by the mature writer. The first person refers sometimes to Sartre, sometimes to Poulou, but abrasive adult comment is regularly insinuated into the narrative: 'I liked to please and wanted to give myself baths of culture; I recharged myself every day with holiness.'[3] 'I take society to be a strict hierarchy based on merit and power.'[4] 'I never stop creating myself; I am the giver and the gift.'[5] The present tense (lost in Irene Clephane's English translation) belongs to the stratagem of infiltrating mature reflections into an immature mind; the claim of self-generation, which is regularly reiterated throughout the book, belongs to Sartre's obsessive denial of parentage – the mother is presented as a sister-figure – while the idea of being giver and gift has obviously less to do with Poulou's attitudes than with Sartre's wish to substitute an anthropological for a psychological perspective.[6] The book contains many echoes of Mauss's *Essai sur le don*; this is the most undisguised.

One of the mains points is that the child was putting on an act, developing the role he was expected to play in the family. But Sartre uses none of his dramatic skill to make us identify with the child as he picks up the adults' hints about the behaviour they want. This is partly inability to identify and partly refusal. Not wanting us to sympathize with Poulou, Sartre is driven by his hatred for his own childhood, and for the idea of childhood most adults have. He digresses into an anecdote about an American friend in a dogs' cemetery. 'Outraged, he kicked out at a cement dog and broke its ear. He was right: to love children and animals *too much* is to love them as an alternative to men.'[7] Sartre did not love children or animals enough, but not because he loved men too much. The book is informed by hatred of the bourgeois family. As he said in a prefatory note when *Novy Mir* published an excerpt from the book, 'I do not hold the child responsible but the period which had formed him. And above all I detest the well-worn myth of childhood perfected by the adults. I'd like this book to be read for what it really is: the attempt to destroy a myth.'[8]

It is also an attempt to create a myth about self-creation and freedom from guilt.

> Among the Aeneases who carry their Anchises on their back, I cross from one bank to the other alone and detesting these progenitors mounted invisibly on their sons throughout life; I left behind a young corpse who had no time to be my father and who today might be my son. Was this bad or good? I don't know, but I subscribe willingly to the verdict of an eminent psychoanalyst: I have no superego ... the hasty retreat of my father had supplied me with a very incomplete Oedipus complex: no superego, agreed, but no aggressivity either. My mother was mine, no-one disputed my quiet possession of her ... Against whom, against what would I have rebelled? Never did the whim of another claim to be my law.[9]

This bland assertion is never explicitly contradicted by the narrator, but the narrative has already begun to contradict it. The bearded patriarchal grandfather is compared with God the father and with Moses. Charles Schweitzer rules despotically over his daughter, who is not allowed to return later than ten in the evening, even when she goes out to dinner, while he implants such a ferocious superego in Poulou that fifty years later his conscience still speaks in his grandfather's voice, 'this recorded voice which wakes me up with a start and throws me to my table, I wouldn't listen to it if it were not my own'.[10] No superego? Not agreed.

In the myth Sartre creates about the origins of his literary neurosis, the grandfather plays the main role: he is the villain who implants it. The book is divided into two halves, 'Reading' and 'Writing'. The first half, which centres on Poulou's experience of stories and books, ends with the sentence: 'I was saved by my grandfather: he threw me, without wanting to, into a new imposture which changed my life.'[11] Between the ages of nine and ten, we are told in the second part, the boy becomes entirely 'posthumous'; the imaginary child turns into a real knight errant whose exploits will be real books. The mother buys exercise books for him to write stories; the boy comes to believe he has two voices: one dictates what the other should say. He is learning how to achieve immortality by turning himself into books; for centuries he will sit indestructibly on other people's shelves. 'My bones are leather and cardboard, my parchment flesh smells of glue and mildew ... I'm taken, opened, spread out on a table, opened with the flat of the hand and sometimes made to crack.'[12] The mother says: 'This child will write'; the grandfather, feeling the boy's skull, confirms: 'He's got the bump of literature',[13] but advises him to become a teacher. Famous writers have died of hunger, it is better to choose a second calling.

If Charles had called out from afar, opening his arms: 'Here's the new Victor Hugo, here's the budding Shakespeare!' I should today be an industrial designer or a teacher of literature. He was careful not to: for the first time I was facing the patriarch ... this was Moses dictating the new law. My law. He had mentioned my vocation only to underline the disadvantages: I conclude that he was taking it for granted ... I did not doubt for an instant that this was my lot; I tell myself at the time: 'That's all there is to it' and 'I'm talented.'[14]

Of all the characters in the narrative Charles Schweitzer is the liveliest. The brightest sequences have the frozen vividness of snapshots, and Charles never comes to life more than when he is striking poses, as if for a camera. Photographs of him fill the house. He is the victim of two recently discovered techniques – photography and the art of being a grandfather, as outlined by Victor Hugo in *L'Art d'être grandpère*. A reactionary old man, he has stopped reading new books in 1885, the year of Hugo's death. Now he only re-reads. As a teacher he values novels only for their vocabulary; as a translator he lives by cutting dead men into slices. But is this the real Charles Schweitzer or just a caricature grandfather, a figure in an anti-bourgeois myth? Though Sartre told Leiris that he wanted to write the autobiography as if he were a historian or a biographer of someone else, the real Charles Schweitzer was progressive both in his 'direct method' of teaching language and in his attitude to literature. In *La Vie et les oeuvres de Hans Sachs* he attacks 'la littérature de la bourgeoisie' which he defines as 'now purely didactic, now morose and corrosive'. Sartre's characterization seems to be based partly on his grandfather but partly on Victor Hugo's book. As in his novels, which contain more pastiche and parody than is immediately apparent, Sartre is writing anti-literature, a book designed to invalidate previous books. *Les Mots* mocks at Gide's autobiographical *Si le grain ne meurt* and involves a complex pattern of contrasts between low culture and high culture, comics, films, and boys' adventure stories versus the classics of literature. The classics are discreditable because they have served to bolster middle-class complacency, while their champion, the grandfather, is disconcertingly similar to the archetypes of bourgeois paternalism satirized in *La Nausée* – incarnated in a gigantic bronze statue Gustave Impetraz clutches a top hat in one hand, resting his other on a pile of folio volumes, which is reassuring to black-clad housewives, who can regard him as guardian of the values they grew up with.

This is only one of the dialectical axes in the book, which is structured around contrasts. Constantly moving between the present and the past, the narrative treacherously cultivates the appearance of chronological progression. Sartre is either forgetting or counting on the reader to forget the caveat embedded so deeply into the narrative of *La Nausée*. 'To make the most banal event become an adventure, you have – and you have only – to start making it into a story.'[15] Surrounded by your own and other people's stories, you look at your life through them and live it as if you were telling it. Though exceptionally alert to this tendency, Sartre was exceptionally prone to it. Had he tried to tell the truth about his attempts to cope with it, while trying, without any conjuring tricks, to test how far he could reconstruct himself by making his past into a narrative, the autobiography might have been a superb totalization, but he is too contentious, too manipulative.

In *La Nausée* he makes Anny uninterested in the details of what happens to Roquentin: she cares only about his 'eternal essence'. In his autobiography, as in his biographies, Sartre, more aprioristic than existentialist, concerns himself with the eternal essence of his subject but camouflages his indifference to facts and chronology. In *Les Mots* his dating is vague and inaccurate. We are left in uncertainty about when the crucial commitment was made to becoming a writer – sometimes it is between seven and eight, sometimes between eight and ten, and he asserts confidently that he was seven when his golden curls were cut off, which (as we have seen) contradicts what he had told Toulouse.[16] But this incident is climactic in the first half of the book, as it could not have been if he was only five at the time. What the story needs is a mythical moment of disenchantment when the idyll of childhood beauty dissolves into realistic awareness of his ugliness. He is betraying himself by telling the story, but his technique is to let one level of self-betrayal overlay another. The resemblance to Genet is nowhere stronger than in this habit of treachery. In a curious footnote he writes: 'Be satisfied with yourself and other self-satisfied people will love you; tear your neighbour to pieces and your other neighbours will laugh. But if you punish your soul, all the souls will cry out.'[17] No autobiography has hit out more vindictively at the author's soul, but not content with betraying himself, Sartre even betrays the habit of self-betrayal. The reader is left wondering whether at the end of the book he is meant to agree that Sartre has no superego or to recognize that the narrative has betrayed its starting point.

When Sartre's mother read the book she was so upset that she said: 'Poulou has understood nothing about his childhood', and to put the record straight she sat down to write her own memoir. She is not portrayed unsympathetically in *Les Mots* though, as characterized, she has a great deal in common with Lucien's mother in 'L'Enfance d'un chef' and with Flaubert's mother in the biography. But it is not her that Sartre is trying to betray: it is himself.

The premiss of *Jean-sans-terre* is visible when he says that he had inherited neither property nor any sense of destination from his father. But the grandfather gives him his destiny. 'He flung me into literature by the efforts he made to guide me away from it.'[18] Docile, unmasculine, malleable, the little boy is trapped into writing for the sake of writing. The fifty-eight-year-old Sartre is more tolerant – and more amusing – when he describes how the boy fantasized about being a man of action, rescuing heroines from vengeful janissaries with curved swords, but he convinces himself that even his adult habit of leaving work unfinished had its roots in childhood. He wrote fast, hated re-reading his stories, lost the exercise books he dropped on the floor, saw no point in finishing a story when the first episodes were missing.[19]

The style of *Les Mots* is grounded in ambivalence. The prose is quite different from that of the *Critique*. 'The sentences are among the most carefully polished I've ever written. And I took time on it. I wanted there to be implications in every phrase, one or two implications ... It was full of tricks, stratagems, belles-lettrism, almost wordplay.' Wanting the book to be literary, he claimed that the reason was: 'it was in some fashion a way of saying goodbye to a certain kind of literature ... I wanted to be literary in order to show the error of being literary.' His intention was to bring the autobiography up to middle age and then to concentrate on political writing;[20] he wrote a long essay on Patrice Lumumba, the Congolese leader whose assassination ended his short career of advocating non-violence,[21] but the autobiographical project would be cut short and for the next fifteen years the bulk of Sartre's working time would be given to Flaubert. On the other hand, the writing of *Les Mots* may have fed Sartre's disinclination to think of himself as a writer and his willingness to undertake commitments that took him away from his study.

In the summer he and de Beauvoir accepted another invitation from the Soviet Writers' Union – this time for a congress of COMES, the Community of European Writers, which had been set up in 1958 to encourage *détente*. The president was the poet Guiseppe Ungaretti. Held in Leningrad, the meeting was attended by writers from all over Europe, including Angus Wilson, Nathalie Sarraute, Alain Robbe-Grillet, Hans Magnus Enzensberger and Tibor Déry.[22] But Khrushchev had reverted to a more Stalinist cultural policy since his attack on the progressive art exhibited at the Manège, and Ilya Ehrenburg was under attack. Khrushchev believed he had exerted a harmful influence on Sartre, encouraging him to leave the Party; it was useless to point out that he had never joined it.

At the congress other Soviet writers tried to show their loyalty to the leadership by attacking Proust, Joyce and Kafka. Afterwards Sartre and de Beauvoir were among the delegates Khrushchev received at his country house in Georgia. When his guests had been shown the new swimming pool, surrounded by a glass wall which disappeared at the touch of a button, they were harangued about the evils of capitalism and the beauties of socialism. At lunch Khrushchev scarcely spoke, and the non-Russian guests afterwards had to sit in uncomprehending silence for forty-five minutes while Alexsandr Tvardovsky read a poem. Apparently Khrushchev had been visited earlier in the day by Maurice Thorez, who had denounced the anti-communists he was about to receive.[23]

From Moscow, Sartre and de Beauvoir went on to the Crimea, where they stayed for a week before going on to Georgia and Armenia. Lena Zonina spoke no Georgian, and when a dinner party was thrown for them by the president of the Writers' Union, who also acted as a *tamada*, or master of ceremonies, everything he said had to be translated first into Russian and then into French.

Sartre and de Beauvoir returned to Paris in September, and in November left again to visit Czechoslovakia. There too they were guests of the Writers' Union. They had seen little of the country on their 1954 visit, but the cultural climate had obviously improved. Kafka's books were on sale, as were many foreign books in Czech translation, including some by Sartre and de Beauvoir. In Prague Antonin Liehm, Sartre's translator, acted as their guide and interpreter, together with the writer Adolf Hoffmeister, who had been ambassador in Paris at the end of the forties. At a press conference, where one of his interlocutors was Milan Kundera, Sartre attacked the idea of decadence as an obstacle to communication between Eastern and Western intellectuals. In Leningrad Freud, Kafka and Joyce had been denounced, but these three writers, said Sartre, had helped to make him into a Marxist.[24] From Prague they went on to Bratislava. Later Sartre published one of Kundera's stories in *Les Temps modernes*. According to Liehm, Sartre's influence had contributed to the relaxation of pressure on Czech intellectuals.[25] In Prague he took part in a debate about decadence, gave a talk on the radio, attended the Czech premiere of *Les Séquestrés d'Altona*; he also gave three lectures – in Prague, Bratislava and Brno.

Les Mots, which was published in January 1964, was widely and favourably reviewed. Many critics welcomed it as a return to literature, but in an April interview Sartre said: 'In comparison with the death of one child, *La Nausée* isn't up to scratch.' This provoked a good deal of controversy,[26] but Sartre's remark needs to be seen in the perspective of what he had already written in the Fanon preface about Western culture: the only true culture was the revolution.[27] The Western intellectual should not be allowed to use cultural monuments as a justification for a civilization which had been murderous towards the colonized population: in the past the Parthenon, Chartres cathedral, the Rights of Man and the swastika had all served as floats on the fishing-line,[28] but this period was over. What had to come now was violence. It may have been anomalous for Sartre to concern himself with autobiography so soon after advancing this argument, but his life had long been full of anomalies. He said that his object in talking about a child's death had been to question what significance literature can have in a world where people are hungry, but the remark shows the same tendency to disparage his first great literary achievement as to disparage his childhood. Sartre's method of moving forward was to move violently against his earlier self, rather like an angry Jewish father turning his back on the grown-up child who has married out of the faith. Sartre could never quite afford to let his self-hatred catch up with him, but he gave it *carte blanche* to play against his past.

His partial acceptance of Freudianism had done nothing to make him feel warmer towards writers or friends who had been influential in the past, and he had not been in touch with René Maheu since the thirties, but Maheu had been director of UNESCO since 1962, and when it organized a colloquium under the title *The Living Kierkegaard*, to be held in Paris during April, Sartre was invited to give a lecture. Though Kierkegaard had been the first philosopher to use the word 'existentialism', Sartre had previously had little to say about him, and the invitation constituted a challenge, partly because Kierkegaard was such a champion of individuality, partly because he had laid so much stress on the insignificant accidents of his life. Looking at him in the perspective of the *Critique*, Sartre would have to question both how much of his private experience had entered into history and how much of this man could be known. Like Freud, Kierkegaard believed that self-knowledge was the passport to knowledge of others; unlike Sartre he detested the masses: his existentialism was a programme for attaining existential subjectivity while rising above the men who had let themselves be made into things.

At the colloquium, held in the UNESCO auditorium, recorded messages from Heidegger and Jaspers were relayed. Sartre was such a star attraction that an uninvited group of students arrived from the Sorbonne. 'We're philosophers too.' Some sat on the floor, others squeezed onto benches where well-dressed UNESCO luminaries crowded closer together.[29]

Kierkegaard, said Sartre, had a special relationship with history: 'as the Kierkegaardian adventure unfolded, it revealed itself as known in advance'[30] and, like Nietzsche, he made philosophy coextensive with the personal experience of the philosopher. Wanting to designate himself as a trans-historical absolute, he ceaselessly fabricated himself by writing. His life crystallized around the problem of the relationship between history and lived experience: how much of this is recuperable? Kierkegaard had been formed by a series of biographical accidents, but what was their historical meaning? Sartre uses the term 'singular universal' for the significance acquired as the insignificant accidents are subsumed. Man is the creature who transforms his being into meaning.[31] Kierkegaard was 'perhaps the first to show that the universal enters history as a singular, in so far as the singular institutes itself in it as a universal'.[32] In this dialectical formulation, Sartre was preparing the position he would take in his Flaubert biography.

He would often make elaborate preparations for a lecture, knowing that some of the work would filter into a book. After accepting an invitation to speak on morality and society at another colloquium – this time in Rome during May at the Istituto Gramsci – Sartre wrote about two hundred pages of notes.[33] Proceeding from the premisses of his *Critique*, he attacked ethical imperatives, social customs and moral norms as attempting to curb the individual's freedom to produce himself as a subject and as imposing a predetermined future which belongs to the past. Each social system produces moral-seeming pressures which are conducive to its own survival but give no clue about the behaviour that will be requisite after its demise. Capitalism cannot determine the future of the working class.[34]

Invited to join the celebrations in Kiev for the 150th anniversary of the Ukrainian poet Shevchenko's birth, Sartre and de Beauvoir hesitated because an anti-semitic pamphlet had been published by a professor at Kiev. Finally urged by their friends to accept, they left Paris at the end of May. From Kiev they went on to Moscow, where more modern blocks were being built and the number of taxis had doubled in twelve months, while food was more plentiful.[35] Next they visited Vladimir, Tallinn, the capital of Estonia, Leningrad and Novgorod. After a few more days in Moscow, they flew back to Paris on 10 July, to stay only briefly before leaving for another Roman summer.

Sartre had abandoned his version of *Alcestis* but he began to work in Rome on what was to be his last play, an adaptation of Euripides' *The Trojan Women*. He had become interested in the play when a 1961 performance of a literal translation had impressed an audience that obviously favoured negotiations with the FLN. Euripides was hostile both to war and to colonial expeditions, but the play struck Sartre as more like an oratorio than a tragedy, and he gave a sharper dramatic edge to the conflicts.[36] He also sharpened the denunciation of colonialism. And, as in *Les Mouches*, he emphasized the weakness of the gods, who will disappear alongside the humans.

After being in Paris when Maurice Thorez died on 12 July Sartre was in Rome when Palmiro Togliatti died at the end of August. Like the two parties they led, the two men were vastly different. It was Sartre's misfortune not to live in a country where the Party was led by a man like Togliatti. If he had, he might have joined it. The statement he had sent to the PCF was polite but cool, paying tribute to Thorez's intelligence, energy, courage and persistence.[37] But after attending Togliatti's funeral, Sartre wrote enthusiastically in *Les Temps modernes* about 'the man who has forged with his own hands a party of men who are tough and free ... My friend Togliatti.'[38]

At the beginning of the autumn Sartre was approached by an Italian acquaintance, the philosopher Enzo Paci, who surprised him by asking for a text of the speech he would make when he was awarded the Nobel Prize for Literature. This was the first he heard of the judges' decision. *Les Mots* had brought him back into the international literary limelight. His decision to reject the prize was not quite immediate. Some people urged him to accept, but when de Beauvoir canvassed opinion among students and friends she was confirmed in her feeling that he ought to refuse. One of those consulted was Nizan's daughter, now married to Olivier Todd. What concerned him deeply was the political implications of the decision he had to make. The prize had been given to Pasternak but not to any non-dissident Soviet writer; to Camus but not to any Western communist – not even Neruda. Were the Swedes trying to show that Sartre could be aligned with the right?

On 15 October an article appeared in *Le Figaro littéraire* written by the Swedish correspondent: Sartre might be this year's winner. The next morning he wrote to warn the Swedish Academy that he did not want the prize. His letter was received but ignored, and on 22 October the prize was awarded to him. He was having lunch with de Beauvoir in a café near her flat when a journalist came over to tell them the news. Not wanting to use the French press as his means of conveying a refusal to the Swedish Academy, Sartre made a statement to a Swedish journalist who passed it to Stockholm through Gallimard's representative. Translated back into French, the statement then appeared in *Le Monde* and other newspapers. The writer should not make himself into an institution, he maintained: his attitude to Venezuelan guerrillas, for instance, should involve only him, not those who awarded him the prize. In any case he could not accept an award that could be offered only to Western writers or Soviet dissidents: 'It's regrettable that the prize was given to Pasternak before Sholokhov, and that the only Soviet work to be honoured should be a work published abroad and banned at home.'[39] As soon as the statement was released, Sartre was pursued by crowds of journalists. He took refuge, thoughtlessly or disingenuously, in de Beauvoir's flat, where they had no difficulty in tracking him down. The scandal lasted for months, and many well-known writers joined in. Gabriel Marcel called Sartre a 'licensed corrupter'.[40] André Breton diagnosed 'a perfectly gauged political action, a propaganda operation in support of the Eastern bloc'.[41] A Marxian ideologist, Kostas Axelos, wrote that Sartre could have as readily lived under Hitler as under Stalin.[42] Sartre's worldwide fame was enhanced more by the rejection of the prize than it would have been by acceptance, but what embarrassed him was letters from people asking him to accept the prize and pass on the money (twenty-six million old francs) to them.[43]

Sartre's relationship with Arlette Elkaïm (as she now spelled her surname) had progressively become more important. A keen amateur musician, she had learned to sing and to play the flute and the piano. After lunching with her at the Coupole he loved to sit down at the piano in her flat and accompany her or play duets or sing to her, accompanying himself.[44] He spent a good deal of time there, sleeping there on average perhaps twice a week. At the end of January 1965 he applied formally to adopt her as his daughter, and in March this was granted. Most people would have expected him to want de Beauvoir at least as his literary executrix if not as his heiress. To adopt Arlette as his daughter was to make her both – a betrayal in line with the offers of marriage to Dolorès and Wanda. For a lifetime of devotion de Beauvoir's reward would be to see the youngest of her rivals given unchallengeable ownership of everything Sartre had written, everything he had possessed.

If the gesture was partly symbolic, the symbolism was complex. By a legal act Sartre was approximating to the realization of a fantasy he had entertained throughout his life. The relationship between Frantz and Léna in *Les Séquestrés d'Altona* consummates the incest already hinted at in the relationships between Boris and Ivich and between Orestes and Electra. Arlette was not a younger sister, but by adopting a young mistress as his daughter he was aiming a sacrilegiously mocking blow at the institution of the family while acting out a variation on a favourite fantasy. Also behind the gesture was a mixture of generosity and aggression. It was an act of solidarity with the underprivileged. Arlette was in four ways an incarnation of victimization: she was a woman, she was Jewish, she was Algerian, she was lacking in self-confidence. As Sartre's adopted daughter she would be given a new identity that would certainly bring civic and financial security, together, possibly, with a greater degree of emotional and ontological security. By guaranteeing a future in which she would be in a position of wealth and power, it might give her a stronger grip on the present. At the same time, if Jankélévitch was right to think that Sartre still had residual guilt feelings towards the Jews, here was a grandiose gesture of atonement. It was also a magnificently impertinent but practically effective way of forging a permanent link with a mistress, more original and more defiant of convention than the non-marital pact with de Beauvoir.

As an act of aggression it was directed mainly against de Beauvoir, who had been so insufferably loyal for so unconscionably long to a man who could not bear to be in anyone's debt – not even a woman's. She had had relationships with Algren and Lanzmann, but she was nearly always available. Loyal, discreet, unselfish, steady, cool, disciplined, a good organizer, she had succeeded extraordinarily well in replacing the lost mother and deputizing for the sister he had always wanted. Though she enjoyed saying 'we' about herself and Sartre, she was not proprietorial. But she was still emotionally dependent. She once said to Henriette Nizan: 'If Sartre died, I wonder what I'd do. Perhaps I'd commit suicide.' But as an act of vengeance against her, the adoption of Arlette was open-ended. There was no need to decide yet about whether to leave a will or whether to appoint de Beauvoir as his literary executrix. Whatever he did, she would go on being known as the woman who had shared his life. But if he made no will, Arlette would inherit everything, including his literary estate.

Les Troyennes was due to open at the Théâtre National Populaire on 10 March in a production by the Greek film director Michael Cacoyannis, who had just made *Zorba the Greek*. Influenza prevented Sartre from attending rehearsals, and when he saw the production with de Beauvoir only a few days before the opening, he was appalled. The music (by John Prodromides) made much of the text inaudible, and the choruses had been badly choreographed. Sartre persuaded Cacoyannis to cut some of his theatrical effects, but it was too late to make any radical changes.[45]

It was the Algerian War which had first prompted the idea of adapting the play, but the Vietnam War had been worsening during the summer of 1964, while he was working on it. In February 1965 the American air force bombed North Vietnam, and on 8 March, 3,500 US marines landed in the South. Sartre had been due to give a series of lectures at Cornell University in April on Flaubert and on ethics. Continuing the work done for his contribution to the 1964 colloquium in Rome, he had written notes extending over several hundred pages, but in March, to protest against the intervention in Vietnam, he rescinded his acceptance of the invitation. Earlier his Cuban friends had been encouraging him to go: he could tell the Americans about Cuba. Since the raids they had been saying: 'What do you want to do down there?'[46]

At the beginning of May he sent a long telegram to the organizers of a teach-in on Vietnam at Boston University: he hoped they would have more success than French intellectuals had had in opposing the Algerian War; in any case their activities would show the world that the rising generation in America disapproved of its leaders' policies.[47]

TWENTY-FIVE · *Half Way to Revolution*

During the run-up to the presidential elections of December 1965 it was obvious that the PCF was impotent against de Gaulle's authoritarian leadership. The need for a social-democratic party was obvious; the chances of uniting the left were remote. Since the 1920 Congress of Tours, hostility between communists and socialists had been interrupted with short-lived alliances, but in 1963 hopes of rapprochement dwindled in face of the initiative taken by Gaston Defferre, mayor of Marseille and temporarily a presidential candidate, as he made a strong effort to unite all the non-communist socialists into a new federation. Except that he was operating from inside the party system, he was attempting almost exactly what David Rousset and Sartre had attempted fifteen years earlier, but he could not expect any support from Sartre. In two interviews with *Le Nouvel Observateur* Sartre admitted that the left was moribund but declared that it could not be revived by 'defeatists' like Defferre, who offered poison labelled as medicine. The right would be the only possible beneficiary of any attempt to form a coalition that excluded the communists.[1]

It was not only that Sartre had moved further to the left since the days of the Rassemblement démocratique révolutionnaire; his horizons were different. After his encounters with Castro and Fanon, after countless conversations with members of the Russell Tribunal, politicians, intellectuals, dissidents, militants, students in Italy, Cuba, China, Egypt, Israel, Brazil, Russia and Eastern Europe, he was more cosmopolitan in outlook. In France he was less interested in party politics, more oriented towards the students, addressing himself primarily to them as the only true socialists and the only people genuinely concerned with Third World victims of colonialism. This probably tended to make French students more like what he took them to be.

Though the main explosion was not to occur until May 1968, the pressure was building steadily. The student population, only 175,000 in 1958, grew to 330,000 by the summer of 1964, and little had been done to adjust the antiquated educational system. Everyone who passed the *baccalauréat* was entitled to a place at a university, but almost fifty per cent of the students were dropping out by the end of the first year. Attempts were being made to recruit new teachers. Four new universities had been created (at Amiens, Orléans, Rheims and Rouen) while in Paris extensions were built to the Sorbonne – faculties in the rue de Censier and on the quai St-Bernard, halls of residence at Orsay and Nanterre. But unhappiness about overcrowding, poor amenities, shortage of money, inefficient administration and sexual segregation in the halls of residence was compounded by anxiety about future unemployment. One reason for the popularity of the student union, the UNEF, which had 100,000 members by the summer of 1964, was that students felt alienated from a system which did not meet their needs. The men who had power – de Gaulle, the professors, the bureaucrats (French universities were controlled directly by the state) – seemed old, traditionalistic, remote, dictatorial, unsympathetic.

In 1964 the Minister of Education, Christian Fouchet, produced his plan for a two-tier system in the universities: some students would stay for only two years. This provoked both hostility and resistance. UNEF campaigned in the streets for a uniform student grant, winning support from both students and the general public, while the union was pushed further to the left, partly by pressure from a hostile government, partly by internal pressure from the militant radicals.

This double movement was characteristic of what was happening in the mid-sixties; the growth of militancy was fomented by unsympathetic efforts to impose discipline. The government, the catholic church and the PCF were unwittingly collaborating to provoke the rebellion. In failing to stop the police in May 1968 from dealing viciously with students who were protesting peacefully, the government was to go on making the same mistake it had already made, together with the Church and the Party, which had both expelled dissidents from youth organizations. These grievances could not be contained by discipline. From 1963 onwards the militants who dominated the catholic students union JEC (Jeunesse étudiante chrétienne) and the communist students union UEC (Union des étudiants communistes) took over leadership of the UNEF.

The new secretary general of the PCF was Waldeck Rochet, a man of Burgundian peasant origin, more flexible than his predecessor, Thorez, but not flexible enough for the dangerous situation. The defeat of Defferre's plans for a federation and his withdrawal from presidential candidacy made a communist-socialist alliance look feasible again, and Rochet pledged the PCF to support Mitterrand in the election, expelling the UEC rebels who objected. Sartre was the ally of these rebels, who had been inspired by the ideas of Togliatti, filtered to them through *Les Temps modernes*. His supporters in the UEC were known as the *italiens* and at the congress of 1963 they won control of the union. After this, Sartrean ideas and terms were noticeable in its manifestos.[2]

This was not the only way in which Sartre's ideas were influencing the students. One of the key figures was André Gorz, who since 1956 had been working to steer the review into vociferous support for revolutionary movements adapted to local conditions; from 1961 onwards the articles he introduced conducted a tough campaign against 'neo-capitalism'. Scrutinizing the French educational system in contributions to the review he showed his faith in the revolutionary potential of the economically oppressed students, and when he started writing regularly for *Le Nouvel Observateur*, using the name Michel Bosquet, he had a platform from which he could address a much bigger public. *Les Temps modernes* meanwhile, with the aim of appealing to militant student readers, commissioned leaders of UNEF to write on student *gauchisme*,[3] and in 1964 Gorz published his book *Stratégie ouvrière et néo-capitalisme*: since poverty could no longer be counted on to act as a sufficient incentive to revolution, the concept of alienation should be used to radicalize the better-paid workers, creating solidarity between them and the underpaid proletariat. Sartre not only encouraged Gorz but helped directly to promote the idea of a new working class, privately subsidizing Serge Mallet while he wrote *La Nouvelle Classe ouvrière*, which appeared in 1963; Pierre Belleville's book *Une Nouvelle Classe ouvrière* was published the same year in the *Temps modernes* collection.[4]

Politics was more prominent than ever in Sartre's motivation, but this made it still harder for him to decide on how to allocate his time. Since 1963 China and the USSR had been dangerously at loggerheads and the hostility was exacerbated by the Soviet refusal to help the North Vietnamese with ammunition. Both the Russians and the Chinese were due to attend the peace congress at Helsinki in July, and when Ehrenburg, who was briefly in Paris, asked Sartre to attend so that he could speak up for the Russians, he was uncertain whether his presence could really have much effect, but it was not an invitation he could refuse. He went to Moscow with de Beauvoir at the beginning of July, planning to fly from Leningrad to Helsinki for a couple of days in the middle of the month. Khrushchev had been replaced in October 1964 by Brezhnev and Kosygin; when Sartre and de Beauvoir arrived in Moscow the cultural situation seemed more relaxed. Kafka's work was still unavailable, but Pasternak's was on sale again, Solzhenitsyn's stories were coming out in *Novy Mir*, and Tvardovsky had issued a manifesto asking writers to speak their mind openly. Sartre and de Beauvoir travelled to Lithuania and Pskov, where they visited Pushkin's estate. In Moscow and Leningrad they were free to do as they pleased, but in other towns they were received by delegations of writers who were reluctant even to let them take a walk by themselves.[5]

In Helsinki on 13 and 14 July 1965 the Chinese delegates, who applauded none of the speakers except the Vietnamese, accused the Russians of deviationism, revisionism and a return to capitalism. Ehrenburg not only lost his temper with the Chinese but got upset with Sartre when he seemed to be siding with them by asking for total solidarity with the North Vietnamese and proposing a motion to ask for the immediate withdrawal of all American troops.

In Moscow, acting on Ehrenburg's suggestion, Sartre sent a letter through the Writers' Union to Anastas Mikoyan (president of the USSR since July 1964) asking him to pardon the young Jewish poet Brodsky, who had been accused of 'parasitism' (a charge normally used only against prostitutes) and sentenced to five years of forced labour. Shortly afterwards Brodsky was pardoned.[6]

But in October Andrey Sinyavsky (who used the nom-de-plume Avram Tertz) and Yuli Daniel (who called himself Arzhak) were arrested and charged with publishing anti-Soviet works abroad. When Sartre and de Beauvoir went to Rome at the beginning of October for a COMES meeting, they found Tvardovsky, Ehrenburg and other Russian writers alarmed at this new development. Defying the censor who had condemned them to silence, some Soviet writers were circulating work in typescript, and it looked as though the authorities were about to clamp down on all this clandestine activity.[7]

The theme of the congress was 'The European Avant-Garde Yesterday and Today', and when Sartre made his speech on 6 October, he launched a surprising attack on what he called the phoney avant-garde: Solzhenitsyn, James Joyce, Céline, Breton and Robbe-Grillet, he said, were concerned 'simply to exploit all the possibilities of a given language, experimenting with the limits of the language or introducing a new mode of reading'. All these writers were basically 'traditionalist' and were carrying on a 'dialogue with the dead'. Genuinely avant-garde writers did not just play with language: they created it, giving it to the people. Today it was only outside Europe, Sartre concluded, that avant-garde writing could thrive.[8]

Had he been living in Italy, Sartre might have felt less isolated, but in the perspective of de Gaulle's France, Europe appeared to be tainted with Americanism. In an interview with Mikis Theodorakis, addressing himself to the Greek left which had staged demonstrations during the summer, he attacked American investment in European states: 'For you, as for us, these objectives are inseparably linked: democracy, national sovereignty, autochthonous culture.'[9]

If de Gaulle won the election of 1965, he would have another seven years as president. His popularity had been seriously reduced by the anti-strike legislation and the austerity programmes designed to build up gold reserves and to pay for nuclear weapons. But when Defferre withdrew from the race François Mitterrand was unchallenged as the left's candidate, and it was obvious that he stood no chance against de Gaulle. In the November issue of *Les Temps modernes* the editorial was mainly negative towards Mitterrand, but on the day before the elections Sartre issued a statement: 'To give Mitterrand your vote is not to vote for him but *against* personal power and *against* the drift of socialists to the right.'[10] On the first ballot de Gaulle failed to win an absolute majority, and in the second, a fortnight later, he polled only 55 per cent of the vote.

Had Sartre tried to keep the promises made when *Les Temps modernes* was launched, the review would have forced him to keep in touch with intellectual life in Paris. During 1965 Lévi-Strauss, Foucault, Barthes, Lacan and Althusser had all published major books, but Sartre, though his own reputation was in decline, still took no initiative to define his position in relation to structuralism. In the November 1966 issue of the review Jean Pouillon was to make a valiant, if belated, effort to show that Sartrean ideas were not incompatible with it, but Sartre himself replied polemically and superficially when interviewers questioned him on the subject. In a 1965 interview with Pierre Verstraeten he defined the signifier as the the speaker and the signified as the object, accusing the structuralists of a literary positivism which sank pessimistically to the level of Flaubert: the function of the 'literary object' was to compensate for the inadequacy of language.[11] In an interview about 'anthropology' for *Cahiers de Philosophie* he attacked the structuralists for trying to abstract structure from historical *praxis*: the linguistic model was misleading because it led towards a separation of the practico-inert from the historical forces which constituted it.[12] And in an interview with Bernard Pingaud he baldly condemned Lévi-Strauss, Lacan, Althusser and the *Tel Quel* writers as unhistorical and neo-positivistic. They were all guilty of approaching philosophical and historical problems with a scientific method.[13]

Too busy to engage seriously with the issues, Sartre could not protect his reputation, which was eclipsed. No longer living the professional life of a Paris intellectual, he was no longer felt to be in the avant-garde. If he had been spending more time in Paris, he could have defended himself better, but this is not to say that he would have. Though his popularity mattered to him enormously, changes in intellectual fashion did not.

His increasingly frequent, increasingly protracted absences from Paris, where his life consisted mainly of interruptions, helped him to make headway with the Flaubert biography, spurring himself on once again with reckless doses of corydrane. Since boyhood he had felt more affinity with

Stendhal but more stimulated by Flaubert, who seemed like a cautionary nineteenth-century paradigm of everything Sartre might have become had he not put himself under oath to hate the bourgeoisie, and not resisted the lure of *l'imaginaire*. If he still had lingering regrets about his undeveloped talent as a novelist, he could fight them by characterizing Flaubert as an idiot who became a genius while propelled pathologically into a creativity which was no more than an alibi for passivity, an escape from reality. Henry James noticed that in making Emma Bovary 'the victim of the imaginative habit' Flaubert must have been 'far from designing or measuring the total effect which renders the work so general, so complete an expression of himself'.[14] But the book, for James, is a masterpiece, fortified by Flaubert's ability to project his 'irritated sensibility' into hard facts; Sartre cannot forgive his incapacity for hard action.

As so often before, the question of literary tradition is evaded. Is the work of Homer, Sophocles, Shakespeare, Molière, Tolstoy, Dostoevsky, Kafka, to be dismissed as imaginative and therefore valueless? Once again the two main questions for Sartre are 'How did this man become a writer?' and 'Does his life have a single intelligible meaning?' Sartre had already been worrying at the second question when he wrote *La Nausée*. However reasonable Roquentin's hypotheses about Rollebon appear to be, 'They are simply a way of unifying my pieces of information – not a glimmer comes from Rollebon's direction. Slow, lazy, disagreeable, the facts adapt themselves reluctantly to the order I want to impose, but it remains outside them.'[15] His conclusion is that 'Fictional characters would be more convincing or in any case more entertaining.' The Sartre of the sixties offers *L'Idiot de la famille* as 'a true fiction', but he is obliged to assume that all the necessary illumination is coming from Flaubert's direction, while his approach to both questions is conditioned by the period in which he finally arrives at this project which has so long been inevitable. After abandoning the *Critique*, he gave himself up to long sessions of intensive work on Flaubert. The promise he could not redeem in the *Critique* was to explain the relationship between the individual and history; he now tries to compensate by explaining the relationship between one individual and history. The personal pressures that shaped Flaubert must be shown to have impersonal sources; correspondences must be found between public events and private crises. If Sartre devotes an inordinate amount of space to Flaubert's juvenilia, postponing *Madame Bovary* for one of the two final volumes he will never write, it is because he is working less as a literary critic than as psycho-analyst of a dead patient, and the unrevised prose reads like an uninterrupted free-associating monologue. The early fiction is full of symptoms: here, surely, at least a glimmer is coming from Flaubert.

If Roquentin is both more convincing and more entertaining than the semi-fictional Flaubert who emerges from this *roman vrai*, one reason is that in the thirties Sartre, not yet a public figure, was writing for a public. When his friends accused him of overwriting, he worked hard to trim his prose. In the sixties he was living the other half of his life in public but writing for himself. Any intelligent friend could have advised him, if asked, that the book ought to be no longer than six hundred pages, but he was not open to suggestions of this kind, even from de Beauvoir or Robert Gallimard. He also lacked what Keats called 'negative capability' when he praised Shakespeare as a man 'capable of being in uncertainties, mysteries, doubts, without any irritable reaching after fact and reason'.[16] Determined 'to leave nothing in the dark',[17] Sartre probes persistently into corners that other writers on Flaubert had been obliged to leave obscure.

At the beginning of the fifties Sartre had shown in *Saint Genet* that he was capable of writing a Freudian biography without having made a serious study of Freud; now that he has, he produces what could be called the most Freudian biography ever written. It was Freud who pushed biography decisively away from fact towards speculation. Deeply interested in the art and contemptuous of the insights achieved by nineteenth-century biographers, who knew little and said less about the sexuality of their subjects, Freud wrote several biographical essays, but his ideas about Moses, Leonardo and Dostoevsky have exerted less influence on subsequent biographers than his discoveries about the unconscious and his explorations of his patients' sexual past. In any evolutionary account of biography as an art, space should be given to the way Freud's case histories have prized certainty out of the biographer's grasp. 'Dora' never succeeds in making Freud accept her version of what happened; he never succeeds in making her accept his. During the traumatic lakeside experience she underwent at the age of fourteen, when 'Herr K.' forcibly kissed her, did she feel his erect penis pressing against her? The analyst-narrator is easily able to upstage the subject-patient, whose narrative may distort memories which may themselves distort what actually happened. In effect Freud has redefined the object of biographical enquiry. The goal is now situated at the far end of a swampy field and there can no longer be any rules for what constitutes foul play. But no-one has been more intrepid than Sartre in playing on the swamp.

Perhaps he never had any dreams or fantasies in which he was an analyst with Flaubert's putrefying corpse on his couch, but he makes no secret of wanting to write a case history. 'For this difficult test-case I think it permissible to select a compliant subject who yields himself easily and unconsciously.' The analysable material is plentiful, but is a highly intelligent, highly articulate, highly sophisticated writer such a good subject for what Freud calls 'pathography' as an inhibited, undeveloped girl? It is true that writers – to adapt Kafka's remark about the Jews – 'have always experienced their joys and sorrows at more or less the same time as their Rashi commentary on them', but while the psycho-analyst is intent on bringing to the surface something which has previously sheltered in the timeless silence of the unconscious or the coded language of dreams and physical symptoms, a biography of Flaubert (or of Sartre) will be mainly concerned with translating the written word into the written word. Is the hidden content of Flaubert's fictions really so different from their apparent content? Undeniably there is more difference in the juvenilia than in the mature work, and this is why Sartre postpones his confrontation with *Madame Bovary* for one of the two final volumes he will never write. Analysis of the juvenilia is less interesting to the general reader, but this is not a book for the general reader.

Flaubert once said that his fiction was 'the response to a deep and always hidden wound'. Sartre joyfully takes up the challenge. What had always been hidden must be uncovered, especially if Flaubert wanted to hide it. But can it be uncovered? The importance of Sartre's gigantic, unbalanced, unfinished, almost unreadable book may turn out to reside in the sheer quantity of the energy it throws into a raid on the unknowable. If Sartre had previously seemed peremptory in claiming a knowledge more accurate than Genet's about whether or not his first experience of homosexuality preceded his first experience of stealing, the new biography is still more uncompromising in its refusal to be confined either by ignorance of the facts or by knowledge of facts which contradict the hypotheses. Sartre holds back from speculating about the pre-natal life of the foetus in Caroline Flaubert's womb, but he constructs an elaborate fiction to fill the gap that previous biographers had been obliged to leave for the first six years of Gustave's life. If the family is at fault – as all families are, according to Sartre – this is the time to show it. What Sartre hated most about Flaubert was what he hated most about himself – the bourgeois conditioning, the inclination to passivity, the habit of confusing words with things, the cognate tendency to prefer the imaginary to the real. With himself Sartre fights ferociously against these proclivities; with Flaubert he fights by trying to prove that the child was pathologically propelled towards art by damage that the family inflicted. The main theme of *L'Idiot de la famille* is close to the main theme of *Les Mots*. Sartre's theory is that the passivity Flaubert acquired between the ages of five and nine had foundations laid for it during the second year of his life as he absorbed his mother's rhythms. In the oral phase of sexuality, filial love is determined by the mother's handling of the baby, and without denying that all he can offer us is guesswork, Sartre tells us in detail about Caroline Flaubert's behaviour and baby Gustave's thumb-sucking.

The more a biographer speculates, the more he is liable to slip into disguised autobiography – Achille-Cléophas Flaubert is unmistakably modelled on Charles Schweitzer – and speculations about the subject's infancy can serve as a pretext for smuggling in the biographer's suspicions about his own. Had Sartre ever admitted to himself the possibility that his mother would have preferred a girl? Having claimed that the early death of his father was liberating, he puts the opposite interpretation on the early death of Caroline Flaubert's mother. The baby girl, he insists, must have felt rejected, guilty. Ten years later her father died. His terminal illness was induced, according to Sartre, by an irresistible urge to take revenge on little Caroline for killing her mother in childbirth. When it was her turn to have babies, she gave birth to three boys, two of whom died. After this, how could she possibly have wanted another boy? No, if Gustave had been a girl, Caroline could have used her to compensate for memories of her own unhappy childhood. She could have lived vicariously through the child. Yes, disappointed that Gustave was a boy, she must have been dutiful but unloving in bringing him up. Once again Sartre is intent on forging a myth. In reality there are more grounds for supposing that Anne-Marie Sartre would have preferred a daughter. At the beginning of 1905 she was saying that her baby would be either 'a little Annie' or 'a little Paul'.[18] This helps to account for Poulou's long hair and the habit of dressing him in smocks. And whereas Caroline Flaubert gave birth to a daughter less than a year after Gustave was born – she would then have no reason to go on treating the boy as a girl – Anne-Marie gave birth to no other child.

But in *L'Idiot de la famille* Caroline Flaubert is severely reprimanded for the damage inflicted on the infant who imaginatively tried to be the daughter she wanted. 'Putting her imprint on him she has condemned him for ever to have only an *imaginary* sexual life. An unreal woman in men's hands he will be an unreal man in his relations with women.' It would have been interesting to have this thesis tested out in an objective analysis of the evidence about Flaubert's relationship with Louise Colet, but Sartre has little to say about this.

The title *L'Idiot de la famille* points to his central assumption that Flaubert's development was retarded. According to his niece Caroline Commanville, who was reminiscing in old age, her uncle once told her that he could not read when he was nine. This is patently untrue. He was born on 12 December 1821 and in a letter written before the end of December 1830 to his school friend Ernest Chevalier, he offers with alarmingly precocious sophistication to send his comedies and some of his 'political and constitutional liberal speeches'. Undaunted, Sartre decides that the old lady's memory must have been unreliable and that what Flaubert actually said was that he could not read when he was seven. Perhaps someone then told him that he was 'the idiot of the family'.

The rising of May 1968 has sometimes been called a Sartrean rebellion, and Lévi-Strauss interpreted it as triumph of Marxian existentialism over structuralism. 'In France, you know,' he said at the end of 1969, 'structuralism is not longer a fashion. Since May 1968 all objectivity has been repudiated. The position of the youth corresponds to that of Sartre.'[19] This is misleadingly simplistic. Though Sartre had done a great deal towards making students more politically aware, he was co-operating with a trend which owed more to the Vietnam War, and from 1966 to 1968, while Louis Althusser and Henri Lefebvre were in daily contact with students, lecturing at the ENS and at Nanterre, Sartre was leading the cosmopolitan life which had become normal for him. In 1966 he spent five weeks in Russia during the late spring, travelled to Greece in the summer and in the autumn spent a month in Japan, followed by a week in Russia, later going to London for a meeting of the Russell Tribunal. During February and March 1967 he would be in Egypt and Israel, going to Stockholm in May and to Denmark for two weeks of the autumn.

Ideology played a major role both in the 1968 rebellion itself and in the preliminary build-up of pressure, but underlying the appeal of the various radical ideologies was a huge undertow of resentment. If French students could identify better than any other section of the population with the Vietnamese, it was partly through empathic generosity but partly because the remote, persecuted Asians seemed to reflect their own fate as victims of the establishment's indifference. Nobody cared about them. Overcrowded, under-subsidized, condescendingly treated and inefficiently organized while they were in the university, they would probably be unemployed when they graduated. While Sartre's *tiers-mondisme* was helping to consolidate all these heterogeneous feelings of resentment, the aggressive foreign policy of the US was helping to recruit support for French Maoism. Not only students but lycéens were joining the action committees formed as branches of the Comité Vietnam national (CVN), but the PCF was as myopically hostile to the committee as it had been to the *italiens*, and as half-hearted about the Vietnamese as it had been about the Algerians. The students cared; the Party pretended to care. Whereas the CVN's slogan was 'The FLN (Front de libération nationale) will win', the PCF's slogan was 'Peace in Vietnam'.

The pro-Chinese journal *Révolution* had been founded in 1963, with funding from Peking, and since then Maoism had gathered momentum in France. In Paris its principal ideological stronghold was the ENS, where Althusser was recognized as the leader of a faction strongly critical towards the PCF. Since 1960 he had been austerely opposed to rapprochement with the non-communist left. Roger Garaudy, now one of the Party's chief theorists, had been moving towards Sartrean existentialism, a tendency Althusser denounced most outspokenly in his 1964 essay on Marxism and humanism. Referring frequently to Mao, Althusser insisted on the need to retain all the revolutionary purity of Marxist theory; the masses must be indoctrinated with Marxist-Leninist ideas. Ideological purity obviously mattered more in Maoist China than in Brezhnev's Russia, and, thanks partly to Althusser, this helped to split the French student left. His disciples demanded that the communist student union (UEC) should affiliate to the French Communist Movement (Marxist-Leninist) – the MCF(ML) – France's new pro-Chinese organization, funded by Peking. Intending to counter the danger of disruption, the UEC leaders then expelled about six hundred students in October and November 1966. In December many of these joined to form the Union des jeunesses communistes marxistes-léninistes, the UJC(ML).

This accelerated the fragmentation that was already under way. The Jeunesse communiste révolutionnaire (JCR) had been founded on 2 April 1966 when about 120 young people met in a Paris hall. Trotskyist in ideology but Leninist in organization, the group consisted of 'circles': each new recruit would be kept under observation by other members of his circle for three trial months. One of the leaders was Alain Krivine, a tall dark eloquent student of history at the Sorbonne, the son of a Jewish dentist. The JCR played a prominent part in creating the CVN and encouraging demonstrations against the Vietnam War.

Of the student 'groupuscules' the most obviously Sartrean was the situationists, whose manifestos bristled with his jargon and derived from his ideas. Positive action and theory, they held, must ensue on the negative liberty acquired during the act of revolt. As in the manifestos of other groups, the borrowings from the *Critique* sometimes look like disguised pieces of plagiarism in student essays, but, unlike Althusser and Lefebvre, Sartre was not trying to keep *au courant* with radical student writing. In 1966 he was more ambivalent than they were about wanting a revolution.

When he and de Beauvoir went back to Russia at the beginning of May 1966, they found Ehrenburg and their other friends depressed and anxious about the outlook for the intellectuals. Tried in February, Daniel and Sinyavsky had been sentenced to re-education in a labour camp for five and seven years respectively. Sixty-two writers had put themselves at risk by signing a petition for their release and offering themselves as surety, but at the twenty-third Party Congress, Sholokhov deplored the leniency of the sentence.

Three of Solzhenitsyn's stories had been published in *Les Temps modernes* and it was suggested that he should meet Sartre and de Beauvoir, but after parleying with Solzhenitsyn for an hour, Lena Zonina came back with a refusal. According to her, he had said he would suffer too much if he met a writer who was free to publish his work. But in *The Oak and the Calf* Solzhenitsyn explains his reason for refusing: Sartre had insulted Russian literature by saying that a Nobel prize ought to be awarded to the 'hangman' Sholokhov.

Sartre and de Beauvoir stayed in Russia over a month, visiting Yalta, Odessa, Lvov and Kishinev. After returning to Paris on 6 June, Sartre left again in July to stay in Greece before going on to Rome. In the middle of September he and de Beauvoir went to Japan, accepting an invitation from his publisher there, Watanabe, and the University of Kyoto. They flew over the North Pole, and, when they landed in Tokyo, about two hundred photographers and journalists and over a thousand students were waiting for them. But the first meal of raw fish made Sartre violently sick; afterwards he could swallow nothing for two days.[20] Mr Watanabe arranged for them to see a private performance of a Noh play and a *kyogen*. But after the performance the meal was cut short: a typhoon was expected. They were awakened in the night by the wind. Their rooms were full of dust and uprooted trees lay in the street.[21] From Tokyo they went on to visit Kyoto and Nagasaki; they lectured, appeared on television and, on their last day in Japan, they both addressed a big rally in Tokyo against the Vietnam War. After a month in Japan (18 September to 16 October) they went on to Moscow, staying from 17 to 22 October.

In November they left Paris again, this time to visit London for a meeting convened by the ninety-two-year-old Bertrand Russell, who during the summer had formed an 'International Tribunal against War Crimes in Vietnam', the idea being to use the Nuremberg trials as a model for judging the American tactics in Vietnam. In July Sartre had been approached by a chief secretary of the Russell Foundation, and had agreed to be involved. At the two-day meeting in mid-November Sartre was elected executive president of the tribunal. On 23 November, when an anti-war meeting was held at the Mutualité, the huge audience of young people gave Sartre's speech an enormous ovation.[22] After the writer Alejo Carpentier had headed a commission to visit Vietnam for the tribunal, he reported that planes were bombing schools, hospitals, leper colonies and churches, which were all better targets than straw huts. In January 1967 Sartre and de Beauvoir went back for a meeting in London to formulate questions for the tribunal to investigate and at a Paris press conference on 2 February, Sartre and his former ally Laurent Schwartz, one of the '121' who had been dismissed from his chair at the Ecole Polytechnique, presented a report on the commission's findings. The tribunal was planning to hold most of its meetings in Paris, but a key member, the Yugoslav historian Vladimir Dedijer, who had fought with Tito in the resistance, was refused a visa to attend the meeting convened for February.

Sartre and de Beauvoir did not go to Vietnam, but they had been planning for more than a year to visit Egypt and Israel in the hope of starting a dialogue between left-wingers in the two countries. Writing on anti-semitism in 1945, Sartre had said that so long as there was a single Jew who could not feel safe in the world, Christians would also be in danger, and he had disapproved of all the obstacles Britain put in the way of founding a Jewish state. But since the Algerian War had brought him close to so many Arabs, friendships and loyalties had been pulling him in opposite directions. In December 1965 he had announced that after visiting Egypt and Israel he would bring out an issue of *Les Temps modernes* presenting both viewpoints.[23] He had planned to make the journey with de Beauvoir in December 1966, but they postponed it to February 1967.

Before leaving for Cairo, they were asked to approach Nasser on behalf of eighteen young men who had been imprisoned without a trial for attempting to reconstitute a communist party. Together with Lanzmann and an Egyptian journalist, Ali el-Saman, who had both contributed to reports in *Les Temps modernes* about the situation in the two countries, Sartre and de Beauvoir flew to Cairo on 25 February for three weeks in Egypt. They saw the City of the Dead, visited temples, floated down the Nile on a boat, cruised over it in a plane.[24] When Nasser received them at Heliopolis, Sartre asked whether the eighteen young men could be put on trial soon. If they were, said Nasser, they might get a ten-year sentence. It would be better to keep them a little longer and release them quietly.

Visiting the Palestinian refugees in a crowded Gaza camp, Sartre had the impression that the display of misery had been carefully staged, and at a banquet laid on, not far from the starving refugees, by the Egyptian governor of the Gaza zone, the Palestinian leaders tried to convince him that the Jews should be expelled from Israel.[25] Back in Cairo it was good to learn that the eighteen young communists had been released.

Lanzmann could stay for only the first three days of the seventeen in Israel, but Arlette Elkaïm came out to join Sartre and de Beauvoir. Though they had been invited by a group which included political and intellectual figures, the visit was less official than the one to Egypt. They travelled all over the country, visiting kibbutzim, where the division of labour between men and women struck de Beauvoir as unfair. Sartre spoke at a meeting called against the Vietnam War. They met a number of Arabs, not one of whom felt satisfied with his rights or with the life he had in Israel, and they met Israeli Jews who were campaigning to give the Arabs a better deal. In one kibbutz they met survivors of the Warsaw ghetto risings. On their last day they were received by the Prime Minister, Levi Eshkol, and Sartre held a press conference. He was now convinced that Israel's right to national existence was incompatible with the right of a million Palestinian refugees to live in the country from which they had been expelled.

After two days in Athens,[26] the three of them arrived back in Paris only a few days before war broke out between Israel and Syria. At the end of May Sartre was one of the French signatories of a statement that though they felt hostile to American imperialism and friendly towards the Arab peoples, Israel should be guaranteed its sovereignty, its independence and its right to use international waterways. For many Arabs this was enough to mean that Sartre had sided with Israel.[27]

On 13 April he despatched a letter – handwritten on squared paper – to de Gaulle asking whether the refusal to give Vladimir Dedijer a visa meant that the government intended to stop the Russell Tribunal from meeting in Paris. De Gaulle's reply, which started 'Mon cher Maître', confirmed this ban. 'You will not be the one', wrote de Gaulle, 'to teach me that all justice, in principle as well as practice, belongs to the state.' Sartre then gave an interview to say that the government must be afraid of the tribunal.[28] It met on 2 May at Stockholm. The judges, who had been recruited by Russell's secretary, Ralph Schoenman, from all over the world, included the historian Isaac Deutscher and the American pacifist Dellinger, editor of *Liberation*; the playright Peter Weiss, secretary general of the Swedish committee, was co-opted as a judge. The languages used were English, French and Spanish. Dedijer presided, assisted by Schwartz. Altogether there were about 200 people in the hall.[29] In his opening speech Sartre made the point that the tribunal could enforce its verdict only through public opinion. Unlike the Nuremberg tribunal, it was not backed by a victorious government, but impotence was a guarantee of independence.[30] Two American international lawyers argued that America had disregarded the Geneva Convention and artificially established a South Vietnamese state; a French physicist demonstrated that the anti-personnel bombs – which could not be used against targets protected by sandbags – were designed to kill civilians. Photographs and films showed burnt and mutilated corpses, children who had lost limbs, others who had been disfigured by napalm burns. The mutilated Vietnamese civilians who appeared before the tribunal included a twelve-year-old boy who took off his clothes to reveal hideous burns.[31] The evidence was examined in hearings that continued until 10 May, when the tribunal concluded unanimously that the Americans were guilty of aggression against the Vietnamese and of terroristic bombing to destroy the people's morale. 'What has been important for me', said Sartre, 'is the progress from this vague, already intolerable idea: "Children, women and elderly people are being killed in Vietnam" to this precise and odious idea: "It is being done deliberately".'[32] At a press conference in the Mutualité on 19 May he presented the tribunal's verdict.

Since 1962 he and de Beauvoir had travelled eight times to Russia, but in May 1967, to protest against the treatment of Sinyavsky and Daniel, they refused an invitation to the tenth Congress of the Soviet Writers' Union. Their only regret, retrospectively, was to have missed their last chance of meeting Ilya Ehrenburg, who died on 31 August. 'We liked his intelligence, his courage, the charm of his old, tired face.'[33]

In May Sartre was also involved in writing the preface for a special issue of *Les Temps modernes* dealing with the Arab–Israeli conflict. Over the opening of the Gulf of Akaba he supported Israel, offending Frantz Fanon's widow, who refused to allow *Les Damnés de la terre* to go on being reprinted with his preface.

Another session of the Russell Tribunal was to be held during November in Denmark. In September Sartre and de Beauvoir went to Brussels for a preliminary discussion. Dellinger, who was going to lead a big pacifist march in America on 21 October, asked for the session to start late in November. He hoped to bring some American servicemen to testify. The pacifist march culminated in the siege of the Pentagon at which Norman Mailer was arrested. He was sentenced to thirty days imprisonment.

On 19 November Sartre and de Beauvoir flew to Copenhagen. The sessions were to be held in a trade union building, Fjord-Villa, at Roskilde, twenty miles from the capital. The hall was used as a ballroom on Saturday evenings, and the judges sat behind a long table on a stage, with the dance-floor shut off by railings.[34] One question was whether the Americans were attempting genocide. A Japanese delegate revealed that rice, sugar-cane and vegetables were being sprayed with poison: it was not only the guerrillas who were harmed. A twenty-three-year-old American, an ex-member of the 'special services', testified that he taught Vietnamese government troops how to torture, and had seen American officers pushing pieces of bamboo under prisoners' nails. Senior American officers knew that torture was being used, and a lieutenant or captain was invariably present.[35] Another American described how the wounded were finished off and how tanks and machine-guns would fire for what was called a 'crazy moment' at everyone and everything in a village. Another described the 'strategic hamlets' into which Vietnamese civilians were herded and kept without beds, water, latrines or adequate food. His evidence was substantiated by a French journalist's film. A beautiful Vietnamese woman told the tribunal how she had been hung up by her wrists and had been tied half naked to a tree swarming with ants that could bite. She also described how soldiers had poured over a woman's head a bowl full of pus, the sputum of consumptives, vomit and water in which a leper had washed.[36] A West German surgeon gave evidence about peasants machine-gunned from the air and about depopulated tracts of country – four million Vietnamese had been relocated in the South. There was film, most of it shot by American servicemen, to confirm the stories of gratuitous killing and torture. When Bost arrived to report the hearing for *Le Nouvel Observateur*, he was against using the word 'genocide'; three days later he agreed it was unavoidable.

The sessions lasted from 20 November to 1 December. To prepare for the statement he was to make as executive president at the final session, Sartre had to work at night after the long exhausting sessions, but he produced a cogent indictment of the Americans. When Dean Rusk, the American secretary of state, had said: 'It is ourselves we are defending', he had meant that the first aim was military – to encircle communist China. But since 1965 there had been more evidence of racism – anti-negro, anti-Asiatic, anti-Mexican – among American soldiers, and as there was no possibility of inflicting a military defeat on thirty-one million Vietnamese, systematic bombing of crowded cities like Hanoi and Haiphong was insidiously calculated to prepare world opinion for the idea of genocide. To denounce what the Americans were doing in Vietnam was the only alternative to being their accomplice.[37] What Sartre could not resolve was the fundamental ambiguity in his own position as executive president. His Marxist condemnation of the violence as indispensable to neo-colonialism had to be reconciled with his condemnation of it for violating international law – a bourgeois concept. In any event his speech was effective: afterwards the tribunal unanimously upheld the charge of genocide. But the press systematically ignored the proceedings, and the world remained ignorant of what was going on until March, when the My Lai massacre was exposed.

Sartre returned to Paris at the beginning of December, intending to leave again in January 1968 for a cultural congress in Havana, but he succumbed to an inflammation of the arteries. On the telephone to a Cuban journalist, he expressed admiration for the example Cuba was setting: 'I believe that for a European today it is in Vietnam, in Cuba and in Latin America that his fate is sealed.'[38] But it was rumoured in Cuba that Sartre's illness was a fiction, that he was absenting himself from the congress to avoid confrontations with Arab journalists.[39]

In his address to the nation at the beginning of 1968 de Gaulle had greeted the new year 'with serenity', and during the spring *Le Monde*'s analysis of the political situation was headlined 'France is bored'. In the universities a proliferation of strikes suggested that students were becoming less tractable, while their demonstrations were more violent. Bombs were exploded outside the offices of American organizations.

Lefebvre, who believed in confrontation and resistance to all forms of alienation, allowed classroom discussion to become militant, and one of his most vociferous sociology students, an excitable young German, Daniel Cohn-Bendit, helped a demonstration to form itself into a movement. What happened on 22 March was that news about the arrest of local CVN militants arrived during a meeting in a lecture hall. The group proceeded to invade the administration building, occupying the council room on the top floor. The Mouvement du 22 mars (M22M) was formed by spontaneous combustion. Later Cohn-Bendit, who called himself not the leader but the spokesman of the movement, would say that some of its members had read Marx, 'perhaps Bakunin, and of the moderns, Althusser, Mao, Guevara, Lefebvre. Nearly all the militants of the M22M have read Sartre.'[40]

To prevent a teach-in on the struggle against imperialism, the campus was closed for three days, and the tension was exacerbated by news that in West Berlin an attempt had been made to kill Rudi Dutschke, the student leader, and by rumours that attacks were to be expected from right-wing commando groups. On 3 May, when all teaching was suspended at Nanterre, a demonstration was staged at the Sorbonne. The police were called in to evacuate the buildings. The students agreed to leave quietly, but about 500 of them were put into police vans, watched by a crowd of about 2,000 people, who jeered and yelled. Soon paving-stones were being hurled at the police, who fought back with tear-gas and truncheons. They were brutal not only with demonstrators but with passive onlookers. Three days later there were twelve hours of vicious fighting between police and students.

On 6 May, when Cohn-Bendit and other student leaders were due to appear before the Sorbonne's disciplinary council, the students' union (UNEF) organized a demonstration, and in the Latin Quarter throughout the day students, using paving-stones as weapons, clashed with police using truncheons, tear-gas and fire-hoses. The ferocity of the police, which amazed onlookers, generated extra sympathy for the students. Barricades were built, cars set on fire, students taken off in police vans and beaten up. The next day a procession of perhaps 35,000 demonstrators marched from Denfert-Rochereau to the Etoile, some waving red or black flags, some singing the *Internationale*.[41] This was the day Sartre appeared in the foreground. He condemned the police and together with de Beauvoir, Colette Audry, Michel Leiris and Daniel Guérin, signed a manifesto calling on all workers and intellectuals to give the students moral and material support.[42] More demonstrations followed. The students were demanding that the Sorbonne should be reopened, that the arrested students should be released, that the police should withdraw from the Latin Quarter. On

9 May, the day that de Gaulle made the education minister, Alain Peyrefitte, announce that the Sorbonne would remain closed, Sartre, Lefebvre and Jacques Lacan signed a manifesto: 'It's scandalous not to recognize what this movement is aimed at and what is at stake: the wish to escape at any price from an order which is alienated but so strongly structured and integrated that it can turn the simplest dispute to its advantage.'[43]

Taking sides against the students, *Humanité* had attacked 'the German anarchist Cohn-Bendit'. It was obvious that the unions were not going to let the students lead the workers into a revolution but on 8 May the two biggest unions, the CGT and the CFDT, began talks with UNEF and the university lecturers' union SNESup and the teachers', FEN. The two students' unions, UNEF and UEC called for a twenty-four-hour general strike starting on the 13th and a demonstration against repression. In the evening the Latin Quarter was again a battlefield with barricades in the rue Gay-Lussac and vicious fighting between riot police and students. The CS gas and the tear-gas had their effect, but the students were throwing Molotov cocktails as well as paving-stones.

Interviewed for Radio Luxembourg on Sunday 12 May, Sartre reiterated what he had written in his preface to *Aden-Arabie*: 'These youngsters don't want the future of their fathers – our future – a future which has proved we were cowardly, worn out, weary, stupefied by total obedience ... Violence is the one thing that remains, whatever the regime, for the students ... The only relationship they can have to this university is to smash it.'[44] This message, which was printed in a leaflet and distributed in the Latin Quarter, was in line with the revolutionary slogans that had appeared in the corridors of the Sorbonne and on the walls outside, predicting a violent death for consumer society. Bureaucracy, alienation, capitalism, industrialism, boredom were all anathematized.[45] Every day new slogans and messages appeared.

On 11 May de Gaulle promised to meet the students' demands, but the concession came too late to stave off the twenty-four-hour general strike. Relations between students and workers did not improve when Cohn-Bendit described communist leaders as Stalinist filth; but there was massive support for the demonstrations, both in Paris and in the provinces. Leaders of left-wing parties marched with students and workers, chanting slogans, and though the CGT, using loudspeaker vans in the place Denfert-Rochereau, tried to make the workers disperse, some of them joined with the students to rally in the Champ-de-Mars.

In the Sorbonne red flags flew over the chapel and the statues; the look of the place gave de Beauvoir the impression of an enormous party. Bands were playing jazz and dance music. Hot meals, sandwiches and fruit juice were brought by sympathizers for the students, many of whom were spending the night there in sleeping-bags. There was a crèche in the attic. Press offices were set up in lecture rooms, debate raged endlessly, much of it about the Arab–Israeli conflict. The 'Left-wing Zionists' had a stall next to the Palestinians and a huge variety of leaflets was being distributed.[46]

On 15 May the students swarmed into the place de l'Odéon and occupied the theatre. Soon their black flag was flying from its roof. Passers-by were friendly, and the atmosphere must have been similar to that of Berlin during November 1918 after the abdication of Kaiser Wilhelm. Power appeared to be in the hands of the people. In Paris, though de Gaulle had not abdicated, people had at least momentarily the impression that they were no longer to be excluded from decision-making. Strangers entered into long conversations about education or public transport or taxation as if consensus between private citizens could from now on make itself felt. When cafés were raided by the police it seemed to confirm that the government was nervous of free discussion. The rebels may have got only half way to revolution, but they had shown that revolution was feasible.

Two days later students carried the Sorbonne's red flag to the huge Renault factory at Billancourt with a placard declaration: 'The working class takes the battle flag from the students' frail hands.' The next day strikes began to paralyse France. In Paris public transport stopped and banks closed. Petrol and cigarettes were in short supply. Ambulance drivers had to appeal for fuel; dustbins overflowed onto pavements.[47] Factories were occupied by workers. Soon it was the biggest strike in the history of France, but the rebels were not trying to take power. They were fighting for a fair deal.[48] Different factions made different demands. Workers were asking for participation in management, and middle-class rebels supported them. In her despatch to the *New Yorker* Janet Flanner pointed out that in the past de Gaulle had offered the French people a choice between him and chaos. Now they had both.[49]

By interviewing Cohn-Bendit, Sartre helped him to improve his image. He could not be just a hot-headed radical student if the *Nouvel Observateur* was printing in its special supplement a rational conversation between him and a great thinker. At the end Sartre praised him and the students for 'putting the imagination in power'. The slogans on the walls of the Sorbonne proved how imaginative they were. 'This is what I'll call extending the field of the possible.'[50] On the same day that the interview appeared, 20 May, Sartre, who had been briefed by the secretary of SNESup, Alain Geismar, in a two-hour session during the small hours of the morning, debated in the great hall of the occupied Sorbonne with the leaders of the rebellion. He praised Cohn-Bendit, and derided the CGT for having to follow his lead. From then on Sartre kept in close touch with the rebels. Many of his young supporters were members of action committees, sold the paper

Action, distributed leaflets.

On the night of the 23rd, in protest against the expulsion of Cohn-Bendit, students again built barricades and fought with the riot police. The next day two demonstrations were organized by the CGT to drum up support for the strikers.

At least nine million people were on strike by 24 May, when de Gaulle broadcast on television and radio to promise a referendum, offering to resign if it went against him. Students with transistors, listening *en masse* outside the Gare de Lyon, booed, and afterwards, led by Alain Geismar, marched to the stock exchange, where they started fires.[51] The prime minister, Georges Pompidou, formerly de Gaulle's private secretary, offered substantial concessions over wages, working hours and workers' rights on the shop floor, but the strike went on.

On 27 May, at a meeting in the Stade Charléty, the two socialist leaders Mendès-France and Mitterrand were reconciled, and on the 29th the CGT, which had been absent from the meetings, held a demonstration. The disunity of the left added to the pandemonium. To the middle classes it looked as though France might be on the verge of another revolution: panic-stricken parents moved with their children from Paris to the country, and on 29 May, when de Gaulle vanished, the panic increased. It looked as though he had run away in despair of bringing the situation under control. An evening paper carried the headline: 'French President lost for seven hours.' In fact he knew that, as in the Algerian troubles, he was safe so long as the army remained loyal, and he had gone to consult General Massu in Baden-Baden. Reappearing on 30 May he cleverly regained control by dissolving the Assembly and announcing that he would hold an election. When a large Gaullist procession marched down the Champs-Elysées the same evening, the unions opted against countering it with an anti-Gaullist demonstration. From now on the split between workers and students would be increasingly apparent; the students would try in vain to convince voters that they should boycott the elections. The occupation of the Sorbonne and the Odéon lasted only till the middle of June.

Defending student violence in an interview, Sartre called it 'counter-violence' provoked by the police. It was not desire for disorder but desire for a different order: the intellectual must be willing to fight for his political and social ideals. Inevitably the rift widened between Sartre and more conservative intellectuals, such as his old friend Raymond Aron: Aron's question, formulated in *Le Figaro*, was 'Do you expect a bourgeois state to finance a Cuban university?' To Sartre reasoning and reasonableness of this kind seemed antiquated. His riposte was that because Aron had never become embattled, he was not fit to teach.[52] Sartre also defended the students against communist criticism. Whether they were bourgeois or not, they had stood up for a truly socialist democracy.[53] The rebellious students approximated closely to what he had described in the *Critique* as a group-in-fusion. Later he would call the rebellion 'the first large-scale social movement which has realized, momentarily, something close to liberty, and which, from then on, has tried to devise liberty in action. And this movement has produced people – me among them – who have decided that it is now necessary to try to describe positively what liberty is when conceived as a political objective.'[54] After the election had given the Gaullists 358 of the 485 seats, Sartre categorically blamed the communists for the failure of the rebellion. 'In this crisis I think the Communist Party had an attitude which was not at all revolutionary, or even reformist.'[55] The PCF's official explanation of its inaction was that the conflict could not have been genuinely revolutionary since it had been initiated by neither the revolutionary class nor its accredited organization. Unimpressed by this argument, Sartre still gave no sign of regret at having refused to support Defferre.

Though it is easy to overestimate the influence of Sartre on the events of May to June, it would be hard to overestimate their influence on him. He had never been closer to a revolution, and it changed his life. The most apparent change was that he never again wore a suit or a tie: even for formal occasions he would turn up informally dressed. This was superficial but symptomatic.

What had been happening in Czechoslovakia during April 1968 was what had failed to happen in France during May: workers and intellectuals joined forces. For twenty years no-one had been able to tell the truth about the alienation, the bureaucracy, the nationwide depression caused by an imported, prefabricated socialism, but suddenly the democratic impulse had robustly reasserted itself. A reformist Party leadership was outstripped by popular experiments in electing workers' councils and by solidarity between workers and intellectuals clamouring for the right to unrestricted information. In March, after the resignation of the Stalinist president, Antonin Novotny, parliamentary elections were announced. In June the workers' right to self-management was conceded, and 'committees for the freedom of expression' were set up by factory workers. But on 1 July the 'Letter of the Five Powers' was signed by Russia, Hungary, Poland, Bulgaria and East Germany, calling on Czech communists to oppose the policies of Alexander Dubček, who had become first secretary of the Party in January and taken bold liberalizing initiatives. Lenin had said of the Soviet masses that the new society could be built only by them and with them, but in 1968 the Soviet system was still intent on keeping tight control over the masses in Eastern Europe, and in August the Russian tanks arrived in Prague.

Sartre, who had gone on to Rome after holidaying in Yugoslavia, found himself at a point on the spiral visibly in line with the point he had reached in 1956 during the Soviet attack on Budapest. He had spoken out then against the 'crime' which 'had been made possible and perhaps necessary (from the Soviet viewpoint) by twelve years of terror and imbecility'. The slaughter of Hungarian workers proved 'the complete failure of socialism as merchandise imported from the USSR'. The terror and imbecility had continued: the same merchandise was being exported during Sartre's eight years of friendship with Russia, but he had forgotten the lesson which, as he had said, 'the Hungarians are teaching us with their blood'. Thanks to the new lesson, taught with Czech blood, his break with the Kremlin would be final. The Soviet aggression, he told the communist paper *Paese Sera*, was 'what is called in international law a war crime... It is because I have profound respect for the history of the Soviet Union and am by no means an anti-communist that I feel obliged to condemn unreservedly the invasion of Czechoslovakia... Today the Soviet example, smothered as it is with bureaucracy, is no longer valid.'[56] Disappointingly, Castro applauded the Soviet action, as did most of the prominent Soviet writers except Tvardovsky; the PCF, which had supported the aggression against Hungary, dissociated itself from the new aggression but expelled Roger Garaudy for criticizing it too vigorously.

In another interview for *Paese Sera*, published four days earlier, on 17 August, Sartre spoke to four young Italian film makers about the Venice Film Festival which was to open in September. The National Association of Italian Cineastes (ANAC) had demanded that the festival should be radically changed and the industry restructured. Siding with them, Sartre declared himself hostile not only to prizes and competitions but to evaluative film criticism. This is in line with his attitude to literary criticism. Even in the communist countries, he said, competitive festivals were 'symptomatic of a reformism which is no longer revolutionary', while 'the critics' function should be expository, informative. They should not pass judgment on merit, because it is for the mass audience to judge. The juries are only super-critics and therefore represent the opposite of what culture ought to be.'[57]

For ten years since his narrow escape from a stroke in 1958, Sartre's health had been holding up well, but one day in Rome he had an ominous attack of giddiness. He was with de Beauvoir and her schoolteacher friend Sylvie Le Bon. In the Piazza Santa Maria in Trastevere his legs gave way and he clutched hold of the two women as if he had been drinking heavily, but he had not.[58]

He soon recovered, and, back in Paris, resumed his normal routine. He did not attend the meeting on 11 October at the Mutualité but sent a message which was read out. Denouncing all forms of oppression, he condemned Soviet surveillance of the Czechs and police repressiveness towards the French working class.[59]

He had begun to suspect, as Bertrand Russell did, that the shifting balance of power might bring Russia and America into alliance against China. Together with Schwartz and Dedijer, Sartre and Russell signed a letter in *Le Monde* occasioned by Soviet and Bulgarian threats against Yugoslavia: 'The secret diplomacy of the rulers of the USSR and the US is a threat to the liberty and sovereignty of men, wherever they are. It is essential that in order to safeguard truth this identity of interest between American capitalism and Soviet bureaucracy should be clearly understood and fought.'[60] Later in the month Sartre and Russell again collaborated as signatories – this time with Herbert Marcuse – in an appeal for Soviet troops to be withdrawn immediately from Czechoslovakia, where intellectuals and militant workers were being intimidated and blacklisted.

When Sartre was invited by the Czech Writers' Union to the Prague premiere of *Les Mouches*, he spent three days in the city (28 November to 1 December) without going to see *Les Mains sales*, which was also receiving a Czech premiere. Interviewed on television and by journalists, he was encouraging though cautious. 'Those who believe the Czechs are defeated may find they are making a mistake.'[61] But after the Soviet aggression and the 1968 rebellion, he no longer felt loyal to international communism, no longer believed in the Party as an organization capable of representing the interests of the working class. What was needed was a force capable of uniting the disparate groups, which had crystallized radical opinion to the left of the Party, and they showed that he was in no danger of isolation. Without offering any of them his exclusive allegiance, he could believe what he badly needed to believe – that, unlike most left-wingers of his generation, he was in touch with the young.

His mother was now eighty-six and in poor health, with rheumatism, headaches, high blood pressure and a weak heart. Since 1962 she had been living at the Hôtel L'Aiglon in the boulevard Raspail, not far from Sartre and de Beauvoir, who had both been calling in on her. Nervous of giddiness in the street, she stayed in her room nearly all the time. On Christmas Day Sartre and de Beauvoir went to drink champagne with her, but on New Year's Eve and New Year's Day she was unwell, and on 3 January 1969 she had a heart attack. She was taken into the Fernand-Widal hospital in the rue du Faubourg St Denis, where she stayed for a week, sharing a room with another woman, but after a serious attack of uraemia, she was moved to the Lariboisière hospital, in the rue Ambroise-Paré, where she had a stroke with hemiplegia. Sartre found her unconscious in a cubicle, surrounded by instruments; she was taken back to the Fernand-Widal, given a room to herself and again covered with instruments. For two weeks she was comatose, her right side paralysed, her lower lip twisted. Sartre spent hours at her bedside; twice she put her good hand on his wrist, squeezed it, signalled to him to go away. On 30 January he was summoned to the hospital, but half an hour before he and de Beauvoir arrived, she died quietly. The body was very white; the lips, slightly apart, had resumed their normal shape.[62]

Believing that Sartre had cut his autobiography short for fear of upsetting her, she had expected him to resume it after her death, but he no longer had any desire to analyse the personal factors that had fomented his hatred of the bourgeoisie. In his biography of Flaubert he was co-ordinating social and familial pressures, but he did not want to deal directly with the hostility he still felt towards Charles Schweitzer and Joseph Mancy. Nor did he resume work on his 'dialectical morality'. After writing copious notes during 1964–5 for the Cornell lecture he cancelled, and adding to them before delivering his 1966 lecture at the Istituto Gramsci, he had the feeling that a new book on ethics existed inside his head: all he would have to do was put it down on paper.[63] But for this there was no time. He was not only giving priority to the Flaubert biography but allowing it, like *Saint Genet*, to absorb material that had been prepared or half-prepared for more philosophical work.

He was also trying to arrive at a new compromise – necessary after his rapprochement with Freud – over the unconscious. The new term Sartre introduced was *le vécu*, lived experience. He had previously used a distinction, borrowed from Jaspers, between knowing and comprehending. Knowledge is factual and analytic; comprehension involves intuition and empathy. A biography which merely depicts the subject's experience factually cannot be adequate: the biographer must use his imagination if he is to convey an impression of emotional living. No longer so hostile to *la vie intérieure*, Sartre deduces subjectivity from external events. Like his earlier term 'bad faith', *le vécu* gives him an alternative to Freud's way of dealing with the kind of consciousness that can always elude the torchbeam that consciousness throws on itself. 'What I call *le vécu* is the accumulation of the dialectical process of psychic life in so far as this process remains obscure to itself as a constant totalization. It is impossible to be conscious of a totalization which also totalizes consciousness. *Le vécu*, in this sense, is permanently susceptible of comprehension but never of knowledge.'[64] The experience of the moment always consists of an attempt to unify whatever is confronting consciousness with the residue of all previous experiences. In family life the hierarchical conventions and values create pressures which are interiorized by the child, who subsequently exteriorizes them. His actions reflect what the family has made of him. Sartre's emphasis is no longer on freedom but on conditioning: the child is only choosing to be what he has been made to be.

The overall purpose of the book is to show that Flaubert was the victim of a double conditioning. He was what he was partly because of the family, partly because of literature and language in the state they had reached by the nineteenth century. The phenomenon of Flaubert's art is only a neurotic reaction to his subjective malaise and to the disturbed state of French literature. To describe the cultural situation Sartre brings out his old notion of the practico-inert – literature and language as the residue of past *praxis*. This idea is combined with the argument he had developed in dealing with Mallarmé, depicting the French nineteenth-century writers as 'knights of nothingness'. Flaubert is guilty because he developed ideas which were then taken to their logical extreme by Mallarmé. This use of one writer to denigrate another is characteristic of Sartre's methodology. His quarrel with Flaubert is only part of his quarrel with literature, and having spent so much time with Flaubert, after deriding him as a man you would not want to spend much time with, Sartre widens the focus of his attack. Even Kafka comes under fire. He too had a bullying father; for him too remorse and resentment are indistinguishable. 'Gustave's intention – we guess at it when we re-read *Metamorphosis* ... Something is going to happen to him, something atrocious – death, old age, the name doesn't matter: the point is that he will be *other*. Different and degraded ... In horror Gustave sees the time and place approaching for his metamorphosis into vermin.'

Sartre was seeing himself as a spokesman. Conducting a literary battle against literature without using literary criteria, he was a spokesman for active involvement in contemporary history; returning in the spring to activism he spoke out against the *Loi d'orientation*, the law based on a prescription by Edgar Fauré, the former radical premier, for a structural reorganization of higher education. Nervous of the radicals, de Gaulle was supporting him against the more reactionary Gaullists, and Fauré was expected to compromise between preserving and democratizing the antiquated educational system. The problem of overcrowding, which had prompted the rioting, concealed the more fundamental problem of objectives, and the rebels had challenged French society's tendency to use the educational system as a means of teaching the skills and cultivating the attitudes it needed for its own existence to continue undisturbed. The *Loi d'orientation*, which had been passed in October 1968, involved students and non-teaching staff in electing councils to govern the new 'teaching and research units' which replaced the faculties, but the Ministry of Education kept control over

awarding degrees, and while administration remained centralized, the autonomy of the individual universities was more apparent than real. In February, after thirty-four students had been expelled from the University of
Paris, Sartre and Foucault both spoke at a protest meeting in the Mutualité.
Sartre, who attacked the *Loi d'orientation*, was given a huge ovation by the
students, and in a March interview for the *Nouvel Observateur* he said that
a university should not create an elite but should bring culture to everybody
– students and non-students alike. If he were still a philosophy teacher,
he said, he would let students decide both the topics for discussion and
whether they wanted him to be present. He would support them in their
struggle and above all teach them 'that they aren't petty bourgeois nihilists
but simply youngsters caught in a trap, refusing an education designed
to make them servile'.[65] This provoked a heated controversy, and Fauré
replied in the *Nouvel Observateur*.

During the May rebellion one of the slogans painted on the walls of the
Sorbonne was 'Analysed of the earth, arise', and in the early spring of
1969 the editorial board of *Les Temps modernes* was acrimoniously divided
over whether to publish the transcript of a quarrel between an analyst and
a patient who after twelve years of analysis had taken a tape-recorder into
the consulting room and terrorized the doctor by refusing either to switch
it off or to leave. Prefacing the 'document' entitled 'L'Homme au magnétophone', in the April issue of the review, Sartre describes himself as a 'critical
fellow-traveller' of psycho-analysis. Though he does not go back to denying
the existence of the unconscious, he supports the patient's insurrection
against the doctor who never looks him in the face. How can he be cured
when there is no reciprocity, when he is constantly being judged by a
man who sees him without being seen? Only by rebelling can the object
turn himself into a subject. Granted, the doctor is being threatened with
violence, but the 'inversion of *praxis* demonstrates clearly that the psycho-
analytical relationship is *intrinsically* violent'.[66] This conclusion was unacceptable to both Pontalis and Pingaud, who formulated their reservations
in short statements printed after the dialogue. Pontalis recognized the affinity between Sartre's attitude and that of the student revolutionaries;
Pingaud concedes that there can be no equality in the relationship until
the moment of cure, but defends the situation as contrived to de-centre
the subject in such a way that the process will culminate in the restitution
of reciprocity.[67]

By using his editorial authority to get the transcript into print Sartre
was resuming his warfare against Freud at a moment when France's greatest
representative of authoritarianism was about to topple. After surviving the
crisis of 1968, de Gaulle was defeated in the spring of 1969 by a smaller

crisis which was largely of his own making. It is still hard to be sure whether he was trying to consolidate his strength or to duck out of his economic problems by committing political suicide. Wanting to rob the senate of its legislative powers, and to arrange that in future only half of it would be elected, the other half being nominated by interest groups, he decided, cavalierly, to present the nation with a referendum, making it vote both on this issue and on a plan for a limited degree of decentralization to regional government. To these two dissimilar questions voters had to respond with a single yes or no, knowing that unless de Gaulle got a majority of affirmatives, he would resign. In the past none of his referenda had been rejected, but this time just over fifty-three per cent of the voters refused to support him, and he resigned on 24 April.

In the presidential elections which followed, Sartre, de Beauvoir, Colette Audry, Marguerite Duras and Michel Leiris were among those who signed a letter in *Le Monde* urging voters to support the Communist League candidate, Alain Krivine. But in the ensuing campaign, Sartre gave Krivine no active support, and in June, when the only candidates left in the field were Pompidou and Alain Poher, the president of the senate, neither Sartre nor de Beauvoir voted. They were not alone in abstaining: only sixty-nine per cent of the electorate voted, so Pompidou, who won fifty-eight per cent of the votes cast, had only thirty-seven and a half per cent of the voters behind him.

Beyond Communism (1968–80)

It was obvious that the *gauchistes* who had shown their strength in 1968 would be powerless in the new political situation unless a degree of unity could be achieved and it was natural that Sartre should want to help by using *Les Temps modernes* as a forum for the young leaders of radical groups. Natural, that is, in so far as it had become second nature for him to ignore the lessons of his own writing. The group, he had written in the *Critique*, can achieve cohesion and dynamism unavailable to the collective. But the group, which starts out with a genuine dedication to its class interests, develops vested interests of its own. The Party is a group which takes its power from the class it represents but survives by letting the class fall into passive seriality. Born from the heat of conflict, the group proceeds to snatch defeat from its own victory. This is what the student groupuscules had done, and when, after holidaying in Yugoslavia during the summer of 1969, Sartre went on with de Beauvoir to Rome, where they had a meeting with Daniel Cohn-Bendit and his brother, with Marc Kravetz, with François George, and with others, the young extremists were hostile both towards each other and towards *Les Temps modernes*, which, according to them, had become an institution.

On the night of 1–2 January 1970 five immigrant African workers were asphyxiated in their huts at Aubervilliers when they were trying to use gas as a source of heat. Sartre was present on the 10th when the corpses were carried out of the building. To demonstrate against the deaths a group of people occupied the offices of the employers' organization, the CNPF. The group included Roland Castro, an activist belonging to Vive la révolution (VLR), a libertarian movement trying to preserve the fighting spirit of May, Maurice Clavel, Genet and Michel Leiris. The riot police were called in to remove the demonstrators, which they did brutally, pushing Genet and Clavel down a staircase and herding them all into police vans. Castro, who tried to escape when a van stopped at a red light, was beaten up and held when the others were released. He was charged with assaulting a police officer. At the trial Sartre appeared as a witness for the defence.

In May 1968 Castro had been editing *La Cause du peuple* for the union of young Maoists, who called themselves Marxist–Leninists UJC(ML). The paper's object was to help anyone contemplating subversive action. It published information about strikes, sabotage, squatting and other militant actions which might be emulated, and in interviews and articles it let the workers speak in their own language to other workers about the bosses. Twenty-one issues had come out between May and June 1968, and it reappeared in November, after being taken over by the Gauche prolétarienne (GP) which had evolved out of the UJC(ML) and Cohn-Bendit's M22M. The GP was Maoist, hierarchical and traditionally Leninist in its methods of organizing activism. To Michel Contat, who knew Sartre well, it seemed odd that he should have sided with the GP in preference to VLR.[1] *La Cause du peuple* would now serve as an organ of liaison between factories where the GP had a base.

In the first months of 1970, Sartre, who was close to completing the third volume of his Flaubert biography, was giving a lot of time to activism directed against a government that since 1968 had tightened its grip and against the residue of colonial oppression. On 13 January he signed a statement on Biafra: 'After the assassination of Biafran hope, the reign of political gangsterism has spread all over the planet.'[2] Thanks partly to Russell, he had come to feel strongly, *pace* de Gaulle, that the state had no monopoly of legality, that illegal means must be used to fight legalized gangsterism. Two days later he addressed a meeting at the Mutualité on the situation in Brazil. In February he gave a filmed interview to an international committee formed to support the Mexican people. In March he joined the Israel–Palestine committee formed by the independent revolutionary militants of the *gauchiste* groups. Though his Maoist friends complained about the time he was devoting to a biography which could appeal only to a small minority, he refused to abandon it. He was still a writer, and his quarrel with Flaubert had not been settled.

In the middle of April he had lunch at La Coupole with the two leaders of the GP, Geismar and Benny Lévy, and with other leading *gauchistes*. He had only a rough idea of the GP's policies or principles and had recently come under acid attack in the paper, but the impression he gave Geismar was that he felt honoured by the invitation to become involved. *La Cause du peuple* was in danger of being suppressed. It had not been banned, but two successive editors, Jean-Pierre Le Dantec and Michel Le Bris, had been arrested; as soon as copies of the paper came off the press, they were regularly, though illegally, confiscated by the police. When de Gaulle said: 'You don't arrest Voltaire', Sartre had been irked by his immunity, but now he could use it as a weapon. Within two weeks he had agreed to take over nominal responsibility for the paper and its supplements, together with the Maoist-communist *La Parole au peuple* and *Révolution*, which was published by a dissident group from the Communist League. He was not being asked to edit the papers, but to let his name be used. From May onwards *La Cause du peuple* gave him a back page credit as managing director, and, together with de Beauvoir's, his name appeared on every other page. Printed in red and black on cheap beige paper, *La Cause du peuple* proclaimed itself to be a communist, revolutionary, proletarian newspaper. The issue dated 1 May printed Sartre's declaration: 'I affirm my solidarity with all the acts which, like those which have been indicated, will translate the violence which *actually* exists today among the masses, to underline its revolutionary character.' But the issue of 8 May carried a correction: the word 'articles' should have appeared instead of the word 'acts'.

Once again Sartre's continuing movement leftwards was dividing the editorial committee at *Les Temps modernes*. The April issue contained a demand by André Gorz for the system of higher education to be scrapped – 'Détruire l'université'. After 'L'Homme au magnétophone' Pontalis and Pingaud had been persuaded not to resign, but there was no persuading them now.

For twenty years Sartre had been ambivalent about revolution. The ideal had been present in the name 'Rassemblement démocratique révolutionnaire' but it had not been a revolutionary organization, and it was only after May 1968 that Sartre felt in no doubt: a revolution was what he wanted. In May, after the twenty-second issue of *La Cause du peuple* had been confiscated, he said: 'What this is about is making it possible through prolonged effort, extending over years, for ninety-seven per cent of the French people one day to make a revolution.'[3] If the interview of May 1968 had helped to confer respectability on Cohn-Bendit, Sartre performed the same service for Alain Geismar, interviewing him about the GP for the *Nouvel Observateur*.[4] The next day, 25 May, Sartre took the chair and Geismar was one of the speakers at the Mutualité in a protest organized by the *gauchiste* groups about the arrest of Le Dantec and Le Bris. About five thousand people attended. Except during the Occupation, said Sartre, it was the first time since 1881 that two editors had been imprisoned. The only one of the speakers to be arrested was Geismar, who said nothing more inflammatory than the others.[5]

While the two editors were being tried on 27 May the Palais de Justice was surrounded by police vans, and there were two rows of plain-clothes policemen in the court. Appearing as a witness for the defence, Sartre complained about the police. 'Threats, searches and arrests have been on the increase for months. This land of liberty has the most conspicuous police force in the world.' And the principal victims were young people.

'The government is framing laws to protect us against the younger generation.'[6] The public prosecutor asked for *La Cause du peuple* to be suspended
for a year. The judge refused but sentenced Le Dantec to a year in prison
and Le Bris to eight months. When Sartre, going up to the bench, expressed
surprise at being free, the judge said there was nothing he could do about
it.[7]

On the same day, Raymond Marcellin, the minister of the interior,
announced that he was dissolving the GP. He was expecting the militants
to put themselves on the wrong side of the law by trying to reorganize
it. The same evening there was a demonstration in the Latin Quarter:
the police threw tear-gas grenades and the demonstrators responded by
throwing back the pins. No-one was injured, but Geismar, who was
illogically held responsible, was sentenced to eighteen months.[8]

At the beginning of June, when Sartre proposed to form a new association,
the 'friends' of *La Cause du peuple*, the police refused to authorize it until
legal action was brought against them: the new association could subsequently be dissolved, but they could not stop him forming it. With ironical
opportunism he was using his fame as a strategic weapon.[9] His thirst for
martyrdom, wrote François Mauriac in *Le Figaro littéraire*, was 'no reason
for putting this incurably offensive person in prison'.[10]

The creation of the 'friends' was followed a week later by the creation
of the Secours rouge. On 18 June Sartre gave a press conference. The
object was to provide legal, moral and material support for victims of oppression and their families. But the organization was soon to extend its political
activities, trying to co-ordinate *gauchiste* groups and organize demonstrations. What Sartre wanted, above all, was to encourage solidarity between
workers and intellectuals. Useful though he was, the radical leaders thought
him politically naive.[11]

On 20 June, together with the film director François Truffaut, he was
distributing *La Cause du peuple* in the marketplace on the rue Daguerre
when a policeman, taking him by the arm, told him to come along to the
station. Someone in the crowd shouted: 'You're arresting a Nobel Prize'
(sic). Immediately the policeman let go and hurried away. Sartre followed
him, and people yelled 'Stop, thief!' but the policeman got away.[12] Six
days later, when Sartre, accompanied by twenty-seven other people including the film directors Louis Malle and Alexandre Astruc and the actor
Sami Frey, was distributing copies in the Grands Boulevards, a summons
was issued, but he was released after an hour and a half.

But the summer brought its usual reprieve from agitprop activity. In
July he travelled in Scandinavia with Arlette and Vladimir Dedijer, going
on to join de Beauvoir in Rome. They came back to Paris in September.
The holiday had not given him any regrets about his involvement with

the *gauchistes*: he was willing to go still further. In his view the role of the intellectual had changed since May 1968: what he should do now was re-educate himself by putting himself directly in the service of the masses.[13] In *La Cause du peuple* Sartre was signing articles he had not written and giving his name to ideas he consciously disagreed with. This was in line with his old antipathy to individual personality, but he was trying harder than he ever had when adding his signature to Merleau-Ponty's in *Les Temps modernes* to make himself plural. On the 11th, when the distributors of *La Cause du peuple* had to appear in court, he did not attend but sent written testimony: 'If they are guilty, I am more guilty than they are; if they are innocent, they are more innocent than I am.' He had decided to make himself available for any 'politically just task' he was asked to perform. He announced this in an interview with *L'Idiot international* and after taking over the editorship of the Maoist *Tout*, which had been started by militants of Vive la révolution, he declared in the first issue: 'I am making myself available to any revolutionary newspaper in order to make the middle classes either bring me to a political trial which will be clearly concerned for once with the freedom of the press or – by not bringing charges against me – reveal the deliberate illegality of its repression.'[14] The result was that he nominally became editor of at least a dozen extremist papers, but he was not always told when his name was being used. Nor was he even prepared to defend the quality of these papers. He told *L'Idiot international* that the bourgeois papers were more truthful and generally superior.[15]

Despite all this strenuous activism and despite the two packs of Boyards he smoked every day, his health had not let him down since the moment of near-collapse in Rome during the summer of 1968. But one Saturday evening in September, after he had drunk a lot of vodka while having dinner with de Beauvoir and Sylvie Le Bon at a restaurant, he fell asleep at de Beauvoir's flat, dropping his cigarette. In the morning he seemed well enough, but when they arrived to fetch him for lunch at La Coupole, he bumped into the furniture at each step he took, and after the meal he was staggering. They called in Sartre's doctor, Dr Zaidmann, who returned with a specialist, Dr Lebeau, who said that the disequilibrium might be caused by the inner ear or the brain. An encephalogram revealed nothing abnormal. On 8 October, when the third volume of the biography was delivered to Gallimard, Sartre had an abscess in his mouth, and felt as though flu was beginning. He was half way through a series of eleven consultations with specialists. The circulation in the left hemisphere of his brain was found to be seriously impaired and his arteries, congenitally narrow, had been narrowed further. It was important for him to smoke less. A series of injections was prescribed and on 15 October the doctors made him cancel a journey organized by the Maoists for him to observe the living conditions of the workers in Fossey-sur-Mer and other industrial towns. But he refused to rest. On the 16th he helped to move copies of *La Cause du peuple* from the printer to the bookshop La Joie de Lire, and he distributed the paper in the rue St-Séverin. In the boulevard St-Michel two of the young people distributing the papers were arrested and escorted to a waiting police van by two policemen, who ignored the questions of the journalists: 'What have they done? Why are you arresting them?'[16]

On the 21st, when Geismar was tried, Sartre, instead of appearing in court, went to address the Renault workers at Billancourt. With Georges Michel and two Maoists he waited outside the main entrance but the trade union had been alerted about his plans and had arranged for the workers to leave by a side entrance. The four men went to the place Bir-Hakeim. With his leg paining him, Sartre climbed on an empty barrel and spoke through a hand-microphone to a small crowd consisting partly of activists, journalists and plain-clothes police. He was not at the trial, he said, because class justice had already decided to punish Geismar. The intellectuals, he said, should be the allies of the people, as they had been in the nineteenth century; this was why he wanted to testify in the street.[17] 'Geismar,' he said, 'the man on trial, he is the people himself'[18] – which is reminiscent of his 1952 equation of the Party with the people. He went on talking to the tiny audience as if he were beginning, there and then, to revive the alliance between workers and intellectuals. Meanwhile, Geismar was sentenced to eighteen months in prison.

Together with Jean-Luc Godard, André Glucksmann (a former student of Althusser and author of two books, *Le Discours de la guerre*, 1967, and *Stratégie et révolution en France*, 1968) and some other friends, Sartre was setting up another paper, *J'accuse*, which appeared on 1 November. He was suffering from bouts of drowsiness, but these were probably caused by the medicines and, when consulted, Dr Lebeau reduced the dosage. After another encephalogram had been taken on the 22nd, Lebeau declared that his patient was cured.[19]

Sartre's next idea was to test whether the premiss of the Russell Tribunal could be used against injustice inside France. In an accident during February 1970 sixteen miners had been killed by a carburetted hydrogen explosion at Hénin-Liétard. In protest, Molotov cocktails were thrown into the offices of the management, causing a fire, for which four Maoists and two ex-convicts – probably not the men responsible – were arrested, but the trial was not due to be held till 14 December. Secours rouge therefore organized a 'people's tribunal' in the town hall at Lens. Since responsibility for the explosion lay with the state, Sartre concluded: 'the state-proprietor is guilty of the murder committed on 4 February 1970 ... They consciously gave output priority over safety; in other words they valued the production of material objects higher than human life.'[20] Two days later the six men were acquitted.

At the beginning of 1971 his health was still standing up to the strain. On 7 January, speaking at a Mutualité protest meeting about the situation of the Jews in Russia, he demanded the release of Kuznetsov and ten others who had tried to escape by hijacking a plane and had been severely sentenced in December. Sartre also wrote for the first issue of *J'accuse*, which appeared on 15 January: analysing the concept of popular justice as compared with class justice, he told the story of the people's tribunal at Lens.

In February he narrowly escaped violence at the hands of the police when he took part in a Maoist occupation of the Sacré Coeur. The idea was to publicize the injury done to a boy, Richard Deshayes, who had been disfigured by a tear-gas grenade during a Secours rouge demonstration. Together with the photographer Liliane Siegel, some other Maoist friends and about 200 militants, Sartre asked to see the rector, Mgr Charles, who was expected to be sympathetic. But all the doors were shut, trapping the demonstrators inside the church until the riot police arrived, hitting out indiscriminately. Sartre hid in a corner; one man had his thigh pierced by a spike from a railing. On 15 February, together with Jean-Luc Godard, Sartre held a press conference about the incident, but three days later, resenting the unfair Maoist domination over Secours rouge, he resigned from the management committee.

To any casual observer in the Paris streets it was obvious that the police were prepared for outbreaks of violence, and sometimes there were scuffles between leftists and members of the right-wing group L'Ordre nouveau. When a lycéen called Guiot was arrested after being charged with hitting a policeman, thousands of lycéens protested by sitting down on pavements in the Latin Quarter. Eventually Guiot was acquitted.[21]

In April Sartre took a holiday in St-Paul-de-Vence with Arlette, de Beauvoir and Sylvie Le Bon, staying with Arlette in the annexe of a hotel while the others slept in a building at the bottom of a garden. They went for walks and visited Cagnes, going back to the hotel where he had stayed with de Beauvoir in 1949. When, after returning to Paris, he found advance copies of the first two volumes of *L'Idiot de la famille*, he said he was as glad to see it in print as he had been to see the first copies of *La Nausée*.

Since Fidel Castro's support for the Soviet invasion of Czechoslovakia, Sartre had not been in touch with Cuba, but in April he was asked to sign an appeal for the release of Heberto Padilla, a poet who had been arrested on Castro's orders. The charge was sodomy. After he was released, he and his wife wrote such violent letters of self-criticism that torture may have been used to extort them. Sartre wrote to Castro asking him to 'spare Cuba from dogmatic obscurantism, cultural xenophobia and systematic repression such as Stalin imposed on the socialist countries'.[22] From now on Castro regarded him as an enemy, but Sartre made no attempt to repudiate the influential eulogies he had published in *France-Soir*, such as: 'Castro is at the same time the island, the men, the cattle, and the earth... he *is* the whole island because he refuses to take it or keep a single patch of ground for himself. The Cubans must win, or we shall lose everything, even hope.'

Sartre was still spending time with Wanda and Michelle but his routine was to pass the evening with de Beauvoir except on the two days each week when he stayed overnight with Arlette.[23] On Monday 17 May he was feeling unwell when he arrived at her flat, and during the night he had a slight stroke. The next day he was walking with difficulty and speaking indistinctly out of a twisted mouth. In the evening, with de Beauvoir, he insisted on drinking whisky, which made him worse, and on Wednesday morning Liliane Siegel went with him to Dr Zaidmann, who found that in the left side of the brain the circulation of the blood had deteriorated since October. For the last two months Sartre had not been taking his medicine and sometimes, when the lift was out of order, he had walked up ten flights of stairs. The doctor now ordered him to do no walking.

In the evening his cigarette kept dropping out of his lips, and when de Beauvoir unthinkingly played a recording of Verdi's *Requiem*, he murmured: 'How apt!'[24] When he woke up in the morning, his right arm felt heavy and numb. Dr Lebeau could not come but sent another specialist, Dr Mahoudeau, who attributed the stammer to the twist in the mouth and the lower blood pressure to the medicines. But Sartre still found it difficult to hold a cigarette, and four days later Dr Zaidmann told Arlette that he might never be entirely cured. Within two days, though, he seemed just like his old self, and one day, lunching with de Beauvoir at La Coupole, he pointed at a blue-eyed girl with dark hair and a round face: 'Do you know who she reminds me of?' 'No.' 'You at her age.'[25]

He did not give himself leave to take things easy. On 4 June he assumed control of the Maoist paper *Révolution*, and in the middle of the month, together with Maurice Clavel, he launched the Libération press agency, intending to produce a daily news bulletin. The agency was to be 'a new platform for journalists who want to tell the whole truth to people who want to hear the whole truth'. Calling him 'the nation's red cancer', the right-wing weekly *Minute* said he should be in prison.[26]

By the end of the month he could neither speak nor eat without hurting his tongue. 'Oh it makes no difference', he said. 'When you're old it doesn't matter ... It can't go on much longer ... It's natural to get gradually bogged down.' To his friends he seemed detached, unconcerned. But he was cheerful when he spent the evening with de Beauvoir and Sylvie, especially on 21 June, when they celebrated his sixty-sixth birthday.[27]

Without expecting to live long, he was intending to carry on the fight for an alternative justice powered by public opinion. The next project was to investigate police activity since the beginning of the year.[28] Two hundred and thirty-seven intellectuals signed an appeal for the police to be given a 'people's trial'. It was scheduled for the Cité universitaire, but then banned by the police, and on 19 June Sartre was summoned to court and informed that Pleven and Marcellin, ministers of justice and of the interior, were bringing charges against him for libel of the police department and the police system. The evidence against him consisted mainly of two unsigned articles in *La Cause du peuple* (16 June and 23 June) and the article on drugs in *Tout* (1 February 1971).

The tribunal was replaced by a combination of meeting and press conference at the Mutualité on 30 June. Sartre was not well enough to attend, but he sent a letter and an interview which he had just recorded for Luxembourg radio and television.

Still sectioning his summer holiday, he was planning to spend three weeks with Arlette and two with Wanda before joining de Beauvoir in Rome. But in the middle of July, while in Switzerland with Arlette, he had another minor stroke during his sleep. When he woke up his mouth was still more twisted than before, his speech indistinct, his arm insensitive to heat and cold. When Arlette telephoned Dr Zaidmann, she was told: 'If he's having spasms like that, the arteries must be exhausted.'[29]

With Wanda in Naples he went for long walks and revisited Pompeii. When he arrived in Rome his face was swollen because of an abscessed tooth, but he was cheerful and full of vitality. He took his medicine obediently, drank no coffee or tea, enjoyed one glass of wine at lunch time, slept for a couple of hours in the afternoon, drank beer at dinner, followed by two glasses of whisky on the terrace of the hotel.[30]

No longer needing to sleep in the afternoon when he was back in Paris he went to bed about midnight and got up at half past eight. His mouth was still partly paralysed, making it hard for him to chew, but he started on the fourth volume of the biography, which was to deal with *Madame Bovary* and he toyed with the notion of writing something for the theatre or a new novel. Another possibility was to write a 'political testament'. Benny Lévy, the GP leader, wanted him to write a popular novel, and what tempted him about the idea was the possibility of writing a political testament as a continuation of his autobiography. 'It's time that I finally told the truth. But I could only tell it in a work of fiction.'[31] The novel remained unwritten.

On 24 September he had to appear in court before two judges. He was immediately released, but he said: 'From now on an article constitutes a problem for the rulers, and there is no more freedom in France.'[32] On 27 October in the Goutte d'Or district, which was inhabited mainly by North Africans, a fifteen-year-old Algerian boy, Djelalli, was shot dead by his concierge, who said that he was making too much noise. In November Sartre took part in two anti-racist demonstrations in the area, making speeches through a megaphone. Genet, Foucault and the writer Claude Mauriac, François Mauriac's son, were also involved. A Djelalli Committee was set up. Sartre volunteered for a stint of work at the committee's head-quarters, but Genet persuaded him that he wasn't well enough, and at the beginning of December he abruptly told de Beauvoir: 'I've spent all the health in my account. I shan't get past the age of seventy.'[33] He asked to be cremated and not to be buried between his mother and step-father in the Père Lachaise cemetery. The ceremony should be simple but he hoped that a lot of Maoists would follow his coffin.[34]

Early in 1971, after Geismar had been involved in a hunger strike at the Santé, demanding better conditions for prisoners, Pleven had made promises, but not honoured them, and at the end of the year, at a prison in Nancy, there was an eight-day revolt by the prisoners. At a meeting held on 5 January 1972, to present the public with the facts about the revolt, Sartre made a statement: 'We're law-abiding citizens only because we've given in and given up; they're in prison only because they've rebelled.' Sartre, Foucault and the critic Gilles Deleuze were among those who asked for a committee of the Prisoners' Information Group to investigate the uprising, and in the middle of January Sartre went with Michelle Vian, Foucault, Deleuze, Claude Mauriac and other members of the Secours rouge to hold a press conference about the prison system inside the Ministry of Justice. Quickly evicted, they adjourned to the Libération press agency (APL) where Sartre and Foucault spoke.

At the end of February Sartre went back to Brussels. Lallemant, a lawyer who had helped Algerians to cross the frontier and had arranged for Sartre to lecture there on the Algerian War, had now had him invited to lecture as a guest of the Jeune Barreau de Bruxelles, the Brussels Young Lawyers' Association. Appearing in a black pullover to speak on 'Justice and the State', he found himself facing a fashionably well-dressed audience. Un-deterred, he explained the difference between bureaucratic justice, which 'ties the proletariat to its condition' and wild justice, which he defined as 'the profound movement by which the proletariat and the plebs assert their freedom against proletarianization'.[35] The audience would have been unconvinced even if it had not been distracted by Alexandre Astruc, who was making a film about Sartre. He caught his trousers against something while crawling along the floor with his camera, and suddenly his bottom was exposed.[36]

On the same day the unrest at the Renault factory in Billancourt culminated in a killing. Since the end of January Maoist militants had been distributing leaflets at the factory gates. Some militants were sacked, and two of them, a Tunisian and a Portuguese, started a hunger strike, sheltering in a Boulogne church. On 14 February, Sartre, together with Michelle Vian and some journalists, had been taken inside the factory hidden in a van, only to be thrown out when they started distributing leaflets about the dismissals. In protest against these a demonstration was called for 25 February, and when the workers were beginning to come out, Pierre Overney, who had been sacked a year earlier and now worked as a truck-driver, was shot in a scuffle between Maoists and eight armed security guards.

Back in Paris after the killing, Sartre, together with Clavel, called on all democratic citizens to accompany him to Billancourt on the 28th to investigate what had happened. The investigation yielded little, but more than 30,000 people took part in a protest march the same day, and six days later, before Overney's funeral, Sartre was one of about 160,000 people who marched in protest, though his legs were too weak for him to go more than part of the way. When Renault's personnel chief, Robert Nogrette, was kidnapped, Sartre and Maurice Clavel declared that this reprisal 'was only a normal response to the repression rampant at Renault'. The inadequacy of the PCF's response to the killing provoked Sartre into the most hostile statement he had yet made about the Party. Together with de Beauvoir and Philippe Sollers, a novelist and critic associated with *Tel Quel*, he put his name to the statement: 'The real struggle against the capitalist slave system is from this point on inseparable from the struggle against the PCF in its effort to pervert the communist idea.' He also accused the communists of being 'in league with the government against the Maoists'.[37]

Privately Sartre had misgivings about the kidnapping,[38] which had been carried out by the Nouvelle Résistance populaire, a militant section of the GP which had gone underground, but, having felt sympathetic towards terrorism since the fifties, he was now closer to involvement in it, and prefacing Michèle Manceaux's book *Les Maos en France*, he wrote: 'Revolutionary violence is immediately *moral* because workers become the subject of their history.' (This parallels Sartre's argument about the patient who rebels against being an object to the analyst.) According to the Maoists, wrote Sartre, it was desire for freedom that gave a festive mood to the actions of the masses fighting for 'a moral society' in which 'man, overcoming his alienation, can find himself in his true relationships with the group'. Behind this sentence is an understandable nostalgia for the gaiety that had erupted during the violence of May 1968. Sartre's activism during the seventies was part of a desperate attempt to revive the revolution that had stopped. He was still theorizing but he had shifted from the generalizations of the *Critique* to collaboration with activists who had been influenced by it. He could not have moved further from his earlier view that violence was an immoral interference with other people's freedom.

After another spring visit to St-Paul-de-Vence with Arlette, de Beauvoir and Sylvie, he threw himself energetically back into radical politics, protesting against police treatment of squatters in the 165,000 unoccupied buildings of Paris – especially in the Goutte d'Or district. On 11 April he took part, with Roland Castro and Claude Mauriac, in a Secours rouge press conference about squatters. He also contributed a preface to a book published in Heidelberg by a group of therapists who were carrying out what he called 'the only possible radicalization of anti-psychiatry'.[39] The relationship with the patient should be dialectical, he said. But he was becoming more critical of both the Maoists and *La Cause du peuple-J'accuse* – as it had been called since the papers had merged. After a murder committed at Bruay-en-Artois at the beginning of April, the paper suggested that Leroy, the lawyer accused of the crime, ought to be lynched. 'He must be taken by the balls.' 'Give him to us and we'll cut him to pieces with a razor.' The language of violence upset Sartre who – perhaps thinking of mob justice at the Liberation of Paris – retorted in the issue dated 17 May that popular justice should assume that a man is innocent until proved guilty. But the same issue contained an article signed 'La Cause du peuple' insisting that it was wrong to stand in the way of the people's natural instinct for justice. In the next issue (21 June) Sartre formulated his misgivings about the didactic and working-class orientation of the paper, which was 'less and less democratic'. He accused it of ignoring such minorities as the young, women, intellectuals and homosexuals. In 1970 it had given new voices a chance to be heard, but now it was becoming 'as edifying as a bosses' newsletter ... it's becoming factional and it reflects today's struggles in a very narrow way'.[40] But when the paper, which was doing badly, suspended publication, Sartre went every morning to discussions on how to keep it alive.[41]

He did his best to ignore his own disabilities but the impaired circulation of the blood in his brain was making his memory defective, while his gums were troubling him, he was sleeping badly at night and was often dropping off to sleep during the early evening. A single glass of whisky could reduce him to talking nonsense and lurching when he walked. One evening when

André Puig, who had replaced Claude Faux as his secretary, arrived just before midnight at Arlette's flat, he found Sartre lying on the floor drunk. On the way back to his flat, accompanied by Puig, Sartre fell, bruising his nose and lips.[42]

Before leaving Paris in July for a holiday with Arlette in Austria he signed nineteen appeals and protests, including a statement in support of a hunger strike by Basque political refugees in Paris and a demand that General Massu should be prosecuted for championing torture in his memoirs of the Algerian War. From Austria Sartre went on to meet de Beauvoir in Rome on 12 August. (Wanda was sometimes and Michelle was always being left out of his summer holiday plans, though his friendship with both continued.) Alone on the train to Rome he drank too much wine in the restaurant car, but the holiday in Rome was free from the fits of absent-mindedness that had afflicted him in June.[43] De Beauvoir noticed, though, that eating ice cream would make him hurry to the lavatory, and one afternoon in October, when they were passing the Pantheon with Sylvie on the way back to the hotel, he was walking in front of the two women when he stopped. 'Some cats have just pissed on me', he said. 'I went close to the balustrade and they wetted me.' Sylvie laughed but de Beauvoir knew he had become incontinent. They did not talk about it until October. Twice in her flat he left a mark on her chair before going to the lavatory. When she said he should speak to the doctor, he was surprisingly resigned: 'I've told him. It's been going on for a long time. It's those cells I lost.' In the morning, asked whether he found it embarrassing, he answered: 'You have to be modest when you're old.'[44]

The trouble with his gums had continued: he was suffering constantly from painful abscesses, and the only cure was to have all his teeth pulled out. What scared him was the prospect of being unable to speak in public, but, once accustomed to wearing a plate, he was glad to know abscesses would never trouble him again. As the year ended he was quite cheerful.[45] *La Cause du peuple* was resurrected, and in October he contributed to 'We accuse the President of the Republic', which was printed as a poster. In December he was among one hundred and thirty-seven intellectuals who denounced 'The New Racism' in an appeal published in both *La Cause du peuple* and in the *Nouvel Observateur*.

The most important of all these projects was the creation of a new newspaper, *Libération*. When he had admitted to *L'Idiot international* that revolutionary journalism was inferior to that of the establishment, he was implicitly recognizing the need for a revolutionary paper of higher quality. As he said in a broadcast, 'We believe in direct democracy and we want the people to speak to the people ... If a means could be found of using what's arresting in popular speech, this would be a new form of writing ... we need to reinvent gestures and intonations... if we find this style, which should be the style of all the articles in *Libération*, I think we'll pass muster.'[46] This is Rimbaudian both in its fervour and in its formulation about the need for a new language. After admiring the way *La Cause du peuple* addressed the workers in their own language, Sartre was envisaging a colloquial journalism liberated from the academic prose used in the conventional papers.[47] This idea excited him so much that he was willing to put the Flaubert biography aside for six months to devote all his energy to bringing *Libération* into existence. To raise money for it he started in November 1972 on a series of conversations with Benny Lévy and Philippe Gavi which were to be published under the title *On a raison de se révolter* (*It's Right to Rebel*). It was this book more than any other that displaced his critique of *Madame Bovary*. Lévy, an Egyptian Jew, was using the pseudonym Pierre Victor; he had been at the ENS. A member of Vive la révolution, Gavi had contributed to *Les Temps modernes*. It was Gavi who set out the programme for the new paper. Sartre excitedly took part in planning it; and his original intention was to write a daily editorial.[48]

The spiral of his development was bringing him back to a new emphasis on freedom. Between 1958, when he wrote the *Critique*, and the rising of 1968, the word had almost dropped out of his vocabulary, but his involvement with the *gauchistes* renewed his faith in 'conceiving a political struggle centred on freedom', though he recognized that he was now concerned less with the freedom of the individual than with 'the freedom of the militant'.[49] He had always had strong anarchist leanings, but while he had vigorously contested de Gaulle's claim to a state monopoly of justice, he would not have declared in 1967, as he did in 1973, 'I believe in illegality'.[50]

At the same time his resistance to parliamentary democracy had hardened. As a student he had not troubled to vote, and, much later, he attributed this reluctance to an obscure feeling 'that a vote could never represent a man's concrete thought'.[51] *Les Temps modernes* had often advised readers either not to vote or to feel that they were voting against one candidate rather than for another. De Gaulle's cynical and repeated use of the referendum had shown that autocracy could be given a democratic veneer, and in the January 1973 issue of the review Sartre advanced a reasoned attack on the voting system: 'When I vote I abdicate my power – that's to say the opportunity each person has of forming with everyone else a sovereign group which has no need of representatives – and I affirm that we, the voters, are always other than ourselves and that none of use can rise out of seriality into the group, except through intermediaries.' To vote is above all 'to vote for voting, as Kravetz puts it, that is to vote for the political institution which keeps us in a state of serial impotence'.[52] As in many similar statements, Sartre was using his own *Critique* as his theoretical model and the May rebellion as his practical model.

In February he was doing all he could to prepare for the launching of *Libération*. He disliked television – he had no set in his flat and, not wanting to collaborate with a state-controlled organization, he had consistently refused to appear on television – but he did agree to appear in the series *Radioscopie*. On 7 February 1973 he was to be seen fending off the interviewer's questions about his life and his books to talk about the new paper. He also travelled to Lyon and Lille, for meetings about *Libération*; he went with a team of *Libération* journalists to investigate housing complexes at Villeneuve-la-Garenne.[53]

Anxiety about his health caught him in odd ways. Once he said: 'They'll end up by cutting my legs off... Oh, my legs! I could manage without them.' At the end of February he caught bronchitis, and though he seemed to recover quickly, he overtaxed his strength working on an article for the first issue of *Libération* about the first round of the presidential elections on 4 March. At about ten on the evening of the 5th, while he was watching a film on television at Arlette's flat, his face twisted and his cigarette fell from his fingers. His arm was paralysed. Dr Zaidmann prescribed a course of injections, which restored the use of his arm, but he had enormous difficulty in remembering who people were or what had just happened. When Dr Lebeau arranged for him to see a neurologist, her encephalogram was reassuring, but, disobeying her instructions, he went on drinking and smoking. He would mistake one friend for another, and, even after a doctor at the Salpêtrière had diagnosed anoxia – asphyxia of the brain – caused partly by smoking, partly by the state of his arteries and arterioles, he obstinately refused to stop drinking or smoking, and, the lift in his block of flats being out of order, he once again climbed the ten flights of stairs to carry on with an article he had started about the Greek Resistance.[54]

He let himself be persuaded to take a holiday with Arlette at Junas in the south of France, where he read detective stories, became confused about why he was there, expected Hercule Poirot to arrive, and mistook André Puig, who came for two days, for Vladimir Dedijer. When he went on to join de Beauvoir in Avignon, he was uncertain which of the two women was which. Later he talked about feeling invisible and about having relations with people only if he caused them to exist. Twice he said: 'I'm going to be sixty-eight.' Back in Paris he did not notice that Sylvie had diluted the whisky by pouring water into the bottle.[55] After examining Sartre again, the doctor from the Salpêtrière warned de Beauvoir that another stroke could be fatal; Sartre, who had not overheard the conversation, was aware of the danger: 'One will have to end up by ending up. After all, I've done what I could. I've done what I had to do.'[56]

TWENTY-SEVEN · *Fading Vision*

In April 1973 Sartre seemed better, though not well enough to work much. He wrote a letter to the *New York Review of Books* asking for American deserters from Vietnam to be amnestied.[1] He went back to Junas for a few days with Arlette. After motoring down, de Beauvoir and Sylvie drove them both on to St-Paul-de-Vence, where Sartre, who was listless, complained of being gaga.

Back in Paris he alternated between liveliness and lethargy, lucidity and confusion. What looked like a perpetual smile was due to partial paralysis of the muscles in his face.[2] Once, when Arlette said she had seen a private screening of a film by Lanzmann about Israel, he told her: 'You aren't the only one. Arlette went too.'[3] On 21 May he was well enough to resume the conversations with Gavi and Lévy, but an ophthalmic examination revealed that he had lost forty per cent of the vision in his one good eye. Even with a magnifying glass he found it difficult to read newspaper articles. In July, after another attack of giddiness, he was found to have a thrombosis in a temporal vein and a triple haemorrhage at the back of the eye, but a course of treatment cured two of the three haemorrhages and restored twenty per cent of his vision.[4] He went on trying to write, knowing he would not be able to read what he had written, not knowing that no-one else would. 'I was heartbroken when I looked at this scribble', wrote Georges Michel. 'Totally illegible lines. His handwriting was barely recognizable. Overlapping letters heaped together, lines not straight, rising, falling, like the handwriting of some people who are mentally ill.'[5]

The launching of *Libération* had been delayed, but the first issue had appeared on 22 May and he participated in a discussion with workers at Villeneuve-la-Garenne: extracts were published in four issues of the paper during the third week of June.[6] He signed an appeal for an Ordre nouveau meeting to be banned, and, when it went ahead, published an attack on Marcellin's decision to authorize it.[7]

In July he spent another three weeks with Arlette in Junas, doing very little. He would sit on her balcony for hours, gazing at the village. At the end of the month de Beauvoir and Sylvie collected him in the car for the four-day journey to Venice, where he was to stay with Wanda. He was lucky to have retained the devotion of women who made themselves available whenever he needed them, though he was mostly unavailable when they needed him. Michelle Vian had been his mistress since 1945.[8] Despite jealousy, rivalry and quarrels the relationships survived. Though Arlette, the youngest and newest of the long-term mistresses, was in the most favoured position, the tolerance of the others was boundless. Eating lunch at Menton with de Beauvoir and Sylvie he overturned a plate of fish soup and seemed unconcerned when the two women mopped at his feet. They drove him to a hotel on the Grand Canal, and he went in a motorboat to meet Wanda at the airport.[9]

Wanda was not an early riser, and until de Beauvoir left Venice about two weeks later, he would often meet her in the mornings – he went for walks with Wanda in the afternoon, and spent a great deal of time listening to music on the transistor de Beauvoir and Sylvie had given him. On 16 August, when he flew to meet them in Rome, his eyesight had noticeably deteriorated since the beginning of the month. The oculist recommended by the hotel found a haemorrhage in the middle of the eye, together with the beginnings of glaucoma, for which he prescribed pilocarpine. There was also too much pressure within the eye, though this was soon alleviated by doses of diamox. In the morning de Beauvoir read to Sartre – mostly books about Flaubert. After lunch he slept for a couple of hours. She read to him from the newspapers when he woke up, and they usually had dinner with Sylvie. No longer incontinent, Sartre drank only the prescribed rations of alcohol, coffee and tea, but he did not like de Beauvoir to cut up his food for him. With his impaired vision, his false teeth and his partially insensitive lips he could not help eating messily, but grew irritable when told to wipe away traces of food from around his mouth.[10]

Sitting on the balcony of his hotel room, he could enjoy the sunlight: as he described it later, it was a beautiful white light, very bright, very luminous.[11] He went on hoping that he would be able to resume work, but uncertainty about his eyesight was torture, and, as de Beauvoir noticed, the need to sleep during the day was mainly need for respite from it. He was no longer capable of living on his own, and when they returned to Paris Arlette and Liliane Siegel found him a flat with two bedrooms in a large ugly modern block on the rue Edgar-Quinet. The bedrooms looked out on an inner garden, and the Eiffel Tower was visible from the window of the study. Like his flat on the boulevard Raspail, the new flat was on the tenth floor, but there were two lifts in the block. But before he moved, the lift in his old block again went wrong, and again he insisted on climbing ten flights of stairs. After this he stayed at de Beauvoir's flat most nights until the new flat was ready. He was having injections twice a day and was still sleeping heavily in the afternoons, still uncertain whether he would ever again read and write. Dr Zaidmann explained that he had a thrombosis which made haemorrhages inevitable; the oculist warned him that he would never get his sight back entirely and that he would have to go for a long time without reading.[12] Depressively he let the women make all the arrangements for his move into the new flat, showing interest neither in the furniture nor in what they did with his papers.[13]

In October he was finally brought to trial by the right-wing paper *Minute*. It was nearly two and a half years since it had demanded a prison sentence for him. Attacked by *La Cause du peuple*, which had called its editorial staff 'a bunch of thugs, unpurged at the Liberation, part-time members of the OAS and professionals in the art of inciting murder',[14] *Minute* then sued *La Cause du peuple* for 800,000 francs as damages for libel and intimidation; Sartre employed Gisèle Halimi as his defence counsel. The line of argument had to be that *Minute* had provoked the denunciation. At the trial Gisèle Halimi spoke for more than an hour about *Minute*'s hardline support for the OAS and its encouragement of racist murders. The judge in the end fined Sartre 400 francs, ordering him to pay damages of one franc.

After the trial he went with Arlette to the oculist, who told him that his retina was incurably damaged towards the centre; with special apparatus he might be able to read for an hour a day, using lateral vision. But the apparatus turned out to be useless: the words went by much too slowly. Another examination at the Salpêtrière revealed that he was now diabetic.[15] De Beauvoir took him to a specialist, who diagnosed mild glycaemia, prescribed pills and a sugarless diet without even the fruit juice Sartre had been drinking in the evening. He tried to go on working at the Flaubert biography but when de Beauvoir read *Madame Bovary* out loud he fell asleep. Irrationally he went on believing that his sight would improve within three months.[16]

When he had moved into the new flat de Beauvoir regularly spent the evening there with him, sleeping there five nights a week, while Arlette slept there the other two. One morning, when de Beauvoir wiped some saliva off the front of his shirt, he remarked with an equanimity that looked like indifference: 'Yes, I dribble. I've been dribbling for two weeks.' When with friends he was mostly silent and listless. On 23 November, when he saw a new doctor at the Bicêtre, Dr Lapresle, he was strongly advised to give up smoking. At first he intended to disobey, but soon made up his mind to cut down by rationing himself to a diminishing daily quota.

De Beauvoir and Arlette both spent a great deal of time reading to him until this function was taken over by Benny Lévy, who had given up the

GP. A refugee from his native Cairo, Lévy was stateless. Known to the police as a *gauchiste*, he was making his life still more dangerous by going around like a spy in a comic, wearing dark glasses and a false beard. It occurred to Geismar that Lévy's life would be less insecure if Sartre employed him, and when Liliane Siegel broached the question, Sartre agreed immediately. Arlette was apprehensive that Lévy would take unfair advantage of the ailing man, and de Beauvoir was ambivalent, though she would no longer have to give up so much of her working day. Sartre went on sleeping a great deal of the time while Lévy was reading to him.

In December 1973 de Beauvoir took him to see a new ophthalmologist, Dr Ciolek, who reported that the haemorrhage had left permanent scars on the middle of the retina, which was now dead tissue. On the way back Sartre asked: 'So I'll never be able to read again?' But then he dropped off to sleep in the taxi. In the next few days he went on talking as if he could still read. He dozed during *Temps modernes* editorial meetings, and often sank into bouts of depression. He disliked the flat, he said. 'It's the place where I no longer work.' Accustomed to a chaotic proliferation of books, periodicals, typescripts and files in his study, friends were saddened to see immaculate order. Like a prisoner in privileged solitary confinement, he moved only from his leather armchair to his telephone or his radio and back to his leather armchair.[17] Sometimes he forgot that he was in Paris; often he had the impression that his sight was improving. He said: 'Obviously it's unbearable unless one takes it to be temporary.' Throughout his life of dismissing the past and giving the future priority over the present, it had been hard to recognize that his future was dwindling; it was harder still to admit that it was crumbling into sightlessness. On 8 January 1974, when Lanzmann, saying goodbye, kissed him on the cheek, Sartre remarked: 'I don't know whether you're kissing a bit of a tomb or a living man.' Later on in the evening he asked de Beauvoir: 'I'll never get my eyes back?' She was afraid not, she said, and went on weeping all night.[18]

Though Sartre impressed all his friends by his uncomplaining matter-of-factness, it took him a long time to realize that his eyesight was not going to improve. In another consultation at the end of January 1974 Dr Ciolek assured him that his sight had not deteriorated; Sartre said: 'He doesn't seem to think I'll be able to read and write again', and couldn't help adding: 'for a long time'.[19] Two days later, picking up a paperback in his flat, he held it near the lamp to see whether he could read the title. He could, but often failed to read newspaper headlines. A side-effect of the medicines was to make him lose control of his bladder again, and of his bowels too.[20] De Beauvoir was tactful and self-effacing in helping him to clean up.

After the final conversations in the series with Gavi and Lévy he left on 17 March for a few days with Arlette in Junas, going on to meet de

Beauvoir and Sylvie in Avignon. They travelled by train to Milan, spending a night at the Hotel di La Scala, where they had stayed in 1946, and went on to Venice, where they had rooms at the Hotel Monaco on the Grand Canal. Last year's routine was resumed: de Beauvoir read to him in the morning; he slept in the afternoon; the three of them went for a walk in the early evening. At a Donizetti opera, *Maria di Rohan*, Sartre could see almost nothing of the action on stage.

Back in Paris, he went for check-ups to Ciolek, to the diabetes specialist and to Dr Lapresle, who were all satisfied that his condition was stable. He was becoming more resigned, but there was little that gave him pleasure. 'I have the feeling of living through the same day again and again', he told de Beauvoir. 'I see you, I see Arlette, doctors, and then it starts all over again.'[21] But for urgent persuasion from her he would often have absented himself from editorial meetings of *Les Temps modernes*.

Over the presidential elections which ensued on the death of Pompidou (2 April 1974) the editorial board was divided. Together with de Beauvoir, Bost and Lanzmann wanted to support Mitterrand, while Sartre, like Pouillon and Gorz, favoured 'revolutionary abstention'.[22] If the activist Charles Piaget had been a candidate, Sartre would have voted for him, he told *Libération*, but only because he'd have stood no chance of getting in.[23]

When *On a raison de se révolter* was published, Herbert Marcuse, who was in Paris, took part in a discussion with Sartre, Gavi and Lévy. This was reported for *Libération* by an attractive young Greek girl Sartre had befriended, Hélène Lassithiotakis. Marcuse, who was meeting Sartre for the first time, admitted privately: 'Sartre has always been my super-ego. He may not want to be the world's conscience, but that's what he is.'[24]

Though unable to write by dictating into a tape-recorder, he still enjoyed being interviewed, and the indefatigable de Beauvoir suggested that during the summer holidays she should question him about his life, so that he could approximate to the autobiography he had never completed. Towards the end of June he went with Arlette to Junas, and then travelled to Florence for a holiday with Wanda. When de Beauvoir, who was going to Rome with him on the train, collected him from the hotel, the reunion was reminiscent of her 1939 visit to the army camp in Brumath. Once again he was almost unrecognizable behind a mossy beard, only this time it was white. He could no longer shave and he disliked going to the barber. But in Rome de Beauvoir helped the hotel barber to win his confidence, and when Sylvie arrived a few days later, she bought him an electric shaver.[25]

In Rome de Beauvoir began the long interview which was to continue after their return to Paris. Her motivation, naturally, was mixed. She wanted above all to rally his flagging interest in life, helping him to produce an oral continuation of *Les Mots*. This was how he regarded the interview;[26]

he also told another interviewer that he would like it 'to constitute *our* biography, that of our relationship' as well as an account of his life, but he says little about the relationship. Even if he had been in better health she would have been an indulgent interviewer, more concerned to reassure than to challenge. In detail, many of his memories are inaccurate – he now thought that in the Stalag the Germans had presented him with Heidegger's *Sein und Zeit* after an officer had enquired whether he needed anything,[27] and he claimed that he had not read Kafka until after writing *La Nausée*. In fact he read *Der Prozess* (*The Trial*) in 1934 while still working on the novel.

Essentially a writer, Sartre could not feel fully alive when unable to write, and, back in Paris, could not stop himself from making such remarks as 'You've come to see the dead man's house?' and 'Well yes, I'm a living corpse.'[28] Sometimes the idea of suicide occurred to him.[29] After a routine, stretching over fifty years, of writing for nearly ten hours nearly every day, it was not easy to face a future with no writing in it. In conversation he was slower than before but lucid, though he still had nominal aphasia and he tired easily. The brain was softening because the blood was not circulating sufficiently.[30]

Though the salaried job had produced a permit for Lévy to live in France, he was still stateless; the principal of the Ecole Normale, Robert Flacelière, had made several unsuccessful attempts to obtain French nationality for his gifted pupil. But when Sartre wrote to the new president, Giscard d'Estaing, he received a handwritten reply and naturalization followed promptly. He sent only a brief letter of thanks, but it led to a correspondence with the president: 'Though I'm not on his side', Sartre told an interviewer in 1978, 'this doesn't mean I don't sympathize with him.' But after adding that he had been having a 'dialogue by letters' with Giscard, he stipulated that the interview should not be published until after his death.[31]

Sartre had been waging a lifelong war against himself – not only thinking against himself but persecuting his body, not so much to pleasure his mind as to make it more productive. With his tough constitution he had survived without paying the full price for rejecting moderation and ignoring the doctors' advice, but his period of impunity was over. The war, of course, went on, but for the rest of his life he would be paying a young ally to fight with him against himself. Benny Lévy's task was exceedingly tricky. His main battle was against the apathy which had been encroaching on Sartre – it has left its mark on the long interview with de Beauvoir – and the enemy forces were so formidable that Lévy thought seriously of giving up. When he arrived in the morning he would ring the bell – like Cau and the two other secretaries he was given no key – and Sartre often failed to hear, especially if the radio was on.[32] For the work Sartre had done

Lévy had unbounded admiration, but his task was to maintain a lively rapport with a somnolent old man who in losing his sight had lost what had always mattered to him most – his future as a writer. It was not easy to make Sartre live in the present. In conversation he was obliged to concentrate, but when Lévy read aloud, as he did for much of the time they were together, he could not always be sure whether Sartre was half asleep.

Sartre could not afford to be realistic about his condition. 'My mind is probably as clear', he claimed in 1975, 'as it was ten years ago, and my sensitivity has remained the same ... I feel neither sad nor melancholy about what I've lost.'[33] His emotional dependence on Lévy would increase proportionately to Lévy's success in making him believe he still had a future, if not as a solo writer at least as a duettist. They could collaborate. Though many of those who disliked Lévy would have agreed with Pierre Goldmann that he was a Talmudist who had strayed into Maoism,[34] he appeared to correspond with Sartre's lifelong fantasy of himself as a man of action. The old man who had always detested privacy and interiority could make a fresh attempt, collaborating with a young ex-leader, to write in the first personal plural. Thirty years ago he had started *Les Temps modernes* with the ideal of involving readers, co-editors and himself in thinking that was done collectively; about Merleau-Ponty he had written: 'He showed me what my own thoughts were.' Now Lévy could not only show him but help him to develop them in the direction of a new socialism. 'Of all the people I've known he's the only one who from this point of view gives me complete satisfaction.'[35] While still accepting Marx's ideas about the class struggle and surplus value, Sartre no longer trusted Marxism as a philosophy of power: what was needed now was 'another way of thinking which takes account of Marxism to go beyond it, to reject it and take it up again, to subsume it'.[36]

In some ways Lévy's inconsiderateness was advantageous. Instead of making tiresome allowances for Sartre's frailty, he carried on as if there were nothing wrong with him, sometimes reading in a provocative tone, sometimes posing a demanding question when Sartre appeared to be on the point of succumbing to fatigue.[37] Like an intellectual nurse, Lévy needed to have control over his patient, but the stronger his control became, the more his presence was resented by the women who surrounded Sartre. The only one to be won over was Arlette, who not only typed out transcripts of their conversations but began to study Hebrew with Lévy. What they had in common, apart from Judaism and their North African background, was their youth. They were the last young couple to arouse the jealousy of their seniors, as Olga and Bost once had when Sartre had preferred their company; now the Bosts were among the seniors.

It was unpleasant for friends and colleagues in *Les Temps modernes* to watch a loving interdependence develop between the blind old man and the young Jew. The others could not be sure whether Lévy was abusing his position of trust, controlling the direction of the old man's thinking, using him as a mouthpiece for his own ideas, which had been changing rapidly. During the triangular conversations with Gavi, the differences of opinion had been small in comparison with the consensus. But Lévy had been drifting from Maoism towards Judaism. To de Beauvoir Sartre could say that he did not consider the Torah to be the source of all morality, but his conversations with Lévy had become inseparable from readings in which Lévy did the selecting. One day, when Georges Michel called, he saw an enormous book on Sartre's table – Baron's *Histoire d'Israël*. 'It's not uninteresting', said Sartre. 'It teaches me things I didn't know.' According to Michel he spoke 'like a punished child putting on a good face against misfortune'.[38]

To a large extent, though, Sartre was responsible for Lévy's fanatical pursuit of his Jewishness. A Sartrean idea was boomeranging ironically back. According to *Réflexions sur la question Juive*, a Jew cannot be authentic unless he lives out fully his condition as a Jew. The young Sartre who wrote this did not know that the old Sartre would be in the hands of a young man who would rebound from fanatical Maoism into the equally fanatical pursuit of his Jewish identity.

Sartre could no longer take any important decisions independently. When he was approached about appearing on television in a series about his life, his first instinct was to refuse, but conversations with Lévy and Gavi led to the idea of programmes about twentieth-century history as he had experienced it. Marcel Jullian, the controller of the channel Antenne Deux, agreed to a series of ten programmes. Discussing it in an interview, Sartre said: 'We'll see how far we can go.'[39]

The March 1974 issue of *Les Temps modernes* had contained an article on 'torture by sensory deprivation' inflicted in prison on members of the Baader–Meinhof group, and an article by their lawyer, Klaus Croissant, about torture by isolation. After this Croissant asked Sartre to go and see for himself how members of the group, the Rote Armee Fraktion, were being treated in prison. At the beginning of November 1974 he applied to the German authorities for permission to interview Andreas Baader in prison, and eventually this was granted. In an interview which appeared in *Der Spiegel* on 2 December, Sartre explained that though he disapproved of the group's violence, he wanted to show solidarity with an imprisoned revolutionary militant.[40] On 4 December, accompanied by Lévy, Croissant and Cohn-Bendit, who was to be his interpreter, Sartre visited Baader in the Stammheim prison at Stuttgart, where he was in the fourth week of a hunger strike. Afterwards Sartre gave a press conference and later, together with Heinrich Böll, appeared on German television to appeal for the creation of an international committee to protect the interests of political prisoners. But, as Sartre realized, his efforts were ineffectual or possibly counter-productive: it was useless to explain that he was not condoning what Baader had done, only protesting against the conditions of his imprisonment. The intervention was treated abusively by the German press.

Sartre gave another press conference in Paris on 10 December, with Croissant and Geismar on the platform. By then he was having three meetings a week with de Beauvoir, Lévy and Gavi to plan for the ten television programmes. Each programme was to last for ninety minutes, with the final fifteen minutes devoted to present-day problems. In December Gavi made a serious tactical mistake, writing in *Libération* that if Sartre agreed to work for television it was only in order to make it look ridiculous, but during the first three months of 1975, preparations for the series went ahead. To do the research, a team of young historians was recruited, mostly by Lévy and Gavi. After preliminary meetings on 5 January and 1 February, they settled down to a routine of monthly meetings. They were divided into groups, working separately on the themes Sartre, de Beauvoir, Lévy and Gavi had planned. Jullian made preliminary payments on 22 January and 6 March, but no contract had been signed. The historians did not want to be mere researchers with no control over how their contributions were used, and Sartre was in no state to dominate meetings. Unable to see other people, he tended to remain silent, while Lévy did most of the talking, authoritatively but not always tactfully.

In March Sartre left Paris to stay with Arlette at Junas, where they were joined by Michel Contat, who tape-recorded a long interview, spanning three days. Contat, who had written a study of *Les Séquestrés d'Altona*, was doing a lot of underpaid bibliographical work on *Les Ecrits de Sartre*, which was to be published by Gallimard, and Sartre agreed to his proposal that they should have equal shares in earnings from the interview, which could be sold all over the world. It yielded each of them about 50,000 francs.

Nothing had been settled about the television programmes when Sartre left Paris again on 23 March for a visit with de Beauvoir to Portugal. What had originally been planned as a holiday turned into a fact-gathering tour; they were joined by Lévy and the editor of *Libération*, Serge July. In April 1974 the fascistic Portuguese government had been overturned by a military coup and the Armed Forces' Movement (MFA) had gained popular support. Sartre and de Beauvoir stayed at a hotel in the centre of Lisbon near a noisy open-air market. Generally the mood of the city seemed cheerful. Sartre met members of the MFA, lectured to unresponsive students, visited a democratic factory near Oporto. In a series of five interviews published between 22 and 26 April in *Libération*, Sartre came out on the side of the MFA. As during his visit to Cuba, he was naively optimistic about the 'creativity of the masses' and even about the prospect that genuine democracy could spread to France. 'They have self-management there; groups create entire hospitals by occupying buildings and even palaces and mobilizing the whole district. They are taking action with the support of the population and are forming a people's power ... It is such a people's power that we would like to encourage through the television programmes.'[41]

Discussion about the series was continuing inconclusively. Much time was spent on planning for it, while Sartre made headway in collaborating with Lévy on a book to be called *Pouvoir et liberté* (*Power and Liberty*). The object, as Sartre summarized it in 1976, was to show that there could be no ethics without freedom and no freedom until both the concept and the reality of power had been demolished. 'A society without power starts to become an ethical society.'[42]

In June a contract for the television programmes was drafted, but Jullian procrastinated so long over signing that Sartre had to take his summer holiday in a state of uncertainty. He started the holiday with Arlette, continuing it with Wanda, and finishing it with de Beauvoir and Sylvie, this time – since he wanted to be with Hélène – in Greece instead of Rome. The two women, who had driven southwards, collected him at the airport in Athens. Hélène was working at the university there and Sartre, de Beauvoir and Sylvie divided their time between Crete, Rhodes and Athens.

Back in Paris, they had an angry confrontation with Jullian, who had asked them to make a pilot programme. Behind this disingenuous proposal was the fact that their synopses for the series had been submitted to the prime minister, Jacques Chirac, who wanted the idea to be dropped. Two days after the meeting with Jullian Sartre gave a press conference. 'I have been made to give up: it's a case of formal indirect censorship.' He would never again appear on television either in France or abroad, he promised.[43] He did take part in a programme put out by Radio-Télévision Luxembourgeoise to explain what had happened, but he was depressed and exhausted.

At times the corner of his mouth and the tip of his tongue were partially paralysed, and early in October he collapsed or lost his balance several times. Dr Zaidmann gave him injections. His blood pressure had risen from 140 to 200, and he could not walk even from his bed to the lavatory without help. De Beauvoir stayed in his flat to nurse him. Two days later his blood pressure was 215. Dr Zaidmann and Dr Lapresle called together and prescribed medicines which reduced the blood pressure to 160 within a week at the cost of reducing his control over bladder and bowels. Seeming indifferent, he declared his intention of continuing to smoke but relented, either because of de Beauvoir's protest or because of an article Michelle read: with arteritis, smoking could make it necessary for a leg to be amputated.[44]

He was in no state to be interviewed, and when Gavi persuaded him to talk about Spain for *Libération* he made the mistake of describing Franco, who was on his deathbed, as having 'the foul face of a Latin swine'.[45]

When Sartre woke in the morning his mouth and his throat were partially paralysed: it took him half an hour to drink a cup of tea or a glass of juice. He also had difficulty in walking even short distances, and on 20 October Dr Lapresle told de Beauvoir that physically Sartre had sunk to a level from which he would never again rise.[46] Mentally he was lucid enough to work regularly with Lévy on *Pouvoir et liberté*. Arlette rented a television set for him and, sitting close to the screen, he could enjoy watching films.

When a threatening letter had arrived from an extreme right-wing group that claimed to have blown up Photo-Libération, the picture library offshoot of the press agency, he seemed unperturbed; but de Beauvoir had an armoured door installed. Before the year ended he had recovered sufficiently to take a short holiday with her and Sylvie in Geneva.

During 1976 he was able, without too much exertion, to support demonstrations and appeals that struck him as important. In January he declared his solidarity with a group of Paris militants who had been imprisoned for occupying an annexe of the Soviet embassy in protest against oppression in Russia; in March, to help the dissident Dr Mikhail Stern, who was in prison there, Sartre and de Beauvoir arranged for fifty Nobel prize-winners to join them in signing a *Libération* appeal for his release. In March, after thinking for some time about the murder of Pier-Paolo Pasolini, Sartre took only three hours to produce an article about him. After writing it out illegibly, he dictated it from memory to de Beauvoir, and it was published in the *Corriere della Sera*.[47]

Later in the month he left for Venice with de Beauvoir and Sylvie. Though he could take only short steps, he willingly went on long walks with de Beauvoir. 'It doesn't bore you having a little friend who walks so slowly?' he asked her. But when, suffering from a neuralgic pain in her right arm, she was talking about old age and said: 'There's always something wrong somewhere', he retorted with conviction: 'Not me. There's nothing wrong with me.' She had to laugh, and so, after a moment, did he.[48]

He had not been back in Paris for long when the news broke about the death of Ulrike Meinhof in a German prison. Sartre expressed his 'horror at a tragic end'.[49] Nor did he stay in Paris long. He left to stay with Arlette in Junas and with Wanda in Venice, dividing a month between them before spending nearly three weeks with de Beauvoir and Sylvie in Capri. After driving to Rome, he stayed there with de Beauvoir for nearly a fortnight before flying to Athens, where he passed the days with her and the evenings with Hélène.

In the autumn he stayed away from editorial meetings but resumed his routine of working three hours a day with Lévy. When new members were needed for the editorial committee at *Les Temps modernes* – Bost was becoming too deaf and Lanzmann too busy – Lévy was co-opted, together with François George, Pierre Rigoulot, Pierre Goldmann and Claire Etcherelli. Because of Lévy Sartre started coming to the meetings again.[50]

In November he accepted an honorary degree from the University of Jerusalem, but not without declaring – in a speech which he learned by heart – his concern about the Palestinian refugees and his willingness to accept a degree from Cairo University, should he be offered one.[51]

By January 1977 he could hardly walk. He had pains in his left leg and when he went with de Beauvoir to the Brazilian restaurant – a short journey which had been easy in December – he had to stop three times on the way, arriving breathless and in pain. Of the women who were seeing him regularly Michelle had always been the least strict about letting him drink, but de Beauvoir and Arlette saw no danger in letting her sleep in his flat on Saturday nights. On Saturday evenings Wanda was with him until eleven and it was not easy for de Beauvoir or Arlette to take over from her so late. One Sunday evening at nine he was so ill that de Beauvoir dialled SOS on the telephone to call a doctor. Sartre's blood pressure was 250 but it dropped to 140 after an injection. Told that she could no longer sleep in the flat on Saturday nights, Michelle said she had been trying to let him die cheerfully, believing this to be what he wanted.[52]

In the middle of February he was well enough to fly with Lévy to Athens for a week. Hélène had arranged for him to give a lecture at the university there on the 22nd. After six days of lunching with Lévy, dining with Hélène and thinking about the lecture, he spoke on 'What is philosophy?' to an audience of about 1,500.[53]

Just over two weeks later Hélène came to Paris, but on her first evening, after taking her to the Brazilian restaurant, Sartre collapsed on the way back. In the morning his blood pressure was 220, although he had drunk very little, and Dr Cournot, who came in the evening, discovered there had been a spasm in his leg. The next day he had several falls, and when he was taken into the Hôpital Broussais, it was found that his blood-pressure, good on the right side, was poor on the left. After inspecting the results of an extensive X-ray examination, Dr Housset delivered an ultimatum: unless he gave up smoking it would be necessary to cut off first his toes, then his feet, then his legs. Visibly disconcerted, Sartre promised to think it over. Two days later he sadly handed his cigarettes and lighters to de Beauvoir.[54]

At the next consultation Housset prescribed a series of intravenous injections, warning Sartre that any cramp meant he must immediately stop walking to avert the danger of a stroke or heart attack. Housset was not in favour of a holiday in Junas and he gave de Beauvoir a bulky envelope for Dr Cournot. Together with Liliane Siegel she steamed it open, but most of the contents were incomprehensible to them. Liliane took them to a medical friend, who explained that Sartre had only thirty per cent circulation in his legs. 'If he's careful', she said, 'he can live for a few more years.'[55]

Dr Cournot advised Sartre to walk very little during the next few weeks, and, arriving with him in Venice, de Beauvoir persuaded him to ask for a wheelchair. From the hotel, where they were given the same rooms as before, he seldom went further than the bar on the other side of the street. Most of his time was spent either sleeping or listening to music.[56]

When they arrived back in Paris, Hélène was there, and in her company, he said, he felt thirty-five. He was still suffering a lot of pain in his legs, but he celebrated his seventy-second birthday with an eloquent protest against Soviet oppression. While President Giscard d'Estaing was receiving Brezhnev at the Elysée, Sartre was one of the intellectuals receiving a group of dissidents at the Théâtre Récamier. He sat next to Mikhail Stern, who had been released after the appeal on his behalf. But as Sartre's health went on deteriorating, his need for alcohol was increasing; at the end of each session with Lévy he insisted on whisky.[57]

At the beginning of July Sartre motored to Junas with Arlette, Puig and his girlfriend. After going on, as usual, to spend a fortnight with Wanda in Venice, he was collected by de Beauvoir and Sylvie, who drove him to Rome, stopping en route to spend a night in Florence. He and de Beauvoir stayed for thirty-five days in Rome, where Bost and Olga came to visit them. It was hard for Sartre to walk, but he gave a long interview to a left-wing paper, *Lotta continua*. His progressive disillusionment with Marxism now culminated in the explicit declaration: 'I am no longer a Marxist.'[58] It was at about this time that Hélène lost her power to rejuvenate him: he decided that he neither wanted her to visit him in Rome nor to visit her in Athens, but he would go on giving her money to live in Paris. When she came to see him there after his return, he reduced her to tears by telling her that he no longer loved her; he told de Beauvoir that he had never been so surrounded by women.[59]

His feelings about terrorism were ambivalent. In the September interview he had said: 'Each time the state police shoots at a young militant, I'm on the young militant's side.'[60] And after Baader and his group had, according to official bulletins, shot themselves in prison, Sartre, while reiterating his disapproval of the Baader–Meinhof gang's terrorism, had no doubt that they had been assassinated, and he protested vigorously.

After years of trying to encourage peace between Israel and the Arab countries, he was pleased when the courageous Egyptian President Sadat took the initiative of visiting Israel. Early in December Sartre published an approving article,[61] and in February 1978, together with Lévy and Arlette, he travelled to Jerusalem so that he could find out what was going on and perhaps even contribute to a *détente*. After five days of interviewing Palestinians he and Lévy both put their names to a piece written mainly by Lévy about the situation. When it was sent to the *Nouvel Observateur*, Bost rang de Beauvoir: 'It's horribly bad. At the paper we're all quite appalled. Do persuade Sartre to withdraw this piece.' Equally appalled when she read it, de Beauvoir passed on Bost's request. Sartre was quite willing to comply, but Lévy was furious, and at a *Temps modernes* editorial meeting he insulted Pouillon and Gorz when they told him what they thought of the article. After pronouncing them all to be corpses, Lévy never again came to an editorial meeting, and never again spoke to de Beauvoir, who kept away from Sartre's flat while he was there. Nor did she ever go with Sartre to what Lévy called his 'community', a suburban house he and his wife shared with another couple.[62]

Sartre was now under serious pressure. Besides Hélène, Wanda and Michelle were receiving a monthly allowance, while he owed money to Gallimard. When de Beauvoir told him to buy himself new shoes, he said he couldn't afford them.[63] But he took an Easter holiday with her and Sylvie at Sirmione, where they had hotel rooms on the shores of Lake Garda. After returning to Paris he went on working with Lévy. They were accumulating an enormous amount of material on tape – the conversations had been going on since 1975 – but Sartre was increasingly unrealistic about the outcome, believing that the resultant book would contain the tension of disagreements between him and Lévy, whom he still called Pierre. Some passages would be

> written by both of us: the beginning of the sentence will be Pierre's, I'll add a secondary proposition which will introduce a detail; perhaps I'll finish the sentence, or Pierre. The written sentence in these passages will have the value of registering a deeper research than that of one person, because the other will not enter easily into the sentence, he'll want to change it a bit, so that both make every effort to put the best of themselves into the form which has emerged. It will therefore be *better written* by two people than the same ideas could have been by one.[64]

It is not hard to see why Sartre wanted to believe this. His habit was to take less pride in what he had achieved than in what he was going to achieve. To a man who had been proving his freedom by refusing to accept the limitations his body tried to impose, what Lévy appeared to be offering was irresistible: at the same time as breaking down the barriers of the private self, Sartre could feel that he was still active as a writer, still living when he was half dead. More than anyone else Lévy personified the future. But he was no altruist. When he had been a Maoist leader, Sartre had said explicitly that he had no objection to being used and no illusion that the Maoists had approached him for any other reason than his usefulness. He was still useful to Lévy but in different ways.

One result of the unlikely partnership was an Israeli–Palestinian conference. As an Egyptian Jew Lévy had an almost congenital interest in reconciliation between Israel and the Arab countries, and, since accompanying Sartre to Jerusalem in February 1978, he had kept in touch with Eli Ben Gal, an Israeli journalist Sartre had met during his 1967 visit. Another liberal Israeli journalist, Flapan, had taken the chair in 1978 at an Arab–Israeli conference and had kept a record of the discussion, but he was asking Les Temps modernes an exorbitant price for the rights to publish this. Lévy's counter-proposal was to hold a similar conference in Paris. Gallimard agreed to pay the delegates' travelling expenses, and Foucault allowed his large flat to be used for the discussions. On 14 March 1979 Sartre made the opening speech, but said little subsequently, and it would have been impossible anyway for the delegates to reach any useful conclusions or to provide Les Temps modernes with the 'international scoop' Lévy had promised.[65]

For the Easter holiday de Beauvoir and Sylvie drove Sartre to Provence, but soon after their return to Paris he was attacked and wounded in the hand by a half-mad Belgian poet, Gérard de Clèves. Sartre had often given him a hundred-franc note or two when, between periods of confinement in an asylum, de Clèves came to his door asking for money. Eventually wearying of this, Sartre told him not to come any more, and when he did come, refused to let him in, opening the door only on the chain. De Clèves then produced a knife, slashed at Sartre's hand and battered so vigorously at the armoured door that it began to give way. Arlette, who was in the flat, telephoned for the police, who took Clèves away, but Sartre refused to prefer charges. There was a deep gash in his thumb and he had to wear a bandage for weeks.[66]

It was at this time that Françoise Sagan became a friend. After obtaining his permission through an intermediary, she had published in L'Egoiste a 'Lettre d'amour à Jean-Paul Sartre', eulogizing him as the only contemporary 'man of justice, honour and generosity', the only great writer who was equally admirable as a man. 'In short you have loved, written, shared, given all you had to give, which was important, at the same time as you rejected everything offered to you, which was importance.'[67] He asked to meet her and they went out to lunch at the Closerie des Lilas. They had not seen each other for twenty years and she was stammering with nervousness but as they walked she held his hand to stop him from falling. After this they ate together at intervals of about ten days. When she went to collect him at his flat, he would be waiting in his duffel-coat. Though the food travelled unsteadily on his fork, journeying blindly to his mouth, his voice was still bright and brave. She enjoyed listening to music with him, making tea for him, cutting up his meat, especially when he managed to joke about it: 'You're beginning to cut my steak into pieces that are too big. Are you losing respect for me?' He had been embarrassed, he said, to ask for her 'love letter' to be read to him more than once, so she made a recording which he played during evenings of depression.[68]

Before leaving Paris for the summer holidays he took part in a press conference to raise money for aid to Vietnamese who were running away from the pressure put on the South by the North. Many refugees had been collected in a boat, the *Ile-de-Lumière*, anchored off Pulo-Bidong, and the organizing committee now wanted to create an air-lift. André Glucksmann took Sartre to the press conference at the Hôtel Lutétia,[69] where he shook hands with Aron in front of newspaper photographers. But later, after a visit to the Elysée, he recoiled when Aron tried to embrace him. To his former friend's nostalgic 'Bonjour, mon petit camarade!' Sartre replied only: 'Bonjour'.[70]

In the summer he went to Aix with de Beauvoir and Sylvie before flying to Rome with de Beauvoir; in the autumn he resumed the conversations with Lévy. In 1976 he had been confident the book would be published by 1979; he now said they needed another two or three years for readings, followed by two years for writing the book.[71]

At the beginning of February 1980 a check-up at the Broussais hospital confirmed that his condition was unchanged. He was still enjoying life and still finding it easy to make friends with young girls who were glad to spend time with him. Freedom now meant freedom to forget the restrictions imposed by his deteriorating body. In the same way that he had fought fatigue by swallowing corydrane, he fought back against the doctors' regime and the surveillance of the loyal de Beauvoir. Michelle had been wrong to think he wanted to die but right about his antipathy to discipline. The caring de Beauvoir seemed like a reactionary enemy who could be outwitted by subversive friends willing to smuggle in cigarettes, whisky, vodka, which he hid behind books. One Saturday night early in March he spent the night alone in the flat, and in the morning Arlette found him lying on his bedroom floor with a hangover. When de Beauvoir arrived, the two women searched the flat and confiscated the alcohol they found. After scolding Sartre, who tried to laugh it off, de Beauvoir telephoned the girl-friends to warn them of the danger.

At the beginning of 1980 Lévy started to prepare three instalments of excerpts from their dialogue to be published in *Le Nouvel Observateur*. Sartre had always enjoyed quarrelling with his earlier self, but there was no precedent for this attack on the sincerity of his philosophical statements. 'I talked about despair, but it's nonsense. I talked about it because it was being talked about; it was fashionable. People were reading Kierkegaard ... I've never experienced despair, nor seen it as a quality that could be mine. It was Kierkegaard's influence on me.' *Angst* had been 'one of the key notions of philosophy from 1930 to 1940 ... one of the notions I made use of all the time but which didn't correspond to anything for me'. In November 1976 he had said 'anguish and flight from anguish are one and the same for me',[72] but while the earlier statement prefigures the later, the two remain irreconcilable.

Not content with excerpting statements of self-accusation, Lévy made it appear that Sartre would have tended, had he been more honest, to be less relativistic: 'What I did not say in *L'Etre et le Néant*, at least not in this form, is that each man ... has an end which I'd call ... transcendent or absolute, and all these practical ends have no meaning except in relation to it ... and hope is attached to this absolute end.' Lévy presents a Sartre who displays all the contrition of a convert: 'I kept the idea that a man's life manifests itself as a failure: what he has attempted he has not achieved. He doesn't even think what he wants to think or feel what he wants to feel. That leads in sum to an absolute pessimism. Which I did not say in *L'Etre et le Néant* but which I'm forced to affirm now.'

Questioned about morality, Sartre answers: 'Each consciousness has a dimension I have not studied in my philosophical works ... the dimension of obligation ... a sort of requirement which goes beyond the actual and which makes the action I intend conform to an interior constraint.' Sartre also blames himself for placing too much emphasis on individual freedom: 'Other people are always there and they condition me – I left people too independent in *L'Etre et le Néant*. Each individual is dependent on every other.'[73]

Dutifully optimistic, he now holds out humanistic hopes in solidarity: 'What a morality needs is to extend the idea of fraternity until it becomes a unique and evident connection between everybody.' Lévy also led him to a remorseful recantation about Jews: 'What precisely was lacking was the reality of the Jew. Notice that this kind of reality, which is on the whole metaphysical, did not figure much in my philosophy ... I now see men differently.' Sartre's final declaration of faith in history borders on the religious: 'Revolutionaries want a society which would be humane and satisfying to men but they forget that a society of this kind is ... a society in which relations between men are moral ... Well, this idea of ethics as the ultimate end of revolution ... it's by a sort of messianism that you can truly conceive it.'

Reading Lévy's excerpts from the conversations before they were published in *Le Nouvel Observateur* de Beauvoir was aghast, but Sartre brushed her protests aside: he wanted the interview to appear in exactly this form. The first instalment was published on 10 March, the second a week later. On Wednesday 19 March before going to bed he asked her whether anyone at *Les Temps modernes* had talked about the published conversation. No, she said.

In the morning, when she went to wake him at nine, he was sitting on the edge of the bed, gasping. For four hours, since the attack had started, he had been too weak to reach the door of the other bedroom. De Beauvoir tried to telephone for help, but the line had been cut off because of an unpaid bill. Using the concierge's telephone, she rang a nearby doctor, who came immediately, and, after seeing Sartre, called from a neighbour's flat for the emergency service. Blood was taken and an injection given, followed by a treatment which lasted almost an hour. With an oxygen mask over his head, Sartre was wheeled on a stretcher trolley to an ambulance which took him to the Broussais hospital, where he was put into intensive care. The newspapers were quick to pick up the news and, disguised as male nurses, two photographers tried to get into his room. They were ejected and the photograph in *Match* showing Sartre asleep in a hospital bed was presumably taken with a telescopic lens from a neighbouring rooftop.[74]

He had a pulmonary oedema, which had been caused by an arterial blockage that stopped his lungs from being irrigated adequately. He had a high temperature and he was delirious. In the morning, thinking that both he and Arlette were dead, he asked her what it had felt like to be cremated. Once his pulmonary circulation had been restored, he recovered his lucidity. The doctors would allow him only one visitor at a time, so Arlette spent the mornings with him, de Beauvoir the afternoons, and Arlette came again in the evenings, sometimes alternating with Lévy. Sartre sat in an armchair to eat his meals and receive de Beauvoir, but spent the rest of the time in bed. She had already booked rooms for a holiday they had planned in Belle-Ile, but it was clear he would not be well enough. He was moved to a bigger, brighter room, but he had begun to develop bedsores and his bladder was functioning badly. When he got out of bed he trailed a small plastic bag of urine. No longer adequately supplied with blood, his kidneys could not eliminate urea, and he was too weak for an operation to save one of them. His circulation was so poor that his bed-sores became gangrenous.

When Pouillon came to see him, Sartre, after asking for a glass of water, promised: 'Next time we have a drink it'll be whisky at my place.' But the next day he asked de Beauvoir: 'How will we pay for the funeral?' The following day, with his eyes closed, he took her by the wrist and told her: 'I love you very much my dear Beaver.' When she came on Monday 14 April he murmured a few words without opening his eyes and when he pursed his lips to be kissed, she kissed both his mouth and his cheek. By the evening he was in a coma and he did not recover consciousness, though it was about twenty-four hours before he died. Arlette, who was with him, rang de Beauvoir, who rang Sylvie, who rang Bost, Lanzmann, Pouillon and Gorz. The seven of them stayed overnight with the body, but when de Beauvoir, asking to be left alone with it, tried to lie down next to him under the sheet, a nurse warned her that the gangrene was dangerous. She lay down on top of the sheet and slept – or thought she slept – for a while. In the middle of the night press photographers tried to enter the room. At five a.m. male nurses covered the body and took it away.

He was to be buried in the afternoon of Saturday 19 April and disinterred four days later for cremation. Wanting to see the body again on Friday, de Beauvoir went with Bost to the lecture theatre of the hospital, a large, cold room with a tiled floor, and the double coffin was brought in. Inside it Sartre was dressed in the clothes Sylvie had found in de Beauvoir's flat, clothes he had worn for a visit to the opera, a maroon corduroy suit, a light shirt, a tie with an abstract pattern on it. The spectacles were missing, the hair carefully combed, the well-shaved face made up.[75]

On Saturday morning he was again brought to the lecture theatre. The lid of the coffin was placed to reveal the upper half of his body. His hands were clasped; a red rose rested against his neck. De Beauvoir asked Pingaud to take some photographs. Embarrassed, he dropped the camera, which hit the coffin and then the tiled floor. He picked it up, stood on a chair, took about four shots.

De Beauvoir had already dosed herself heavily with valium, and when she asked for more, Sylvie refused at first, only to give in. De Beauvoir swallowed two tablets. She could hardly see. When she was unable to hold her tears back she let them flow, trying neither to conceal them nor to wipe them away. From time to time she put her hand on Sartre's cold forehead. Dr Housset came to bow in front of the body. So did the actor François Périer. The president of the Republic, Giscard d'Estaing, had already come to pay his tribute and had stayed for an hour, alone with the coffin. When people approached de Beauvoir to console her, she said: 'He didn't suffer', as if she were consoling them. When four black-clad men approached the coffin she leaned over to give Sartre a final kiss on the mouth. An official from the police commissariat put seals on the inner coffin, which would go into the furnace at the cremation; the men in black arranged the straps which would be used to lift it from the outer coffin. This too was sealed. Eventually the sheet was folded back over his face, the coffin closed and taken away.

The hospital, which is in the middle of the 14th arrondissement, is not far from the cemetery in Montparnasse, but the hearse had to travel through narrow streets which were more than usually congested. Outside the hospital a woman in black had been waiting for hours, carrying a red rose in silver paper. Before the hearse emerged about 20,000 people were crowding round her. Inside the hearse de Beauvoir, Arlette, Sylvie and de Beauvoir's sister sat with the coffin. Traffic was halted as the procession, moving slowly through the streets, doubled in size and went on growing till about 50,000 people were following the coffin. It was like a demonstration, bigger than any he had attended while alive. For days the newspapers had been publishing articles about Sartre, and Parisians who had not turned out into the streets were watching the procession on television. Hundreds of people had brought their cameras and around the hearse friends linked hands to protect de Beauvoir from being photographed.

Forced by the enormous mass of people to move extremely slowly, the cortége filed past the cafés, the restaurants, the brasseries he had used. Outside his flat in the boulevard Edgar-Quinet, it had to slow down because the mass of people following the hearse had met up with the mass waiting at the cemetery. Many were standing on top of tombstones; those who were straddling crosses had the best view. At the approach of the procession, applause broke out and it continued until the hearse stopped. Around it the crowd was so dense that it was impossible to take out the coffin until several appeals had been made for the crowd to move back. Packed tightly together and struggling to catch a glimpse of what was going on, people trampled on the neighbouring graves. One man was taken to hospital after being knocked to the ground and another, pushed from behind, fell into the grave dug for Sartre. There was no ceremony, no speech. De Beauvoir did not get out of the hearse until the coffin had been lowered into the grave. After asking for a chair, she sat at the edge of the open grave for at least ten minutes surrounded by the vast mass of people. All around her camera shutters never stopped clicking.[76] Sartre could not have pictured anything like this when at the age of twenty he had written the one-act comedy *J'aurai un bel enterrement* (*I'll Have a Nice Funeral*).

Not a Conclusion:
Sartre's Continuing Life

In *Les Séquestrés d'Altona* the action goes on after the principal character has made his final exit: not yet resigned to a future without him, the women listen to the monologue he has tape-recorded for posterity. Apart from the work he left to be published posthumously, including the war diaries and the second part of his *Critique*, Sartre was also the author of a remarkable drama to be improvised after his death. Without knowing what form it would take, he had been mischievously aware that conflict would break out between de Beauvoir and Arlette. By making a will he could have arbitrated, but this would have been to make his intentions clear. He preferred ambiguity. To die intestate was to leave everything, including his literary estate, in the hands of his adopted daughter, but at least it might look as if he had not been deliberate in giving her control – even over the letters he had written to de Beauvoir. The pieces of paper still belonged to her, but she could not publish them legally without Arlette's consent. This was not forthcoming, so she published them illegally.

She had tried not to be proprietorial sexually, but as an autobiographer she had enjoyed writing in the first person plural. The world would go on thinking of him and her as a couple, and in 1983, when she defiantly brought out two volumes of his letters, she was showing the world how ardently he had declared his love to her during the first sixteen years of their relationship. What followed the appearance of the book was an undignified quarrel with Arlette, who took no legal action but reviled her in the press. They were fighting over Sartre as they never could when he was alive.

This is only one of the ways in which Sartre survived himself. His influence is still enormous, but it cannot be analysed because it cannot be isolated. Particles of Sartre are in the blood that flows through our brains; his ideas, his categories, his formulations, his style of thinking are still affecting us. Ripples are still spreading from pebbles he threw into the water.

Even contemporary feminism would not be quite what it is but for the initiative he took in encouraging de Beauvoir to analyse the extent to which her life had been conditioned by an upbringing different from a boy's. *Le Deuxième Sexe* (1949) is very much more than an answer to that question, but it is also an extremely Sartrean book. The first paragraph of the second volume begins: 'You are not born a woman: you become one. The figure presented in society by the human female is not determined by biological, psychological or economic fatality; it is civilization as a whole which produces this creature, half way between male and eunuch, which is called female.' This is a direct application of Sartre's idea about our freedom to recreate ourselves.

No-one has been more directly or deeply influenced than de Beauvoir; his effect on other leading contemporary thinkers is less definable but, to take, as an example, a man twenty-one years his junior, Michel Foucault would probably not have worked in quite the same way but for Sartre's example. Much of Foucault's work turns on a challenge, not unlike Sartre's, to the conventional categorizations of knowledge, and on the problem of the subject. As Foucault defines it himself, his objective has been 'to create a history of the different modes by which human beings, in our culture, are made subjects'. People are reduced to object status by being classified and segregated as criminal or insane, by being studied as objects suitable for scientific classification or by being subjected to processes of domination by a class or group in a stronger position. Foucault is by no means Sartrean in either his approach or his methodology, but it is doubtful whether, without Sartre as his precursor, he would have taken the same kind of interest in insanity or made the same kind of attempt as he does in *L'Archéologie du savoir* (1969) to subvert the traditions of dealing with history in terms of period, with culture in terms of totality and with literature in terms of the individual writer's oeuvre.

It is easier to demonstrate the indebtedness of R.D.Laing, who draws openly, gratefully and fruitfully on Sartre's proposals for an existentialist psycho-analysis and on his ideas about the reduction of people to object status. Sartre, Foucault and Laing have been among the most influential of those who have taught us to distrust the idea of a boundary between sanity and madness, and to listen more sympathetically to the 'insane' discourse of those who might formerly have been dismissed as incapable of communicating with us.

A major part of Sartre's achievement rests on his courage and obstinacy in asserting that we are what we make of ourselves. The idea which de Beauvoir handed, like a flag, to the feminists is essentially the same idea that was later handed by Sartre first to the working class and then to Third World victims of colonialism. *Les Communistes et la paix* tells us that 'classes do not exist; they are made'. In his preface to Fanon's *Les Damnés de la terre* he explains that the native is free to cure himself from the 'colonial neurosis' by using violence against the oppressive intruder. The problem of violence is central in Sartre's work and to say that he has altered our thinking about violence is to say that he has altered our violence. He was the greatest and most influential of all the thinkers who sanctioned the concept of 'counter-violence' as the only effective retaliation against the legalized violence of the state. No great mind has ever been tugged more painfully between the Western moral tradition and the homicidal mania of contemporary terrorism.

Since the American massacres in Vietnam and the communist invasions of Hungary, Czechoslovakia, Cambodia and Afghanistan, after the wars, massacres and famines in India and Africa, where the apathy of governments with the power to distribute supplies has been matched only by the apathy of richer countries with the power to send more help, it has been impossible to go on believing in the state as guardian of morality. Before the end of the nineteenth century Nietzsche had already shown that the concept of goodness did not originate from neighbourly altruism. The evolution of language had been determined by the dominant groups who used their name-giving prerogatives to glorify themselves and their qualities while denigrating those of weaker rivals. 'Good' had been cognate with 'noble', 'evil' with 'plebeian'. But even Sartre, who was familiar with Nietzsche's work, could not simply carry on as a moral philosopher from where Nietzsche had left off. The ideas of good and evil established by the Judaeo-Christian tradition were not easily overturned, and we are rightly reluctant to abandon our belief in the rule of law, even when the laws are made by a government we distrust. We also distrust terrorists. Sartre was in the same quandary and though, like Nietzsche, he failed to find a satisfactory escape route, we cannot ignore the discoveries he made while looking for one.

Situations is the right title for his essays because his ideas changed with changing circumstances and he was constantly propelled into what he called thinking against himself by what Marxists call contradictions in the situation. Despite his precocity he did not come of age as a philosopher until the war, when the quarrel between his instincts and his ideas about violence was precipitated by the situation of France in defeat. As a passionate advocate of individual liberty he was bound to condemn violence as theft of the other person's freedom: by using force we are making him into an object. But what about the freedom-fighters who were sabotaging German freight trains? Obviously counter-violence was the only effective way of fighting back against the nazis, whose power was founded on violence.

Violence is not a crucial issue in most of the fiction Sartre had written or sketched out before the war, but from *L'Engrenage* onwards he is preoccupied with the question of whether power can be wielded without violence, and, if not, whether violence can be humane. *Les Mains sales* plunges him deeper into the problem. Like Jean in *L'Engrenage*, Hoederer understands that a leader cannot expect to keep his hands clean. Violence is the only available route to a future in which freedom may be available to everybody. In spite of the sympathy Sartre felt towards the communists, the play turned out to be a powerful weapon in the hands of anti-communists, and by banning performances of his text he was in effect denying himself freedom of expression. It was almost irrelevant that his self-censorship involved him in financial sacrifices.

The word 'freedom' does not disappear from his vocabulary, but instead of being designated as something which is destroyed when force is used, it reappears as something which can flicker only briefly into life during moments of collective violence. There can be no true freedom for the individual until there is freedom for everyone. The *Critique* looks forward to the initiative taken collectively by the students in 1968: they will seize hold of their own liberty in the same way as the crowd that marched on the Bastille in 1789.

It is easy to understand how Sartre, who never said that he was a Maoist and sometimes said that he wasn't, came to join forces with extremist ex-students after the rebellion failed. When, at the end of the war, he wrote that France had never been so free as during the Occupation, he meant that moral decisions had never been so clear-cut. But they had been almost equally clear-cut during the period of tension that preceded the rebellion. Against a government that allowed Algerians to be tortured in Algeria and murdered in France, counter-violence was hardly less attractive than it had been when the nazis were in control. But in the seventies, when Sartre sided with the militants, he baulked at the mindless anarchic violence they would have welcomed in their hatred of the *status quo*. The hunger for the justice of the lynch-mob was as erratic as the clamour for vengeance against collaborators after the Liberation of Paris when mobs prowled savagely through the streets.

From 1968, when he appeared on Czech television trying to encourage movement towards liberalization, to 1979, when he was still trying to promote peace between Israel and the Arab countries and to help the Vietnamese boat people, he was pragmatically siding with the forces of good against evil, though he was still unable to formulate any adequate moral theory. After he helped to launch *Libération* and helped it to weather a major financial crisis, it is still in existence – tangible evidence of his power. But between his writing and his activism, the lack of co-ordination was more debilitating than it had been when he launched *Les Temps modernes* and tried to rally support for the RDR. In the forties and fifties the public he had addressed in his writing was the same public he was trying to involve in political action: the tone, the style, and the level of his Baudelaire biography are no different from those of *Qu'est-ce que c'est que la littérature?* which made its first appearance in *Les Temps modernes*. But the Flaubert biography is not written for the same public as *Libération*. It had been dangerous to cultivate two styles of writing, one depending on careful revision, the other depending on drugs, haste and disregard for style, and it had been dangerous to regard abstraction as a cleansing force.

We can sum up the inadequacy of his writing throughout the latter half of his life by saying that he never observed anything with the abrasively honest tenacity with which he had once observed the chestnut tree: his genius for nauseated description had to abdicate. The conviction that loser wins was so deep-seated that he gambled confidently against himself. The anti-Proustian devaluation of the past collaborated with an impatient scepticism about the present – these instants of consciousness are almost valueless. Trying to renovate Marxism or to co-ordinate French Maoism, he let the passing moment pass unnoticed. Personal experience and writing drift further apart. He becomes addicted to consciousness of his influence as a substitute for consciousness of his consciousness. If his name, his face, his image are useful to the causes he believes in, the public image must be allowed to separate from the private Sartre, who still enjoys smoking, drinking and chatting with young girls.

If the whole of his postwar career was bedevilled by the difficulty of integrating literary and political activity, he not only failed to solve the problem but let the two halves of his life become progressively separated. But his importance rests more on this failure, I believe, than on any of his successes. He could not have clung more tightly to both sides of the dilemma; his main achievement is the trajectory of his life. Undeniably, he ends up in a position of error, a non-Maoist editor of Maoist papers, a blind writer collaborating verbally for five years with an ex-Maoist Talmudist on a book which will never be finished, but there is something heroic in Sartre's indomitable persistence, in his boundless willingness to be wrong. This is most evident of all in the Flaubert biography, where he is engagingly open about the possibility that his guesswork is inaccurate: perhaps the actual course of events was quite different from the course of his narrative. But this is not the fundamental error. He is erecting an enormous monument to nineteenth-century culture, which he despised, while his work is based on a premiss which belongs more to that culture than to ours – that words, logic and narrative can contain the whole truth. Though at other times he wrote about language as he had once written about nausea – language is not inside us, we are inside it – he never lost faith in his ability to make the signifier transparent and the signified perfectly visible.

During the nineteenth century, biography tended to emulate the pattern of the *Bildungsroman*: the heroic subject would progress from the romantic excesses of youth to wisdom and maturity. He would learn from each adventure, each mistake, ending up at dignified peace with a society that appreciates and rewards him. Sartre's life was less a pilgrimage towards the truth than a series of intellectual and political adventures in which he strenuously entangled himself in self-deception and angrily extricated himself. But if he has survived himself it is because he came so close, while living autobiographically, to giving his experiences the quality of myth. In his UNESCO lecture he quoted Kierkegaard's remark: 'My own untruth is something I can discover only by myself because it is discovered only when I have discovered it, even if the rest of the world knew it already.' Here the word 'untruth' points to what is predictable and confounding in the situation from which he starts, trapped within a historical progression. He can liberate himself only by experiencing his subjective truth.

Together with Nietzsche, Kierkegaard inaugurates a phase of philosophy in which truth and experience are tightly intertwined. Sartre quotes from Antoine de Waelhens: 'When Kierkegaard, Nietzsche and Bergson arrived on the scene, philosophy ceased to be *detached explanation* and claimed from now on to be *at one* with experience.' It was necessary 'to give up the ideal of philosophy as a rigorous science'. Instead of illuminating human life it 'aspired to become this life in its complete consciousness of itself'. Sartre was a philosopher of this kind. Judged by the standards of rigorous science or even of academic philosophy, his thinking may fail to pass muster, but, like Kierkegaard and Nietzsche, he has succeeded in 'designating himself as a transhistorical absolute' – this is the phrase he uses of Kierkegaard. His discovery of his own untruth was so complete that the resonance is still audible. Like Nietzsche and Kierkegaard he cannot be reduced to what he wrote. When we try to extrapolate the statements from the situations, the pronouncements about liberty and violence merely contradict each other and eventually cancel each other out, but when we put the texts into their context, we see that each volte-face, each failure to fulfil a promise or complete a work, is only superficially an interruption of the progress he is making. Without these discontinuities the movement itself is unthinkable. Which is not to say that he should never have attempted it. But it was essential for him to assert his freedom repeatedly in the way Roquentin had: by abandoning the book he was writing. No less ambitious than Nietzsche in the tasks he set himself – to write a phenomenological ethic, to prove that history has a single meaning, to create a dialectical morality, to reconcile psycho-analysis with Marxism – he cannot possibly fulfil them. But he could not have done what he did if he had been realistic about what he could do.

Sartre's life will continue indefinitely; less forcefully, though, since Simone de Beauvoir's death on 14 April 1986, almost exactly six years after his on 15 April 1980. In many ways their relationship had continued throughout the six years. In April 1980 she had been thrown into a depression from which she never recovered fully. Like him, she believed in the therapeutic value of work and eventually she settled down to write *La Cérémonie des adieux*, which was ready to be published by the end of 1981. The first 150 pages, a disturbingly honest account of the last ten years in his life, are closely based on the diaries she had kept; the remaining 400 pages comprise an almost unedited transcript of the interviews she had conducted with him in Rome during the summer of 1974. In 1982 she published his letters to her but not hers to him, and she had no wish to make any other use of the material in her diaries. After her moving 1964 book about the death of her mother, *Une Mort très douce* (*A Very Easy Death*), and her 1970 book on old age (*La Vieillesse*), it might have seemed natural to write about her own experience of old age in a sequel to the four volumes of autobiography, but she had lost the one man who could possibly have persuaded her to write another book.

Like Sartre, she adopted a grown-up daughter. Thirty-four years her junior, Sylvie Le Bon had shared her life for more than eight years before his death and went on sharing it until the end. But, without him, de Beauvoir had only a limited interest in staying alive. At first she took an active part in running *Les Temps modernes*, and she went on supporting the causes she believed in. In 1972 she had repudiated the statement made at the end of *Le Deuxième Sexe* – that she was not a feminist – and she went on, generously and judiciously, being helpful to the movement. But in 1984, when Claude Chabrol's film of her second novel, *Le Sang des autres*, was shown in Paris, she had no desire to see it, and though her mind was still quick, active, lucid, it had become apparent that no-one had paid sufficient attention to the first sentence in her preface to *La Cérémonie des adieux*: 'Here is the first of my books – no doubt the only one – that you will not have read before it was printed.'

Their partnership had been extraordinary, not only as an experiment in personal relationships but as a literary phenomenon. The voice of Sartre's 'little judge' survives in his work, just as his voice survives in her work.

Notes

ABBREVIATIONS

Ast.	Transcript of interview film directed by Astruc and Contat called 'Sartre par lui-même'
Carnets	Sartre, *Les Carnets de la drôle de guerre*
Cér	de Beauvoir, *La Cérémonie des adieux*
Critique 1	Sartre, *Critique de la raison dialectique* part 1 (1960)
Critique 2	Sartre, *Critique de la raison dialectique* part 2 (1986)
Ecrits	Contat & Rybalka, *Les Ecrits de Sartre*
FA	de Beauvoir, *La Force de l'âge*
FC	de Beauvoir, *La Force des choses*
HD	Howard Davies, '*Les Temps Modernes* and Anthropology 1945–81: a contribution to the analysis of the Sartrean notion of "anthropologie synthétique"', doctoral thesis (unpublished)
Idiot	Sartre, *L'Idiot de la famille*
JFR	de Beauvoir, *Mémoires d'une jeune fille rangée*
LC	Sartre, *Lettres au Castor et à quelques autres*
LTM	*Les Temps modernes*
M	Sartre, *Les Mots*
OR	Sartre, *Oeuvres romanesques*
repr.	reprinted in
Sits	Sartre, *Situations*
TCF	de Beauvoir, *Tout compte fait*

An author's name followed by a page number refers the reader to an entry in the Bibliography on pages 471–6. Where a title is given without the author's name, the book is by Sartre. See pp. 471–2.

INTRODUCTION

1 Michel Contat and Michel Rybalka *Le Monde* 17.4.80
2 *Qu'est-ce que c'est que la littérature?*
3 *Questions de méthode*
4 Scriven p. 6
5 Cau p. 234
6 Interview, *New Left Review* Nov.–Dec. 1969
7 Roland Barthes, *Le Degré zéro de l'écriture* (Paris 1953) p. 43
8 Cau pp. 233–4
9 Michelle Vian interview with RH 2.7.85
10 Cau pp. 233–7
11 Nietzsche, *Jenseits von Gut und Böse* Section 6
12 *Cér* interview p. 368
13 *Critique* p. 332
14 *Carnets* p. 175
15 Jean Cau interview with RH 6.7.85
16 *Idiot* II p. 1488
17 Marcel Péju interview with RH 28.6.85

CHAPTER 1
Poulou

1 *M* pp. 11–12
2 *OR* p. 1728
3 Cohen-Solal pp. 17–33
4 p. 36
5 pp. 45–6
6 p. 73
7 *M* p. 14
8 James Brabazon, *Albert Schweitzer: a Biography* (London 1976)
9 *M* p. 27
10 de Beauvoir, *La Vieillesse* pp. 346–7. M. Durand is actually Charles Schweitzer.
11 *M* pp. 16–17
12 pp. 17–18
13 *Idiot*
14 Ibid.
15 *Carnets* p. 93
16 Ibid.
17 p. 94
18 *M* p. 76
19 Ibid.
20 'L'Enfance d'un chef'
21 *M* p. 73
22 p. 84
23 p. 85
24 p. 30
25 Cohen-Solal p. 40
26 p. 45
27 *Carnets* p. 100
28 Cohen-Solal p. 56
29 *M* p. 55
30 p. 60
31 p. 109
32 *Carnets* pp. 320–1
33 *M* p. 47
34 p. 136
35 'Erostrate' *Le Mur*
36 p. 164
37 p. 174
38 p. 182
39 Ibid.
40 p. 186
41 Ibid.
42 *Ecrits* p. 22
43 *M* p. 189
44 p. 190

45 Cohen-Solal p. 26
46 *Ecrits* p. 22
47 *M* p. 191

CHAPTER 2
Nitre and Sarzan

1 *Baudelaire* p. 21
2 Interview with J. Gérassi, *OR* p. xxxviii
3 Ast. p. 16
4 Ibid.
5 Interview, 'Autoportrait à 70 ans', *Sits* 10
6 Ast. p. 18
7 *Cér* p. 1974
8 p. 192
9 p. 403; interview also repr. Chapsal
10 Ast. p. 19
11 Michel Guillet, 'Jean-Paul Sartre au lycée', *Sud-Ouest Dimanche* 25.10.64
12 *Cér* p. 416
13 Jeanson (1974) p. 291
14 Ibid.
15 *Cér* p. 193
16 Jeanson (1974) pp. 291–2
17 *Ecrits* p. 511
18 Ast. p. 27
19 *Cér* p. 188
20 Ast. p. 24
21 *Cér* p. 374
22 *Carnets* pp. 325–6
23 *Saint Genet* p. 13
24 p. 14
25 p. 21
26 *Cér* p. 186
27 Ast. p. 20
28 *Cér* p. 167
29 p. 195
30 *Carnets* pp. 326–7
31 *LC* vol. 1 p. 25
32 *Cér* p. 374
33 Cohen-Solal/H. Nizan p. 33
34 Ast. p. 30
35 *Cér* p. 167
36 p. 174
37 p. 167
38 p. 166
39 *Sits* 4
40 'Paul Nizan', *Sits* 4

41 Ibid.
42 Cohen-Solal/H. Nizan p. 34
43 *Ecrits* p. 507
44 *Libération* édition spéciale Sartre (supplement to no. 1932) p. 18
45 *Ecrits* p. 22
46 Interview in Schilpp
47 *Ecrits* p. 22
48 *Carnets* p. 194
49 *Ecrits* p. 502
50 p. 503
51 Jeanson (1974) p. 285

CHAPTER 3
At the Lycée Louis-le-Grand
1 Nizan, *La Conspiration* p. 46
2 Chapter 1 of *La Semence et le scaphandre, Magazine littéraire* 12.71
3 *Cér* p. 193
4 Merleau-Ponty (1961), Introduction
5 Canguilhem interview in *Arts* 11–17.1.61
6 *La Semence et le scaphandre*
7 *Cér* p. 375
8 JFR pp. 440–4
9 Register of results, archive of Lycée Louis-le-Grand
10 *La Semence et le scaphandre*
11 *Obliques* 18–19 p. 66
12 Ast. p. 24
13 *Cér* pp. 178–9
14 p. 178
15 p. 179
16 Cohen-Solal/H. Nizan pp. 34–5
17 pp. 37–8
18 Archive of Lycée Louis-le-Grand
19 *Libération* édition spéciale Sartre p. 3
20 Ast. p. 40
21 Archive of Lycée Louis-le-Grand
22 *Arts* 11–17.1.61
23 *Cér* p. 375
24 Aron (1983) p. 35
25 p. 34
26 p. 35
27 *Cér* p. 181
28 'Paul Nizan', *Sits* 4
29 *Le Mur*
30 *Cér* p. 375; pp. 378–9

CHAPTER 4
School for Superiors
1 Jeanson (1974) p. 289
2 *Sits* 4 p. 149
3 Cohen-Solal p. 95
4 Canguilhem in *Arts* 11–17.1.61; 'Paul Nizan', *Sits* 4
5 *Cér* p. 329
6 *Cér* p. 315
7 Jean Fabre, *Revue d'histoire littéraire de la France* no. 6, 11–12.75
8 Canguilhem in *Arts* 11–17.1.61
9 Lagache in *Arts* 11–17.1.61
10 *Cér* p. 409
11 Library register of loans at the Ecole
12 'L'Enfance d'un chef' *Le Mur*
13 Ibid.
14 Library register
15 'Paul Nizan', *Sits* 4
16 Cited by Jacqueline Leiner in *Le Destin littéraire de Paul Nizan* (Paris 1970) p. 40
17 Advertisement in *Europe* Jan. 1925 cited by N. Racine, *Les Ecrivains communistes en France 1920–36* p. 213
18 Letter from Aragon and Breton to Jacques Doucet 2.22 cited R. Garaudy, *L'Itinéraire d'Aragon* (Paris 1961) p. 132
19 Henri Lefebvre, *La Somme et le reste* p. 389
20 *Cér* pp. 234–5
21 Breton, *Les Pas perdus* (Paris 1924), p. 206
22 Lefebvre p. 373
23 Notebook in H. Nizan's archives, Leiner p. 49
24 *L'Oeuvre* 22.3.26 cited Cohen-Solal p. 97
25 *Cér*
26 *LC* vol. 1 pp. 28–9
27 Ibid.
28 *LC* vol. 1 p. 30
29 Ibid.
30 Cohen-Solal/H. Nizan p. 48
31 *JFR* p. 321
32 *FA* pp. 72–3
33 Interview, *OR* p. 1791
34 Ibid.

35 *LC* vol. 1, pp. 15–16
36 p. 10
37 pp. 10–11
38 p. 12
39 pp. 12–13
40 p. 13
41 pp. 12–14
42 Ibid.
43 p. 15
44 pp. 16–17
45 Ibid.
46 Ibid.
47 Ibid.
48 p. 18
49 p. 20
50 p. 22
51 Ibid.
52 pp. 23–4
53 p. 24
54 p. 25
55 p. 26
56 Aron (1983) p. 32
57 'Paul Nizan', *Sits* 4
58 Ibid.
59 *FA* pp. 47–8 (Guille is called Pagniez)
60 pp. 39–40
61 *LC* vol. 1 pp. 33–5
62 *FA* p. 40
63 *LC* vol. 1 p. 27
64 Ast. p. 38
65 Alain, *Système des beaux arts* (Paris 1920), p. 16
66 Dumas, *Nouveau traité de la psychologie*, vol. 2 p. 594
67 Binet, *L'Ame et le corps* (Paris 1908)
68 *LC* vol. 1 p. 27
69 p. 886
70 p. 888
71 H. Nizan in *Arts* 11–17.1.61
72 *FA* pp. 73–4
73 *LC* vol. 1 p. 32
74 *Carnets* p. 342
75 'Paul Nizan', *Sits* 4
76 *LC* vol. 1 p. 34
77 *Sits* 4 p. 147
78 Canguilhem in *Arts* 11–17.1.61
79 Lagache in *Arts* 11–17.1.61
80 *Critique* 1 p. 22

81 *FA* p. 47
82 *Carnets* p. 227
83 'Sartre et les femmes', interview in Muchnik
84 *Ecrits* p. 24
85 *FA* p. 41
86 Aron, interview with J. Gérassi, *OR* p. xliv
87 Aron (1983) p. 37
88 *Les Nouvelles littéraires* 2.2.29
89 Ibid.
90 *FA* p. 47
91 pp. 74–8
92 Ibid.

CHAPTER 5
The Beaver

1 *JFR* p. 330
2 p. 335
3 pp. 440–5
4 p. 454
5 *Vogue* 7.65 p. 72
6 *JFR* pp. 458–9
7 p. 471
8 pp. 475–6
9 p. 476
10 p. 477
11 pp. 477–8
12 p. 478
13 p. 480
14 p. 482
15 Maurice de Gandiller in Cohen-Solal p. 116
16 *JFR* p. 482
17 *Cér* p. 206
18 *JFR* p. 484
19 p. 485
20 pp. 488–9
21 Ibid.
22 *FA* p. 17
23 p. 18
24 Ibid.
25 Ibid.
26 p. 19
27 Ibid.
28 Ibid.
29 pp. 19–20
30 p. 21
31 p. 22

32 p. 24
33 pp. 26–7
34 p. 27
35 p. 54
36 *JFR* p. 403
37 *FA* p. 35
38 Ibid.
39 p. 36
40 p. 38
41 p. 43
42 *Carnets* p. 96
43 p. 98
44 *FA* p. 33
45 *LC* pp. 42–3
46 *Cér* p. 408
47 de Beauvoir, *La Vieillesse* p. 347
48 *FA* pp. 44–5
49 *Carnets* p. 109
50 *FA* p. 46
51 pp. 46–7
52 p. 49
53 Ibid.
54 *Ecrits* p. 53
55 *Cér* p. 330
56 p. 551
57 *FA* p. 50
58 Certificate found among the papers
of Mme Mancy, *Ecrits* p. xlviii
59 *FA* pp. 80–1
60 p. 82

CHAPTER 6
Provincial Schoolmaster

1 Aron (1983) p. 82; Ast. p. 49
2 Jean Giustiniani in Cohen-Solal
p. 126; Robert Marchandeau, *Bulletin
des anciens élèves du Lycée François I*
no. 75, Cohen-Solal p. 126
3 A. Dupuis, *OR* pp. 1678–80
4 Cohen-Solal pp. 127–8
5 Albert Palle in *Arts* 11–17.1.61
6 Palle interview with RH 21.6.85
7 Ibid.
8 *Cér* pp. 403 and 410
9 pp. 330–2
10 pp. 252–4
11 *FA* p. 83
12 *Ecrits* pp. 549–50
13 *FA* p. 86 and *Cér* p. 294

14 Letter to de Beauvoir, *OR* pp. 1687–8
15 Ibid.
16 *M* p. 135
17 *OR* p. 1687
18 p. 6
19 pp. 1680–1
20 p. 1681
21 *Cér* p. 394
22 *OR* p. 22
23 *Le Monde* 22.1.82
24 *OR* p. 1682
25 Ibid.
26 p. 1683
27 p. 1684
28 Ibid.
29 *FA* p. 111
30 p. 110
31 *OR* p. 1686
32 p. 5
33 *FA* p. 115
34 *Cér* p. 254
35 *FA* p. 113
36 p. 114
37 Ibid.
38 p. 372
39 p. 119
40 p. 121
41 p. 122
42 Ibid.
43 p. 128
44 *Cér* pp. 406–7
45 *FA* pp. 136–8
46 p. 140
47 Ibid.
48 *Critique* 1 p. 23
49 Ibid.

CHAPTER 7
A German Credo

1 *FA* p. 141
2 Ibid.
3 p. 142
4 Ibid.
5 *Sits* 1 p. 25
6 p. 17
7 pp. 18–22
8 *FA* p. 143
9 p. 145
10 p. 146

11 p. 333
12 p. 149
13 p. 151
14 p. 153
15 p. 154
16 Bost in Ast. p. 50
17 *FA* p. 161
18 *Carnets* p. 100
19 *Sits* 1 p. 31
20 p. 33
21 Ibid.
22 'L'Ecrivain et sa langue', *Revue esthétique* 7–12.65
23 Husserl, 'Cartesian Meditation', tr. Dorian Cairus (The Hague 1960) pp. 24–5
24 *La Transcendance de l'Ego*
25 *FA* pp. 190–1
26 *LC* p. 361
27 *OR* pp. 25–6
28 *La Nausée* p. 141
29 p. 232
30 Heidegger quoted by Sartre in *Esquisse pour une théorie des émotions*
31 *La Nausée* p. 180
32 *Sits* 1 p. 34
33 *La Nausée* p. 182
34 p. 180
35 pp. 182–3
36 p. 185
37 p. 87
38 p. 137
39 p. 31
40 p. 59
41 *Carnets* pp. 225–6
42 Ibid.
43 *La Nausée* p. 84
44 p. 189
45 pp. 121–2
46 *FA* p. 186
47 p. 188
48 pp. 190–1
49 *FA* p. 203
50 *OR* p. 1831
51 *Carnets* p. 320
52 *Cér* p. 396
53 Ibid.
54 'Strictly Personal', *Harper's Bazaar* 146, 1945
55 de Beauvoir, *La Vieillesse* p. 348

CHAPTER 8
Back in Bouville

1 Ast. p. 51
2 *Carnets* pp. 100–1
3 *Cér* pp. 419–20
4 *FA* pp. 209–11
5 Ast. p. 42
6 Ibid.
7 Lagache in *Arts* 11–17.1.61
8 *FA* pp. 216–17
9 Ibid.
10 pp. 217–18
11 Ast. pp. 53–4
12 *FA* p. 218
13 Ibid.
14 *Carnets* p. 102
15 p. 156
16 Ibid.
17 *FA* p. 219
18 p. 224
19 *LC* pp. 60–1
20 *FA* p. 255
21 Interview with Contat, *OR* p. 1803
22 Letter to de Beauvoir 7.35, *LC* vol. 1 pp. 58–9
23 *FA* pp. 226–8
24 *Carnets* p. 102
25 Ibid.
26 *OR* pp. 446–7
27 *FA* p. 240
28 pp. 240–2
29 pp. 248–51
30 p. 253
31 pp. 253–5
32 p. 258
33 *OR* p. 270
34 pp. 258–62
35 pp. 264–5
36 pp. 266–7
37 Chapter 11
38 *FA* pp. 269–70

CHAPTER 9
Intimacy

1 *LC* p. 132
2 *Cér* p. 410
3 *FA* pp. 273–4

4 *LC* p. 70
5 *Ecrits* pp. 555–6
6 *Carnets* pp. 182–3
7 *FA* pp. 279–80 and *Cér* pp. 232–3
8 *LC* p. 90
9 *FA* p. 294
10 pp. 287–9
11 *OR* p. li
12 *Cér* p. 208
13 *FA* p. 298
14 de Beauvoir interview with RH 5.83
15 *Carnets* pp. 14–15
16 *FA* p. 301
17 *LC* p. 96
18 p. 103
19 *LC* pp. 117–18
20 p. 129
21 pp. 117–18
22 p. 136
23 p. 145
24 p. 147
25 *Carnets* p. 234
26 *FA* pp. 311–17
27 *LC* p. 149
28 p. 159
29 p. 157
30 *FA* p. 323

CHAPTER 10
Breakthrough
1 *Carnets* p. 102
2 p. 305
3 pp. 300–2
4 p. 302
5 p. 303
6 *Esquisse*
7 *FA* p. 329
8 pp. 329–31
9 *OR* p. liii
10 pp. 1849–50
11 *Sits* 2 pp. 212–13, cited in *Ecrits* p. 70
12 *FA* p. 335
13 *Ecrits* p. 60
14 *Vendredi* 6.5.38, *OR* p. 1701
15 16.5, *OR* p. 1701
16 *Journal Echo de Paris* 30.5.38, *OR* p. 1703
17 *Nouvelles littéraires* 18.6.38, *OR* p. 1703

18 *Alger républicain* 20.10.38, *OR* p. 1709
19 *FA* p. 336
20 *Sits* 1 p. 29
21 p. 8
22 *FA* p. 337
23 *LC* p. 180
24 p. 184
25 Ibid.
26 p. 185
27 p. 187
28 pp. 188–9
29 pp. 190–5
30 p. 194
31 p. 199
32 p. 204
33 p. 207
34 p. 213
35 *FA* p. 338
36 p. 339
37 *Carnets* p. 234
38 *FA* pp. 339–43
39 pp. 344–5
40 Interview, *Marianne* 7.12.38, *Ecrits* p. 65
41 *Sits* 1 p. 36
42 pp. 37–51
43 *OR* p. 1860
44 Ibid.
45 Interview, *Marianne* 7.12, *OR* p. 1698
46 Interview in Roger Troisfontaines, *Le Choix de Jean-Paul Sartre* (Paris 1946), *Ecrits* p. 145
47 *FA* pp. 356–62
48 *LC* p. 218
49 Sartre's blurb for *Le Mur* (1967), *Ecrits* pp. 69–70
50 *Les Livres littéraires* 6–7.39, *OR* p. 1817; *Le Figaro* 4.3.39, *OR* p. 1812; *Le Temps* 30.3.39, *OR* p. 1815
51 *Alger républicain* 12.3.39, *OR* p. 1814
52 *FA* p. 363
53 *LC* pp. 177–8
54 *OR* p. 402
55 de Beauvoir interview with RH 5.83
56 *OR* p. 436
57 p. 437
58 p. 438
59 p. 442
60 p. 466

61 *FA* p. 367
62 p. 370
63 p. 371
64 *LC* p. 228
65 p. 229
66 pp. 229–30
67 p. 232
68 p. 234
69 p. 235
70 p. 240
71 p. 241
72 p. 239
73 p. 242 and RH interview with de Beauvoir 5.83
74 pp. 242–3
75 *Cér* p. 385, p. 400
76 p. 395, p. 400
77 p. 393
78 Ibid.
79 pp. 398–9
80 *FA* pp. 383–5 and *LC* pp. 246–7
81 *LC* p. 249 and *FA* pp. 383–4
82 *Cér* p. 397
83 *FA* p. 386
84 *LC* p. 270
85 p. 271
86 de Beauvoir's diary 1.9.39, *FA* pp. 390–2
87 2.9 p. 392
88 *LC* p. 274
89 Ibid.

CHAPTER 11
The War Profiteer
1 *Cahiers* p. 14
2 Jules Romains, *Prélude à Verdun*
3 *LC* vol. 1 p. 275
4 p. 277
5 pp. 279–83
6 p. 283
7 pp. 285–91
8 pp. 288–92
9 pp. 291–4
10 pp. 293–300
11 p. 377
12 pp. 302–19
13 *L'Etre et le Néant* pp. 536–7
14 *LC* vol. 1 p. 380
15 Jean Pierre, 'Réponse à Sartre' (unpublished TS)

16 Diary entry 14.9.39, *FA* p. 12
17 *LC* vol. 1 pp. 301–21
18 p. 389
19 'Réponse à Sartre'
20 *LC* vol. 1 p. 336
21 p. 258
22 p. 263
23 *LC* vol. 1 p. 347 letter to Simone Jollivet
24 p. 366
25 p. 358
26 p. 359
27 p. 373
28 Ibid.
29 *OR* p. 446
30 p. 523
31 Interview with Christian Grisoli, *Paru* no. 13, Dec. 43
32 *OR* pp. 507–8
33 *LC* vol. 1 p. 304
34 p. 389
35 *Carnets* p. 51
36 p. 156
37 *LC* vol. 1 p. 337
38 pp. 345–6
39 p. 373
40 p. 382
41 Letter to de Beauvoir 26.10.39, *LC* pp. 377–80
42 *Carnets* p. 175
43 *OR* p. 625
44 *Carnets* p. 175
45 p. 172
46 *LC* p. 341
47 p. 353
48 p. 365
49 p. 375
50 p. 376
51 p. 386
52 p. 376
53 p. 380
54 de Beauvoir's diary 1.11.39, *FA*
55 *LC* p. 391
56 p. 390
57 p. 395
58 p. 396
59 p. 401
60 p. 407
61 p. 440

62 Letter to de Beauvoir 4.12.39, *LC* pp. 457–9
63 9.12
64 Ibid.
65 *Carnets* p. 122
66 Sartre gives the name as Mistler; according to Jean Pierre the clerk's name was Selzer
67 *Carnets* pp. 120–1
68 *LC* p. 407
69 p. 414
70 p. 425
71 p. 427
72 p. 441
73 p. 446
74 p. 447
75 p. 443
76 pp. 465–6
77 p. 467
78 p. 465
79 Jean Pierre, letter to Bernard Poirot-Delpeche (unpublished)
80 *LC* p. 469
81 p. 492
82 p. 496
83 p. 497
84 p. 490
85 p. 500
86 p. 518
87 p. 506
88 p. 518
89 p. 549
90 p. 548
91 p. 533
92 p. 538
93 p. 548
94 p. 478
95 p. 552
96 Jean Pierre, letter to Bernard Poirot-Delpeche (unpublished)
97 *LC* p. 537
98 p. 555
99 pp. 556–7
100 p. 567
101 p. 543
102 Jean Pierre, letter to Bernard Poirot-Delpeche (unpublished)
103 *LC* p. 563
104 *Carnets* p. 240
105 Ibid.
106 p. 241
107 p. 242
108 p. 267
109 p. 247
110 *FA* pp. 443–5
111 *Carnets* pp. 308–9
112 pp. 338–40
113 *LC* p. 588
114 p. 586
115 p. 593
116 *LC* vol. 2 pp. 90–1
117 p. 89
118 p. 94
119 Ibid.
120 p. 98
121 p. 110
122 p. 107
123 p. 111
124 Ibid.
125 *Carnets* p. 413
126 p. 414
127 *LC* vol. 2 p. 145
128 p. 147
129 p. 146
130 p. 147
131 p. 191
132 p. 162
133 p. 201
134 p. 159
135 p. 180
136 Ibid.
137 p. 181 and p. 197; p. 195
138 Jean Pierre, 'Réponse à Sartre'
139 *LC* vol. 2 p. 199
140 pp. 204–5
141 pp. 220–1
142 p. 235
143 p. 221
144 Jean Pierre, 'Réponse à Sartre'
145 *LC* vol. 2 p. 226, p. 230
146 p. 222
147 p. 268
148 p. 229
149 Ibid.
150 p. 231
151 p. 232
152 p. 236
153 p. 240

154 p. 251
155 Ibid.
156 p. 252
157 p. 262
158 p. 268
159 p. 269
160 p. 275; p. 280
161 Ibid.
162 p. 281
163 Ibid.
164 p. 287; 'La Mort dans l'âme',
   10–11.6.40, *Ecrits* pp. 638–49
165 Jean Pierre, letter to Bernard Poirot-
   Delpeche (unpublished)
166 *Cér* pp. 489–90
167 *LC* vol. 2 pp. 286–7
168 'Journal de Mathieu', *LTM*
   9.82
169 *LC* vol. 2 p. 285
170 p. 290
171 Ibid.
172 p. 289
173 p. 294
174 p. 295

CHAPTER 12
Stalag
 1 *Ecrits* p. 642
 2 *Sits* 3 p. 34
 3 *LC* vol. 2 pp. 295–6 and 299
 4 Ibid.
 5 p. 299
 6 Perrin pp. 39–66
 7 p. 91
 8 Ibid.
 9 *Ecrits* pp. 565–633
10 Perrin p. 97
11 Interview with J. Gérassi, *OR* p. lvi
12 Perrin p. III
13 p. 112
14 p. 113
15 *OR* p. lxvi
16 Perrin pp. 115–20
17 pp. 127–8
18 *LTM* 9.82
19 Perrin p. 127
20 'Journal de Mathieu', *LTM* 9.82
   pp. 450–75
21 p. 146

CHAPTER 13
In Occupied Paris
 1 *Sits* 4 p. 348
 2 Ibid.
 3 Pryce-Jones pp. 37–42
 4 p. 164
 5 *FA* pp. 492–4
 6 p. 494
 7 Ast. p. 68
 8 J.B. Pontalis interview with RH 3.7.85
 9 'Merleau-Ponty vivant', *Sits* 4
10 Cohen-Solal p. 232
11 Pryce-Jones p. 118 and pp. 228–9
12 *FA* pp. 495–6
13 Testimony of Simone Debout and
   J.-T. Desanti, Cohen-Solal pp. 234–5
14 *FA* pp. 496–7
15 pp. 497–8
16 pp. 504–5
17 pp. 505–6
18 Interview, *Avant-Scène* 1–15.5.68
19 *Cér* p. 363
20 *FA* pp. 506–9
21 pp. 509–11
22 pp. 511–16
23 *Sits* 3 p. 18
24 p. 22
25 pp. 25–6
26 Ibid.
27 pp. 31–2
28 *FA* pp. 515–20
29 *Carrefour* 9.9.44
30 Pétain, *La France nouvelle* (Paris
   1943) p. 167
31 p. 521
32 p. 511
33 p. 509
34 p. 511
35 Marcel Péju interview with RH
   28.6.85
36 Posthumously published interview,
   Libération 8–9.6 and 10.6.85
37 Testimony of Mme Pierre Kaan and
   Pierre Piganiol, Cohen-Solal
   pp. 266–7
38 *FA* pp. 530–1
39 pp. 533–4
40 pp. 533–5
41 pp. 535–7

42 *L'Etre et le Néant* pp. 561–2
43 p. 563
44 p. 639
45 pp. 640–1
46 *OR* p. 1033
47 *Sits* 4 pp. 34–5
48 *L'Etre et le Néant* p. 134
49 *OR* pp. 1057–8
50 Bergson, *Essai sur les données immédiates de la conscience* (Paris 1889) p. 99
51 *L'Etre et le Néant* p. 300
52 Book review in *New Statesman* 25.5.57
53 George Steiner, *Heidegger* (London 1978)
54 *L'Etre et le Néant* p. 296
55 p. 430
56 p. 451
57 p. 457
58 p. 664
59 p. 660
60 p. 688
61 p. 682
62 p. 684
63 p. 689
64 p. 708
65 Heidegger, *Brief über den Humanismus* (Bern 1947)
66 Ibid.
67 Ibid.
68 *L'Etre et le Néant* p. 85
69 *OR* p. 1094
70 'Un Nouveau Mystique' 10–12.43 repr. *Sits* 1
71 *L'Etre et le Néant* p. 89
72 *Sits* 1 p. 23
73 Heidegger, *Sein und Zeit* (Tübingen, 12th edn 1972) Section 40
74 Section 53
75 *L'Etre et le Néant* pp. 690–1
76 *Sein und Zeit* Section 60
77 *L'Etre et le Néant* p. 695
78 pp. 697–8
79 *OR* p. 1123
80 Camus, *Essais* (Pléiade edition 1965) p. 108
81 *Sits* 1 p. 113
82 p. 115
83 p. 121

CHAPTER 14
The Future Reappears
1 *FA* pp. 540–2
2 pp. 540–2
2 pp. 546–9
3 *Cahiers Charles Dullin* vol. 2, March 1966
4 Ibid.
5 *FA* pp. 552–3
6 p. 553
7 *Paris Soir* 15.6.43
8 Armory in *Les Nouveaux Temps* 13.6.43
9 'Oreste et la cité', *Les Lettres françaises* no. 12 repr. Leiris, *Brisées* (Paris 1966)
10 Dullin, *Ce sont les dieux qu'il nous faut* (Paris 1969)
11 *FA* p. 566
12 Ibid.
13 p. 568
14 *Ecrits* p. 101
15 *L'Etre et le Néant* p. 276
16 pp. 444–5
17 *FA* p. 576
18 *FA* pp. 569–70
19 Maria Casarès, *Résidente privilégiée* (Paris 1980) p. 232
20 *FA* p. 584
21 p. 587
22 p. 590
23 Ibid.
24 pp. 591–3
25 *Sits* 10 p. 196
26 *FC* p. 27
27 Herbert R. Lottman, *Camus* (London 1979) p. 340
28 *Saint Genet*
29 *FA* p. 595
30 Ibid.
31 *Critique* p. 100
32 *Sits* 10 p. 106
33 *Baudelaire* p. 245
34 p. 130
35 *Carnets* p. 381
36 pp. 308–9
37 p. 381
38 p. 391
39 *FA* p. 597

40 Spoken preface to DGG recording of
   Huis clos repr. *Un Théâtre de situations*
41 *FA* p. 598
42 p. 599
43 pp. 599–600
44 'Colère d'une ville', *Combat* 30.8.44,
   Ecrits pp. 103–4
45 'L'Insurrection', *Combat* 28.8.44,
   Ecrits p. 104
46 *FA* p. 608
47 'Toute la ville tire', *Combat* 31.8,
   Ecrits p. 104
48 'La Délivrance est à nos portes',
   Combat 2.9.44, *Ecrits* p. 105
49 'La République du silence', *Sits* 3
   p. 12
50 pp. 12–13
51 *Les Mandarins* p. 15
52 *FC* p. 18
53 *Réflexions sur la question juive*
54 *Nouvel Observateur* 10.3.80
55 Werner Cohn, 'The "Aryans" of
   Jean-Paul Sartre', *Encounter* Dec.
   1981
56 *LA* vol. 2 p. 25
57 Sartre's blurb for *L'Age de raison*,
   Ecrits p. 113

CHAPTER 15
Making a New Start

1 Caute pp. 36–7
2 pp. 44–5
3 *OR* p. 1921
4 pp. 1918–21
5 '"Volcano on Ice" – A Critical
   Portrait of Raymond Aron'.
   Presented by Richard Mayne and
   produced by Judith Bumpus, BBC
   Radio 3, 14.1.85.
6 *FC* p. 27
7 Ibid.
8 *Les Mandarins* pp. 25–6
9 Lottman, *Camus* pp. 184–5 and 346–7
10 *Cér* p. 303
11 *Sits* 3 p. 113
12 p. 114
13 pp. 122–3
14 p. 93

15 p. 118
16 *FC* p. 45
17 *Ecrits* pp. 117–18
18 *FC* p. 45
19 *Sits* 3 p. 75
20 Testimony of Dolorès Vanetti,
   Cohen-Solal p. 314
21 *Le Figaro* 11–12.3.45, *Ecrits* p. 119
22 *Sits* 3 p. 108
23 p. 81
24 p. 85
25 *Sits* 2 pp. 246–7

CHAPTER 16
Chief Existentialist

1 *FC* p. 50
2 *Les Mandarins* pp. 204–5
3 'Présentation des *Temps modernes*',
   Sits 2 p. 13
4 p. 14
5 pp. 15–16
6 'La Fin de la guerre', *Sits* 2
7 *Ecrits* p. 131
8 pp. 129–30
9 pp. 128–9
10 Interview, *Paru* 12.45, *OR* p. 1912
11 p. 1916
12 Jean Pouillon interview with RH
   22.6.85
13 Lévi-Strauss, inaugural lecture at
   the Collège de France, published as
   Leçon inaugurale (Paris, 1960)
14 *Sits* 2 pp. 22–3
15 Lévi-Strauss *op. cit.*
16 *HD* p. 75
17 *LTM* 1.46
18 'Merleau-Ponty vivant', *Sits* 4
19 *Cahiers* p. 120
20 *Vogue* article, *OR* p. 1919
21 'Merleau-Ponty vivant'
22 *LC* vol. 2 p. 332
23 pp. 850–1
24 Cohen-Solal p. 365
25 *FC* p. 82
26 p. 87
27 André Gorz, *Le Traître* (Paris 1958)
28 Ibid.
29 *Cér* pp. 346–7, 361
30 Cau p. 176

31 'Matérielisme et révolution', *Sits* 3
32 *LC* vol. 2 p. 337
33 Janet Flanner (1966) p. 73
34 *TCF* p. 105
35 Olivier Todd interview with RH 1.7.85
36 Cau pp. 234–7
37 Jean Pouillon interview with RH 22.6.85
38 de Beauvoir interview with RH 4.7.85
39 *FC* p. 123
40 Arthur & Cynthia Koestler, *Stranger on the Square* (London 1984) pp. 68–70
41 *FC* pp. 123–5
42 *Ecrits* p. 157
43 *FC* p. 128
44 pp. 128–9
45 *LC* vol. 2 p. 338
46 *FC* p. 129
47 p. 132
48 Jean Cau interview with RH 6.7.85
49 Cau p. 133
50 *FC* pp. 125–6
51 *LC* vol. 2 p. 336
52 *Sits* 2 p. 196
53 *FC* pp. 140–2
54 *Qu'est ce que c'est que la littérature?* *Sits* 2
55 *Sits* 2 p. 290
56 p. 280
57 p. 285
58 p. 305
59 p. 308
60 *Cahiers* p. 120
61 Interview, *Mondes nouveaux* 21.12.44
62 *Cahiers* p. 90
63 pp. 90–7
64 p. 61
65 p. 101
66 p. 86
67 p. 155
68 p. 39
69 p. 169
70 p. 191
71 p. 212
72 *Cér* p. 512
73 *FC* pp. 147–8
74 pp. 149–50

CHAPTER 17
Democratic Revolutionist

1 Aron (1983) p. 317
2 Interview, *Combat* 18.10.47, *Ecrits* pp. 169–70
3 p. 170
4 p. 171
5 p. 172
6 Aron (1983) p. 318
7 *Ecrits* pp. 195–7
8 *FC* pp. 124–5
9 pp. 155–7 and Arthur & Cynthia Koestler, *Stranger on the Square* pp. 70–1
10 'Pour un théatre de situations', *La Rue* 11.47 repr. *Un Théâtre de situations*
11 Nathalie Sarraute, *International Herald Tribune* 17.3.84
12 *FC* p. 158
13 Juliette Greco, *Jujube* (Paris 1982)
14 *FC* p. 159
15 p. 161
16 *Ecrits*, p. 205
17 'Appel', *Ecrits* p. 198
18 p. 200
19 Janet Flanner (1966) p. 84
20 *La Gauche* 15–30.5.48
21 Interview, *New York Herald Tribune* (Paris edn) 2.6.48
22 *La Gauche* 7.48
23 Burnier p. 55
24 *Les Lettres françaises* 10.2.49
25 *Le Monde* 17.4.80
26 Interview, *OR* p. 1915
27 p. 1323
28 p. 1337
29 p. 1425
30 *Cahiers* pp. 211–15
31 p. 265
32 p. 268
33 *OR* p. 1426
34 p. 1284
35 G. Idt in *Obliques* 18–19 p. 90
36 *OR* p. 1160
37 *LC* vol. 2 p. 340
38 *FC* p. 179
39 *LC* vol. 2 pp. 340–4

40 *FC* pp. 180–1
41 David Rousset interview with RH
    5.7.85
42 *Ecrits* p. 209
43 Ibid.
44 *OR* p. 2147
45 p. 1596
46 p. 1498
47 p. 1520
48 p. 1522
49 *Cahiers* pp. 332–4
50 pp. 309–20
51 pp. 338–44
52 p. 352
53 p. 390
54 Ibid.
55 p. 403
56 p. 409
57 p. 280
58 p. 169
59 pp. 183–8
60 p. 189
61 p. 188
62 *The Nation* 9.4.49 cited by Burnier
63 'Défense de la culture française par
    la culture européenne' in *Politique
    etrangère* 6.49, *Ecrits* pp. 212–15
64 Note by Sartre published by de
    Beauvoir in *FC* p. 194

CHAPTER 18
Communist Values
1 Mary Welsh Hemingway, *How It
   Was* (New York 1951) pp. 280–1
2 Interview, *Franc-tireur* 24.10.49,
   Ecrits p. 219
3 *Franc-tireur* 21.10.49, *Ecrits* p. 218
4 Cohen-Solal pp. 437–8
5 Letter to Simone Jollivet, *LC* vol. 2
   p. 346
6 *Cahiers* p. 501
7 Aron (1983) p. 198
8 Interview in Chapsal (1960)
9 'L'Engagement de Mallarmé',
   Obliques 18–19 p. 192
10 p. 177
11 p. 190
12 p. 182
13 p. 190
14 p. 188
15 p. 186
16 'Merleau-Ponty vivant', *Sits* 4
17 Ibid.
18 *Le Monde* 27.10.49 cited by Burnier
    p. 64
19 Arthur & Cynthia Koestler, *Stranger
    on the Square* p. 71
20 Letter to Simone Jollivet, *LC* vol. 2
    pp. 348–9
21 *FC* p. 230
22 pp. 230–1
23 p. 233
24 Todd p. 106
25 *FC* p. 250
26 'Merleau-Ponty vivant', *Sits* 4
27 Ibid.
28 *Sits* 4 p. 240
29 *Lebensbeschreibung Herrn Götzens von
    Berlichingen* (Nuremberg 1731)
30 Jouhandeau quoted by Sartre, *Saint
    Genet* p. 213
31 Interview, *L'Avant-Scène* 1–15.5.68
32 Ibid.
33 Interview, *New Left Review* no. 58
    (1969)
34 Interview, *Samedi-Soir* 2–8.6.51,
    Ecrits p. 237
35 'Merleau-Ponty vivant', *Sits* 4
36 Note by Sartre quoted in *FC* p. 262
37 Cau p. 251
38 *FC* p. 256
39 Ibid.
40 p. 258
41 Cau p. 239
42 The passage from Odo of Cluny is
    quoted in *Un Théâtre de situations* but
    is omitted from the standard
    translation of Huizinga's *The Waning
    of the Middle Ages*
43 *FC* p. 260
44 Jeanson (1947) p. 159
45 'Merleau-Ponty vivant', *Sits* 4
46 *FC* p. 268
47 Todd p. 58
48 Marcel Péju interview with RH
    28.6.85
49 Lottman, *Camus* p. 496
50 p. 500

51 *Saint Genet* p. 265
52 p. 341
53 p. 512
54 *Sits* 1 p. 31
55 *Saint Genet* p. 363
56 pp. 364–5
57 p. 512
58 p. 421
59 Ibid.
60 p. 500
61 p. 289
62 pp. 304–5
63 p. 81
64 Angelo Hesnard, *L'Univers morbide* (Paris 1948) p. 180 quoted Collins p. 95
65 *Le Mur* p. 165. The relevance of this was spotted by Pacaly p. 246.
66 *Saint Genet* p. 487
67 p. 491
68 p. 487
69 p. 486
70 p. 488
71 p. 516
72 p. 550
73 Ibid.
74 Cocteau, *Journal* pp. 314–18
75 *FC* p. 275
76 p. 273
77 Cau p. 234
78 pp. 229–57

CHAPTER 19
Under Oath to Hate
1 *Ecrits* p. 261
2 *L'Affaire Henri Martin* (1953)
3 Lottman, *Camus* p. 498
4 *FC* p. 279
5 Lottman, *Camus* p. 500
6 *FC* p. 279 and *Ecrits* p. 250
7 Ibid.
8 *LTM* 5.52
9 Casarès cited by Lottman, *Camus* p. 502
10 *FC* p. 278
11 Michelle Vian interview with RH 2.7.85
12 'Merleau-Ponty vivant', *Sits* 4
13 Jeanson (1955)
14 *Cér* p. 217

15 *Sits* 4 p. 249
16 *FC* p. 281
17 *Sits* 6 p. 85
18 p. 96
19 Poster cited by Aronson p. 219
20 Burnier p. 76
21 *LTM* 8.52 repr. *Actuelles* 2 and *Essais*
22 Jeanson's testimony cited by Lottman, *Camus* p. 503
23 'Réponse à Albert Camus', *LTM* 8.52 repr. *Sits* 4 p. 90
24 pp. 91–2
25 pp. 108 and 100, footnotes
26 pp. 95–6
27 p. 107
28 p. 106
29 p. 111
30 pp. 122–5
31 p. 125
32 Camus, *Diary* (Pléiade edition)
33 *Ecrits* pp. 251–2
34 *Sits* 6 pp. 208–10
35 p. 247
36 Trotsky, *Terrorism and Communism: A Reply to Karl Kautsky* (Ann Arbor 1961) p. 60
37 *Sits* 4 p. 251
38 pp. 253–4
39 *HD*
40 *Ecrits* pp. 251–2
41 Marcel Péju interview with RH 28.6.85
42 *Ecrits* p. 257
43 *FC* p. 310
44 *Ecrits* p. 255
45 *FC* p. 311
46 Cau pp. 253–4
47 *Sits* 4 pp. 257–9
48 *LTM* 4.53 pp. 1541–1629
49 *Sits* 6 pp. 259–60
50 Marcel Péju interview with RH 28.6.85
51 'Les Animaux malades de la rage', *Libération* 22.6.53 repr. *Ecrits* pp. 704–8
52 Aron (1983) p. 308
53 Jeanson (1955) p. 78
54 Programme note repr. *Ecrits* p. 268

55 Interview, *Les Lettres françaises* 12–19.11.53, repr. *Un Théâtre de situations*
56 Ibid.
57 Interview repr. *Un Théâtre de situations*
58 *FC* p. 319
59 Ibid.
60 *Combat* 31.10–1.11.53, *Ecrits* p. 266
61 Ast. pp. 110–11
62 *Cér* p. 275
63 Proust, *Jean Santeuil* p. 198
64 Interview, *Le Monde* 1.6.55, *Ecrits* p. 386
65 Interview, *The Listener* 6.6.57
66 *Cér* p. 275
67 p. 274
68 Interview, *Le Monde* 1.6.55
69 *Cér* p. 275
70 Interview, *Le Monde* 18.4.64, *Ecrits* p. 387
71 *Sits* 6 pp. 279–80
72 p. 283
73 pp. 372–3 footnote
74 p. 350
75 p. 382
76 p. 334
77 p. 353
78 p. 351
79 p. 352
80 Merleau-Ponty, *Les Aventures de la dialectique* (Paris 1955), p. 138
81 *FC* p. 327
82 'A nos lecteurs', *LTM* 5.54, *Ecrits* p. 277
83 *Libération* 17.5.54, *Ecrits* p. 277
84 Julius Fucik, *Ecrit sous la potence* (Paris 1954)
85 *FC* p. 327
86 pp. 328–9
87 *Libération* 5–19.7.54, *Ecrits* p. 279
88 *Ecrits* p. 280
89 *Cér* p. 462 (and Cau interview)
90 *FC* p. 331
91 p. 333
92 *Ecrits* pp. 288–9
93 *Sits* 7 p. 112
94 *Ecrits* p. 303
95 Shusha Guppy in conversation with RH 1985
96 *FC* p. 347
97 p. 348
98 *Ecrits* pp. 287–8
99 *FC* p. 354
100 'La Chine que j'ai vue', *France-Observateur* 18.12.55, *Ecrits* pp. 292–3
101 Ibid.
102 *FC* pp. 355–6
103 pp. 356–7
104 pp. 357–8
105 March Péju interview with RH 28.6.85
106 'Colonialisme et guerre d'Algérie', *LTM* 3–4.56, *Sits* 5 and *Ecrits* p. 297
107 Todd p. 143
108 *Sits* 7 p. 109
109 p. 113
110 p. 111
111 Ibid.
112 p. 113
113 pp. 110–11
114 p. 117
115 The *Observer* 25.3.56 cited by Caute p. 224
116 Roger Garaudy, 'A propos d'un article de Jean-Paul Sartre sur Pierre Hervé', *La Nouvelle Critique* 5.56, cited by Caute p. 255
117 *LC* vol. 2 p. 327
118 *Sits* 4 p. 280
119 Ibid.
120 *Ecrits* p. 301
121 Ibid.
122 p. 304
123 p. 303
124 *FC* p. 373
125 András Hegedüs, *Memoirs*
126 *LTM* Nos. 129–31 (1956–7) p. 678
127 *FC* p. 382
128 *L'Express* 9.11.56, *Ecrits* pp. 305–6
129 *FC* p. 384
130 *Sits* 7 p. 158
131 p. 219
132 p. 217
133 p. 191
134 p. 188
135 p. 193
136 p. 257

137 pp. 162–3
138 p. 271
139 'Le Fântome de Staline', *Sits* 7
140 Caute p. 227
141 Burnier p. 105
142 *Sits* 7 p. 290
143 p. 307
144 *Humanité* 5.11.56, Caute p. 230

CHAPTER 20
Back to Philosophy
 1 Preface to *Critique* I
 2 *LTM* 2–3.57
 3 5.57 repr. *Sits* 5
 4 *FC* p. 392
 5 *Le Monde* 14.5.71
 6 See p. 157
 7 Olivier Todd interview with RH
    16.6.57
 8 'Le Séquestré de Venise', *Sits* 4
 9 Ibid.
10 'Des Rats et des hommes', *Sits* 4
11 Ibid.
12 *Critique* I p. 48
13 p. 47
14 9–10.57 repr. as 'Questions de
    méthode' in *Critique*
15 *Word, Journal of the Linguistic Circle
    of New York* 8.45
16 *Sits* 10 pp. 149–50
17 *Critique* I p. 28
18 p. 40
19 Ibid.
20 p. 17
21 Ibid.
22 p. 18
23 p. 28
24 pp. 41–2 footnote
25 Henri Lefebvre, 'Perspectives de
    sociologie rurale', *Cahiers de
    sociologie* 1953
26 *L'Etre et le Néant* p. 537
27 p. 536
28 'Histoire et éthnologie', *Revue de
    métaphysique et de morale* nos. 3–4
    (1949), repr. as Introduction to
    Anthropologie structurelle
29 Marx, *Das Kapital* III
30 *Critique* I p. 32

31 Burnier p. 120
32 p. 114
33 *Sits* 5 p. 52
34 p. 55
35 Ibid.
36 *FA* p. 403
37 p. 404
38 *Sits* 5 p. 70
39 p. 86
40 *FA* p. 407
41 *Cér* pp. 404–6
42 Interview repr. Chapsal
43 *Critique* I p. 142
44 p. 125 footnote
45 p. 369
46 pp. 453–4
47 p. 144
48 p. 442
49 p. 431
50 p. 454
51 *Critique* I p. 74 including footnote
52 Lévi-Strauss, *La Pensée sauvage*
    chapter 9
53 HD p. 261
54 *La Pensée sauvage* chapter 4
55 Ibid.
56 HD p. 266
57 p. 308
58 p. 290
59 *Cér* p. 418
60 'Le Prétendant', *Sits* 5
61 de Beauvoir diary 27.5.58, *FC* p. 414
62 'Le Théâtre peut-il aborder
    l'actualité politique?', *France-
    Observateur* 13.2.58, repr. Arthur
    Adamov, *Ici et maintenant* (Paris
    1964)

CHAPTER 21
Freudian Interlude
 1 de Beauvoir diary 4.6.58, *FC* p. 428
 2 de Beauvoir diary 16.6.58, *FC*
    p. 437
 3 *Sits* 10, p. 150
 4 'Le Théâtre peut-il aborder
    l'actualité politique?'
 5 *FC* p. 475
 6 de Beauvoir diary 17.8.58, *FC* p. 455
 7 *Le Scénario Freud* p. 531

8 de Beauvoir diary 23.9.58, *FC* pp. 466–7

9 29.9.58, *FC* p. 470

10 pp. 473–5

11 p. 476

12 *Le Scénario Freud* p. 535

13 Interview, 'L'Ecrivain et sa langue', *Revue d'esthétique* 7–12.65; interview repr. Chapsal

14 Ibid.

15 *Ecrits* p. 728

16 H. Hamon and P. Rotman, *Les Porteurs de valise* (Paris 1981) p. 158

17 *FC* p. 491

18 Cohen-Solal p. 495

19 Interview with Bernard Dort repr. *Un Théâtre de situations*

20 Interview with A. Koehler ibid.

21 *LC* vol. 2 p. 360

22 Ibid.

23 p. 563

24 p. 361 and *FC* p. 498

25 John Huston, *An Open Book* (New York 1980) pp. 289–96

CHAPTER 22
Unofficial Ambassador

1 Janine Gallimard's testimony, Lottman, *Camus* pp. 661–4

2 'Albert Camus', *Sits* 4

3 *Sartre on Cuba* p. 7

4 pp. 8–10

5 *France-Soir* 12.7.60, *Ecrits* p. 349

6 9.7.60, p. 348

7 *Sartre on Cuba* p. 94

8 p. 98

9 *France-Soir* 14.7.60, *Ecrits* pp. 349–50

10 *Sartre on Cuba* pp. 137–9

11 *Cér* p. 503

12 Interview, *Nouvel Observateur* 19.11.64, *Ecrits* p. 407

13 *FA* p. 514

14 p. 515

15 Merleau-Ponty (1961) Introduction

16 *Le Semeur* 7–8.2.60, *Ecrits* pp. 352–3

17 *Les Cahiers libres de la jeunesse* 15.2.60

18 'Paul Nizan', *Sits* 4

19 Ibid.

20 Ibid.

21 Merleau-Ponty (1961) Introduction

22 Ibid.

23 *FA* p. 516

24 p. 522

25 J.G. Weightman, *Encounter* 6.61; *FA* p. 523

26 *Critique* 2, typescript p. 20

27 *Critique* 1 p. 131

28 *Critique* 2 typescript p. 20

29 p. 59

30 p. 78; p. 102; p. 41

31 p. 291

32 p. 212

33 p. 317

34 p. 379

35 pp. 393–4

36 p. 409

37 p. 415 and p. 450

38 p. 460

39 p. 435

40 p. 466

41 p. 471 and p. 488

42 p. 490

43 p. 505

44 p. 526

45 p. 500

46 Ibid.

47 Ibid.

48 Michel pp. 52–3

49 p. 24

50 Interview, *Obliques* 18–19 p. 14

51 Interview, *New Left Review* no. 58

52 *Ecrits* p. 359

53 *FA* p. 526

54 p. 534

55 Interview, *Verité-Liberté* 7–8.60, *Ecrits* p. 356

56 *FA* p. 536

57 p. 540

58 p. 541

59 p. 543

60 pp. 541–6

61 p. 554

62 p. 559

63 p. 563

64 pp. 563–4

65 Hamon and Rotman, *Les Porteurs de valise* pp. 300–6

66 *Le Figaro* 21.9.60

67 *FA* p. 574
68 Ibid.
69 p. 577
70 p. 579
71 p. 594
72 p. 597
73 Interview with Laszlo Robert, *The New Hungarian Quarterly* 10–12.82

CHAPTER 23
Kill Sartre
1 Michel p. 64
2 *FA* p. 603
3 Ibid.
4 *LTM*
5 Introduction, *L'Express* 4.1.61 repr. *Sits* 5
6 *L'Arc* no. 30, 1966
7 Interview, *France-Observateur* 8.5.61, *Ecrits* p. 366
8 *FA* p. 617
9 p. 618
10 p. 620
11 p. 622
12 p. 624
13 *Cahiers* p. 191
14 Preface to *Les Damnés de la terre*, *Sits* 5 p. 174
15 Régis Debray cited by Cohen-Solal p. 576
16 Flanner (1966) p. 512
17 *FC* pp. 626–7
18 'Merleau-Ponty (I)', tr. William S. Hamrick in *The Review of Metaphysics* (Washington DC), March 1984 1984
19 *FC* p. 631
20 p. 633
21 p. 636
22 p. 639
23 p. 647
24 'Albert Schweitzer 1875–1975', Catalogue of Exhibition at National and University Library of Strasbourg, *OR* p. lxxxii
25 *FC* p. 640
26 p. 641
27 pp. 646–7
28 p. 650

29 Interview, *La Voie communiste* 6–7.62, *Ecrits* pp. 378–9
30 *Sits* 5 pp. 176–85
31 *Sits* 10 p. 221
32 *FC* 654–7
33 p. 662
34 p. 665
35 pp. 665–6
36 'La Démilitarisation de la culture', *Sits* 7 pp. 326–7
37 *Le Figaro* 20.11.62, *Ecrits* p. 367
38 *TCF* p. 320
39 Jean Pouillon interview with RH 22.6.85

CHAPTER 24
Writing is Neurosis
1 *Cér* p. 275
2 Interview, *Le Monde* 18.4.64, *Ecrits* p. 387 and p. 398
3 *M* p. 57
4 p. 23
5 p. 22
6 This point has been made by Howard Davies in Jameson (1985)
7 *M* p. 21
8 *Novy Mir* 10.10.64, *Ecrits* p. 388
9 *M* p. 11
10 p. 137
11 p. 111
12 p. 161
13 pp. 127–8
14 pp. 131–2
15 *La Nausée* pp. 60–1
16 *M* p. 84
17 p. 136
18 p. 113
19 p. 125
20 *Cér* 276; *M* p. 275 and *Novy Mir* 10.10.64
21 'La Pensée politique de Patrice Lumumba', *Présence africaine* 7–9.63, *Sits* 5
22 *TCF* pp. 321–2
23 pp. 322–6
24 Interview, *La Nouvelle Critique* 6–7.64, *Ecrits* pp. 399–400
25 'Kafka 10 ans après', *LTM* 7.73 cited *OR* p. lxxxiv

26 *Ecrits* p. 399
27 *Sits* 5 p. 172
28 p. 189
29 Flanner (1966) pp. 589–90
30 Speech repr. *Kierkegaard vivant* (Paris 1966)
31 Ibid.
32 Ibid.
33 *Ecrits* p. 425
34 'Détermination et liberté', *Ecrits* pp. 735–45
35 *TCF* pp. 338–9
36 *Un Théâtre de situations*
37 *L'Humanité* 16.7.64, *Ecrits* p. 400
38 *LTM* 10.64
39 *Le Monde* 24.10.64, *Ecrits* p. 403
40 *Nouvelles littéraires* 29.10.64, *Ecrits* p. 405
41 *La Brèche* 12.64, *Ecrits* p. 405
42 *TCF* p. 138
43 Interview, *Nouvel Observateur* 24.10.64, *Ecrits* pp. 405–6
44 Cohen-Solal p. 585
45 *TCF* p. 216
46 'Pourquoi je refuse d'aller aux Etats-Unis', *Nouvel Observateur* 1.4.65, *Ecrits* pp. 412–13
47 'Up All Night', *The Nation* 31.5.65, *Ecrits* p. 416

CHAPTER 25
Half Way to Revolution
1 *Nouvel Observateur* 17.6.65, *Ecrits* p. 417; *Nouvel Observateur* 24.6.65
2 Johnson p. 65
3 HD p. 283
4 Hirsh pp. 143–5, p. 155
5 *TCF* pp. 351–3
6 p. 351
7 p. 356
8 'Avant-garde? de quoi et de qui?' *Nouvel Observateur* 20.9–6.10.65, *Ecrits* pp. 421–2
9 Interview in various Greek daily papers 9.11.65 and in *Le Monde* 10.11, *Ecrits* p. 422
10 *Le Monde* 4.12.65, *Ecrits* pp. 422–3
11 *Sits* 9 pp. 48–9

12 *Cahiers de philosophie* 2.66, *Ecrits* pp. 429–30
13 *L'Arc* 10.66, *Ecrits* pp. 433–4
14 Henry James, *The Art of Fiction* (New York 1948) p. 126 and p. 131
15 *La Nausée* p. 26
16 Letter to George and Thomas Keats 22.12.1817
17 *Idiot* p. 657
18 Cohen-Solal p. 42
19 *New York Times* 31.12.69, cited by Poster p. 386
20 *TCF* pp. 279–84
21 pp. 285–96
22 p. 377
23 Interview, *Al Ahram* (Cairo) 25.12.65, *Ecrits* pp. 440–1
24 *TCF* pp. 403–15
25 pp. 415–23
26 pp. 423–42
27 *Le Monde* 1.6.67, *Ecrits* p. 444
28 *Nouvel Observateur* 26.4–3.5.66, *Ecrits* p. 447
29 *TCF* pp. 383–4
30 *Tribunal Russell: Le jugement de Stockholm* (Paris 1967), *Ecrits* pp. 447–8
31 *TCF* pp. 385–9
32 Interview, *Nouvel Observateur* 24–30.5.67, *Ecrits* p. 448
33 *L'Unità* 3.9.67, *Ecrits* p. 451
34 *TCF* pp. 391–2
35 p. 393
36 p. 395
37 'Le Génocide', *LTM* 12.67
38 *Granma* (Havana) 1.68, *Ecrits* pp. 459–66
39 *Ecrits* p. 460
40 Daniel Cohn-Bendit, *The French Student Revolt*, tr. B. Brewster (New York 1968) p. 58
41 *TCF* pp. 469–70
42 *Le Monde* 8.5.68, *Ecrits* pp. 462–3
43 *Le Monde* 10.5.68, *Ecrits* p. 463
44 *Ecrits* pp. 463–4
45 J. Besançon, *Les Murs ont la parole* (Paris 1948), cited Hirsh p. 140
46 *TCF* pp. 469–70
47 p. 470

48 *Sits* 10 p. 184
49 Flanner (1971) p. 255
50 *Nouvel Observateur* special supplement 20.5.68, *Ecrits* p. 464
51 *TCF* p. 474
52 *Le Figaro* 14.6.68; *Nouvel Observateur* 19–25.6.68, *Ecrits* pp. 467–8
53 *Nouvel Observateur* 26.6–2.7.68, *Ecrits* pp. 466–7
54 *Sits* 10 p. 184
55 *Der Spiegel* 15.7.68, *Ecrits* pp. 467–8
56 *Paese Sera* 25.8.68, *Ecrits* p. 470
57 21.8.68, *Ecrits* p. 469
58 *Cér* p. 8
59 *Nouvel Observateur* 4–10.11.68, *Ecrits* pp. 471–2
60 *Le Monde* 17.10.68, *Ecrits* p. 471
61 3.12.68, *Ecrits* pp. 472–3
62 *TCF* pp. 108–11
63 *Ecrits* p. 426
64 *Idiot* vol. 3 p. 1753
65 *Nouvel Observateur* 17–23.3.69, *Ecrits* p. 477
66 'L'Homme au magnétophone', *Sits* 10
67 Ibid.

CHAPTER 26
With the Maoists
1 *Sits* 10 pp. 184–5
2 *Le Monde* 13.1.70, *OR* p. xcii
3 *Le Monde* 17–18.5.70
4 *Nouvel Observateur* 24.5
5 Lecture 25.2.72 to Jeune Barreau, Brussels, 'Justice et Etat', *Sits* 10 p. 67
6 *Sits* 8
7 Lecture 25.2.72, *Sits* 10
8 Ibid.
9 Ibid.
10 *Le Figaro littéraire* 15–21.6.70
11 Roland Castro interview with RH 1.7.85
12 *TCF* p. 481
13 *L'Idiot internationale* 9.70 repr. *Sits* 8
14 *Tout* 23.9.70
15 *L'Idiot internationale* 9.70
16 Michel p. 84
17 pp. 86–7

18 *L'Idiot internationale* 11.70
19 *Cér* p. 11
20 p. 12
21 p. 14
22 *Le Monde* 22.5.71
23 *Cér* p. 7
24 p. 32
25 p. 34
26 *Minute* 16.6.71 cited in Contat & Rybalka (eds), *The Writings of Sartre*
27 *Cér* p. 34
28 *Le Monde* 24.6.71
29 *Cér* p. 35
30 *Cér* p. 36
31 *OR* p. xcv
32 *Le Monde* 26–7.9.71
33 *Cér* pp. 37–8
34 p. 38
35 *Sits* 10 p. 52
36 *Cér* p. 26
37 p. 28
38 Ibid.
39 p. 48
40 *La Cause du peuple-J'accuse* no. 25
41 *Cér* p. 49
42 Ibid.
43 *Cér* pp. 50–1
44 *Cér* pp. 51–2
45 pp. 52–3
46 Broadcast of 7.2.73 cited in Contat & Rybalka (eds), *The Writings of Sartre*
47 Serge July interview with RH 5.7.85
48 Ibid.
49 *On a raison de se révolter* pp. 17–18
50 Interview *Actuel* 2.73, *Obliques* 18–19 p. 336
51 *On a raison* pp. 23–4
52 *Sits* 10 p. 81
53 *Cér* pp. 38–9
54 pp. 39–42
55 pp. 42–6
56 pp. 67–8

CHAPTER 27
Fading Vision
1 *New York Review of Books* 19.4.73, *Obliques* 18–19 p. 336
2 *Cér* p. 49
3 p. 69

4 pp. 48–51
5 Michel p. 102
6 *Libération* 15, 18, 19 and 20.6, *Obliques* 18–19 p. 336
7 *Libération* 29.6
8 Michelle Vian interview with RH 17 and 19.6.85
9 *Cér* pp. 51–3
10 pp. 53–4
11 Michel p. 103
12 *Cér* pp. 77–8
13 Cohen-Solal p. 621
14 *Cér* p. 77
15 pp. 79–81
16 pp. 82–3
17 Michel pp. 104–5
18 Remark to Contat; *Cér* 87 pp. 85–7
19 p. 89
20 Ibid.
21 p. 94
22 *Sits* 10 p. 214
23 Interview, *Libération* 13–14.4.74
24 Remark to Contat, *OR* p. xlviii
25 *Cér* 96–7
26 *Sits* 10 p. 152
27 Charlesworth p. 143
28 *Cér* 97
29 Sagan p. 134
30 Michel p. 107
31 *Le Monde* 17.4.80
32 Cohen-Solal p. 631
33 Interview, *Nouvel Observateur* 23 and 30.6 and 7.7.75, *Sits* 10
34 Pierre Goldmann, *Souvenirs d'un juif polonais né en France* (Paris 1975)
35 *Sits* 10 p. 193
36 Ibid.
37 Cohen-Solal p. 636
38 Michel p. 188
39 *Cér* p. 99
40 *Der Spiegel* 2.12.74, *Obliques* p. 338

41 Schilpp p. 26
42 Interview in Silverman and Elliston (eds) p. 233
43 *Cér* p. 114 and *Obliques* 18–19 p. 340
44 *Cér* pp. 116–17
45 *Libération* 28.10.75, *Obliques* 18–19 p. 350
46 *Cér* p. 118
47 *Corriere della Sera* 14.3.76, *Cér* p. 120
48 p. 121
49 *Le Monde* 12.5.76, *Obliques* 18–19 p. 342
50 *Cér* pp. 125–6
51 pp. 124–5
52 pp. 127–8
53 pp. 128–9
54 pp. 129–30
55 pp. 130–1
56 pp. 131–2
57 p. 133
58 *Lotta Continua* 15.9.77, *OR* p. cii
59 *Cér* p. 136
60 *Lotta Continua* 15.7.77, *Obliques* 18–19, p. 343
61 *Le Monde* 4.5.12.77
62 *Cér* p. 140
63 p. 139
64 Interview, *Obliques* 18–19 p. 16
65 *Cér* pp. 143–5
66 pp. 145–6 and Michel pp. 121–2
67 Sagan p. 129
68 pp. 131–4
69 *Cér* p. 115
70 Todd pp. 267–8
71 Michel p. 27
72 Interview in Silverman and Elliston (eds) p. 239
73 *Nouvel Observateur* 10.3.80
74 *Cér* p. 157
75 Michel p. 30
76 pp. 30–8; *Cér* pp. 157–9

Bibliography

SARTRE'S WORK IN FRENCH
(*The publisher is Gallimard except where another name is given.*)

1936   *L'Imagination* (Presses universitaires de France)
1937   *La Transcendance de l'Ego* (Vrin)
1938   *La Nausée*
1939   *Le Mur* (In addition to the title story this contains 'L'Enfance d'un chef',
        'Intimité', 'La Chambre' and 'Erostrate')
        Esquisse d'une théorie des émotions (Hermann)
1940   *L'Imaginaire*
1943   *L'Etre et le Néant*
        Les Mouches
1944   *Huis clos*
1945   *L'Age de raison*
        Le Sursis
1946   *L'Existentialisme est un humanisme* (Nagel)
        Morts sans sépulture
        La Putain respectueuse
        Réflexions sur la question juive
        Baudelaire
1947   *Situations I*
        Les Jeux sont faits (Nagel)
1948   *Les Mains sales*
        L'Engrenage (Nagel)
        Situations II
1949   *La Mort dans l'âme*
        Situations III
        Entretiens sur la politique (with David Rousset and Gérard Rosenthal)
1951   *Le Diable et le Bon Dieu*
1952   *Saint Genet, comédien et martyr*
1953   *L'Affaire Henri Martin*
1954   *Kean*
1955   *Nekrassov*
1959   *Les Séquestrés d'Altona*
1960   *Critique de la raison dialectique* (prefaced by *Questions de méthode*)
1963   *Les Mots*
1964   *Situations IV*

Situations V

Situations VI

1965   Les Troyennes

Situations VII

1970   Ecrits de Sartre (ed. Michel Contat and Michel Rybalka. In addition to
the bibliography this contains the play Bariona and several previously
uncollected pieces)

1971   L'Idiot de la famille vols I and II

1972   Situations VIII

Situations IX

1973   Un Théâtre de situations

1974   On a raison de se révolter (with Philippe Gavi and Pierre Victor)

1976   Situations X

1977   'Sartre par lui-même' (transcript of sound track from an interview film
directed by Alexandre Astruc and Michel Contat)

1981   Oeuvres romanesques (ed. Michel Contat and Michel Rybalka with
Geneviève Idt and George H. Bauer)

1983   Les Carnets de la drôle de guerre

Cahiers pour une morale

Lettres au Castor et à quelques autres (2 vols)

1984   Le Scénario Freud (ed. J.B. Pontalis)

1986   Critique de la raison dialectique Part 2

SARTRE'S WORK IN ENGLISH

FICTION

The Age of Reason, tr. Eric Sutton (New York and London 1947)

The Reprieve, tr. Eric Sutton (New York and London 1947)

Nausea, tr. Lloyd Alexander (New York and London 1949; London title: The Diary
of Antoine Roquentin)

Intimacy (Le Mur), tr. Lloyd Alexander (New York and London 1949)

Iron in the Soul (La Mort dans l'âme), tr. Gerard Hopkins (London 1950, New
York 1951; New York title: Troubled Sleep)

PHILOSOPHICAL AND PSYCHOLOGICAL WORKS

Existentialism, tr. Bernard Frechtman (New York 1947; Existentialism and
Humanism, tr. Philip Mairet, London 1948)

Outline of a Theory of the Emotions, tr. Bernard Frechtman (New York 1948; Sketch
for a Theory of the Emotions, tr. Philip Mairet, London 1962)

Psychology of the Imagination, tr. Bernard Frechtman (New York 1948; London 1949)

Being and Nothingness, tr. Hazel Barnes (New York 1956; London 1957)

The Transcendence of the Ego, tr. Forrest Williams and Robert Kirkpatrick (New
York 1957)

Search for a Method, tr. Hazel Barnes (New York 1963; The Problem of Method,
London 1964)

Critique of Dialectical Reason, tr. Alan Sheridan Smith, vol I: Theory of Practical
Ensembles (London 1976)

BIOGRAPHICAL AND AUTOBIOGRAPHICAL WORKS

Baudelaire, tr. Martin Turnell (New York 1950)

Saint Genet: Actor and Martyr, tr. Bernard Frechtman (New York 1963)
The Words, tr. Bernard Frechtman (New York 1964; *Words*, tr. Irene Clephane, London 1964)
The Idiot of the Family, tr. Hazel Barnes (New York and London 1982)
War Diaries, tr. Quintin Hoare (London 1984)

PLAYS
The Flies and *In Camera* (*Huis clos*) tr. Stuart Gilbert (London 1946); *The Flies* (New York 1947); *No Exit* (*Huis clos*) (New York 1947)
The Respectful Prostitute, tr. Kitty Black (London 1947; tr. Lionel Abel, New York 1949)
Men without Shadows, tr. Kitty Black (London 1949); *The Victors*, tr. Lionel Abel (New York 1949)
Dirty Hands, tr. Lionel Abel (New York 1949); tr. Kitty Black (London 1949)
Lucifer and the Lord, tr. Kitty Black (London 1953); *The Devil and the Good Lord* (New York 1960)
Kean or Disorder and Genius, tr. Kitty Black (London 1954; New York 1960)
Nekrassov, tr. Sylvia and George Leeson (Toronto 1957; London 1958; New York 1960)
Loser Wins, tr. Sylvia and George Leeson (London 1960); *The Condemned of Altona* (New York 1961)
The Trojan Women, tr. Ronald Duncan (New York and London 1967)

SCREENPLAYS
The Chips Are Down, tr. Louise Varèse (New York 1948; London 1951)
In the Mesh (*L'Engrenage*), tr. Mervyn Savill (London 1954)
The Freud Scenario, tr. Quintin Hoare (London 1985)

ESSAYS AND INTERVIEWS
Anti-Semite and Jew, tr. George J. Becker (New York 1948); *Portrait of the Anti-Semite*, tr. Eric de Mauny (London 1948)
What is Literature?, tr. Bernard Frechtman (New York 1949)
Literary and Philosophical Essays, tr. Annette Michelson (New York and London 1955)
Literary Essays, tr. Annette Michelson (New York 1957)
Sartre on Cuba (New York 1961)
Essays in Aesthetics, tr. Wade Baskin (New York 1963)
Situations, tr. Benita Eisler (New York 1965)
The Communists and Peace, tr. Martha H. Fletcher with John R. Kleinschmidt (New York 1968)
The Spectre of Stalin, tr. Irene Clephane (London 1969)
Politics and Literature, tr. J.A. Underwood and John Calder (London 1973)
Between Existentialism and Marxism, tr. John Mathews (London and New York 1974)
Sartre on Theater, tr. Frank Jellinek (New York and London 1976)
Life/Situations: Essays Written and Spoken, tr. Paul Auster and Lynda Davis (New York 1977)
Sartre by Himself, tr. Richard Seaver (New York 1978)
Simone de Beauvoir, *Adieux*, tr. Patrick O'Brian (New York 1984)

BIBLIOGRAPHIES IN FRENCH AND ENGLISH

Contat, Michel and Rybalka, Michel, *Les Ecrits de Sartre* (Paris 1970)

Contat, Michel and Rybalka, Michel (eds), tr. Richard McCleary, *The Writings of Sartre*, 2 vols (Evanston, Illinois 1974)

Lapointe, François and Claire, *Jean-Paul Sartre and His Critics: An International Bibliography (1938–75)* (Bowling Green, Ohio 1975)

Wilcocks, Robert, *Jean-Paul Sartre: A Bibliography of International Criticism* (Edmonton, Alberta 1975)

SELECT BIBLIOGRAPHY OF WORK ON SARTRE AND HIS BACKGROUND

Alleg, Henri, *La Question* (Paris 1961)

Aron, Raymond, *L'Opium des intellectuels* (Paris 1955); *Les Marxismes imaginaires* (Paris 1970); *Histoire et dialectique de la violence* (Paris 1973); *Mémoires* (Paris 1983)

Aronson, Ronald, *Sartre: Philosophy in the World* (London 1980)

Barnes, Hazel, *Sartre* (New York 1973); *Sartre and Flaubert* (New York 1982)

de Beauvoir, Simone, *L'Invitée* (Paris 1943); *Les Mandarins* (Paris 1954); *La Longue Marche* (Paris 1957); *Mémoires d'une jeune fille rangée* (Paris 1958); *La Force de l'âge*, 2 vols (Paris 1960); *La Force des choses*, 2 vols (Paris 1963); *La Vieillesse* (Paris 1970); *Tout compte fait* (Paris 1972); *La Cérémonie des adieux* (Paris 1981)

Boschetti, Anna, *Sartre et les temps modernes* (Paris 1985)

Bree, Germaine, *Camus and Sartre* (New York 1972)

Burnier, Michel Antoine, *Les Existentialistes et la Politique* (Paris 1966)

Camus, Albert, *Essais* (Paris 1965)

Casarès, Maria, *Résidente privilégiée* (Paris 1980)

Cau, Jean, *Croquis de mémoire* (Paris 1985)

Caute, David, *Communism and the Intellectuals* (London 1964)

Caws, Peter, *Sartre* (London 1979)

Cazalis, Anne-Marie, *Les Mémoires d'une Anne* (Paris 1976)

Chapsal, Jacques, *La Vie politique sous la V*ᵉ *république* (Paris 1981)

Chapsal, Madeleine, *Les Ecrivains en personne* (Paris 1960)

Charlesworth, Max, *The Existentialists and Jean-Paul Sartre* (Brisbane 1975)

Charmé, Stuart L., *Meanings in the Studies of Lives: Sartre as Biographer* (Harvard 1984)

Chiodi, Pietro, tr. Kate Soper, *Sartre and Marxism* (Hassocks, Sussex 1976)

Cocteau, Jean, *Journal: Le Passé défini* (Paris 1984)

Cohen-Solal, Annie, with Nizan, Henriette, *Paul Nizan: Communiste impossible* (Paris 1980)

Cohen-Solal, Annie, *Sartre 1905–80* (Paris 1985)

Collins, Douglas, *Sartre as Biographer* (Cambridge, Mass. and London 1980)

Colombel, Jeannette, *Sartre ou le parti de vivre* (Paris 1981)

Cranston, Maurice, *Sartre* (Edinburgh 1962)

Fišera, Vladimir (ed.), *Writing on the Wall: May 1968, a Documentary Anthology* (London 1978)

Flanner, Janet, *Paris Journal 1944–65* (London 1966); *Paris Journal 2 1965–71*, ed. William Shawn (New York 1971); *Uncollected Writings* (New York 1979)

Frears, J.R., *France in the Giscard Presidency* (London 1981)

George, François, *Sartre* (Paris 1976)

Goldmann, Pierre, *Souvenirs d'un juif polonais né en France* (Paris 1975)

Goldthorpe, Rhiannon, *Sartre: Literature and Theory* (Cambridge 1984)

Gorz, André, *Le Traître* (Paris 1958); *Adieux au prolétariat* (Paris 1980)

Greco, Juliette, *Jujube* (Paris 1983)

Grisoni, Dominique (ed.), *Politiques de la philosophie* (Paris 1976)

Halpern, Joseph, *Critical Fictions: The Literary Criticism of Jean-Paul Sartre* (New Haven and London 1976)

Hanley, D.L., Kerr, A.O. and Waites, N.H., *Contemporary France: Politics and Society since 1945* (London 1979)

Heller, Gerhard, *Un Allemand à Paris* (Paris 1981)

Hirsh, Arthur, *The French Left: A History and Overview* (Quebec 1982)

Hollier, Denis, *Politique de la prose: Jean-Paul Sartre et l'an quarante* (Paris 1982)

Idt, Geneviève (ed.), *Etudes sartriennes I* (Paris 1984)

Jameson, Frederick, *Sartre: The Origins of a Style* (New Haven 1961); *Marxism and Form* (Princeton 1971); (ed.), *Sartre after Sartre*, Yale French Studies No. 68, (Binghamton, N.Y. 1985)

Jeanson, Francis, *Le Problème moral et la pensée de Sartre* (Paris 1947); *Sartre par lui-même* (Paris 1955); *Sartre dans sa vie* (Paris 1974)

Johnson, Richard, *The French Communist Party versus the Students. Revolutionary Politics in May–June 1968* (New Haven and London 1972)

Lecarme, Jacques, *Les Critiques de notre temps et Sartre* (Paris 1973)

Lejeune, Philippe, *Le Pacte autobiographique* (Paris 1975)

Lévi-Strauss, Claude, *La Pensée sauvage* (Paris 1962)

Lévy, Benny, *Le Nom de l'homme: Dialogue avec Sartre* (Paris 1984)

Lottman, Herbert, *Left Bank* (London 1982)

McCarthy, Patrick, *Camus: A Critical Study of His Life and Work* (London 1982)

McMahon, Joseph H., *Humans Being: The World of Jean-Paul Sartre* (Chicago and London 1971)

Marcuse, Herbert, *Studies in Critical Philosophy* (Boston 1973)

Merleau-Ponty, Maurice, *Les Aventures de la dialectique* (Paris 1955); *Signes* (Paris 1961)

Michel, Georges, *Mes Années Sartre* (Paris 1981)

Muchnik, Nicole (ed.), *De Sartre à Foucault: Vingt ans de grands entretiens dans le Nouvel Observateur* (Paris 1984)

Murdoch, Iris, *Sartre* (Cambridge 1953)

Nizan, Paul, *Le Cheval de Troie* (Paris 1935); *La Conspiration* (Paris 1938)

Obliques (review), two special issues with Michel Sicard as guest editor: *Sartre* and *Sartre et les arts*, nos 18–19 and 24–5, both undated

Pacaly, Josette, *Sartre au miroir* (Paris 1980)

Perrin, Marius, *Avec Sartre au Stalag XIID* (Paris 1980)

Poster, Mark, *Existential Marxism in Post-War France: From Sartre to Althusser* (Princeton 1975)

Pryce-Jones, David, *Paris in the Third Reich* (London 1981)

Sagan, Françoise, *Avec mon meilleur souvenir* (Paris 1984)

Schilpp, Paul-Arthur (ed.), *The Philosophy of Jean-Paul Sartre* (La Salle, Illinois 1982)

Schwarzer, Alice, *Simone de Beauvoir Today* (London 1984)

Scriven, Michael, *Sartre's Existential Biographies* (London 1984)

Seale, Patrick and McConville, Maureen, *French Revolution 1968* (London 1968)

Sendick-Siegel, Liliane, *Sartre: images d'une vie* (Paris 1978)

Silverman, Hugh J. and Elliston, Frederick J. (eds), *Jean-Paul Sartre: Contemporary Approaches to his Philosophy* (Brighton 1980)

Singer, Daniel, *Prelude to Revolution: France in May 1968* (London 1970)

Steiner, George, *Heidegger* (London 1978)

Suhl, Benjamin, *Jean-Paul Sartre: The Philosopher as Literary Critic* (New York 1970)

Thody, Philip, *Jean-Paul Sartre: A Literary and Political Study* (London 1960)

Thompson, Kenneth and Margaret, *Sartre: Life and Works* (New York and Bicester 1984)

Tint, Herbert, *France since 1918* (London 1970)

Todd, Olivier, *Un fils rebelle* (Paris 1981)

Touraine, Alain, tr. Leonard F.X. Mayhew, *The May Movement: Revolt and Reform* (New York 1979)

Verdès-Leroux, Jeannine, *Les Intellectuels au service du Parti* (Paris 1983)

Verstraeten, Pierre, *Violence et ethique* (Paris 1972)

Vian, Boris, *L'Ecume des jours* (Paris 1963)

Warnock, Mary, *The Philosophy of Jean-Paul Sartre* (London 1965); (ed.), *Sartre: A Collection of Critical Essays* (New York 1971)

Webster, Paul and Powell, Nicholas, *Saint-Germain-des-Près: French Post-War Culture from Sartre to Bardot* (London 1984)

Index